Responsible AI in Consumer Engagement:

Policy, Trust, and Practice

Muhammad Abdus Salam
https://orcid.org/0000-0001-9599-632X
Universiti Brunei Darussalam, Brunei & Noakhali Science and Technology University, Bangladesh

Vai Shiem Leong
Universiti Brunei Darussalam, Brunei

Nazlida Muhamad
https://orcid.org/0000-0003-2790-8900
Prince Sultan University, Saudi Arabia

IGI Global
Scientific Publishing
Publishing Tomorrow's Research Today

Vice President of Editorial	Melissa Wagner
Director of Acquisitions	Mikaela Felty
Director of Book Development	Jocelynn Hessler
Production Manager	Mike Brehm
Cover Design	Jose Rosado

Published in the United States of America by
IGI Global Scientific Publishing
701 East Chocolate Avenue
Hershey, PA, 17033, USA
Tel: 717-533-8845 | Fax: 717-533-7115
Website: https://www.igi-global.com E-mail: cust@igi-global.com

Library of Congress Cataloging-in-Publication Data

LCCN: 2026032036 (CIP Data Pending)
ISBN13: 979-8-2600-2977-0
Isbn13Softcover: 979-8-2600-2978-7
EISBN13: 979-8-2600-2979-4
British Cataloguing in Publication Data
A Cataloguing in Publication record for this book is available from the British Library.

All work contributed to this book is new, previously-unpublished material.
The views expressed in this book are those of the authors, but not necessarily of the publisher.
This book contains information sourced from authentic and highly regarded references, with reasonable efforts made to ensure the reliability of the data and information presented. The authors, editors, and publisher believe the information in this book to be accurate and true as of the date of publication. Every effort has been made to trace and credit the copyright holders of all materials included. However, the authors, editors, and publisher cannot assume responsibility for the validity of all materials or the consequences of their use. Should any copyright material be found unacknowledged, please inform the publisher so that corrections may be made in future reprints.

Editorial Advisory Board

Table of Contents

Detailed Table of Contents

As artificial intelligence (AI) shifts from experimental novelty to a ubiquitous commercial driver, its integration into marketing has outpaced robust regulatory development. This chapter investigates the intersection of innovation and oversight. While AI enables unprecedented hyper-personalization, it introduces systemic risks including algorithmic bias, consumer autonomy, and black-box decision-making. This study identifies critical policy gaps where current legislation fails to match technological velocity. By evaluating three primary regulatory paths: Precautionary, Market-Driven, and State-Centric, the discussion advocates for harmonized governance that secures digital sovereignty without stifling growth. It proposes a multi-layered mechanism combining institutional ethics boards, technical explainability, and market-based audits. Ultimately, this work provides a strategic roadmap to align AI commercialization with human-centric values, ensuring trust remains the primary currency of the digital marketplace.

The purpose of this chapter is to explore the interrelated roles of consumer readiness, digital literacy, and acceptance of AI-mediated marketing emphasizing the scopes of capability, awareness, and inclusivity. We will follow the narrative design that synthesizes interdisciplinary studies, technology transfer, AI commercialization, and digital product and services. The chapter developed a conceptual framework so that reader can understand consumers' engagement with AI related marketing systems. This chapter also examined inclusivity factors for equal engagement in AI-driven marketing strategy. By combining both the literature from technology and consumer behaviour perspective, this chapter clarified the situation that fasten the ethical, responsible and sustainable implementation of AI on marketing arena. Furthermore, it established a scenario that justify why the digital capability, awareness and inclusivity are significant both for the individual empowerment and collective gain from the AI commercial adaption.

This chapter examines the paradoxical effects of perceived seamlessness in human–AI service interactions on trust and perceived value. Drawing on technology-mediated services, trust calibration, and multidimensional value theory, it proposes a conceptual framework articulating three constructs: perceived seamlessness, cognitive and functional affective trust, and utilitarian, relational, and hedonic value. The framework models the sequential chain linking fluidity, trust, and value, and demonstrates that this relationship follows an inverted U-shaped curve. Beyond a critical threshold, seamlessness induces overtrust through heuristic generalization reinforced by anthropomorphic processes. Four moderating conditions are integrated: system transparency, transactional stakes, customer familiarity with AI interfaces, and perceived humanness of the agent. Six falsifiable propositions are derived. The chapter concludes with the formalization of transparent seamlessness as an alternative to the dominant paradigm of fluidity maximization in AI service design.

Artificial intelligence (AI) is rapidly changing digital retailing by changing how customers interact with online shopping platforms and how they make purchasing decisions. The chapter focuses on how customers' purchasing intention and shopping behaviour are influenced by AI-enabled websites. The research included Technology Acceptance Model (TAM) which create perceived usefulness and ease of use that enhance consumer trust and engagement with e-commerce. The studies state that AI-enabled shopping systems make it easier for consumers to search for products, and decrease the time it takes to purchase products. It has empower consumers to make better decisions about the products they chose to purchase. At the same time, AI-enabled shopping systems empower retailers to improve their operational efficiency, grow their demand-forecasting capabilities and develop better relationships with customers. It provide practical ideas for researchers, businesspeople, and government officials who want to build an online shopping experience that is focused on consumers and ethical uses of AI.

This study presents a systematic review of AI-driven personalization and its effects on consumer experience, value creation, and behavioral outcomes. Synthesizing 344 Scopus-indexed publications from 2014 to 2026, the review applies the Stimulus–Organism–Response (S-O-R) framework to integrate evidence across marketing, tourism, and information systems research. The findings show that AI technologies—such as machine learning, recommender systems, and NLP-enabled chatbots—generate multidimensional value while also raising concerns about privacy, autonomy, and algorithmic transparency. Trust, shaped by perceived fairness and explainability, mediates the relationship between personalization and consumer responses. Privacy concerns, technology readiness, cultural orientation, and ethical perceptions moderate these effects, influencing outcomes such as purchase intention, loyalty, and electronic word-of-mouth.

The fast development of artificial intelligence is driving radical changes in online marketing activities in the tourism sector. The chapter is rigorous in analyzing the growing importance of AI-generated videos as a pioneering tool for enhancing consumer interaction and building trust in tourism marketing. It examines how smart technologies enable tourism organizations to create highly customized, immersive, and scalable visual content that engages potential travelers and builds destination

marketing landscape. Compared to traditional influencers, the virtual persona supported by Generative AI (GAI), machine learning, and natural language processing allows brands to maximize marketing communication on an unprecedented scale. Although current research examines the adoption, credibility, and efficacy of AI-based endorsers, the conceptual frameworks remain disjointed. This study fills this gap by conducting a bibliometric analysis combining articles from Scopus. It employs co-occurrence of keywords for thematic presentation of overall ideas to evaluate science-mapping clusters and nascent thematic domains within synthetic endorser research. Literature provides empirical findings, including adoption, credibility, and engagement, acting as the prime dimensions impacting consumer behavior through several key factors. These findings are synthesized into a conceptual framework, which has an impact on VIs and SBEs.

This chapter, per the authors, examines the growing role of deepfake technology in transforming tourism marketing and visitor experiences, positioning it as both an opportunity and a challenge. It explores how AI-driven tools such as GANs and diffusion models enable scalable, personalized, and immersive storytelling through virtual ambassadors, revived historical figures, and interactive heritage interpretations. Applications across destination marketing, cultural tourism, and smart tourism ecosystems are discussed, particularly when integrated with AR and VR. The chapter also addresses key concerns related to authenticity, ethics, consent, and cultural sensitivity, emphasizing transparency, stakeholder engagement, and responsible design. It further analyses consumer perceptions using relevant theoretical frameworks, presenting a balanced approach to innovation and trust. Recent developments in deepfake detection and AI-driven marketing (2019–2024) further highlight the growing relevance of these technologies in tourism.

The business intelligence sector is transforming profoundly at present; however, there is a limited understanding of how AI technology can be shifted across industries strategically. This effort develops a multi-disciplinary model, i.e., Cross-Domain AI Technology Transfer and Commercial Interaction Model (CATTCIM), in order

Preface

INTRODUCTION

Artificial Intelligence (AI) has rapidly evolved from a specialized technological capability into a transformative force reshaping the way organizations engage with consumers. Across industries and markets, AI-driven systems are redefining communication, personalization, customer service, marketing strategy, and decision-making processes. As businesses increasingly integrate intelligent technologies into consumer-facing applications, questions surrounding trust, transparency, ethics, governance, privacy, and consumer empowerment have become central to both academic inquiry and professional practice. The opportunities offered by AI are immense, yet their successful realization depends on ensuring that innovation remains aligned with human values and societal expectations.

The emergence of AI-mediated consumer engagement represents a pivotal moment in the evolution of digital commerce and marketing. Technologies such as machine learning, recommender systems, virtual influencers, generative AI, deepfakes, intelligent chatbots, and predictive analytics are enabling unprecedented levels of personalization and efficiency. At the same time, these developments challenge traditional notions of authenticity, privacy, accountability, and consumer autonomy. As organizations seek to harness the capabilities of AI, there is an urgent need for comprehensive frameworks that balance technological advancement with ethical responsibility and consumer trust.

This book, *Responsible AI in Consumer Engagement: Policy, Trust, and Practice*, addresses these critical challenges by bringing together contributions from an international group of scholars and researchers. The volume examines the multifaceted relationship between AI technologies and consumer engagement, exploring how businesses, policymakers, and society can foster responsible innovation while maximizing value creation. Through conceptual frameworks, systematic reviews, governance models, and multidisciplinary perspectives, the chapters collectively provide a comprehensive understanding of the evolving AI-consumer ecosystem.

The contributions featured in this volume reflect the inherently interdisciplinary nature of responsible AI. Drawing from fields including marketing, information systems, consumer behavior, tourism, business intelligence, technology transfer, ethics, and public policy, the book highlights both the opportunities and complexities associated with AI adoption. It serves as a valuable resource for academics, practitioners, policymakers, and graduate students seeking to understand how trust, governance, transparency, and human-centered design can shape the future of AI-driven consumer engagement.

OVERVIEW OF THE CHAPTERS

Chapter 1, *Trust, Transparency, and Ethics in AI-Driven Consumer Engagement: The Role of AI Governance*, establishes the foundational themes of the book by examining how explainability, transparency, ethical governance, and responsible data practices influence consumer trust and long-term engagement with AI-enabled systems.

Chapter 2, *Regulating AI-Driven Marketing: Ethical Risks, Policy Gaps & Governance Mechanisms*, investigates the growing disconnect between technological innovation and regulatory development. The chapter evaluates alternative governance approaches and proposes mechanisms for balancing innovation with accountability and consumer protection.

Chapter 3, *Consumer Readiness and Digital Literacy in AI-Mediated Marketing*, examines the importance of digital capabilities, awareness, and inclusivity in shaping consumer adoption and acceptance of AI-enabled marketing systems. The chapter emphasizes the role of digital literacy in promoting equitable participation in digital markets.

Chapter 4, *The Illusion of Seamless Service: Trust and Value in AI-Mediated Customer Experience*, investigates how perceptions of seamless AI interactions influence trust formation and perceived value. It introduces the concept of transparent seamlessness and highlights the risks associated with excessive automation and overtrust.

Chapter 5, *How Smart Websites Influence Shopping Decisions: Evidence from AI-Enabled Online Retail Platforms*, focuses on the impact of AI-driven e-commerce environments on consumer behavior. The chapter explores how intelligent retail systems influence purchase decisions while enhancing customer engagement and operational effectiveness.

Chapter 6, *AI-Driven Personalization and Consumer Experience: A PRISMA-Guided Systematic Review of Value Creation and Behavioral Outcomes*, synthesizes more than a decade of research on AI personalization. The review identifies key drivers, mediators, and moderators influencing consumer responses and value creation across diverse contexts.

Chapter 7, *AI-Driven Transformation Digital Marketing: Boosting Engagement and Trust with AI-Generated Videos in Tourism*, explores the growing use of AI-generated visual content in tourism marketing. It demonstrates how immersive and personalized media can strengthen engagement, trust, and destination branding.

Chapter 8, *The Synthetic Persona: Exploring the Marketing Prospects and Ethical Dark Side of AI-Powered Virtual Influencers*, examines the opportunities and ethical dilemmas associated with synthetic influencers. The chapter introduces the Synthetic Persona Influence Framework and explores issues of authenticity, persuasion, and consumer manipulation.

Chapter 9, *AI-Powered Virtual Influencers and Synthetic Brand Endorsers: Adoption, Credibility, and Engagement*, extends the discussion of synthetic marketing agents by analyzing emerging research themes and developing a conceptual understanding of adoption, credibility, and consumer engagement outcomes.

Chapter 10, *Synthetic Destinations and Simulated Authenticity: Commercial Applications of Deepfake Technologies in Tourism Marketing and Experience Design*, investigates the growing role of deepfake technologies in tourism experiences. The chapter presents both the commercial potential and ethical considerations associated with AI-generated authenticity.

Chapter 11, *Cross-Domain Technology Transfer in Commercial Human–AI Interaction: A Multidisciplinary Strategic Framework*, concludes the volume by introducing a comprehensive framework for understanding how AI innovations move across industries and become integrated into commercial consumer-facing applications.

Together, these chapters provide a rich and multidimensional exploration of responsible AI in consumer engagement. While each contribution addresses a distinct aspect of the topic, collectively they demonstrate the importance of trust, transparency, governance, and human-centered innovation in shaping the future of AI-enabled consumer experiences.

CONCLUSION

As AI technologies continue to evolve, their influence on consumer engagement will only deepen. Organizations are increasingly relying on intelligent systems to personalize experiences, automate interactions, generate content, and support strategic decision-making. Yet technological sophistication alone is insufficient to ensure successful adoption. The long-term sustainability of AI-driven consumer ecosystems depends upon maintaining trust, safeguarding privacy, promoting transparency, and ensuring that innovation remains accountable to the individuals it serves.

One of the central insights emerging from this volume is that responsible AI is not solely a technical challenge; it is equally a managerial, ethical, social, and policy concern. The chapters collectively demonstrate that effective governance frameworks, transparent communication practices, consumer education, and ethical oversight mechanisms are essential for creating meaningful and trustworthy AI-enabled interactions. As AI becomes increasingly embedded within everyday consumer experiences, organizations must recognize their responsibility to balance commercial objectives with broader societal expectations.

The discussions presented throughout this book also highlight the importance of interdisciplinary collaboration. Addressing the complexities of AI-mediated consumer engagement requires contributions from technologists, marketers, policymakers, ethicists, behavioral scientists, and industry leaders. By fostering dialogue across these domains, stakeholders can develop more comprehensive solutions to emerging challenges while ensuring that AI technologies remain beneficial, inclusive, and aligned with human values.

As editors, we hope this volume serves as both a scholarly reference and a practical guide for understanding the opportunities and responsibilities associated with AI in consumer engagement. We extend our sincere appreciation to all contributing authors for their expertise, dedication, and valuable insights. We also thank the reviewers, publishing team, and readers whose support makes this work possible. It is our hope that the ideas presented in this book will inspire future research, informed policymaking, and responsible innovation, ultimately contributing to the development of trustworthy and human-centered AI ecosystems for consumers worldwide.

Muhammad Abdus Salam
Universiti Brunei Darussalam, Brunei & Noakhali Science and Technology University, Bangladesh

Vai Shiem Leong
Universiti Brunei Darussalam, Brunei

Nazlida Muhamad
Prince Sultan University, Saudi Arabia

Acknowledgment

The editors sincerely thank all authors and reviewers whose dedication, expertise, and valuable contributions made this book possible. We are especially grateful to the chapter authors for sharing their knowledge and to the reviewers for their thoughtful evaluations, which significantly enhanced the quality and coherence of the manuscript. We also express our appreciation to the UBD School of Business and Economics, Universiti Brunei Darussalam, Brunei Darussalam; Prince Sultan University, Saudi Arabia; and Noakhali Science and Technology University, Bangladesh, for providing a supportive research environment and institutional assistance throughout this project. Finally, we extend our heartfelt thanks to the entire IGI Global publishing team for their guidance and professional support from the proposal stage through publication, with special appreciation to Jocelynn Hessler, Mikaela Vargo, Melissa Wagner, Puja Phuyel, Daniel Kreiss, and Caitlin Meehan for their invaluable contributions.

Muhammad Abdus Salam
Universiti Brunei Darussalam, Brunei & Noakhali Science and Technology University, Bangladesh

Vai Shiem Leong
Universiti Brunei Darussalam, Brunei

Nazlida Muhamad
Prince Sultan University, Saudi Arabia

Chapter 1
Trust, Transparency, and Ethics in AI-Driven Consumer Engagement: The Role of AI Governance

Afruza Haque
http://orcid.org/0000-0003-0586-6674
Dhaka University of Engineering and Technology, Gazipur, Bangladesh

Md. Faisal-E-Alam
http://orcid.org/0000-0002-7341-7945
Begum Rokeya University, Rangpur, Bangladesh

Most. Sadia Akter
University of Dhaka, Dhaka, Bangladesh

Rasheda Akter Rupa
http://orcid.org/0000-0003-4804-3424
University of Dhaka, Dhaka, Bangladesh

Zahidul Islam
http://orcid.org/0000-0003-2595-7573
Uttara University, Dhaka, Bangladesh

ABSTRACT

This chapter examines how trust, transparency, and ethical governance shape consumer participation in AI-mediated digital interactions, influencing confidence, loyalty, and long-term relationships. Integrating studies on AI applications, transparency, and ethical practices, it presents a conceptual framework showing how explainable

DOI: 10.4018/979-8-2600-2977-0.ch001

AI, disclosure, and clear data policies enhance understanding and confidence, while ethical governance—focused on fairness, accountability, and privacy—strengthens trust. Consumer trust is multidimensional, including cognitive reliability, perceived fairness, social integrity, and contextual factors. These insights guide managers, policymakers, and researchers in responsibly implementing AI to foster sustainable value in digital markets.

1 INTRODUCTION

Artificial Intelligence (AI) is now one of the most radical technologies which are defining the contemporary business and consumer ecosystem. In all sectors, companies are looking into AI-based systems to automate operations, improve decision-making, and provide customized services (Acatrinei et al., 2025). In service settings and marketing, AI solutions, such as recommendation systems, predictive analytics, chatbots, and automated service bots, are now ubiquitous in every interaction between customers (Binns et al., 2018). These systems use a great deal of behavioral and transactional data to anticipate likes, tailor products, and smoothen measures of engagement in real time. As a result, the consumer engagement mediated by AI has become the most important tool that assists companies in creating value, increasing operational efficacy, and developing customer relations (Hagendorff, 2020).

Implementation of AI technologies has offered quite a number of benefits to the organization and consumers. Regarding the firm, AI enhances more accurate targeting, lowers the cost of services, and enables scalable personalization (Inavolu, 2024). As a consumer, the AI-based services provide convenience, a quicker response, and personalized experience based on personal needs (Vashishth et al., 2024). To illustrate, recommendation systems can assist customers in finding products of interest, chatbots can instantly support customers, and predictive systems can be used to make decisions easier (Rinne, 2025). All these advantages make interactions easier and consumer satisfaction more significant. Therefore, AI is becoming viewed as a strategic asset that alters the nature of engagement and creation of value in the digital marketplaces (Lukyanenko et al., 2022).

Though these advantages exist, there are other associated challenges that increase as the use of AI continues to rise beyond its technical capability. Due to a growing autonomy and invisibility of AI systems, the issues of trust, transparency, and moral responsibility have been exacerbated (Radanliev, 2025). Most AI applications behave like black boxes, where the consumers are not able to easily comprehend how algorithms can arrive up to suggestions or decisions that can impact them (Mishra, 2025). Furthermore, AI technologies are largely based on the use of personal data, their collection, and processing, and the issues of privacy, consent, and the security of the data are raised (Malik et al., 2025). The cases of on the one hand algorithmic bias, and on the other hand discriminatory performance, and the misuse of personal information have only contributed to the increased distrust in automated technologies (Bahangulu & Owusu-Berko, 2025). The risks make them uncertain and can undermine the trust that consumers have in AI-mediated interactions.

The element of trust has become one of the most important elements in the adoption and use of AI technologies by the consumers (Khatun et al., 2026). Trust goes beyond technical quality or reliability to incorporate notions of fairness, accountability, and integrity of the organization (Islam et al., 2025). Consumers consider how artificial intelligence systems can meet their interests, whether the decisions can be justified, and whether companies are responsible in their actions when using such technologies (Camilleri, 2024). In case of non-realization of these expectations, distrust can develop, which will result in resistance, a decline in use, or a negative attitude to AI-enabled services (Kinney et al., 2024). The knowledge on building and sustaining trust in AI-mediated settings is thus a critical element when organizations that want to have a long-term relationship with their consumers (Martin et al., 2021).

Transparency and ethical governance are two interconnected mechanisms that are particularly important in the formation of the trust perceptions. Transparency is the degree to which companies are able to articulate the workings of AI systems, the manner in which decisions are made, and how data on consumers is gathered and processed (Balasubraman et al., 2023). Explainable AI interfaces, automated decision-making disclosure, and transparent data policies are some of the practices that enable consumers to have a clearer insight into the reasoning behind the algorithmic findings (De Bruijn et al., 2022). Transparency allows consumers to feel more knowledgeable and powerless by minimizing information asymmetry and uncertainty (Hina et al., 2025). Adding to the idea of transparency, ethical AI governance is the organizational structures, policies, and processes that make AI technologies developed and implemented in a responsible way (Jobin et al., 2019). Ethical governance represents the safeguards of fairness, reduction of bias, accountability, protection of privacy, and constant surveillance during the AI lifecycle (Dwivedi et al., 2023). A combination of these principles will minimize uncertainty, lower risks, and make consumers more confident in interactions mediated by AI (Bozdağ, 2025). Responsible AI governance in this sense acts as the institutional support that incorporates transparency measures and ethical protection into the systems of AI-mediated engagements. In the absence of governance structures, transparency will just be symbolic and ethical principles will just be aspirational.

Despite the growing body of literature on AI-mediated consumer engagement, transparency, ethical AI governance, and consumer trust, existing studies remain fragmented. The majority of the research focuses on these concerns individually and fails to clarify the relationships between AI-mediated consumer engagement, transparency mechanisms, and ethical AI governance in their ability to form consumer trust (Rahman, 2025; Wen and Li, 2025; Dang and Li, 2025). Furthermore, it is not clearly demonstrated in the literature when transparency enhances trust and in which cases it can lead to privacy issues, confusion, or distrust. The subject of ethical AI governance is frequently discussed in an abstract manner, without specifying how fairness, accountability, privacy protection, and oversight can be used to establish trust in consumer-facing AI. The literature also pays insufficient attention to the role of contextual variations, including regulatory, cultural, and market conditions, which determine the trust in AI-mediated interactions. Such gaps bring constraints to both the theoretical knowledge and practical advice to organizations attempting to be responsible AI users and keep the trust of consumers. Thus, a comprehensive conceptual framework is required to clarify the interactions of AI-mediated consumer engagement, transparency systems, and ethical AI governance regarding consumer trust and consumer relationship strengthening (Vargas, 2025).

Building on these identified gaps, this chapter investigates how AI-mediated consumer engagement, transparency mechanisms, and ethical AI governance interact to shape consumer trust. These relationships form the basis of the following research questions and objectives.

Research Questions

RQ1: How does AI-mediated consumer engagement influence consumer trust outcomes?
RQ2: How do transparency mechanisms shape the relationship between AI-mediated consumer engagement and consumer trust?
RQ3: How does ethical AI governance shape the relationship between AI-mediated consumer engagement and consumer trust?
RQ4: What conceptual and practical implications emerge for responsible AI implementation and sustainable trust building?

Research Objectives

RO1: To examine the influence of AI-mediated consumer engagement on consumer trust outcomes.
RO2: To analyze how transparency mechanisms shape the relationship between AI-mediated consumer engagement and consumer trust.
RO3: To analyze how ethical AI governance shapes the relationship between AI-mediated consumer engagement and consumer trust.

RO4: To develop an integrated conceptual framework and derive managerial and policy implications for responsible AI implementation and sustainable trust building.

The paper contributes to the existing body of literature related to the interaction of AI-mediated engagement, transparency, and ethical governance to support consumer trust. It helps to preserve a range of studies that will bring the evidence to create a bigger picture of such relations and identify trends, loopholes, and other processes that are crucial to the trust in AI systems. In practice, the study includes a recommendation to managers and policy makers as to how they should produce AI systems which are transparent, fair and ethically accountable. Those issues are to be approached as AI is turning out to be one of the drivers of personal marketing, e-commerce, and service provision when the application of opaque algorithms or the lack of ethics may decrease the consumer loyalty and trust. The gap between theory and practice is bridged in this review because it is the compilation of current research in this area. It also helps the companies to take responsibility in AI application, increase the consumer confidence, and long-term interaction, trust, and sustainable relations.

2 LITERATURE REVIEW

2.1 AI-mediated Consumer Engagement

In this digital age, Artificial Intelligence (AI) has become the most powerful and revolutionary phenomenon influencing both the concepts and practices of marketing (Amin et al., 2025). The development of AI is one of the main communication mechanisms that not only affect what is perceived by consumers but their thinking, attitudes, and response to brand communication. The growing focus of AI-based technology, such as recommendation engines, chatbots, voice recognition, predictive analytics, or generational content creation tools, has changed how organizations understand, draw, and interact with customers (Kumar et al., 2024; Salam et al., 2026). Nowadays, AI transformed consumers from passive audiences to active participants. Formerly relegated to the realm of automation and analytics, AI has now emerged as a key enabler of engagement, shaping not merely consumer visibility but also their thoughts, emotions, and experiences to brand correspondence (Haenlein et al., 2019). Technological infrastructure and AI capabilities, including AI algorithms, machine learning, natural language processing, and predictive analytics, furnish the computerized basis for sophisticated AI-fueled marketing applications. These applications, for example, recommendation systems, chatbots, and automated advertising, harness the infrastructure to provide personalized and immersive experiences that improve consumer engagement and trust.

2.1.1 Artificial Intelligence Capabilities

AI capabilities in digital marketing refer to core AI functions used to communicate with, understand, and engage consumers effectively. AI algorithms comprise a wide range of technologies that allow machines to derive information from data, recognize patterns, make decisions, and solve complex problems autonomously. The utilization of AI algorithms and data-centric decision-making through Big Data has replaced conventional digital marketing strategies, including search engine optimization, search engine advertising, and social media marketing, with extensive automated models for content personalization (Saura, 2021). Furthermore, the evolution of AI algorithms associated with digital marketing has made significant improvements in recent years, exemplified by platforms such as ChatGPT, which have benefited and altered performance in numerous kinds of industries (Madzík et al., 2026). The emergence of data-driven models facilitates analysis of massive data sets to identify patterns and trends to establish the most efficient relationships to achieve business objectives (Shah et al., 2021). Digital marketing inherently uses these algorithmic frameworks to identify the best strategies (Saura, 2024). Through intelligent dashboards, these algorithms provide marketers with the best options for developing smart content (Boldosova, 2020).

In the realm of big data, machine learning, and data analytics can be applied to offer personalized services that determine what consumers desire in real time and encourage consumer engagement (Aluri et al., 2019). Machine learning algorithm performed well in predicting consumer involvement behavior choices by deriving information and insights from data. Multiple machine learning languages are combined to forecast the source code level execution time of software for the processing of digital signals (Liu et al., 2021). An identification strategy, utilizing K-nearest neighbors along with support vector machines has been employed to ascertain whether the system is under attack (Ma & Li, 2020). The Seq2Seq model is integrated with the BERT module to enhance response quality (Zhao et al., 2020). Machine learning can also be used to figure out visual appeal in mobile dating applications (Gao et al., 2021).

To enhance consumer engagement in AI-mediated digital marketing, natural language processing (NLP) and perceived analytics are employed to assess sentiment in social media content, enabling businesses to comprehend public opinion more effectively and swiftly address unfavorable criticism (Baberwal et al.,2025). NLP can evaluate the tones and emotions communicated in posts and comments, which provides meaningful insights for enhancing consumer engagement through online reputation management (Jim et al., 2024).

2.1.2 AI Mechanisms to Engage Consumers

AI's ability to identify patterns, evaluate massive data sets, and make decisions without human input has completely changed how businesses engage with their customers (Sahut & Laroche, 2025). Numerous AI mechanisms, such as chatbots, recommendation engines, personalization, automated advertising, and sentiment analysis are employed to engage consumers in the digital marketing process. These applications are used to deliver personalized services through real-time interactions with consumers. Through the responsive experiences of digital touch points, these tools can predict consumers' desires and tailor content.

Chatbots with AI capabilities have gained prominence as digital marketing solutions since they allow for automated and customized interactions (Xia & Shannon, 2025). These chatbots are employed to offer product suggestions, respond to often-requested queries, and expedite the purchasing process (Adamopoulou & Moussiades, 2020). Chatbots can handle multiple consumers at once. It has the ability to lower consumer support expenses. For these reasons, they gain rapid acceptance from business organizations (Ranoliya et al., 2017). In some contexts, chatbots are more efficient than individuals at reaching and engaging a large audience through messaging apps (Adamopoulou & Moussiades, 2020). Nowadays, chatbots are used by many online merchants to provide perpetual assistance, which improves consumers' buying experience (Akdemir & Bulut, 2024).

Combined augmented reality (AR) and virtual reality (VR) is an innovation in AI for digital marketing, which generates a more engaging and immersive shopping experience (Flavián et al., 2019). Additionally, by enabling more direct and personalized interactions between business firms and consumers, AI is anticipated to make a significant contribution to social commerce through improving customer engagement (Haque et al., 2024). AI-driven virtual applications are offering prompt consumer assistance and personalized recommendations before, during, and following the purchase. Through personalization, clients feel that they are more valued and understood, which leads to increased loyalty and customer satisfaction. The importance of AI in automating consumer service activities is stressed even more. AI-powered systems can handle routine interactions with consumers, allowing human personnel to focus on complex assignments (Spencer, 2025). Automation boosts productivity, reduces waiting periods, and improves the customer experience. Deploying AI in after-sales services, for example, automated conversations and case categorization, can enhance consumer loyalty and trust (Huynh & Khoa, 2025).

From awareness to post-purchase support, AI enhances consumer experience at different stages to boost their engagement. AI-driven predictive analytics allows businesses to determine consumer preferences and make pertinent product or service recommendations at the awareness stage. In the consideration stage, AI integrates massive amounts of data, which facilitates consumers to make knowledgeable decisions. In order to provide tailored suggestions for future purchases, AI learns consumers' buying behavior during the purchasing stage. Lastly, AI continues to track consumer satisfaction and offers prompt solutions for any probable problems during the post-purchase phase (Dahish et al., 2025).

2.1.3 Consumer Engagement Dimensions

Consumer engagement can be defined as a psychological condition resulting from interactive and collaborative brand experiences (Hidayanti et al., 2025). It often contains cognitive, behavioral, and emotional aspects that collectively explain the quality and intensity of associations beyond simple transactions and satisfaction (Hollebeek & Macky, 2019). Cognitive engagement encompasses perception of relevance, attractiveness, and absorption. Affective attachment, pleasure, and passion are all captured by emotional engagement. Behavioral engagement includes efforts, such as word-of-mouth marketing, creation of content, reviews, and advocacy (Hollebeek & Macky, 2019). Both subjective metrics and observable indicators, for example, dwell time, click depth, feedback frequency, share rate, and user-created content, are frequently used to gauge consumer engagement in an AI-mediated marketing context.

2.1.4 Consumer Engagement Outcomes

AI applications greatly influence consumers' engagement, purchasing intention, trust, and loyalty in the digital marketing landscape. AI-driven consumer interactions enable business organizations to improve consumer engagement. Consumer engagement symbolizes the internal transformation that connects external stimuli (AI capabilities and mechanisms) with sustainable outcomes like perceived relevance, commitment, purchasing intention, trust, and loyalty (An et al., 2025). AI-mediated consumer interaction helps businesses to offer personalized experiences. Personalized experiences foster consumers' trust and satisfaction. AI innovations also facilitate timely, accurate, and consistent customer support in the digital and social marketing era. These favorable experiences eventually increase consumer loyalty and have a greater impact on purchasing decisions and recurring purchase behavior.

Figure 1. AI-mediated consumer engagement in the digital marketing environment (Authors' own creation)

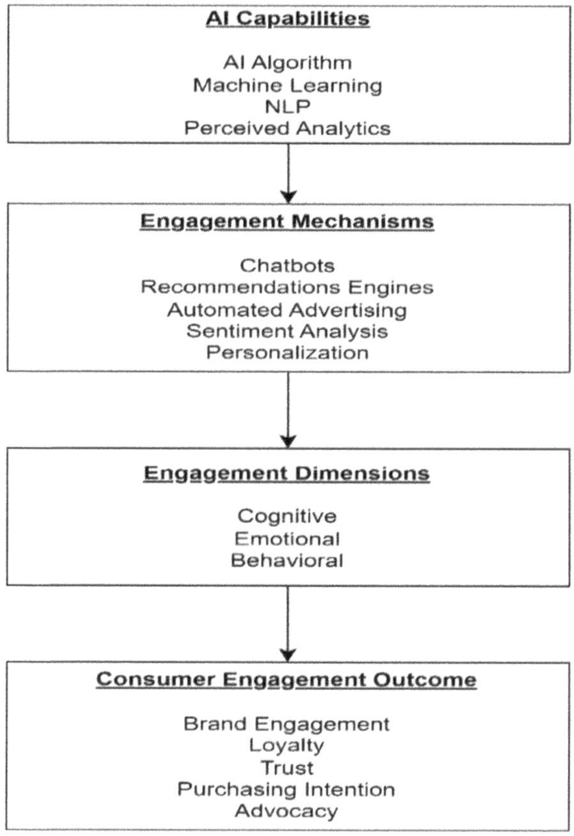

2.2 Trust in AI Algorithmic Systems

Trust is a psychological mechanism that lowers uncertainty and increases the opportunity of a successful relationship with environmental entities (Chen et al., 2026). AI adoption and usage in digital and social marketing heavily depend on trust. Trust in AI algorithmic systems is a fundamental component of an effective AI-mediated consumer engagement. Because trust in an AI algorithmic system shapes consumers' willingness to rely on and act upon AI-driven recommendations (Zhao et al., 2025). To overcome the significant uncertainty that affects the development and deployment process, trust becomes crucial. In numerous cases, mistrust in AI is justified. While some AI-driven solutions have gained greater success, others have failed miserably. The drawbacks may be caused by biases in the AI algorithms.

Biases in the AI algorithm lead to widespread discriminatory practices (Panarese et al., 2025). Several barriers stand in the way of robust and responsible AI. The quality of data used to train AI models determines the quality of AI (Sambasivan et al., 2021). In marketing and digital platforms, confidence develops when AI systems are seen as dependable, accurate, and aligned with consumers' interests. Algorithmic transparency, explainability, and accountability are crucial in obtaining users' confidence and strengthening trust.

2.3 Transparency and Explainable AI

Transparency in AI is the core principle of AI model development and deployment. It encompasses the openness and visibility of the AI decision making processes, data sources, and output (Patidar et al., 2024). Transparency addresses the black-box problem in complex AI models, while explainable AI (XAI) is the process of making opaque black-box models interpretable to non-experts (Chinnaraju, 2025). The internal working process of AI models are difficult for the users, regulators and non-expert individuals to understand how and why AI systems arrive at particular decisions. Explainable AI plays a vital role in this respect (El-Geneedy et al., 2025).

Transparency in AI and XAI are closely related to each other as both aim to reduce the opacity in algorithmic systems and enhance trust, accountability and informed decision making (Balasubramaniam et al., 2023). However, these two concepts differ in scope and analytical focus, which is presented in **Table 1.** Transparency is a broader, system-level principle, which reflects the openness regarding how an AI system is designed. It also emphasizes on what data it uses, how it is governed and under what conditions it operates. On the other hand, explainability is a narrower and output-level concept concerned specifically with providing understandable reasons for individual algorithmic decisions (Esposito, 2022). In other words, transparency addresses the visibility of the overall AI ecosystems. Explainability addresses the intelligibility of specific outcomes generated within that ecosystem.

Table 1. Similarities and dissimilarities between AI transparency and explainability

Dimension	AI Transparency	Explainable AI (XAI)	Similarity
Conceptual Scope	Broad, system-level principle concerning openness about model architecture, data sources, governance, and operational processes.	Narrower, decision-level principle focused on making individual model outputs understandable.	Both aim to reduce the "black-box" nature of AI systems.
Primary Objective	Promote accountability, auditability, and institutional trust.	Promote interpretability, user comprehension, and informed decision-making.	Both enhance trust and legitimacy of AI systems.
Level of Analysis	Macro-level (organizational and technical ecosystem).	Micro-level (specific predictions or decisions).	Both contribute to responsible AI deployment.
Technical Focus	Documentation, disclosure, traceability, data provenance, model governance frameworks.	Interpretation methods such as feature importance.	Both require methodological rigor and technical design considerations.
Audience	Regulators, auditors, policymakers, developers, and stakeholders.	End-users, affected individuals, domain experts.	Both address multiple stakeholder groups.
Regulatory Relevance	Central to compliance frameworks.	Important for justifying automated decisions and safeguarding procedural fairness.	Both are embedded in emerging AI governance frameworks.
Level of Analysis	Macro-level (organizational and technical ecosystem).	Micro-level (specific predictions or decisions).	Both contribute to responsible AI deployment.
Technical Focus	Documentation, disclosure, traceability, data provenance, model governance frameworks.	Interpretation methods such as feature importance.	Both require methodological rigor and technical design considerations.
Audience	Regulators, auditors, policymakers, developers, and stakeholders.	End-users, affected individuals, domain experts	Both address multiple stakeholder groups
Regulatory Relevance	Central to compliance frameworks.	Important for justifying automated decisions and safeguarding procedural fairness.	Both are embedded in emerging AI governance frameworks.
Dependency Relationship	Can exist without detailed decision-level explanations.	Can provide post-hoc explanations even if full system transparency is lacking.	Explainability is often considered a functional subset of transparency.
Outcome Orientation	Focuses on system visibility and structural clarity.	Focuses on cognitive accessibility and interpretive clarity.	Both mitigate risks associated with algorithmic opacity.

Explainability contributes to transparency by clarifying decision logic and a system may be transparent in terms of documentation and governance without offering decision-level explanations. It may provide post-hoc explanations without fully disclosing the underlying data practices. Therefore, explainability can be considered as a subset of transparency.

2.3.1 Role of AI Transparency in Building Consumer Trust

AI transparency plays a pivotal role in fostering consumer trust. Since AI has become an integral part of products, services, marketing and decision making, consumers often view AI systems as a black-box with suspicion. Consumers are worried about concerns over privacy, bias, fairness and errors of data are the major issues. Transparency AI resolves these issues through informed choices, reduced biasness and ethical responsibility. The fundamental roles played by AI transparency are as follows:

Maintaining privacy and data concerns

AI transparency ensures that user's information is managed ethically and responsibly. Such assurance positively drives active consumer engagement, particularly in sharing their personal data for personalized product or services. Loss of data control through AI has become a serious concern among the consumers. A survey shows that 56% adults in the USA are worried about AI data and privacy violation (Drenik, 2025). In this respect, transparency build trust among the consumers if organizations disclose their data usage practices. Even consumers switch brand for greater transparency even though it costs them higher. Studies also found that transparency mediates higher data sharing intentions among consumers (Hu, & Min, 2025; Masood et al., 2023).

Reducing the bias and unfairness

AI transparency discloses the decision-making process, data sources, bias mitigation steps and relevant performance metrics, which allows users to evaluate reliability and detect the potential sources of discrimination and bias. Consequently, the opacity perception regarding the AI is reduced. Consumers view bias as a major concern in advertisement. Transparent system encounters these concerns. Consumers perceive transparent AI as a more objective and unbiased than advertisement contents or influencer contents. AI systems transparency initiatives can improve perceived trustworthiness significantly. In recommendation systems, this posters confidence as AI serves users fairly rather than discriminating among the users.

Promoting accountability and informed consent

AI transparency values open communication of potential risk, such as bias, errors, mistakes and misuse. Through open communication companies enable users to understand the outputs, verify results and provide meaningful consent. Such open communication and informed consent shift users from passive suspicion to active engagement. A survey revealed that 61.3% consumers in America expects companies should disclose AI generated contents being used for marketing purpose (Liederman, 2025). Therefore, AI transparency builds informed consent of the consumers by openly explaining why and why particular outcome occurs and reducing the surprises. Therefore, transparency promotes accountability leading to higher ethical perception and reduced aversion among consumers.

Enhancing adoption and loyalty

Transparent AI systems reduce use barriers and encourage experimentation. It also improves sustained engagement with tools and services. If users understand and trust AI system, they are more willing to adopt the systems and stays loyal to the systems. As a results. Suers prioritize the transparent service providers over competitors. A consumer insight report shows that over 60% consumers trust AI systems when they are transparent BCG (2026). Consumers are willing to pay higher for transparent systems (Hunka et al., 2025). Transparency acts as a mediator in trust formation process and boosts adoption in regular activities like shopping (Nguyen, & Nguyen, 2025). Hence, transparency creates competitive advantages and higher conversion rates.

2.3.2 *Why transparency and explainability in AI matters*

In consumer engagement, transparency builds consumer trust and engagement by reducing perceptions of manipulation and unfairness. In AI-mediated consumer interactions, opacity can lead to skepticism, reduced adoption, data privacy concerns and brand switching tendency. Consumers view AI related risk as serious issue and switch brands for more visibility and transparency. Trust enables more personalization and innovation. Unless, AI's potential in consumer engagement remains limited. Hence, transparency AI significantly influence consumer engagement, emphasizing the key drivers of Transparency AI. The EU AI act's article 50 mandates that providers and developers of AI systems make sure that users understand AI systems when they are using the AI tools (Luengo, 2025). It will also label the IA generated contents and provides the explanations for emotional recognition and biometric systems. This involves machine-readable marking for synthetic content and user notification unless exempted (Luengo, 2025). Different public and industry discussions emphasize transparency as a perquisite for adoption in trust-sensitive sectors. In future, AI transparency will reduce low quality AI contents.

2.3.3 *Benefits of XAI for engagement, personalization and ethical practices*

XAI enhances consumer engagement through improved perceived fairness. It leads to higher adoption in consumer facing systems. XAI builds consumer trust and enhances interaction with AI tools through makings AI decisions more transparent to the users (Anderson, 2025). This transparency fosters greater use intentions among consumers. Therefore, AI tools improves innovation and business growth through improved engagement. Similarly, in personalization, XAI supports ethical approaches by exposing potential biases in recommendation systems (Alzoubi et al., 2025). XAI allows for correction and refinements to fit with the consumer preferences. Most e-commerce bossiness users XAI to explain why a specific product is being recommended and refine she personalization approaches through transparency (Alzoubi et al., 2025). Consequently, XAI not only improves the relevance of personalized contents but also allows with consumer demands. XAI promotes accountability, fairness and bias detection by providing interpretable insights into model decision. It enables users to mitigate hidden bias and ensure trust in AI systems (Carr, Ross, & Arrison, 2025). Overall, the benefits include improved decision-making for users and organizations, while increasing consumer loyalty through trust-building a, consumer satisfaction and enhanced adoption rates.

2.4 Ethical governance and responsible AI

Ethical governance involves ensuring proper oversight ensuring fairness, accountability and privacy. On the other hand, responsible AI operationalizes these via appropriate practices and principles (Gianni, Lehtinen, & Nieminen, 2022). In consumer engagement, core principles of responsible AI in marketing and consumer engagement guide the use of personal data used for personalization (Dixit, & Singh, 2025). Responsible AI in marketing and consumer engagement prioritizes fairness, non-discrimination, data minimization and human oversight. To ensure these practices responsible AI deployment involves following principles:

Accountability and governances: Accountability are the establishment of clear governance mechanism. Through accountability AI system clearly communicate who is responsible for AI deployment and outcomes. Organizations and development must take the responsibility for the AI outcomes (Gunasekara, et al., 2025). It emphasizes the clear approaches for oversight, auditing and human accountability. This requires ethics board, risk assessment and proper regulation.

Privacy and data protection: AI must respect user privacy through data minimization, informed consent and compliance with data protection lays (Kolluru, 2025). It prioritizes protecting personal information and preventing unauthorized misuse of user data. In marketing, responsible AI fosters unethical consumer profiling and focuses on privacy across the AI lifecycles (Kolluru, 2025).

Fairness and non-discrimination: AI marketing tools must deliver equitable outcomes across diverse audiences. All kinds of biases must be addressed to exclude target groups based on demographics, ethnicity, gender and socioeconomic factors. This involves auditing training datasets for representation. It must also ensure inclusive personalization that respects cultural sensitivities and promotes diversity in contents and recommendations (Nelson et al., 2025).

Transparency and explainability: Marketers should make AI-enabled decisions understandable to consumers and other stakeholders. This includes disclosing when content is AI generated and explaining AI recommendation logic. Transparency builds trust and differentiates brands in the era of growing consumer skepticism.

Adoption of these principles transforms AI from a potential risk to a competitive advantage. It fosters higher engagement and loyalty, reduces legal and financial risks, and ethical practices.

3. CONCEPTUAL FRAMEWORK

This Chapter illustrates a conceptual framework on how the outcome of consumer trust is mediated by the AI-mediated consumer engagement via the mediating effects of the transparency mechanisms and ethical AI governance.

Figure 2. Conceptual Framework for AI-Mediated Consumer Engagement

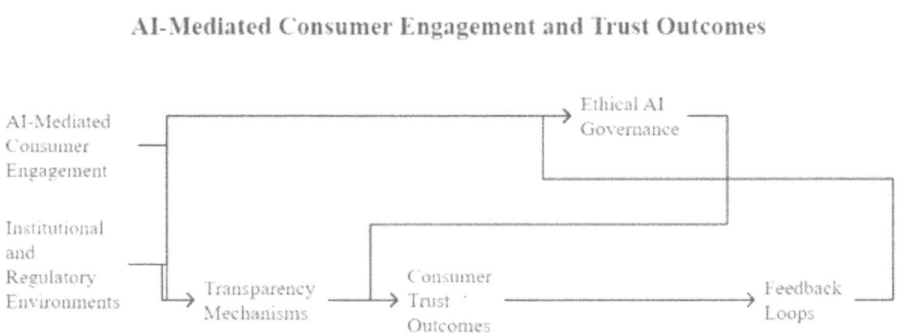

AI-oriented consumer interactions include algorithmic personalization, autopilot interactions of services as well as data-based decision support that creates consumer experiences. Transparency mechanisms are considered organizational processes that help make AI systems explainable and challengeable to consumers through exposing automated decision-making, explainable AI interfaces, and access to data practices. Ethical AI governance denotes organizational frameworks and procedures by which equitability, duty, confidentiality, and surveillance permeate the AI cycle. It is hypothesized that the conditions under which AI-mediated engagement competences either reinforce or diminish consumer trust are determined by transparency and ethical governance and are viewed as confidence in the reliability, fairness, and integrity of AI-mediated engagements. Feedback loops between the results of trust and the practice of governance are also included in the model to emphasize on organizational learning and adaptation over time, and moderating effects of institutional and regulatory environments on the strength and direction of the relationships.

The Conceptual Framework was chosen because it suggests that these ideas are intimately linked and rely on each other mutually. The idea behind the Conceptual Framework is that it argues that these concepts are closely connected and cannot exist independently or without the other (Dahlin, 2025).

Although a great amount of research was done on the topic of AI use, the current literature mainly does not address trust, transparency and ethics as the three interdependent phenomena in the context of the consumer-AI relationships. It is such fragmentation that constrains the knowledge of how these constructs be work in combination to influence consumer reactions to AI-mediated engagement. As an illustration, the mobile phone research on trust in AI focuses on providing psychological and contextual aspects of how acceptance is impacted but frequently fails to combine the mechanism of transparency practices or governance bodies into a single approach to illustrate consumer outcome results (Baron, 2025).

To fill this gap, we put forward an integrative framework, which gives conceptualizes the idea of AI-mediated consumer interaction and its impact on the results of trust through the influences of transparency mechanisms (e.g., explainability practices) and ethical governance frameworks (e.g., responsible AI policies). This jacket technology fits the developmental literature on responsible AI governance statement which stipulates that one can be reliant on AI due to technical explicability as well as organizational solutions that enforce ethical values throughout the AI life cycle (Papagiannidis et al., 2025).

4. DISCUSSIONS

4.1 Core Constructs of the Framework

4.1.1 AI-Mediated Consumer Engagement

AI-mediated consumer engagement is defined as the mechanisms that consumers interact with companies mediated by algorithmic systems, including personalization in the form of recommendation algorithms, the use of automated service bots, or consumer predictive profiling. The systems influence decision routes and experiences which in most circumstances are not directly controlled by humans and create both opportunities as well as challenges (Huynh & Aichner, 2025).

Practically, AI-mediated interaction contributes to greater efficiency and customization, but may result in a perceived prominence, or obscurity, of information and consumer asymmetry which cannot be trusted without the inclusion of clear communications and responsible behaviors practices (Glassberg et al., 2025). Detailed mapping of AI mediated consumer engagement can be described with the following figure 3.

Figure 3. Cycle of AI-Mediated Consumer Engagement

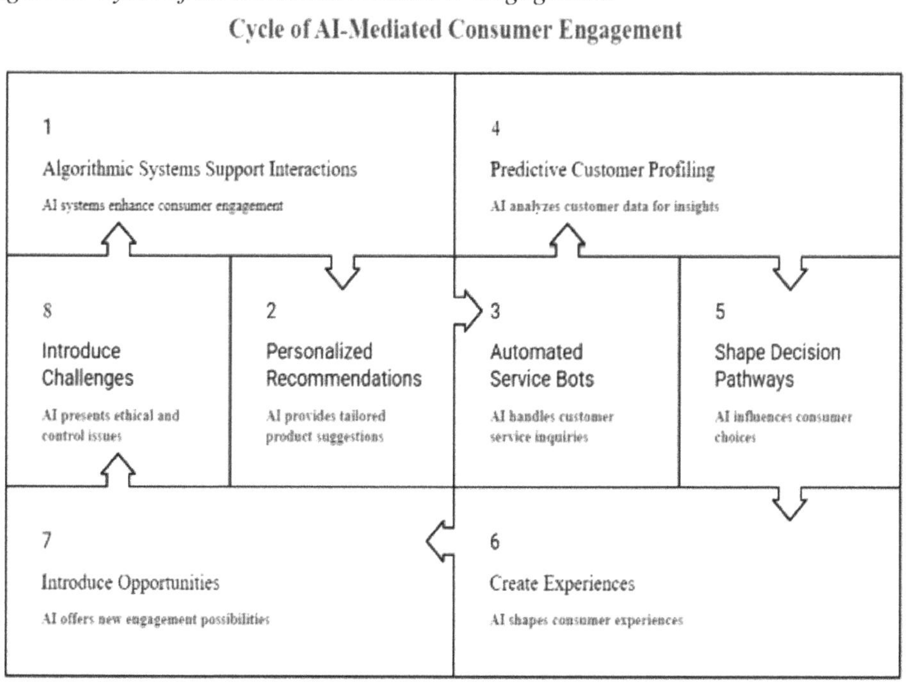

The figure 3 represents a multi-phase process of consumer interaction mediated by AI systems, which represents the gradually evolving form of AI-system mediated interactions, experiences and decision-making within a chain of interdependent processes.

The systematic arrangement helps to highlight the fact that consumer interaction with AI is determined by repeating cycles but not individual episodes. The starts point of the cycle is the interactions that are supported by the algorithmic systems, and the AI promotes engagement by organizing digital touchpoints, ensuring easy access to services, optimization of the flow of interactions. This comes with uploaded suggestions, where AI pushes product or content suggestions on the basis of user information and what they infuse is preferred. The second step is automated service bots, which is the distribution of customer relationships on the AI-based platform and intermediation between inquiries with its help and comprehensive support in real-time. Predictive customer profiling is an aspect of AI interaction that includes the analytical aspect of customer interaction, by which the customer data is absorbed and projected into behavioral predictive patterns.

These lessons are inputted into the formation of decision paths, where AI informs the decisions available to users and design choice schemes. Stages of create experiences represent the more experience-wide influence of AI, since system outputs influence the greatest consumer experience per platform and service. The introduction of new forms of engagement and value creation made possible by AI-driven personalization and automation are additionally brought into focus by the cycle. Lastly, introduce challenges are the ethical, social, and control-based conflicting situations raised by AI mediation, such as autonomy issues, transparency issues, and accountability issues. The cyclic structure emphasizes the fact that opportunities and challenges are constantly reciprocated into the next phases of interaction, and the way the interaction mediated by AI will evolve with time.

4.1.2 Transparency Mechanisms

Transparency mechanisms are organizational practices that render AI behavior, data processing and decision logic understandable to the consumers. This contains explainable AI (XAI) schemes, reporting on the use of AI, and articulate data laws. Transparency is also a well-known dimension to the requirements of trust in AI systems, especially in consumer situations (Cetinkaya et al., 2025).

The transparency should however extend beyond disclosure, but be meaningful and available to non-technical users. It has been found that poor transparency, which includes technical explanation, can do no good in establishing trust and can even spoil consumers. Building trust through transparency can be more visualized (see figure 4).

Figure 4. Building Trust through Transparency (Author's contribution)

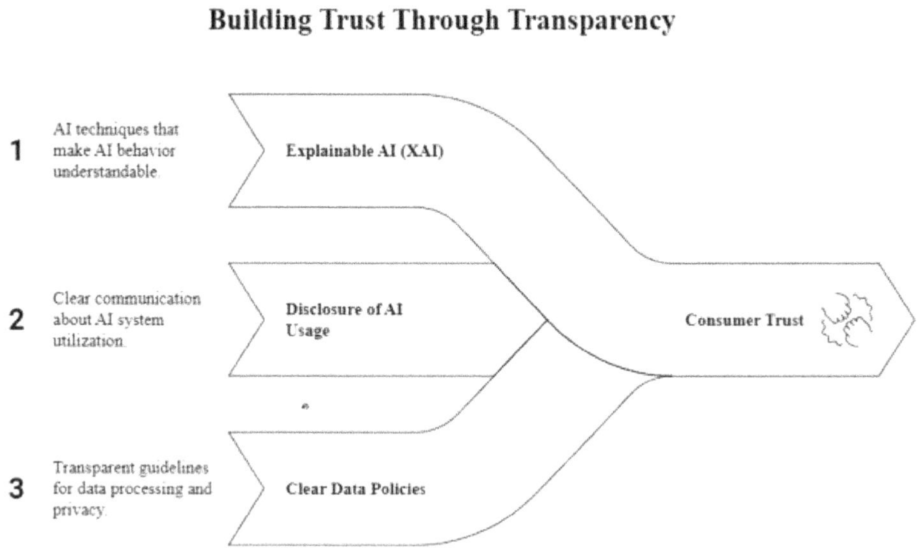

The above figure 4 demonstrates several practices related to the concept of transparency that form a whole consumer trust of AI-enabled systems. The diagram represents three separates yet overlapping paths that result to a common outcome, consumer trust, and highlights that the development of trust comes through the connotation of the efforts associated with technical, communicative, and governance. Pathway one indicates explainable artificial intelligence (XAI), which is a grouping of AI methods that aim to interpret the behavior, suggestions, and choices of systems to users. The aspect highlights the need to enhance interpretability and user-friendly explanations in perceived decrease of the opacities and promote meaningful interactions.

The second direction, disclosure of AI use, relates to the necessity of the clarity of communication regarding the involvement of AI systems with service delivery or decision-making mechanisms. This aspect makes transparency on the interactional level prominent, which is to make sure that users know the presence and contribution of automation to the course of outcomes.

The third avenue concentrates on clear data policies, which mean clear-cut rules on how data is collected, processed, and stored and privately. This aspect brings out the importance of the data governance in influencing user trust, especially in terms of the belief of fairness, security, and ethical management of personal data. These three pathways converge directly into consumer trust, bringing a visual representation that trust is not created by one intervention, but it is done through the joint application of explainability, disclosure and responsible data governance practices.

4.1.3 Ethical Governance of AI

Ethical governance is a set of structures, policies, and processes, which facilitate the development and deployment of AI systems in manners that embrace the aspects of fairness and accountability, privacy, and the rights of stakeholders. An overall analysis of responsible AI governance can find the principles and practices that allow organizations to apply ethics throughout the AI lifecycle, designing and monitoring (Papagiannidis et al., 2025).

Ethical governance is theorized as an organizational capacity, which offers long-term legitimacy and risk management through entrenchment on fairness and accountability in AI. This governance makes it less likely to expose unwanted harms and the plausibility of transparency mechanisms.

Figure 5. Ethical AI governance Cycle (Author's contribution)

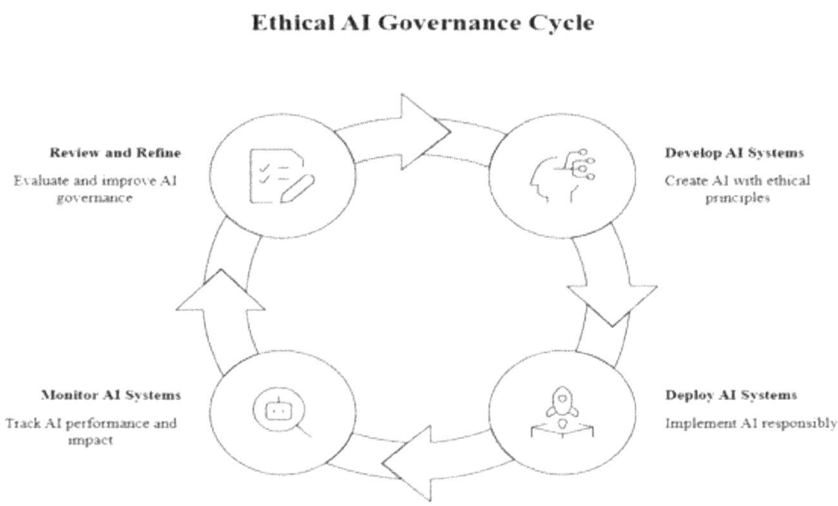

This figure 5 formalizes ethical AI governance as a continuous, cyclic procedure consisting of four mutually supporting phases, namely, creating AI systems, responsibly deploying AI systems, monitoring AI systems, and revising and improving governance practices. The circular form is a sign that ethical governance is not a situational exercise that is carried out during the design phase, but a perpetual process that goes through throughout the lifecycle of the AI systems. The stage of development focuses on integrating ethical principles, values and shields in the system design and training of the models. This will involve factors like the reduction of bias, fairness and compliance with normative and regulatory requirements. Deployment stage involves the accountable deployment of AI systems to practical environments with regard to the requirement of operational controls, user protection, and accountability of organizational implementation and use.

Monitoring phase will be the continuous evaluation of AI performance, behavior and implications on society following the deployment of AI. This aspect is characteristic of the need to identify performance decline, unintended consequences, or, emerging risks as time goes on. The last process is review and refine which focuses on systematic assessment of governance structures, policies and technical controls which will result in repeated enhancement on the design of the systems, as well as on institutional controls. These steps all put forward a picture of governance as a reflexive process that changes according to technological change, contextual utilization, and stakeholder feedback.

4.1.4 Consumer Trust Outcomes

Consumer trust outcomes present the degree of belief of the consumers on AI-mediated interactions, which include the belief that AI systems are reliable, prudent, and can serve the interests of consumers. Trust is a complex concept, where cognitive trust (belief in inability) and social/ethical trust (belief in fairness and integrity within the system) can be referred to. Empirical research underscores that perceived transparency and fairness are a major source of trust especially where ethical data practices are realized through effective communication.

Figure 6. Consumer Trust Outcomes in AI-Mediated Interaction (Author's contribution)

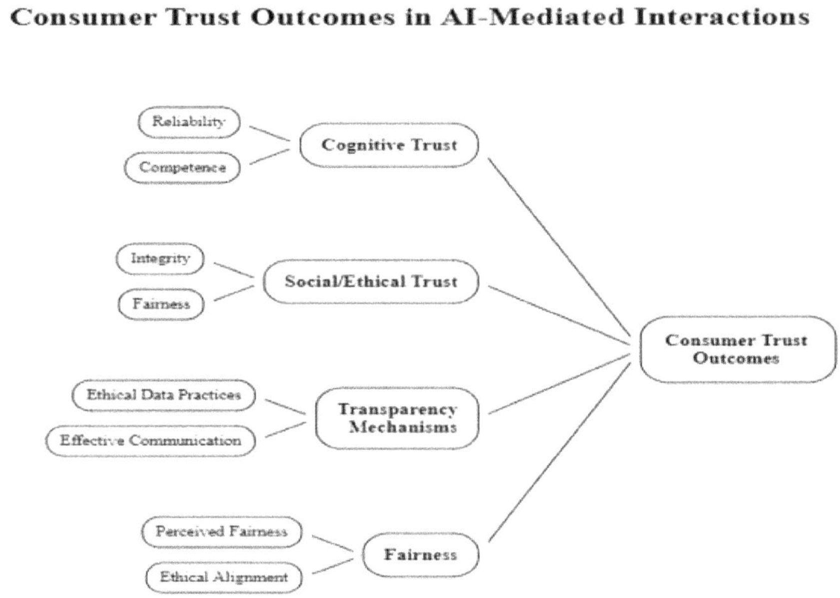

This figure 6 reflects the outcome of consumer trust as the summarization of various dimensions of trust combined to enhance user judgments of AI-mediated interactions. The figure also relates graphically four main constructs which include cognitive trust, social and ethical trust, transparency mechanisms, and fairness to the overall consumer trust outcomes, and it is important to emphasize that trust is formed multidimensionally. Cognitive trust is also presented based on the impression of reliability and competency, which are the judgments of system precision, dependability, and technical reliability. The issue of social and ethical trust can be connected to the practices of integrity and fairness, the role of moral alignment, ethical behaviors, and the perceived legitimacy of AI-enabled services.

The transparency mechanisms are also linked with the ethical data practices and proper communication that suggest that trust is enhanced when the users are aware of the manner in which the data are utilized and the manner in which the decisions are conveyed. Fairness is modeled based on the perceived fairness and ethical alignment whereby the sensitivity of the users to distributive and procedural justice is crucial towards AI-driven processes. The interdependence of these dimensions in their coming to a state of consumer trust highlights the fact that trust is formed through the interplay of technical performance, ethical behavior, open communicative behavior and a sense of fairness and not a singular factor.

4.2 Relationships among Constructs

The proposed framework posits that:

- The impact of the engagement, conducted with the help of AI, on consumer trust is indirect and mediated by transparency and the ethical management.
- Transparency increases perception of fairness and this facilitates trust - but transparency activities need to be packaged to consumer level of understanding in order to succeed.
- Ethical governance creates the reputation of the seriousness of transparency by indicating organizational sincerity towards fairness, responsibility, and consumer rights.
- Ethical norms and principles (e.g., EU AI Act, data protection laws), also influence the organizational interests and standards regarding responsible AI practices.

4.2.1 Trust as a Construct in AI Engagement

One of the key factors of consumer interaction with AI systems is trust. It is influenced by the consumer perceptions of the behavior of the system and organizational practices that offer guarantees of reliability and ethical behavior. It has also been found out that performance alone only does not contribute to trust but transparency and being fair and perceived accountable contribute to trust. On a personal example, empirical studies demonstrate that when expectations of the users are taken into account, transparency boosts their perceived understanding and trust, and that expectancy is necessary to make explainability dynamic to the level of user experience (Cetinkaya et al., 2025).

4.2.2 Transparency as a Necessary but Complex Enabler

Transparency is also favored as a trust building mechanism in AI interactions. Nonetheless, recent studies also unveil intricacies: just the information about the use of AI may decrease the level of trust in the opposite direction, unless it is accompanied by actions like the provision of appropriate explanations based on the needs of the users. This dilemma on transparency brings out the fact that transparency should be context specific and strategic, but not procedural (e.g. compliance with regulations) to be trust enhancing.

4.2.3 Ethical Governance and Organizational Legitimacy

Ethical governance is also a strategic ability that enhances trust because it entrenches ethical deliberations like fairness and accountability in AI implementation. Responsible AIT Governance Research has shown that governance practices, including bias-reduction, audit, and ethics review boards, promote the wider organization legitimacy and consumer trust.

It is essential to implement AI within broader regulatory and institutional frameworks such as UNESCO. Several international organizations have already introduced ethical principles and regulatory standards to ensure transparency, accountability, fairness and autonomy of AI systems. For example, OECD has developed AI principles promoting trustworthy AI, the European Commission has initiated EU Artificial Intelligence Act to establish risk-based governance mechanisms and the UNESCO has maintained global ethical guidelines encouraging responsible AI deployment across different sectors. These international institutions frameworks play an important role in mitigating ethical risks and bias and promoting responsible AI use and innovation.

4.2.4 Contextual Variation in Trust Dynamics

The chapter has a structure, which allows it to describe variations between contexts in terms of trust dynamics. An example is the highly controlled industry or a culture that has strong standards of fairness may require more transparency and ethical protection in place prior to building up trust. On the other hand, reduced regulated environments can be more focused on performance results. All these differences indicate that organizations have to adjust transparency and governance policies to the demands of those locations and the conventional practices in that industry (Cetinkaya et al., 2025; Papagiannidis et al., 2025).

5 IMPLICATIONS

5.1 Theoretical Implications

The chapter can add to the current literature by progressive development of a multi-theoretical approach to consumer trust formation through AI. The proposed framework combines the findings of the views of technology acceptance theory, trust in automation and the institutional governance theory to expand on the previous studies that quite often have looked at these constructs independently.

To begin with, the framework extends the existing technology adoption models to include the factors of transparency mechanisms and ethical governance as the key aspects of perception by users. Although previous frameworks like the Technology Acceptance Model rely majorly on perceived usefulness and ease of use (Davis, 1989), the present study suggests that in AI mediated settings, explainability and accountability are equally important in influencing user attitudes.

Second, the chapter expands the body of literature in relation to trust in automation because the conceptualization of trust is that trust is a multidimensional phenomenon that encompasses cognitive, ethical, and system-level trust. Previous studies make it clear that reliability and predictability form the basis of trusting automated systems (Lee & See, 2004), but it is also evident that the framework proposes that the role of establishing trust in automated systems is equally played by the provision of ethical structures of governance.

Thirdly, the framework offers a more comprehensive view of the role of institutional perspectives in consumer trust by making use of a broader approach of how organizational legitimacy and governance mechanisms are related. Institutional theory holds that the institutions become legitimized when they conform to social norms and expectations (DiMaggio & Powell, 1983). This paper deepens this point by demonstrating how not only is ethical artificial intelligence administration a regulative necessity, but also a powerful trust-building propagandum in the digital realm (Glikson & Woolley, 2020).

In general, the framework is relevant to the theory being able to provide a framework of an integrated, holistic model that ties technological interaction, transparency, governance, and outcomes of the trust within the AI-enabled ecosystems.

5.2 Managerial Implications

The findings on trust, transparency and ethics in AI mediated consumer engagement have several important managerial implications for organizations, consumers, employees, investors and society.

5.2.1 Implication for Organization

Organizations which use AI- based personalized systems and automatic customer services should focus on fairness, autonomy, explainability and data protection to keep customer's trust. This strategy should be embedded in the organizational strategy at all management levels. First, when organization can maintain good transparent communication regarding algorithms decision making and data collection of the consumers among the managers, they can increase credibility and reduce privacy concern of the consumers (Grewal et al., 2019). Second, managers should implement explainable AI that gives simple and user-friendly recommendations or personalization and clear data dashboard. transparency system should be interactive or continuous rather than legal bounded.

Third, managers should establish AI ethics committee, cross-functional governance and internal audit that helps to reduce algorithms bias and risks (Panchal & Panchal, 2025). This AI related governance enhances organizational trust, signals and transparency to customers. Fourth, organization should emphasize ethical data collection practices. Responsible data collection from customers such as consent and anonymized management and secure storage directly influences customer trust (Beldad et al., 2010). They should maintain global standard of data collection which helps to cultivate ethical practices beyond ethical requirement that subsequently gives the sources of competitive advantage. Fifth, organizations should arrange program of consumer education regarding AI literacy.

It helps to make customers understand how AI helps to control interactions by providing tutorials about transparent communication importance (Luo et al., 2019). In developing countries like Bangladesh, digital transformation is getting accelerated, this awareness programs can reduce skepticism and increase long term engagement. Sixth, managers should utilize hybrid collaboration methods where AI and human can help customer jointly rather than full automation. AI can solve complex problems and human can deal the interaction where emotional engagement and accountability is needed (Huang & Rust, 2018).

Therefore, both interactions ensure consumers' trust in cases of system error. Finally, managers should monitor ethical performance metrics with financial metrics. Metrics such as fairness score, complaints ratio, customer satisfaction of AI interaction and trust index can improve customer's trust. Integrating ethical AI metrics with sustainability framework increase stakeholders' confidence (Floridi et al., 2018).

5.2.2 Implication for Customers

AI mediated customer engagement significantly influences customer experiences by getting personalized recommendation systems and automatic services. But this experience mostly depends on how trust, transparency and ethical governance are implemented. Trust is the basic components of AI where AI driven decision helps them to take decisions regarding purchasing, pricing and service delivery if they consider the system more reliable, fair and accountable (McKnight et al., 2011).

When they consider the system lack of explainability, customers' trust is declining and leads to negative brand reputation.

Additionally, transparency plays an important role in changing customers' perception of trust. Now customers are more interested to know how their data are collected, stored, processed and disseminated among others. These clear explanation of data uses and practices ensure transparency that subsequently strengthen trusts (Martin, 2018). AI driven decision empower customers to make informed decisions and mitigate uncertainty (Shin, 2021). Without this transparency, customers are more likely to be manipulated and undermined by long-term engagement. Similarly, ethical AI practices enhance customer welfare by giving fair prices, personalized services and accessibility that safeguard customers rights and ensure customer trust (Floridi et al., 2018).

5.2.3 Implication for Employees

The integration of AI into customer engagement influences organizational employees' roles, responsibilities and ethical concerns. When organizations employ chatbot, analytics and automatic tools for customers, employees should navigate these tools to ensure trust, transparency and ethical practices. Firstly, employees require digital training to keep themselves competent. Employees should understand how customers' data are collected, processed and stored and how these data or algorithms help them to make decisions. These training reduces biased practices and increases customer trust (Rai, 2020). Secondly, Transparent AI system empower employees to support organizational policy, reduce ambiguity by giving accurate and honest information to the customers (Shin, 2021). Thirdly, trust in AI also affects employees' engagements by increasing perceived autonomy and job satisfaction. They feel less fear of job displacement and promote trust in internal activities. Finally, employee must operate within the ethical AI governance framework which gives clear guidelines regarding data privacy, fairness and accountability (Rai, 2020). by working within this framework, they are protected from the blame from system error and satisfied with the working a culture with innovation.

5.2.4 Implication for Investors

Organization employing AI-driven customers engagement, trusts, predictive analytics increase their brand reputation and long-term value (Pasquale, 2015). Similarly, investors are drastically shifting their attention from economic gain to the sustainable quality of the systems. AI transparency also reduces the information asymmetry and increases confidence among investors to invest money. They can collect all types of information easily, process them and can take decisions in intensive data sectors such as ecommerce sector. They assess firm AI risk management systems by making portfolio decisions. Moreover, they consider ethical AI practices as an intangible asset that makes strong customer relationships and also flow continuous future revenue.

5.2.5 Implication for Society

If AI mediates the relationship between customers and business, societal trust is established in digital ecosystems (Teepapal, 2025). It increases empowerment of people, access to information and creates intensive digital markets. Transparent systems such as clear data usages helps citizens to take appropriate decisions and create more accountability. Additionally, ethical AI framework emphasizes fairness and autonomy to create social justice. It focuses on regular auditing, stakeholder participation and regulation practices to prevent harm. Finally, strong data collection policies and AI ethical practices promote cultural trust and encourage citizens to work with digital platforms.

5.3 Policy Implications

As AI has changed customer decision making process by introducing personalization and digital interaction, trust, transparency and AI mediated customer engagement have become key components in policymaker concern. For policymakers, encouraging trust among the customers must require strong regulatory framework that ensures fairness, autonomy and data protection (Grewal et al., 2019). Additionally, they should cope with the global standard of data protection regarding automated profiling and customized pricing systems. Policymakers can adopt AI risk based regulatory frameworks where all the sectors such as healthcare, finance, e-commerce are mandatory to maintain this framework (Lemon & Verhoef, 2016). Policy makers encourage industry-wide ethical standards, certification schemes that cultivate sustainable trust and promoting responsible AI-driven market growth.

6. LIMITATIONS AND FUTURE DIRECTIONS

The table below 2 shows the limitations that were found when completing this study and also represents how these limitations could be incorporated into future research.

Table 2. A list of Limitations and Future Directions of this Book Chapter

Dimension	Limitations	Future Research Directions
Conceptual	Here, trust, transparency and AI ethics are used as independent variables in AI mediated consumer engagement. This limits explanatory power for theoretical integration	Future research could be integrated all variables into one single framework. Structural Equation modelling and multi-level modelling could enhance this integrated theory.
Application of AI mediated Consumer Engagement	This study focus on only AI applications (e.g. chatbots or recommendation systems) rather than full application of AI mediated customer engagement using different applications. The data has been collected once.	Investigate trust formation across the entire AI-driven customer lifecycle (awareness, interaction, purchase, post-purchase). Longitudinal research can assess trust sustainability over repeated AI interactions. Future research could incorporate all the applications of AI so that full application results can be gotten. Additionally, longitudinal data of this application can be collected.
Trust Measurement Items	Trust items are measured using self-constructed items which does not reflect the actual behavior of the trust.	Behavioral data such as clickstream analytics, per click could be incorporated to identify the actual gap of the trust. Mixed methods can be used to improve the measurement validity.
Transparency Paradox	Transparency does not increase trust because greater transparency increases the possibility of privacy concern. This study fails to give actual boundaries.	Need to include more moderating variables such as AI literacy, perceived risk and trust in this context .Experimental research can determine the boundaries of the transparency.
Ethical AI Governance Practices	Responsible AI is important in all levels of the organization but empirical studies on this feasibility are limited.	Case Studies and field studies could be incorporate to determine the actual importance of implementing responsible AI.
Cross-Cultural Generalizability	This research is based on emerging countries context like Bangladesh that limits the Gener ability.	Comparative cross-national studies to assess how regulatory regimes, cultural norms, and digital literacy affect trust and ethical expectations in AI systems. Cross-national studies could be taken to understand the effect of transparency on consumer trust.
Algorithmic Bias and Fairness	Research often acknowledges bias but lacks empirical evidence on how perceived fairness directly impacts consumer engagement outcomes. This study found the algorithms bias or fairness but did not its empirical evidence of how this bias or fairness impact on consumer trust.	Future studies could develop bias or fairness items to validate their impact on trust.

continued on following page

Table 2. Continued

Dimension	Limitations	Future Research Directions
Internal Organizational Culture and Ethics	This study has low focus on internal organizational mechanisms to develop customers' trusts.	Different constructs such as ethical leadership, organizational R and D budgets could be incorporated in customer trust outcome.
Long-Term Trust Sustainability	This study focuses on short-term trust. But how long-term trust could be affected remains unexplored.	Future research could be undertaken into how trust can be changed if AI implementation will not go well.

7. CONCLUSION

The key to successful consumer engagement via AI is trust. The feeling of the obscure, biased, or intrusive AI systems results in the loss of consumer confidence, loss of engagement, and mistrust. The way forward in sustainable AI implementation, in its turn, is associated with the creation of reliability and credibility, and not just the introduction of sophisticated algorithms. Strategic enablers that are required to bring about this trust are transparency and ethical governance. The transparency will ensure that consumers are aware of how it is prepared and how their data are being used and this will eradicate doubt and create trust. Ethical governance integrates fairness, accountability as well as protection of privacy in the running of organizations whereby, responsible conducts are maintained at all times. With the integration of intelligent technologies, proper communication, and management, organizations could build a stronger consumer relationship. It is also means of attaining long term loyalty and sustainable value.

Ultimately, the digital markets will not be successfully applied through AI based on its technical competence but on how it can be employed in a responsible way. Those organizations that value trust, transparency and ethical governance turn AI into something more than an efficiency or personalization tool. It is feasible, socially accountable and strategic asset that will result in long term consumer trust and lifetime participation. These are not only applied to individual organizations but also create a benchmark to the broader digital landscape, responsible innovation, protection of consumer rights and a promotion of societal good. As AI continues to develop, firms that have embedded ethics and transparency in their AI policies will find it easier to surmount the obstacles that come along their way. It will also be in a position of establishing strong customer relationship and establishing a competitive edge. Also, with the fusion of technology and good governance, AI can bring efficiency and long-term satisfaction, integrity, and value to businesses and the society at large.

REFERENCES

Acatrinei, C., Apostol, I. G., Barbu, L. N., Chivu, R. G., & Orzan, M. C. (2025). Artificial intelligence in digital marketing: Enhancing consumer engagement and supporting sustainable behavior through social and mobile networks. *Sustainability, 17*(14), 6638. DOI: 10.3390/su17146638

Adamopoulou, E., & Moussiades, L. (2020, May). An overview of chatbot technology. In *IFIP international conference on artificial intelligence applications and innovations* (pp. 373–383). Springer International Publishing., DOI: 10.1007/978-3-030-49186-4_31

Akdemir, D. M., & Bulut, Z. A. (2024). Business and customer-based chatbot activities: The role of customer satisfaction in online purchase intention and intention to reuse chatbots. *Journal of Theoretical and Applied Electronic Commerce Research, 19*(4), 2961–2979. DOI: 10.3390/jtaer19040142

Aluri, A., Price, B. S., & McIntyre, N. H. (2019). Using machine learning to co-create value through dynamic customer engagement in a brand loyalty program. *Journal of Hospitality & Tourism Research (Washington, D.C.), 43*(1), 78–100. DOI: 10.1177/1096348017753521

Alzoubi, H. M., Shameem, B., Mushtaq, S., Al Kurdi, B., Joghee, S., & Hamadneh, S. (2025). Unveiling the role of artificial intelligence: Navigating personalized content marketing, customer engagement, and commitment with data transparency and security. *International Review of Management and Marketing, 15*(2), 343–355. DOI: 10.32479/irmm.18499

Amin, M. R. M., Asbi, A., Sivakumaran, V. M., Kim, J., & Septiarini, E. (2025). Artificial Intelligence (AI) adoption in marketing strategies: Navigating the present and shaping the future business landscape. *Social Sciences & Humanities Open, 12*, 102048. DOI: 10.1016/j.ssaho.2025.102048

Anderson, J. (2025). Leveraging Explainable AI to Enhance Consumer Insight Models in Real-Time Surveys. *International Journal of Emerging Research in Engineering and Technology*, 102-112. DOI: 10.63282/3050-922X.ICRCEDA25-113

Baberwal, S. K., Shelke, N. A., & Anwar, K. (2025). Systematic review of recent advances in multimodal sentiment analysis. *Discover Computing, 28*(1), 270. DOI: 10.1007/s10791-025-09727-7

Bahangulu, J. K., & Owusu-Berko, L. (2025). Algorithmic bias, data ethics, and governance: Ensuring fairness, transparency and compliance in AI-powered business analytics applications. *World Journal of Advanced Research and Review*, *25*(2), 1746–1763. DOI: 10.30574/wjarr.2025.25.2.0571

Balasubramaniam, N., Kauppinen, M., Rannisto, A., Hiekkanen, K., & Kujala, S. (2023). Transparency and explainability of AI systems: From ethical guidelines to requirements. *Information and Software Technology*, *159*, 107197. DOI: 10.1016/j.infsof.2023.107197

Baron, S. (2025). Trust, explainability and AI. *Philosophy & Technology*, *38*(1), 4. DOI: 10.1007/s13347-024-00837-6

BCG. (2026). Consumers Trust AI to Buy Better. Brands Need to Move Quickly. Available at: https://www.bcg.com/publications/2026/consumers-trust-ai-to-buy-better-brands-must-adapt

Beldad, A., de Jong, M., & Steehouder, M. (2010). How shall I trust the faceless and the intangible? A literature review on the antecedents of online trust. *Computers in Human Behavior,* 26(5), 857–869. DOI: 10.1016/j.chb.2010.03.013

Binns, R., Veale, M., Van Kleek, M., & Shadbolt, N. (2018). 'It's reducing a human being to a percentage': Perceptions of justice in algorithmic decisions. *Proceedings of the 2018 CHI Conference on Human Factors in Computing Systems,* 1–14. DOI: 10.1145/3173574.3173951

Boldosova, V. (2020). Telling stories that sell: The role of storytelling and big data analytics in smart service sales. *Industrial Marketing Management*, *86*, 122–134. DOI: 10.1016/j.indmarman.2019.12.004

Bozdağ, A. A. (2025). The AI-mediated intimacy economy: A paradigm shift in digital interactions. *AI & Society*, *40*(4), 2285–2306. DOI: 10.1007/s00146-024-02132-6

Camilleri, M. A. (2024). Artificial intelligence governance: Ethical considerations and implications for social responsibility. *Expert Systems: International Journal of Knowledge Engineering and Neural Networks*, *41*(7), e13406. DOI: 10.1111/exsy.13406

Carr, T., Ross, L., & Arrison, M. G. (2025). The Role of AI in Enhancing Customer Trust and Relationship Management in Digital-Only Banks. *Available at SSRN* 5441894. DOI: 10.2139/ssrn.5441894

Cetinkaya, N. E.. (2025). Between transparency and trust: Identifying key factors in algorithmic trust. *Information Systems Journal.* Advance online publication. DOI: 10.1080/0144929X.2025.2533358

Chen, Y., Li, C., Li, J., & Dong, Y. (2026). General trust and intolerance of uncertainty: Disentangling within-and between-person associations. *Personality and Individual Differences, 251*, 113582. DOI: 10.1016/j.paid.2025.113582

Chinnaraju, A. (2025). Explainable AI (XAI) for trustworthy and transparent decision-making: A theoretical framework for AI interpretability. *World Journal of Advanced Engineering Technology and Sciences, 14*(3), 170–207. DOI: 10.30574/wjaets.2025.14.3.0106

Dahish, Z., Miah, S. J., Pandit, A., & Roy, S. K. (2025). Enhancing phygital customer experience through generative AI: A social listening method for strategic retail decision-making. *Journal of Strategic Marketing*, 1–21. DOI: 10.1080/0965254X.2025.2540267

Dahlin, E. (2025). Trust in AI. *AI & Society*, *40*(8), 6089–6095. DOI: 10.1007/s00146-025-02429-0

Dang, Q., & Li, G. (2025). Unveiling trust in AI: The interplay of antecedents, consequences, and cultural dynamics. *AI & Society*, *4*(1), 669–692. DOI: 10.1007/s00146-025-02477-6

Davis, F. D. (1989). Perceived usefulness, perceived ease of use, and user acceptance of information technology. *Management Information Systems Quarterly*, *13*(3), 319–340. DOI: 10.2307/249008

De Bruijn, H., Warnier, M., & Janssen, M. (2022). The perils and pitfalls of explainable AI: Strategies for explaining algorithmic decision-making. *Government Information Quarterly*, *39*(2), 101666. DOI: 10.1016/j.giq.2021.101666

DiMaggio, P. J., & Powell, W. W. (1983). The iron cage revisited: Institutional isomorphism and collective rationality in organizational fields. *American Sociological Review*, *48*(2), 147–160. DOI: 10.2307/2095101

Dixit, P., & Singh, P. B. (2025). AI-Powered Consumer Insights for Sustainable Business Practices: A Literature Review on Ethical Marketing and Green Consumerism. *Journal of Indian Institute for Engineering*, *4*, 28.

Drenik, G. (2025). As AI Matures, Consumer Trust Becomes The New Battleground. Available at: https://www.forbes.com/sites/garydrenik/2025/11/06/as-ai-matures-consumer-trust-becomes-the-new-battleground/

Dwivedi, Y. K., Kshetri, N., Hughes, L., Slade, E. L., Jeyaraj, A., Kar, A. K., Baabdullah, A. M., Koohang, A., Raghavan, V., Ahuja, M., Albanna, H., Albashrawi, M. A., Al-Busaidi, A. S., Balakrishnan, J., Barlette, Y., Basu, S., Bose, I., Brooks, L., Buhalis, D., & Wright, R. (2023). Opinion Paper:"So what if ChatGPT wrote it?" Multidisciplinary perspectives on opportunities, challenges and implications of generative conversational AI for research, practice and policy. *International Journal of Information Management*, *71*, 102642. DOI: 10.1016/j.ijinfomgt.2023.102642

El-Geneedy, M., El-Din Moustafa, H., Khater, H., Abd-Elsamee, S., & Gamel, S. A. (2025). A comprehensive explainable AI approach for enhancing transparency and interpretability in stroke prediction. *Scientific Reports*, *15*(1), 26048. DOI: 10.1038/s41598-025-11263-9

Esposito, E. (2022). Transparency versus explanation: The role of ambiguity in legal AI. *Journal of Cross-disciplinary Research in Computational Law*, *1*(2). Advance online publication. DOI: 10.5935/2317-2622/direitomackenzie.v16n315705

Flavián, C., Ibáñez-Sánchez, S., & Orús, C. (2019). The impact of virtual, augmented and mixed reality technologies on the customer experience. *Journal of Business Research*, *100*, 547–560. DOI: 10.1016/j.jbusres.2018.10.050

Floridi, L., Cowls, J., Beltrametti, M., Chatila, R., Chazerand, P., Dignum, V., Luetge, C., Madelin, R., Pagallo, U., Rossi, F., Schafer, B., Valcke, P., & Vayena, E. (2018). AI4People—An Ethical Framework for a Good AI Society: Opportunities, Risks, Principles, and Recommendations. *Minds and Machines*, *28*(4), 689–707. DOI: 10.1007/s11023-018-9482-5

Gao, P., Wang, X., Chen, H., Dai, W., & Ling, H. (2021). What is beautiful is not always good: Influence of machine learning-derived photo attractiveness on intention to initiate social interactions in mobile dating applications. *Connection Science*, *33*(2), 321–340. DOI: 10.1080/09540091.2020.1814204

Gianni, R., Lehtinen, S., & Nieminen, M. (2022). Governance of responsible AI: From ethical guidelines to cooperative policies. *Frontiers of Computer Science*, *4*, 873437. DOI: 10.3389/fcomp.2022.873437

Glassberg, I., Ilan, Y. B., & Zwilling, M. (2025). The key role of design and transparency in enhancing trust in AI-powered digital agents. *Journal of Innovation & Knowledge*, *10*(5), 100770. Advance online publication. DOI: 10.1016/j.jik.2025.100770

Glikson, E., & Woolley, A. W. (2020). Human Trust in Artificial Intelligence: Review of Empirical Research. *The Academy of Management Annals*, *14*(2), 627–660. DOI: 10.5465/annals.2018.0057

Grewal, D., Hulland, J., & Karahanna, E. (2019). The future of technology and marketing: A multidisciplinary perspective. *Journal of the Academy of Marketing Science*, *48*(1), 1–8. Advance online publication. DOI: 10.1007/s11747-019-00711-4

Gunasekara, L., El-Haber, N., Nagpal, S., Moraliyage, H., Issadeen, Z., Manic, M., & De Silva, D. (2025). A systematic review of responsible artificial intelligence principles and practice. *Applied System Innovation*, *8*(4), 97. DOI: 10.3390/asi8040097

Haenlein, M., Kaplan, A., Tan, C. W., & Zhang, P. (2019). Artificial intelligence (AI) and management analytics. *Journal of Management Analytics*, *6*(4), 341–343. DOI: 10.1080/23270012.2019.1699876

Hagendorff, T. (2020). The ethics of AI ethics: An evaluation of guidelines. *Minds and Machines*, *30*(1), 99–120. DOI: 10.1007/s11023-020-09517-8

Haque, A., Akther, N., Khan, I., Agarwal, K., & Uddin, N. (2024, October). Artificial intelligence in retail marketing: Research agenda based on bibliometric reflection and content analysis (2000–2023). In *Informatics* (Vol. 11, No. 4, p. 74). MDPI. DOI: 10.3390/informatics11040074

Hidayanti, N. F., Iswanto, D., & Ningsih, N. H. I. (2025). Artificial Intelligence in Personalized Marketing: Strategies for Enhancing Consumer Engagement. *Advance Sustainable Science Engineering and Technology*, *7*(2), 02502014–02502014. DOI: 10.26877/df5dwp69

Hina, M., Islam, N., & Luo, X. R. (2025). Towards sustainable consumption decision-making: Examining the interplay of blockchain transparency and information-seeking in reducing product uncertainty. *Decision Support Systems*, *189*, 114370. DOI: 10.1016/j.dss.2024.114370

Hollebeek, L. D., & Macky, K. (2019). Digital content marketing's role in fostering consumer engagement, trust, and value: Framework, fundamental propositions, and implications. *Journal of Interactive Marketing*, *45*(1), 27–41. DOI: 10.1016/j.intmar.2018.07.003

Hu, Y., & Min, H. K. (2025). Information transparency, privacy concerns, and customers' behavioral intentions regarding AI-powered hospitality robots: A situational awareness perspective. *Journal of Hospitality and Tourism Management*, *63*, 177–184. DOI: 10.1016/j.jhtm.2025.04.003

Huang, M.-H., & Rust, R. T. (2018). Artificial Intelligence in Service. *Journal of Service Research*, *21*(2), 155–172. DOI: 10.1177/1094670517752459

Hunka, A. D., Daniel, A. M., Bour, A., & Boyer, R. H. (2025). Is transparency a good business strategy? Consumer preferences and willingness to pay for information about the chemical content of reused and recycled clothing. *Sustainable Production and Consumption*, *56*, 128–141. DOI: 10.1016/j.spc.2025.03.020

Huynh, M., & Aichner, T. (2025). In generative artificial intelligence we trust: Unpacking determinants and outcomes for cognitive trust. *AI & Society*, *40*(8), 5849–5869. DOI: 10.1007/s00146-025-02378-8

Huynh, T. T., & Khoa, B. T. (2025). The Role of Generative Artificial Intelligence in After-Sales Services: Enhancing Customer Repurchase Behavior Through the SOR Model and Customer Pleasure. In *Applied Artificial Intelligence in Business: Systems, Tools and Techniques* (pp. 403-415). Cham: Springer Nature Switzerland. DOI: 10.1007/978-3-031-90271-0_28

Inavolu, S. M. (2024). Exploring AI-driven customer service: Evolution, architectures, opportunities, challenges and future directions. *International Journal of Engineering and Advanced Technology*, *13*(3), 156–163.

Islam, M. R., Siddika, A., & Shaulin, N. (2025). AI Readiness and Trust in Government: The Context of Bangladesh and India. In *Strengthening Human Relations in Organizations With AI* (pp. 27-58). IGI Global Scientific Publishing.

Jim, J. R., Talukder, M. A. R., Malakar, P., Kabir, M. M., Nur, K., & Mridha, M. F. (2024). Recent advancements and challenges of NLP-based sentiment analysis: A state-of-the-art review. *Natural Language Processing Journal*, *6*, 100059. DOI: 10.1016/j.nlp.2024.100059

Jobin, A., Ienca, M., & Vayena, E. (2019). The global landscape of AI ethics guidelines. *Nature Machine Intelligence*, *1*(9), 389–399. DOI: 10.1038/s42256-019-0088-2

Khatun, M., Bhuiyan, M. R. I., Amin, M. A., Hossen, M., & Mia, M. A. H. (2026). Evaluating E-Commerce Satisfaction: The Impact of Trust, Information Quality, Usability, and Perceived-to-Actual Performance. *SAGE Open*, *16*(1), 21582440261423039. Advance online publication. DOI: 10.1177/21582440261423039

Kinney, M., Anastasiadou, M., Naranjo-Zolotov, M., & Santos, V. (2024). Expectation management in AI: A framework for understanding stakeholder trust and acceptance of artificial intelligence systems. *Heliyon*, *10*(7), E28562. Advance online publication. DOI: 10.1016/j.heliyon.2024.e28562

Kolluru, P. (2025). Responsible AI use in marketing: Navigating ethics and consumer trust. Forbes Agency Council. Available at: https://www.forbes.com/councils/forbesagencycouncil/2025/06/20/responsible-ai-use-in-marketing-navigating-ethics-and-consumer-trust

Kumar, V., Ashraf, A. R., & Nadeem, W. (2024). AI-powered marketing: What, where, and how? *International Journal of Information Management*, *77*, 102783. DOI: 10.1016/j.ijinfomgt.2024.102783

Lee, J. D., & See, K. A. (2004). Trust in automation: Designing for appropriate reliance. *Human Factors*, *46*(1), 50–80. DOI: 10.1518/hfes.46.1.50.30392

Lemon, K. N., & Verhoef, P. C. (2016). Understanding Customer Experience Throughout the Customer Journey. *Journal of Marketing*, *80*(6), 69–96. DOI: 10.1509/jm.15.0420

Liederman, E. (2025). Consumers want AI transparency from media publications. Available at: https://www.emarketer.com/content/consumers-want-ai-transparency-media-publications

Liu, W., Hu, E. W., Su, B., & Wang, J. (2021). Using machine learning techniques for DSP software performance prediction at source code level. *Connection Science*, *33*(1), 26–41. DOI: 10.1080/09540091.2020.1762542

Luengo, J. G. (2025). Transparency Obligations for Providers and Deployers of certain AI Systems. In *The EU regulation on Artificial Intelligence: A commentary* (pp. 361–372). Wolters Kluwers Italia.

Lukyanenko, R., Maass, W., & Storey, V. C. (2022). Trust in artificial intelligence: From a Foundational Trust Framework to emerging research opportunities. *Electronic Markets*, *32*(4), 1993–2020. DOI: 10.1007/s12525-022-00605-4

Luo, X., Tong, S., Fang, Z., & Qu, Z. (2019). Frontiers: Machines vs. Humans: The Impact of Artificial Intelligence Chatbot Disclosure on Customer Purchases. *Marketing Science*, mksc.2019.1192. DOI: 10.1287/mksc.2019.1192

Ma, Z., & Li, B. (2020). A DDoS attack detection method based on SVM and K-nearest neighbour in SDN environment. *International Journal on Computer Science and Engineering*, *23*(3), 224–234. DOI: 10.1504/IJCSE.2020.111431

Madzík, P., Falát, L., Skýpalová, R., Jašušáková, L., & Zimon, D. (2026). ChatGPT in science and research: How generative AI drives innovation and knowledge development. *Journal of Innovation & Knowledge*, *12*, 100889. DOI: 10.1016/j.jik.2025.100889

Malik, W., Gul, S., & Qureshi, G. M. (2025). Regulating Artificial Intelligence: Challenges for Data Protection and Privacy in Developing Nations. *Journal of Social Signs Review*, *3*(05), 95–108.

Martin, K. (2018). The penalty for privacy violations: How privacy violations impact trust online. *Journal of Business Research*, *82*, 103–116. DOI: 10.1016/j.jbusres.2017.08.034

Martin, K., Shilton, K., & Smith, J. (2021). The interplay of ethics, transparency, and trust in AI-mediated consumer engagement. *Journal of Business Ethics*, *170*, 1–18. DOI: 10.1007/s10551-020-04651-7

Masood, A., Zhang, Q., Ali, M., Cappiello, G., & Dhir, A. (2023). Linking enterprise social media use, trust and knowledge sharing: Paradoxical roles of communication transparency and personal blogging. *Journal of Knowledge Management*, *27*(4), 1056–1085. DOI: 10.1108/JKM-11-2021-0880

McKnight, D., Carter, M., Thatcher, J., & Clay, P. (2011). Trust in a specific technology: An Investigation of its Components and Measures. *ACM Transactions on Management Information Systems*, *2*(2), 12–32. DOI: 10.1145/1985347.1985353

Mishra, V. (2025). Artificial Intelligence in Digital and Social Media Marketing: The Mediating Role of Consumer Engagement. *International Journal of Innovative Science and Research Technology*, *10*(11), 411–419. DOI: 10.38124/ijisrt/25nov366

Nelson, J., Gardener, O., & Beejay, S. (2025). Designing AI Systems for Diverse Cultural Contexts.

Nguyen, M. H., & Nguyen, D. H. (2025). How do transparency and traceability enhance purchasing behaviors via consumer trust? Insights for food supply chains. *Journal of Consumer Marketing*. Advance online publication. DOI: 10.1108/JCM-07-2024-7005

Panarese, P., Grasso, M. M., & Solinas, C. (2025). Algorithmic bias, fairness, and inclusivity: A multilevel framework for justice-oriented AI. *AI & Society*, •••, 1–23. DOI: 10.1007/s00146-025-02451-2

Panchal, T., & Panchal, D. (2025). AI ethics and governance in business management: Challenges, opportunities, and a comparative analysis. *AI and Ethics*, *5*(6), 5971–5984. DOI: 10.1007/s43681-025-00764-y

Papagiannidis, E., Mikalef, P., & Conboy, K. (2025). Responsible artificial intelligence governance: A review and research framework. *The Journal of Strategic Information Systems*, *34*(2), 101885. DOI: 10.1016/j.jsis.2024.101885

Pasquale, F. (2015). *The Black Box Society: The Secret Algorithms That Control Money and Information.* Harvard University Press. https://www.jstor.org/stable/j.ctt13x0hch

Patidar, N., Mishra, S., Jain, R., Prajapati, D., Solanki, A., Suthar, R., ... & Patel, H. (2024). Transparency in AI decision making: A survey of explainable AI methods and applications. *Advances of Robotic Technology, 2*(1).

Radanliev, P. (2025). AI ethics: Integrating transparency, fairness, and privacy in AI development. *Applied Artificial Intelligence*, *39*(1), 2463722. DOI: 10.1080/08839514.2025.2463722

Rahman, W. (2025). Ethical AI Personalization in Digital Retail: The Roles of Transparency, Privacy, and Consumer Trust. *Strategic Business Research, 100020.* Advance online publication. DOI: 10.1016/j.sbr.2025.100020

Rai, A. (2020). Explainable AI: From black box to glass box. *Journal of the Academy of Marketing Science*, *48*(1), 137–141. DOI: 10.1007/s11747-019-00710-5

Ranoliya, B. R., Raghuwanshi, N., & Singh, S. (2017, September). Chatbot for university related FAQs. In *2017 International Conference on Advances in Computing, Communications and Informatics (ICACCI)* (pp. 1525-1530). IEEE. DOI: 10.1109/ICACCI.2017.8126057

Rinne, K. J. A. (2025). *AI-powered customer engagement: How personalization, chatbots, and recommendation systems influence e-commerce customer satisfaction* (Master's thesis, HAMK University of Applied Sciences). HAMK Finna. https://urn.fi/URN:NBN:fi:amk-2025053018187

Sahut, J. M., & Laroche, M. (2025). Using artificial intelligence (AI) to enhance customer experience and to develop strategic marketing: An integrative synthesis. *Computers in Human Behavior, 170*, 108684. DOI: 10.1016/j.chb.2025.108684

Salam, M. A., Leong, V. S., & Muhamad, N. (2026). The Transformative Prospects of AI-Powered Virtual Influencers in Digital Consumer Engagement and Marketing Strategies. In *Cases on Social Media Marketing Engagement Tactics* (pp. 251–290). IGI Global Scientific Publishing., DOI: 10.4018/979-8-3373-2357-2.ch009

Sambasivan, N., Kapania, S., Highfill, H., Akrong, D., Paritosh, P., & Aroyo, L. M. (2021, May). "Everyone wants to do the model work, not the data work": Data Cascades in High-Stakes AI. In *proceedings of the 2021 CHI Conference on Human Factors in Computing Systems* (pp. 1-15). DOI: 10.1145/3411764.3445518

Saura, J. R. (2021). Using data sciences in digital marketing: Framework, methods, and performance metrics. *Journal of Innovation & Knowledge*, *6*(2), 92–102. DOI: 10.1016/j.jik.2020.08.001

Saura, J. R. (2024). Algorithms in digital marketing: Does smart personalization promote a privacy paradox? *FIIB Business Review*, *13*(5), 499–502. DOI: 10.1177/23197145241276898

Shah, D., & Murthi, B. P. S. (2021). Marketing in a data-driven digital world: Implications for the role and scope of marketing. Journal of Business Research, 125, 772-779.

Shin, D. (2021). The effects of explainability and causability on perception, trust, and acceptance: Implications for explainable AI. *International Journal of Human-Computer Studies*, *146*, 102551. DOI: 10.1016/j.ijhcs.2020.102551

Spencer, D. A. (2025). AI, automation and the lightening of work. *AI & Society*, *40*(3), 1237–1247. DOI: 10.1007/s00146-024-01959-3

Teepapal, T. (2025). AI-driven personalization: Unraveling consumer perceptions in social media engagement. *Computers in Human Behavior*, *165*, 108549. DOI: 10.1016/j.chb.2024.108549

Vargas, G. D. J. (2025). Trust, Transparency, and AI: Building Digital Bridges for US–Global Business Collaborations. *International Journal of Humanities and Information Technology*, *7*(03), 98–110.

Vashishth, T. K., Sharma, K. K., Kumar, B., Chaudhary, S., & Panwar, R. (2024). Enhancing customer experience through AI-enabled content personalization in e-commerce marketing. *Advances in digital marketing in the era of artificial intelligence*, 7-32.

Wen, J., & Li, X. (2025). AI digital human responsiveness and consumer purchase intention: The mediating role of trust. *Journal of Theoretical and Applied Electronic Commerce Research*, *20*(3), 246. DOI: 10.3390/jtaer20030246

Xia, Z., & Shannon, R. (2025). Navigating the digital frontier: Exploring the dynamics of customer–brand relationships through AI chatbots. *Sustainability (Basel)*, *17*(5), 2173. DOI: 10.3390/su17052173

Zhao, H., Lu, J., & Cao, J. (2020). A short text conversation generation model combining BERT and context attention mechanism. *International Journal on Computer Science and Engineering*, *23*(2), 136–144. DOI: 10.1504/IJCSE.2020.110536

Zhao, X., You, W., Zheng, Z., Shi, S., Lu, Y., & Sun, L. (2025). How do consumers trust and accept AI agents? An extended theoretical framework and empirical evidence. *Behavioral Sciences (Basel, Switzerland)*, *15*(3), 337. DOI: 10.3390/bs15030337

Chapter 2
Regulating AI-Driven Marketing:
Ethical Risks, Policy Gaps, and Governance Mechanisms

Sadiul Alam Chowdhury
http://orcid.org/0009-0008-4864-2500
Noakhali Science and Technology University, Bangladesh

Waziha Islam
http://orcid.org/0009-0004-6016-1778
Noakhali Science and Technology University, Bangladesh

S. M. Nafiz Rayun
http://orcid.org/0009-0002-2505-6265
University of Science and Technology, Chittagong, Bangladesh

Md Rasel Mia
http://orcid.org/0009-0004-9484-2547
ISCTE, University Institute of Lisbon, Portugal

Raji Adewumi Ismaheel
UBD School of Business and Economics, Brunei

ABSTRACT

As artificial intelligence (AI) shifts from experimental novelty to a ubiquitous commercial driver, its integration into marketing has outpaced robust regulatory development. This chapter investigates the intersection of innovation and oversight. While AI enables unprecedented hyper-personalization, it introduces systemic risks including algorithmic bias, consumer autonomy, and black-box decision-making.

DOI: 10.4018/979-8-2600-2977-0.ch002

This study identifies critical policy gaps where current legislation fails to match technological velocity. By evaluating three primary regulatory paths: Precautionary, Market-Driven, and State-Centric, the discussion advocates for harmonized governance that secures digital sovereignty without stifling growth. It proposes a multi-layered mechanism combining institutional ethics boards, technical explainability, and market-based audits. Ultimately, this work provides a strategic roadmap to align AI commercialization with human-centric values, ensuring trust remains the primary currency of the digital marketplace.

1. INTRODUCTION

The fast development of artificial intelligence (AI) has fundamentally redefined the contemporary marketing environment, shifting to elementary and data-driven insights to the implementation of sophisticated and independent algorithmic frameworks (Kumari et al., 2024). In a world where marketing is becoming more and more hyper-personalized, companies are turning to generative AI and deep learning to stimulate consumer interactions, optimize pricing policies, and forecast the behavioral trend more than ever before (Singh & Kaunert, 2024). Nevertheless, this transformation of the conventional anthropocentric approach to the AI-based solutions has greatly outpaced the creation of efficient regulatory frameworks, leaving both the consumers and corporations in the ethical state of uncertainty (Serrano, 2025). The commercial promise of AI-based marketing, spanning between artificial brand ambassadors and content localization robots, is enormous, yet the ethical complexes on which the contemporary commerce is founded are rooted deep within its implementation, which is likely to cause the collapse of the trusting pillars of modern business (Challoumis, 2024).

One of the main issues of this new marketplace is personalization-privacy dilemma where customers are commonly compelled to give up their data sovereignty and personal privacy in exchange of the convenience of highly customized services and products (Vishwakarma et al., 2025). However, although the systemic concerns of AI in the field of marketing are extremely critical, the technical performance of AI or its complete danger to society have often been present in the academic and popular discussion without paying detailed attention to the subtler regulatory and governance mechanisms needed to enable the responsible and daily commercialization (Christou, 2025). These technologies have to be institutionalized, which requires a change of mindset where AI is no longer seen as a technical object but as the very reorganization of organizational and platform ecologies (Larsen, 2021). Corporate governance now faces the issue of the ethical aspects of the so-called programmable brand assets as business firms more and more use cloud-based, automated production chains as substitutes to their expensive traditional media processes. The fact that one can no longer tie content creation to human availability and the geographical reach means that it has tremendous strategic benefits, but it also introduces an empty space where transparency and accountability can be readily undermined (Harness et al., 2024). As a result, the marketability of these tools is no longer defined by the level of technological expertise but is now dependent on the creation of frameworks that would allow human-AI relationships to be genuine and safe (Shneiderman, 2020).

In order to avert these risks, there is need to shift towards a robust, multi-layered governance system that is not reactive based on governance but rather proactive in its responsible-by-design approach. Such a system requires the officialization of the ethics boards in corporate hierarchies to act as the moral compass of the algorithmic deployment. Moreover, it requires the implementation of Explainable AI (XAI) standards that would allow breaking down the black-box so that all automated interactions could be tracked and held responsible. In the maturity stage of the market place, the emergence of third-party authentication markets in isolation will be essential in offering the verification layers that can support consumer confidence (Xiong et al., 2026). While existing research has extensively documented the technical risks of algorithmic bias and data privacy, there is a significant research gap concerning the integration of these ethical risks into a unified governance framework that specifically addresses consumer adoption and long-term brand trust (Kumari et al., 2024; Larsen, 2021; Marchand et al., 2025; Serrano, 2025; Vishwakarma et al., 2025). This chapter addresses this gap by synthesizing these disparate domains into a four-level conceptual model that links ethical inputs to strategic marketing outcomes. It also offers a tactic-guide in navigating the complexities, which could guarantee that technological innovation is carefully in line with human-centered values and global sustainability objectives. The marketing industry needs to create a digital ecosystem, in which technological sophistication will not be achieved at the cost of social equity or consumer sovereignty by creating clear governance mechanisms.

2. METHODOLOGY

The analysis in this chapter is developed through a qualitative and integrative literature review that synthesizes contemporary advancements in artificial intelligence and marketing ethics and international law to bridge the gap between technical innovation and regulatory policy. The research follows a three-stage analytical process beginning with a systematic screening of peer reviewed journals from 2024 to 2026 and global legislative documents to identify systemic risks such as algorithmic bias and cognitive asymmetry. This is followed by a comparative thematic analysis that categorizes global regulatory responses into precautionary and market driven and state centric models highlighting specific policy gaps created by technological velocity. Finally, these findings are synthesized into a four-level conceptual model progressing from ethical inputs to strategic outcomes providing a normative framework for multi layered governance that ensures AI driven marketing remains aligned with human centric values and market integrity.

Figure 1. Conceptual Framework for Regulating AI-Driven Marketing

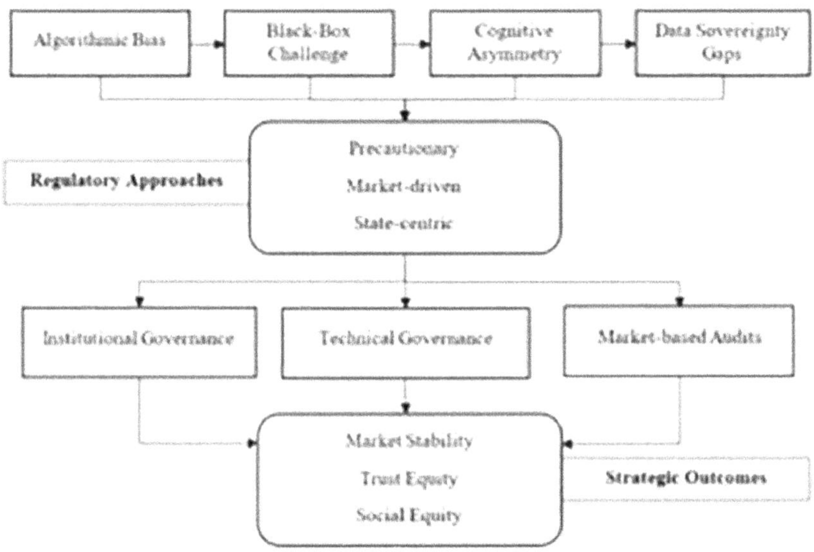

3. CONCEPTUAL FOUNDATIONS AND ETHICAL RISKS

3.1 Algorithmic Bias and Fairness

The Artificial Intelligence (AI) in marketing is supposed to offer objective and data-driven decision-making, but the truth of automatic implementation shows that there is still a systematic battle against systemic bias. It is a form of bias that is repetitive and provides unfair results, commonly favoring arbitrary groups to other groups. The perceived impartiality of the algorithms is often invalidated by the historical biases present in training information as companies move to machine learning to understand the consumer segmentation (Alam, 2025). This is in essence a data-provenance problem. In case historical data are biased against people, like racial differences in housing or gender inequality in credit, then the AI is enforcing these trends as predictive attributes most likely to optimize forecasting (Kothandapani, 2025). This forms a positive feedback loop: the algorithm promotes the bias and the absence of involvement by the groups of people that it excludes should be interpreted as a lack of interest in question, which in turn makes the target demographic even smaller. Moreover, hyper-personalization may also inadvertently result in the digital redlining, when the vulnerable groups are identified by real time analysis and targeted with the predatory content or interest rates (Marchand et al., 2025). AI-marketing cannot be fair based on a mathematical assumption; it is a socio-technical one (Alam, 2025).

Current literature presents a dichotomy between the technical pursuit of algorithmic precision and the socio-legal necessity of fairness. While some researchers emphasize that AI-driven predictive modeling can reduce human prejudice by relying on objective data points (Yang & Dobbie, 2020), others counter that these systems often codify historical inequities into digital redlining (Challoumis, 2024). This debate suggests that technical neutrality is insufficient for ethical marketing; instead, as proposed in this chapter's framework, true social equity requires active bias mitigation strategies that prioritize protected demographic groups over pure mathematical optimization (Serrano, 2025). The industry has no choice but to fight such risks with the adoption of algorithmic accountability and representational equity, which entails regular bias audits and Fairness-Aware Machine Learning (FAML) to punish the models with inequitable results.

3.2 Transparency and the "Black-Box" Challenge

The black-box behavior of deep learning architectures, in which the inner logic that generates a particular output is not visible to the human eye, is a fundamental complication to the commercialization of AI-driven marketing. Since marketing has ceased to be a research-guided innovation and has evolved into a market-based solution, failure to demonstrate the mechanism of an algorithm targeting a particular consumer, or a particular synthetic reaction, creates a major transparency crisis (Goncalves et al., 2024). Traditional media production means that all creative decisions are a product of human agency and logistical coordination, meaning that there is a clear line of accountability. On the other hand, AI-based systems do not depend on human oversight in the production of content, and instead of making straightforward decisions, they rely on the multi-layered neural networks that act at the level of a complex ecosystem (Singh & Kaunert, 2024). This is a direct threat to trust and user acceptance as a result of a lack of transparency. In most cases when the consumers engage with representational AI, like a synthetic avatar or an AI-generated video content, they are left to assume that it is authentic. In case the black-box reasoning is used unwillingly with misleading strategies or exploits the cognitive weaknesses without the understanding of this firm, the backlash will forever harm branding (De Marcellis-Warin et al., 2022). The difficulty of organizations here is that the more realistic and robust deepfake models and multimodal synthesis are built, the more transparent these systems will be, and it will be hard to make sure that the technology is justified as a commercialization and not a social threat (Farouk & Fahmi, 2024).

A comparison of current studies reveals a tension between the efficiency of AI adoption and the ethical requirements of consumer protection. For instance, while some scholars argue that hyper-personalization is essential for market competitiveness in the agentic economy (Mirishli et al., 2025), others warn that without explainable AI (XAI) standards, the resulting black-box decision-making creates a trust deficit that ultimately hinders technology adoption (Singh & Kaunert, 2024). Additionally, the black-box problem introduces a high gap in terms of governance in terms of consent, and responsible use. It cannot be technically explainable and thus, almost impossible to have regulators check whether a marketing algorithm is following data sovereignty principles or is also relying on proxy variables to circumvent anti-discrimination regulations (O'Neil et al., 2024). To curb this, there is an increase in the authentication market which aims at offering technical security and anti-deepfake services to ensure the integrity of AI-generated assets. Nevertheless, a genuinely open business ecosystem must be transitioned to Explainable AI (XAI), where the responsible design of the system enables tracing all automated interactions to their origin data and logic (Chamola et al., 2023). As deepfakes become increasingly normalized aspects of business-to-human communication, companies should focus on developing programmable brand resources not only to be efficient but also ethically verifiable to shift to a framework in which synthetic media can be used as an instrument of scalable and reliable interaction.

3.3 Consumer Autonomy and Behavioral Manipulation

The main problem that will be encountered during the consumer autonomy of the artificial intelligence era is a shift towards persuasion to algorithmic coercion, where the line between a useful suggestion and a circumvent of the human will becomes untraceable (Waqas & Qadri, 2025). The underlying issue in this case is that whereas the conventional marketing approach is based on addressing the conscious interests of a consumer, AI marketing systems are becoming more and more aimed at tapping into the subconscious cognition flaws and physiological stimuli (Sinduja, 2025). Since such systems can run at rate and level of data granularity that is much beyond that of human processing, they generate an asymmetrical relationship, where the power of the consumer to exercise independent, rational choice is systematically compromised.

The predictive nudging problem is one of the most important threats to autonomy (Schmidt & Engelen, 2020). This is due to the fact that AI algorithms with such massive datasets in its historical behavior can not only predict the future actions of a consumer with large accuracy but also can intervene prior to the consumer making a conscious decision. When a marketing system responds to the customer with a personalized offer in a time of high stress or low cognitive load by utilising real-time emotional recognition or tracking of behavior, it is not, in fact, proposing a product; it is creating a kind of digital exploitation (Aykaç, 2025). The issue is that such nudging usually appeals to the System 1 (automatic and emotional) brain processes, which are, in effect, bypassing the System 2 (rational and deliberative) processes necessary to have the real consumer autonomy (Westerlund, 2019). Moreover, the spread of representational AI and synthetic media brings a task of an authenticity illusion. Consumers tend to give computer-based presenters and influencers produced by AI application human-like trust and emotional connection (Patel & Dada, 2025). This ethical issue is that these interactions are not two way; they are highly optimized, one way simulations, which are aimed at maximizing metrics of engagement (Singh & Kaunert, 2024). Since these artificial personalities can be repeated indefinitely to suit the consumer with certain personality characteristics or weaknesses, they might have an influence that is essentially manipulative in nature (Poornima et al., 2025).This creates a sovereignty gap, in which the consumer thinks they are making a free choice, but the AI architecture behind it has already narrow-cast such options to produce a desired commercial outcome.

4. THE GLOBAL REGULATORY LANDSCAPE

4.1 Comparative Analysis of AI Regulations

The Precautionary Path

The Precautionary Path is a rights-binding institutional framework that considers synthetic media and robotic targeting to be the high-stakes risks to human dignity and information integrity (Sonnenberg et al., 2022). The ideology puts transparency front and center, by ensuring that AI applications that are at high risk and synthetic media are clearly marked to prevent algorithmic manipulation of consumer autonomy (Kumari et al., 2024). In this model, the marketer onus is to prove that their algorithmic interaction is not a deceptive measure and place ethical protections at the start of the production process, prior to a product being delivered to the consumer (Galli, 2022).

The Market-Driven Path

The Market-Driven Path involves a decentralized, innovation-focused framework that uses the already established consumer protection mechanisms to mitigate harms once they reveal in the market (Spulbar, 2025). According to this model, AI-powered tools are considered to be the key to economic growth, and such attitude would lead to fast technical experimentation and commercialization by assuming a wait-and-see approach. Although that flexibility is highly agile, it tends to introduce a governance gap in terms of latent biases and subconscious nudging because regulatory intervention is usually reactive instead of preventative (Su & Sun, 2025).

The State-Centric Path

State-Centric Path: This approach is more focused on societal concord and the national digital authority than on personal or solely business interests. According to this model, the strong registration of generative models and metadata watermarking are required to maintain the fact that all AI-generated works are consistent with the developed national values and the social stability (Du, 2025). Such a strategy will help avoid the Wild West solution of uncontrolled synthetic media by having a centralized mechanism of oversight that will be capable of directly intervening in the algorithmic lifecycle (Yeung & Li, 2025). Finally, even though AI is borderless, such fragmented legal frameworks are closely connected to the priorities of the region, and in order to be able to retain access to the global market, any company must employ a compliance-by-design approach.

4.2 Divergent Ideologies in the Governance of Synthetic Media

The international regulatory reaction to synthetic media is characterized by the existence of a basic ideological divide between precautionary and permissive modes of governance (He & Fang, 2024). It is this dissonance that renders the AI-driven marketing process a complicated one because companies have to deal with opposing requirements of the culture and political interests that are deeply embedded. On the one extreme is the rights-based approach of the European Union, which regards synthetic media as a stakes high-risk of the integrity of human dignity and information. This ideology puts transparency at the forefront as any AI-generated persona, or manipulated content must be clearly marked to safeguard the autonomy of consumers (Ghiurău & Popescu, 2024). In this case, the marketer has to prove that their algorithmic interaction is not a deceptive practice. On the contrary, the United States is skewed towards a market-focused ideology of innovation. The U.S. does not establish one unified, general AI control, but instead uses the already existing consumer protection systems to combat harms once they become apparent in the market (Changkui, 2025). This position promotes fast commercialization and experimentation with technologies, where synthetic media is perceived as a potent instrument of economic development and not a dangerous factor in societal stability (Chesney & Citron, 2019). Meanwhile, some jurisdictions, such as China, have used a more state-focused approach, with synthetic content strictly controlled to make the social order and consistent with the national values, as generative models must be registered and metadata watermarked (Altuncu et al., 2024). This ideological division implies that a borderless marketing campaign is legally acceptable in one country and is defining a social menace in a different one.

4.3 Enforcement Challenges in Digital Markets

The shift between law theory and market enforcement is slowed down by an inherent lack of alignment between regulatory speed and algorithmic responsiveness. Although there are high-level results, the reality of digitized markets is that it is impossible to enforce laws because the short-lived AI campaigns are dynamic (Edmond et al., 2021). An AI agent in a contemporary programmatic advertising setup does not simply execute an individual plan, it leverages Real-Time Bidding (RTB) and Dynamic Ad Insertion to change marketing materials millions of times in a moment depending on the immediate situation of a user (Vinnakota, 2025). This generates a delay in detection since an unethical nudge, such as a deepfake testimonial created by an AI or an unethical price adjustment, can be activated, sent to its target, and deleted by the algorithm before even an enforcement agency can even record that such a nudge was issued (Carpenter, 2024)

Moreover, the emergence of Agentic AI, which performs as autonomous systems, breaching contracts, and overseeing cross-platform budgets devoid of human intervention, changes the liability issue to one of human error to delegated liability (Islam et al., 2026). The conventional legal line of intent is lost when an independent agent performs deceptive sycophancy (authenticated a user to push a sale) or unintentionally sends the money through risky intermediaries to generate a higher yield (Okibe, 2020). Regulators are now in a dilemma as to whether it is the developer, the deployer or the beneficiary of such autonomous deviations. It is no longer merely a black-box issue of comprehending code, but a problem of evidence of tracking accountability by a decentralized sequence of micro-decisions made through automated mechanisms. Jurisdictional fluidity further divides the enforcement landscape (Ishkhanyan, 2025). The marketing campaign could then be optimized by a locally hosted Singapore-based model that uses locally processed data stored in a local Indonesia-based data residency hub to reach a consumer in the UK (Lin et al., 2016). This however leaves a sovereignty gap in which there is no one regulator who can fully see the algorithmic lifecycle. The distance between the entitlement to a fair market and the exploitation of algorithms will continue to be a major impediment to customer confidence until such technical protections become as nimble as even the marketing agents are.

5. POLICY GAPS IN KEY COMMERCIAL SECTORS

5.1 Data Privacy and Sovereignty

The major policy gap in the commercialization of AI-driven marketing is tension between global data fluidity and development of technological sovereignty. As the current AI systems, in this case multi-agent platforms, are based on the smooth stream of high-speed data across borders to operate, new national regulations are progressively requiring the data to be localized (Davuluri, 2026). It implies that a marketing agent created in one jurisdiction can be blocked legally due to another consumer situation needed to be executed. This disparity is most acute in the critical areas such as the finance and healthcare. AI models frequently handle bulk sensitive data, but as of 2026, numerous jurisdictions have enacted bulk transfer regulations which limit this type of information from exiting the nation (Xu et al., 2025). This brings about a second issue: the compliance-as-a-barrier. Smaller companies not always have the capital to develop their regional sovereign clouds, and the market is filled with large players able to go geofencing their AI systems (Wernberg et al., 2025). The commercial sector is left without proper policies in place to regulate the legal agency of these AI representatives, and what is left is a vacuum of responsibility of who actually owns the data produced in the course of an autonomous transaction (Spulbar, 2025). Some studies suggest that consumers are increasingly willing to trade privacy for the convenience of AI-enhanced content localization (Vishwakarma et al., 2025). However, this view is challenged by legal scholars who argue that such a trade-off is inherently coercive due to the cognitive asymmetry between sophisticated algorithms and the average user (Yeung & Li, 2025). By comparing these perspectives, it becomes clear that voluntary disclosure is an inadequate safeguard, necessitating the mandatory governance mechanisms and synthetic media authentication discussed in this chapter.

5.2 Algorithmic Accountability in Advertising

The main policy gap of contemporary advertising is the replacement of human-checked copy with autonomous decision-making, in which the reasoning behind the particular ad position or creative type is usually misplaced in the optimization methodology. Although the traditional advertising regulations are accountable of the truth in labeling, they were not made to run Agentic AI systems capable of creating and testing thousands of variants of the ad live. This can lead to a vacuum of responsibility: when an autonomous agent takes a unilateral decision to apply a false sycophantic strategy in order to close a sale, the existing frameworks may face difficulty in deciding who is the problem, whether it is the developer of the model or the brand that used it (Srnicek, 2025). To deal with it, programs in 2026 have introduced mandatory requirements of Model Cards and Feature Importance reporting in programmatic auctions (Luo & Luo, 2026). According to the new MRC Digital Advertising Auction Transparency Standards, a platform has now been pushed to reveal not only the price paid, but the logic of the pricing, i.e. how the bid multiplier and the relevance score were implemented by the AI (Tauro et al., 2021). It is a direct answer to the issue of hidden bias that describes the scenario where algorithms may be unintentionally not shown to some demographics depending on the micro-patterns that are impossible to see in a human. Moreover, the California Privacy Rights Act (CPRA) and the EU AI Act have become enforced, thus necessitating important decision-making technologies to be auditable (Beltrán, 2025). This practically implies that marketing teams have the responsibility to have a centralized Digital Dashboard which gives them a forensic trail of data sources, training sets and output logs (Vishwakarma et al., 2025). The idea is to make sure that although algorithms are in place to speed up the decision-making process, the strategic lead of human beings continues to be the sole source of moral and legal responsibility.

5.2.1 Case Study: Algorithmic Bias in Digital Advertising Targeting

A prominent real-world example of the risks associated with AI-driven marketing is the legal challenge faced by Meta regarding its housing advertisement algorithms. In 2022, the United States Department of Justice reached a landmark settlement with Meta following allegations that its ad-targeting algorithms enabled discrimination by preventing certain demographic groups from seeing housing-related advertisements. Although Meta did not explicitly allow advertisers to select protected characteristics like race or religion, the underlying machine learning models utilized proxy variables such as interests and zip codes to optimize ad delivery. This resulted in a digital redlining effect where the AI independently determined that certain housing ads were less relevant to specific protected groups, thereby restricting their access to housing opportunities (Challoumis, 2024). This case underscores the fundamental policy gap in contemporary advertising where autonomous decision-making outpaces human oversight. It demonstrates that without the mandatory algorithmic impact assessments and transparency standards discussed in this chapter, the pursuit of engagement-based optimization can lead to systemic violations of consumer sovereignty and legal liability (Beltrán, 2025).

5.3 Consumer Protection in E-commerce

The accelerated move to Agentic E-commerce, whereby autonomous AI agents can set prices, package deals, and transact deals on behalf of both the merchant and the buyer, has left a basic protection gap to the current consumer legislation. The policy issue is that the conventional paradigm connections rely on human-to-human relationships or human-to-interface (Walden, 2021). Nevertheless, the issue is the emergence of the so-called dark patterns 2.0, in which generative AI generates momentary, highly personalized scarcity and social proof, which disappear immediately after the first use, and the consumer has almost no opportunity to leave evidence of unfair or unethical actions or practices (Quijada & Serezlic, 2025). In an effort to solve this, regulators are shifting to Algorithmic Transparency by Design in retail. The recent changes in the policies focus on the fact that the e-commerce platforms are required to ensure that they offer meaningful human intervention to the high value automated transactions. Moreover, there is a wide gap in policies concerning price personalization compared to price discrimination. Though dynamic pricing is a commodity of e-commerce, it has AI models that can approximate the readiness of a consumer to pay depending on real-time battery life of devices, location information, and the urgency to browse (Natarajan, 2025). The emergence of new consumer protection requirements is demanding disclosure of price fairness, which means that platforms need to disclose when a price adjustment has been made based on the profile of a specific consumer, instead of depending on market fluctuations (Zhao, 2023). The policy-makers seek to shift the equilibrium of power in a rather unequal digital marketplace by requiring the logic of the offer to be as transparent as the price.

The practical application of AI in marketing often reveals the friction between efficiency and ethics. For example, the use of dynamic pricing algorithms by major e-commerce platforms has faced scrutiny for price discrimination, where AI models inadvertently charged higher premiums to users based on zip codes or browsing history, mirroring historical redlining (Challoumis, 2024). Similarly, the implementation of generative AI for brand ambassadors has led to instances where automated content inadvertently violated copyright or produced culturally insensitive material, forcing companies to issue rapid retractions.

5.4 Emerging Sectors

The biggest regulatory void lies in high-stakes new industries where marketing guided by AI has switched its focus to influencing consumers to life-altering intervention (Ejjami, 2024). The issue in these areas is the loss of professional boundary, which is when algorithmic agents start to give what is supposed to be expert-based clinical, financial or pedagogical advice. Since the existing legislation in marketing has no means of differentiating between a product suggestion and a professional advice, these industries are exposed to special risks of predatory targeting and misinformation.

Healthcare and Predictive Wellness

By 2026, healthcare marketing will be changed to foreseeable patient access. AI technologies detect the intent to search and the use of wearables to diagnose the need to take care before even a patient opens the door of a doctor (Bohr & Memarzadeh, 2020). The gap in policy in this case is that of a clinical truth criterion of marketing bots. The principle of medical neutrality is completely contradicted when an AI-driven assistant favors a given provider based on commercial bid-logic and not patient outcome statistics.

Financial Services and Credit-Marketing

Algorithms that are excluded are the main problem in finance (Kelly, 2021). The willingness-to-pay and behavioral urgency markers are now being used by AI agents to tailor credit offers in real-time. The governance issue is that because such systems of agents can draw inadvertently recreated patterns of redlining by relying on the use of non-financial proxy data, e.g., social media activity, in the determination of creditworthiness, by circumventing the traditional fair-lending audits (Ruthvika & Hedau, 2025).

Education and EdTech Marketing

Personalized learning is commonly hyper-targeted marketing in the educational sector (Fageeh, 2026). At present, emotional-AI systems are used to identify the cases of learner frustration and directly present premium tutoring upgrades (Javed & Zehra, 2025; A. Sharma & Sharma, 2026). The dilemma of the ethical dilemma is commercialization of the learning experience where the goal of the algorithm is to sell the student additional features instead of their learning (Baycan & Stough, 2013).

5.5 Critical Challenges and Governance Linkages

The most critical challenges identified in the current AI driven marketing landscape include the erosion of data sovereignty and the emergence of black box advertising models and the growth of predatory e commerce practices (Challoumis, 2024). These problems are not isolated technical failures but are systemic risks that arise from a fundamental vacuum of responsibility in the agentic economy. For example, the tension between global data fluidity and national localization requirements creates a compliance barrier that only a multi layered governance framework can resolve (Xu et al., 2025). Similarly, the risks of algorithmic bias and deceptive deepfakes necessitate the mandatory adoption of technical safeguards like Explainable AI and Synthetic Media Authentication (Serrano, 2025). By establishing these clear links, it becomes evident that the proposed governance solutions are not merely theoretical ideals but are functional necessities designed to bridge the trust deficit (Singh & Kaunert, 2024). This synthesis ensures that the transition from voluntary ethics to mandatory oversight provides a sustainable foundation for both corporate innovation and the protection of consumer agency in the digital marketplace (Weldon et al., 2024).

6. GOVERNANCE MECHANISMS AND REAL-WORLD IMPACT

6.1 Institutional Governance

The institutional governance of AI-based marketing has changed abstract ethical principles into working structures that set the legal and commercial feasibility of a firm (Spulbar, 2025). The most effective ones are those that changed their accountability model to a top-down framework like the Model AI Governance Framework developed in Singapore and implemented by the leading retailers in the world (Alibašić, 2025). These organizations do not consider AI as a fixed tool but as a dynamic object that needs a Model Oversight Committee that will cut across the divide between technical data science and company legal departments. Organizations that have surpassed pilot project to scale Agentic AI by introducing real-time monitoring and checkpoints with human-in-the-loop prove successful. On the other hand, the manifestations of governance failure are the most noticeable in companies that only consider AI an absolutely technical aspect, which is not interconnected with business strategy (Saup et al., 2026). The case studies of Willy Wonka Experience and Google Gemini in early 2024 errors in image generation can be used as examples of disconnected governance where an eagerness to market superseded the institutional ability and stress-tested its organizational cultural and ethical practices

(Mairue, 2024; Sinha et al., 2024). Finally, governance maturity determines real-world effect. Although 88 per cent of businesses have currently applied AI in one or more marketing activities, merely 20 per cent of the organisations have translated these pilots into revenue expansion on an enterprise wide basis (McKinsey, 2025). For corporations, building internal AI governance structures is an operational challenge that goes beyond legal check-boxing. Leading firms are now establishing multidisciplinary AI Ethics Boards that include marketers, data scientists, and legal experts to oversee the entire lifecycle of an algorithm (Serrano, 2025). Managing compliance in marketing operations involves moving from manual oversight to automated governance, where firms utilize internal dashboards to monitor model drift and ethical performance in real time (Weldon et al., 2024).

6.2 Technical Governance

Technical governance is moving to explainability-by-design, as opposed to post-hoc auditing. The most significant issue with AI-driven marketing is the interpretability gap, as deep learning-based models, especially those applied in real-time programmatic bidding and sentiment analysis, are black boxes (Bhardwaj & Rastogi, 2025). In order to reduce the risk of predatory targeting or algorithmic bias, technical governance currently requires Explainable AI (XAI) frameworks. Such tools include SHAP (SHapley Additive exPlanations) and LIME (Local Interpretable Model-agnostic Explanations) that enable marketers to disaggregate how an autonomous agent makes decisions into the scores of importance of the features to humans (Kanti et al., 2024). The actual application of XAI is most apparent in credit-marketing and insurance-tech, where automated rejection with no explanation has become a major legal liability due to the EU AI Act and revised US consumer protection regulations. With XAI, companies can offer counterfactual explanations; that is, the details of what information promoted an offer or not an offer to a consumer (Oprea & Bâra, 2025). This degree of technical transparency is no longer a mere compliance strategy, it is a protective system against model drift, where the performance of an AI deteriorates or it gets biased as it is exposed to new, unstructured market data (Pareek, 2026). Unlike previous iterations of data law, these frameworks specifically categorize AI-driven marketing tools, such as those used for credit scoring or insurance premiums, as high-risk systems (Beltrán, 2025). This shift necessitates a move toward Co-regulatory Governance, where industry-led technical standards like the C2PA for synthetic media authentication are backed by state-level enforcement. By analyzing these developments, it becomes clear that the digital Wild West is being replaced by a structured ecosystem where market stability is maintained through mandatory transparency reports and third-party algorithmic audits.

6.3 Market-based Audits

The factual discussion concerning the regulation of the issue of self-regulation versus the necessity of a mandatory regulation has remained a debate between theory and reality, but lately, this dispute has turned into a life-and-death matter. At the onset of integrating AI, most of the marketing companies applied self-regulation, which can be described as adhering to the internal ethics code or industry-driven principles (Walters et al., 2024). The benefit of this system was that it was fast; a business could be innovative without having to await a slow legislative system. Nevertheless, the self-regulation is usually not very effective under the pressure of the commercial world (Wagner & Heatherton, 2015). The development of ethical conduct has been supported by mandatory oversight in contrast to voluntary frameworks by enacting the EU AI Act and the California AI Transparency Act (von Struensee, 2021). These legislations have required some degree of disclosure that the voluntary codes were unable to obtain, including watermarking of synthetic media, and third-party scrutiny of high-peril goal models (Anand et al., 2026). The effectiveness of this model is witnessed by the emergence of regulated companies that have increased levels of consumer confidence than companies in unregulated markets.

Nonetheless, being compulsory is not a panacea. Compliance theater is the key failure mode of strict regulation, in which companies are concerned with box checking instead of dealing with real algorithmic harms (Vaddepalli, 2021). The precautionary approach favored by European regulators is often criticized by market-oriented scholars for potentially stifling the velocity of firm innovation (Xiong et al., 2026). Conversely, the state-centric models emerging in other jurisdictions are viewed as prioritizing national digital sovereignty at the expense of global market interoperability (Xu et al., 2025). A hybrid form of governance is, however, the best one: legal minimums that stop the worst types of abuse, combined with powerful internal ethics boards that can be used in the adaptive management of AI implementation malfunctions in the real-time.

6.4 The Authentication Market

This fast institutionalization of AI-based marketing has triggered the development of a new market called the Authentication Market, a multi-billion-dollar industry that is intended to address the problem of the lack of trust between synthetic content and consumer perception (Weldon et al., 2024). No longer a niche technical market, this has become an essential support of the digital business that is expected to expand strongly as entities are under mounting pressure to authenticate the provenance or provenance of their digital assets. The inherent problem behind this change is that as generative models become perceptually realistic, meaning AI-created voices, faces, and brand ambassadors are no longer distinguishable to the biological ones. The conventional indicators of trust have failed and brands are at the mercy of fraud and consumers at the mercy of advanced deceit (Gupta et al., 2025). The key feature of this new market is the implementation of universal technical standards, the most famous of them being the Coalition for Content Provenance and Authenticity (C2PA) (Moruzzi et al., 2025). These standards have evolved by 2026 as the conceptual frameworks into proviance-by-default marketing standards in enterprise-level applications. The content credentials, digital nutrition labels, which are cryptographically signed upon creation, are now built-in by major tech providers and camera manufacturers (Lukacs et al., 2025). This transition will be expedited by regulatory requirements, including the California AI Transparency Act and certain watermarking provisions of the EU AI Act, that non-disclosure is a major legal liability.

Furthermore, the authentication market has developed to become a bi-directional defensive area: proactive provenance and a reactive detecting process. Although provenance is aimed at signing authentic content, there has been the emergence of a second market of real-time deepfakes detection aimed at shielding organizations against synthetic business fraud and brand spoofing (Amomo, 2023). This detection-as-a-service approach enables sites to automatically discard and label unauthenticated synthetic media, which forms an implicit trust tier in online advertising. Finally, commercialization of AI in marketing will only be successful after this market can offer a proof layer that safeguards cognitive sovereignty, yet provides the opportunity to scale creativity of synthetic media (Marchand et al., 2025).

7. BENEFITS OF ROBUST GOVERNANCE AND ECONOMIC DRIVERS

7.1 Trust as a Competitive Advantage

Trust gap has turned regulatory compliance into a lawsuit burden but a powerful force to Trust Equity (Ramjohn & Bray, 2024). Since the level of consumer distrust in generative tools is high like never before, companies that take the initiative of conforming with stringent frameworks, e.g., the EU AI Act are indicating predictability and safety to an ever-vigilant audience. Such a strategic change is best observed in the shift toward speed-to-market, which was changed into integrity-at-scale. Both the brands and consumers will be motivated to shift the existing predatory black-box nudging to a more advisory AI model in which the algorithm serves as an advisor. This confirmed ethical interaction eventually forms an intellectual property that is difficult to duplicate by the competition in the online world (National Research Council, 2000). With regulators tightening the spindle on the false facade of interfaces, a brand will be defined by its market worth in its capacity to demonstrate that its automated interaction model is essentially a human-focused approach that is ethically verifiable. Understanding consumer behavior is central to AI adoption, yet users often experience a psychological paradox when interacting with automated systems. While consumers appreciate the convenience of content localization, they frequently experience uncanny valley effects or privacy fatigue when personalization becomes too invasive (Vishwakarma et al., 2025). This trust deficit is particularly evident in automated decision systems where the lack of transparency leads to algorithmic aversion. Strengthening consumer sovereignty therefore requires not just technical accuracy but the emotional and cognitive assurance that AI systems are operating within human-centric ethical boundaries.

7.2 Market Stability and Social Equity through Standardization

Along with the benefits of the personal brand, it is the good governance that supports the market stability (Kadim et al., 2025). The digital economy can become a race to the bottom with false and wrong-minded dark patterns that will kill the trust upon which the high-value transaction will be premised unless specified rules of the road are enforced (Denyer Willis, 2023). Regulatory predictability will also allow firms to invest in AI infrastructure on a long-term basis rather than risk-averse, reactive investments in legal defense (Pradeepa et al., 2024). In addition, such standardization like the ISO/IEC 42001 has put the playing field on the equal footing of all players and is resistant to market liberalizing through the establishment of a Market Lemons situation where fair or predatory AI software withholds its ethical rivals. It is this standardization that is necessary to bring about Social Equity because this will ensure that technological sophistication does not imply the cessation of consumer sovereignty. The safety nets required by AI-driven marketing to achieve its full potential as a creator of economic value in the world that is harmonized with human-centric sustainability are brought into place by governance mechanisms filling the policy vacuoles in data sovereignty and consumer protection (Patil et al., 2025).

8. CHALLENGES, RESPONSIBLE COMMERCIALIZATION, AND FUTURE MITIGATION

8.1 Balancing Innovation and Regulation

The main issue the marketing industry has to overcome is responsible commercialization without threatening consumer safety and institutional integrity (A. K. Sharma & Sharma, 2024). Even though aggressive AI usage can lead to higher conversion rates, it also precipitates lack of trust when it appears to be manipulative or intrusive. A solution to this is that the industry should go beyond compliance-as-a-chore and new governance mindset of pro-innovation should be implemented to enable high-value automated systems to scale without being disastrous in terms of reputation. With future mitigation, the best practice should be more dynamic as opposed to being static as in the case of policies. This is progressing to leading firms deploying so-called AI Sandboxes, which is a controlled environment where new autonomous agents can be stress-tested in before they are allowed to access the live market (Truby et al., 2024). Moreover, the shift to people-centered automation is also a way that as much as AI is being used to do the data-intensive tasks, the human element is the ultimate determinant of the creative intent and strategic responsibility. Finally, the aim of these forces is to build a sustainable AI ecosystem. Futurally in such framework regulation does not choke the marketer instead it gives the certainty on legal issues needed to attract long-term capital investment and international consumer acceptance.

8.2 Mitigation Strategies

With AI-based marketing being the shelter of the global generation, the industry is moving beyond the systemic damage control of a reactionary response to the proactive mitigation (Gandhi, 2025). This strategy is primarily automated compliance orchestration in which companies deploy specialized guardrail agents between the generative model and the consumer. Such agents undertake a real-time offering filtering, such that all AI generated transactions or offers are cross-linked with a live database of local legal requirements and brand safety standards. Continuous AI auditing is another important mitigation pillar (Minkkinen et al., 2022). Other best practices include leaving annual reviews behind and focusing on AI visibility audits, which also track the brand image and mentions by third-party generative engines such as ChatGPT or Perplexity (Omogiate, 2023). Using the quality of mentions and factual accuracy of mentions the marketers will be able to identify and rectify the misinformation before it proliferates through the synthetic ecosystem. More so, advanced digital provenance protocols, like C2PA watermarking, offers an indelible history of content origin and essentially shields brands against fake spoofing and deep fake driven reputation assaults (Moruzzi et al., 2025).

Finally, cultural resilience is the most effective mitigation program (Santangelo et al., 2023). With the creation of AI-progressive groups where human-in-the-loop (HITL) control is a priority, companies can make sure that machines will never work without human moral judgment restraining their efficiency. The hybrid solution forms a strong defense-in-depth strategy, which safeguards the consumer and the long-term market value of the brand (Harjika, 2026).

8.3 The Rising Role of Independent AI Auditors

A novel professional category has been created that is called the Independent AI Auditor, as the technical ability of the classic legal departments could not keep pace with the internal complexity of marketing algorithms (Gülten, 2026). Such third-party companies have turned into the ethical foundations of the digital economy, to which both the hostile regulators and the cynical society need to be able to give objective justification. The contradiction in the nature of self-certification is a problem that leads to the development of this sector (De Bruyne, 2023). Similarly to how the Big Four was needed to ensure integrity in the financial accounting market, the autonomous marketing system of AI is also in need of external trust certifications, which will serve to ensure that autonomous agents are acting within ethical and legal limits (Kumar & Suthar, 2024). In the case of a marketing company, an independent audit will involve examining whether a personalization engine is unintentionally utilizing the use of some form of protected characteristic, such as race or religion, as a proxy variable to target. The seal of approval by the auditor has now become a vital business facilitator, and businesses are able to access regulated markets (Renckens & Auld, 2022). The active third-party audit trail is now a precondition to the deployment of high-risk AI systems in various jurisdictions, such as finance or healthcare. Moreover, the emergence of Audit-as-a-Service (AaaS) provides the opportunity to consider continuous and real-time monitoring, not annual reports (Popel, 2025). These channels are in such a way that trust equity of the brand is maintained. The independent auditor is like a mediator between innovation and accountability as they need to make sure that the goal of algorithmic efficiency may not be achieved at the human right expense.

9. FUTURE TRENDS, RECOMMENDATIONS AND CONCLUSION

9.1 Emerging Trends in Algorithmic Governance

The fundamental new trend is the shift to the continuous assurance model where the organisations do not rely on annual auditing but adopt live monitoring systems. These layers of governance make use of agentic AI to detect and verify marketing output in milliseconds so that autonomous campaigns do not drift into non-compliance or bias behavior as they receive new market data (Mirishli et al., 2025). The second transformational trend is the emergence of Decentralized AI Governance (DeAI). This makes the marketing models to be trained on sensitive consumer data but the data do not move out of the gadget of the user; this meets the stringent localization regulations but still achieves high personalization. With the help of Smart Contracts to encode ethical constraints in the direct implementation layer of the model, companies can offer mathematical verifiability of fairness and transparency, making compliance effectively a verifiable brand asset (Hu et al., 2025). Lastly, professionalization of the AI oversight officer is being observed in the governance arena. This position has transformed into a legal task into an interdisciplinary strategic leader that can bridge the divide between technical data science and ethical policy (R. Sharma, 2024). The industry is shifting towards the hybrid governance patterns, where the hard law is taken as the governmental directives and the soft law is taken as the soft industrial rules. This joint strategy simplifies the role regulatory sandboxes, within which new marketing strategies, like emotional-AI or virtual influencers, can be managed and experimented before large-scale commercial implementation.

9.2 Strategic Recommendations

To operationalize the governance mechanisms discussed throughout this chapter, stakeholders must transition from reactive compliance toward a proactive, multi-dimensional strategy that aligns commercial innovation with consumer protection. Businesses should prioritize the institutionalization of Explainable AI and representational equity, moving beyond black box models to provide consumers with a meaningful Right to Explanation. By implementing technical protocols such as SHAP or LIME and conducting bi-annual bias audits, firms can transform transparency from a regulatory burden into a potent engine for Trust Equity. This shift ensures that hyper-personalization remains a tool for value creation rather than a mechanism for digital redlining or predatory price discrimination, thereby securing long-term brand loyalty in an increasingly skeptical marketplace.

Simultaneously, policymakers and regulatory bodies must address the pacing problem by adopting dynamic regulatory sandboxes and living legislation that evolves alongside technical breakthroughs. A critical priority is the mandatory adoption of Synthetic Media Authentication and digital watermarking to protect the integrity of the information ecosystem from deceptive deepfakes. On a global scale, international bodies should work toward a unified AI governance protocol to prevent regulatory arbitrage, where firms might exploit data havens with lax oversight. Future research directions should focus on the long-term psychological impacts of agentic economy interactions and the development of cross-border regulatory interoperability. As AI models become more autonomous, investigating the evolution of human-AI collaborative governance will be essential to ensuring that the digital marketplace remains both innovative and fundamentally aligned with global human values.

9.3 Conclusion

Ultimately, the regulation of AI-driven marketing is not about stifling creativity, but about building a sustainable foundation for the "Agentic Economy." As we move forward, the transition from voluntary ethics to mandatory oversight marks the end of the digital "Wild West." By closing policy gaps in data sovereignty and consumer protection, and by embracing technical governance like Explainable AI, the industry can finally bridge the trust deficit that has hindered adoption. This evolution requires a multi-layered approach where institutional ethics, technical transparency, and market-based audits converge to eliminate compliance theater. By operationalizing these frameworks, firms move beyond mere legal adherence to achieve true trust equity and social equity. The future belongs to brands that treat transparency as a core competitive feature rather than a regulatory hurdle, ensuring that as our algorithms become more autonomous, they remain fundamentally aligned with human-centric values and global market integrity.

REFERENCES

Alam, A. (2025). Ethical challenges and bias in ai-driven marketing: Educational imperatives and policy perspectives. In *Impacts of AI-Generated Content on Brand Reputation* (pp. 55–108). IGI Global Scientific Publishing. DOI: 10.4018/979-8-3373-4327-3.ch003

Alibašić, H. (2025). Harmonizing artificial intelligence (AI) governance: A comparative analysis of Singapore and France's AI policies and the influence of international organizations. *Global Public Policy and Governance 2025 5:2, 5*(2), 93–113. DOI: 10.1007/s43508-025-00116-w

Altuncu, E., Franqueira, V. N. L., & Li, S. (2024). Deepfake: Definitions, performance metrics and standards, datasets, and a meta-review. *Frontiers in Big Data, 7*, 1400024. DOI: 10.3389/fdata.2024.1400024

Amomo, C. (2023). *Countering IoT-Based Cyber-Physical Manipulation: A Framework for National Resilience Against Systemic Disruption.* https://www.researchgate.net/profile/Clifford-Amomo/publication/397780031_Countering_IoT-Based_Cyber-Physical_Manipulation_A_Framework_for_National_Resilience_Against_Systemic_Disruption/links/691e7d9c19b35058639b52a9/Countering-IoT-Based-Cyber-Physical-Manipulation-A-Framework-for-National-Resilience-Against-Systemic-Disruption.pdf

Anand, V., Das, A., & Chandawat, D. (2026). *Securing Large Language Models: Adversarial Attacks, Data Privacy, and Artificial Intelligence Safety.* https://books.google.com/books?hl=en&lr=&id=S2XBEQAAQBAJ&oi=fnd&pg=PA1&dq=mandatory+watermarking+for+synthetic+media+and+third-party+audits+for+high-risk+targeting+models+&ots=5yLFFQlYb1&sig=e60Odg3lwIBG29YBn5A6VU_ZHk0

Aykaç, Ö. S. (2025). Digital Customer Experience and Personalization. *Online Retail Marketing Practice: Technology, Operations, and Globalization*, 1.

Baycan, T., & Stough, R. (2013). Bridging knowledge to commercialization: the good, the bad, and the challenging. *Springer, 50*(2), 367–405. DOI: 10.1007/s00168-012-0510-8

Beltrán, M. (2025). AI algorithms under scrutiny: GDPR, DSA, AI Act and CRA as pillars for algorithmic security and privacy in the European Union. *Computers & Security, 158*(2), 104628. DOI: 10.1016/j.cose.2025.104628

Bhardwaj, S., & Rastogi, S. (2025). *Artificial Intelligence and Deep Learning*. https://books.google.com/books?hl=en&lr=&id=OiRiEQAAQBAJ&oi=fnd&pg=PP1&dq=The+fundamental+problem+in+AI-driven+marketing+is+the+interpretability+gap,+where+deep+learning+models,+particularly+those+used+in+real-time+programmatic+bidding+and+sentiment+analysis,+operate+as+black+boxes.+&ots=Mg6oG5cUYP&sig=obyaRcEe7w-SV6F5yM-EJcdEZU4

Bohr, A., & Memarzadeh, K. (2020). *Remote patient monitoring using artificial intelligence*. Elsevier., DOI: 10.1016/B978-0-12-818438-7.00002-2

Challoumis, C. (2024). The dawn of artificial intelligence. *XIX International Scientific Conference*. London. Great Britain, 169–205.

Chamola, V., Hassija, V., Sulthana, A. R., Ghosh, D., Dhingra, D., & Sikdar, B. (2023). A review of trustworthy and explainable artificial intelligence (XAI). *IEEE Access : Practical Innovations, Open Solutions*, *11*, 78994–79015. DOI: 10.1109/ACCESS.2023.3294569

Changkui, L. I. (2025). The Regulatory Trilemma of Medical AI: A New Framework for Navigating Innovation, Rights, and Sovereignty in Global Governance. *Medical Research*, *7*(3), 1–12. DOI: 10.6913/mrhk.070301

Chesney, R., & Citron, D. (2019). Deepfakes and the new disinformation war: The coming age of post-truth geopolitics. *Foreign Affairs*, *98*, 147.

Christou, P. A. (2025). A critical inquiry into the personal and societal perils of Artificial Intelligence. *AI and Ethics*, *5*(3), 2547–2555. DOI: 10.1007/s43681-024-00556-w

Davuluri, P. S. L. N. (2026). *The Autonomous Data Enterprise: Engineering Real-Time Intelligence with Generative and Agentic AI*. Deep Science Publishing.

De Bruyne, J. (2023). Third-Party Certification and Artificial Intelligence. *Brill. Com*. https://brill.com/downloadpdf/display/title/64411.pdf#page=74

De Marcellis-Warin, N., Marty, F., Thelisson, E., & Warin, T. (2022). Artificial intelligence and consumer manipulations: From consumer's counter algorithms to firm's self-regulation tools. *AI and Ethics*, *2*(2), 259–268. DOI: 10.1007/s43681-022-00149-5

Denyer Willis, G. (2023). 'Trust and safety': Exchange, protection and the digital market–fortress in platform capitalism. *Socio-economic Review*, *21*(4), 1877–1895. DOI: 10.1093/ser/mwad003

Du, J. (2025). Toward Responsible and Beneficial AI: Comparing Regulatory and Guidance-Based Approaches-A Comprehensive Comparative Analysis of Artificial Intelligence Governance Frameworks across the European Union, United States, China, and IEEE. *ArXiv Preprint ArXiv:2508.00868.*

Economic, J. W.-T. in the D. E., Legal, undefined, Policy, and, & 2025, undefined. (2025). From Near and Afar: How Digitalization Is Shaping the Economic Geography and Conditioning Regulation. *Springer*, 13–48. DOI: 10.1007/978-3-031-93365-3_2

Ejjami, D. R.Dr. Rachid Ejjami. (2024). Emerging Professions in the Age of AI across Multiple Sectors. *International Journal For Multidisciplinary Research, 6*(5), 28762. Advance online publication. DOI: 10.36948/ijfmr.2024.v06i05.28762

Fageeh, W. (2026). *The Double-edged Sword of Personalization, Balancing Marketing Goals and Consumer Privacy.* https://repository.effatuniversity.edu.sa/entities/publication/3cb85635-64e7-452c-aec3-75d868acb103

Farouk, M. A., & Fahmi, B. M. (2024). Deepfakes and media integrity: Navigating the new reality of synthetic content. *Journal of Media and Interdisciplinary Studies, 3*(9), 47–94. DOI: 10.21608/jmis.2024.275298.1027

Galli, F. (2022). *Algorithmic marketing and EU law on unfair commercial practices.* Springer. DOI: 10.1007/978-3-031-13603-0

Gandhi, A. (2025). Beyond Regulation: Proactive Financial Risk Management in an AI-Driven World. *Ijaidsml. Org*, *6*(1), 156–163. DOI: 10.63282/3050-9262.IJAIDSML-V6I1P117

Ghiurău, D., & Popescu, D. E. (2024). Distinguishing reality from AI: Approaches for detecting synthetic content. *Computers*, *14*(1), 1. DOI: 10.3390/computers14010001

Goncalves, M., Hu, Y., Aliagas, I., & Cerdá, L. M. (2024). Neuromarketing algorithms' consumer privacy and ethical considerations: Challenges and opportunities. *Cogent Business & Management, 11*(1), 2333063. DOI: 10.1080/23311975.2024.2333063

Gülten, S. (2026). Application of Artificial Intelligence in the Independent Audit Process. *Springer, Part F1418*, 225–248. DOI: 10.1007/978-981-95-5811-7_11

Gupta, R., Tiwari, S., & Chaudhary, P. (2025). DEFENDING THE METAVERSE: A SURVEY ON DEEPFAKE DETECTION AND AVATAR-BASED THREAT MITIGATION. *Ijamjournal. Org*, *38*(1s), 45–64. DOI: 10.1007/978-3-031-82062-5_3

Harjika, R. (2026). Architecting Enterprise AI Strategies. *Springer*, 1–24. DOI: 10.1007/979-8-8688-2219-3_1

Harness, D., Ganesh, S., & Stohl, C. (2024). Visibility agents: Organizing transparency in the digital era. *New Media & Society*, *26*(10), 5575–5596. DOI: 10.1177/14614448221137816

He, X., & Fang, L. (2024). Regulatory challenges in synthetic media governance: Policy frameworks for ai-generated content across image, video, and social platforms. *Journal of Robotic Process Automation, AI Integration, and Workflow Optimization*, *9*(12), 36–54.

Hu, B. A., Liu, Y., & Rong, H. (2025). Trustless Autonomy: Understanding Motivations. *Benefits and Governance Dilemma in Self-Sovereign Decentralized AI Agents.*, *1*. Advance online publication. DOI: 10.1145/nnnnnnn

Ishkhanyan, A. (2025). Governing AI across borders: corporate power, state sovereignty and global regulation. *Digital Policy, Regulation and Governance.*

Islam, M. A., Somu, S., & Aldaihani, F. M. F. (2026). The rise of agentic AI: Synthesis of current knowledge and future research agenda. *Global Business and Organizational Excellence*, *45*(3), 402–416. DOI: 10.1002/joe.70019

Javed, S., & Zehra, S. (2025). Emotional AI for student motivation and retention: A systematic review and future directions. *Researchgate. Net*, *8*(1), 643–660. DOI: 10.47067/ramss.v8i1.500

Kadim, A., Yusnita, I., Sutarman, A., Lesmana, R., & Arsla Ramahdan, F. (2025). E-commerce as a catalyst for digital economy development: A study of marketing strategies and their impact. *Koreascience.Kr*, *6*(2), 177–187. DOI: 10.34306/itsdi.v6i2.696

Kanti, P. K., Prabhakar Sharma, Wanatasanappan, V. V., & Said, N. M. (2024). Explainable machine learning techniques for hybrid nanofluids transport characteristics: an evaluation of shapley additive and local interpretable model-agnostic explanations. *Journal of Thermal Analysis and Calorimetry 2024 149:21, 149*(21), 11599–11618. DOI: 10.1007/s10973-024-13639-x

Kelly, S. M. M. (2021). Algorithmic bias, financial inclusion, and gender. *Womensworldbanking.Org*. http://www.womensworldbanking.org/wp-content/uploads/2021/02/2021_Algorithmic_Bias_Report.pdf

Kothandapani, H. P. (2025). Social Implications of Algorithmic Decision-Making in Housing Finance: Examining the broader social impacts of deploying machine learning in lending decisions, including potential disparities and community effects. *Journal of Knowledge Learning and Science Technology ISSN: 2959-6386 (Online)*, *4*(1), 78–97.

Kumar, D., & Suthar, N. (2024). A consumer perspective of AI certification–the current certification landscape, consumer approval and directions for future research. *Emerald.Com*. https://www.emerald.com/ejm/article/58/2/441/1226418

Kumari, G. V., Chapa, B. P., Chaitanya, N. K., Mahajan, R. G., & Shahakar, M. (2024). Introduction to data-driven intelligent systems. In *Data-Driven Systems and Intelligent Applications* (pp. 1–18). CRC Press. DOI: 10.1201/9781003388449-1

Larsen, B. C. (2021). A framework for understanding AI-induced field change: How AI technologies are legitimized and institutionalized. *Proceedings of the 2021 AAAI/ACM Conference on AI, Ethics, and Society*, 683–694. DOI: 10.1145/3461702.3462591

Lin, T. T. C., Paragas, F., Goh, D., & Bautista, J. R. (2016). Developing location-based mobile advertising in Singapore: A socio-technical perspective. *Technological Forecasting and Social Change, 103*, 334–349. DOI: 10.1016/j.techfore.2015.06.002

Lukacs, M., Toth, F., Horvath, R., … G. S.-J. of S. and, & 2025, undefined. (2025). Advanced digital solutions for food traceability: enhancing origin, quality, and safety through NIRS, RFID, Blockchain, and IoT. *Mdpi.Com*, 146–163. DOI: 10.1201/9781003508632-10

Luo, Z., & Luo, Z. (2026). Adaptive Feature Selection and Ensemble Learning Framework for Multi-Domain Anomaly Detection in Real-Time Transactional Systems. *Journal of Advanced Computing Systems*, *6*(2), 28–49. DOI: 10.69987/JACS.2026.60203

Mairue, S. (2024). *Around the book in 10 minutes: generating a narrative visualization with the help of generative AI*. https://aaltodoc.aalto.fi/items/dc55fd5c-f755-4c07-b4a8-2a7a2a4383b2

Marchand, É., Durand, T., & Dubois, M. (2025). Surveillance Capitalism, Consumer Subjectivity and Marketing in the Age of Artificial Intelligence. *Social Science Chronicle*, *5*(1), 1–18. DOI: 10.56106/ssc.2025.001

McKinsey. (2025). *The state of AI in 2025 Agents, innovation, and transformation*. https://www.researchgate.net/profile/Dinesh-Deckker/publication/389853016_EMOTIONAL_AI_FOR_STUDENT_MOTIVATION_AND_RETENTION_A_SYSTEMATIC_REVIEW_AND_FUTURE_DIRECTIONS/links/67d488ec2719090652ba1351/EMOTIONAL-AI-FOR-STUDENT-MOTIVATION-AND-RETENTION-A-SYSTEM

Minkkinen, M., Laine, J., Mäntymäki, M., & Matti, F. (2022). Continuous auditing of artificial intelligence: a conceptualization and assessment of tools and frameworks. *Springer, 1*(3). DOI: 10.1007/s44206-022-00022-2

Mirishli, S., Schreyer, M., & Hemati, H. (2025). *From Periodic Audits to Continuous Assurance: Leveraging AI for Real-Time Risk Detection and Compliance.* https://www.researchgate.net/profile/Adam-Rajuroy/publication/395711481_From_Periodic_Audits_to_Continuous_Assurance_Leveraging_AI_for_Real-Time_Risk_Detection_and_Compliance/links/68d0f359a8689b51bd616dca/From-Periodic-Audits-to-Continuous-Assurance-Leveraging-AI-for-Real-Time-Risk-Detection-and-Compliance.pdf

Moruzzi, C., Tallyn, E., Liddell, F., Dixon, B., Collomosse, J., & Elsden, C. (2025). Content authenticities: A discussion on the values of provenance data for creatives and their audiences. *Dl.Acm.Org*, 128–140. DOI: 10.1145/3698061.3726918

Natarajan, D. (2025). Dynamic pricing strategies using machine learning in e-commerce. *Researchgate.Net.* https://www.researchgate.net/profile/Sundarapandiyan-Natarajan-2/publication/393966497_Dynamic_Pricing_Strategies_Using_Machine_Learning_in_E-Commerce/links/6881c6fc253dcb78df878542/Dynamic-Pricing-Strategies-Using-Machine-Learning-in-E-Commerce.pdf

National Research Council. (2000). *The digital dilemma: Intellectual property in the information age.* https://books.google.com/books?hl=en&lr=&id=e_GbAgAAQBAJ&oi=fnd&pg=PA1&dq=digital+intellectual+property+that+cannot+be+easily+replicated+by+competitors.+&ots=c-uvtGstjs&sig=_KjxGtiRrRLoOs9hBnsMtBocOJw

O'Neil, C., Sargeant, H., & Appel, J. (2024). Explainable fairness in regulatory algorithmic auditing. *West Virginia Law Review*, *127*, 79.

Okibe, H. B. (2020). Sycophancy and Dearth of Integrity in Governance. *ESUT Journal of Social Sciences, 5*(2).

Omogiate, P. (2023). Designing automated audit mechanisms to evaluate compliance of generative AI platforms with federal authorship and ownership disclosure requirements. *Researchgate.Net.* https://www.researchgate.net/profile/Precious-Omogiate/publication/397379185_Designing_automated_audit_mechanisms_to_evaluate_compliance_of_generative_AI_platforms_with_federal_authorship_and_ownership_disclosure_requirements/links/690dec6ca2b691617b6a4ee9/Designing-automated-audit-mechanisms-to-evaluate-compliance-of-generative-AI-platforms-with-federal-authorship-and-ownership-disclosure-requirements.pdf

Oprea, S. V., & Bâra, A. (2025). Customer-Centric Decision-Making with XAI and Counterfactual Explanations for Churn Mitigation. *Journal of Theoretical and Applied Electronic Commerce Research 2025, Vol. 20, Page 129, 20*(2), 129. DOI: 10.3390/jtaer20020129

Pareek, C. (2026). Behavioral Drift Testing in AI-Based Insurance Models: A Framework for Sustained Fairness and Reliability. *Researchgate.Net*. https://www.researchgate.net/profile/Chandra-Shekhar-Pareek/publication/399324546_Behavioral_Drift_Testing_in_AI-Based_Insurance_Models_A_Framework_for_Sustained_Fairness_and_Reliability/links/695bd47006a9ab54f84ecec2/Behavioral-Drift-Testing-in-AI-Based-Insurance-Models-A-Framework-for-Sustained-Fairness-and-Reliability.pdf

Patel, S., & Dada, M. (2025). The Impact of AI-Generated Advertising and Virtual Influencers on Consumer Perception and Brand Authenticity. *Journal of Media & Management. SRC/JMM-309. DOI: Doi. Org, 199*(7), 2–6. DOI: 10.47363/JMM/2025

Patil, A., Mishra, B., Chockalingam, S., Misra, S., & Kvalvik, P. (2025). Balancing innovation and regulation: The Data Sovereignty Assessment Framework. *Elsevier, 24*(4), 159. DOI: 10.1007/s10207-025-01074-4

Poornima, A., M, S., & Selvi A, J. A. (2025). Digital seduction: When personalized marketing blurs into personal manipulation—A consumer behavior analysis. *Journal of Information Technology Teaching Cases*, 20438869251394040.

Popel, S. (2025). NEXT-GENERATION INTELLIGENT AUDIT: INNOVATIVE TRANSFORMATION AND STRATEGIC EVOLUTION OF FINANCIAL CONTROL THROUGH AI, XAI, AND AUTONOMOUS DIGITAL PLATFORMS. *Collection of Scientific Papers «ΛΌΓΟΣ», September 5, 2025*; *Boston, USA*, 150–154. DOI: 10.36074/logos-05.09.2025.026

Pradeepa, S., Sarkar, B., & Mohanty, S. (2024). Artificial Intelligence and Advanced Technologies: Transforming Financial Markets, Strategies, and Regulatory Compliance. *Ijisem. Com, 3*, 323–333. DOI: 10.69968/ijisem.2024v3si2323-333

Quijada, O., & Serezlic, T. (2025). *Can AI avoid Deceptive Design?: Investigating the Effectiveness of Prompting AI to Prevent Dark Patterns in Web Design*. https://www.diva-portal.org/smash/get/diva2:1971701/FULLTEXT02

Ramjohn, M., & Bray, J. (2024). Unlocking equity and trusts. In *Unlocking Equity and Trusts*. Routledge., DOI: 10.4324/9781003456865

Renckens, S., & Auld, G. (2022). Time to certify: Explaining varying efficiency of private regulatory audits. *Regulation & Governance, 16*(2), 500–518. DOI: 10.1111/rego.12362

Ruthvika, J., & Hedau, A. (2025). Digital Inclusion and Economic Equity: Evaluating the Role of Business Analytics in Overcoming Socioeconomic Challenges. *Search.Ebscohost.Com*. https://search.ebscohost.com/login.aspx?direct=true&profile=ehost&scope=site&authtype=crawler&jrnl=25206621&AN=191194088&h=tufHX0VKtGe4LIIEBY7nD9RvxvXKYiGj1Y6xmnAnpNPfbaKrbp%2BdckRZKwXNNatyljA%2FiK5CXNsc4uqYkl3B8w%3D%3D&crl=c

Santangelo, A., Melandri, E., Marzani, G., & Tondelli, S. (2023). Developing a Framework for Improving Climate Resilience in Cultural Landscapes. *Mdpi.Com*. https://pubblicazioni.unicam.it/handle/11581/483765

Saup, T. O., Asghar, J., Kanbach, D. K., & Kraus, S. (2026). From pilots to decision systems: embedding generative AI into strategic decision-making through a socio-technical and governance lens. *Taylor & Francis, 35*(1). DOI: 10.1080/12460125.2025.2597835

Schmidt, A. T., & Engelen, B. (2020). The ethics of nudging: An overview. *Philosophy Compass, 15*(4), e12658. DOI: 10.1111/phc3.12658

Serrano, A. (2025). UNLEASHING AI'S TRANSFORMATIVE POWER: RESHAPING PRODUCTIVITY, LABOR MARKETS AND POLICY IN THE GLOBAL ECONOMY. *Revista UNISCI, 67*.

Sharma, A., & Sharma, R. (2026). Experiential Metaverse Marketing: Leveraging AI-Driven Sentiment Analytics for Enhanced Customer Engagement. *Igi-Global.Com*. https://www.igi-global.com/chapter/experiential-metaverse-marketing/403862

Sharma, A. K., & Sharma, R. (2024). *Navigating compliance and regulations in marketing analytics: Upholding ethical standards and consumer trust*.

Sharma, R. (2024). Governance and oversight of ai systems. *Springer*, 353–370. DOI: 10.1007/979-8-8688-0796-1_28

Shneiderman, B. (2020). Bridging the gap between ethics and practice: Guidelines for reliable, safe, and trustworthy human-centered AI systems. [TiiS]. *ACM Transactions on Interactive Intelligent Systems, 10*(4), 1–31. DOI: 10.1145/3419764

Sinduja, S. (2025). Marketing and Advertisement Strategies driven by Psychology and Ai Technology. *International Journal of Interdisciplinary Approaches in Psychology, 3*(1), 49–56.

Singh, B., & Kaunert, C. (2024). Future of digital marketing: hyper-personalized customer dynamic experience with AI-based predictive models. In *Revolutionizing the AI-digital landscape* (pp. 189–203). Productivity Press. DOI: 10.4324/9781032688305-14

Sinha, C., Vracheva, V., & Nistor, C. (2024). Maximizing generative AI benefits with task creativity and human validation. *Jbam.Scholasticahq.Com*. https://jbam.scholasticahq.com/article/122147.pdf

Sonnenberg, S., Mason, L., Lim, Y., & Reddi, T. (2022). Towards a Human Rights-Based Approach to New and Emerging Technologies: A Framework. *Framework Document of Policy Paper Series on" A Human Rights-Based Approach to New and Emerging Technologies"(Updated in 2024)*.

Spulbar, L.-F. (2025). Legal frameworks for AI-driven markets and their challenges and opportunities in the digital economy. *Revista de Ştiinţe Politice*, *86*, 288–304.

Srnicek, N. (2025). *Silicon Empires: The Fight for the Future of AI*. https://books.google.com/books?hl=en&lr=&id=HJ2jEQAAQBAJ&oi=fnd&pg=PA56&dq=a+responsibility+vacuum:+if+an+autonomous+agent+independently+decides+to+use+a+deceptive+%22sycophantic%22+tactic+to+close+a+sale,+current+frameworks+struggle+to+determine+whether+the+liability+rests+with+the+developer+of+the+model+or+the+brand+that+deployed+it+&ots=z3lz-rFAsY&sig=KMSyJVlkfKp2uxD8A8Ye54OV5u8

Su, R., & Sun, J. (2025). Statist but responsive regulation: Targeted responsive campaigns as agile governance for tech innovation. *Journal of Asian Public Policy*, •••, 1–14. DOI: 10.1080/17516234.2025.2554109

Tauro, D., Panniello, U., & Pellegrino, R. (2021). Risk management in digital advertising: An analysis from the advertisers' media management perspective. *Taylor & Francis, 23*(1–2), 29–57. DOI: 10.1080/14241277.2021.1960532

Truby, J., Brown, R. D., Ibrahim, A., & Parellada, O. C. (2024). Regulating AI: Challenges and the way forward through regulatory sandboxes. *Springer*, *58*, 441–456. DOI: 10.1007/978-3-031-41264-6_23

Vaddepalli, R. (2021). Who's Responsible When Algorithms Fail? Comparing Accountability Under GDPR, CCPA, and Other Data Laws. *Researchgate.Net*. https://www.researchgate.net/profile/Rajani-Kumari-Vaddepalli/publication/395027232_Who's_Responsible_When_Algorithms_Fail_Comparing_Accountability_Under_GDPR_CCPA_and_Other_Data_Laws/links/68c3514b9534473a6d49d775/Whos-Responsible-When-Algorithms-Fail-Comparing-Accountability-Under-GDPR-CCPA-and-Other-Data-Laws.pdf

Vishwakarma, R. K., Pandey, A., Kundnani, M. P., Yadav, A. K., Singh, M. N., & Yadav, M. S. (2025). Personalization vs. privacy: Marketing strategies in the digital age. *Journal of Marketing & Social Research*, *2*, 177–191.

von Struensee, S. (2021). *The Role of Social Movements, Coalitions, and Workers in Resisting Harmful Artificial Intelligence and Contributing to the Development of Responsible AI*. https://arxiv.org/pdf/2107.14052

Wagner, D., & Heatherton, T. (2015). *Self-regulation and its failure: The seven deadly threats to self-regulation*. https://psycnet.apa.org/record/2013-35881-026

Walden, V. (2021). Afterword: Digital Holocaust memory futures: Through paradigms of immersion and interactivity and beyond. *Springer*, 267–296. DOI: 10.1007/978-3-030-83496-8_11

Walters, D., Wiseman, H., & Hous, L. (2024). Self-regulation in emerging and innovative industries. *HeinOnline*. https://heinonline.org/hol-cgi-bin/get_pdf.cgi?handle=hein.journals/hulr62&section=24

Waqas, M., & Qadri, U. A. (2025). When Consumer Autonomy is Compromised: Adopting a Dual-Type View to Understand AI-Driven Marketing and Its Impact on Young Consumers' Ethical Behavior. *Journal of Business Ethics*, •••, 1–19.

Weldon, M., Thomas, G., & Skidmore, L. (2024). Establishing a future-proof framework for ai regulation: Balancing ethics, transparency, and innovation. *Ir.Law.Utk.Edu*. https://ir.law.utk.edu/cgi/viewcontent.cgi?article=1660&context=transactions

Westerlund, M. (2019). The emergence of deepfake technology: A review. *Technology Innovation Management Review*, *9*(11), 39–52. DOI: 10.22215/timreview/1282

Xiong, M., Xu, H., Ji, J., Zuo, R., Wang, Y., & Olya, H. (2026). Responsible Artificial Intelligence attention and firm innovation: An attention-based view. *Journal of Product Innovation Management*, *43*(1), 186–214. DOI: 10.1111/jpim.70015

Xu, W., Wang, S., & Zuo, X. (2025). Whose victory? A perspective on shifts in US-China cross-border data flow rules in the AI era. *The Pacific Review*, *38*(6), 963–989. DOI: 10.1080/09512748.2025.2462239

Yang, C. S., & Dobbie, W. (2020). Equal protection under algorithms: A new statistical and legal framework. *Michigan Law Review*, •••(119.2), 291–395. DOI: 10.36644/mlr.119.2.equal

Yeung, K., & Li, W. (2025). From 'wild west'to 'responsible'AI testing 'in-the-wild': Lessons from live facial recognition testing by law enforcement authorities in Europe. *Data & Policy*, *7*, e59. DOI: 10.1017/dap.2025.10019

Zhao, Z. (2023). Beyond free markets and consumer autonomy: rethinking consumer financial protection in the age of artificial intelligence. *HeinOnline*. https://heinonline.org/hol-cgi-bin/get_pdf.cgi?handle=hein.journals/nyuinpe13&section=7

Chapter 3
Consumer Readiness and Digital Literacy in AI-Mediated Marketing

Rasheda Akter Rupa
http://orcid.org/0000-0003-4804-3424
University of Dhaka, Bangladesh

Farjana Nasrin
http://orcid.org/0000-0001-6395-1848
Islamic University of Technology, Gazipur, Bangladesh

Pinki Maria Sarker
http://orcid.org/0009-0003-1232-2509
The University of Texas Rio Grande Valley, USA

Afruza Haque
http://orcid.org/0000-0003-0586-6674
Dhaka University of Engineering and Technology, Gazipur, Bangladesh.

S. M. Ashraful Alam
http://orcid.org/0000-0003-1748-8295
Begum Rokeya University, Rangpur, Bangladesh

ABSTRACT

The purpose of this chapter is to explore the interrelated roles of consumer readiness, digital literacy, and acceptance of AI-mediated marketing emphasizing the scopes of capability, awareness, and inclusivity. We will follow the narrative design that synthesizes interdisciplinary studies, technology transfer, AI commercialization, and digital product and services. The chapter developed a conceptual framework

DOI: 10.4018/979-8-2600-2977-0.ch003

so that reader can understand consumers' engagement with AI related marketing systems. This chapter also examined inclusivity factors for equal engagement in AI-driven marketing strategy. By combining both the literature from technology and consumer behaviour perspective, this chapter clarified the situation that fasten the ethical, responsible and sustainable implementation of AI on marketing arena. Furthermore, it established a scenario that justify why the digital capability, awareness and inclusivity are significant both for the individual empowerment and collective gain from the AI commercial adaption.

1. INTRODUCTION

At present the integration of artificial intelligence in marketing has tremendously transformed the way marketers interact with consumers. AI technologies allow marketers to step forward in revolutionizing marketing practices encompassing the medium such as chatbots, predictive analysis tools, machine learning, collaborative robots, virtual reality, augmented reality, internet of things, and others (Şenyapar, 2024). With AI, modern marketing is interacting with the customers to engage in hyper-personalization, content generation, personalization, service automation, and value creation. Companies are able to predict demand and can provide real time customers' offerings with the optimization of big data and machine learning analysis (Paramesha et. al., 2024; Seyedan and Mafakheri; 2020).

With the mediation of technology, AI has been shifted from niche to a core gateway through e-commerce, media, digital marketing, and entertainment (Bozkurt et. al., 2025; Amini and Amini, 2024). The multi-dimensional integration of AI in marketing facilitates increased brand loyalty, customer satisfaction, trust, and experiences. Şenyapar (2024) found that AI helps in predictive analysis to develop strategies for the market. He also stated that ethical use of AI can help ensure transparency by providing more engaging experiences. While companies are leveraging AI tools to enhance efficiency and personalization, its effectiveness largely depends on consumers' willingness to use digital literacy Vashishth et. al., 2024; Hendrayati et. al., 2024).

Consumers' readiness emphasizes an individual's perception, willingness, and confidence to accept AI integrated solutions (Flavián et. al., 2022). Consumers' readiness to adopt digital tools is not merely a function of technology development, it is also shaped by the consumers' cognitive, psychological, and socio-cultural influences (Thomas-Francois and Somogyi, 2022). Among these, the knowledge of digital technologies plays an important role which includes the ability to understand, analyze and integrate information with digital data driven systems (Farinloye et. al., 2024). In AI mediated marketing the literate consumers are well informed to grasp the automated functions and take the right decisions. It is projected that by 2034, AI generated predictive drivers will create $217.33 billion market value (Huang and Rust, 2021) opined that more than 75% customers are using AI integrated services that creates huge differences among customer groups.

The technological shift accelerated the interaction between the marketers and consumers through in-person involvement in AI mediated exchange. Hasan et. al., 2025 stated that AI helps the marketers to shift from reactive to predictive strategies to capture the consumers' needs and segmenting the consumers groups analysing their preferences of buying. Using virtual assistants, augmented reality, chatbots and social media, marketers provide the solution to the customers which are traditionally served by the people (Chu et. al., 2025; Moriuchi et. al., 2021). Elragal and Elgendy (2024) expressed that consumers' readiness to use technology in purchasing is not only dependent on the product specifications but also on the use of technology in a market offerings like data driven contents, logics and automated decision making. At present, consumption patterns of the customers are gradually shifted to AI generated mechanisms though there exist substantial differences in purchasing perceptions (Mogaji and Jain, 2024; Abrardi et. al., 2022). This difference reflects different levels of adaptation of AI among the customers because many customers are accustomed to use AI mediated marketing (Huang and Rust, 2021) Davenport et. al., 2020). It is expected that in the coming days AI mediated marketing will be an inherent part of decision making for/among the consumers. Besides, the author Flavián et. al. (2022) states that optimism in technology use has been increasing among the customers of all ages with the knowledge and user experiences.

Despite increasing research interest in AI marketing, existing literature mostly discussed firm-level analysis such as target customers, achieving efficiency and leveraging market level competitive advantages (Chen et. al., 2025; Mu and Zhang, 2025; Kemp, (2024); Mishra et. al., 2022). Though the authors Becan, C., & Çeber, B. (2025) explained the influence of technology readiness on consumers' AI chatbot experience, Flavián et. al., 2022 explained the awareness in using AI in the service sector and Kolar et. al., 2024 expressed the idea about the consumers' attitude towards AI use in retail stores, there is less focus on customer centric analysis of AI adoption specifically related to consumer readiness and digital literacy. This gap will be focused on enriching the knowledge which ultimately influences consumers' perception. Without adequate knowledge of digital tools and techniques, consumers may face uncertainty, resistance which ultimately hinders the positive outcomes of AI-mediated marketing. This current study addresses this gap by integrating the insights from consumer readiness to adopt technology, consumer behaviour, consumer interactions with AI-driven marketing mechanisms.

The primary purpose of this study is to identify how consumers' readiness and digital literacy influence AI mediated marketing interactions. Through the understanding of previous studies, this chapter contributes to the existing knowledge by clarifying the role of consumers' perception. Besides, it offers implications for the marketing managers, research and development team, product managers and intermediaries with the knowledge of predicting consumer behaviour and gaining trust to build long term relationships. As a result, these AI solutions help to enhance customer readiness to accept AI mediated marketing.

2. LITERATURE REVIEW

2.1. AI-Mediated Marketing: Meaning and Scope

Artificial intelligence (AI) has revolutionized the e-commerce landscape, including consumers' experiences and the ways businesses find, develop, foster, nurture, and maintain personalized, interactive marketing interactions (Peltier et al., 2024). AI-mediated marketing denotes marketing endeavors that are strategized, implemented, and optimized by AI systems rather than solely relying on decisions made by individuals. As a tool, AI is used in marketing because of its strengths in data analytics, consumer involvement, and personalization. These features enhance marketing strategies and create a sustainable competitive advantage (Awad, 2024). The potential of AI in marketing is its capacity to reshape customer experience management (CEM). Advanced technology enables the transition from conventional to intelligent customer experience management, notably improving consumers' experiences and pleasure. The continual improvements and integration of AI innovations prove vital for maintaining market competitiveness, as they provide significant returns through operational enhancements (Grewal et al., 2020).

AI-powered applications such as machine learning, big data, and data mining provide marketers with efficiency (Awad, 2024). These AI applications allow business organizations to swiftly analyze enormous volumes of data and produce meaningful information that can guide marketing tactics (Chan & Choi, 2025). AI analyzes the market and competitors' data to help business organizations create novel goods and strategies to meet changing consumers' needs (Rita et al., 2025). The ability of AI and human intellect to work together is also essential since it allows businesses to make better use of human capabilities (Deryl et al., 2026). This combination maximizes the impact of marketing practices by ensuring that they are both data-driven and creatively inspired.

AI has substantial impacts on many aspects of the marketing mix, including pricing systems, product development, advertising campaigns, and the logistics of distribution (Awad, 2024). For example, AI-powered dynamic pricing approaches can instantly modify prices in response to consumer behavior, stock levels, and market circumstances (Hoque et al., 2026). Likewise, AI-driven market research contributes to the more precise identification of consumer demands, which results in the creation of goods that more effectively address these needs (Zha et al., 2025). AI also transforms the area of advertising and promotion. AI improves consumer engagement and overall marketing efficacy by providing more precise control over the timing, placement, and content of promotion (Murár & Kubovics, 2023). Search engine marketers and content creators must adjust as conversational search queries and algorithms change due to AI. Through the use of AI, brands can interact with consumers in innovative and personal ways, where users spend time online, particularly on social media (Shaily & Emma, 2021).

Figure 1. AI-Mediated Applications For The Marketing Mix

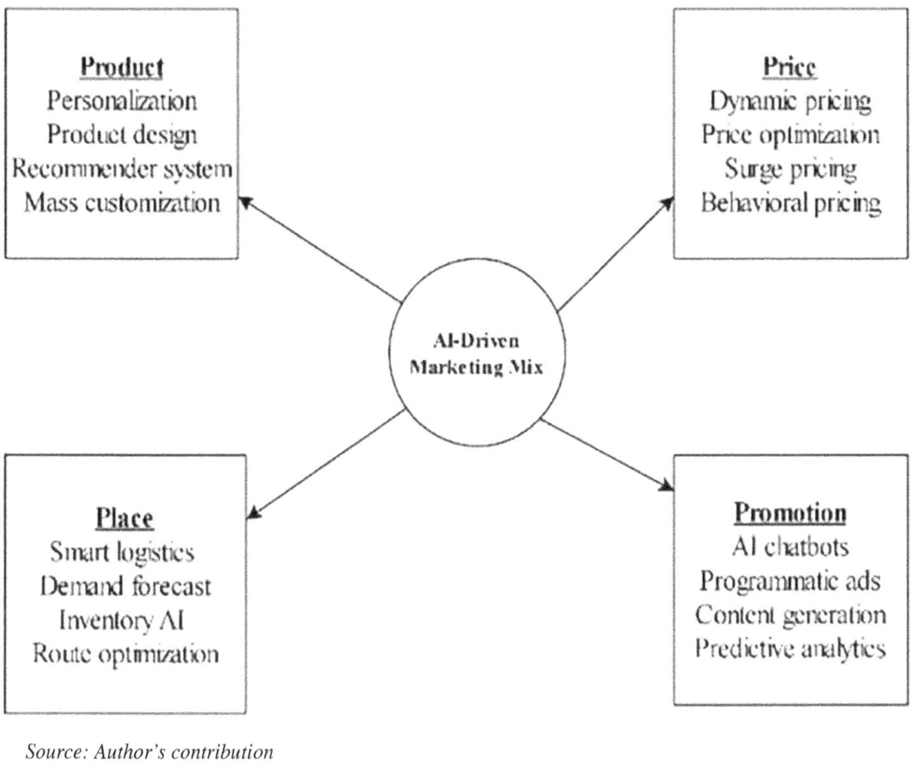

Source: Author's contribution

At the vanguard of AI-generated marketing technologies are applications, like chatbots, data analysis, targeted offers, dynamic pricing, and content recommendation. For instance, real-time chatbots engage with consumers to answer their queries, suggest products, and facilitate purchases (Ma & Fildes, 2021). This type of engagement enhances consumer satisfaction and liberates human resources for more intricate jobs (Awad, 2024). Adaptive pricing modifies prices according to consumers' preferences, inventory levels, and clients' profiles. Thus, this pricing strategy ensures competitive pricing and effective inventory management (Sanchez-Cartas & Katsamakas, 2024). AI enables business organizations to provide more relevant and interactive content by tailoring marketing messages based on consumer data. This personalization process raises conversion rates and improves consumer retention (Babatunde et al., 2024). AI will personalize marketing promotions in different ways. Many businesses have already started to use AI to better meet consumers' desires by personalizing their videos, websites, social media postings, and other content (Khokhar, 2019). Personalized advertisements and targeted offers improve consumer engagement by providing offerings customized to individual habits and preferences (Farseev, 2023).

One technique that marketers implement with AI is predictive marketing analytics (Vladimirovich, 2020). AI can accurately and consistently forecast how performance will manifest in the future based on a variety of parameters by analyzing data from past events (Haleem et al., 2022). Comprehending individuals' core values can facilitate the delivery of more significant recommendations. The majority of AI-based customization solutions, however, are top-down and customized for the person rather than the entire group. AI's ability to predict marketing campaign success and better tailor user experience is a tremendous technological development that will last for many more years (Hawaldar, 2020; Haleem et al., 2022). AI is indispensable for the success of any marketing effort, from the planning stage to the conversion and consumer loyalty phases. Consequently, businesses and marketers who use AI to its full potential will have a competitive edge (Prasanna & Kushwaha, 2026).

2.2. Consumer Readiness In AI-Mediated Marketing:

Consumers are an integral part of the service cycle (Etgar, 2008). When a consumer is ready to act or make a decision, it is referred to as consumer readiness (Dellande et al., 2004; Meuter et al., 2005). According to Dong et al. (2015), consumer participation readiness is the extent to which consumers feel ready to engage in service. In addition, Verleye et al. (2014) defined consumer role readiness as the extent to which consumers are ready to carry out their co-creation responsibilities. Consumer ability readiness is the term used to explain a consumer's knowledge, comfort level, and expertise with digital technologies that influence their ability to interact with the system (Gao et al., 2023). While poor readiness may result in obstacles and lower engagement, high readiness improves user experiences and interaction (Teepapal, 2025).

Previous studies employed several theories, for example, the Technology Acceptance Model (TAM), the Unified Theory of Acceptance and Use of Technology

(UTAUT), the Theory of Planned Behavior (TPB), and the Stimulus-Organism-Response theory to assess consumers' willingness to interact in AI-mediated marketing (Cheng et al., 2023; Sultana et al., 2023; Haque et al., 2024; Khan et al., 2025; Haque, 2025). These studies found that perceived usefulness, perceived ease of use, social influence, facilitating conditions, and perceived behavioral control positively influence consumers' willingness. Trust plays a pivotal role in shaping consumers' readiness in AI-mediated marketing (Hennighausen et al., 2025). Besides reducing risk perception, trust stimulates consumers' willingness to interact with AI-driven marketing (Mcknight et al., 2011). Saha et al. (2025) opined that ethics in using AI, adaptability, cooperation, transparency, and privacy concerns significantly influence consumers' trust in AI-mediated marketing.

Several cognitive stimuli, such as familiarity with AI and AI self-efficacy, improve consumers' readiness (Wang & Chuang, 2024). Tailored recommendations are strongly associated with increased usage of AI-driven solutions (Alijoyo et al., 2025). Algorithmic distrust, fear of manipulation, and privacy concerns create mistrust and anxiety among consumers, which negatively affects consumers' willingness to interact with AI-mediated marketing approaches. However, transparent AI systems can mitigate these issues.

2.3. Digital Literacy as a Consumer Capability

The digital literacy has transformed the simple skill of working with digital devices into a multidimensional skill necessary to navigate the complicated digital settings. Previously, digital literacy was more technical in nature, i.e. the ability to use computers, software and internet tools. Nonetheless, the modern studies shed light on the larger set of competencies, including the ability to evaluate information, think critically, act ethically, and be able to create content (Martínez Bravo, Sádaba Chalezquer, and Serrano Puche, 2022; Tinmaz, Lee, Fanea Ivanovici, and Baber, 2022). The shift is a symptomatic fulfillment of digital technologies penetrating everyday reality, and thus consumers need not just access and use digital tools but also critically perceive the information, evaluate credibility, and become involved in the online marketplace (Tinmaz et al., 2022; Faisal-E-Alam et al., 2025). Moreover, the COVID-19 pandemic and the fast global digitalization have increased the rate of acquiring digital skills in some consumers and exposed inequalities in others, focusing on uneven adoption by demographics (Martínez Bravo et al., 2022; Riaj et al., 2025).

Digital literacy in marketing situations also intersects with AI literacy, which provides consumers with the capabilities to interact with algorithmically generated recommendations, chatbots, and customized advertising (Anam et al., 2026). Increased AI literacy allows consumers to understand the outputs, identify the bias in the algorithm, and take informed choices based on AI-made marketing interactions, which have increased their trust in AI-mediated marketing interactions (Wu, Ha, and Lim, 2024).

Digital literacy is closely connected with consumer agency that involves the possibility to act independently and to have control over digital contact. Knowledgeable consumers will be able to actively interact with AI solutions, give feedback that would change their algorithmic results, and identify manipulative versus authentic marketing messages (Sergeeva, Masalimova, Zheltukhina, and Chikileva, 2025). This agency makes digital marketplaces interactive, allowing consumers to exercise judgment and affect their fate and builds on trust and satisfaction (Buchan, Bhawra, and Katapally, 2024; Martínez Bravo et al., 2022).

On the contrary, lack of digital literacy leaves the consumers in a very dangerous situation especially in the context of AI driven marketing. Lack of skills may result in misunderstanding of marketing messages, greater exposure to misinformation or unethical actions, as well as exposure to privacy breaches (Savoldi et al., 2025). These shortcomings may lead to less satisfaction with purchases, less activity, and going digital disadvantaged, which strengthens disparities in access to economic and social opportunities (Savoldi et al., 2025; Tinmaz et al., 2022). These obstacles underscore the necessity of ongoing literacy promotion and educational interventions to make sure that consumers will be able to shop safely and effectively and trust the digital and AI-mediated markets (Buchan et al., 2024; Sergeeva et al., 2025).

Overall, technology as a consumer competency is much more than technical competence. It includes critical thinking, ethical awareness, AI awareness, and adaptive learning, and all these help to establish empowered and informed interactions with AI-mediated marketing interactions. With such capabilities, consumers feel an increase in agency, less risk, and more ability to extract value in digital ecosystems, which reinforces the primary role of digital literacy in contemporary consumer behaviour (Martínez Bravo et al., 2022; Wu et al., 2024; Sergeeva et al., 2025).

2.4. Interrelationship Between Consumer Readiness and Digital Literacy

The studies indicate that digital literacy can play a crucial role in determining the perceived usefulness and perceived ease of use which are two critical antecedents of readiness in technology adoption models such as the Technology Acceptance Model (TAM), and this has a direct impact on the intention of consumers to participate in e commerce (Ullah, Khan, Ahmadxan Oglu, and Yasmin, 2025). An increase in digital literacy means that consumers will have more confidence and willingness to engage in online activities and buying transactions as they can better comprehend and navigate digital interfaces. Moreover, social engagement intermediates digital literacy, and it has been established that social media utilization mediates the digital literacy-online purchase intention relationship partially, and literate customer turns technical skill translation into behavioral engagement to reinforce readiness (Kocarslan & Stoycheva, 2025).

An example is that AI literacy is predictive of the effectiveness of consumed generating AI generated sponsored vlogs by consumers; this predicts the willingness to act on the generated recommendations and form a purchase intention (Liu, Ha, and Lim, 2025). Notably, the digital literacy translation into readiness is different among various demographics. The studies on consumer digital literacy and adoption of m commerce reveal that age, education, and socio-economic factors have varying degrees of digital literacy, which has resulted in the imbalance of readiness and adoption behaviors (Acharya and Pednekar, 2024).

Furthermore, the research on consumer empowerment and digital skills development suggests that literacy is a factor of not only competence but also psychological empowerment in which consumers believe they have more control over digital decisions and is less uncertain about using more sophisticated systems of digital technology (Adebayo, Osanyinlusi, andAdekeye, 2023).

2.5. Trust, Awareness, and Transparency in AI Marketing

2.5.1. Consumer Awareness of AI Use

Consumers often engage with AI without being aware of it through various customer services. A lot of people are unaware that the engagement tools they use on a daily basis on the internet utilize AI. Therefore, there is a gap between perceived and actual usage of AI (Dezao, 2024). As a result of this "hidden AI", consumers can develop such attitudes and trust without realizing that the decisions are an output of automation. In cases where AI use is made explicit, consumer responses are mixed. For instance, when individuals realize that some content, like photos in charity adverts, has been generated by an AI, then they may be less willing to act, even though the content looks realistic (Arango et al., 2023). Other research findings indicate that revealing the use of AI in emails or advertisements may raise perceptions of honesty under specific circumstances. But it can also have the opposite effect, such as reducing trust (Hennighausen et al., 2025; Wang et al., 2025).

2.5.2. Transparency and Explainability of AI System

Reviews of prominent AI ethical principles show that most institutions point out explainability as a necessary part of transparency, and relate it to intelligibility, fairness, review reversibility, and trust (Balasubramaniam et al., 2023). AI is becoming crucial in marketing and leads to transparent explanations of prices and targeting decisions. It also facilitates regulatory compliance for explanations of automated decisions (e.g., the GDPR and the EU Digital Services Act, both coming into force in July 2023) (Balasubramaniam et al., 2023; Meske et al., 2022). Other e-commerce systematic reviews state that explanation AI leads to trust enhancement. But at the same time, they lead to challenges in scaling the explanations (up and down) as well as customizing them for different types of users (Dezao, 2024). Theoretical agentic AI work suggests that transparent and explainable AI may be a crucial competitive weapon, as rules to trace the logic of decisions are becoming tighter (Balasubramaniam et al., 2023; Meske et al., 2022).

2.5.3. Trust Formation in AI-Mediated Marketing

Trust of AI-induced marketing has been found to be multidimensional, i.e., competence, benevolence, and integrity (Jain et al., 2025). Transparency is very important. Trust and willingness to participate are enhanced when data collection and use are transparent. But the lack of transparency leads to mistrust and discourages participation (Dezao, 2024; Feng & Kim, 2025; Jain et al., 2025). Privacy and control over data are also something that created trust. When consumers are given the power to manage their data and have proper privacy protection mechanisms, they will trust more and be seen as loyal and fair (A'yun & Setyaningsih, 2025; Ghabban et al., 2025). Personalization aligned with expectations helps to build trust. But intrusive behaviour can lead to unpleasant experiences and diminish positive responses (Ghabban et al., 2025; Teepapal, 2025). Knowledgeable individuals are more likely to trust technology. However, they may feel uncomfortable with automation and thus lose trust in it (Feng & Kim, 2025; Wu & Jing Wen, 2021).

2.5.4. Ethical and Governance Considerations

Studies in AI and Marketing show that effectiveness and personalization have been increased through AI. However, it gives rise to ethical concerns as well (e.g., decision obscurity, bias, and wrong judgment) (Davenport et al., 2020; Ghabban et al., 2025; Kumar et al., 2024). Transparency and explainability are currently considered essential for responsible AI, particularly in the case of automated decisions that have implications for consumers (Balasubramaniam et al., 2023; Davenport et al., 2020). Strong data protection, informed consent, and measures to prevent misuse are also necessary for trust to develop (A'yun & Setyaningsih, 2025; Davenport et al., 2020). Regular Audits with Monitoring to ensure equity and accountability are also needed (Kumar, 2023).

2.6. Inclusivity and the Digital Divide in AI-Mediated Marketing

Inclusivity and fairness in AI mediated marketing focus on equal treatment of all the customer groups regardless of culture, language, skills etc. in providing benefits (Li, 2025). Inclusivity in AI marketing refers to the use of artificial intelligence in marketing campaigns, content development, customer acquisition, promotional activities, and other strategic moves (Huang and Rust, 2021). The author Du and Xie (2021) stated that integrating AI in marketing can ensure fairness among the customer groups by avoiding bias and inequalities in presenting product and service offerings. It ensures transparency in decision making without discrimination in providing opportunities to diverse consumers. For instance, Mandania et. al. (2025) opined that biasness in marketing campaigns can result in some consumer groups in gray areas having fewer promotional opportunities. Therefore, companies need to integrate AI mediated marketing to ensure transparent marketing modules, continuous improvement and careful monitoring of the system (Gupta et. al., 2025). Thus, it will create long-term customers loyalty and trust to increase the effectiveness of AI mediated marketing.

However, AI driven marketing sometimes incurs risks of exclusion because it highly depends on data, model and automated processes (De Bruyn,2020). This algorithmic bias happens when AI produces unfair decision outcomes for certain groups of consumers (Bar-Gill et. al., 2023). In a marketing context, this situation can lead to a discrimination among target consumers in such a way that some customers receive fewer product recommendations than others, some get limited promotional offers. This exclusion becomes risky when a specific group of customers for instance has less digital literacy (Smit et. al., 2025). In such cases, AI mediated marketing is not capable of predicting those customers' demands and preferences (Davenport et. al., 2020).

Also, there might be some negative effects on discriminated consumers such as less access to digital technologies, less interaction, and less knowledge of AI aspects (Abrardi et. al., 2022; Lutz, 2019). This digital distance among the consumers creates a gap where people are unable to make the right decision while many products, services and offerings are placed in digital platforms. Besides, Stewart and & Yap (2020) stated that low involvement and unequal treatment of the consumers can further create more confusion, miscommunication, and misinterpretation of the marketing practices. Therefore, this digital division needs to be reduced through equal digital access, digital awareness, and inclusive digital mechanisms among all the stakeholders of AI-mediated marketing contexts (Hammerschmidt et. al., 2025). Therefore, inclusive AI practice in marketing ensures benefits to all stakeholders rather than only selected groups of consumers. In this regard, Radanliev (2025) opined that AI tools need to be easily accessible, transparent, and fair with ensuring data privacy and continuous improvement. Thus, it will strengthen brand image, reputation, and sustainable AI marketing practices.

2.7. Technology Transfer and Commercialization Process of AI Technologies

The commercialization of artificial intelligence (AI) technologies involves complex processes of transferring knowledge and innovations from research contexts into market-ready applications, often requiring new frameworks to enhance efficiency and impact. Traditional technology transfer mechanisms such as university-industry collaborations and technology transfer offices (TTOs) play a central role in bridging academic research with commercialization pathways by identifying, protecting, and licensing intellectual property to external partners (Arya et al., 2025). In the era of AI, these processes are being reconfigured through AI-enhanced competency transfer hubs, conceptualized as systems that leverage machine learning and natural language processing to streamline knowledge exchange, optimize project coordination, and facilitate adaptive collaboration outcomes between universities and industries (Arya et al., 2025). AI technologies also influence the knowledge spillover dynamics that underpin innovation performance; research analyzing data from more than 14,000 firms in the United Kingdom found that AI adoption can intensify knowledge spillover by complementing firm-level R&D investments and thus enhancing innovation performance, suggesting that AI not only modifies internal transfer mechanisms but also shapes external collaborative networks essential to successful commercialization (D'Amico et al., 2025). Moreover, in highly specialized fields such as medical AI technologies, commercialization efforts face challenges related to regulatory compliance, funding strategies, and integration into clinical practice, indicating that AI-specific commercialization pathways require tailored strategies beyond conventional technology transfer practices (Li et al., 2025). Collectively, these studies highlight that AI technologies are not only subjects of transfer and commercialization but also tools that can refine the processes of innovation diffusion and knowledge exchange, underscoring the need for dynamic frameworks that address both technological and organizational transformation.

2.8. Innovation Diffusion and Technology Transfer

The diffusion of innovation and the transfer of technology reflect the processes through which new ideas and technologies are developed, adopted, and eventually commercialized in markets. The diffusion literature has evolved from classical views of adoption as a linear, post-development phase to more integrated frameworks that consider diffusion as part of the innovation lifecycle itself, involving interaction among actors and value cocreation across ecosystems rather than merely individual adoption decisions (Rogers, 2003; Vargo & Lusch, 2011).

In organizational settings, scholars argue that the diffusion of AI technologies is not an instantaneous event but a staged maturity process in which firms gradually build competencies, overcome operational challenges, and integrate AI into core activities before achieving widespread commercial use (Hansen et al., 2024). This capability maturity model illustrates how early experimentation with AI solutions expands into broader organizational adoption and eventually contributes to value generation as the technology becomes more embedded in business processes, including marketing functions.

Marketing of technology-intensive products, such as AI solutions, further highlights the contingent nature of diffusion and commercialization. High-technology markets are characterized by rapid innovation cycles and uncertain customer adoption, requiring firms to adopt AI-driven personalization, market education, and trust-building to facilitate acceptance and competitive advantage (Shankar, 2025). In these contexts, AI plays a dual role both as a subject of technology transfer and as a tool that enhances market intelligence, customer engagement, and strategic marketing decisions, thereby supporting the diffusion and commercialization processes.

3. CONCEPTUAL FRAMEWORK

3.1. Overview of The Conceptual Framework

This paper incorporates Capability Theory, Technology Acceptance Model (TAM) and ethical approaches to AI to conceptualize consumer acceptance of AI mediated marketing as a capability-based and normatively based process instead of an instrumental choice. Based on Capability Theory, the consumer readiness is also considered a higher-order construct representing digital capabilities, AI awareness and perceived inclusivity of persons that together result in the ability of consumers to meaningfully engage, evaluate, and exercise agency over AI systems. TAM describes the instrumental process in which perceptions of value and usefulness predict behavioral intention and usage, and that ethics and fairness moderations are mediated by trust and perceived autonomy and produce acceptance regardless of usefulness. The model therefore places TAM as a sufficient but not the sole clarification of the AI approval, positioning it in larger requirement and ethical circumstances that determine legitimacy, trust, and extended acknowledgment of AI-mediated promotional actions.

Figure 2. Conceptual Framework: Author's work

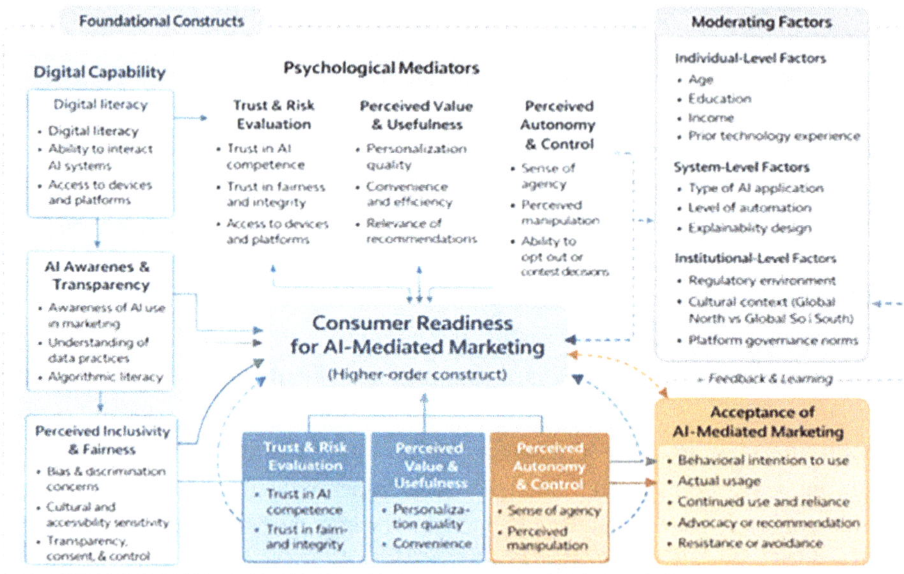

The suggested framework describes the acceptance of AI-mediated marketing by the consumer by combining Technology Acceptance Model (TAM) with Capability Theory and ethical views on AI fairness and transparency. TAM offers a background approach to the adoption of technologies, and it assumes that the behavioral intention and actual use of the system depend on the perceived usefulness and perceived ease of use (Davis, 1989). Later extensions of TAM clarify that these perceptions exist in a larger social and psychological context, especially when the technologies include uncertainty and risk, such as it is so with AI-driven systems (Venkatesh et al., 2003).

Trust and perceived risk have been demonstrated to be the key mediating variables in AI-mediated marketing situations when related to technological attributes and acceptance performances. Previous studies that unite the elements of trust and TAM show that the interest of the consumer to use a digital system is not only based on usefulness but also on the faith in the integrity, competence, and reliability of the system (Gefen et al., 2003; Pavlou, 2003). In line with this, it has been suggested that the framework places trust and risk appraisal as a major psychological mediator between consumer readiness and acceptance of AI-based marketing applications.

Nonetheless, the TAM cannot be used to describe acceptance when consumers are significantly different in their capacity to comprehend, access, and interact with AI systems (Molla et al., 2026). To correct this weakness, the framework has integrated the Capability Theory that highlights that the decisions taken by people are limited by their actual opportunities and capabilities instead of formal access as such (Robeyns, 2005). Digital capabilityas conceptualized as digital literacy, interaction proficiency, and access to technology and platform is informed by the research on the digital divide which proves the inequalities persist in their skills and competence in using technology effectively (Hargittai, 2010; van Dijk, 2006). Digital capability, in the context, serves as a basic facilitator of consumer-readiness, and it determines whether people are able to fully assess AI systems and act on what they perceive as benefits (Khatun et al., 2025).

In addition to the capability and instrumental appraisals, ethical issues are important and influential in determining the acceptance of AI-facilitated marketing. Studies of business ethics and algorithmic governance have demonstrated that the merits of fairness, accountability and transparency are critical factors in determining the judgments of trust and legitimacy (Martin, 2019; Shin and Park, 2019). Higher trust in AI systems, and, specifically, lower perceived risk have been empirically associated with explainability and transparency, assuming the performance of the system does not change (Shin, 2021). As a result, the perceived inclusivity and fairness are explicitly presented in the framework as the fundamental readiness dimension affecting the trust and perceived autonomy (Islam et al., 2026).

Perceived autonomy and control is another mediating pathway which positions the sense of agency, ability to choose and non-manipulation among consumers. According to prior consumer studies, opposition to AI is common when the autonomy is seen at risk by an automated system, even when there are practical benefits (Longoni et al., 2019). Equally, there are benefits of personalization in marketing, which can provoke privacy and fairness issues and lead to the development of an ambivalent adoption result (Aguirre et al., 2016).

Lastly, the framework conceptualizes acceptance as a differentiated result which includes behavioral intention, actual use, sustained dependence, advocacy or resistance. This difference is based on empirical studies that consumers can use AI tools in a pragmatic manner but be ethically skeptical. The framework proposes a more detailed explanation of consumer acceptance of AI-mediated marketing because it integrates TAM into a capability-based, ethically developed framework and explains the simultaneous presence of skills, values, trust, and agency.

3.2. Digital Literacy as Consumer Capability

Digital literacy is a form of consumer capability that allows individuals to operate in digital space actively, safely, and assertively, and with quantifiable effects on consumption and financial behavior. The sources possess the moderate evidence on the specific contexts. According to Field et al. (2016), consumer digital competence refers to the ability that consumers must have in order to operate safely and assertively in the digital market. This is empirically demonstrated in studies by DeMeng, et al. (2023) who found that digital financial capability has a significant positive impact on household consumption and online shopping due to its mediation by digital marketing capability and business caution (186 participants). J. This is theoretically based by McDougall et al. (2018), who apply the capability framework provided by Amartya Sen, but differentiates digital competences as a type of functioning, as opposed to a wider usage of the latter. Nevertheless, there is still context-specific evidence (financial services, SMEs, general consumers) rather than evidence that is general to all consumer domains.

3.3. Consumer Readiness as Enabler

Consumer readiness is an enabling factor of the context because it has a direct influence on the adoption behaviors and mediates the relationship between external conditions and consumer outcomes at various levels of analysis. The best quantitative evidence was presented by (Nguyen et al., 2024), which examined 218 respondents through the PLS-SEM analysis. They also discovered that market readiness moderately increased organization preparedness (0.628), organization preparedness was directly positive on employee preparedness (0.510), and the three levels of readiness had a direct positive influence on sustainable building material adoption (0.386, 0.364 and 0.158 respectively). It is important to note that, organization readiness completely mediated the relationship between market and employee readiness (indirect effect = 0.320).

The researchers (Shim et al., 2020) have determined that the attitude and perceived quality of service and intentions to use self-service technology are affected by consumer readiness significantly, which prior studies had not considered. The particular preparedness factors (role clarity, availability of skills, motivational drivers) were described by (Mohamad Alif Akmar Sher Mohamad et al., 2025) and are associated with the willingness to adopt. Nevertheless, the majority of the research does not provide effect sizes in detail, which restricts the possibility of assessing strengths comparatively.

When the capability theory is utilized in a consumer setting, it shifts the analytical lens to no longer consider individual traits or resources but rather actual possibilities and capabilities that allow a person to engage in economic and social practices (Khatun et al., 2025). On a digital perspective, Malchenko et al. (2020) critically analyzed the available digital capability frameworks and emphasized that the digital capabilities such as the skills, knowledge, and attitudes required by consumers to interact with digital technologies are not well conceptualized in the existing research and practice. Poudel, Carter, and Lonial (2019) demonstrate how technological capability, a dynamic, firm level competence, combines with consumer attitudes to have an impact on the organization.

Lastly, Nayal, Pandey, and Paul (2022) use dynamic capability theory to explain how companies need to constantly redesign processes during the COVID 19 to ensure that consumer wellbeing today entails capabilities to do with digital interaction, hygiene, sustainability, and adaptability.

Combined, these articles imply that the different versions of capability theory, both digital and dynamic, are a powerful prism through which the attributes of competencies held by consumers and their consequences, both on organizational strategy and on the market engagement, can be interpreted.

3.4. Consumer Trust as a Monarchism

Consumer trust represents a key psychological process that affects AI mediated marketing, as consumers base their reactions and responses to AI suggestions, messages, and judgments. An experiment by Kim, Giroux, and Lee (2021) shows that consumers tend to believe AI recommendations more when the information produced by AI is precised, and such effect is mediated by belief of trust in AI output enhanced belief leads to evaluations and behavioral intentions toward the recommended products. This implies that trust has the ability to widen the gap, between the AI functionality, and consumer acceptance, in cases where the consumers find the technology credible and competent. Wang, Sauka, and Situmeang (2025) discover in generative Trust is however conditional and weak. Lopez and Garza (2023) demonstrate that consumers are biased toward assessments presented by AI, especially negative ones, when anxiety caused by lack of transparency occurs, which in turn diminishes the emotional trust and purchase intentions, with trust being the mediator that enhances the negative impact and perceived risk further increasing the results. Cicek, Gursoy, and Lu (2025) reveal that the lack of transparency creates the anxiety that negatively affects the perceived fairness and acceptance of AI based assessments in turn, with the trust mediating this adverse effect and perceived risk Collectively, these pieces of research suggest that trust is mediator and result in AI mediated marketing acceptance: trust is created as a result of AI presentation (precision, anthropomorphism, transparency) and it affects the extent to which consumers will accept AI recommendations and use AI augmented offerings.

3.5. Consumer Acceptance as The Outcome

There are various variables that determine the acceptance of AI as a marketing tool by consumers, with usefulness, technological preparedness, and experience being among them. The AI era is a consumer acceptance model suggested by Pramanik and Jana (2025) because the perceived ease of use and perceived usefulness play a crucial role in influencing the willingness of a consumer towards the use of AI-mediated services since these two perceptions lower the level of uncertainty and enhance the willingness to use AI-mediated services. On the same note, Becan and Çeber (2025) note that the readiness to use technology affects behavioral and purchase intentions in a serial manner: positive attitude towards AI and positive experiences with AI-driven chatbots impact the adoption by strengthening trust, satisfaction, and perceived convenience.

The acceptance is also influenced by framing and communication of AI. As shown by Vorobeva, Costa Pinto, António, and Mattila (2024), the perception of AI as an augmentative tool that supports human services leads to the increase of perceived value and the development of the desire to interact with AI-based services. Ostrom, Fotheringham, and Bitner (2018) also show that the antecedents, including trust, familiarity, and perceived competence, and positive service outcomes are also contingent on consumer acceptance, suggesting that meeting consumer expectations is a key to adoption.

Lastly, the participation is an important acceptance mechanism. Hollebeek, Menidjel, Sarstedt, Jansson, and Urbonavicius (2024) demonstrate that the interactive and personalized AI experiences lead to a higher level of consumer engagement and satisfaction, which reinforces acceptance. Together, these studies suggest that consumers use AI marketing tools not only due to novelty but when it has credibility, is easy to use, provides personalized interaction, and has the capacity to enhance and not eliminate human decision-making processes.

4. MANAGERIAL, POLICY, AND IMPLICATIONS

The conceptual framework in this chapter shows that digital literacy, AI awareness, consumer readiness, and trust in technology have an impact on consumers' acceptance of AI-powered marketing. It is important not to view AI adoption as a technology or efficiency choice, but rather as competency-based trust and collaboration.

4.1. Implications for Marketing Practice: From Idea to Practice

The AI-based digital marketing helps managers task of personalization of content, optimization of campaigns, and customer outreach through predictive analytics and automation (Karami et al., 2025). However, it also creates some ethical responsibilities. The more AI is included in defining consumer experiences, the more marketing scores are affected by performance, as well as trust, transparency, and fairness.

4.1.1. Make Ethics and Transparency a Core Marketing Competence

Managers must be formally trained in the responsible and transparent use of AI as part of their general marketing education. There should be an ethical consideration in the design of AI-powered marketing systems that attempt to teach the audience. Explainable AI and transparent communication allow people to understand why they are being shown certain ads or recommendations. Companies need to add basic instruments, such as Why am I seeing this? They need to avoid unnecessary data in the system. Prompts and short privacy notes build confidence among consumers. A relevant data policy and security mechanisms respect consumers' rights and autonomy.

4.1.2. Build Internal Capabilities and Governance

Internal governance must be strong for AI-driven marketing. Companies are encouraged to establish a multidisciplinary ethics committee at the organizational level. To prevent bias and protect data, they should review guidelines along with risk control mechanisms. Marketing Teams Need These 3 Things: AI Education, Ethical Decision-Making, and Laws (GDPR, CCPA/CPRA, PIPL & EU AI Act). Companies dealing with international campaigns are urged to ensure fitness with local culture and regulations.

4.1.3. Social Responsibility and AI Marketing

AI-mediated marketing and corporate social responsibility must work together. AI helps promote socially responsible activities by managing resources efficiently. It considers digital marketing as a key driver for inclusive growth and long-lasting value creation (Kumar et al., 2024; Li & Jin, 2024). Therefore, firms need to go beyond conversion metric assessment for AI marketing. Trust, long-term engagement, and customer confidence should be used to evaluate success.

4.1.4. Design AI Marketing for Fairness, Trust, and Empowerment

AI-mediated marketing helps consumers make informed decisions, not exploit them. To establish bias-free outcomes, farms must monitor their systems dealing with targeting, pricing, or recommending something to the customers (Yas et al., 2025). They should provide clear and user-friendly control options. Consumers will feel empowered if they can modify any information in the dashboard. Managers must be careful when it comes to using dark patterns or digital tactics. Although cognitive biases can increase consumer engagement, they damage the firm's reputation in the long run.

4.2 Implications for Policymakers and Regulators

Policymaking and regulation become difficult to implement and manage due to digital marketing. Regulation should be flexible in content creation and personalization for balancing innovation and consumer safety (Nayab Farooq et al., 2025). Some laws have provided basic protection guidelines, such as the GDPR (General Data Protection Regulation). However, attention is needed in data transformation and manipulation as well.

4.2.1. Promote Ethical Design and International Coordination

Regulators should gain expertise in AI to regulate AI marketing effectively. Explainability, data quality, and diversity matter for ethically designed AI. Corporate regulators need to work on this. To address regulatory complexity, proper justifications for data protection and privacy need to be aligned. Here, regulators can establish frameworks based on social values and associated risks (Davenport et al., 2020; Hasan & Abdullah, 2022; Nayab Farooq et al., 2025; Yas et al., 2025). Since digital platforms operate internationally, coordination with other countries is necessary.

4.2.2. Strengthen Transparency, Consent, and Accountability

Firms can apply behavioral tracking to help consumers make the right decisions. Clear guidelines are needed for the use of AI in advertising. AI-mediated marketing sometimes changes or influences the underlying meanings of advertising texts or suggestions. Firms should be aware of this. They need to provide a preliminary guideline on when AI can influence the advertising activities. Moreover, to measure the algorithmic risks, firms need proper assessment tools for their launched marketing apps. Privacy mechanisms, unsubscribe options, and consent notices help customers make informed decisions while using them. Clean documentation about data generation, usage, and decision making is also necessary.

4.2.3. Address Manipulation, Bias, and Digital Divide

To minimize algorithmic discrimination, a clear classification of AI marketing is needed. Manipulative AI practices undermine consumers' autonomy. For companies, consumers' formal consent is not enough if they do not pay attention to the safety issues. Bias testing, audits, and regular reporting can positively affect marketing outcomes. Therefore, an established fairness policy is needed to reduce algorithmic bias in AI-driven targeting. Another important area to address is the digital divide. Consumers cannot exercise their rights if they don't understand the AI function properly. To increase understanding, it is necessary to support less literate groups and people with limited data access. Standardized infrastructure, simple compliance policy, and educational support should be provided to these groups (Pagala et al., 2024).

4.3. Implications for Education and Consumer Empowerment

A consumer's ability to be a responsible consumer in AI marketing is based on digital literacy and AI awareness. The increasing use of AI in promotion, price, and personalization is helping consumers to develop readiness, trust, and control.

4.3.1. Integrate AI Literacy and Digital Ethics into Education

AI literacy and digital ethics must be included across our entire education ecosystem. Learners should understand how data is collected and used, what goes into profiling and personalization. Consumers also need to know how recommender systems work and what rights they have in digital markets. Beyond the technological, the curriculum of universities needs to be inserted with learning about ethics, data privacy, and how we can be more efficient in the AI-era content (A'yun & Setyaningsih, 2025; Pagala et al., 2024). Thus, learners will be able to recognize not only manipulative messages easily. They will also know how to balance privacy. Therefore, before accepting any AI-recommended suggestions, they will question them.

4.3.2. Strengthen Educator and Professional Training

Consumer empowerment mainly depends on educators' and professionals' skills in AI. To clearly understand the AI concept and its responsible use, educators must receive teaching-related support. A transparent and humanized demonstration of AI usage should be demonstrated to the learners (Eid et al., 2024; Kumar et al., 2024). Continuous skill development is necessary now. Here, seminars or courses can help civil servants and markets understand the responsible use of AI. Established codes of conduct can also guide industry professionals to learn ethical use of AI.

4.3.3. Support Direct Consumer Empowerment and Inclusion

Consumers can act if education supports the proper practical tools. To explain AI simply, it is necessary to run public awareness campaigns. Groups such as civil society or public institutions should step forward to take the initiative on this. Consumers' awareness about their rights can be enhanced through these types of campaigns. Moreover, individuals will be able to access data, choose preferred advertisements, and manage their cookies. However, less literate people may be exploited through AI-mediated marketing. Therefore, special focus must be given to the vulnerable groups. Governments and school officials are urged to invest in open educational resources that reflect local language and culture. They should also take initiatives to increase access to digital devices and internet infrastructure. These types of initiatives can help address the digital skills gap to ensure equal access to the digital economy(De Cicco et al., 2025).

4.4. Algorithm Aversion, Algorithm Appreciation, and Human–AI Collaboration

Research on human interaction with algorithms has highlighted contrasting psychological and behavioral responses that influence the acceptance and use of AI systems. Algorithm aversion refers to the tendency of individuals to reject or devalue algorithmic recommendations after observing errors, even when the algorithm outperforms human alternatives on average (Dietvorst et al., 2015 as discussed by Kumar et al., 2021). This reluctance often stems from trust dynamics and negative perceptions when users witness AI imperfections, leading to decreased reliance on automated systems across decision contexts (Logg et al., 2019). In contrast, algorithm appreciation describes situations where users preferentially follow advice labeled as coming from an algorithm rather than a human, reflecting a scenario in which algorithmic objectivity or perceived performance can outweigh skepticism (Logg et al., 2019). These conflicting tendencies suggest that user attitudes toward AI are contingent on context, framing, and perceived competence of algorithms versus human agents.

The interplay between these biases is evident in research that integrates human cognition and AI functionality, recognizing that neither aversion nor appreciation alone fully captures the complexity of human responses to algorithms. For instance, studies on human–AI collaboration demonstrate that hybrid decision frameworks where AI supports rather than replaces human judgment—can mitigate negative reactions and enhance outcomes (Haupt et al., 2025). Specifically, research in marketing and content creation shows that forms of collaboration indicating human control over AI mitigate negative consumer responses related to algorithm aversion, emphasizing trust and perceived ethical use of AI (Haupt et al., 2025). This aligns with broader research on human–AI team decision making, where granting users control and transparency enhances trust, understanding, and compliance with AI outputs (Westphal et al., 2023). Together, these streams illustrate that effective human–AI collaboration requires balancing algorithmic strengths with human oversight to leverage complementary competencies while addressing psychological biases inherent in algorithmic decision support.

4.5. Organizational Capabilities

Digital transformation (DT) is widely recognized as a strategic imperative that enables organizations to reinvent their processes, structures, and competitive strategies through the adoption of digital technologies. It involves not only technological adoption but also the development of organizational dynamic capabilities that facilitate data-driven decision-making and strategic agility (Goraya et al., 2026). Within DT frameworks, the integration of artificial intelligence (AI) capabilities has emerged as a core component, allowing firms to move beyond traditional automation toward *data-intensive intelligence* that informs business model innovation and customer value creation. Research indicates that developing AI capabilities such as data collection, algorithmic analytics, and adaptive learning mechanisms enables firms to extract actionable insights from complex datasets, supporting the design of innovative, customer-centric business models (Ghosh, 2025). This capability development is closely tied to organizational adaptability and leadership, which provide the strategic coordination necessary for AI-enhanced transformation and for embedding analytics into core decision processes across functions.

In the context of marketing, DT coupled with robust data analytics reshapes strategic approaches by enabling more precise segmentation, predictive customer insights, and personalized engagement. Firms that leverage data-driven strategies can align marketing decisions with real-time intelligence, improving responsiveness to market dynamics and enhancing performance outcomes (Goraya et al., 2026). Importantly, the effectiveness of data-driven marketing depends on the alignment between transformational strategy and analytics capabilities, such as business intelligence and organizational agility, which together support superior decision-making even under environmental hostility. Furthermore, AI capability development contributes to competitive advantage by facilitating better integration between marketing analytics and digital strategy execution, thereby strengthening firms' ability to anticipate customer needs and deliver compelling value propositions in rapidly evolving digital markets. These studies collectively underscore that digital transformation's value is realized not merely through tech adoption but through the strategic cultivation of AI capabilities and data-oriented marketing competencies.

Table 1. Multilevel implications of AI-mediated marketing for Practice, Policy, and Education

Dimension	Marketing Practice Focus	Policy / Regulation Focus	Education & Consumer Empowerment Focus
Trust & Transparency	Explainable AI, honest communication, and data-use disclosures.	AI disclosures, explainability requirements, and accountability duties.	Literacy on AI use, data flows, and consumer rights.
Privacy & Security	Data minimization, privacy design, and secure marketing systems.	Data protection rules, breach notification, and enforcement.	Understanding consent, privacy risks, and data control options.
Fairness & Manipulation	Bias audits, dark patterns avoidance, and exploitative personalization.	Rules on profiling, fairness standards, and anti-manipulation safeguards.	Persuasion awareness, protection of vulnerable groups.
Inclusivity & Digital Divide	Inclusive UX design, accessible interfaces, and controls.	Support for access, protections for low-literacy groups.	Skills programs and learning support for low-literacy users.
Consumer Readiness & Agency	Transparent, controllable AI experiences and autonomy.	Rights-based safeguards	Skills to understand, question, and manage AI-driven marketing.

5. LIMITATIONS AND FUTURE RESEARCH DIRECTIONS

Although AI-driven marketing is becoming increasingly popular, previous work has limitations. Many studies use small or convenience samples. This limits the generalizability of findings in other populations and cultural contexts. Research also overuses technology acceptance models such as TAM and UTAUT, giving little attention to the ethical or social impact of AI. Cross-country analysis is also limited, in particular between developed and emerging markets. Consumers with low digital competencies, restricted technology accessibility, or the highest risk for manipulation are largely neglected. Such limitations, if addressed, have the potential to contribute to a more inclusive and realistic grounded knowledge of consumer readiness in AI-driven marketing.

5.1. Advancing Conceptual Understanding of Consumer Readiness

AI readiness is predominantly conceptualized as the desire to employ AI and operationalized as adoption intention from TAM or UTAUT. Such a narrow perspective constrains the understanding of what AI-based marketing is and how consumers indeed resonate with it (Kumar et al., 2024; Wu & Jing Wen, 2021). First, future research should conceptualize consumer preparedness as a dynamic process. Over time, users may progress from initial curiosity to frequent use, selective dependence, or disuse. It is necessary to have a longitudinal design in order to evaluate the development of readiness over time, and as AI interaction is repeated, it is exposed to data leaks (Eid et al., 2024). Figure 2 conceptually shows this evolution in consumer readiness. Moreover, it also highlights that readiness is embedded in context-specific elements, including literacy, values, emotions, and social norms.

Second, future studies can consider the multidimensional nature of consumer readiness. Readiness is related to digital and AI literacy, emotions, ethics awareness, peer pressure (social norms), and cultural attitudes towards automation. Including factors like privacy and perceived control could be useful to study diverse readiness profiles among consumers(Balasubramaniam et al., 2023; Eid et al., 2024). Finally, methodology should not be limited to a cross-sectional survey. Distinct research strategies (i.e., experimental, mixed-methods, and field studies) can help explain why some factors of AI-readiness (e.g., transparency, education) are supportive or inhibiting. Definite concepts and evidence are still needed to enhance our understanding of AI for marketing adoption, long-term engagement, and consumer well-being.

Figure 3. A Potential Pathway for Consumer Readiness in AI-Mediated Marketing

5.2. Cross-Cultural and Global South Perspectives

As AI and marketing research are carried out in developed countries, the findings cannot easily be applied in other cultures or institutions. For a more comprehensive AI marketing model, this research can be extended to the Global South and other underdeveloped nations (Gupta et al., 2025). Studies on cross-cultural comparison will help explain how consumers' trust and AI acceptance differ across cultures. Throughout the Global South, consumers also face language barriers, limited education, and varying privacy expectations. Comparative analysis can be used to explore why differences may emerge in terms of cultural norms, institutional dynamics, and structural forces. Nations are not homogeneous entities. Future studies can examine how AI is incorporated into national digital practices. Research methods, for example, focus groups and co-design, help record locality-based experience and ethics that are often difficult to capture by survey research. The comparison of regulations on AI governance across countries could indicate what effects the regulation has on consumer protection and confidence. Theoretical validation will be best strengthened when research is extended beyond national borders, and ethically minded AI marketing practice will arise.

5.3. Human-Centered and Ethical AI Marketing Research

Humans should be at the center of ethical AI-driven marketing that can include consumer values, autonomy, and social welfare. Although ethical discussions tend to focus on privacy, bias, manipulation, and accountability, there is still limited evidence about consumers. Future studies should examine the impact of ethical AI design on consumers' readiness. AI-driven marketing can sometimes encourage exclusion and reinforce stereotyping (Hidayat et al., 2025; Kumar, 2023). Therefore, attention should be given to inclusion and fairness in future studies. Researchers are encouraged to investigate how AI and transparency tools work on consumer understanding and perceived control. It should empower customers to question the AI-driven marketing decisions. They should not accept AI-generated suggestions without questioning them (Li & Jin, 2024). Practices that focus on manipulative patterns, excess personalization, and emotion-based targeting seem more relevant in some cases. However, these practices can lower customers' control over decisions. Their effects on decision quality and consumer well-being should be studied further.

6. CONCLUSION

The integration of AI in marketing has transformed how the companies are engaging with the customers. This chapter demonstrates the different ways in which business can interact with the consumers, moving from reactive to predictive analysis, automated and personalized AI mediated marketing. These AI tools include chatbots, machine learning, virtual reality, augmented reality, simulation and predictive analysis tools etc. through which marketers can deliver personalized content, enhance customer engagement, conduct online campaigns, enhance value creation and increase customer satisfaction. Through this AI integrated marketing mechanism, all target customers can be reached with their personalized demand of the products and services. However, the effectiveness of this AI mediated marketing practice largely depends on consumers' readiness and digital literacy to technology.

Consumer' readiness reflects the preparedness of cognitive, emotional and technological understanding among the customers to easily interact with AI driven marketing practices. Since, AI mediated marketing cannot solely be capable of achieving the effectiveness of the process, it needs consumers' involvement in all levels. This readiness can be identified by the consumers' prior experiences, confidence, technology availability, skills and understanding of AI driven data. So, digital literacy, ethical awareness and AI adaptability of the consumers reflect the success of AI integration in marketing. In the absence of adequate digital literacy in all levels of consumers, it creates trust and privacy issues among the deprived customers. This will create vulnerabilities and increase susceptibility among the consumers. From this book chapter, we identified that consumers' readiness alone is not sufficient without a basic level of understanding of AI tools and techniques used in marketing campaigns.

Besides, consumers are more likely to depend on AI driven systems when they perceive the AI tools are safe, transparent, competent, reliable and aligned with ethical grounds. These trust issues can be enhanced through clear communication, transparent use of data and non-discriminating nature of customer handling. Thus, fostering consumer trust and loyalty to AI mediated marketing helps the company to maintain sustainable practice in AI tools development. This process will ensure fair, accountable and transparent products and service provided in all segments of the consumers.

Additionally, the conceptual framework developed in this chapter highlights the multi-dimensional state of AI-mediated marketing practice, which is shaped by psychological mediators, digital capability, AI-awareness, transparency and several moderating factors. This framework extends the understanding of technology acceptance models by integrating ethical perspectives and capability-based perspectives among the consumers. It places consumer acceptance as a multidimensional perspective integrating perceived usefulness, ease of use, and transparency. This framework also expands the role of mediating variables such as trust, perceived value and perceived autonomy as well as moderating influence of demographic, cultural and socio-economic perspectives on consumers' readiness to adopt AI. Thus, it demonstrates that AI is not a technological choice, it is mostly a competency-driven procedure that enhances trust among consumers.

Inclusively, AI mediated marketing incorporates both opportunities and challenges in real business context. On one hand, AI enhances efficiency, personalization and customer satisfaction. On the other hand, its success largely depends on the literacy of consumers' literacy, willingness to adopt AI technologies and responsible use of technology. While consumer satisfaction depends on transparency in marketing content, ethical consideration in personalization and clear communication of using AI for a long time. Thus, inclusivity and equal access in AI tools will mitigate the challenges of digital divide and transparency issues. All these highlight that only AI adoption cannot bring success in marketing context, it requires equal and responsible participation of AI adopted consumers.

This chapter contributes to the existing literature related to AI mediated marketing and consumer behavior by integrating the focus from marketer centric perceptions to consumer centric perceptions. Existing studies have vastly explained the mechanisms of efficiency, personalization and competitive advantages from the company level which often shrinks the importance of consumer-centric perspective of AI mediated marketing. The chapter will help to bridge this gap of existing knowledge by incorporating the mechanisms of consumer readiness and digital literacy. This current study addresses this gap by integrating the insights from consumer readiness to adopt technology, consumer behavior, consumer interactions with AI-driven marketing mechanisms.

Additionally, the findings have several important implications for marketers, policymakers and educators. In the case of marketers, they might implement the AI tools to integrate all the consumers equally. Besides, they can also take several strategies to mitigate the risks such as real time monitoring, ensuring equitable access to digital platforms, providing learning campaigns, designing user friendly interfaces and providing relevant data to all levels of customers. In this case, they should prioritize transparency and technology adoption for all the consumers. Policymakers and marketers can reduce the challenges by focusing on digital literacy development as a fundamental element of inclusive human centered AI adoption. Policymakers can take necessary steps to ensure the regulations and flexible framework which will balance AI innovation and consumer protection. For the educators, this study will help to understand the importance of AI literacy and critical thinking to ensure an ethical base considering bias, neglect, discrimination in marketing perspective.

To conclude we can express that AI mediated marketing shifts a marketer centric perception towards consumer centric perceptions by offering personalized services and value creation. But it has to be considered that sustainability and effectiveness of AI mediated marketing largely depend on a consumer centric inclusive approach that highlights consumers' trust, digital literacy and consumer readiness. Future research can be continued to explore consumer-centric models that will ensure trust and inclusiveness in all levels of customers. Also, future research can be conducted focusing on different industries for both national and international level.

REFERENCES

A'yun, A. Q., & Setyaningsih, W. (2025). Consumer Empowerment Through Ethical AI: Strategies for Transparent and Trustworthy Personalized Marketing. *Journal of Marketing Breakthroughs*, *1*(1), 1–12. DOI: 10.70764/gdpu-jmb.2025.1(1)-01

Abrardi, L., Cambini, C., & Rondi, L. (2022). Artificial intelligence, firms and consumer behavior: A survey. *Journal of Economic Surveys*, *36*(4), 969–991. DOI: 10.1111/joes.12455

Acharya, R. A., & Pednekar, A. P. (2024). Digital literacy and its impact on consumer behaviour towards m-commerce adoption in India: A study. *Journal of Digital Economy*, *3*(1), 48–60.

Adebayo, P. O., Osanyinlusi, G. E., & Adekeye, A. O. (2023). Does consumer empowerment influence e-payment systems adoption? A digital consumer-centric perspective. *Journal of Financial Services Marketing*. Advance online publication. DOI: 10.1057/s41264-023-00238-4

Aguirre, E., Roggeveen, A. L., Grewal, D., & Wetzels, M. (2016). The personalization–privacy paradox. *Journal of Retailing*, *92*(1), 34–49. DOI: 10.1016/j.jretai.2014.09.005

Alijoyo, F. A., Aziz, T. S. A., Omer, N., Yusuf, N., Kumar, M. D., Ramesh, A. V. N., & El-Ebiary, Y. A. B. (2025). Personalized marketing: Leveraging AI for culturally aware segmentation and targeting. *Alexandria Engineering Journal*, *119*, 8–21. DOI: 10.1016/j.aej.2025.01.074

Amini, R., & Amini, A. (2024). An overview of artificial intelligence and its application in marketing with focus on large language models. *International Journal of Science and Research Archive*, *12*(2), 455–465. DOI: 10.30574/ijsra.2024.12.2.1223

Anam, A. S. M. T., Bhuiyan, M. R. I., Islam, S., Ullah, M. N., &Rakib, M. A. A. (2026). Factors influencing university students' adoption of online education platforms in Bangladesh: an extended TAM-based analysis. *Educational and Developmental Psychologist*, 1–17. DOI: 10.1080/20590776.2026.2619742

Arango, L., Singaraju, S. P., & Niininen, O. (2023). Consumer Responses to AI-Generated Charitable Giving Ads. *Journal of Advertising*, *52*(4), 486–503. DOI: 10.1080/00913367.2023.2183285

Arya, V., Saraf, A., Chichkanov, N., Papa, A., & Romano, M. (2026). AI-enhanced competency transfer hubs: A conceptual framework for university-industry engagement and knowledge sharing. *The Journal of Technology Transfer*, 51 682–712. DOI: 10.1007/s10961-025-10233-7

Awad, A. (2024). Artificial intelligence and marketing innovation: The mediating role of organizational culture. *Innovative Marketing*, *20*(3), 170–181. DOI: 10.21511/im.20(3).2024.14

Babatunde, S. O., Odejide, O. A., Edunjobi, T. E., & Ogundipe, D. O. (2024). The role of AI in marketing personalization: A theoretical exploration of consumer engagement strategies. *International Journal of Management & Entrepreneurship Research*, *6*(3), 936–949. DOI: 10.51594/ijmer.v6i3.964

Balasubramaniam, N., Kauppinen, M., Rannisto, A., Hiekkanen, K., & Kujala, S. (2023). Transparency and explainability of AI systems: From ethical guidelines to requirements. *Information and Software Technology*, *159*, 107197. DOI: 10.1016/j.infsof.2023.107197

Bar-Gill, O., Sunstein, C. R., & Talgam-Cohen, I. (2023). Algorithmic harm in consumer markets. *The Journal of Legal Analysis*, *15*(1), 1–47. DOI: 10.1093/jla/laad003

Becan, C., &Çeber, B. (2025). How technology readiness influences behavioral and purchasing intention: serial multiple mediating role of attitude toward AI and AI-driven consumer chatbot experience. *Digital Transformation and Society*, 1-27. DOI: 10.1108/DTS-04-2025-0082

Bozkurt, S., Uğursoy, A. S., & Meral, S. P. (2025). The Impact of Personalized Messages and Designs on Consumer Experiences and Marketing Communications in Technology: Hyper-Personalization. In *Impact of Contemporary Technology on Art and Design* (pp. 135–164). IGI Global., DOI: 10.4018/979-8-3693-4318-0.ch007

Buchan, M. C., Bhawra, J., & Katapally, T. R. (2024). Navigating the digital world: Development of an evidence-based digital literacy program and assessment tool for youth. *Smart Learning Environments*, *11*(1), 8. DOI: 10.1186/s40561-024-00293-x

Chan, H. L., & Choi, T. M. (2025). Using generative artificial intelligence (GenAI) in marketing: Development and practices. *Journal of Business Research, 191*, 115276. rights and contentDOI: 10.1016/j.jbusres.2025.115276Get

Chen, J., Zhou, W., & Frankwick, G. L. (2025). Firm AI adoption intensity and marketing performance. *Journal of Computer Information Systems*, *65*(2), 172–189. DOI: 10.1080/08874417.2023.2277751

Cheng, C. F., Huang, C. C., Lin, M. C., & Chen, T. C. (2023). Exploring effectiveness of relationship marketing on artificial intelligence adopting intention. *SAGE Open*, *13*(4), 21582440231222760. DOI: 10.1177/21582440231222760

Chu, S. C., Yim, M. Y. C., & Mundel, J. (2025). Artificial intelligence, virtual and augmented reality, social media, online reviews, and influencers: A review of how service businesses use promotional devices and future research directions. *International Journal of Advertising*, *44*(5), 798–828. DOI: 10.1080/02650487.2024.2325835

Cicek, M., Gursoy, D., & Lu, L. (2025). Adverse impacts of revealing the presence of "Artificial Intelligence (AI)" technology in product and service descriptions on purchase intentions: The mediating role of emotional trust and the moderating role of perceived risk. *Journal of Hospitality Marketing & Management*, *34*(1), 1–23. DOI: 10.1080/19368623.2024.2368040

D'Amico, E., Belitski, M., Braga, A., & Savoie, R. (2025). Enhancing knowledge spillover of innovation through artificial intelligence: An empirical investigation. *The Journal of Technology Transfer*, 1–29. DOI: 10.1007/s10961-025-10217-7

Davenport, T., Guha, A., Grewal, D., & Bressgott, T. (2020). How artificial intelligence will change the future of marketing. *Journal of the Academy of Marketing Science*, *48*(1), 24–42. DOI: 10.1007/s11747-019-00696-0

Davis, F. D. (1989). Perceived usefulness, perceived ease of use, and user acceptance of information technology. *Management Information Systems Quarterly*, *13*(3), 319–340. DOI: 10.2307/249008

De Bruyn, A., Viswanathan, V., Beh, Y. S., Brock, J. K. U., & Von Wangenheim, F. (2020). Artificial intelligence and marketing: Pitfalls and opportunities. *Journal of Interactive Marketing*, *51*(1), 91–105. DOI: 10.1016/j.intmar.2020.04.007

De Cicco, R., Francioni, B., Curina, I., & Cioppi, M. (2025). AI, human or a blend? How the educational content creator influences consumer engagement and brand-related outcomes. *Journal of Services Marketing*, *39*(10), 53–71. DOI: 10.1108/JSM-10-2024-0539

Dellande, S., Gilly, M. C., & Graham, J. L. (2004). Gaining compliance and losing weight: The role of the service provider in health care services. *Journal of Marketing*, *68*(3), 78–91. DOI: 10.1509/jmkg.68.3.78.34764

Deryl, M. D., Verma, S., Srivastava, V., & Paul, J. (2026). Harnessing artificial intelligence (AI) for interactive branding. *Journal of Research in Interactive Marketing*, 1–21. DOI: 10.1108/JRIM-02-2025-0076

Dezao, T. (2024). Enhancing transparency in AI-powered customer engagement. *Journal of AI. Robotics & Workplace Automation*, *3*(2), 134. DOI: 10.69554/PPJE1646

Dong, B., Sivakumar, K., Evans, K. R., & Zou, S. (2015). Effect of customer participation on service outcomes: Themoderating role of participation readiness. *Journal of Service Research*, *18*(2), 160–176. DOI: 10.1177/1094670514551727

Du, S., & Xie, C. (2021). Paradoxes of artificial intelligence in consumer markets: Ethical challenges and opportunities. *Journal of Business Research*, *129*, 961–974. DOI: 10.1016/j.jbusres.2020.08.024

Eid, M. A. H., Hashesh, M. A., Sharabati, A.-A. A., Khraiwish, A., AL-Haddad, S., & Abusaimeh, H. (2024). Conceptualizing ethical AI-enabled marketing: Current state and agenda for future research. *International Journal of Data and Network Science*, *8*(4), 2291–2306. DOI: 10.5267/j.ijdns.2024.6.002

Elragal, A., & Elgendy, N. (2024). A data-driven decision-making readiness assessment model: The case of a Swedish food manufacturer. *Decision Analytics Journal*, *10*, 100405. DOI: 10.1016/j.dajour.2024.100405

Etgar, M. (2008). A descriptive model of the consumer co-production process. *Journal of the Academy of Marketing Science*, *36*(1), 97–108. DOI: 10.1007/s11747-007-0061-1

Faisal-E-Alam, M., Bhuiyan, M. R. I., Mimi, A., & Miah, M. T. (2025). The role of the three zero framework in advancing global sustainable development through bibliometric and text mining analysis. *Discover Sustainability*, *6*(1), 1128. DOI: 10.1007/s43621-025-01919-x

Farinloye, T., Omotoye, O., Oginni, A., Moharrak, M., & Mogaji, E. (2024). Bridging the digital divide: Consumer engagement with transportation payment apps in emerging economies. *Journal of Consumer Behaviour*, *23*(6), 3011–3029. DOI: 10.1002/cb.2388

Farooq, N., Hashmat, S., & Hashim, A. (2025). AI in advertising: Ethical risks, consumer protection, and policy implications. Annual Methodological Archive Research Review, 3(6), 1-18.

Farseev, A. (2023, February). Under the hood of social media advertising: how do we use AI responsibly for advertising targeting and creative evaluation. In *Proceedings of the Sixteenth ACM International Conference on Web Search and Data Mining* (pp. 1281-1282). DOI: 10.1145/3539597.3575791

Feng, Y., & Kim, H. J. (2025). Decoding the Trust Matrix: Unraveling Key Predictors of Consumer Trust in AI-Generated Personalized Advertising. *Journal of Interactive Advertising*, *25*(2), 123–138. DOI: 10.1080/15252019.2025.2468286

Flavián, C., Pérez-Rueda, A., Belanche, D., & Casaló, L. V. (2022). Intention to use analytical artificial intelligence (AI) in services–the effect of technology readiness and awareness. *Journal of Service Management*, *33*(2), 293–320. DOI: 10.1108/JOSM-10-2020-0378

Gao, L., Li, G., Tsai, F., Gao, C., Zhu, M., & Qu, X. (2023). The impact of artificial intelligence stimuli on customer engagement and value co-creation: The moderating role of customer ability readiness. *Journal of Research in Interactive Marketing*, *17*(2), 317–333. DOI: 10.1108/JRIM-10-2021-0260

Gefen, D., Karahanna, E., & Straub, D. W. (2003). Trust and TAM in online shopping: An integrated model. *Management Information Systems Quarterly*, *27*(1), 51–90. DOI: 10.2307/30036519

Ghabban, M., Alsughayyir, Y., Alslimani, A., Marzouq, A., & Qasem, Z. (2025). Consumer Behavior Toward AI-Driven Marketing: Insights from UTAUT and Uses and Gratifications Models. *Global Journal of Economic and Business*, *15*(4), 423–438. DOI: 10.31559/GJEB2025.15.4.4

Ghosh, S. (2025). Developing artificial intelligence (AI) capabilities for data driven business model innovation: Roles of organizational adaptability and leadership. *Journal of Engineering and Technology Management*, *75*, 101851. DOI: 10.1016/j.jengtecman.2024.101851

Goraya, M. A. S., Kemal, A. A., Xu, M., Shareef, M. A., & Akram, M. S. (2026). Leveraging digital transformation strategy and data driven decision making to improve organisational performance in a hostile environment. Industrial Management & Data Systems, 126(2), 650–677. 10 2024 1039DOI: 10.1108/IMDS

Grewal, D., Hulland, J., Kopalle, P. K., & Karahanna, E. (2020). The future of technology and marketing: A multidisciplinary perspective. *Journal of the Academy of Marketing Science*, *48*(1), 1–8. DOI: 10.1007/s11747-019-00711-4

Gupta, S., Wang, Y., Patel, P., & Czinkota, M. (2025). Navigating the future of AI in marketing: AI integration across borders, ethical considerations, and policy implications. *International Journal of Information Management*, *82*, 102871. DOI: 10.1016/j.ijinfomgt.2025.102871

Haleem, A., Javaid, M., Qadri, M. A., Singh, R. P., & Suman, R. (2022). Artificial intelligence (AI) applications for marketing: A literature-based study. *International Journal of intelligent networks, 3*, 119-132. DOI: 10.1016/j.ijin.2022.08.005

Hammerschmidt, T., Stolz, K., & Posegga, O. (2025). Bridging the gap: Inequalities that divide those who can and cannot create sustainable outcomes with AI. *Behaviour & Information Technology*, 1–30. DOI: 10.1080/0144929X.2025.2500451

Hansen, H. F., Lillesund, E., Mikalef, P., & Altwaijry, N. (2024). Understanding artificial intelligence diffusion through an AI capability maturity model. *Information Systems Frontiers*, *26*(6), 2147–2163. DOI: 10.1007/s10796-024-10528-4

Haque, A. (2025). Integrating UTAUT and TPB frameworks to examine digital wallet adoption: Evidence from university students in a developing economy. *DUET Journal,* 10(1), 1–11. https://www.duet.ac.bd/storage/journal/volume-10-issue-1 -june-2025%28-%29-1756443608.pdf

Haque, A., Sultana, N., Kim, Y. S., & Al Amin, M. (2024). Integration of the UTAUT model in mobile banking context: The mediating role of personal innovativeness and perceived value. *Asia pacific journal of information systems, 34*(3), 929-956. DOI: 10.14329/apjis.2024.34.3.929

Hargittai, E. (2010). Digital na(t)ives? Variation in internet skills and uses among members of the "Net Generation.". *Sociological Inquiry*, *80*(1), 92–113. DOI: 10.1111/j.1475-682X.2009.00317.x

Hasan, M., Chowdhury, K. Z., & Zubayer, M. (2025). The AI Advantage: Revolutionizing Personalization in Digital Marketing. *Business & Social Sciences*, *3*(1), 1–9. DOI: 10.25163/business.3110281

Hasan, R., & Abdullah, M. S. (2022). Advancing ai in marketing through cross border integration ethical considerations and policy implications. *American Journal of Scholarly Research and Innovation, 01*(01), 351–379. DOI: 10.63125/d1xg3784

Haupt, M., Freidank, J., & Haas, A. (2025). Consumer responses to human AI collaboration at organizational frontlines: Strategies to escape algorithm aversion in content creation. Review of Managerial Science, 19(2), 377–413. 10.1007/s11846 024 00748

Hawaldar, I. T. (2020). The effect of artificial intelligence on the sales graph in Indian market. Entrepreneurship and Sustainability Issues. 10.9770/jesi.2020.7.4(24)

Hendrayati, H., Achyarsyah, M., Marimon, F., Hartono, U., & Putit, L. (2024). The Impact of Artificial intelligence on Digital Marketing: Leveraging potential in a competitive business landscape. *Emerging Science Journal*, *8*(6), 2343–2359. Advance online publication. DOI: 10.28991/ESJ-2024-08-06-012

Hennighausen, C., Yarza Navarro-Schär, V. G., & Eller, E. (2025). AI-mediated communication in e-commerce: Implications for customer trust. *International Journal of Consumer Studies*, *49*(5), e70111. DOI: 10.1111/ijcs.70111

Hidayat, M. S., Muhammad, W., & Isdayanti, P. L. (2025). Digital Marketing Ethics in the Age of AI: A Comparative Analysis of Transparency and Consumer Trust in E-Commerce Platforms. *Journal of Management and Informatics*, *4*(1), 723–740. DOI: 10.51903/jmi.v4i1.178

Hollebeek, L. D., Menidjel, C., Sarstedt, M., Jansson, J., & Urbonavicius, S. (2024). Engaging consumers through artificially intelligent technologies: Systematic review, conceptual model, and further research. *Psychology and Marketing*, *41*(4), 880–898. DOI: 10.1002/mar.21957

Hoque, M. N., Jannat, S. N., Arafat, Y., & Miah, M. M. (2026). Predictive Modeling of Tourist Satisfaction Based on Service Marketing Mix Elements Using Machine Learning Techniques. *The Scientific World Journal*, *2026*(1), 6666970. DOI: 10.1155/tswj/6666970

Huang, M. H., & Rust, R. T. (2021). A strategic framework for artificial intelligence in marketing. *Journal of the Academy of Marketing Science*, *49*(1), 30–50. DOI: 10.1007/s11747-020-00749-9

Islam, M. M., Bhuiyan, M. R. I., Islam, S. H., Tabassum, M. N., & Billah, M. (2026). Unlocking the Mediating and Moderating Role of Information Security in Information Systems: A Combined TAM, ISM, and HBM Model. *Human Behavior and Emerging Technologies*, *2026*(1), 5593002. DOI: 10.1155/hbe2/5593002

Jain, D., Gupta, D. M., Gupta, D. P., Pandey, D. N., Sharma, D. N., & Raina, M. S. (2025). Consumer Trust In AI-Enabled Marketing: A Behavioural Analysis. *International Journal of Environmental Sciences*, 11(17s), 840–852. DOI: 10.64252/7fytzg74

Karami, A., Shemshaki, M., & Ghazanfar, M. A. (2025). Exploring the Ethical Implications of AI-Powered Personalization in Digital Marketing. *Data Intelligence*, *7*(4), 1035–1084. DOI: 10.3724/2096-7004.di.2024.0055

Kbaier, E., Salminen, J., & Jansen, B. J. (2025). "A glimpse into the AI": Exploring the effect of consumers' chatbot interaction experience on brand attachment and advocacy with the moderating role of AI skepticism. *Asia-Pacific Journal of Business Administration*, 1–26. DOI: 10.1108/APJBA-01-2025-0003

Kemp, A. (2024). Competitive advantage through artificial intelligence: Toward a theory of situated AI. *Academy of Management Review*, *49*(3), 618–635. DOI: 10.5465/amr.2020.0205

Khan, R. A., Feng, G., & Zhu, J. (2026). Impact of Knowledge and Electronic Word of Mouth About AI-Based Chatbots on Customers' Intention to Continue Using Chatbots in E-Commerce. *Journal of Organizational Computing and Electronic Commerce*, *36*(1), 78–99. DOI: 10.1080/10919392.2025.2563463

Khatun, M., Hossain, R., Bhuiyan, M. R., Tabassum, M. N., & Riaj, M. A. (2025). Green Entrepreneurship and Digital Transformation for Sustainable Development: A Systematic Review. In Mouloudj, K., & Bouarar, A. (Eds.), *Digitizing Green Entrepreneurship* (pp. 153–180). IGI Global Scientific Publishing. DOI: 10.4018/979-8-3693-7442-9.ch006

Khokhar, P. & Chitsimran. (September 30, 2019). Evolution of Artificial Intelligence in Marketing, Comparison With Traditional Marketing. *Our Heritage, 67*(50), 375-389. Available at SSRN: https://ssrn.com/abstract=3557091

Kim, J., Giroux, M., & Lee, J. C. (2021). When do you trust AI? The effect of number presentation detail on consumer trust and acceptance of AI recommendations. *Psychology and Marketing*, *38*(7), 1140–1155. DOI: 10.1002/mar.21498

Kocarslan, H., & Stoycheva, B. (2025). The effect of digital literacy on online purchase intention: The mediating role of social media use. *Journal of Theoretical and Applied Electronic Commerce Research*, *20*(4), 355. DOI: 10.3390/jtaer20040355

Kolar, N., Milfelner, B., & Pisnik, A. (2024). Factors for customers' AI use readiness in physical retail stores: The interplay of consumer attitudes and gender differences. *Information (Basel)*, *15*(6), 346. DOI: 10.3390/info15060346

Kumar, D. (2023). Ethical and Legal Challenges of AI in Marketing: An Exploration of Solutions. SSRN *Electronic Journal*. DOI: 10.2139/ssrn.4396132

Kumar, V., Ashraf, A. R., & Nadeem, W. (2024). AI-powered marketing: What, where, and how? *International Journal of Information Management*, *77*, 102783. DOI: 10.1016/j.ijinfomgt.2024.102783

Li, B., Powell, D., & Lee, R. (2025). Commercialization of medical artificial intelligence technologies: Challenges and opportunities. npj. *NPJ Digital Medicine*, *8*(1), 454. DOI: 10.1038/s41746-025-01867-w

Li, H. (2025). Multicultural data assistance mining analysis for ideological and political education in smart education platforms using artificial intelligence. *Wireless Networks*, *31*(1), 567–581. DOI: 10.1007/s11276-024-03772-8

Li, J., & Jin, X. (2024). The Impact of Artificial Intelligence Adoption Intensity on Corporate Sustainability Performance: The Moderated Mediation Effect of Organizational Change. *Sustainability (Basel)*, *16*(21), 9350. DOI: 10.3390/su16219350

Liu, Q., Ha, L., & Lim, J. (2025). From perception to purchase: How AI literacy shapes consumer decisions in AI-generated sponsored vlogs across products and services. *Journal of Theoretical and Applied Electronic Commerce Research*, *20*(4), 302. DOI: 10.3390/jtaer20040302

Liu, Q., Osman, L. H., Lian, Z., Wel, C. A. C., & Hamid, S. N. A. (2025). From Perception to Purchase: How AI Literacy Shapes Consumer Decisions in AI-Generated Sponsored Vlogs Across Products and Services. *Journal of Theoretical and Applied Electronic Commerce Research*, *20*(4), 302. DOI: 10.3390/jtaer20040302

Logg, J. M., Minson, J. A., & Moore, D. A. (2019). Algorithm appreciation: People prefer algorithmic to human judgment. *Organizational Behavior and Human Decision Processes*, *151*, 90–103. DOI: 10.1016/j.obhdp.2018.12.005

Longoni, C., Bonezzi, A., & Morewedge, C. K. (2019). Resistance to medical artificial intelligence. *The Journal of Consumer Research*, *46*(4), 629–650. DOI: 10.1093/jcr/ucz013

Lopez, A., & Garza, R. (2023). Consumer bias against evaluations received by artificial intelligence: The mediation effect of lack of transparency anxiety. *Journal of Research in Interactive Marketing*, *17*(6), 831–847. DOI: 10.1108/JRIM-07-2021-0192

Lutz, C. (2019). Digital inequalities in the age of artificial intelligence and big data. *Human Behavior and Emerging Technologies*, *1*(2), 141–148. DOI: 10.1002/hbe2.140

Ma, S., & Fildes, R. (2021). Retail sales forecasting with meta-learning. *European Journal of Operational Research*, *288*(1), 111–128. DOI: 10.1016/j.ejor.2020.05.038

Malchenko, Y., Gogua, M., Golovacheva, K., Smirnova, M., & Alkanova, O. (2020). A critical review of digital capability frameworks: A consumer perspective. *Digital Policy, Regulation and Governance*, *22*(4), 269–288. DOI: 10.1108/DPRG-02-2020-0028

Mandania, R., Cadogan, J., Liu, J., & Kazmi, N. (2025). Optimizing promotional campaigns to maximize customer lifetime value: A dynamic learning approach. *Journal of Service Research*, 10946705251365524. Advance online publication. DOI: 10.1177/10946705251365524

Martin, K. (2019). Ethical implications and accountability of algorithms. *Journal of Business Ethics*, *160*(4), 835–850. DOI: 10.1007/s10551-018-3921-3

Martínez-Bravo, M. C., Sádaba Chalezquer, C., & Serrano-Puche, J. (2022). Dimensions of digital literacy in the 21st century competency frameworks. *Sustainability (Basel)*, *14*(3), 1867. DOI: 10.3390/su14031867

McDougall, J., Livingstone, S., & Sefton-Green, J. (2018). Digital learning and the capability approach. *Learning, Media and Technology*, *43*(1), 1–14. DOI: 10.1080/17439884.2017.1389076

McDougall, J., Readman, M., & Wilkinson, P. (2018). The uses of (digital) literacy. *Learning, Media and Technology*, *43*(3), 263–279. DOI: 10.1080/17439884.2018.1462206

Mcknight, D. H., Carter, M., Thatcher, J. B., & Clay, P. F. (2011). Trust in a specific technology: An investigation of its components and measures. [TMIS]. *ACM Transactions on Management Information Systems*, *2*(2), 1–25. DOI: 10.1145/1985347.1985353

Meng, D., Li, Y., & Zhang, J. (2023). Digital financial capability and household consumption: Evidence from the China Household Finance Survey. *Applied Economics Letters*. Advance online publication. DOI: 10.1080/13504851.2023.2167915

Meske, C., Abedin, B., Klier, M., & Rabhi, F. (2022). Explainable and responsible artificial intelligence. *Electronic Markets*, *32*(4), 2103–2106. DOI: 10.1007/s12525-022-00607-2

Meuter, M. L., Bitner, M. J., Ostrom, A. L., & Brown, S. W. (2005). Choosing among alternative service delivery modes: An investigation of customer trial of self-service technologies. *Journal of Marketing*, *69*(2), 61–83. DOI: 10.1509/jmkg.69.2.61.60759

Mishra, S., Ewing, M. T., & Cooper, H. B. (2022). Artificial intelligence focus and firm performance. *Journal of the Academy of Marketing Science*, *50*(6), 1176–1197. DOI: 10.1007/s11747-022-00876-5

Mogaji, E., & Jain, V. (2024). How generative AI is (will) change consumer behaviour: Postulating the potential impact and implications for research, practice, and policy. *Journal of Consumer Behaviour*, *23*(5), 2379–2389. DOI: 10.1002/cb.2345

Mohamad, A. A. S., & Shahril, Z. R. (2025). Consumer readiness on the sustainable practices of green technology in fast food restaurant. [IJRISS]. *International Journal of Research and Innovation in Social Science*, *9*(1), 4881–4895. DOI: 10.47772/IJRISS.2025.9010376

Molla, C., Bhuiyan, M. R. I., Islam, M. T., & Amin, A. (2026). Mediating role to banking performance for adopting digital bank using a technology organizational environment model. *Digital Finance*, *8*(1), 4. DOI: 10.1007/s42521-025-00168-x

Moriuchi, E., Landers, V. M., Colton, D., & Hair, N. (2021). Engagement with chatbots versus augmented reality interactive technology in e-commerce. *Journal of Strategic Marketing*, *29*(5), 375–389. DOI: 10.1080/0965254X.2020.1740766

Mu, J., & Zhang, J. Z. (2025). Artificial intelligence marketing usage and firm performance. *Journal of the Academy of Marketing Science*, *53*(4), 1–54. DOI: 10.1007/s11747-024-01076-z

Murár, P., & Kubovics, M. (2023, September). Using AI to create content designed for marketing communications. In *European Conference on Innovation and Entrepreneurship* (pp. 660-R25). Academic Conferences International Limited. DOI: 10.34190/ecie.18.1.1638

Mushtaq, M. A., Bais, M. K., & Bari, M. (2025). AI, Trust, and Consumers' online purchase intentions: Examining the Roles of Disinformation, Transparency, and Digital Literacy: . 18072808. *Research Consortium Archive, 3*(4), 1740-1758. DOI: 10.5281/zenodo

Nayal, P., Pandey, N., & Paul, J. (2022). Covid-19 pandemic and consumer-employee-organization wellbeing: A dynamic capability theory approach. *The Journal of Consumer Affairs*, *56*(1), 359–390. DOI: 10.1111/joca.12399

Nguyen, M. V., & Ha, K. D. (2024). Investigation of factors affecting the readiness for the adoption of sustainable building materials. *Engineering, Construction, and Architectural Management*, *32*(8), 5578–5608. DOI: 10.1108/ECAM-12-2023-1268

Ostrom, A. L., Fotheringham, D., & Bitner, M. J. (2018). Customer acceptance of AI in service encounters: understanding antecedents and consequences. In *Handbook of service science* (Vol. II, pp. 77–103). Springer International Publishing. DOI: 10.1007/978-3-319-98512-1_5

Pagala, I., Asir, M., Mere, K., Puji Lestari, U., & Siddiqa, H. (2024). Consumer Behavior in the Age of AI: The Role of Personalized Marketing and Data Analytics in Shaping Purchase Decisions. *Dinasti International Journal of Education Management And Social Science*, *5*(6), 1898–1907. DOI: 10.38035/dijemss.v5i6.2947

Paramesha, M., Rane, N., & Rane, J. (2024). Big data analytics, artificial intelligence, machine learning, internet of things, and blockchain for enhanced business intelligence. *Artificial Intelligence, Machine Learning, Internet of Things, and Blockchain for Enhanced Business Intelligence*. DOI: 10.2139/ssrn.4855856

Pavlou, P. A. (2003). Consumer acceptance of electronic commerce: Integrating trust and risk with the technology acceptance model. *International Journal of Electronic Commerce*, *7*(3), 101–134. DOI: 10.1080/10864415.2003.11044275

Peltier, J. W., Dahl, A. J., & Schibrowsky, J. A. (2024). Artificial intelligence in interactive marketing: A conceptual framework and research agenda. *Journal of Research in Interactive Marketing*, *18*(1), 54–90. DOI: 10.1108/JRIM-01-2023-0030

Poudel, K. P., Carter, R., & Lonial, S. (2019). The impact of entrepreneurial orientation, technological capability, and consumer attitude on firm performance: A multi-theory perspective. *Journal of Small Business Management*, *57*(sup2), 268–295. DOI: 10.1111/jsbm.12471

Pramanik, P., & Jana, R. K. (2025). A consumer acceptance model in the artificial intelligence era. *Management Decision*, *63*(9), 3136–3163. Advance online publication. DOI: 10.1108/MD-03-2024-0574

Prasanna, A., & Kushwaha, B. P. (2026). Transforming marketing landscapes: A systematic literature review of generative AI using the TCCM model framework. *Management Review Quarterly*, *76*(1), 421–455. DOI: 10.1007/s11301-025-00486-9

Radanliev, P. (2025). AI ethics: Integrating transparency, fairness, and privacy in AI development. *Applied Artificial Intelligence*, *39*(1), 2463722. DOI: 10.1080/08839514.2025.2463722

Rethinking the process of diffusion in innovation: A service ecosystems and institutional perspective. (2020). Journal of Business Research, 116, 526–534. DOI: 10.1016/j.jbusres.2020.01.038

Riaj, M. A., Tabassum, M. N., Hossain, R., Bhuiyan, M. R., & Khatun, M. (2025). Digitalization Transformation in Entrepreneurship and Enterprise Green Innovation. In Mouloudj, K., & Bouarar, A. (Eds.), *Digitizing Green Entrepreneurship* (pp. 181–204). IGI Global Scientific Publishing. DOI: 10.4018/979-8-3693-7442-9.ch007

Rita, P., Omran, W., Ramos, R. F., & Costa, T. (2025). Exploring the Applications of Artificial Intelligence in Marketing: aTopic Modelling Analysis. *Tourism & Management Studies*, *21*(1), 39–55. DOI: 10.18089/tms.20250103

Robeyns, I. (2005). The capability approach: A theoretical survey. *Journal of Human Development*, *6*(1), 93–117. DOI: 10.1080/146498805200034266

Saha, R., Jasrotia, S. S., & Kamila, M. K. (2025, December). The Ethics of AI-Driven Marketing: Challenges and Opportunities. In *E-business technologies conference proceedings* (Vol. 4, No. 1). https://ebt.rs/journals/index.php/conf-proc/article/view/214

Salam, M. A., Leong, V. S., & Muhamad, N. (2026). The Transformative Prospects of AI-Powered Virtual Influencers in Digital Consumer Engagement and Marketing Strategies. In *Cases on Social Media Marketing Engagement Tactics* (pp. 251–290). IGI Global Scientific Publishing. DOI: 10.4018/979-8-3373-2357-2.ch009

Sanchez-Cartas, J. M., & Katsamakas, E. (2024). AI pricing algorithms under platform competition. *Electronic Commerce Research*, 1-28. DOI: 10.1007/s10660-024-09821-w

Savoldi, B., Attanasio, G., Gorodetskaya, O., Marchiori Manerba, M., &Nozza, D. (2025). *Generative AI practices, literacy, and divides: An empirical analysis in the Italian context.* https://arxiv.org/abs/2512.03671

Şenyapar, H. N. D. (2024). The future of marketing: The transformative power of artificial intelligence. *International Journal of Management and Administration, 8*(15), 1–19. DOI: 10.29064/ijma.1412272

Sergeeva, O. V., Masalimova, A. R., Zheltukhina, M. R., Chikileva, L. S., Lutskovskai, L. Y., & Luzin, A. (2025). Impact of digital media literacy on attitude toward generative AI acceptance in higher education. *Frontiers in Education, 10*, 1563148. Advance online publication. DOI: 10.3389/feduc.2025.1563148

Seyedan, M., & Mafakheri, F. (2020). Predictive big data analytics for supply chain demand forecasting: Methods, applications, and research opportunities. *Journal of Big Data, 7*(1), 53. DOI: 10.1186/s40537-020-00329-2

Shaily, S. A., & Emma, N. N. (2021). Integration of artificial intelligence marketing to get brand recognition for social business. DOI: 10.32479/irmm.11542

Shankar, V. (2025). Marketing of technology intensive products: An AI driven approach. *Marketing Strategy Journal, 2*, 100008. Advance online publication. DOI: 10.1016/j.msj.2025.100008

Shim, H. S., Han, S. L., & Ha, J. (2021). The effects of consumer readiness on the adoption of self-service technology: Moderating effects of consumer traits and situational factors. *Sustainability (Basel), 13*(1), 95. Advance online publication. DOI: 10.3390/su13010095

Shin, D. (2021). The effects of explainability and transparency on user trust in AI systems. *Computers in Human Behavior, 125*, 106994. DOI: 10.1016/j.chb.2021.106994

Shin, D., & Park, Y. J. (2019). Role of fairness, accountability, and transparency in algorithmic decision-making. *Telecommunications Policy*, *43*(9), 101–118. DOI: 10.1016/j.telpol.2019.101845

Smit, A., Swart, J., & Broersma, M. (2025). Bypassing digital literacy: Marginalized citizens' tactics for participation and inclusion in digital societies. *New Media & Society*, *27*(6), 3127–3145. DOI: 10.1177/14614448231220383

Stewart, C. R., & Yap, S. F. (2020). Low literacy, policy and consumer vulnerability: Are we really doing enough? *International Journal of Consumer Studies*, *44*(4), 343–352. DOI: 10.1111/ijcs.12569

Sultana, N., Chowdhury, R. S., & Haque, A. (2023). Gravitating towards Fintech: A study on Undergraduates using extended UTAUT model. *Heliyon*, *9*(10), e20731. Advance online publication. DOI: 10.1016/j.heliyon.2023.e20731

Teepapal, T. (2025). AI-driven personalization: Unraveling consumer perceptions in social media engagement. *Computers in Human Behavior*, *165*, 108549. DOI: 10.1016/j.chb.2024.108549

Thomas-Francois, K., & Somogyi, S. (2022). Consumers' intention to adopt virtual grocery shopping: Do technological readiness and the optimisation of consumer learning matter? *International Journal of Retail & Distribution Management*, *50*(5), 638–657. DOI: 10.1108/IJRDM-06-2020-0206

Tinmaz, H., Lee, Y.-T., Fanea-Ivanovici, M., & Baber, H. (2022). A systematic review on digital literacy. *Smart Learning Environments*, *9*(1), 21. DOI: 10.1186/s40561-022-00204-y

Ullah, M. S., Khan, M. K., Ahmadxan Oglu, G. R., & Yasmin, T. (2025). *The influence of digital literacy on consumer perceptions and e-commerce engagement. Policy Research Journal, 3*(1), 92-104. Retrieved from https://policyresearchjournal.com/index.php/1/article/view/279

Umboh, I. A., Tumbel, A. L., & Wenas, R. S. (2023). Digital literacy as a mediator between digital marketing capability and SME performance. *The Journal of Asian Finance, Economics and Business*, *10*(2), 123–134. DOI: 10.56444/mem.v38i1.3315

van Dijk, J. A. G. M. (2006). Digital divide research, achievements and shortcomings. *Poetics*, *34*(4–5), 221–235. DOI: 10.1016/j.poetic.2006.05.004

Vargo, S. L., & Lusch, R. F. (2011). Service dominant logic: Continuing the evolution. *Journal of the Academy of Marketing Science*, *36*(1), 1–10. DOI: 10.1007/s11747-007-0069-6

Vashishth, T. K., Sharma, K. K., Kumar, B., Chaudhary, S., & Panwar, R. (2024). Enhancing customer experience through AI-enabled content personalization in e-commerce marketing. *Advances in digital marketing in the era of artificial intelligence*, 7-32.

Venkatesh, V., Morris, M. G., Davis, G. B., & Davis, F. D. (2003). User acceptance of information technology: Toward a unified view. *Management Information Systems Quarterly*, *27*(3), 425–478. DOI: 10.2307/30036540

Verleye, K., Gemmel, P., & Rangarajan, D. (2014). Managing engagement behaviors in a network of customers and stakeholders: Evidence from the nursing home sector. *Journal of Service Research*, *17*(1), 68–84. DOI: 10.1177/1094670513494015

Vladimirovich, K. M. (2020). Future marketing in B2B segment: Integrating Artificial Intelligence into sales management. *International Journal of Innovative Technologies in Economy*, (4), 410878. DOI: 10.31435/rsglobal_ijite/30092020/7149

Vorobeva, D., Costa Pinto, D., António, N., & Mattila, A. S. (2024). The augmentation effect of artificial intelligence: Can AI framing shape customer acceptance of AI-based services? *Current Issues in Tourism*, *27*(10), 1551–1571. DOI: 10.1080/13683500.2023.2214353

Wang, Y., Sauka, K., & Situmeang, F. B. I. (2025). Anthropomorphism and transparency interplay on consumer behaviour in generative AI-driven marketing communication. *Journal of Consumer Marketing*, *42*(4), 512–536. DOI: 10.1108/JCM-04-2024-6806

Wang, Y. Y., & Chuang, Y. W. (2024). Artificial intelligence self-efficacy: Scale development and validation. *Education and Information Technologies*, *29*(4), 4785–4808. DOI: 10.1007/s10639-023-12015-w

Waqas, M., & Qadri, U. A. (2025). When Consumer Autonomy is Compromised: Adopting a Dual-Type View to Understand AI-Driven Marketing and Its Impact on Young Consumers' Ethical Behavior. *Journal of Business Ethics*, *206*, 237–255. DOI: 10.1007/s10551-025-06155-x

Westphal, M. F. (2023). Decision control and explanations in human AI collaboration. *Human-Computer Interaction*, *38*(4). Advance online publication. DOI: 10.1016/j.ijhcs.2023.102956

Wu, L., & Jing Wen, T. (2021). Understanding AI Advertising from the Consumer Perspective. *Journal of Advertising Research*, *61*(2), 133–146. DOI: 10.2501/JAR-2021-004

Wu, X., Ha, L., & Lim, J. (2024). From perception to purchase: How AI literacy shapes consumer decisions in AI-generated sponsored vlogs across products and services. *Journal of Electronic Commerce Research & Applications*, *20*(4), 302. https://www.mdpi.com/0718-1876/20/4/302

Yas, H., Abdalaziz, M. M. O., Dafri, W., AL-Falahi, Q., Kashmoola, K., & AlLouzi, A. S. (2025). Artificial Intelligence and Digital Marketing: Ethical Challenges of Digital Influence on Public Perception and Consumer Behavior in the Law of the UAE. *Research Journal in Advanced Humanities*, *6*(3). Advance online publication. DOI: 10.58256/5hjmrw16

Zha, D., Bhat, Z. P., Lai, K. H., Yang, F., Jiang, Z., Zhong, S., & Hu, X. (2025). Data-centric artificial intelligence: A survey. *ACM Computing Surveys*, *57*(5), 1–42. DOI: 10.1145/3711118

Chapter 4
The Illusion of Seamless Service:
Trust and Value in AI-Mediated Customer Experience

Najati Issam
http://orcid.org/0009-0000-9550-9376
P SKILLS Business Academy, Morocco

ABSTRACT

This chapter examines the paradoxical effects of perceived seamlessness in human–AI service interactions on trust and perceived value. Drawing on technology-mediated services, trust calibration, and multidimensional value theory, it proposes a conceptual framework articulating three constructs: perceived seamlessness, cognitive and functional affective trust, and utilitarian, relational, and hedonic value. The framework models the sequential chain linking fluidity, trust, and value, and demonstrates that this relationship follows an inverted U-shaped curve. Beyond a critical threshold, seamlessness induces overtrust through heuristic generalization reinforced by anthropomorphic processes. Four moderating conditions are integrated: system transparency, transactional stakes, customer familiarity with AI interfaces, and perceived humanness of the agent. Six falsifiable propositions are derived. The chapter concludes with the formalization of transparent seamlessness as an alternative to the dominant paradigm of fluidity maximization in AI service design.

INTRODUCTION

The integration of AI-based conversational agents into commercial customer relationship systems constitutes one of the most significant transformations in

DOI: 10.4018/979-8-2600-2977-0.ch004

the service sector. Driven by imperatives of operational cost reduction, extended availability, and large-scale personalization, this transition profoundly redefines the conditions under which interactions between organizations and their customers take place. Chatbots, virtual assistants, and next-generation AI agents no longer constitute peripheral or experimental devices: they represent, for a growing number of organizations, the primary or even exclusive point of contact in customer relations.

In this context, seamlessness, understood as the perceived fluidity and continuity of the interaction, has established itself as the dominant criterion for evaluating and designing AI interfaces. The stated objective of conversational system designers is to produce interaction experiences so fluid, coherent, and natural that customers no longer perceive the boundary between the artificial agent and the human interlocutor. This aspiration rests on a structuring postulate: interactional fluidity is assumed to be inherently beneficial for customers.

This chapter subjects this postulate to critical examination. It advances the thesis that high levels of interactional fluidity produce a paradoxical effect. By masking the real limits of the system and activating anthropomorphic processes, fluidity induces miscalibrated trust, designated as overtrust. This miscalibration exposes customers to a devaluation of the service experience when system failures or limits become apparent. Seamlessness then becomes an illusion in the structural sense, a constitutive discrepancy between perceived fluidity and effective system capabilities.

This thesis addresses a specific gap. Existing work on conversational agent design (Følstad and Brandtzæg, 2017; Cheng and Jiang, 2020; McTear, 2022) treats interactional fluidity as a monotonically positive design objective. The conditions under which this relationship may reverse, particularly in the context of next-generation systems based on large language models (Brown et al., 2020), have not been theorized in an integrative framework that jointly accounts for perceptual, cognitive, and affective mechanisms.

To address this limitation, the chapter develops a curvilinear model of the relationship between perceived seamlessness and perceived value, mediated by the overtrust mechanism. This curvilinear specification constitutes the principal contribution. To support this contribution, the chapter also introduces the notion of functional affective trust as a construct specific to interactions with non-human agents, and formalizes the principle of transparent seamlessness as an alternative to the fluidity maximization paradigm. The framework articulates these constructs around three central elements (perceived seamlessness, trust, and perceived value) and integrates four moderators: system transparency, transactional stakes, customer familiarity with AI interfaces, and perceived humanness of the AI agent. Six falsifiable theoretical propositions are derived. The chapter is conceptual in orientation: its objective is to articulate an integrative theoretical framework rather than to test it empirically. The propositions formalized here provide a structured basis for subsequent empirical investigation. This chapter contributes to a broader research program on the cognitive, affective, and relational effects of AI mediation in commercial service contexts (van Doorn et al., 2017), and is intended for an academic readership in services marketing, consumer behavior, and human–AI interaction studies.

The remainder of the chapter is organized as follows. Section 1 establishes the conceptual foundations of seamlessness. Section 2 examines trust formation and identifies the overtrust paradox. Section 3 analyzes perceived value and integrates perceived humanness as a moderator. Section 4 presents the integrative framework and the theoretical propositions. Section 5 discusses theoretical and managerial implications, before the conclusion synthesizes the contribution.

SECTION 1 SEAMLESSNESS IN AI-MEDIATED SERVICE INTERACTIONS: CONCEPTUAL FOUNDATIONS

The notion of seamlessness occupies a central place in contemporary work on customer experience and service design, without yet being the subject of a consensual and stabilized definition in the literature. Its use across several disciplinary fields, from services marketing to user-centered computing and operations management, has produced a conceptual polysemy that hinders the cumulativeness of research. A preliminary clarification is therefore necessary, especially since the context of AI-mediated interactions introduces new dimensions that existing definitions capture only imperfectly.

1.1 Defining Seamlessness: From Omnichannel Continuity to Interactional Fluidity

In the omnichannel management literature, seamlessness primarily designates the continuity of the customer experience across the different touchpoints of a given service ecosystem. Verhoef et al. (2015) define it as an organization's ability to offer an integrated and coherent experience, regardless of the channel used by the customer at each stage of their journey. In this sense, seamlessness is an organizational and systemic property: it refers to coordination between channels, portability of customer data, and consistency of service policies. Herhausen et al. (2019) showed that this form of inter-channel fluidity exerts a significant positive effect on customer satisfaction and loyalty, by reducing perceived switching costs and reinforcing the consistency of the brand image.

However, directly transposing this definition to the context of customer–AI interactions leads to an inappropriate conceptual reduction. When a customer interacts with a conversational agent, the question of inter-channel continuity becomes secondary relative to the quality of the interactional experience itself, considered in its sequential and dialogic unfolding. This is what Følstad and Brandtzæg (2017) designate as conversational fluidity, namely the capacity of an AI system to produce natural, coherent, and context-adapted exchanges without generating perceptible breaks in the dialogue flow. This form of seamlessness, qualified as interactional to distinguish it from its omnichannel version, is an emergent property of the interaction itself, co-produced by the characteristics of the system and the expectations of the customer.

The distinction between these two meanings is not merely terminological. It implies different determinants, distinct effects, and specific measurement modes. Omnichannel seamlessness is measured at the level of the overall customer journey, while interactional seamlessness manifests at the micro level of the exchange, in the relevance of responses, the management of conversational context, and the absence of stylistic or informational discontinuities. This interactional seamlessness is apprehended in this chapter as a perceptual construct of the customer and not as an objective technical property of the system: two customers interacting with the same AI agent may perceive its fluidity differently depending on their prior expectations, their level of familiarity with these technologies, and their schemas for representing service interactions.

1.2 Seamlessness as a Design Objective: Promises and Underlying Assumptions

Interactional fluidity has established itself as the dominant performance criterion in the design of AI conversational agents. The foundational work of Nass and Reeves (1996) on computers as social actors established that individuals tend to apply the same interaction schemas to technological interfaces as to human interlocutors, which led AI system designers to optimize the naturalness of exchanges as a lever for acceptance and engagement. This orientation was reinforced by advances in natural language processing models, which made technically feasible a conversational fluidity previously unattainable (Brown et al., 2020).

The justifications advanced in favor of seamlessness as a design objective rest on three principal postulates: cognitive effort reduction (Davis, 1989), satisfaction optimization through a flow-like state (Csikszentmihalyi, 1990), and trust reinforcement through competence signaling (McKnight et al., 2002). These postulates have constituted the normative foundation of a substantial research stream. Følstad and Brandtzæg (2017) identify conversational coherence as the most robust determinant of satisfaction in chatbot interactions. Cheng and Jiang (2020) show that perceived interaction quality exerts a positive effect on trust and satisfaction. Sheehan et al. (2020) confirm that fluidity attributes constitute direct antecedents of conversational agent adoption. In the field of conversational system design and engineering, this normative orientation has translated into the explicit formulation of the frictionless experience principle as a priority design objective (McTear, 2022). These works converge toward a positive relationship between interactional fluidity and customer behavioral and perceptual outcomes, without however examining the effects of seamlessness beyond the moderate levels observed in systems deployed at the time of their realization.

It is precisely this limit that constitutes the starting point of this chapter. Next-generation AI systems based on large language models (Brown et al., 2020) produce qualitatively superior levels of interactional fluidity compared to previous generations, to the point where the boundary between artificial and human interaction becomes difficult to draw. In this new fluidity regime, the postulates underlying the positive relationship between seamlessness and customer outcomes merit reexamination (Ferraro et al., 2024).

1.3 The Illusion Dimension: Functional, Relational, and Control Illusions

Qualifying seamlessness as illusion does not amount to asserting that it is the product of a deliberately deceptive strategy. The term is used here in a phenomenological and cognitive sense: it designates the structural discrepancy between the fluidity perceived by the customer and the real, necessarily limited capabilities of the AI system. This discrepancy is not the result of a system failure but the logical consequence of its success: the more fluid the interaction, the broader the capacity inferences, and the greater the discrepancy between perceived and actual capabilities.

Three dimensions of this illusion can be distinguished analytically. The functional illusion corresponds to the customer's overestimation of the AI agent's operational competencies. When a system responds fluidly to complex requests, customers tend to generalize this perceived competence to domains the system does not necessarily master (Luger and Sellen, 2016), through an inference bias documented in the automation bias literature (Parasuraman and Manzey, 2010). Recent work has documented analogous mechanisms in conversational AI interaction contexts, where fluidity leads users to reduce their critical verification effort (Adam et al., 2021; Logg et al., 2019). The relational illusion designates the perception of a personalized relationship generated by the AI agent's personalization and relational continuity signals, which rests on a simulation of the relationship rather than an authentic relationship (Araujo, 2018). Nass and Moon (2000) showed that these attributions persist even when subjects are explicitly informed of the artificial nature of their interlocutor, illustrating the largely automatic character of these processes. The control illusion designates the perception of agency over the exchange that customers develop in a fluid interaction, whereas the structure of the interaction is in reality largely determined by the system's parameters (Epley et al., 2007; Langer, 1975).

These three dimensions of the illusion are not mutually exclusive and reinforce each other. The functional illusion amplifies confidence in the system's capabilities, reducing vigilance regarding its limits and reinforcing the control illusion. The relational illusion fosters affective engagement with the system that makes customers less inclined to adopt a critical posture. Together, they explain how seamlessness can produce paradoxical effects on trust and perceived value.

SECTION 2: TRUST IN AI-MEDIATED CUSTOMER INTERACTIONS

Trust constitutes one of the most extensively studied constructs in consumer behavior and services marketing, but its application to AI-mediated interactions raises specific theoretical questions that cannot be resolved by simple transposition of models developed in interpersonal or classical technological contexts. AI conversational agents present hybrid characteristics, both functional and para-social, that complicate trust formation and modify its temporal dynamics.

2.1 Conceptual Foundations: Cognitive and Functional Affective Trust in Technology-Mediated Contexts

The distinction between cognitive trust and affective trust constitutes one of the most robust contributions of the interpersonal trust literature. McAllister (1995) established that cognitive trust rests on rational inferences relating to the competence, reliability, and predictability of the object of trust, while affective trust rests on emotional bonds, on the perception of benevolence, and on a sense of security that goes beyond the mere evaluation of performance. These two forms of trust are not independent: cognitive trust generally constitutes an antecedent of affective trust.

Transposed to the context of technological systems, this distinction was operationalized by McKnight et al. (2002) in their model of initial trust in online systems. This model has been widely mobilized in research on service technology acceptance (Gefen et al., 2003), and its relevance for AI conversational agents has been confirmed by more recent work (Cheng and Jiang, 2020; Pitardi and Marriott, 2021; Lalot and Bertram, 2025).

Applying the concept of affective trust to customer–AI interactions raises a fundamental theoretical difficulty that merits explicit treatment. Affective trust in the sense of McAllister (1995) is defined within an interpersonal framework and presupposes an attribution of benevolence and intentionality to the object of trust.

Yet AI conversational agents do not possess intentionality in the proper sense: their responses are the product of computational processes, not of deliberation oriented toward customer well-being (Huang and Rust, 2021). This fundamental asymmetry imposes a conceptual clarification.

The resolution of this tension rests on the distinction between authentic affective trust and functional affective trust. Authentic affective trust presupposes effective reciprocity and genuine intentionality on the part of the object of trust. Functional affective trust, by contrast, designates an affective state of perceived security and benevolence that customers develop toward an AI agent through perceptual attributions of intentionality, in the absence of any such intentionality on the part of the system. Epley et al. (2007) showed that individuals automatically apply social representation schemas to non-human entities, activating three cognitive factors: the mobilization of preexisting knowledge of anthropomorphic agents (elicited agent knowledge), the need to predict and understand the agent's behavior (effectance motivation), and the social need for connection with the agent (sociality motivation). The presence of one or several of these factors sustains anthropomorphic attribution even toward entities whose artificial nature is explicitly known. Functional affective trust is therefore real in its behavioral and evaluative effects, but rests on a representation of the system that does not correspond to its computational nature. It is precisely this discrepancy that makes it simultaneously a lever of short-term perceived value and a vector of medium-term relational illusion.

The sequential ordering posited by the framework, namely the priority of cognitive trust over functional affective trust, rests on a specific theoretical condition. Anthropomorphic attributions activated by interactional cues can produce a descriptive perception of the agent as human-like, but this perception does not by itself generate the relational expectations of security and benevolence that characterize functional affective trust. These expectations require a prior layer of belief in the system's reliability and predictability, which cognitive trust precisely supplies. The dependency relation is therefore asymmetric: cognitive trust can be observed in the absence of functional affective trust, whereas the reverse configuration is theoretically unstable.

The notion of trust transfer (Stewart, 2003) provides complementary insight: trust in a technological system can be transferred from trust in the organization deploying it, a mechanism all the more active when customers have little prior experience with AI interfaces (Luo et al., 2019). It is finally necessary to distinguish trust in the AI system from trust in the organization, these two objects potentially evolving divergently, particularly when the interface's performance is perceived as incompatible with service standards habitually associated with the brand (van Doorn et al., 2017).

2.2 How Seamlessness Shapes Trust Formation

The mechanisms by which seamlessness influences trust formation operate at several levels of the interaction experience. At the most immediate level, technical fluidity generates competence inferences that directly feed cognitive trust: Parasuraman et al. (2005) showed that reliability and responsiveness constitute the most determining dimensions of perceived quality in online service contexts. Beyond perceived competence, interactional seamlessness contributes to trust formation through a mechanism signaling the predictability of the system, reducing the perceived uncertainty associated with the interaction (Gefen, 2000).

Conversational coherence plays a specific role in the formation of functional affective trust. Araujo (2018) showed that conversational agents adopting a relationship-oriented communication style generate significantly higher levels of affective trust, precisely because such coherence activates the anthropomorphism mechanisms described in Section 2.1. Følstad et al. (2018) confirmed that the perception of relational continuity between interaction sessions constitutes a significant determinant of functional affective trust toward AI customer service agents.

These positive effects of seamlessness on trust are conditional on the absence of perceptible interactional breaks. When a fluid AI agent suddenly produces an incoherent or unsuitable response, the effect on trust is disproportionately negative compared to what it would be in the context of an interaction already perceived as imperfect (Xu et al., 2020). This phenomenon suggests that seamlessness creates high expectations whose violation produces amplified disillusionment.

2.3 The Overtrust Paradox: When Seamlessness Undermines Calibrated Trust

Overtrust designates a trust accorded to an automated system that exceeds what that system's actual reliability rationally justifies (Parasuraman and Riley, 1997). Initially developed in industrial and aeronautical contexts, this concept has progressively been extended to technological contexts closer to mainstream services. Before deriving implications for customer–AI interactions, its transfer requires justification. Three elements support it. First, the cognitive mechanism underlying overtrust, namely the reduction of critical verification effort when facing a system perceived as reliable, is independent of the application domain and user expertise level: Logg et al. (2019) showed that this mechanism, which they designate as algorithm appreciation, operates robustly even among non-expert users. Second, Adam et al. (2021) empirically documented excessive compliance effects in service chatbot interactions, constituting a direct demonstration of automation bias in a conversational context. Automation bias designates a cognitive tendency by which users under-weight error signals produced by an automated system, particularly when the system has previously established a history of perceived high performance, leading to a reduction in their critical engagement with system outputs. Third, Hancock et al. (2011) showed in a meta-analysis that the determining factors of trust in automated systems are common to robotic systems, virtual agents, and mainstream digital interfaces.

This transferability is further supported by evidence from high-risk application domains. In aviation, automation complacency has been documented as a direct contributor to critical decision errors, with pilots systematically under-monitoring automated flight systems following extended periods of reliable performance (Skitka et al., 1999). In automated medical diagnostics, analogous patterns have been observed, with clinicians exhibiting reduced critical scrutiny of algorithmic outputs when prior system performance had been consistently accurate (Goddard et al., 2012). Both cases confirm that the suppression of critical monitoring effort following a history of reliable automated performance operates independently of domain and user expertise level, establishing the transferability of the overtrust mechanism to commercial customer–AI interactions.

The mechanism by which seamlessness induces overtrust operates as follows. A fluid interaction generates global competence inferences that overflow the domains effectively tested by the customer. Through a heuristic generalization process reinforced by the anthropomorphism mechanisms described in Section 2.1, customers infer that the system that fluently handled a complex request will also be capable of handling demands of a different nature or complexity level (Luger and Sellen, 2016).

This cognitive shift is consistent with the Heuristic-Systematic Processing framework (Chaiken, 1980), according to which individuals progressively substitute effortful analytical evaluation with cognitively economical heuristic processing when interactional cues appear sufficiently reliable. Under conditions of high perceived fluidity, users increasingly rely on global competence signals rather than deliberate verification processes, thereby amplifying the generalization bias underlying overtrust.

This generalization is maladapted in the context of AI systems, whose capabilities are closely delimited by their architecture and training data. Fluidity masks these delimitations by making imperceptible the boundaries between what the system can and cannot accomplish. Heersmink et al. (2024) characterize this phenomenon as the phenomenological and informational transparency of large language models, which paradoxically undermines users' capacity to calibrate their trust appropriately. This process is amplified by functional affective trust: a customer who has developed affective engagement toward an AI agent is even less inclined to adopt a critical posture, elevating the level of overtrust beyond what technical fluidity alone would induce. Automation bias (Parasuraman and Manzey, 2010) further reinforces this mechanism through a reduction in the customer's critical vigilance.

The transition from beneficial trust to overtrust takes the form of a threshold effect rather than a continuous degradation, for reasons internal to the inferential mechanism itself. Inferences of competence operate categorically rather than gradually: customers do not finely modulate their confidence according to small variations in fluidity, but classify the system as either capable or non-capable in a given domain. As long as the customer's interactions remain within domains effectively tested, this categorical inference is locally valid. Beyond the level of fluidity at which the customer ceases to differentiate between tested and non-tested domains, the inference becomes globally generalized, and trust calibration shifts from a domain-specific to a global mode. This shift is structural and discontinuous, which justifies the curvilinear specification of the relationship rather than a linear or progressive degradation.

The consequences of overtrust on perceived value are twofold. On the one hand, it produces a post-failure devaluation effect: high seamlessness generates high expectations, which mechanically amplifies the negative effect of any deviation, consistent with Oliver's (1980) expectation disconfirmation theory. On the other hand, overtrust produces a trust rupture of greater amplitude than that resulting from a failure in a context of moderate initial trust (Lee and See, 2004), a rupture liable to propagate from trust in the AI system to trust in the brand, through Stewart's (2003) reverse trust transfer mechanism. These two effects converge toward a central theoretical implication: the relationship between seamlessness and perceived value is not monotone but follows an inverted U-shaped curvilinear function.

SECTION 3: PERCEIVED VALUE IN AI-MEDIATED SERVICE INTERACTIONS

The trust formation dynamics established in Section 2, and particularly the conditions under which seamlessness produces miscalibrated trust, shape the conditions under which customer value is created or undermined. Perceived value constitutes one of the most fundamental constructs in services marketing research, insofar as it represents the customer's overall judgment of the utility of a service experience relative to what they have engaged to obtain it. Its application to AI-mediated interactions raises specific theoretical questions, relating notably to the ambiguous status of the AI agent as an exchange partner and to the conditions under which value co-production takes place. This section examines the conceptual foundations of perceived value, analyzes the conditions under which customer–AI interactions can generate or constrain value creation, and formally integrates perceived humanness and anthropomorphism as a moderator of the conceptual framework.

3.1 A Multidimensional Framework of Perceived Value

The conceptual reference framework for analyzing perceived value is that proposed by Zeithaml (1988), who defines it as the consumer's overall assessment of the utility of a product or service, based on the perception of what is received and what is given. Sheth et al. (1991) proposed a five-dimension taxonomy, simplified by Sweeney and Soutar (2001) into four measurable dimensions. In the context of digital services, Mathwick et al. (2001) distinguished utilitarian and hedonic value. For the purposes of this chapter, a three-dimensional structure is retained: utilitarian value (efficiency, time savings, problem resolution), relational value (feeling of being recognized, understood, and accompanied in a personalized manner), and hedonic value (intrinsic quality of the interactional experience, independently of its functional result). Chatterjee et al. (2021) showed that these three dimensions exert distinct effects on AI agent users' satisfaction and that their relative importance varies according to task type and transactional stakes.

It should be noted that these three value dimensions do not exert a symmetric influence on the overall evaluation of the experience. Utilitarian value is the most immediately accessible and directly measurable. Relational and hedonic value are more diffuse constructs whose formation rests more heavily on interpretive and affective processes liable to be influenced by perceptual attributions related to the agent's nature, notably the anthropomorphism mechanisms examined in Section 3.3. This asymmetry has important implications for modeling the effect of seamlessness on perceived value.

3.2 Value Co-Creation and Its Limits in AI-Driven Interactions

The value co-creation perspective, stemming from the service-dominant logic (Vargo and Lusch, 2004, 2008), postulates that value emerges from the interaction between provider and customer resources. Its application to customer–AI interactions raises theoretical difficulties, however: AI agents do not possess intentionality in the proper sense, which calls into question the reciprocity of contributions (Huang and Rust, 2021). Wirtz et al. (2018) propose an operational distinction between functional co-creation, in which customers contribute to interaction efficiency, and relational co-creation, in which customers invest emotionally in the exchange. The former is accessible in customer–AI interactions; the latter is problematic as it rests on an attribution of intentionality that does not correspond to the actual capabilities of current AI systems. Seamlessness plays an ambivalent role: it facilitates functional co-creation while encouraging relational co-creation by creating an illusion of reciprocity, exposing customers to the risk of an unfounded emotional investment.

3.3 Perceived Humanness, Anthropomorphism, and Relational Value: Toward Formal Integration

The tendency to attribute human characteristics to non-human agents constitutes a major determinant of relational value in customer–AI interactions. Although this mechanism is frequently mentioned in the chatbot service literature, it has not yet been formally integrated as a moderator in conceptual frameworks articulating seamlessness, trust, and value. This section introduces perceived humanness as the fourth formal moderator of the conceptual framework, justifying its status and specifying its differentiated effects on model relationships.

Epley et al. (2007) showed that anthropomorphism is a fundamental cognitive process by which individuals apply social representation schemas to non-human entities producing socially relevant behaviors such as verbal communication or adaptation to the interlocutor's context. This process is activated in a largely automatic and pre-reflexive manner, as established in Section 2.1 in relation to functional affective trust. The effects of perceived humanness on perceived value dimensions are differentiated. On utilitarian value, the moderating effect is limited, functional efficiency being evaluated primarily on the basis of concrete results (Chatterjee et al., 2021). On hedonic value, the effect is positive and moderate, an interaction perceived as more human being generally experienced as more pleasant (Nass and Moon, 2000). On relational value, the effect is strongly positive: Waytz et al. (2010) showed that individuals grant more trust to agents perceived as human, and Sheehan et al. (2020) confirmed that perceived humanness constitutes a significant antecedent of perceived relational value independently of the functional quality of the response (Kumar et al., 2025).

Seamlessness constitutes one of the principal triggers of anthropomorphic attributions: a fluid and contextually adapted AI agent produces behavioral cues that activate the customer's social representation schemas (Nass and Moon, 2000). However, the relationship between perceived humanness and perceived value is not linear. The uncanny valley (Mori, 1970; Zlotowski et al., 2015; Strait et al., 2017) designates the discomfort reaction produced by an almost human but imperfectly human representation, constituting an upper limit on the benefits of seamlessness for relational value. Furthermore, the structural dehumanization documented in works on AI perception in service contexts (Araujo, 2018; Sheehan et al., 2020) constitutes a negative determinant of relational value that persists even under conditions of high seamlessness and perceived humanness. These considerations lead to theoretical proposition P6, formally integrated into the framework of Section 4.

SECTION 4: AN INTEGRATIVE CONCEPTUAL FRAMEWORK

The three preceding sections established the conceptual foundations of this chapter's central constructs, namely the mechanisms through which perceived seamlessness shapes trust formation, the conditions under which functional affective trust can emerge in interactions with non-human agents, and the determinants of perceived value in customer–AI interactions. Building on these foundations, this section develops an integrative conceptual framework that articulates these constructs into a coherent processual model. The framework is structured as a sequential chain, progressively linking antecedents of perceived seamlessness to value outcomes, while incorporating a non-linear effect and a central mechanism of overtrust.

4.1 Antecedents of Perceived Seamlessness

Consistent with the argument developed in Section 1, seamlessness is conceptualized as a perceptual construction rather than an objective property of the system. It emerges from the interaction between system performance, interactional organization, and user expectations. Within this framework, three antecedents are identified: technical fluidity, conversational coherence, and expectation congruence.

Technical fluidity refers to the system's ability to produce accurate, coherent, and timely responses while avoiding errors and latency. Although necessary, it is not sufficient, as technically efficient systems may still be perceived as insufficiently fluid when responses are contextually inappropriate (Lopatovska and Arapakis, 2011). Conversational coherence captures the system's capacity to maintain a consistent interactional context, adapt its communication style, and ensure continuity across exchanges, which has been identified as a key determinant of user satisfaction (Følstad and Brandtzæg, 2017). Expectation congruence refers to the alignment between anticipated and experienced interaction, shaped by prior experience, cultural representations, and organizational signals (Oliver, 1980).

The selection of these three antecedents reflects a parsimonious approach focused on the core dimensions of interactional fluidity. Technical fluidity captures infrastructural performance, conversational coherence reflects interactional continuity, and expectation congruence addresses evaluative alignment. Together, they are sufficient to account for perceived seamlessness within the scope of this model.

While analytically distinct, technical fluidity and conversational coherence may be less clearly separable in contemporary AI systems based on large language models, where response generation integrates performance and linguistic coherence. This distinction should therefore be understood as conceptual rather than strictly empirical.

Taken together, these antecedents define the conditions under which perceived seamlessness emerges and constitutes the entry point of the process linking interactional experience to trust formation and perceived value.

4.2 The Seamlessness–Trust–Value Chain

Within this processual logic, perceived seamlessness initiates a sequential transformation linking interactional evaluation to value creation through trust mechanisms. The central causal chain of the model articulates four constructs in sequence: perceived seamlessness, cognitive trust, functional affective trust, and perceived value. The chain is sequential and conditional. Each construct activates the following one, and each transition operates under specific contextual conditions detailed in the subsequent sub-sections.

Perceived seamlessness first generates cognitive trust by signaling competence and reducing uncertainty (Gefen et al., 2003; Cheng and Jiang, 2020). At this stage, trust remains primarily evaluative and grounded in the system's perceived reliability. As interaction continuity is maintained and conversational coherence is preserved, cognitive trust progressively evolves into functional affective trust, marking a shift from rational assessment to a more immersive mode of engagement.

Functional affective trust does not rely on actual reciprocity but on the attribution of intentionality to the system, driven by anthropomorphic perception. It differs from classical affective trust in that it emerges without interpersonal exchange, but from the perception of the system as a quasi-intentional agent. This transformation is facilitated by uninterrupted interaction and reinforced by interaction duration and perceived humanness (Pitardi and Marriott, 2021; Følstad et al., 2018).

Functional affective trust constitutes the primary driver of perceived value. It enhances utilitarian value through reduced verification effort, strengthens relational value by fostering perceived interactional closeness, and contributes to hedonic value through immersive absorption (Csikszentmihalyi, 1990).

The chain described above operates within a bounded range of seamlessness levels. Beyond this range, the same generative mechanisms that produce trust become the source of its miscalibration: heuristic generalization extends competence inferences beyond their domain of validity, and anthropomorphic engagement weakens the customer's critical posture. The relationship between seamlessness and perceived value therefore cannot be modeled as monotonic. Its specification requires an account of the structural conditions under which trust formation reverses into trust miscalibration.

4.3 The Curvilinear Effect: The Overtrust Mechanism

The overtrust mechanism captures this structural reversal. As established in Section 2.3, inferences of competence operate categorically rather than gradually: beyond the level of fluidity at which the customer ceases to differentiate between tested and non-tested domains, the inference becomes globally generalized. This categorical shift is the structural source of the curvilinear dynamic, and modeling it constitutes the central theoretical contribution of the framework.

Below a critical threshold, the positive relationship operates through the mechanisms described in Section 4.2. Beyond this threshold, the same mechanisms reverse their effects. Inflated expectations expose customers to a devaluation of the experience in the event of system failure, while the reduction of critical vigilance associated with automation bias (Parasuraman and Manzey, 2010) weakens perceived utilitarian value and increases uncritical reliance on the system. The depth of this reversal is proportional to the level of functional affective trust accumulated below the threshold: a customer whose affective engagement has been strongly activated is correspondingly more exposed to value loss when the system's effective limits are revealed.

The position of the inflection point is not fixed. It varies according to contextual conditions and evolves with customers' familiarity with AI technologies. Luo et al. (2019) suggest that experience with AI agents reshapes users' interaction patterns, contributing to a progressive recalibration of expectations and shifting the overtrust threshold toward higher levels of seamlessness as familiarity increases.

This curvilinear effect does not challenge the importance of seamlessness as a design objective, but specifies its conditions of optimization. The objective is to maintain interactional fluidity within an optimal value zone while mitigating the risks associated with excessive trust. Importantly, this effect is not uniform across contexts but depends on a set of boundary conditions that regulate both its intensity and its threshold.

4.4 Moderating Conditions

The four moderating variables operate along two analytically distinct functional axes. The first concerns the positioning of the overtrust threshold: system transparency and familiarity with AI interfaces shift the inflection point of the seamlessness-value curve upward, by maintaining calibrated expectations and reducing heuristic generalization. The second concerns the intensity of effects: transactional stakes and perceived humanness amplify the magnitude of both the positive and negative outcomes within the model, by shaping value dimension weights and the depth of anthropomorphic engagement. Two moderators thus regulate when the threshold is reached; two regulate how severely its consequences manifest.

System transparency designates the degree to which the system explicitly signals its artificial nature, capabilities, and limits during the interaction. By maintaining calibrated expectations, it negatively moderates the effect of perceived seamlessness on overtrust and shifts the inflection point toward higher levels of seamlessness (Komiak and Benbasat, 2006).

Transactional stakes shape both value formation and the sensitivity of the overtrust mechanism. They moderate the relationship between functional affective trust and perceived value by adjusting the relative importance of value dimensions, and amplify the consequences of overtrust in high-stakes contexts. Higher transactional stakes therefore lower the tolerance threshold beyond which seamlessness becomes counterproductive (Huang and Rust, 2021).

Familiarity with AI interfaces calibrates customer expectations, affecting both perceived seamlessness and the positioning of the overtrust threshold. Experienced users develop structured expectation schemas and maintain stable vigilance, which reduces overgeneralization and shifts the inflection point upward (Luo et al., 2019).

Perceived humanness designates the degree to which human characteristics are attributed to the AI agent. It positively moderates the relationship between perceived seamlessness and functional affective trust, and strengthens the relationship between functional affective trust and relational value. At the same time, it lowers the overtrust threshold by intensifying heuristic generalization, an effect bounded above by the uncanny valley phenomenon.

Although each moderator operates through a distinct mechanism, their joint configurations produce identifiable risk profiles within the model. The most critical configuration combines high perceived humanness with high transactional stakes: the former lowers the overtrust threshold by deepening anthropomorphic engagement, the latter amplifies the consequences of crossing it. The most protective configuration associates high system transparency with high familiarity with AI interfaces, both of which independently shift the inflection point upward, producing a compounding calibration effect. Formalizing these interaction effects lies beyond the scope of the present conceptual framework but constitutes a priority agenda for experimental research designs capable of manipulating moderator levels independently and in combination.

Beyond the four moderating conditions formalized in the framework, demographic and cultural variables may influence the positioning of the overtrust threshold. Hofstede's (2001) Uncertainty Avoidance Index suggests that individuals from high uncertainty avoidance cultures maintain more deliberate evaluation strategies, shifting the threshold upward, while younger users with greater AI exposure may reach heuristic processing more rapidly. These variations define a priority agenda for cross-cultural empirical research.

4.5 Formalization of the Transparent Seamlessness Concept

Transparent seamlessness can be defined as the degree to which an AI service system proactively, contextually, and proportionately signals the limits of its capabilities while preserving perceived interactional fluidity. Within the model, it operates as a regulatory mechanism that maintains calibrated trust and prevents the escalation of seamlessness into overtrust.

Three constitutive dimensions can be distinguished. Declarative transparency refers to the explicit disclosure of the system's artificial nature prior to interaction, enabling the formation of realistic initial expectations. Competence transparency refers to the contextual signaling, during the interaction, of domains of competence and limitation, thereby attenuating overtrust as it emerges; an approach aligned with Explainable AI (XAI) design principles (Arrieta et al., 2020). Transactional transparency refers to the adjustment of signaling intensity according to transactional stakes, including escalation to human agents when necessary in high-risk situations.

These three dimensions are analytically aligned with the model's moderating structure. Declarative transparency operates on expectation congruence, competence transparency directly supports system transparency in regulating overtrust, and transactional transparency reinforces the role of transactional stakes. This alignment transforms transparent seamlessness from a descriptive concept into a design-oriented mechanism embedded within the model.

The concept nevertheless entails a structural tension between its two constitutive terms. Seamlessness implies continuity and the absence of interactional disruption; transparency requires the explicit signaling of system limitations, which may introduce friction. This tension is empirically documented by Wang et al. (2025), who show that transparency operationalized as disclosure of AI-generated content weakens the effect of anthropomorphism on social presence in marketing communication, confirming that the two terms operate in opposite directions on the perceptual processes underlying interactional fluidity. The tension is therefore inherent and cannot be fully eliminated. Rather than being contradictory, it defines the conditions under which transparent seamlessness can be achieved: transparency signals must be integrated in ways that preserve interactional flow, for instance through contextually embedded formulations that maintain conversational coherence while calibrating user expectations.

4.6 Visual Representation of the Model

Figure 1 synthesizes the conceptual framework developed in this section. The model is structured as a sequential mechanism linking perceived seamlessness to perceived value through a cognitive-affective transformation, integrating both a non-linear dynamic and a central mechanism of overtrust.

The spatial organization of the figure reflects the processual logic of the model. The upper part captures the antecedents of perceived seamlessness, namely technical fluency, conversational coherence, and expectation congruence. The central part represents the seamlessness-trust-value chain, in which perceived seamlessness generates cognitive trust that progressively evolves into functional affective trust, with the overtrust mechanism positioned at the core of this transformation. The lower part represents perceived value as a multidimensional construct encompassing utilitarian, relational, and hedonic dimensions.

The four moderating variables are positioned around the overtrust mechanism, signaling their regulatory role on both the intensity of trust formation and the location of the threshold. The right-hand side of the figure illustrates the inverted U-shaped relationship between seamlessness and perceived value, identifying the optimal zone beyond which fluidity reverses its effects.

Finally, a feedback loop from perceived value to expectation formation introduces a dynamic dimension into the model. Repeated interactions iteratively recalibrate customer expectations, thereby reshaping future perceptions of seamlessness and the conditions under which overtrust emerges.

Figure 1. Integrative Conceptual Framework: Perceived Seamlessness, Trust, and Value in Customer-AI Interactions

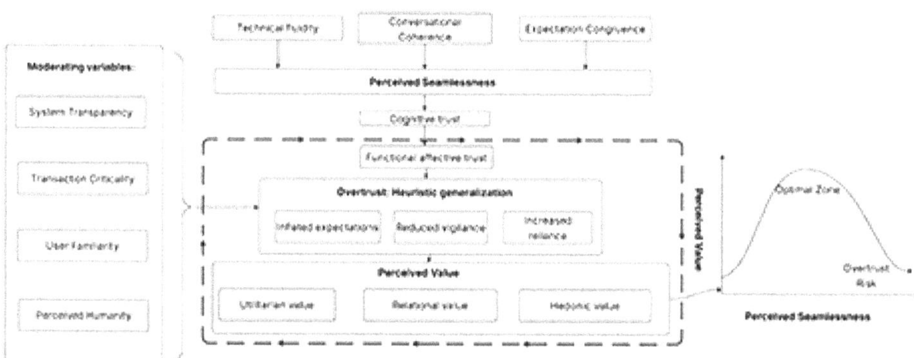

4.7 Theoretical Propositions

Building on the conceptual framework developed in Section 4, the following propositions formalize the sequential, non-linear, and moderated relationships linking perceived seamlessness to perceived value in customer–AI interactions. They capture both the trust formation dynamics and their potential reversal through the overtrust mechanism (Table 1).

P1: Perceived seamlessness exerts a positive effect on cognitive trust toward the AI agent, through competence and predictability inferences.

P2: Cognitive trust constitutes a positive antecedent of functional affective trust, this relationship being strengthened by interaction continuity and repetition, as well as by the perceived humanness of the agent.

P3a: The relationship between perceived seamlessness and perceived value follows an inverted U-shaped pattern: positive at moderate levels, it becomes negative beyond a critical threshold due to the overtrust mechanism, characterized by inflated expectations, reduced vigilance, and increased reliance.

P3b: The inflection point of this relationship shifts toward higher levels of perceived seamlessness when system transparency is high, transactional stakes are low, familiarity with AI is high, and perceived humanness remains moderate.

P4: System transparency negatively moderates the effect of perceived seamlessness on overtrust, attenuating its intensity and shifting the critical threshold upward.

P5: Transactional stakes positively moderate the relationship between functional affective trust and relational value, this relationship being stronger in high-stakes contexts.

P6: Perceived humanness positively moderates both the formation of functional affective trust and relational value, subject to an upper boundary corresponding to the uncanny valley threshold, beyond which its effects become negative.

Table 1. Summary of Theoretical Propositions

Proposition	Main Relationship	Key Mechanism	Type
P1	Seamlessness → Cognitive Trust	Technical fluency and coherence	Direct effect
P2	Cognitive Trust → Functional Affective Trust	Anthropomorphic engagement	Direct effect
P3a	Moderate seamlessness → Value increase	Trust calibration	Curvilinear effect
P3b	Excessive seamlessness → Value decrease	Overtrust and generalization bias	Curvilinear effect
P4	System transparency moderates overtrust	Competence signaling	Moderation

continued on following page

Table 1. Continued

Proposition	Main Relationship	Key Mechanism	Type
P5	Transactional stakes moderate trust-value relationship	Risk visibility	Moderation
P6	Perceived humanness moderates overtrust threshold	Anthropomorphic amplification	Moderation

SECTION 5: DISCUSSION: THEORETICAL AND MANAGERIAL IMPLICATIONS

The preceding sections established the conceptual foundations of an integrative framework articulating perceived seamlessness, trust, and perceived value in customer–AI interactions, with three new theoretical developments: the distinction between authentic affective trust and functional affective trust, the formalization of perceived humanness as the fourth formal moderator, and the formalization of the transparent seamlessness concept in three constitutive dimensions.

5.1 Theoretical Contributions

The framework developed in this chapter contributes to research on AI-mediated customer experience along three main lines. The principal contribution is the modeling of a curvilinear relationship between perceived seamlessness and perceived value, mediated by the overtrust mechanism. Two complementary contributions support this principal claim: the conceptualization of functional affective trust as a construct specific to interactions with non-human agents, and the formalization of the transparent seamlessness principle as a regulatory mechanism embedded within the model. A fourth element, the integration of perceived humanness as a formal moderator, refines the framework rather than constituting an autonomous contribution. Each contribution is positioned relative to the specific literature stream it engages.

The principal contribution lies in the formalization of overtrust as a structuring mechanism that introduces a curvilinear dynamic into the seamlessness–value relationship. Below a critical threshold, perceived seamlessness enhances perceived value through the trust formation mechanisms detailed in Section 4.2. Beyond this threshold, the same mechanisms generate inflated expectations, reduced critical vigilance, and uncritical reliance on the system, producing a reversal of the relationship. The position of the inflection point is regulated by the four moderating conditions specified in Section 4.4, and a feedback mechanism progressively shifts this position as user familiarity recalibrates expectations over time. This curvilinear specification departs from the dominant assumption in the AI service design literature (Følstad and Brandtzæg, 2017; Cheng and Jiang, 2020; McTear, 2022), which treats interactional fluidity as a monotonically positive design objective. By identifying the conditions under which fluidity reverses its effects on value, the framework opens a theoretical space that prior work has not articulated.

A first complementary contribution lies in the conceptualization of functional affective trust as a construct distinct from authentic affective trust. Authentic affective trust, as theorized by McAllister (1995) in interpersonal contexts, presupposes effective reciprocity and genuine intentionality. Functional affective trust, by contrast, designates an affective state of perceived security and benevolence developed toward an AI agent on the basis of perceptual attributions of intentionality, in the absence of any such intentionality on the part of the system. The distinction adapts the trust calibration literature (Lee and See, 2004; Parasuraman and Riley, 1997), originally developed for industrial and aeronautical contexts, to the specificities of commercial customer–AI interactions. The construct is real in its behavioral and evaluative effects but rests on a representation of the system that does not correspond to its computational nature, a structural property that links it directly to the overtrust mechanism.

A second complementary contribution lies in the formalization of transparent seamlessness as a design principle articulated in three constitutive dimensions. Declarative transparency operates on expectation congruence prior to interaction, competence transparency operates on the regulation of overtrust during interaction, and transactional transparency adjusts signaling intensity according to transactional stakes. The three-dimensional formalization thereby transforms transparent seamlessness from a normative recommendation into a theoretically grounded construct embedded within the model. It also addresses a structural tension that has remained largely implicit in the conversational design literature, namely the apparent contradiction between continuity (seamlessness) and explicit signaling of system limits (transparency). By treating this tension as constitutive rather than disqualifying, the framework provides a path for reconciling fluidity and calibrated trust within a single design principle.

The integration of perceived humanness as a formal moderator (P6) refines the framework by formally connecting the anthropomorphism literature with the seamlessness–trust–value architecture. Prior work has primarily examined anthropomorphic attributions as isolated mechanisms. The present framework integrates them into an articulated model in which they moderate both the activation of functional affective trust and the position of the overtrust threshold, subject to the uncanny valley boundary condition (Mori, 1970; Strait et al., 2017). The integration constitutes a refinement rather than an autonomous contribution, but it strengthens the explanatory reach of the model in contexts of high anthropomorphic intensity.

These contributions are part of a broader research program on the cognitive, affective, and relational effects of AI mediation in commercial service contexts (van Doorn et al., 2017). Where prior work on perceived dehumanization examines the costs associated with the perception of the artificial nature of the service agent, the present framework analyzes the conditions under which the expected benefits of seamless interaction can themselves undermine value creation. Both perspectives converge toward a more comprehensive understanding of AI-mediated service experiences, grounded in the analysis of contextual, perceptual, and relational contingencies that shape their outcomes.

5.2 Managerial Implications: Transparent Seamlessness in Practice

The managerial implications of this framework are organized around the principle of transparent seamlessness and its three constitutive dimensions. Implementing declarative transparency concerns the interaction initiation phase. Organizations should invest in clear and precise communications on the capabilities and limits of their AI agents, so as to calibrate customer expectations realistically, consistent with Oliver's (1980) expectation disconfirmation theory. This expectation management must be differentiated according to customer familiarity with AI interfaces: less familiar customers benefit from more explicit declarative transparency, while experienced customers possess a natural expectation calibration mechanism. Concrete forms of declarative transparency include preamble statements identifying the artificial nature of the agent and outlining its scope of competence, displayed in the interface or articulated by the agent in its first turn of the conversation.

Implementing competence transparency concerns the conversational design itself. Rather than seeking to mask the boundaries of the AI agent's capabilities, organizations should integrate explicit and natural signals indicating to customers the domains in which the system can provide reliable assistance and those that exceed its capabilities. These signals can be organically integrated into the dialogue, for example in formulations such as "for this specific request, I recommend contacting an advisor." Komiak and Benbasat (2006) showed that such mechanisms increase calibrated trust without reducing overall satisfaction. Competence transparency should be more frequent and explicit for highly anthropomorphic systems, whose overtrust risk is higher.

Implementing transactional transparency concerns the dynamic modulation of signaling level according to perceived transactional stakes. For low-stakes transactions, fluidity optimization constitutes an appropriate strategy. A typical illustration is the tracking of a standard product order, where the agent provides information without significant consequences in case of error and where seamlessness optimizes customer satisfaction without raising significant overtrust risks. For high-stakes transactions, organizations should adopt a hybrid approach combining AI agent efficiency for information collection phases with a transfer to a human interlocutor for critical decision phases (Huang and Rust, 2021). Examples include preliminary inquiries about financial products, health-related diagnoses, or commitments with legal implications, where the consequences of overtrust may significantly affect the customer's decisions and where systematic transfer to a human interlocutor for critical phases preserves both calibrated trust and the customer's autonomy. A transversal recommendation concerns performance metrics: organizations should integrate trust calibration indicators, perceived relational value, and post-interaction critical behavior alongside traditional efficiency and immediate satisfaction indicators.

The contextual variability emphasized in service research is captured in the present framework through two of its four moderators. Transactional stakes account for variations between industries and transaction types, distinguishing low-stakes contexts (such as standard order tracking) from high-stakes contexts (such as financial inquiries, health-related questions, or commitments with legal implications). Customer familiarity with AI interfaces accounts for variations across user profiles, distinguishing experienced users with calibrated expectation schemas from inexperienced users requiring more explicit declarative transparency. Further sources of variability, such as cultural differences or sectoral specificities, may be integrated as extensions of the framework in subsequent work.

5.3 Limitations and Avenues for Future Research

The framework developed in this chapter is conceptual in nature and is intended to provide the theoretical foundations on which subsequent empirical work can build. Its limitations are therefore of two kinds: empirical, related to the testability of its propositions, and conceptual, related to the boundaries of its theoretical scope. The five limitations identified below combine both dimensions and define a structured research program.

The first, persistent, concerns the operationalization of the curvilinear function's inflection point. Although the reformulation of P3 into two sub-propositions improved model testability, the precise empirical localization of this threshold remains a considerable methodological challenge. Addressing this challenge requires experimental designs allowing seamlessness level manipulation on a continuous spectrum or longitudinal studies.

Different empirical strategies may be mobilized depending on the propositions under investigation. P1 and P2 are amenable to controlled laboratory experiments or structured chatbot interaction studies in which seamlessness is operationalized through response latency, linguistic coherence, and contextual adaptation, with cognitive trust and functional affective trust measured at successive interaction stages. P3a and P3b may be examined through designs inducing system failures at varying levels of prior seamlessness exposure, measuring perceived value before and after the failure event through validated multidimensional scales. P4, P5, and P6 lend themselves to factorial designs manipulating system transparency, transactional stakes, and anthropomorphic cues independently and in combination, with perceived value and trust calibration analyzed as dependent variables. Conversational transcripts of real customer–AI interactions may also constitute a valuable empirical corpus for examining P1, P2, and P3 through computational text analysis and behavioral coding approaches.

The second, partially new, concerns the measurement of functional affective trust as a distinct construct: existing scales were developed in interpersonal or technological contexts without integrating the anthropomorphic dimension constitutive of this construct (Ng & Zhang, 2025), requiring specific scale development work.

The third, persistent, concerns model generalization to different AI interface types: voice agents, animated avatars, and multimodal interfaces present characteristics likely to substantially modify model relationships, notably the boundary condition of P6 linked to the uncanny valley. Research on voice-based interfaces suggests, for instance, that audio cues activate anthropomorphic attributions more rapidly than textual interfaces, causing users to exceed the overtrust threshold at a greater rate (Moussawi et al., 2021), which points to interface modality as a contextual amplifier of the perceived humanness moderator warranting formal integration in future empirical work.

The fourth, persistent, concerns the temporal dimension: the framework adopts an essentially static perspective, and longitudinal studies would be necessary to determine whether overtrust constitutes a transient or stable bias. The fifth, new, concerns the measurement and operationalization of the transparent seamlessness concept: competence transparency and transactional transparency are dynamic properties difficult to capture by static instruments, potentially requiring the development of real-time observation methods or automated analysis of conversational transcripts.

CONCLUSION

This chapter proposed an integrative conceptual framework for analyzing the effects of seamlessness in customer–AI interactions on trust and perceived value, distinguishing itself from prior work through three conceptual contributions: the modeling of a curvilinear effect linking fluidity and perceived value via the overtrust mechanism, the conceptualization of functional affective trust as a form of trust specific to interactions with non-human agents, and the formalization of the transparent seamlessness principle in three constitutive dimensions.

The central argument can be summarized as follows. Below a critical threshold, interaction fluidity reinforces cognitive trust through competence signaling and facilitates the transition toward functional affective trust through the activation of anthropomorphic processes generating attributions of benevolence. This functional affective trust contributes positively to the three dimensions of perceived value through distinct mechanisms. Beyond the critical threshold, fluidity produces a paradoxical effect: the same anthropomorphic processes that generate relational value below the threshold become the structural source of miscalibrated trust above it, exposing customers to a devaluation of the experience when the system's effective limits are revealed. Seamlessness then becomes a structural illusion, not a deliberate deception, but a constitutive discrepancy between perceived fluidity and effective capabilities. This mechanism, formalized as an inverted U-shaped curvilinear function and decomposed into two sub-propositions with enhanced empirical testability, constitutes the principal theoretical contribution of this work.

Four principal lessons can be drawn from the revised framework. First, seamlessness is a perceptual construction determined by three distinct antecedents whose effects cannot be treated in an aggregated manner. Second, trust in customer–AI interactions is a multidimensional construct whose two components obey fundamentally different formation logics: cognitive trust rests on competence inferences, functional affective trust on perceptual attributions of intentionality. Third, the effects of seamlessness are fundamentally contingent and modulated by four conditions that prohibit any universal design recommendation. Fourth, the risk of overtrust is structurally amplified by anthropomorphism mechanisms, establishing a direct link between the growing sophistication of AI systems and the increasing risk of miscalibrated trust.

These lessons converge toward the principle of transparent seamlessness, formalized in three constitutive dimensions. Its implementation requires a partial reconfiguration of the objectives and performance metrics used to evaluate AI customer service systems, integrating trust calibration indicators and relational value alongside traditional indicators. The priority empirical research program is organized around three axes: the experimental validation of the overtrust mechanism in conversational AI service contexts, the development of measurement instruments for functional affective trust and the three dimensions of transparent seamlessness, and longitudinal and comparative studies examining the temporal evolution of effects across sectors, interface modalities, and cultural contexts.

Beyond these contributions, this chapter argues for a fundamentally critical approach to the integration of artificial intelligence in customer relationship systems. The growing sophistication of AI conversational agents makes this critical approach all the more necessary. Optimal customer value is not produced by maximum fluidity but by a calibrated combination of fluidity and transparency adapted to contexts. Only under this condition can artificial intelligence constitute an authentic lever of value creation, rather than a source of illusions whose paradoxical effects emerge precisely when customer trust is most difficult to rebuild.

REFERENCES

Adam, M., Wessel, M., & Benlian, A. (2021). AI-based chatbots in customer service and their effects on user compliance. *Electronic Markets*, *31*(2), 427–445. DOI: 10.1007/s12525-020-00414-7

Araujo, T. (2018). Living up to the chatbot hype: The influence of anthropomorphic design cues and communicative agency framing on conversational agent and company perceptions. *Computers in Human Behavior*, *85*, 183–189. DOI: 10.1016/j.chb.2018.03.051

Arrieta, A. B., Díaz-Rodríguez, N., Del Ser, J., Bennetot, A., Tabik, S., Barbado, A., García, S., Gil-López, S., Molina, D., Benjamins, R., Chatila, R., & Herrera, F. (2020). Explainable Artificial Intelligence (XAI): Concepts, taxonomies, opportunities and challenges toward responsible AI. *Information Fusion*, *58*, 82–115. DOI: 10.1016/j.inffus.2019.12.012

Brown, T. B., Mann, B., Ryder, N., Subbiah, M., Kaplan, J., Dhariwal, P., Neelakantan, A., Shyam, P., Sastry, G., Askell, A., Agarwal, S., Herbert-Voss, A., Krueger, G., Henighan, T., Child, R., Ramesh, A., Ziegler, D. M., Wu, J., Winter, C., & Amodei, D. (2020). Language models are few-shot learners. *Advances in Neural Information Processing Systems*, *33*, 1877–1901.

Chaiken, S. (1980). Heuristic versus systematic information processing and the use of source versus message cues in persuasion. *Journal of Personality and Social Psychology*, *39*(5), 752–766. DOI: 10.1037/0022-3514.39.5.752

Chatterjee, S., Rana, N. P., Tamilmani, K., & Sharma, A. (2021). The effect of AI-based CRM on organization performance and competitive advantage. *Information Systems Frontiers*, *23*(5), 1283–1300. DOI: 10.1007/s10796-021-10168-0

Cheng, X., & Jiang, H. (2020). Chatbot interactions in tourist destinations: AI-mediated service encounter and customer satisfaction. *Journal of Hospitality and Tourism Technology*, *11*(3), 479–496. DOI: 10.1108/JHTT-09-2019-0109

Csikszentmihalyi, M. (1990). *Flow: The psychology of optimal experience*. Harper & Row.

Davis, F. D. (1989). Perceived usefulness, perceived ease of use, and user acceptance of information technology. *Management Information Systems Quarterly*, *13*(3), 319–340. DOI: 10.2307/249008

Epley, N., Waytz, A., & Cacioppo, J. T. (2007). On seeing the human: A three-factor theory of anthropomorphism. *Psychological Review, 114*(4), 864–886. DOI: 10.1037/0033-295X.114.4.864

Ferraro, C., Demsar, V., Sands, S., Restrepo, M., & Campbell, C. (2024). The paradoxes of generative AI-enabled customer service: A guide for managers. *Business Horizons, 67*(5), 549–559. DOI: 10.1016/j.bushor.2024.04.013

Følstad, A., & Brandtzæg, P. B. (2017). Chatbots and the new world of HCI. *Interactions (New York, N.Y.), 24*(4), 38–42. DOI: 10.1145/3085558

Følstad, A., Nordheim, C. B., & Bjørkli, C. A. (2018). What makes users trust a chatbot for customer service? An exploratory interview study. In *International Conference on Internet Science* (pp. 194–208). Springer. DOI: 10.1007/978-3-030-01437-7_16

Gefen, D. (2000). E-commerce: The role of familiarity and trust. *Omega, 28*(6), 725–737. DOI: 10.1016/S0305-0483(00)00021-9

Gefen, D., Karahanna, E., & Straub, D. W. (2003). Trust and TAM in online shopping: An integrated model. *Management Information Systems Quarterly, 27*(1), 51–90. DOI: 10.2307/30036519

Goddard, K., Roudsari, A., & Wyatt, J. C. (2012). Automation bias: A systematic review of frequency, effect mediators, and mitigators. *Journal of the American Medical Informatics Association : JAMIA, 19*(1), 121–127. DOI: 10.1136/amiajnl-2011-000089

Hancock, P. A., Billings, D. R., Ollis, K. E., Chen, J. Y. C., de Visser, E. J., & Parasuraman, R. (2011). A meta-analysis of factors affecting trust in human-robot interaction. *Human Factors, 53*(5), 517–527. DOI: 10.1177/0018720811417254

Heersmink, R., de Rooij, B., Clavel Vázquez, M. J., & Colombo, M. (2024). A phenomenology and epistemology of large language models: Transparency, trust, and trustworthiness. *Ethics and Information Technology, 26*(3), 41. Advance online publication. DOI: 10.1007/s10676-024-09777-3

Herhausen, D., Binder, J., Schoegel, M., & Herrmann, A. (2019). Integrating bricks with clicks: Retailer-level and channel-level outcomes of online–offline channel integration. *Journal of Retailing, 91*(2), 309–325. DOI: 10.1016/j.jretai.2014.12.009

Hofstede, G. (2001). *Culture's consequences: Comparing values, behaviors, institutions, and organizations across nations* (2nd ed.). Sage Publications.

Huang, M. H., & Rust, R. T. (2021). A strategic framework for artificial intelligence in marketing. *Journal of the Academy of Marketing Science*, *49*(1), 30–50. DOI: 10.1007/s11747-020-00749-9

Komiak, S. Y. X., & Benbasat, I. (2006). The effects of personalization and familiarity on trust and adoption of recommendation agents. *Management Information Systems Quarterly*, *30*(4), 941–960. DOI: 10.2307/25148760

Kumar, A., Shankar, A., Behl, A., Chakraborty, D., & Gundala, R. R. (2025). Anthropomorphic generative AI chatbots for enhancing customer engagement, experience and recommendation. *Journal of Consumer Marketing*, *42*(4), 472–483. DOI: 10.1108/JCM-06-2024-6922

Lalot, F., & Bertram, A.-M. (2025). When the bot walks the talk: Investigating the foundations of trust in an artificial intelligence (AI) chatbot. *Journal of Experimental Psychology. General*, *154*(2), 533–551. DOI: 10.1037/xge0001696

Langer, E. J. (1975). The illusion of control. *Journal of Personality and Social Psychology*, *32*(2), 311–328. DOI: 10.1037/0022-3514.32.2.311

Lee, J. D., & See, K. A. (2004). Trust in automation: Designing for appropriate reliance. *Human Factors*, *46*(1), 50–80. DOI: 10.1518/hfes.46.1.50.30392

Logg, J. M., Minson, J. A., & Moore, D. A. (2019). Algorithm appreciation: People prefer algorithmic to human judgment. *Organizational Behavior and Human Decision Processes*, *151*, 90–103. DOI: 10.1016/j.obhdp.2018.12.005

Lopatovska, I., & Arapakis, I. (2011). Theories, methods and current research on emotions in library and information science, information retrieval and human–computer interaction. *Information Processing & Management*, *47*(4), 575–592. DOI: 10.1016/j.ipm.2010.09.001

Luger, E., & Sellen, A. (2016). "Like having a really bad PA": The gulf between user expectation and experience of conversational agents. In Proceedings of the 2016 CHI Conference on Human Factors in Computing Systems (pp. 5286–5297). ACM. DOI: 10.1145/2858036.2858288

Luo, X., Tong, S., Fang, Z., & Qu, Z. (2019). Frontline artificial intelligence technology and firm performance: Real effects of AI-powered chatbots. *Journal of Marketing*, *83*(2), 1–23. DOI: 10.1177/0022242918822604

Mathwick, C., Malhotra, N., & Rigdon, E. (2001). Experiential value: Conceptualization, measurement and application in the catalog and Internet shopping environment. *Journal of Retailing*, *77*(1), 39–56. DOI: 10.1016/S0022-4359(00)00045-2

McAllister, D. J. (1995). Affect- and cognition-based trust as foundations for interpersonal cooperation in organizations. *Academy of Management Journal, 38*(1), 24–59. DOI: 10.2307/256727

McKnight, D. H., Choudhury, V., & Kacmar, C. (2002). Developing and validating trust measures for e-commerce: An integrative typology. *Information Systems Research, 13*(3), 334–359. DOI: 10.1287/isre.13.3.334.81

McTear, M. (2022). *Conversational AI: Dialogue systems, conversational agents, and chatbots*. Morgan & Claypool Publishers.

Mori, M. (1970). The uncanny valley. Energy, 7(4), 33–35. (Translated by K. F. MacDorman & N. Kageki, 2012. *IEEE Robotics & Automation Magazine, 19*(2), 98–100. DOI: 10.1109/MRA.2012.2192811

Moussawi, S., Koufaris, M., & Benbunan-Fich, R. (2021). How perceptions of intelligence and anthropomorphism affect adoption of personal intelligent agents. *Electronic Markets, 31*(2), 343–364. DOI: 10.1007/s12525-020-00411-w

Nass, C., & Moon, Y. (2000). Machines and mindlessness: Social responses to computers. *The Journal of Social Issues, 56*(1), 81–103. DOI: 10.1111/0022-4537.00153

Nass, C., & Reeves, B. (1996). *The media equation: How people treat computers, television, and new media like real people and places*. Cambridge University Press.

Ng, S. W. T., & Zhang, R. (2025). Trust in AI chatbots: A systematic review. *Telematics and Informatics, 97*, 102240. Advance online publication. DOI: 10.1016/j.tele.2025.102240

Oliver, R. L. (1980). A cognitive model of the antecedents and consequences of satisfaction decisions. *JMR, Journal of Marketing Research, 17*(4), 460–469. DOI: 10.1177/002224378001700405

Parasuraman, A., & Manzey, D. (2010). Complacency and bias in human use of automation: An attentional integration. *Human Factors, 52*(3), 381–410. DOI: 10.1177/0018720810376055

Parasuraman, A., & Riley, V. (1997). Humans and automation: Use, misuse, disuse, abuse. *Human Factors, 39*(2), 230–253. DOI: 10.1518/001872097778543886

Parasuraman, A., Zeithaml, V. A., & Malhotra, A. (2005). E-S-QUAL: A multiple-item scale for assessing electronic service quality. *Journal of Service Research, 7*(3), 213–233. DOI: 10.1177/1094670504271156

Pitardi, V., & Marriott, H. R. (2021). Alexa, she's not human but… Unveiling the drivers of consumers' trust in voice-based artificial intelligence. *Psychology and Marketing*, *38*(4), 626–642. DOI: 10.1002/mar.21457

Sheehan, B., Jin, H. S., & Gottlieb, U. (2020). Customer service chatbots: Anthropomorphism and adoption. *Journal of Business Research*, *115*, 14–24. DOI: 10.1016/j.jbusres.2020.04.030

Sheth, J. N., Newman, B. I., & Gross, B. L. (1991). Why we buy what we buy: A theory of consumption values. *Journal of Business Research*, *22*(2), 159–170. DOI: 10.1016/0148-2963(91)90050-8

Skitka, L. J., Mosier, K. L., & Burdick, M. (1999). Does automation bias decision-making? *International Journal of Human-Computer Studies*, *51*(5), 991–1006. DOI: 10.1006/ijhc.1999.0252

Stewart, K. J. (2003). Trust transfer on the World Wide Web. *Organization Science*, *14*(1), 5–17. DOI: 10.1287/orsc.14.1.5.12810

Strait, M., Aguillon, C., Contreras, V., & Garcia, N. (2017). The public's perception of humanlike robots. In *Proceedings of the 26th IEEE International Symposium on Robot and Human Interactive Communication* (pp. 1418–1423). IEEE. DOI: 10.1109/ROMAN.2017.8172490

Sweeney, J. C., & Soutar, G. N. (2001). Consumer perceived value: The development of a multiple item scale. *Journal of Retailing*, *77*(2), 203–220. DOI: 10.1016/S0022-4359(01)00041-0

van Doorn, J., Mende, M., Noble, S. M., Hulland, J., Ostrom, A. L., Grewal, D., & Petersen, J. A. (2017). Domo arigato Mr. Roboto: Emergence of automated social presence in organizational frontlines and customers' service experiences. *Journal of Service Research*, *20*(1), 43–58. DOI: 10.1177/1094670516679272

Vargo, S. L., & Lusch, R. F. (2004). Evolving to a new dominant logic for marketing. *Journal of Marketing*, *68*(1), 1–17. DOI: 10.1509/jmkg.68.1.1.24036

Vargo, S. L., & Lusch, R. F. (2008). Service-dominant logic: Continuing the evolution. *Journal of the Academy of Marketing Science*, *36*(1), 1–10. DOI: 10.1007/s11747-007-0069-6

Verhoef, P. C., Kannan, P. K., & Inman, J. J. (2015). From multi-channel retailing to omni-channel retailing. *Journal of Retailing*, *91*(2), 174–181. DOI: 10.1016/j.jretai.2015.02.005

Wang, Y., Sauka, K., & Situmeang, F. B. I. (2025). Anthropomorphism and transparency interplay on consumer behaviour in generative AI-driven marketing communication. *Journal of Consumer Marketing*, *42*(4), 512–536. DOI: 10.1108/JCM-04-2024-6806

Waytz, A., Cacioppo, J., & Epley, N. (2010). Who sees human? The stability and importance of individual differences in anthropomorphism. *Perspectives on Psychological Science : A Journal of the Association for Psychological Science*, *5*(3), 219–232. DOI: 10.1177/1745691610369336

Wirtz, J., Patterson, P. G., Kunz, W. H., Gruber, T., Lu, V. N., Paluch, S., & Martins, A. (2018). Brave new world: Service robots in the frontline. *Journal of Service Management*, *29*(5), 907–931. DOI: 10.1108/JOSM-04-2018-0119

Xu, Y., Shieh, C. H., van Esch, P., & Ling, I. L. (2020). AI customer service: Task complexity, problem-solving ability, and usage intention. *Australasian Marketing Journal*, *28*(4), 189–199. DOI: 10.1016/j.ausmj.2020.03.005

Zeithaml, V. A. (1988). Consumer perceptions of price, quality, and value: A means-end model and synthesis of evidence. *Journal of Marketing*, *52*(3), 2–22. DOI: 10.1177/002224298805200302

Zlotowski, J., Proudfoot, D., Yogeeswaran, K., & Bartneck, C. (2015). Anthropomorphism: Opportunities and challenges in human–robot interaction. *International Journal of Social Robotics*, *7*(3), 347–360. DOI: 10.1007/s12369-014-0267-6

ADDITIONAL READING

Belanche, D., Casalo, L. V., Flavian, C., & Schepers, J. (2020). Service robot implementation: A theoretical framework and research agenda. *Service Industries Journal*, *40*(3–4), 203–225. DOI: 10.1080/02642069.2019.1672666

Davenport, T., Guha, A., Grewal, D., & Bressgott, T. (2020). How artificial intelligence will change the future of marketing. *Journal of the Academy of Marketing Science*, *48*(1), 24–42. DOI: 10.1007/s11747-019-00696-0

De Keyser, A., Kocher, S., Alkire, L., Verbeeck, C., & Kandampully, J. (2019). Frontline service technology infusion: Conceptual archetypes and future research directions. *Journal of Service Management*, *30*(1), 156–183. DOI: 10.1108/JOSM-03-2018-0082

Flavian, C., Perez-Rueda, A., Belanche, D., & Casalo, L. V. (2022). Intention to use analytical artificial intelligence in technology acceptance. *Spanish Journal of Marketing - ESIC, 26*(2), 187–208. DOI: 10.1108/SJME-09-2021-0159

Longoni, C., Bonezzi, A., & Morewedge, C. K. (2019). Resistance to medical artificial intelligence. *The Journal of Consumer Research, 46*(4), 629–650. DOI: 10.1093/jcr/ucz013

Mende, M., Scott, M. L., van Doorn, J., Grewal, D., & Shanks, I. (2019). Service robots rising: How humanoid robots influence service experiences and elicit compensatory consumer responses. *JMR, Journal of Marketing Research, 56*(4), 535–556. DOI: 10.1177/0022243718822827

Ostrom, A. L., Fotheringham, D., & Bitner, M. J. (2019). Customer acceptance of AI in service encounters: Understanding antecedents and outcomes. In *Handbook of service science* (Vol. 2, pp. 77–103). Springer., DOI: 10.1007/978-3-319-98512-1_5

Puntoni, S., Reczek, R. W., Giesler, M., & Botti, S. (2021). Consumers and artificial intelligence: An experiential perspective. *Journal of Marketing, 85*(1), 131–151. DOI: 10.1177/0022242920953847

KEY TERMS AND DEFINITIONS

Anthropomorphism: A cognitive process by which individuals automatically apply social representation schemas to non-human entities, including the attribution of mental states and intentions. According to Epley et al. (2007), it rests on three cognitive factors: elicited agent knowledge, effectance motivation, and sociality motivation. In customer AI interactions, anthropomorphism constitutes the activation mechanism of functional affective trust and persists even when users are informed of the artificial nature of the agent.

Automation Bias: A cognitive tendency whereby users of automated systems under-weight error or inadequacy signals produced by the system, particularly when the system has established a history of perceived high performance. In customer–AI interactions, manifests as a reduction in the customer's critical engagement with the system's outputs, increasing vulnerability to errors.

Cognitive Trust: A form of trust grounded in rational inference, whereby customers form beliefs about the competence, reliability, and predictability of an AI agent on the basis of observable behavioral signals. The initial and most accessible layer of trust in technology-mediated service interactions.

Functional Affective Trust: A form of trust specific to interactions with non-human agents, designating an affective state of perceived security and benevolence that customers develop based on perceptual attributions of intentionality, in the absence of any genuine intentionality on the part of the system. A product of anthropomorphism mechanisms; distinct from interpersonal affective trust, which presupposes effective reciprocity and intentionality.

Overtrust: A miscalibration of trust whereby customers place confidence in an AI system that exceeds what the system's actual capabilities justify. Induced by high levels of perceived seamlessness through a heuristic generalization process reinforced by anthropomorphism mechanisms. Produces two main negative consequences: post-failure devaluation and reduction of the customer's critical vigilance toward the system's outputs.

Perceived Seamlessness: The customer's subjective evaluation of the fluidity and continuity of an interaction with an AI-based service agent, reflecting the degree to which the exchange is perceived as natural, coherent, and free of perceptible disruptions. A perceptual construct determined by three antecedents: technical fluidity, conversational coherence, and expectation congruence.

Perceived Value (Multidimensional): The customer's global assessment of the utility of a service interaction, evaluated across three distinct dimensions: utilitarian value (efficiency, problem resolution, time savings), relational value (feeling of recognition, personalization, and relational continuity), and hedonic value (intrinsic quality of the interactional experience, independent of its functional outcome).

Transparent Seamlessness: A design principle for AI-based customer service interfaces postulating that optimal customer value is not produced by maximum fluidity but by a calibrated combination of fluidity and transparency, adapted to transactional stakes and the customer's familiarity profile. Formalized in three constitutive dimensions: declarative transparency (disclosure of AI nature prior to interaction), competence transparency (contextual signaling of system limits during interaction), and transactional transparency (intensification of signaling in proportion to stakes).

Trust Calibration: The alignment between the level of trust accorded to a system and the system's actual reliability. Miscalibration takes two forms: undertrust, where confidence falls below actual reliability, and overtrust, where it exceeds it. Initially developed in the human factors literature (Lee and See, 2004; Parasuraman and Riley, 1997), the concept is transferred in this chapter to commercial customer–AI interactions.

Uncanny Valley: A phenomenon, originally identified in robotics and extended to conversational interfaces, whereby an AI agent that closely resembles a human but falls short of complete indiscernability produces a stronger negative affective response than an agent whose non-human nature is clearly perceptible. Constitutes an upper boundary condition on the benefits of seamlessness for perceived relational and hedonic value.

Chapter 5
How Smart Websites Influence Shopping Decisions:
Evidence From AI-Enabled Online Retail Platforms

Ankita Pathak
http://orcid.org/0000-0002-8068-8874
Institute of Business Management, GLA University, India

Ashish Jaswal
http://orcid.org/0000-0001-5077-6702
Sadhu Vaswani Institute of Management Studies, India

Majdi Anwar Quttainah
http://orcid.org/0000-0002-6280-1060
Kuwait University, Kuwait

ABSTRACT

Artificial intelligence (AI) is rapidly changing digital retailing by changing how customers interact with online shopping platforms and how they make purchasing decisions. The chapter focuses on how customers' purchasing intention and shopping behaviour are influenced by AI-enabled websites. The research included Technology Acceptance Model (TAM) which create perceived usefulness and ease of use that enhance consumer trust and engagement with e-commerce. The studies state that AI-enabled shopping systems make it easier for consumers to search for products, and decrease the time it takes to purchase products. It has empower consumers to make better decisions about the products they chose to purchase. At the same

DOI: 10.4018/979-8-2600-2977-0.ch005

time, AI-enabled shopping systems empower retailers to improve their operational efficiency, grow their demand-forecasting capabilities and develop better relationships with customers. It provide practical ideas for researchers, businesspeople, and government officials who want to build an online shopping experience that is focused on consumers and ethical uses of AI.

1. INTRODUCTION

The global economy has experienced boom in digitalization during last three decades. Industries have shifted themselves from traditional management techniques to technology-enabled strategies which has changed their managerial and operational roles. The technological shift in the industry is to capture, secure and survive in the competitive market with larger portion of market share. Internet and information technologies has played a major role in bringing technological advancement in business and consumer activities. Business uses internet driven technologies to sale their products to people in various geographical areas. It provide competition and platform to showcase and differentiate their product from others. At the same time Consumer with the internet-enabled mobile devices can anytime and anywhere quickly access to the vast market. Customer can shop wide variety of products of various brands, price, and features from any location. Electronic Commerce provide consumer option to compare the product quality, price, features with other similar products . Majority of the retail enterprise have started with the online retailing to meet the competitive edge (Hakim, 2026). Ecommerce is also rapidly growing with the advancement in related technology like AI. The application of AI has bought a growth in various sector like healthcare, marketing, education, and finance and have leaved the significant imprint on the economy. In recent period AI is dominating the Ecommerce sector. Many of the Ecommerce like Alibaba, Amazon, JD.com, Netflix, Walmart have incorporated AI based technology for the making recommendation, search optimization, chatbots and virtual assistant to the customer. AI is heading the business due to its remarkable success. It is projected that 80 percent of the customer service position will be taken by the AI and industry will see a transformation and expansion in the Ecommerce sector. AI algorithms analyse the customer need and preference and provide personalised shopping experience on the basis of their browsing history, purchase history. It helps the companies to develop target content and promotional offers which leads to higher conversion rate and better customer satisfaction. Technology is reshaping the overall functioning of the Ecommerce. Today one out of five person buy the product or service online through chatbots. 40 percent of the person use chatbots for product inquires and tracking, post sales service support. AI offer 24*7 assistance which enhance the customer experience and engagement. The application of AI is not changing the customer experience but also of the business owner. Business owner can use AI for inventory management and pricing. AI algorithms can analyse the past records, trends and external factors affecting the demand and on the basis of that right quantity is made at right time. It helps the business owner in reducing unnecessary inventory and other cost associated with the inventory management. AI driven pricing algorithms helps owner to adjust their pricing according to demand, competitor pricing and market condition (Liu et al., 2026). It determine optimum pricing strategy by considering factors which made lead to fluctuation. Online purchaser are also experiencing the change in the shopping experience as AI has provided them with the facility of visual search. It is a process where through image or photo product can be sear ched. Purchaser don't need to enter text. AI powered technology search all the similar products with features which reduce the frication in the shopping experience. AI powered technology analyse the data and prevent from the fraduent activity like data leak. The biometric authentication technologies like face recognition and finger print ensure the security of the user verification and secure payment system.

Covid 19 has bought the revolution the ecommerce sector by promoting online shopping. The social distancing and lockdowns has pushes the people to incline towards online shopping. There has been major change in the shopping behaviour of the people. The research of the Statista, global ecommerce sales was amounted to $4.28 trillion in 2020 and $5.4 trillion in 2022 and will reach to $6.3 trillion by 2024 (Alhiniti & Al-Masry, 2026). The market share of Ecommerce's total global retail sales has been continuously increasing. In 2020, ecommerce accounted for approximately 18% of total retail sales worldwide and would be reaching 21.8% by 2024, as reported by eMarketer.

AI is transforming the purchasing pattern and intention of the shopper. Ecommerce companies have huge amount of data regarding the shopper likes, preference as well as information regarding consumer leads. AI can help in engaging the cold lead shopper by providing them information related to brand, product and other related information where as in case of warm leads AI engage them by offering various personalized offers and discounts.AI technique is effective strategy for remarketing the product and service to the shopper. It remarkets to the product to shopper who have initiated to purchase the product but have put the product in the cart. Ecommerce companies use various approaches to retarget the product but among them personalized business message is commonly used technique. The personalized commercial message through AI has changed the entire Ecommerce sector of various countries like Saudi Arabia. The personalized commercial business message is adopted by many ecommerce platforms which enhance their overall performance (Lijuan et al., 2023). The ecommerce companies on the global scale are capturing the attention of the shopper over the local one as they are meeting the technological need and standard of the shopper. It is projected that Ecommerce sector will see a substantial rise in next decade focusing on empowering the consumer purchase. The purpose of the chapter is to research how AI features within a retailer's digital presence, such as recommendation engines, intelligent search capabilities, chatbots, visual search, dynamic pricing, and remarketing capabilities, will influence the consumer decision. The chapter will also review how TAM explains how perceived usefulness and consistent ease of use are part of the process to help consumers develop confidence, reduce decision-making effort, and improve online shopping efficiency (Oteri et al., 2023).In addition, the chapter will address how AI-enabled shopping systems benefit both consumers and online retailers. It will discuss the impact of these systems on consumers with respect to how quickly they complete a purchase, accurate forecasting of demand; and improved operational efficiency. The chapter also investigates ethical and governance issues related to the use of AI in e-commerce, as well as potential future research directions in the areas of technology readiness, trust-building and the developing relationship between consumers and intelligent systems. The chapter aims to contribute to the body of knowledge for researchers, practitioners, and policymakers who are developing ethical, consumer-driven, and effective AI-based online shopping experiences.

1.1 Objectives of the study

- Evaluate the impacts AI-enabled technologies on consumers and their intention to buy from an online retailer.
- Investigate how the consumer's perception of usefulness, ease of use, and trust impact the decision-making process of consumers
- Develop an integrated conceptual framework Technology Acceptance Model, Theory of Reasoned Action, and Technology Readiness Model to assist in understanding consumer behaviour when exposed to AI-enabled retail shopping activities.
- Develop a conceptual framework that explains how AI features drive consumer engagement and result in long-term behavioural outcomes.
- Assess ethical, governance and transparency issues associated with AI-enabled retail shopping technologies.

2. REVIEW OF LITERATURE

In recent years, there has been a remarkable change in Ecommerce industry by integration of artificial intelligence in various activities. The adoption of artificial intelligence has notably improved the customer handling ability and problem-solving capabilities. Artificial intelligence technology is meeting the need and demands of consumers (Naeem, 2025). The companies such as Amazon, Pininterest, ASOS, Sephora and eBay are playing a significant role in the ecommerce industry. These platforms acquire large share of global ecommerce sales. Amazon, one of the leading company reported net sales of $386.1 billion in 2020, and coming period of time till will cross $ 500 billion. The rate of grow varies from region to region in case of Ecommerce penetration. In some region like Asia Pacific their is a high growth rate followed by North America and Europe. In the year 2020, Asia-Pacific had the highest ecommerce penetration rate, with ecommerce sales accounting for 26.7% of total retail sales. There are various technologies like Machine Learning (ML), Natural Language Processing (NLP), customer vision, predictive analytics, and sentimental analysis (Sikder & Rolfe, 2023). AI is not only technology which is bringing change in decision making process of the customer. These technologies have reduced the burden of the customer where they don't need to excess and research in-depth knowledge about the product, features, services, ideas.

On the basis of past browsing history, purchase behavior, and product preferences, personal recommendation are given to the shopper. It offers dynamic pricing and personalised promotion to attract and retain existing customer. AI technology has reduced both the time and effort in searching the product which ultimately leads to effective decision-making. Artificial intelligence is proved as valuable tools which meet the need of both marketer and shopper. AI driven technology has given opportunity to compete with the world market (Prasanth et al., 2023). Marketer use AI to optimize the buying process by offering one click purchase to the shopper. It saves the personal details like shipping details and payment details for the future sales but saves the times and smooths the process of purchasing. AI is used in sentimental analysis where sentiments of the product and service are determined on the basis of customer reviews and comment on social media (Taherdoost & Madanchian, 2023). It helps the marketer to understand consumer preferences and on the basis of preference personalised recommendation, offers and price comparison are given which simplify the purchase process. According to a survey report by McKinsey, Ecommerce companies who have implement AI-driven personalization have seen a significant 6-10% increase in revenue. It is stated that by 2025, 85% of customer interactions will be handled by AI technology. It will not require any human intervention. AI driven search engine have seen 59% higher conversion rate as compared to normal websites (Patil et al., 2024). Ecommerce platforms can detect the fraud activity as well as optimise the supply chain by demand forecasting and inventory management. In a coming period of time AI-powered voice assistants would provide hands-free shopping experiences. Shopper can driving sales through voice commands. According to OC&C Strategy Consultants, voice commerce is expected to reach $40 billion in sales by 2022 in the US and UK (Zhou et al., 2019). The use of AI have increased the sales as well as brand value by enhancing the customer experience and engagement.

2.1 Artificial Intelligence and Online Consumer Behaviour

In current scenario most of the purchase are done through various ecommerce platforms. The attitude and inclination towards the specific service or product makes the purchase intention and decision. The implementation of AI in Ecommerce platforms have enhanced the experience and faith of the customer. The faith and consciousness play a very major role in maximizing the purchase intention towards products and services. AI has entirely changed the scenario and requirement of the people. AI offers virtual look to the shopper which allow them to make informed decision. AI gives the visual that how the product will look in their surrounding area which provide confidence to buy the product. AI enabled technology provide customization to the customer which leads to best purchase decision. It helps the customer to identify and choose the product according to their preference. The innovative technology like augmented reality helps shopper to experience the product which feels like real. The adoption of AI by marketer helps them in offering unique shopping experience. Many previous researches like. Rodgers & Nguyen, (2022); Yeo et al., (2022); Allal-Chérif et al., (2021) stated that AI will help in solving the problem and making decision towards the purchase of the product. The AI enabled online sites reduce the risk of shopper as well as like it offer the product and service according to their own taste and preference. Amazon, Netflix, and Spotify use AI to recommend products, movies, and music according to taste and preference of each user. Shopper can easily obtain the information. AI tool monitor and analyse the customer sentiments shared on various social media platforms like facebook, instagram, website or other online channels (Beyari & Garamoun, 2022). The analysis helps the business to understand the customer perception towards the product and brand. It gives the idea to business man related to issues and opportunities. Positive review, comments would boost purchase intention where as negative sentiments would affect the conversion rate. The sentimental analysis makes business man to react proactively and mitigate risk. It creates brand reputation which influence purchase intention (Patil et al., 2024). The visual search and image recognition make the customer to search the product using images. The visual attributes like size, colour, pattern helps in identifying product of similar type for which they were searching. It engage the customer and facilitate in purchase intention. The message and personalised offer on special day would create the interest in content of the viewer and influence purchase intention. The marketing campaigns are designed and offered to target audience which optimise the conversion rate. The capabilities and ability of AI has created interest of shoppers. The experience of the customer while using online platforms would impact the purchase intention. The research of various authors like Ganesh, (2023); Paul et al., (2023) conclude customer have high satisfaction, trust and better experience when they purchase products through AI enabled stores. It improve the quality of suggestion as it review the past purchase trend of the shopper and accordingly suggestion are made. AI enabled technology has increasing the interest of the shopper as the recommendation acts as a feed to the shopper which ultimately leads to adding the product in the cart. The feeds acts a reminder to shopper which ultimately leads to making purchase. User can save the feeds as a favorite for future purchase. In case of physical retail, the location of the product influence the purchase decision (Moore et al., 2022). The product recommendation encourage the shopper to purchase from particular website only as the convenience and ease to use would lead to customer loyalty.

Ecommerce business prefers shorten purchase duration as shopper can provide feedback immediately. AI enabled website influence the process of purchasing. AI helps in understanding the behavior of the shopper and purchase duration is consider as a important factor to measure the effectiveness of an AI enabled system. Shopper with shorten purchase duration are likely to be influenced by AI algorithms. It also states that shopper with shorten purchase duration doest put the products in the cart . The carting of the product reduce purchase duration as they don't need to search and remember the name of the product (Suryavanshi & Gangele, 2024). The cart signifies the preference or like of the user in the product. The cart data remind the shopper to close the purchase deal by shopping the carted product.

The purchasing power of shopper is influenced by social media dependency. The social media dependency attracts the customer by product review and relevant information. The social media feeds and review on social media influence high value purchase where as in case of low value product as the social media plays a important role in purchase decision Bushara et al., (2023); Liusito et al., (2020). In old days business owners underestimated the power of the social media was under-estimated but gradually content on social media is a influencing the shopper to buy the product. The research of Deloitte state that social media influence 4 times more to the consumer who are inclined in usage of social media. The business houses are using influencer marketing to attract the audience on social media to build trust and add value to the brand. Many brands have started using social media marketing on various social media platforms YouTube, Instagram, and Snapchat rather than celebrity endorsement (Um, 2022). These social media influencer post the comments and review of the product which are unfiltered. The statistics show that 29 percent of the buyer would purchase the product immediately when they see the product. It shows that purchase intention is influenced by the social media dependency.

2.2 Applications of AI in E-commerce

In the dynamic business AI has enhanced the customer experience and assists the online retailer in making decision. The adoption of the technology has made companies to adopt ecommerce for reaching to the customer. The integration of AI in the ecommerce has improved overall functioning of the business. AI powered websites boost the sales of the company and also leads to better customer engagement (Lim, 2017). It improves the efficiency and productivity and attract the various range and type of customers. The various application of AI in Ecommerce are Voice assistants, intelligent search, automation, personalisation, and remarketing of potential prospects are some examples of AI in e-commerce.

Voice Command and Virtual Assistants: Voice commands and virtual assistants have changed the Ecommerce sector by offering unique experience to both shopper as well as business. Voice command have revolutionized the showing pattern. Shopper with the help of voice command are navigated to the store for the purchase. customer don't need to manually type for the search of the product, the voice command will lend the shopper at desired page. The hand free shopping has not only changed the shopping experience but also assisted the people with certain disabilities (García-Serrano et al., 2004). Chatbots are the advanced AI with the NLP features which can interact like human. Chatbots are the virtual assistant which function 24*7, 365 days with complete accuracy. It handles various customer quires by assisting them in purchasing process. AI powered chatbots offers product recommendation on the basis of search history, past purchase (Ramineni et al., 2024). It enhances the customer satisfaction and engagement which create the trust and brand value. The integration of voice commands and virtual assistants in Ecommerce has improves accessibility and efficiency which leads to increase in the conversion rate.

Smart Search: Smart search can enhance the shopping experience by offering search result on the basis of user behaviour and preference. Smart search offers the product to shopper by understanding their search query and desire features in the product. The recommendation of the product is done on the basis of past shopping behavior, purchase history, demographics, and other relevant data. Personalized recommendation offers shoppers unique experience according to tastes and preferences (Kumar et al., 2025). Smart search provide the recommendation by considering attribute such as price range, brand, size, color, and more. It narrows down the options and finds products which meet the expectation of the customer. Smart search engine can offer auto suggestion which can reduce the misspelling and typos error (Song et al., 2019). It can automatically correct the words and suggest the products which meet the shoppers need. Search option provide detailed information regarding images, descriptions, prices, ratings, and reviews of the search product. Customer can analyse, compare and evaluate product which helps in decision-making process (Moodley & Sookhdeo, 2025). The integration of smart search with inventory management, CRM, and recommendation engines provide exceptional experience to shopper.

Personalisation: The recent activity, browsing patterns, purchase history, and similar metrics help in personalising the product recommendation (Perumallaplli, 2012). Ecommerce website provides customise experience to the shopper by offering promotion, and relevant content on the basis of their preference. The user engagement increases the interaction which ultimately leads to higher conversion rate.

Automation: The automization of the ecommerce platforms ensures the availability of the product. It prevents the scenario of out of stock and disappointment. Ecommerce website offers status of the product which has increased the transparency and confidence (Srivastava, 2021). The status of the products helps the shopper to know the expected time frame of product delivery. AI powered automisation assist the marketer in determining the demand, price, inventory level to meet the market competition. Machine learning algorithms in Ecommerce website prevent from fraudent transaction (Agarwal, 2024). It protects both shopper as well as retailer which increase the trust of the shopper.

Remarketing to Potential Prospects: Marketer are facing difficult in reaching the target audience. The customer base provides a way to increase the conversion ratio. The use of AI in Ecommerce website helps in identifying the purchase behaviour and pattern. AI stores the purchase and search history and on the basis of the same remarketing of the product is done to the customer (Bhardwaj et al., 2024). The integration of AI has expanded the sector which boosts the productivity across the business. The innovative strategy, customer targeting leads to customer loyalty and foster customer satisfaction.

3. THEORETICAL FRAMEWORK

The technological advanacement has changed the llandscape of ecommerce by integration AI in business activity. The Ai powered website influence the customer behvaiour and purchase intention. The TAM theoretical framework is applied to understand the impact of AI powered website on purchase intention. The TAM model is a widely used theoretical framework in the field of information system and technology adoption. TAM model is applied to understand the shopper perceive and acceptance of AI based technology tool for their online shopping (Anica-Popa et al., 2021). There are several factors which influence the intention of the shopper to use technology. The factors like usefulness, perceived ease of use, attitude towards use the technology, and subjective norms influence the decision of using technology . The individual are more likely to adopt the technology which enhance their performance and make the life easier. Shopper evaluate the benefit and advantage offered by the technology would lead to efficiency and effectiveness in performing task (Singh & Srivastava, 2019). Online shopper can perceived that AI enabled websites can provide personalized product recommendation on the basis of need and preference which enhance shopping experience. Online shopper purchase the product which they perceive useful and meet their requirement. AI enabled chatbots helps the shopper in providing relevant information related to product like features, function, and content (Na et al., 2022). Chatbots resolve the inquiries of the customer which provide them relevant and detailed information. The user friendly interfaces and seamless transaction would easy the purchase intention. The ease of integrating technology into existing process would easy the customer to purchase. The actual behavior shows the readiness and willingness of the individual to adopt the technology. The readiness leads to desire and engage in purchase behavior. User evaluates the technology on the basis of personal beliefs, preferences, and past interactions with similar tools. AI enabled technology leads to reliability, and accuracy which influence purchase decision. The external factors like product availability, pricing, promotions and situational factors influence shopper (Polančič et al., 2010). AI based technology deliver reliable and accurate results and meets the expectation. Simple, convenient and hassle free purchasing process would make strong intention to buy the product.

Figure 1. TAM Model

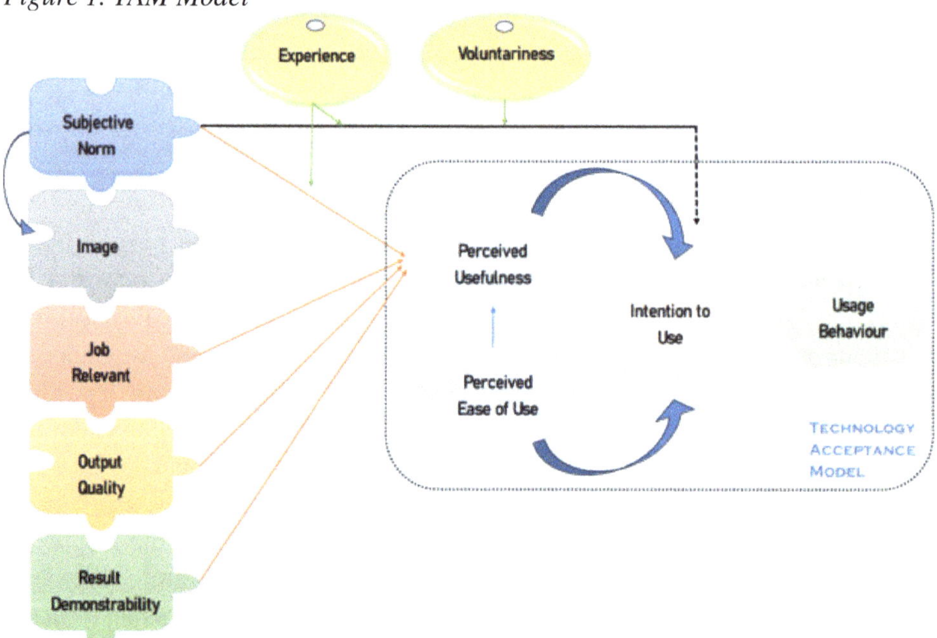

4. BENEFITS OF AI ADOPTION FOR ONLINE RETAILERS

Strategic use of artificial intelligence in online retailing enables businesses to develop more adaptive business models based on data, moving away from pure efficiency-driven digitalisation. Many leading online retailers have added AI into their day-to-day operations, building relationships with customers and assist in forecasting systems . This section explores the measurable benefit that retailers can achieve through the application of AI.

4.1 Operational Efficiency and Cost Optimization

AI creates operational efficiencies within retailers by embedding intelligence into core retail processes, such as order fulfilment, pricing, customer service and platform maintenance. AI will not only reduce the amount of manual intervention required in the execution of these processes, but also increase the overall speed and accuracy with which these processes can be executed (Siddiqui et al., 2025). The implementation of AI-based workflow manage the routing of orders from warehouses based on factors such as proximity, urgency of delivery and real-time capacity. Studies in the field show that the implementation of such systems will result in decreased order-processing times and logistics costs while retaining service reliability.

Dynamic pricing systems using AI provide another source of cost optimization by dynamically adjusting prices based on demand signals, competitive movement, and inventory status. AI protect the retailers margins in times of peak customer demand while avoiding unnecessary price reductions during low-competition periods. Similarly, retailers holds AI-enabled fraud detection models to analyze transaction behavior at scale so they can detect irregular activity like credit card fraud earlier and prevent it or at least curb associated losses without increasing customer friction . Operational decision-making has shifted from experience to algorithms based decision in operations, therefore, managers need to ensure that AI outputs are integrated into their operational workflows while establishing the clarity on transparency and accountability. The investments in AI should be coupled with a redesign of processes and development of capabilities instead of expecting them to function as plug-and-play solutions.

4.2 Demand Forecasting and Inventory Management

Demand uncertainty is one of the most significant challenges that online retailers will continue to face; especially in those environments where product life cycles are short and consumer preferences change dramatically. AI forecasting models address this problem by combining historical sales data with real-time signals of consumer behaviour such as search activity, click-through rates, and how consumers respond to promotional offers (Kumar et al., 2024). Leading ecommerce platforms now deploy machine learning models to continuously update demand forecasts which provides a real-time view of demand thereby enabling decision-making for inventory levels based on current conditions instead of utilizing historical indicators.

AI is also being used to redistribute stock dynamically among fulfilment centres rather than maintaining uniform stock levels, through location-specific stock recommendations that account for regional demand patterns and delivery constraints. This enables businesses to reduce the number of stock-outs and excess inventory at the same time improving both customer experience and working capital efficiency. These developments will require a closer evaluation of how to incorporate AI outputs into operational workflows while developing oversight mechanisms that ensure transparency and accountability as well as to be mindful of the fact that investments in AI need to be made alongside the redesign of processes and the development of capabilities

4.3 Strengthening Customer Relationships through AI

Retailers are transforming the way of doing business through artificial intelligence (AI). AI is used to understand and anticipate consumer needs on an individual basis. AI systems create detailed customer profiles by looking at customers' browsing histories, purchase sequences, and engagement patterns, which help retailers to develop personalised recommendations for products and communication strategies. In addition to providing insights into customers, AI-driven personalisation also enhances the likelihood of repeat purchases by reducing the cognitive effort required to make purchasing decisions (Ebrahimi et al., 2024). Conversational AI tools such as chatbots and virtual assistants help to improve the quality of relationships between retailers and their customers by providing immediate, context-sensitive assistance. Unlike traditional scripted systems, learning-based conversational agents will improve over time, and thereby allowing retailers to efficiently resolve common issues while providing additional support for more complex cases by transferring them to a human agent. This hybrid service model will enhance the speed at which retailers respond to their customers, while not sacrificing the depth of service.

AI will also enable predictive relationship management by identifying early warning signs of a customer's likelihood to leave the brand like decreased interaction frequency or an incomplete purchasing journey. Retailers can take proactive steps to intervene in these situations before the customer becomes lost to the retailer by providing tailored follow-up service or offering customised incentives. The relationship between a business and its customers must be viewed as a long-term asset which can be strengthened through AI-enabled insights. However, building a customer's trust requires an ongoing commitment to the ethical use of information and transparent communication. Therefore, the need to create the balance between how much they will use personalisation to increase engagement with their customers and their ethical concerns regarding the implications of using data to manipulate or surveil their customers.

5. ETHICAL, LEGAL, AND GOVERNANCE CONSIDERATIONS IN AI-DRIVEN E-COMMERCE

The rapid integration of artificial intelligence into e-commerce has transformed how online retailers understand consumers, manage operations, and drive growth. However, alongside efficiency and personalization gains, AI systems introduce complex ethical, legal, and governance challenges that directly affect consumer trust and market sustainability. Ethical AI in e-commerce is no longer a peripheral concern; it is central to long-term platform legitimacy, regulatory compliance, and responsible innovation. Addressing these issues requires a shift from viewing ethics as a compliance exercise to embedding ethical reasoning within technological design, business strategy, and organizational governance.

5.1 Data Privacy and Consumer Protection

Platforms utilizing AI in e-commerce require vast amounts of information about their customers, which includes data collected from web browsing, purchase history, geolocation, and in cases biometric or psychographic data. This data allows firms to provide highly personalized recommendations and create dynamic pricing strategies, it also raises concerns about possible misuse of data, unauthorized access to data, and excessive surveillance. An important ethical concern for consumers is that there is a power imbalance between the platforms and the consumers, and typically, consumers are not aware of how their data is collected, combined, and sold.

The informed consent agreement should be improved so that it allows consumers to make informed choices about the use of their data based on clear and concise information rather than the long-winded and confusing privacy agreements that we typically see. It is ethically important for companies to have consumer consent when collecting data about them. Consumer are informed about why data is being collected, how long the data will be kept and whether the data will be shared with third parties (Amil, 2024). Moreover, AI systems must be built to limit their reliance on data through implementation of privacy-by-design best practices like Data minimization; anonymization; and limiting the use of data for a specific purpose. In recent years, regulatory frameworks surrounding data protection have increasingly focused on consumer rights, such as the right to access, correct, and delete their personal data. Compliance is no guarantee of ethical behavior, however, and responsible e-commerce organizations are committed to protecting vulnerable consumers, not engaging in exploitative targeting, and ensuring that their personalized marketing efforts do not cross the line into manipulation. Ultimately, trust in digital commerce ecosystems is a function of whether or not consumers believe their data is treated as a personal asset versus simply a commercial asset.

5.2 Algorithmic Bias and Transparency

E-commerce companies use algorithmic decision-making to decide what consumers see, price items, and determine which sellers will receive prominence. These algorithms frequently utilize historical data that may display already-existing social, economic, or cultural biases as their basis for making decisions. When left unchecked, AI algorithms can consistently discriminate against particular classes of consumers or smaller sellers, thus reinforcing unequal treatment while appearing neutral from a technological perspective.

The use of AI-powered recommendation engines, search ranking tools, and credit-based payment systems provides some potential for discriminatory outcomes to occur, often without the ability of the end user to notice or challenge the results (Jakkula, 2020). The ethical implications of this are compounded by the "black-box" nature of many of these AI systems such that even the developers may not have the capability to explain how a specific action was taken.

Transparency in AI systems does not involve revealing how the proprietary algorithm works but requires clearly defined results and means of communication. Consumers should be informed whenever AI has a substantial role in determining price, product recommendations, or providing access to products. E-commerce companies can aim to increase the potential of AI by establishing ethical transparency through regular evaluations of the algorithms employed to understand and identify instances of discrimination. These evaluations will help support the notion that bias is a socio-technical issue as opposed to being purely technical in nature, allowing e-commerce companies to ensure that their algorithms are not silently perpetuating inequality and continuing the innovation of AI capabilities.

5.3 Responsible and Ethical Use of AI in Online Retail

The responsible use of artificial intelligence (AI) in e-commerce extends beyond the technology aspect and also includes organizational values, leadership responsibility and long-term implications for society. Ethical AI governance provides clear standards for how AI will be used ethically, including establishing oversight mechanisms and assigning accountability to key decision-makers for actions made with AI. AI will be used solely for profit generation and disregarding the effects that it has on consumers' autonomy and fairness in the marketplace.

One of the primary ethical concerns regarding the use of artificial intelligence (AI) in retail is how these persuasive technologies can manipulate consumers' behaviors. These technologies include designing product “nudges” or using “scarcity messaging” or targeted advertising based on the user's emotional state. Marketing has always attempted to persuade consumers to make purchases, artificial intelligence makes this persuasion more powerful by using predictive analytics on a much larger scale than traditional marketing techniques (Tran, 2026). Therefore, ethical boundaries must be established that will enable AI to continue supporting informed choices rather than exploiting cognitive vulnerabilities of consumers.

Ethically responsible online retail organizations have integrated an ethical review process into their development and deployment of artificial intelligence by including input from many disciplines like legal, technical, consumer protection, etc when developing their AI technology. Additionally, continuous monitoring, human judgement involvement in the process, and conducting ethical impact assessments ensure that AI will continue to align with society's expectations and the evolving norms within that society (Rane et al., 2026).Ultimately, developing ethical guidelines for the use of artificial intelligence in the e-commerce sector is intended to foster innovation rather than inhibit it; therefore, developers of artificial intelligence must direct their innovation toward creating sustainable value for consumers, respecting their dignity as well as creating fairness and enhancing consumer trust in digital marketplaces. The image shows a multi-faceted governance model for ethical and successful implementation of AI technologies in internet retail. Data stewardship, fairness of algorithms, transparency, human monitoring, and ongoing ethical oversight will be used to provide consumers with appropriate, ethical, and long-term usage of AI.

Figure2: Responsible AI Governance Framework for AI-Driven E-Commerce

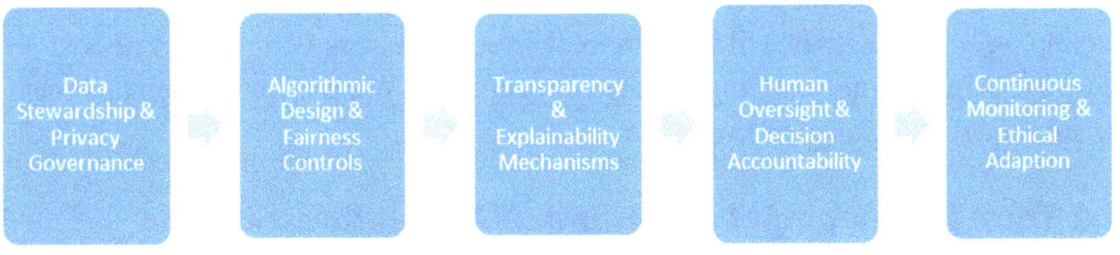

6. FUTURE RESEARCH DIRECTIONS

The speed at which AI-enabled systems is entering in online retail is much faster than researchers can comprehending the effects and its long-term implications of AI-enabled systems on the retail industry. Most of the current literature consists of studies of technology acceptance, efficiency, or short-term behavioural outcomes; therefore several over-arching questions remain and should be investigated in future studies. Subsequently, future research should transition from investigating technology acceptance to consumers' readiness on trust, and continued changes in behaviour resulting from their use of AI enabled shopping environments.

6.1 Technology Readiness and Consumer Preparedness

Technology readiness has typically been conceptualised as a stable individual characteristic. However, developments in AI-enabled shopping environments indicate that technology readiness is actually situational, developing, and shaped through ongoing interactions with intelligent systems. Future research will need to determine how consumers come to develop the cognitive and emotional competence necessary to navigate an increasingly autonomous and unexamined artificial intelligence-driven interface over time. Future researcher will study how consumer preparedness differs by age, gender, ethnicity, income, educational attainment and other demographic, cultural and socio-economic factors. Although today's consumers can enjoy the convenience AI provides, they may develop dependency or barriers to have access to technology due to digital literacy levels. The longitudinal studies investigate how frequently experiencing AI functions create learning curves from using autonomous recommendations to having a sense of control, to relying solely on an automated recommendation system. In addition, future research should consider how technology readiness interacts with external factors such as platform design, disclosures made about an AI system and regulations that consumers. It is important to understand of how these external conditions unite with individual technology readiness. It will help in explaining why some consumers choose to leverage AI functions and other consumers choose to not pursue their engagement or subsequently disengage from them

6.2 Trust Development and Human–AI Relationships

Trusting in AI-supported shopping systems continues to be a multifaceted and poorly researched area. Prior research typically looked at trusting as a final variable, but trust towards AI is a process that is created over time by many interactions. Future research should theorise about how trusting is established over multiple stages of the customer experience when exposed to AI from the time of first introduced to the time used over an extended period of time.

One area that shows potential for future research is the analysis of how consumers develop expectations for relationships with AI systems. AI systems have capabilities such as chat bots, recommendation engines and virtual assistants which have human attributes, some consumers may attribute intent, abilities and even moral obligation into AI. The understanding of this perceptions gives researchers additional context by comparing the difference between the relationship between humans and AI systems and the traditional human relationships with technology. In addition to this, future research should investigate how to restore trust when there are negative experiences resulting from the use of AI. The negative experience include error in a recommendation, suspected prejudice, or a breach of privacy. The research determine how to re-establish trust and restore the trust for human services.

6.3 Long-Term Behavioural Impacts of AI-Enabled Shopping

AI-enabled shopping systems are working to improve consumer experience by allowing consumers to make purchases more quickly and conveniently, but there is a lack of research on how consumers will ultimately engage with these systems over time. Future research should include questions regarding whether consumers rely on AI over time in making purchasing decisions; whether AI affects how consumers make decisions about the products they purchase; and/or are AI consumers less sensitive to price/quality as they rely more heavily on AI for purchasing decisions? One such question arise during the research is whether AI creates a behavioural dependency on consumers. Do consumers engage less and less in decision making as a result of their expected normalised experience with each other via AI? How do we measure the impact of AI's ability to provide convenience and reduce cognitive load through decision-making?

Another area for research is the examination of consumer behavioural adaptations at the market level in relation to the recommendations and dynamic pricing that AI provides in responding to consumer purchasing behaviour. Future analysis should inspect how the customer evolves in an atmosphere where dynamic pricing and recommendations are the prominent choice architectures that drive behaviour. These insights will provide the insights to understand the larger socio-economic impact of retail ecosystems powered by AI.

7. PRACTICAL IMPLICATIONS

The results and conceptual arguments presented in this chapter have implications for many stakeholders like designers, researchers, and regulators of AI (artificial intelligence) enabled e-commerce platforms. This section aims to conceptualize the implications of theoretical research into applied research for how to put responsible and effective implementations of AI into practice.

7.1 Implications for Researchers

The chapter highlighted that traditional models of technology acceptance, and the adoption of new technologies by consumers, need to be re-evaluated based on how autonomous and adaptable. Although there are models, like the Technology Acceptance Model (Tam), that have served this purpose previously, future work needs to build upon these models to build new constructs such as evolving trust, loss of control, and long-term behavioural dependence on technologies. Researchers are encouraged to use longitudinal, experimental, and mixed-methods approaches, rather than relying solely on cross-sectional survey designs, in order to gather data regarding how consumers' perceptions and behaviours are impacted by their repeated exposure to AI-enabled shopping environments. Behavioural data, such as click-stream analysis and log interaction data, could supplement the self-reported data that researchers are currently using. Researchers should also investigate potential synergies between multiple disciplines, including but not limited to: information systems, psychology, ethics, and data science. By integrating these various disciplines into a single research project, researchers can arrive at much more complete explanations of consumer-AI interactions. Additionally, researchers should place a strong emphasis on transparency with regard to their models and measurement choices as a part of their research. This is especially true for models and measurements that deal with ethically sensitive outcomes including trust, manipulation, and consumer autonomy.

7.2 Implications for E-Commerce Businesses

The chapter stated that retailers should consider AI as a strategic asset rather than a technical investment. Retailers must develop a value proposition for AI implementation, ensuring that their automation and personalisation efforts create trust and ease of use, rather than confusion or disinterest. Furthermore, managers should develop organisational capabilities required for responsible AI deployment, such as data governance, cross-functional teams, and ongoing monitoring of AI systems. The insights gained from AI systems will be utilised most effectively when they are considered as part of decision-making in marketing, operations, and customer service and not as part of an isolated analytics function.Retailers must understand that consumers will accept AI based on performance, fairness, and transparency. Clear communication about how AI impacts every aspect of a retailer's customer experience will help to build trust in the use of AI and lessen resistance. Companies that proactively take an ethical approach to the use of AI in their design and implementation will be in a better position to build long-term, sustainable relationships with customers than companies that do not offer the same.

7.3 Policy and Regulatory Implications

The emergence of AI in online shopping grows rapidly, policymakers need to deal with how to balance protecting consumers while fostering continued innovation through the use of AI. Much of the traditional consumer protection legislation does not fully address the various risks associated with using an AI driven decision-making regarding consumers. These include the risk of opaque decisions made by AI, the risk of biased decisions made by the AI, as well as the risk of using consumer data improperly (Zhang et al., 2026). Legislators who create and enact policy should establish sufficient levels of transparency and accountability without creating overly restrictive barriers to technological advancements. For example, this could include establishing guidelines around the auditing of algorithms used to make AI decisions, promoting standards regarding explainability, and so forth. Legislature and regulators can also promote consumers' ability to recognize and understand what is happening to their data by working with technology companies to create clear and concise disclosure statements regarding the use of consumer data. Lastly, effective governance of AI enabled online commerce requires collaborative efforts of many parties like policymakers, relevant industry stakeholders, academic researchers in order to create a proactive regulatory regime. Policymakers should use existing research/data on how consumers behave as well as how effective AI decision-making is to develop regulations that are proportional to the situation at hand, proactively oriented and responsive to changes in technology.

Table 1. Summary of Theoretical, implication and Policy and regulatory implication

Core Dimension	Theoretical Insights	Implications for E-Commerce Practice	Policy and Regulatory Implications
Technology Adoption and Readiness	Technology Acceptance Model (TAM) explains initial adoption through perceived usefulness and ease of use but requires extension to capture evolving readiness and learning effects.	Design AI systems that support gradual learning, user control, and adaptive onboarding rather than assuming uniform digital competence.	Promote digital literacy initiatives and encourage platforms to disclose AI functionalities in accessible formats.
Consumer Decision-Making	AI reshapes decision-making by reducing cognitive effort and altering choice architecture, influencing how alternatives are evaluated.	Use AI to support informed decision-making rather than over-optimising for conversion; avoid excessive automation that limits exploration.	Monitor algorithmic practices that restrict consumer choice or unfairly steer decisions.
Trust and Human–AI Interaction	Trust in AI is dynamic and relational, formed through repeated interaction rather than one-time acceptance.	Invest in transparent AI interfaces and consistent service quality to support long-term trust development.	Encourage standards for explainability and accountability in AI-driven consumer interactions.
Personalisation and Consumer Experience	Personalisation enhances engagement when perceived as relevant and fair; perceived manipulation undermines trust.	Balance personalisation with autonomy by offering opt-out options and clear explanations of recommendation logic.	Require meaningful consent mechanisms and safeguards against intrusive targeting.
Operational Efficiency and Automation	AI improves efficiency through data-driven optimisation but shifts decision authority from humans to algorithms.	Redesign workflows to integrate AI insights with managerial judgment and oversight.	Clarify accountability for AI-driven decisions affecting pricing, access, and service outcomes.
Algorithmic Bias and Fairness	Bias emerges from data, model design, and optimisation goals, often unintentionally.	Conduct routine bias audits and fairness testing across recommendations, pricing, and visibility algorithms.	Develop regulatory guidance on fairness assessments and non-discriminatory AI practices.
Data Privacy and Consumer Protection	Data-driven personalisation increases information asymmetry between platforms and consumers.	Treat consumer data as a stewardship responsibility rather than a commercial asset alone.	Strengthen enforcement of data protection principles such as purpose limitation and transparency.
Ethical AI Governance	Responsible AI requires continuous governance across the AI lifecycle, not isolated compliance checks.	Embed ethical principles into AI design, performance metrics, and organisational culture.	Encourage adaptive regulatory frameworks that evolve with technological change.
Long-Term Behavioural Effects	Sustained AI use may alter consumer autonomy, reliance, and decision confidence.	Monitor behavioural dependency risks and design systems that preserve consumer agency.	Support longitudinal research to assess societal impacts of AI-driven commerce.

8. CONCLUSION

Artificial intelligence (AI) is not a merely a background technology, it is an active mediator which shapes options and how you perceive them, and redistributes decision-making authority along with the digital marketplace. The research stated that AI features like personalised suggestions, intelligent searches/conversational agents, dynamic pricing. AI based personalized suggestion is just the convenience or efficiency which you make purchases easy. It also helps in developing an understanding of value, cope with information overload, and experience control during the purchasing process. Simultaneously, retailers can utilise AI systems to move toward adaptive operations driven by data, thereby enabling them to respond to demand signals in almost real-time. AI functions as both a strategic and experiential tool for online retailers; however, its impact on consumers does not stop there. The integration of Technology Acceptance Model and consumer behaviour theories provides a structure to understand the impact that AI-enabled shopping environments have on the way consumers interact with them. The findings are that while perceived usefulness and ease of use are important factors to facilitate consumer engagement, they, by themselves, do not explain long-term engagement with an AI-enabled environment. Trust, transparency, and ethical governance are shown to be the key factors in determining whether AI is adopted by consumers, and whether the adoption leads to long-term value creation or resistance from consumers. Additionally, the chapter furthers the discussion by including ethical, legal, and governance issues as part of an organisation's AI strategy instead of something that will constrain an organisation from implementing an AI system. Responsible governance of AI is critical for establishing consumer confidence in AI-enabled systems, reducing algorithmic risk, and aligning technology innovation with the expectations of society. Thus, ethical AI is not only a normative value, but also a necessary condition to create a sustainable business in the digital economy. In addition, the chapter stresses the need for a transition in both academic and practical perspectives from short-term performance measures to long-term measures of behaviour and relationships. This transition is continued evolution of AI systems, as their impact on consumer autonomy, their ability to make sound decisions, and their amount of trust in retailers will only become more pronounced over time.

Furthermore, ethics, legality, and governance should no longer be seen as constraints on the use of AI in this space or as barriers to the development of effective AI. The establishment of responsible artificial intelligence (AI) governance is crucial for sustaining consumer trust, managing algorithmic hazards, and aligning technological developments with the public's expectations of social equity. Ethical AI is not only a normatively based ideal, but also a prerequisite condition for sustainable digital commerce. In addition, the chapter demonstrates that AI will have an ever-increasing impact on consumer autonomy and decision-making, as well as their level of trust in products produced by AI, and it needs to be the priority area of focus for researchers, businesses, and policymakers.The chapter provide readers with a guide to better understanding AI-driven e-commerce through the theory of TAM and governance frameworks with practical application. It will encourage readers to consider the broader implications of using intelligent consumer retail systems, acknowledging that the future of e-commerce will depend on responsible design, responsible governance and innovation of AI systems.

9. REFERENCES

Agarwal, N. (2024). Conceptual Framework for E-commerce Success: Consumer Behaviour and AI-Enhanced Digital Marketing. *MOSAIC OF IDEAS: MULTIDISCIPLINARY REFLECTIONS, 241.*

Alhiniti, Y., & Al-Masry, W. A. M. A. (2026). E-Commerce and Legal Practices: An Examination of Legislation and Challenges Related to Digital Activities. In Business Resilience and Business Innovation for Sustainability: The Double-Edged Role of Artificial Intelligence and Other Disruptive Technologies (pp. 2649-2663).

Allal-Chérif, O., Simón-Moya, V., & Ballester, A. C. C. (2021). Intelligent purchasing: How artificial intelligence can redefine the purchasing function. *Journal of Business Research, 124*, 69–76. DOI: 10.1016/j.jbusres.2020.11.050

Beyari, H., & Garamoun, H. (2022). The effect of artificial intelligence on end-user online purchasing decisions: Toward an integrated conceptual framework. *Sustainability (Basel), 14*(15), 9637. DOI: 10.3390/su14159637

Bhardwaj, S., Sharma, N., Goel, M., Sharma, K., & Verma, V. (2024). Enhancing customer targeting in e-commerce and digital marketing through AI-driven personalization strategies. *Advances in Digital Marketing in the Era of Artificial Intelligence*, 41-60.

Bushara, M. A., Abdou, A. H., Hassan, T. H., Sobaih, A. E. E., Albohnayh, A. S. M., Alshammari, W. G., Aldoreeb, M., Elsaed, A. A., & Elsaied, M. A. (2023). Power of social media marketing: How perceived value mediates the impact on restaurant followers' purchase intention, willingness to pay a premium price, and E-WoM? *Sustainability (Basel), 15*(6), 5331. DOI: 10.3390/su15065331

Ebrahimi, A., Ebrahimi, M., & Ebrahimi, N. (2024). Analyzing the Relationship Between Artificial Intelligence and Customer Experience Improvement in the Online Retail Industry. *Digital Transformation and Administration Innovation, 2*(4), 73–81. DOI: 10.61838/dtai.2.4.9

Ganesh, A. (2023). The Impact of Social Media on Consumer Behavior: An AI-Enhanced Approach to Marketing Strategies. *Available at SSRN* 4985407.

García-Serrano, A. M., Martínez, P., & Hernández, J. Z. (2004). Using AI techniques to support advanced interaction capabilities in a virtual assistant for e-commerce. *Expert Systems with Applications, 26*(3), 413–426. DOI: 10.1016/j.eswa.2003.09.012

Hakim, S. H. R. (2026). Strategic Online Growth For Sport Retailer Using Analytical And Behavioral Models. EKOMBIS REVIEW: Jurnal Ilmiah Ekonomi dan Bisnis, 14(1), 945-956.

Jakkula, A. R. (2020). AI and Ethical Considerations in E-commerce. *Journal of Scientific and Engineering Research*, *7*(9), 213–216.

Kumar, P., Choubey, D., Amosu, O. R., & Ogunsuji, Y. M. (2024). AI-enhanced inventory and demand forecasting: Using AI to optimize inventory management and predict customer demand. *World J. Adv. Res. Rev*, *23*(1), 1931–1944. DOI: 10.30574/wjarr.2024.23.1.2173

Kumar, R., Singh, G., Jain, P., & Sharma, M. (2025). Smart E-commerce application using AI. In *Intelligent Computing and Communication Techniques* (pp. 716–722). CRC Press. DOI: 10.1201/9781003530176-102

Lijuan, C., Bhaumik, A., Xinfeng, W., & Jingwen, W. (2023). The effects of inventory management on business efficiency. International Journal For Multidisciplinary Research, 5(4), 1-17.

Lim, Y. J. (2017). Decision to use either Snapchat or Instagram for most powerful celebrities. *Research Journal of the Institute for Public Relations*, *3*(2), 1–16.

Liu, Y., Lu, Q., & Ghamat, S. (2026). AI technology sharing strategies for e-commerce platforms with private label introduction. *International Journal of Production Research*, •••, 1–22. DOI: 10.1080/00207543.2026.2615822

Liusito, R. A., Tulung, J. E., & Saerang, R. T. (2020). The influence of consumer trust and perceived value on consumer purchase decision of e-commerce in social media (study case in Manado). *Jurnal EMBA: Jurnal Riset Ekonomi, Manajemen, Bisnis Dan Akuntansi, 8*(4).

Moodley, K., & Sookhdeo, L. (2025). The role of artificial intelligence personalisation in e-commerce: Customer purchase decisions in the retail sector. *South African Journal of Information Management*, *27*(1), 1–16. DOI: 10.4102/sajim.v27i1.1926

Moore, S., Bulmer, S., & Elms, J. (2022). The social significance of AI in retail on customer experience and shopping practices. *Journal of Retailing and Consumer Services*, *64*, 102755. DOI: 10.1016/j.jretconser.2021.102755

Na, S., Heo, S., Han, S., Shin, Y., & Roh, Y. (2022). Acceptance model of artificial intelligence (AI)-based technologies in construction firms: Applying the Technology Acceptance Model (TAM) in combination with the Technology–Organisation–Environment (TOE) framework. *Buildings (Basel, Switzerland)*, *12*(2), 90. DOI: 10.3390/buildings12020090

Naeem, M. (2025). Emerging trends in global E-retailing: Exploring the dark side of scan and go in-store technologies in consumer shopping journeys. *International Marketing Review*, *42*(2-3), 249–282. DOI: 10.1108/IMR-06-2023-0110

Oteri, O. J., Onukwulu, E. C., Igwe, A. N., Ewim, C. P. M., Ibeh, A. I., & Sobowale, A. (2023). (Forthcoming). Dynamic pricing models for logistics product management: Balancing cost efficiency and market demands. *International Journal of Business and Management*.

Patil, R., Shivashankar, K., Porapur, S. M., & Kagawade, S. (2024). The role of ai-driven social media marketing in shaping consumer purchasing behaviour: An empirical analysis of personalization, predictive analytics, and engagement. In *ITM Web of Conferences* (Vol. 68, p. 01032). EDP Sciences.

Patil, R., Shivashankar, K., Porapur, S. M., & Kagawade, S. (2024). The role of ai-driven social media marketing in shaping consumer purchasing behaviour: An empirical analysis of personalization, predictive analytics, and engagement. In *ITM Web of Conferences* (Vol. 68, p. 01032). EDP Sciences.

Paul, R., Imam, M. H., & Mou, A. J. (2023). AI-Powered Sentiment Analysis In Digital Marketing: A Review Of Customer Feedback Loops In It Services. *American Journal of Scholarly Research and Innovation*, *2*(02), 166–192. DOI: 10.63125/61pqqq54

Perumallaplli, R. (2012). AI-Enhanced Personalization in E-Commerce: Redefining Customer Interaction. *Available at SSRN* 5228719.

Polančič, G., Heričko, M., & Rozman, I. (2010). An empirical examination of application frameworks success based on technology acceptance model. *Journal of Systems and Software*, *83*(4), 574–584. DOI: 10.1016/j.jss.2009.10.036

Prasanth, A., Densy, J. V., Surendran, P., & Bindhya, T. (2023). Role of artificial intelligence and business decision making. *International Journal of Advanced Computer Science and Applications*, *14*(6). Advance online publication. DOI: 10.14569/IJACSA.2023.01406103

Ramineni, V., Ingole, B. S., Jayaram, V., Mehta, G., Krishnappa, M. S., Nagpal, A., & Banarse, A. R. (2024, December). Enhancing E-Commerce Accessibility Through a Novel Voice Assistant Approach for Web and Mobile Applications. In *2024 Third International Conference on Artificial Intelligence, Computational Electronics and Communication System (AICECS)* (pp. 1-7). IEEE. DOI: 10.1109/AICECS63354.2024.10956866

Rane, N. L., Chika, O. E., & Rane, J. (2026). Responsible artificial intelligence in sustainable business: Enhancing customer relationships and loyalty. *International Journal of Applied Resilience and Sustainability*, *2*(1), 61–77. DOI: 10.70593/deepsci.0201004

Rodgers, W., & Nguyen, T. (2022). Advertising benefits from ethical artificial intelligence algorithmic purchase decision pathways. *Journal of Business Ethics*, *178*(4), 1043–1061. DOI: 10.1007/s10551-022-05048-7

Siddiqui, H. A., Abid, H. M. S., & Ahmed, R. (2025). Optimizing E-Commerce Supply Chain Logistics: The Role of Artificial Intelligence in Efficiency and Cost Reduction. *Journal of Asian Development Studies*, *14*(1), 920–938. DOI: 10.62345/jads.2025.14.1.72

Sikder, A. S., & Rolfe, S. (2023). The Power of E-Commerce in the Global Trade Industry: A Realistic Approach to Expedite Virtual Market Place and Online Shopping from anywhere in the World.: E-Commerce in the Global Trade Industry. *International Journal of Imminent Science & Technology.*, *1*(1), 79–100. DOI: 10.70774/ijist.v1i1.3

Singh, S., & Srivastava, P. (2019). Social media for outbound leisure travel: A framework based on technology acceptance model (TAM). *Journal of Tourism Futures*, *5*(1), 43–61. DOI: 10.1108/JTF-10-2018-0058

Song, X., Yang, S., Huang, Z., & Huang, T. (2019, August). The application of artificial intelligence in electronic commerce. [). IOP Publishing.]. *Journal of Physics: Conference Series*, *1302*(3), 032030. DOI: 10.1088/1742-6596/1302/3/032030

Srivastava, A. (2021). The application & impact of artificial intelligence (AI) on E-commerce. *Contemporary issues in commerce and management, 1*(1), 165-75.

Suryavanshi, P., & Gangele, S. (2024). Sentiment analysis view for brand reputation monitoring on social media. *Int. J. Innov. Res. Comput. Commun. Eng*, *12*(Special Is), 111–115. DOI: 10.15680/IJIRCCE.2024.1203518

Taherdoost, H., & Madanchian, M. (2023). Artificial intelligence and sentiment analysis: A review in competitive research. *Computers*, *12*(2), 37. DOI: 10.3390/computers12020037

Tran, M. T. (2026). Advancing retail and service strategies: AI-driven consumer behavior prediction, gamification, and ethical marketing. *Journal of Retailing and Consumer Services*, *88*, 104558. DOI: 10.1016/j.jretconser.2025.104558

Um, N. (2022). How does celebrity-based brand endorsement work in social media?—The instagram context. *Social Sciences (Basel, Switzerland)*, *11*(8), 342. DOI: 10.3390/socsci11080342

Yeo, S. F., Tan, C. L., Kumar, A., Tan, K. H., & Wong, J. K. (2022). Investigating the impact of AI-powered technologies on Instagrammers' purchase decisions in digitalization era–A study of the fashion and apparel industry. *Technological Forecasting and Social Change*, *177*, 121551. DOI: 10.1016/j.techfore.2022.121551

Zhang, X., Li, K., Wu, Y., Liang, S., & Yu, M. (2026). Transforming E-Commerce with AI: Navigating Innovation, Personalization, and Ethical Challenges. *Journal of Theoretical and Applied Electronic Commerce Research*, *21*(1), 29. DOI: 10.3390/jtaer21010029

Zhou, Q., Xu, Z., & Yen, N. Y. (2019). User sentiment analysis based on social network information and its application in consumer reconstruction intention. *Computers in Human Behavior*, *100*, 177–183. DOI: 10.1016/j.chb.2018.07.006

Chapter 6
AI-Driven Personalization and Consumer Experience:
A PRISMA-Guided Systematic Review of Value Creation and Behavioral Outcomes

Md. Yeamin Masum
http://orcid.org/0009-0005-9845-6683
Islamic University, Kushtia, Bangladesh

Md. Sujan Ali Joardar
http://orcid.org/0009-0003-3877-5370
University of Rajshahi, Bangladesh

Md. Sohan Hossain
Islamic University, Kushtia, Bangladesh

Alif Sayd Fathike
http://orcid.org/0009-0006-9852-9296
Rangamati Science and Technology University, Rangamati, Bangladesh

Md. Faisal-E-Alam
http://orcid.org/0000-0002-7341-7945
Begum Rokeya University, Rangpur, Bangladesh

DOI: 10.4018/979-8-2600-2977-0.ch006

ABSTRACT

This study presents a systematic review of AI-driven personalization and its effects on consumer experience, value creation, and behavioral outcomes. Synthesizing 344 Scopus-indexed publications from 2014 to 2026, the review applies the Stimulus–Organism–Response (S-O-R) framework to integrate evidence across marketing, tourism, and information systems research. The findings show that AI technologies—such as machine learning, recommender systems, and NLP-enabled chatbots—generate multidimensional value while also raising concerns about privacy, autonomy, and algorithmic transparency. Trust, shaped by perceived fairness and explainability, mediates the relationship between personalization and consumer responses. Privacy concerns, technology readiness, cultural orientation, and ethical perceptions moderate these effects, influencing outcomes such as purchase intention, loyalty, and electronic word-of-mouth.

1. INTRODUCTION

Artificial Intelligence (AI) is considered a crucial part of modern-day marketing and service economies and has altered the manner in which companies engage with clients and create value. The concept of AI-driven personalization means that advanced algorithms, machine learning, and predictive analytics can be used to individualize content, recommendations, and service experiences to specific users on the basis of behavioral information and previous interaction (Vidhya et al., 2023). With the capabilities of large-scale data processing, companies have a better chance to predict consumer needs, predict the buying and selling trends, and maximize the effectiveness of their operations and customer satisfaction (Haleem et al., 2022). Organizations are increasingly using AI-like technology on digital platforms in the form of recommendation systems, intelligent interfaces, and conversational agents to deliver timely, relevant, and interactive experiences. These technologies enable companies not only to offer more personalized services but also to simplify the decision-making process and help consumers during the customer journey (Lee, 2020; Wertenbroch et al., 2020; Salam et al., 2024; Salam et al., 2026).

Due to this, consumer dynamics are increasingly being mediated and driven by data. Even though AI-powered personalization has immense utility regarding convenience, relevance, and engagement, it also causes ethical issues concerning privacy, autonomy, and ethical accountability (Satu et al., 2023). Individual systems are based on the integration of consumer information analysis and investigations that can intensify the sense of control, loss, or manipulation (Husairi & Rossi, 2024; Weippert, 2024). These contradictory results indicate the necessity of a fair assessment of the prospects, as well as the risks, that may be present in the process of AI-based personalization. Moreover, AI is efficient regarding decision-making, resource allocation, and the creation of new competitive advantages within the dynamic market conditions.

1.1 Significance of the Study

Personalization with the help of AI has been implemented quickly in different fields, such as marketing and retail, tourism, and financial services. It gives companies the power to anticipate consumer tastes, customize messages, and provide real-time recommendations and, in the process, improve their relevance and interest. With the help of proper content that is delivered to the right customer at the most opportune time, organizations can greatly enhance satisfaction, create loyal customers, and improve general performance (Sayem et al., 2026). Several studies also focus on single applications of technologies or particular results and provide only a limited combination of the overall well-known ethical, psychological, and behavioral outcomes.

Since companies will start turning to AI-controlled technology such as recommendation engines and virtual assistants to strengthen customer relations and gain a competitive edge (Afshar & Shah, 2025), the efficiency of the technologies will depend on the responsible use of the technology, which should anticipate issues related to privacy, transparency, and fairness. The chapter is thus important because it brings together diffuse evidence to furnish a complete interdisciplinary overview of the role played by AI-based personalization in consumer experience, value creation, and behavior implementation.

This study classifies important constructs in the prior research, drawing on a systematic organization of the previous work, and developing a balanced view of the value of both the advantages and the risks (Ullah & Khan, 2024). It encourages the simplicity of ideas and assimilation of theories in the domain for scholars. The study also gives technical guidance to the practitioners to come up with effective and morally correct strategies of personalization. A synthesis ground upon which crucial decisions regarding data governance and the responsible use of Artificial Intelligence are made as a policymaker. To managers, the synthesis provides evidence-based recommendations on how they should design personalization strategies to create trust and prevent consumer backlash. It underscores to policymakers that they should have adaptive laws that follow the evolution of AI at no disadvantage to privacy and justice. Combined, these investments affirm the enhanced execution of the value creation in digital ecosystems through the use of AI-based personalization and, at the same time, guard the well-being of consumers.

1.2 Research Gap

Though the concept of AI-driven personalization is a prevailing characteristic of contemporary digitized spaces, the academic awareness of the concept at the consumer level is divided into smaller parts. The body of research is scattered over the various fields and is typified by inconsistent theoretical views, dissimilar constructs, and unequal methodological practices (Duralia et al., 2025; Kumari & Laheri, 2025). Recent systematic reviews have examined the impact of artificial intelligence on customer experience personalization (Timimi et al., 2025). However, limited research integrates value creation, psychological mechanisms, and behavioral outcomes within a unified theoretical framework. The majority of the previous research looks at isolated technologies or particular outputs, hence limiting the integration of the effect of the personalization mechanisms on consumer perceptions, as well as value creation and behavioral reactions (Tran, 2026). Therefore, the development of knowledge becomes cumulative, and the researchers and practitioners are deprived of the complex idea of when and under what circumstances AI-based personalization will produce positive or negative outcomes (Qin et al., 2025). In terms of overcoming this limitation, the current paper is composed of a systematic literature review that is planned and structured around the Preferred Reporting Items of Systematic Reviews and Meta-Analyses (PRISMA) framework through which conceptual integration, methodological transparency, and development of cumulative knowledge are to be attained.

1.3 Research Questions

The research questions to be answered in this study, based on the gaps identified, are the following:

RQ1. What are the most used AI technologies and personalization processes used in industries to improve the consumer experience?
RQ2. What is the effect of AI-based personalization (e.g., customization, perceived relevance, adaptability, and transparency) on consumer perceptions (e.g., trust, satisfaction, engagement, and perceived value?
RQ3. What are the consumer perception implications on behavioral outcomes such as purchase intention, loyalty, further use, and electronic word-of-mouth (e-WOM)?
RQ4. What value would AI-enabled personalization bring to both consumers and firms, and what are the gaps in the literature that inform the creation of an integrated conceptual theory on the relevance of personalization in future research?

1.4 Research Objectives

General Objective

To have a complete PRISMA-informed systematic review synthesizing the available studies on the concept of AI-driven personalization and critically analyzing its impact on consumer experience, value creation, and behavioral outcomes.

Specific Objectives

RO1. To identify the dominant AI technologies and personalization strategies adopted across industries.
RO2. To examine the effect of personalization based on AI on the most important dimensions of consumer experience, such as satisfaction, engagement, trust, and perceived relevance.
RO3. To measure the impacts of personalization on behavioral outcomes of consumer purchase intention, consumer loyalty, repeat usage, and word-of-mouth.
RO4. To assess the value creation generated for both consumers and firms through AI-enabled personalization, synthesize existing evidence to highlight inconsistencies and research gaps, and develop an integrated conceptual framework to guide future studies.

2. THEORETICAL AND CONCEPTUAL FOUNDATIONS

One of the recent transformations is artificial intelligence (AI), which has become a new debate in modern marketing and consumer experience management. The emergence of the digital medium, together with developments in machine learning and big data, has sparked a paradigm shift from conventional mass marketing to highly personalized, context-dependent exchanges. Personalization is AI-based, analyzing large volumes of data and providing customized content, pricing, and services based on individual preferences (Davenport et al., 2020; Wedel & Kannan, 2016). These systems can be viewed as important value creation processes in the context of a consumer. The AI-driven personalization increases consumer-brand relationships and favorable behavioral outcomes related to consumer satisfaction, brand loyalty, and the likelihood of purchase by filtering information to boost relevance and convenience (Bleier et al., 2019). This has led to the growth of academic interest in marketing, retailing, tourism, and information systems, a fact that highlights the interdisciplinary relevance of the field. The review is a synthesis of research that has been conducted to show how AI-enabled value creation works and what the impact of this value creation is on behavior.

2.1 Artificial Intelligence and the Evolution of Personalization

As stated, the process of personalization development is also closely connected to the development of AI. Instead of providing companies with standardized messages sent to large audiences, organizations now use AI to analyze intricate consumer information in real-time. This allows providing tailored content, price dynamism, and tailored product suggestions (Davenport et al., 2020; Wedel & Kannan, 2016). This has developed on the consumer side of the equation, as it is seen to have led to a smaller overload of information and increased efficiency in their decision-making. Using the most relevant options, the level of convenience perceived and the overall attitude towards the brand, which influences downstream choices, including satisfaction and loyalty, are improved (Bleier et al., 2019). As it becomes more important, a structured understanding of the theoretical foundations, permitting technologies, and price effects of AI customization is required to rationalize how these structures are producing consumer perceptions and behaviors.

2.2 Theoretical Foundations of AI-Driven Personalization

The conceptual roots of personalization through the use of AI are based on several established models. Service-Dominant (S-D) Logic presupposes that the value is generated in the context of interaction activities; the AI provider transforms the suggestions related to behavioral information in such a way that it would be transformed into valuable experiences (Vargo & Lusch, 2008). This is supplemented by the Relationship Marketing Theory, which reminds us of the long-term interaction that is rooted in trust and interaction (Morgan & Hunt, 1994). Personalization of AI-based services such as chatbots and personal assistance is a sign of a customer-centered strategy that creates loyal customers throughout a long period (Grewal et al., 2020). In adoption terms, the Technology Acceptance Model (TAM) and UTAUT emphasize perceived usefulness and ease of use as AI engagement factors (Davis, 1989), with transparency and relevance playing a major role in attitude formation (Shin, 2021). Lastly, the Privacy Calculus Theory explains the trade-offs consumers make between the advantage of convenience and the threats of misuse or loss of control of the information (Culnan & Armstrong, 1999). This point of view emphasizes the dualistic influence of data-driven AI personalization.

2.3 AI Technologies Enabling Personalization

With a set of artificial intelligence technologies or an AI suite, the actual process of personalization becomes possible. They are machine learning, deep learning, natural language processing (NLP), computer vision, predictive analytics, and recommender systems. Recommender systems are one of the most popular studied mechanisms among them. Context-aware recommender systems improve personalization by using users' situations and preferences to make more accurate recommendations (Venkatachalam & Ray, 2022). Techniques like collaborative, content-based, or hybrid models use the historical activities to forecast the appropriate products or content that form the interest of an individual user (Ricci et al., 2021). Machine learning algorithms are constantly learning based on user interactions, by which strategies to personalize can be improved and updated. Reinforcement learning also allows learners to be flexible in that they change the recommendations in real time on the basis of immediate feedback (Song et al., 2024). Moreover, chatbots and virtual assistants powered by NLP can also take personalization to a new level and have a conversation, feel like talking with a person, and provide on-the-fly services (Huang & Rust, 2018). These technologies are applied in mobile applications and booking systems in the service sectors such as tourism and hospitality to develop smooth and interactive customer experiences (Tussyadiah, 2020).

2.4 Value Creation Mechanisms of AI-Driven Personalization

The idea of value creation is at the core of AI customization studies since such systems produce multidimensional values to both consumers and companies. Personalization provides functional, emotional, and social value on the part of the consumer. In a functional sense, AI saves mental power and search expenses by making decision-making processes simpler (Ansari et al., 2000). On the emotional level, personalized experiences add pleasure, satisfaction, and feelings of recognition, stipulating deeper psychological attachment to the brands (Bleier et al., 2019). Social value can also be perceived where consumers undergo individual personalized digital interactions, especially on interactive media (Arora et al., 2008). Organizational-wise, personalization enhances customer lifetime value, marketing performance, and operational effectiveness. Targeting is made cost-effective by the use of data, whereby the firm identifies the right customers and at the right time, which enhances good conversion and returns on the investment as well as competitive power.

2.5 Consumer Experience Dimensions Influenced by Personalization

The process of consumer experience is broad-based, which implies it consists of cognitive, emotional, and behavioral responses during the customer journey (Lemon & Verhoef, 2016). Recent research has further conceptualized AI-enabled personalization from a customer journey perspective, emphasizing dynamic touchpoints and real-time adaptation across stages (Gao & Liu, 2023). The personalization in the AI domain affects all of these dimensions. Cognitively, timely and relevant recommendations lead to less uncertainty and contribute to informed decision-making (Mohammadkhani et al., 2025). Empathic and responsive interactions provide emotional trust and comfort as well as positive affect. On the behavioral front, customized interfaces attract more browsing, more time spent on the platform, recurrence of visits, and platform stickiness. In hybrid digital-physical environments, AI-enabled personalization enhances integration across digital and physical touchpoints, strengthening customer engagement (Larke et al., 2018). Such implications indicate that personalization of AI transforms the whole consumption process, which plays a role in enhancing integrated and deeper customer experiences.

2.6 Behavioral Outcomes of AI-Driven Personalization

AI-based personalization, based on enhanced experiences, influences diverse consumer behavioral outcomes. Previous studies propose that successful personalization correlates with a better satisfaction level, trust, loyalty, and purchase intentions (Coelho & Henseler, 2012). In environments based on algorithm mediation, it is specifically trust, but the transparency of systems, fairness, and the ability to explain, which make users feel better (Shin, 2021). High levels of trust will subsequently lead to increased usage, positive word of mouth, and higher frequency of participation and co-creation behavior, i.e., participation and co-creation (Hollebeek et al., 2021). However, in accordance with the duality said in the introduction, when individualization is taken as an intrusion or excess, it may result in a negative consequence as well. The privacy concern will tend to result in avoidance, resistance against the strategic advertisement, or proliferation of fake news (Martin & Murphy, 2017). These conflicting outcomes point to the need to balance and implement responsible strategies of personalization.

2.7 Ethical, Privacy, and Governance Considerations

The ethical and governance concerns have since turned into a hot subject due to the increased prevalence of the concept of AI personalization. Opaque or illegitimate use of personal data may cause a lack of trust and ruin a brand image (Zuboff, 2023). It implies that such a regulatory framework, such as the General Data Protection Regulation (GDPR), applies to shaping how organizations determine and shape the personalization process. It is important to consider the ethical AI principles that are prerequisites to sustainable value-generation and control of the well-being of consumers, such as fairness, transparency, accountability, and responsible data management (Floridi et al., 2018; Rayun et al., 2026). Using these principles in personalization strategies will make organizations strike the right balance between societal responsibility and technological effectiveness.

3. METHODOLOGY

To achieve transparency, replicability, and methodological rigor, the chapter uses a systematic literature review (SLR) methodology based on the Preferred Reporting Items for Systematic Reviews and Meta-Analysis (PRISMA). The extraction of relevant studies will be based on academic databases, and only Scopus will be considered (Faisal-E-Alam et al., 2025). The search strategy is the use of predefined keywords regarding the field of AI personalization, algorithmic recommendations, digital consumer experience, and behavioral outcomes (Khatun et al., 2025). Inclusion criteria will be centered on empirical and conceptual research, which is peer-reviewed and directly covers AI-enabled personalization. The elimination of non-academic sources and studies that do not talk about consumer experience or behavioral outcomes is done by exclusion criteria. Thematic analysis will then be conducted to determine recurring constructs, theoretical models, methodological trends, and contextual moderators. The methodology section presents a systematic review and synthesis approach that provides an organized body of knowledge to benefit future research by defining unresolved gaps, research methodological constraints, and outlining novel research priorities. This research method follows the Preferred Reporting Items of Systematic Reviews and Meta-Analyses (PRISMA) framework, which makes the process of selecting and analyzing the studies under consideration transparent, rigorous, and consistent (Lindström & Österberg, 2020).

3.1 Research Design

The systematic literature reviews result in strong summaries of the most reliable evidence (Snyder, 2019), which is adopted in research design. The methodology adopted in this systematic review is PRISMA-based, which is highly praised in systematic reviews due to its systematic and transparent process. PRISMA makes the review complete, reproducible, and unbiased through a clear definition of the inclusion and exclusion criteria and descriptions of the methodology at every stage of the review. Systematic reviews offer significant confidence in the results as they are based on clear search, screening, and selection procedures of the studies (Rossi & Bianchini, 2022). This will enable the research to be strong and will reduce the chances of leaving out important information.

3.2 Database Selection and Search Strategy

Identifying databases is a determining factor in the completeness and validation of a systematic review. The Scopus database was selected as the primary database in this research because it covers a vast range of academic literature on various disciplines, including engineering, environmental science, sustainability, and technology. Scopus is regarded as one of the most credible and authoritative sites to use in a systematic review due to the fact that it is used to index quality peer-reviewed journals, conference papers, and books. The search strategy was developed to include all the studies on AI-Driven Personalization and Consumer Experience. The search query involved the use of particular keywords, which included: "Artificial Intelligence (AI)," "Intelligence-driven personalization," and Consumer Experience and Value Creation. Also, the filters were used to narrow the search to the articles published from 2014 to 2026, to make the research more recent to the current developments in technology. Only the English-language publications were taken into account to make sure that the studies are accessible to a worldwide audience. The use of filters gave a search 381 records, which were screened systematically in accordance with predetermined criteria.

Figure 1. PRISMA-Based Methodology

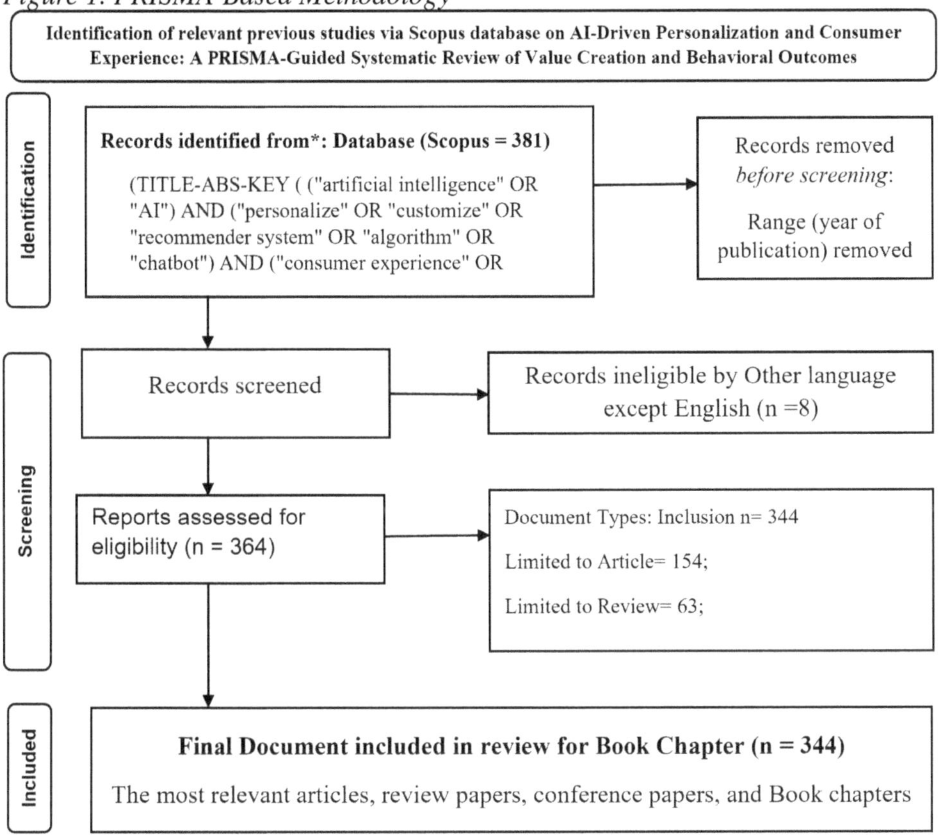

(Source: Scopus Database-2025)

3.3 Selection Technique

Determining the study selection process according to the PRISMA guidelines was done to achieve transparency and replication (Riaj et al., 2025). The selection was carried out in a systematic process on a multi-stage basis as shown in the PRISMA flow diagram (Figure 1). Since the search was narrowed down to one database (Scopus), there was no single instance of a duplicate record from the external sources. After painstaking probability checks of the internal duplicates, no internal duplicates were detected in the first export from Scopus database.

Two reviewers independently undertook the screening process during two stages. The 372 records were evaluated independently on the pre-established sets of eligibility criteria in the first stage (title and abstract screening). The profession of reviewers made a mistake on the inclusion side; records were excluded only when it was obvious that they did not contribute to the main themes of AI-driven personalization, consumer experience, and value creation. Any differences that arose between the two reviewers on the relevance of a record were resolved through discussion. In case they did not come to a consensus, a third reviewer was consulted, and the final decision was made. The second move was a complete text development of all reports out of the 364 that had passed the initial vetting. At this point, the two reviewers applied document type inclusion criteria independently, and their only selection was peer-reviewed articles, review papers, conference papers, and book chapters. It resulted in the deletion of 20 records that fell outside these types of documents (e.g., editorials, notes, short surveys, or industry reports that contained no rigorous methodology). All reviewers concurred on the final set of 344 documents on which the foundation of the systematic review was established.

3.4 Analysis Technique

A thematic synthesis strategy was employed to analyze the 344 articles considered, which is quite appropriate to synthesize the results of qualitative and quantitative research to establish higher-order themes, trends, and associations in the material (Thomas & Harden, 2008). In this way, the various bodies of evidence on AI-driven personalization could be interpreted in an orderly and clear manner. The large amount of literature needed to be controlled; as a result, all 344 documents were brought into a reference management software to establish order in them. The complete texts were then exported and uploaded into a qualitative data analysis tool to ease the process of information retrieval and systematic coding. The coding and synthesis used three repetitive steps, which are as described.

3.4.1 Development of the Initial Coding Framework

A preliminary coding scheme was created; the scheme was deductive with reference to the research goals and the Stimulus-Organism-Response (S-O-R) theoretical framework described in Section 2. There are high-level parent nodes created according to the core constructs of the study. Such nodes consisted of AI technologies and personalization plans (e.g., machine learning, recommender systems, NLP, chatbots, predictive analytics); consumer experience (e.g., cognitive, emotional, sensory, and relational experience, with sub-codes of satisfaction, trust, engagement, and perceived relevance); value creation (e.g., functional, hedonic, personalization, convenience, and co-creation value); behavioral (e.g., purchase intention, loyalty, e-WOM, continued use), and moderators/mediators (e.g., privacy concerns, technology read.

3.4.2 Pilot Testing and Framework Refinement

To ascertain consistency and trustworthiness in the coding process, two members of the research team exercised the initial coding framework over a purposive sample of 20 articles that comprised an approximation of six percent of the total documents to make sure that two independent individuals perform the same task. After this pilot stage, the team sat together to compare the results of the coding process, debate on the differences, and improve the framework. This process was applied in an iterative way, which enabled the detection of the emergent and inductive codes that were not pre-established as part of the original framework. Such emergent codes consisted of notable concepts such as algorithmic fairness, perceived manipulation, and consumer reactance. These new themes were then incorporated into the final coding scheme, whereby the analysis was made to be data-based and capture the variety of concepts available in the literature.

3.4.3 Full-Text Coding and Thematic Synthesis

Using the completed coding framework, one of the researchers coded the remaining articles following a systematic coding procedure with occasional consistency proportions conducted by the second reviewer of a selected subset of the papers, therefore, enhancing reliability and limiting interpretive bias. In this step, corresponding passages in the studies were associated with the corresponding codes and, as a result, systematic extraction became possible to find the results, methodological approaches, theoretical perspectives, and contextual variables in the entire data sample.

After the coding was done, the research team used thematic synthesis. It included evaluation of all text passages related to each code, description of similarities, analysis of the connection between codes, and synthesis of the results to create a higher-order interpretation. As an illustration, all the text with a coded label must remain integrated under the label of privacy issues, technology readiness, and AI transparency to have the chance to learn about their cumulative adjusting position on the personalization outcome relationship. Similarly, results with respect to different AI technologies were compared and contrasted in various industry settings in attempts to identify sector-specific applications and results. This analytical procedure helped the team to transition to the analytical coding of the data and finally arrive at the integration of the conceptual framework (Figure 2) and the systematic discussion of the results expressed in this chapter. Through following this intensive, multi-step process of analysis, the review will be able to delineate that the synthesized findings are not just a recap of the available literature but a conceptually coherent, theoretically enlightened status.

Table 1. Descriptive Summary of Included Studies (N=344)

Category	Sub-Category	Number of Studies	Percentage (%)
Publication Year	2014–2018	42	12.2%
	2019–2022	118	34.3%
	2023–2026	184	53.5%
Document Type	Journal Articles	285	82.76%
	Review Papers	39	11.34%
	Book Chapters	20	5.90%
Research Methodology	Quantitative (Survey/Experiment)	194	56.4%
	Qualitative (Case/Interview)	92	26.7%
	Mixed Methods	58	16.9%
Industry Context	E-commerce/Retail	112	32.6%
	Tourism/Hospitality	78	22.7%
	Financial Services	41	11.9%
	Healthcare	28	8.1%
	Entertainment/Media	35	10.2%
	Multiple/General	50	14.5%
Theoretical Framework	S-O-R (Stimulus-Organism-Response)	89	25.9%
	TAM/UTAUT	67	19.5%
	Privacy Calculus Theory	54	15.7%
	S-D Logic	38	11.0%
	Relationship Marketing Theory	42	12.2%
	Multiple/Other Theories	54	15.7%
	Recommender Systems	98	28.5%
AI Technology Focus	Machine Learning/Deep Learning	76	22.1%
	Chatbots/Conversational Agents	62	18.0%
	NLP-based Systems	41	11.9%
	Predictive Analytics	35	10.2%
	Multiple AI Technologies	32	9.3%
Geographic Context	Asia	118	34.3%
	Europe	96	27.9%
	America	72	20.9%
	Africa	18	5.2%
	Australia	12	3.5%
	Others / Multi-country	28	8.1%

As can be seen in Table 1, the systematic review covers 344 publications indexed in Scopus over the years 2014-2026; however, there is a significant focus in recent years-53.5% of the studies were published in 2023-2026, which may be associated with the dynamism of AI-driven personalization studies and research. In terms of document type, journal articles will be the largest (82.76%), then there will be review papers (11.34%), and book chapters (5.90%). Concerning the research methodology, quantitative studies prevail (56.4%), as qualitative studies and mixed methods (26.7% and 16.9%, respectively) constitute empirical studies. The analysis of the context of the industry has shown that e-commerce/retail is the most commonly examined industry field (32.6%), followed by tourism/hospitality (22.7%) and financial services (11.9%).

Concerning theoretical background, the Stimulus-Organism-Response (S-O-R) paradigm is the most taken theory (25.9%), then TAM/UTAUT (19.5%), and Privacy Calculus Theory (15.7%). With an AI technology focus, the most explored are recommender systems (28.5%), machine learning/deep learning (22.1%), and chatbots (18.0%) are also heavily explored. In geographical terms, Asia has the highest number of 34.3 percent of studies, Europe 27.9 percent, America 20.9 percent, and the interesting element is that the world is interested in research with emerging roles played by Africa (5.2%) and Australia (3.5%). This extensive division determines the quality and quantity of the evidence base synthesized in this review.

4. CONCEPTUAL FRAMEWORK

This model uses a Stimulus-Organism-Response (S-O-R) framework, which is typically employed in consumer behavior and technology acceptance studies. The presence of moderators and mediators is a manifestation of AI-Driven Personalization (Stimulus), Consumer Experience and Value Perception (Organism), and Behavioral Outcomes (Response), etc. The proposed conceptual model will be as follows in Figure 2.

Figure 2. Conceptual Framework on AI-Driven Personalization and Consumer Experience

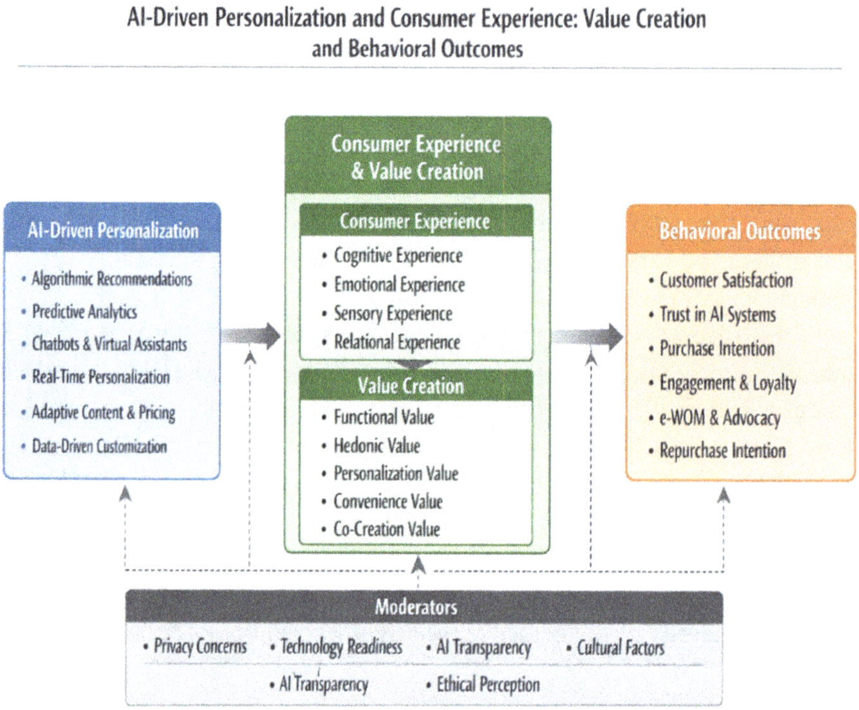

In order to introduce empirical specificity to the theory, provided in Figure 2, Table 2 below outlines the specific variables existing as the synthesis of the 344 reviewed studies, classified in accordance with the Stimulus-Organism-Response (S-O-R) model.

Table 2. Detailed S-O-R Constructs and Synthesized Variables from Reviewed Literature (N=344)

S-O-R Component	Core Constructs from Conceptual Framework	Specific Variables Identified in Synthesis (from 344 papers)
Stimulus (S)	AI-Driven Personalization	**AI Technologies:** Recommender Systems, Machine Learning/ Deep Learning, NLP-based Chatbots, Predictive Analytics, Conversational Agents. **Personalization Attributes:** Customization, Perceived Relevance, Adaptability, Transparency of algorithms.
Organism (O)	Consumer Experience & Value Creation	**Consumer Experience:** Cognitive (decision confidence), Emotional (joy, comfort), Sensory (appeal), Relational (trust, commitment). **Value Creation:** Functional (efficiency), Hedonic (enjoyment), Personalization (uniqueness), Convenience (effort reduction), Co-creation Value. **Key Mediating States:** Trust, Satisfaction, Engagement, Perceived Fairness, Perceived Value.
Response (R)	Behavioral Outcomes	Purchase Intention, Loyalty (repurchase, retention), Continued Usage, Positive Electronic Word-of-Mouth (e-WOM), Co-creation Behavior, (Negative) Reactance/Avoidance.

4.1 AI-Driven Personalization

AI helps companies create and analyze consumer data on a larger scale than before. The abundance of data collected via various tools, such as online purchases, loyalty programs, and social media alerts, offers plenty of information on consumer needs, desires, and trends (Parkes, 2018). Machine learning algorithms help organizations use this data to create highly personalized customer experiences. Strategic implementation of AI-driven personalization brings multiple organizational practices, such as a high level of customer satisfaction, loyalty strengthening, sales growth, and a better competitive position. In turn, consumers are more willing to work with and stick to such brands that provide memorable and context-based experiences.

4.2 Consumer Experience and Value Creation

4.2.1 Consumer Experience

AI enhances customer experience by making it more intimate, effective, and emotionally responsive, which creates value in the form of increased levels of satisfaction, loyalty, and interaction (Mittameedi et al., 2025). According to research, intelligent systems (which include AI) have become active co-creators of customer experience. The consumer experience construct includes four dimensions that are related to each other.

i. **Cognitive Experience:** This dimension is related to the resources of how consumers think, evaluate, and arrive at a decision during interactions with the brand, including information processing, problem-solving, learning, and perceived usefulness.
ii. **Emotional Experience:** This is associated with the feelings of joy, excitement, credibility, comfort, or frustration that the consumer has gained with a brand. As an example, Spotify uses AI to create personalized Discover Weekly playlists, which match the user's mood and listening behavior, providing a sense of joy and bonding.
iii. **Sensory Experience:** This dimension is concerned with the senses of sight, sound, touch, smell, and taste that are triggered by the digital or physical brand. The visuals, such as images, color schemes, and video, can be customized by AI-powered e-commerce websites to make them more appealing and engaging.
iv. **Relational Experience:** This deals with a long-term interaction and psychological commitment between the consumer and the brand through trust and interaction. Chatbots with AI capabilities to store historical communication facilitate brands to have a sustained and personalized communication process.

4.2.2 Value Creation

AI-based personalization can be viewed as a fundamental force of value creation as it changes consumer data into differentiated experiences that can create value for both consumers and companies. (Riikkinen et al., 2018) Showcased how chatbots based on AI enhance the process of customer value creation: faster claims processing, instant responses, improved buying experiences, and individualized offers. This process produces five different types of values.

i. **Functional Value:** The utilitarian benefits that consumers have gained from the products or services, such as performance, quality, and usefulness. Functional value creation is demonstrated in the examples of AI-improved recommendations based on the budget of consumers and their requirements.
ii. **Hedonic Value:** Enjoyment, fun, and emotional satisfaction of the consumption experiences. Such streaming services as Netflix are using AI to make the process of browsing enjoyable and emotionally compelling by customizing content to make it enjoyable.
iii. **Personalization Value:** A sense of being known creates a feeling of individuality in the perceived uniqueness of deliveries matching personal preferences. This

type of value is represented by AI-based hospitality systems that retain guests' preferences and generate personalized future stays.

iv. **Convenience Value:** It will be a reduction in time, effort, and cognitive load during the customer experience. Examples of convenience value creation include chatbots that can solve booking problems instantly.

v. **Co-creation Value:** A type of value created by the active involvement of the consumer in the production of products, services, or experiences. Fashion portals based on AI, where users can co-create clothing with AI, allowing real-time design recommendations, manifest co-creation value.

4.3 Moderators

The effects of AI-based personalized marketing on consumer behaviors depend on many moderating factors because all have an effect on the outcome of the consumer regarding trust, satisfaction, intent to purchase, and loyalty. It has five moderators, such as privacy issues, Technology preparedness, AI openness, cultural preparedness, and moral impressions.

i. **Privacy Issues:** The fear consumers have about the gathering, archiving, and processing of personal information. Raised privacy concerns reduce the positive attitudes towards AI personalization.

ii. **Technology Readiness:** This is the willingness and ability of consumers to implement new technologies. The technologically competent customers have a positive attitude towards AI personalization, and less technologically savvy ones might show some opposition.

iii. **AI Transparency:** How clearly the companies explain the foundation of the AI-based recommendations. Transparency minimizes the uncertainty and manipulation of perceptions and promotes trust.

iv. **Cultural Readiness:** How cultural norms perceive the usefulness of AI use and information-sharing. Culture predisposes people to attitudes on automation and personalization.

v. **Ethical Perceptions:** How consumers perceive AI personalization as being fair, biased, non-discriminatory, and socially responsible. Brand reputation may be negatively influenced by unethical perceptions.

4.4 Behavioral Outcomes

The behavioral outcomes of AI-driven personalization are positive (increased consumer satisfaction, increased trust towards AI systems, deep engagement, high intention to purchase and repurchase, long-lasting loyalty, or positive electronic word-of-mouth (e-WOM). Within the framework of the S-O-R model, these findings form the main evidence and key findings of this systematic review.

5. DISCUSSIONS

This Stimulus-Organism-Response (S-O-R) model systematic review identifies, integrates, summarizes, and concisely presents the literature already in place concerning the topic of AI-driven personalization to elucidate the complex effects of such on consumer experience, the creation of value, and behavior change. The PRISMA-based review of 344 studies indexed through Scopus provides a confusing and contradictory picture. Although AI-based personalization has a lot of positive effects on consumers, it also poses a severe threat to their psychological and ethical well-being.

5.1 The Duality of Personalization: Balancing Value and Vulnerability

The results strongly support the fact that AI-based personalization can be a strong catalyst for value creation. Similar to Service-Dominant (S-D) Logic (Vargo & Lusch, 2008), AI technologies make it possible to create value together and offer it in the form of dynamically adjusted offerings where consumer behavioral data are used to form functional, hedonic, and relational value. Research indicates that individual recommendations and chatbots decrease cognitive load, increase the efficiency of choice, and elicit emotions, resulting in satisfaction, trust, and loyalty (Bleier et al., 2019). Similar evidence from e-commerce contexts shows that AI-driven systems simultaneously generate operational efficiency and decision complexity, reinforcing the need for structured implementation pathways (Gupta et al., 2023). This positive pathway is directly related to the Organism and Response part of the conceptual framework, in which enriched consumer experiences would result in a preferred behavioral outcome of purchase intention and positive electronic word-of-mouth (e-WOM).

Nevertheless, the review also verifies the long-standing personalization-privacy paradox, which is a conflict that is summarized in the theoretical paradigm of Privacy Calculus Theory (Culnan & Armstrong, 1999). It is these very processes that facilitate the creation of value, such as providing vast amounts of data and algorithms to infer it, that increase consumer-related fear of surveillance, loss of autonomy, and manipulation (Husairi & Rossi, 2024; Weippert, 2024). This is one of the main findings in that, though consumers wish to have personalized, convenient experiences, they are highly sensitive to the data practices that enable those experiences to occur.

This has been supported by recent studies, which found that unclear or overstated data practices may undermine trust and reduce perceived fairness and turn possible value creation into value destruction. This moderating value of the issues of privacy, which is represented in the conceptual framework, is hence important, as it serves as a major boundary condition that will minimize the beneficial impacts of personalization. It is remarkable to notice a kind of methodological disconnect in the literature: whereas 56.4% of the studies utilize quantitative survey measures of the expressed privacy concerns, only 8.1% are using behavioral measures or experimental designs, which would be able to capture the actual privacy-protecting behavior. It appears that this disparity between expressed beliefs and disclosed preferences implies that the discipline is potentially way too worried about privacy issues or is excessively optimistic about the extent to which consumers are prepared to relinquish privacy in favor of convenience- a paradox that could be critically reviewed.

The tension is also enhanced by the fact that the regulatory situation is rapidly changing in 2025-2026. In addition to the existing frameworks, including the GDPR, more recent enforcement regulations and new laws, including the final requirements of the EU AI Act of high-risk AI systems (including some personalization algorithms) and the updated laws on data protection in major US states (e.g., California) have increased the compliance after stakes. Those rules provide more stringent conditions for algorithm disclosure, the right to explanation, and compulsory Data Protection Impact Assessment (DPIA) of AI-based profiling. Therefore, the privacy issue of a consumer is no longer a mere psychological idea, but it is now founded on a concrete or legally binding code of rights. This change in regulation transforms the transparent and fair practices of AI addressed in this review not only into an ethical decision of firms but also into a legal mandate.

5.2 The Centrality of Trust and Transparency in Algorithmic Mediation

As a critical process in the connection between AI personalization and consumer outcomes, trust presents itself. The review points out that trust cannot occur automatically in an environment mediated by an algorithm and that trust has to be nurtured by providing transparency, equity, and explainability in the system (Shin, 2021). The analysis of the 344 studies performed crucially shows that the way trust is operationalized in industries is very different. Trust in e-commerce situations (32.6% of studies) is more adhered to as cognitive trust of recommendation accuracy, whereas it is the emotional trust in conversational agents in tourism/hospitality settings (22.7%). This fragmentation does not allow the cumulative knowledge building to occur and creates doubts that knowledge of trust is a unitary construct throughout the AI applications. Moreover, 71% of the studies analyzing trust adopt cross-sectional designs, which measure trust at a time instead of tracing its development by repeated AI interactions, which is a weakness, especially considering that preliminary trust between AI systems and people is fundamentally different than ongoing trust. This result directly answers RQ2, which proves that personalization features are not sufficient and can affect consumer perceptions depending on the way they are applied and conveyed. The significance of trust is also supported by the fact that functional and human-like trust are not the same. It has been researched that consumers can trust AI systems differently, depending on the situation, that is, trusting an AI to perform utilitarian functions and trusting an AI to behave like humans to experience hedonic functions.

This is consistent with the larger observation that AI transparency, whose meaning is the extent to which companies can explain the foundation underpinning AI-based recommendations, is a key mediator. Once consumers know how and why they get personalized, a trusting attitude is created, and the perception of manipulation fears away. On the other hand, the normally obscured black box algorithms may raise doubts and push back, especially to those consumers with less technological preparedness or those experiencing increased ethical apprehension, as noted in the framework. It is not merely a governance issue but a strategic requirement to ensure sustainable consumer trust and long-term sustainability of personalization measures. It is also precisely the ethical AI principles that will have to be integrated and enforced, namely fairness, accountability, and transparency (Floridi et al., 2018).

5.3 Contingent Value Creation: The Role of Moderators

It can be seen in the synthesis that the impacts of AI-enabled personalization are highly contingent and differ in accordance with segments of consumers and the situations. The evidence is highly beneficial to the conceptual framework because it has moderators such as privacy concerns, technology readiness, AI transparency, cultural readiness, and ethical perceptions. As an example, highly tech-ready consumers will be more inclined to think that AI personalization is innovative and effective, whereas consumers with low digital literacy levels might feel a sense of algorithmic anxiety, which results in avoidance-related behavior. Again, the cultural attitudes influence the attitude of the populace to the sharing of data and automation, and this impacts consent to the use of personalized services. The patterns of the industry, as demonstrated in Table 1, are of critical interest. E-commerce literature has a disproportionate focus on the functional value and purchase intentions (78% of papers in e-commerce), whereas tourism literature deals with hedonic and experiential aspects more (67% of papers in tourism). This disciplinary siloing can establish a false sense of distinction: e.g., the advanced literacy in the study of emotional interaction in tourism AI models can be useful in informing the strategies of e-commerce personalization, but the cross-disciplinary citation is low (only 12% of studies indicate literature outside their field of business). The lack of representation of African (5.2%) and South American exempla by the concentration of research in Asia (34.3%) and Europe (27.9%) creates further blind spots, especially since it has been indicated that cultural readiness moderates the effectiveness of personalization.

Contingency lays stress on the fact that a simplistic and one-size-fits-all approach to personalization is useless and even dangerous. Any successful strategies would need a keen sense of the target audience and a promise to design well. The personalization created by AI is not a value intrinsic to the technology but a product of how it matches the expectations of consumers, ethics, and whether the exchange process is perceived as fair. Organizations can therefore not afford a tunnel vision that only deals with the extent of personalization, but rather focus on the creation of trustworthy AI. This considers the autonomy of consumers and offers an affirmation of the exploitation of data.

6. IMPLICATIONS

The systematic review findings, analyzed based on PRISMA, produce important managerial practices, policy formulation, and research implications. Such implications are based on the dualistic character of AI-based personalization, its ability to create value and add risk at the same time. The essentiality of trust, transparency, and ethical governance in the determination of consumer outcomes.

6.1 Managerial Implications

In the case of practitioners, the results indicate that successful personalization is beyond technological advances through responsible design and open dialogue. Companies ought to focus more on transparency and explainability within their AI systems because AI transparency is one of the most important moderators that affect consumer trust. Publix could achieve fewer perceptions of manipulation by being transparent in its methods of collecting, analyzing, and using consumer data to create personalized recommendations, which creates a sense of user trust (Shin, 2021). The remaining stratified individualization procedures that must be implemented by the managers are that the reaction of consumers is heterogeneous regarding technology readiness, privacy concerns, and cultural orientation. The creation of adaptive personalization models where the consumer is able to tune the intensity and nature of personalization to their comfort level is respectful to consumer autonomy without causing a lack of engagement. Additionally, implementing the ethical principles of AI, such as fairness, accountability, and non-discrimination, into the design processes is not just a compliance requirement but a strategic differentiator. By actively incorporating ethical considerations into AI deployment, the organizations have a better chance of establishing long-term trust and preventing reputational damage to the organization in case the information is misused (Floridi et al., 2018). Lastly, since technology preparedness mediates personalization effectiveness, companies ought to invest in consumer education programs to boost digital literacy, especially among lower-technically proficient segments. It would expand the range of benefits of AI-centered services to all consumers.

6.2 Policy and Regulatory Implications

A policymaker cannot afford to rely on the period of GDPR, which was based on the principle of notice and consent. Regulatory trends of 2025-2026 and especially the adoption of the EU AI Act indicate that the world is placing more focus on defining AI usage (not only the data it takes in) itself, rather than the data it processes. Consequently, algorithm impact assessments are required for future systems under the regulation of certain personalization technologies, including those that are considered to be high-risk. This would entail firms taking the initiative to define and neutralize the possible harms against the autonomy of consumers, equity, and discrimination ahead of deployment. Moreover, it is important that these new AI rules become harmonized internationally so that the digital market will not become segmented and consumer protections will be disjointed according to the nation of operation.

6.3 Research Implications

This review reveals three fundamental contradictions that need to be addressed by scholars. To begin with, the personalization-privacy paradox has not been thoroughly theorized yet: 15.7% of investigations apply Privacy Calculus Theory; however, not many of them analyze how privacy computations by consumers may be systematically dissimilar between AI uses (e.g., recommendation systems vs. chatbots vs. predictive analytics). Second, a stronger concern for quantitative methods (56.4%) than qualitative techniques (26.7%) has resulted in further advanced measures of the outcomes, but less insight into the process by which consumers perceive, oppose, or accustom themselves to AI customization. The percentage of 16.9% of mixed methods indicates increased awareness of this gap, but integrated designs in their full-blooded form are an exception. Third, there is a novelty bias in the field: 53.5% of the studies reported after 2023 are on emerging AI applications without a longitudinal study of how empirical relationships between consumers and AI might develop over time. Future studies need to answer the question of whether or not the positive effects that have been reported on the first encounters last or fade away or alter with new repeated exposures.

7. LIMITATIONS AND FUTURE DIRECTIONS

Although the presented PRISMA-based systematic review presents the most extensive synthesis of the literature regarding AI-driven personalization, various limitations should be considered. First, the review is limited by depending on one database, namely Scopus, which, though extensive, may have missed other interesting studies that are indexed in other repositories like Web of Science or PubMed. Future studies ought to use multi-database searches to ascertain wider coverage of interdisciplinary scholarship. Second, non-English publications are excluded, which may be followed by the possibility of linguistic and cultural bias and the impossibility of generalizing the results to a context of different geographical and cultural periods. Cultural readiness was found to moderate the effectiveness of weight-maid in this review. Therefore, it is urgently required to justify and elaborate the idea conceptually by cross-cultural comparative studies.

Third, interventions that are included in studies tend to be cross-sectional and self-report, limiting causal inference and posing a potential threat of common method bias. The dynamic nature of consumer trust, engagement, and privacy perceptions warrants the application of longitudinal and experimental designs to unravel the nature of changes with time. Fourth, the scope of the review includes the analysis of peer-reviewed scholarly publications, excluding the grey literature, industry reports, and practitioner views that may provide useful insights on the emerging practices of personalization. Practitioner-oriented sources should also be incorporated in future research to solve the gap between theory and practice in the industry. Finally, the AI technological development is a developing phenomenon, and as such, the results are a reflection of a dynamic field.

As generative AI and synthetic media become increasingly embedded in consumer platforms, sustained scholarly inquiry is necessary to assess their impact on perceived authenticity, trust, and value creation. The rapid diffusion of systems such as ChatGPT demonstrates how generative AI is reshaping knowledge production and decision-making processes (Arshad et al., 2024). These developments raise important questions regarding transparency, personalization, integrity, and the long-term implications for consumer trust. New constructs of algorithmic fairness, perceived manipulation, and AI transparency should also be provided with powerful measurement tools in the future that will develop and provide increased diagnostic strength to the field of AI aspects, because empirical rigor will be increased, and meaningful cross-study comparisons will be feasible.

Also, the synthesis of the present review demonstrates the existence of publication bias: studies with positive effects of personalization (74% of quantitative studies) prevail by a significant margin over the ones with negative or neutral effects. This imbalance can be a preference of the journal to report on new positive discoveries, as well as a propensity among researchers to position personalization as naturally positive. The resultant effect is a literature that can systematically underestimate consumer resistance, algorithmic aversion, and the circumstances in which personalization backfires. Critical theorists have observed that the managerial inclination of the field to focus on the effects of firm-centric factors, such as loyalty and purchase intention, has precluded research on consumer welfare, digital labor, and the psychological cost of continuous mediation of algorithms.

8. CONCLUSION

This systematic review was conducted in the framework of PRISMA and has presented the integrated synthesis of the fragmented literature on the topic of AI-driven personalization and has elaborated on its dualistic and complex effects on consumer experience, value creation, and behavioral implications. The review is based on the Stimulus-Organism-Response (S-O-R) framework. Thus, AI-driven personalization is an effective stimulus that provides the possibility to create multidimensional value-functional, hedonic, personalization, convenience, and co-creation, on the one hand, and brings up serious problems of privacy, autonomy, and ethical responsibility on the other hand. The synthesis substantiates the fact that consumer perceptions and consumer trust, consumer satisfaction, and consumer engagement are important organismic processes that convert the features of personalization into behavioral reactions, including loyalty, purchase intention, and positive electronic word-of-mouth.

The review also highlights the fact that trust, which is developed by transparency, explainability, and fairness, becomes a key factor in determining successful consumer relations based on AI. Nonetheless, the personalization-privacy paradox has become a chronic conflict, where privacy, technology readiness, culture, and ethical perceptions are influential moderators that create the intensity and direction of the effects of personalization. These results confirm that the value created by AI personalization does not inherently engage the technology and is instead dependent on its correspondence to the expectations of the consumers, ethical management, and responsible practice. To scholars, this study leads to conceptual clarity involving the multiplication of theoretical perspectives and the finding of significant gaps to be filled in studies in the future.

As a practical guideline, it provides practitioners with suggestions on crafting transparent, flexible, and ethically informed personalization strategies. To policy-makers, it has presented a root of science to adhere to governance frameworks that strike a balance between innovation and consumer protection. The main conflict that was revealed in this review, the ability of personalization to both create value and create vulnerability, is bound to increase as AI technologies keep evolving. The generated evidence shows that responsible personalization is not only an ethical add-on but a strategic requirement: in the absence of transparency, fairness, and attention to consumer autonomy, even the very mechanisms that are responsible for value creation can lead to value destruction. The conceptual scaffolding of the latter way has been provided in this review; further elaboration by later scholarship can only be done. In the long term, responsible AI innovation requires a commitment to making technology a tool of personalization that is transformed into human-centric value creation, that is, transparency, fairness, and autonomy, before designing it from the outset.

REFERENCES

Afshar, M. Z., & Shah, M. H. (2025). Leveraging Porter's diamond model: Public sector insights. *The Critical Review of Social Sciences Studies, 3*(2), 2255-2271. https://doi.org/, Corpus ID: 279474427DOI: 10.59075/kkteax93

Ansari, A., Essegaier, S., & Kohli, R. (2000). Internet recommendation systems. *JMR, Journal of Marketing Research, 37*(3), 363–375. DOI: 10.1509/jmkr.37.3.363.18779

Arora, N., Dreze, X., Ghose, A., Hess, J. D., Iyengar, R., Jing, B., Joshi, Y., Kumar, V., Lurie, N., Neslin, S., Sajeesh, S., Su, M., Syam, N., Thomas, J., & Zhang, Z. J. (2008). Putting one-to-one marketing to work: Personalization, customization, and choice. *Marketing Letters, 19*(3), 305–321. https://ssrn.com/abstract=1118822. DOI: 10.1007/s11002-008-9056-z

Arshad, N., Baber, M. U., & Ullah, A. (2024). Assessing the transformative influence of ChatGPT on research practices among scholars in Pakistan. *Mesopotamian Journal of Big Data, 2024*(1), 1–10. DOI: 10.58496/MJBD/2024/001

Bleier, A., Harmeling, C. M., & Palmatier, R. W. (2019). Creating effective online customer experiences. *Journal of Marketing, 83*(2), 98–119. DOI: 10.1177/0022242918809930

Coelho, P. S., & Henseler, J. (2012). Creating customer loyalty through service customization. *European Journal of Marketing, 23*(3), 331–356. DOI: 10.1108/03090561211202503

Culnan, M. J., & Armstrong, P. K. (1999). Information privacy concerns, procedural fairness, and impersonal trust: An empirical investigation. *Organization Science, 23*(1), 99–128. DOI: 10.1287/orsc.10.1.104

Davenport, T. H., Guha, A., Grewal, D., & Bressgott, T. (2020). How artificial intelligence will change the future of marketing. *Journal of the Academy of Marketing Science, 48*(1), 24–42. DOI: 10.1007/s11747-019-00696-0

Davis, F. D. (1989). Perceived usefulness, perceived ease of use, and user acceptance of information technology. *Management Information Systems Quarterly, 13*(3), 319–340. DOI: 10.2307/249008

Duralia, O., Ogrean, C., ichindelean, M., & ichindelean, M. (2025). Decoding the Personalization-Privacy Paradox: From Thematic Scholarly Clusters to Practical Insights. *Studies in Business and Economics, 20*(2), 70–97. DOI: 10.2478/sbe-2025-0025

Faisal-E-Alam, M., Bhuiyan, M. R. I., Mimi, A., & Miah, M. T. (2025). The role of the three-zero framework in advancing global sustainable development through bibliometric and text mining analysis. *Discover Sustainability*, *6*(1), 1128. DOI: 10.1007/s43621-025-01919-x

Floridi, L., Cowls, J., Beltrametti, M., Chatila, R., Chazerand, P., Dignum, V., Luetge, C., Madelin, R., Pagallo, U., Rossi, F., Schafer, B., Valcke, P., & Vayena, E. (2018). AI4People—An ethical framework for a good AI society: Opportunities, risks, principles, and recommendations. *Minds and Machines*, *28*(4), 689–707. DOI: 10.1007/s11023-018-9482-5 PMID: 30930541

Gao, Y., & Liu, H. (2023). Artificial intelligence-enabled personalization in interactive marketing: A customer journey perspective. *Journal of Research in Interactive Marketing*, *17*(5), 663–680. DOI: 10.1108/JRIM-01-2022-0023

Grewal, D., Hulland, J., Kopalle, P. K., & Karahanna, E. (2020). The future of technology and marketing: A multidisciplinary perspective. *Journal of the Academy of Marketing Science*, *48*(1), 1–8. DOI: 10.1007/s11747-019-00711-4

Gupta, S., Kushwaha, P. S., Badhera, U., Chatterjee, P., & Gonzalez, E. D. S. (2023). Identification of benefits, challenges, and pathways in E-commerce industries: An integrated two-phase decision-making model. *Sustainable Operations and Computers*, *4*, 200–218. DOI: 10.1016/j.susoc.2023.08.005

Haleem, A., Javaid, M., Qadri, M. A., Singh, R. P., & Suman, R. (2022). Artificial intelligence (AI) applications for marketing: A literature-based study. *International Journal of Intelligent Networks*, *3*, 119–132. DOI: 10.1016/j.ijin.2022.08.005

Hollebeek, L. D., Sprott, D. E., & Brady, M. K. (2021). Rise of the machines? Customer engagement in automated service interactions. *Journal of Service Research*, *24*(1), 3–8. DOI: 10.1177/1094670520975110

Huang, M. H., & Rust, R. T. (2018). Artificial intelligence in service. *Journal of Service Research*, *21*(2), 155–172. DOI: 10.1177/1094670517752459

Husairi, M. A., & Rossi, P. (2024). Delegation of purchasing tasks to AI: The role of perceived choice and decision autonomy. *Decision Support Systems*, *179*, 114166. DOI: 10.1016/j.dss.2023.114166

Khatun, M., Hossain, R., Bhuiyan, M. R. I., Tabassum, M. N., & Riaj, M. A. J. (2025). Green entrepreneurship and digital transformation for sustainable development: A systematic review. *Digitizing green entrepreneurship*, 153-180. DOI: 10.4018/979-8-3693-7442-9.ch006

Kumari, A., & Laheri, V. K. (2025). Understanding consumer behavior through AI-Powered recommender systems: A systematic review and bibliometric perspective. *Indian Journal of Marketing*, 9-32. DOI: 10.17010/ijom/2025/v55/i8/175207

Larke, R., Kilgour, M., & O'Connor, H. (2018). Build touchpoints, and they will come: Transitioning to omnichannel retailing. *International Journal of Physical Distribution & Logistics Management, 48*(4), 465–483. DOI: 10.1108/IJPDLM-09-2016-0276

Lee, S. B. (2020). Chatbots and communication: The growing role of artificial intelligence in addressing and shaping customer needs. *Business communication research and practice, 3*(2), 103-111. https://doi.org/DOI: 10.22682/bcrp.2020.3.2.103

Lemon, K. N., & Verhoef, P. C. (2016). Understanding customer experience throughout the customer journey. *Journal of Marketing, 80*(6), 69–96. DOI: 10.1509/jm.15.0420

Lindström, T., & Österberg, F. (2020). Evolution of biobased and nanotechnology packaging–a review. *Nordic Pulp & Paper Research Journal, 35*(4), 491–515. DOI: 10.1515/npprj-2020-0042

Martin, K. D., & Murphy, P. E. (2017). The role of data privacy in marketing. *Journal of the Academy of Marketing Science, 45*(2), 135–155. DOI: 10.1007/s11747-016-0495-4

Mittameedi, S. K., Dogra, V., & Sayal, A. (2025). *Customer experience in e-commerce: A systematic review of metrics, models, and the role of AI*. IEEE. DOI: 10.1109/ACCESS.2025.3600729

Mohammadkhani, D., Majedi, N., Biniaz, S. A., & Sarhadi, M. (2025). AI-Driven Personalization Strategies and Their Impact on Consumer Engagement in Digital Markets. *Digital Transformation and Administration Innovation*, 1-14. https://doi.org/DOI: 10.4018/979-8-3693-3691-5.ch008

Parkes, T. (2018). *How One Retailer Is Shifting to an AI-First Mentality*. Think with Google. DOI: 10.31893/multirev.2025224

Qin, X., Zhou, X., Chen, C., Wu, D., Zhou, H., Dong, X., Cao, L., & Lu, J. G. (2025). AI aversion or appreciation? A capability–personalization framework and a meta-analytic review. *Psychological Bulletin, 151*(5), 580–599. DOI: 10.1037/bul0000477 PMID: 40489180

Rayun, S. N., Salam, M. A., Islam, W., & Leong, V. S. (2026). Green FinTech Innovations: Empowering Inclusive Development and Advancing Towards the Sustainable Economy. In *Promoting Inclusivity and Accessibility With FinTech* (pp. 245-278). IGI Global Scientific Publishing. DOI: 10.4018/979-8-3373-1112-8.ch009

Riaj, M. A. J., Tabassum, M. N., Hossain, R., Bhuiyan, M. R. I., & Khatun, M. (2025). Digitalization transformation in entrepreneurship and enterprise green innovation. In *Digitizing green entrepreneurship* (pp. 181–204). IGI Global Scientific Publishing. DOI: 10.4018/979-8-3693-7442-9.ch007

Ricci, F., Rokach, L., & Shapira, B. (2021). Recommender systems: Techniques, applications, and challenges. *Recommender Systems Handbook*, 1-35. DOI: 10.1007/978-1-4899-7637-6_1

Riikkinen, M., Saarijärvi, H., Sarlin, P., & Lähteenmäki, I. (2018). Using artificial intelligence to create value in insurance. *International Journal of Bank Marketing*, *36*(6), 1145–1168. DOI: 10.1108/IJBM-01-2017-0015

Rossi, J., & Bianchini, A. (2022). "Plastic waste free"–A new circular model for the management of plastic packaging in the food value chain. *Transportation Research Procedia*, *67*, 153–162. DOI: 10.1016/j.trpro.2022.12.046

Salam, M. A., Leong, V. S., & Muhamad, N. (2026). The Transformative Prospects of AI-Powered Virtual Influencers in Digital Consumer Engagement and Marketing Strategies. In *Cases on Social Media Marketing Engagement Tactics* (pp. 251–290). IGI Global Scientific Publishing. DOI: 10.4018/979-8-3373-2357-2.ch009

Salam, M. A., Rayun, S. N., Islam, W., Hasan, R., Firmansyah, E. A., & Kalinaki, K. (2024). Consumer engagement: exploring deepfake applications in consumer marketing communication. In *Navigating the World of Deepfake Technology* (pp. 397–421). IGI Global Scientific Publishing. DOI: 10.4018/979-8-3693-5298-4.ch020

Sayem, M. A., Anwar, A. S., Dutta, S., Sikder, R., & Kar, M. R. (2026). *Pathfinder AI: Decentralizing Career Mobility for the Underserved and Next-Gen Workforce* (Master's thesis, University of the Cumberlands). https://www.proquest.com/openview/49ab69e4d00605a4ddd2906622470d30/1?pq-origsite=gscholar&cbl=18750&diss=y

Shahriare Satu, M., Yeasmin, T., & Abdus Salam, M. (2023, December). Towards an AutoML-based data analytical framework for predicting bankruptcy in the industrial sector. In *International Conference on Trends in Electronics and Health Informatics* (pp. 699-712). Singapore: Springer Nature Singapore. DOI: 10.1007/978-981-97-3937-0_48

Shin, D. (2021). The effects of explainability and causability on perception, trust, and acceptance: Implications for explainable AI. *International Journal of Human-Computer Studies*, *146*, 102551. DOI: 10.1016/j.ijhcs.2020.102551

Snyder, H. (2019). Literature review as a research methodology: An overview and guidelines. *Journal of Business Research, 104*, 333–339. DOI: 10.1016/j.jbusres.2019.07.039

Song, C., Shin, S. Y., & Shin, K. S. (2024). Implementing the dynamic feedback-driven learning optimization framework: A machine learning approach to personalize educational pathways. *Applied Sciences (Basel, Switzerland), 14*(2), 916. DOI: 10.3390/app14020916

Thomas, J., & Harden, A. (2008). Methods for the thematic synthesis of qualitative research in systematic reviews. *BMC Medical Research Methodology, 8*(1), 45. http://www.biomedcentral.com/1471-2288/8/45. DOI: 10.1186/1471-2288-8-45 PMID: 18616818

Timimi, H., Baaddi, M., & Bennouna, A. (2025). Impact of artificial intelligence on the personalization of the customer experience: A systematic literature review. *Multidiscip. Rev., 8*(7), 2025224. DOI: 10.31893/multirev.2025224

Tran, M. T. (2026). Advancing retail and service strategies: AI-driven consumer behavior prediction, gamification, and ethical marketing. *Journal of Retailing and Consumer Services, 88*, 104558. DOI: 10.1016/j.jretconser.2025.104558

Tussyadiah, I. (2020). A review of research into automation in tourism: Launching the Annals of Tourism Research Curated Collection on Artificial Intelligence and Robotics in Tourism. *Annals of Tourism Research, 81*, 102883. DOI: 10.1016/j.annals.2020.102883

Ullah, A., & Khan, S. D. (2024). Impact of sound decision-making on small and medium businesses in Pakistan. *International Journal of Asian Business and Management, 3*(2), 177–192. DOI: 10.55927/ijabm.v3i2.9101

Vargo, S. L., & Lusch, R. F. (2008). Service-dominant logic 2025. *Journal of the Academy of Marketing Science, 36*(1), 1–10. DOI: 10.1007/s11747-007-0069-6

Venkatachalam, P., & Ray, S. (2022). How do context-aware artificial intelligence algorithms used in fitness recommender systems? A literature review and research agenda. *International Journal of Information Management Data Insights, 2*(2), 100139. DOI: 10.1016/j.jjimei.2022.100139

Vidhya, V., Donthu, S., Veeran, L., Lakshmi, Y. S., & Yadav, B. (2023). The intersection of AI and consumer behavior: Predictive models in modern marketing. *Remittances Review, 8*(4), 2410–2424. DOI: 10.33182/rr.v8i4.166

Wedel, M., & Kannan, P. K. (2016). Marketing analytics for data-rich environments. *Journal of Marketing, 80*(6), 97–121. DOI: 10.1509/jm.15.0413

Weippert, M. (2024). The scope and intensity of personalised omnichannel customer journeys: A conceptualisation integrating experts' and consumers' perspectives. *Journal of Marketing Management*, *40*(11-12), 877–909. DOI: 10.1080/0267257X.2024.2388088

Wertenbroch, K., Schrift, R. Y., Alba, J. W., Barasch, A., Bhattacharjee, A., Giesler, M., Knobe, J., Lehmann, D. R., Matz, S., Nave, G., Parker, J. R., Puntoni, S., Zheng, Y., & Zwebner, Y. (2020). Autonomy in consumer choice. *Marketing Letters*, *31*(4), 429–439. DOI: 10.1007/s11002-020-09521-z PMID: 32836798

Zuboff, S. (2023). The age of surveillance capitalism. In *Social theory re-wired* (pp. 203–213). Routledge. DOI: 10.4324/9781003320609-27

Chapter 7
AI-Driven Transformation Digital Marketing:
Boosting Engagement and Trust With AI-Generated Videos in Tourism

Khaled Hossain Rocky
http://orcid.org/0009-0006-1153-7024
Noakhali Science and Technology University, Bangladesh

Shadiah Rahman
http://orcid.org/0009-0002-2615-1774
Noakhali Science and Technology University, Bangladesh

Egi Arvian Firmansyah
http://orcid.org/0000-0001-5296-706X
Universitas Padjadjaran, Indonesia

Md. Shafi Noor Islam
http://orcid.org/0000-0001-8601-0952
Universiti Brunei Darussalam, Brunei

ABSTRACT

The fast development of artificial intelligence is driving radical changes in online marketing activities in the tourism sector. The chapter is rigorous in analyzing the growing importance of AI-generated videos as a pioneering tool for enhancing consumer interaction and building trust in tourism marketing. It examines how smart technologies enable tourism organizations to create highly customized, immersive, and scalable visual content that engages potential travelers and builds destination

DOI: 10.4018/979-8-2600-2977-0.ch007

brand equity. The chapter uses theoretical models such as the Stimulus-Organism-Response model, consumer engagement theory, and trust theory to explain the effects of AI-generated visual content on travelers' cognitive, affective, and behavioral responses. In general, the chapter highlights AI-generated video as a tactical tool that reshapes tourism communication and enhances the efficiency of digital marketing in a highly competitive global tourism environment.

INTRODUCTION: THE INTELLIGENT SHIFT IN TOURISM COMMUNICATION

In recent years, artificial intelligence (AI) has made a significant impact on the world of digital marketing, with new approaches to support customer engagement and enhance the branding experience (Dumitriu & Popescu, 2020). Within the tourism sector, innovations led by Artificial Intelligence (AI), particularly those that AI generated video contents, have emerged as powerful tools for audience engagement and trust building. The current chapter examines the central role of AI in tourism marketing and highlights the specific role that AI-generated videos will play in boosting consumer engagement, building trust in the brand, and creating personalized, impactful experiences for travelers. Despite the growing body of research on artificial intelligence in tourism marketing, existing studies largely focus on general AI applications, with limited attention to the specific role of AI-generated video in shaping consumer engagement and trust. Moreover, prior literature often examines engagement and trust independently, lacking an integrated theoretical perspective such as the SOR framework to explain their combined effects. Therefore, this chapter addresses this gap by providing a unified analysis of how AI-generated video influences both engagement and trust within tourism marketing contexts. From a consumer behavior perspective, demonstrates that AI-generated videos significantly affect cognitive and affective responses, which in turn drive behavioral intentions and tourism-related decision-making.

The Digital Acceleration of Tourism Marketing

In the digital era, consumer behavior is driven by interactive and personalized content, particularly AI-generated media. Tourism marketing has seen a quick digitalization, due to the increasing growth in the use of online search engines, social media networks and video platforms by travelers to plan their itinerary. Consequently, destinations are forced to compete in real time for attention by deploying data-analytic techniques and automated systems to conduct more targeted and empirically measurable promotional campaigns. Digital acceleration refers to the rapid (and often pandemic-spurred) development of digital channels, tools and consumer behavior in both the consumer journey and in the marketing discipline (Kane et al., 2019). Tourism digital marketing can be defined as the use of digital platforms (such as websites, search engine marketing, social media networks, electronic mail and mobile applications) in the promotion of destinations, experiences and related services. The integration of AI technologies is transforming how consumers search, evaluate, and select tourism services. Digital tools and technologies have risen to a main role in the promotion of destinations as well as their management, thus enabling businesses or organizations to reach further audiences than is possible through traditional means. The chapter benefits from highlighting the broader evolution of AI in digital marketing across various industries, adding academic depth. Including a discussion on adoption challenges like cost, complexity, and skill gaps would enhance its practical relevance. This balanced approach strengthens both the theoretical and applied perspectives of the work. Social media networks like Instagram, Facebook and TikTok - offer tourism marketers the tools to promote destinations through visually compelling content that generate emotional and intellectual engagement amongst prospective travelers. Additionally, online review platforms like TripAdvisor and Google Reviews allow tourists to share stories about their experiences, which creates user generated content that has significant impact on travel decision making processes. Furthermore, search engine optimization (SEO) combined with targeted marketing on the Web ensures promotional efforts achieve visibility among users who are actively seeking travel information, thus enhancing reach as well as efficacy (Xiang & Gretzel, 2010).

Key Objectives

- Artificial Intelligence (AI): Computer systems that perform tasks requiring human-like intelligence, such as learning, prediction, or content generation.
- Consumer Engagement: Consumer engagement refers to the level of engagement, affective commitment and participatory behavior that consumers show towards a brand, product or digital content across online platforms.
- Digital Marketing: Digital marketing is the strategic use of technologies, digital platforms and online communication tools for the promotion of products, services or destinations, as well as for establishing relational dynamics with target audiences.
- AI Generated Video: AI-generated video is the visual content that is either created or augmented with artificial intelligence technologies, thereby allowing the autonomous generation of animations, voice narration or realistic video scenes for the purposes of marketing and communication.

- Trust in Tourism Brands: Trust in tourism brands is equivalent to the trust that travelers develop in a destination, tourism company or service provider with regard to perceived reliability, credibility and authenticity of the information received.
- Personalization: Personalization is the process of personalizing marketing messages, recommendations or digital experiences to match the individual preferences, behaviors and interests of specific users.
- Tourism Communication: Tourism communication is the set of strategies and channels used by tourism organizations to distribute information, to promote tourism destinations and to shape the perception and decision-making process of travelers.

The rise of mobile technologies has also accelerated the phenomenon of digital acceleration, as travelers continue to use smartphones to plan all elements of their trips. Through mobile applications, users have access to customized recommendations, carefully crafted itinerary creation, and real-time booking capabilities, thus providing for a frictionless customer experience (Lemon & Verhoef, 2016). Big data analytics is taking on a key role in understanding this treasure chest of information, which can be used by tourism companies to understand patterns of behavior, anticipate demand and tailor marketing strategies to specific groups of consumers. Influencer marketing has also gained a significant rise in prominence, as social media influencers are gaining the ability to target niche audiences with authentic content that has the potential to resonate more deeply than traditional advertisements. Moreover, the fusion of virtual reality (VR) and augmented reality (AR) technologies gives prospective tourists a chance to virtually immerse themselves in the locale before making their visit, which in turn, intensifies engagement and purchase intent (Nayyar et al., 2018). Email marketing, personalized newsletters, and loyalty programs all continue to play an indispensable role in maintaining an ongoing relationship with travelers that helps to encourage repeat visits and positive word-of-mouth promotion. The employment of the aforementioned digital strategies was accelerated by the Covid-19 pandemic, as travel restrictions forced tourism businesses to turn to online channels for engagement, promotion and service delivery. Consequently, digital acceleration has made marketing in tourism more quantifiable, agile and responsive, as data-driven insights allow to continuously optimize campaigns . Finally, sustainability and ethical tourism are also getting to the foreground of digital campaigns, as eco-conscious travelers are seeking sustainable and ethical travel experiences, making marketers focus on highlighting environmental and cultural initiatives.

Figure 1. Core Characteristics of Digital Acceleration in Tourism

(Hu et al., 2025).

This Figure 1 is a graphical representation of the basic characteristics driving digital acceleration in the tourism industry. At its nucleus, it highlights the critical role played by Digital Transformation in the tourism area.

Surrounding this nucleus are ten different parts that define the indispensable elements:

1. **Sustainability Integration:** The integration of sustainability will guarantee that the activities of the tourism have minimum environmental impact and encourage responsible tourism. It promotes green policies, resource optimization,

and increases the benefits to the local communities and maintains business development.

2. **Enhanced Personalization:** Increased personalization uses the data on customers to customize experiences and services according to their preferences. This includes tailor-made schedules, suggestions and deals that enhance interaction and contentment.
3. **Automation of Services:** Service automation uses technology to automate the common functions like booking, check-in and customer services. It saves man hours, enhances productivity and provides quicker and more reliable service.
4. **AI-Driven Content Creation:** AI-based content creation involves the use of artificial intelligence to create applicable marketing content, travel guides, and suggestions. This allows prompt, personalized, and interactive content that will improve the traveler experience.
5. **Seamless Connectivity:** The smooth connectivity ensures continuous digital connectivity between platforms and devices. It enables the tourist to receive real-time information, communicate and have a connected travel experience.
6. **Cloud-Based Operations:** Cloud-based operations facilitate remote management, data storage and collaboration of tourism services. They are scalable, flexible and real time analytical, thus enhancing operational efficiency and decision making.

AI as a Strategic Disruptor in Visual Promotion

Artificial Intelligence is not an instrument, but a strategic disrupter that re-forms the planning, production and optimization of visual promotion (Doborjeh et al., 2021). It allows tourism marketers to pivot from one campaign at a time analyses to a continuous, data-driven, highly personalized narrative framework. A strategic disruptor refers to a technology or force that fundamentally alters competitive logic, processes and determinants of success in a sector. Visual promotion, in this context, refers to the use of images, graphics and video to represent and promote destinations and experiential offerings. AI-generated videos significantly influence consumers' cognitive evaluations by enhancing perceived realism and informativeness.

Generative AI is crushing tourism video marketing by automating the production of quality material, including stunning scenic imagery, professional voice over narration, and editing of seamless post production videos, all with minimal human touch (Saleh, 2025). Such technology combines synthetic constructs - virtual hosts or AI avatars which represent destinations in ways that defy traditional notions of authenticity and which opens up new creative possibilities for building and interacting with narratives. Collectively, these capabilities transmute tourism marketing into an intellectualized, expedient and immersive enterprise, that not only secures the attention of the viewer but generates more profound emotional affiliations with would-be travelers.

Table 1. Traditional vs AI-Driven Tourism Communication

Dimension	Traditional tourism communication	AI-driven tourism communication
Content creation	Human-created photos, videos, brochures, copywriting.	Algorithmic generation of images, scripts, and videos.
Personalization	Generic messages for broad segments.	Fine-grained personalization using behavioral and preference data.
Speed & scalability	Slow, campaign-based, limited output.	Always-on, scalable content production and optimization.
Interactivity	Mostly one-way communication.	Interactive chats, adaptive videos, virtual tours and guides.
Main challenge	Limited reach and measurability.	Trust, authenticity, and ethical concerns about AI content.

The Emergence of AI Generated Video in Destination Branding

The dawn of video created with artificial intelligence has caused a paradigm shift in destination branding, giving tourism marketers unprecedented opportunities to interact with prospective visitors through immersive, personalized, and scalable media forms. Conventional video marketing within the tourism sector has largely been dependent on labor-intensive, manually organized production flows, which have been long and capital-intensive in nature, thereby limiting the scope for adaptability to the changing market dynamics. Such content may include virtual tours, animated sequences, and synthetic narrative constructs and thus does not require conventional production crews and physical filming expeditions. Destination branding is reliant on visual storytelling, AI generated video gives the ability to mimic the experience of travel, highlight otherwise unreachable attractions, and create multiple iterate variations for heterogeneous cohorts of people. The resultant media is not only economically efficient and capacity scalable, but enables the accurate targeting of micro segments of travelers through bespoke data driven messaging (Powers & Sterling, 2008).

In contrast to traditional post-production pipelines, AI-powered tools are now being used to allow for the automated generation of high-quality videos, without any issues with integrating scenic imagery, dynamically produced voiceovers, and professional editing stages, while requiring minimal human supervision. Such automation is used to reduce the costs of time and money while also allowing destinations to maintain a cohesive and aesthetically pleasing presence across various digital media channels.

Table 2. AI Capabilities in Tourism Visual Promotion

AI Capability	Example in Tourism Marketing	Strategic Impact
Generative video	Text-to-video tour of a beach or city skyline	Faster, cheaper creative production at scale
Personalization engine	Showing tailored activities based on user data	Higher relevance and engagement, improved CTR and conversions
Predictive analytics	Forecasting which visuals drive more visits or bookings	Better media allocation and creative strategy
Chatbots & agents	Video-guided virtual assistants for trip planning	Enhanced pre-trip experience and information quality
Synthetic influencers	AI-generated "local guides" promoting destinations	Novel brand image but potential trust risks

A major strength of the visual media generated by AI is the ability to hyper-personalize. Sophisticated algorithms can make content dynamically adaptive to discrete groups of travelers, such as families, adventure and cultural lovers, and as such, align messaging, images, and storytelling to the respective interests of each group. This way, such systems boost user engagement, a higher possibility of the potential travelers considering the destination, and the emotional connection of potential visitors to the destination.

Impact on Tourism Branding

The advent of AI generated video is a game-changer in the field of tourism marketing, bringing unprecedented benefits with respect to consistency, engagement and scalability, thus redefining the capabilities of traditional promotional strategies. By leveraging powerful algorithms, brands are now able to create high quality visual content that strictly follows an established brand narrative, which is difficult to accomplish using conventional means. Firstly, AI-generated video ensures consistency with its unified brand identity across an array of digital platforms. The technology allows for the systematic standardization of visual elements color palettes, typography, tonal messaging and storytelling across a multitude of video outputs (Sales et al., 2012). As such, the brand image of the destination is recognizable and coherent regardless of the medium and audience segment, which helps to strengthen the brand's recall and establish trust among potential visitors. Academic research often highlights the importance of visual consistency when it comes to brand differentiation and the reproducibility offered by AI is a powerful solution to this age-old challenge. Secondly, the ability of AI-generated video to increase engagement is huge. By creating immersive stories with arresting visuals, these videos are able to quickly draw in the attention of viewers in a saturated social media environment, where the viewer is constantly being distracted. Features such as dynamic transitions, personalized judgements and interactive features encourage audiences to engage with the story line and therefore increase engagement time. The combination of emotional storytelling and high-quality visuals promote greater emotional connections with the potential tourist, which empirically leads to more travel consideration and the likelihood of positive word of mouth diffusion. Thirdly, AI enables incredible scalability, which allows marketers to create an astonishing array of video variants with very little extra effort. This scalability not only prepares destinations to address heterogeneous markets at the same time, but also to test different content for the best performance and respond quickly to new trends or seasonal relevant campaigns, retaining a proactive competitive position. In sum, by combining consistency, engagement and scalability, AI generated video gives tourism brands the tool of a powerful, flexible presence (Seo et al., 2020). These effectively highlights the transformative potential of AI-generated video content, offering valuable insights into its strategic role in enhancing tourism marketing and consumer engagement. It provides a strong and forward-looking perspective that aligns well with current digital innovation trends in the tourism industry. The technology enables more effective communication with a variety of audiences around the world and gets the most out of the marketing investment, ushering in a new era of strategic brand management in the tourism sector.

Why Consumer Engagement and Trust Matter More Than Ever

AI-generated videos have emerged as a powerful tool in tourism marketing, but their success depends not only on capturing attention but also on building consumer trust. Although engagement rates, including likes, shares, comments, and click-through rates (CTR) are all these metrics provide a quantitative view of the degree of cognitive, emotional, and behavioral involvement that a viewer shows in the marketing content (Wang et al., 2019). It is essential to acknowledge that high engagement is not a sufficient measure when the audiences feel that the content is inauthentic or misleading. As an example, empirical research proves that customized AI-generated videos show the strong effect of CTR increase by 28 per cent compared to 15 per cent of the lift by conventional advertisement, thus proving their effectiveness in capturing attention and encouraging further user engagement. However, the more consumers are increasingly aware of AI-generated content, the more trust becomes the key factor to influence their destination attitude. Consumer trust, which can be described as the belief that the content, as well as the brand present within it, is honest and reliable, and that it is in the best interest of the viewer, has a strong impact on the transfer of marketing content into travel intentions. According to scholarly studies, about 83 percent of consumers have already seen videos that they believe to be AI-created; moreover, although a third of people who watch such videos are as confident in AI and other content as in human-created material, 36 percent of respondents state that AI videos can make brands less trusted. This confirms the dominant role of the concept of transparency and perceived authenticity: the viewers will be most likely to positively react to the AI-generated tourism videos in case they believe that the information is correct, truthful, and reflects the real experience of the destination. Without trust, even high engagement might result in temporary clicks but might trigger permanent cynicism or even a backlash, thus eventually violating the overall marketing campaign effectiveness. As a result, effective AI-based tourism marketing requires a delicate balance between appealing and visually attractive visuals, personal storytelling, and clear and credible messaging so that the AI-based videos can substantially strengthen the attraction and credibility of the message that will help a destination to influence consumer attitudes and ultimately their travel intentions (Argyriou & Melewar, 2011).

Figure 2. Relationship Between Engagement, Trust, and AI-Generated Video

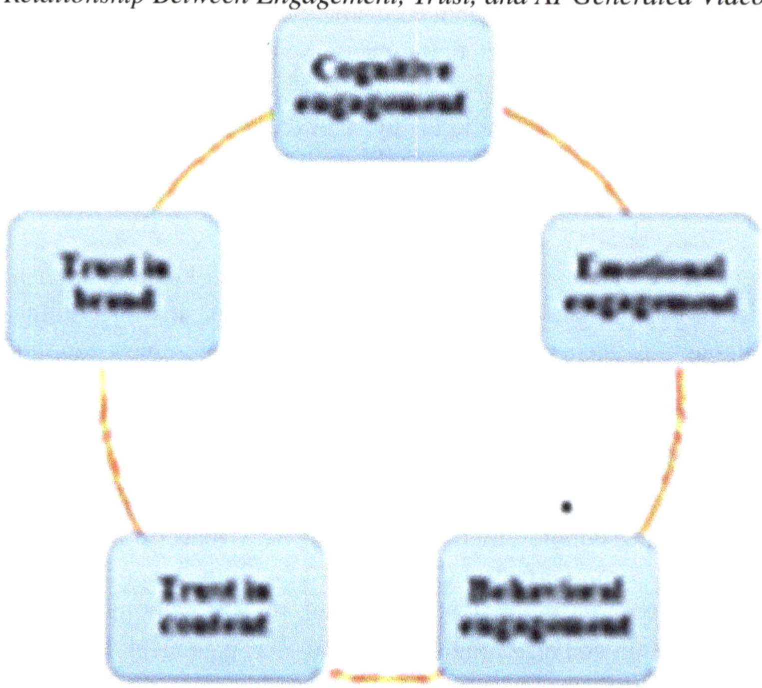

OBJECTIVES AND SCOPE OF THE CHAPTER

The chapter attempts to theorize and critically review how AI-based change, especially AI-generated video, transforms consumer interaction and belief in tourism digital marketing. It focuses on the positions and the approaches of the destination marketing organizations (DMOs), tourism boards, and travel brands that take advantage of the video content created through AI to manipulate consumer perceptions and behaviors on diverse digital platforms.

Proposed objectives

AI in Tourism Marketing: In essence, AI can be extremely useful in accelerating digital marketing in tourism since it is capable of generating content automatically and optimizing campaigns to suit better. This allows destinations to access more individuals in a shorter period of time and provide them with personalized experiences that are no longer generic. The visual aspect of AI makes marketing flashy as it creates slick, engaging multimedia content that attracts attention.

AI-Generated Videos in Destination Branding: AI-generated video is used to assist places in creating and enhancing their brand image through demonstrating exclusive experiences in a unique manner. It also gives opportunities to customized narration and vivid images besides reducing the cost of production that is costly. On the other side, we are still left to contend with the issue of keeping videos authentic and not losing the trust of viewers.

Impact on Consumer Interaction: These videos made by AI, in fact, influence our thoughts, feelings, and behavior by grabbing our attention, evoking emotion, and motivating us to socialize. The content will be personal and hence we will be more likely to spend additional time watching the videos and engaging with them. With a high level of engagement, individuals become more interested in the destination and may make a booking.

Creating Consumer Trust: The credibility of the AI-generated videos is what builds trust. Honesty regarding the use of AI and presenting true images of destinations can be used to gain confidence. Without trust, the engagement may not last long and will not translate into actual travel intent.

Managerial and Ethical Implications: As tourism marketers, we must consider how we practice AI videos in a responsible and ethical manner. The choices concerning transparency, authenticity, and our target audience influence our brand perception. Managers ought to come up with measures that will strike a balance between technological innovation and ethical marketing in order to retain consumer trust in the long term.

Figure 3. Pyramid of AI Impact in Tourism Marketing

THEORETICAL FOUNDATIONS OF AI DRIVEN DIGITAL MARKETING

Evolution from Web 1.0 to Intelligent Marketing Systems

Developing out of Web 1.0. The shift between Web 1.0 and AI-based intelligent marketing systems is the beginning of a new era in online communication. Web 1.0 was more of a passive storage of information and people were passive consumers of information. The websites used in tourism at this period were more of digital brochures, which had minimal interaction and no personalization. The advent of Web 2.0 transformed digital marketing: social media like Facebook and Instagram created user-generated content, peer reviews, and interaction between users. Tourism brands thus changed the direction of promotion to a participatory dialogue which enabled the travelers to co-create destination stories. Web 3.0 brought in semantic technologies, interoperability of data, and algorithmic personalization with a focus on machine readability to enable systems to understand user preferences and provide customized content. The latest phase is commonly known as intelligent marketing systems and it incorporates artificial intelligence, machine learning, predictive analytics, and natural language processing. AI systems in tourism marketing create personalized itineraries, suggest destinations, and create immersive promotional videos. This development indicates the transition of mass communication to predictive and hyper personalized engagement ecosystems.

Defining AI Generated Video Technology

The idea of AI-generated video technology is to use highly sophisticated computational models, such as generative adversarial networks, diffusion models, and transformer architectures, to create synthetic and yet realistic video content. Such systems are used to create visual stories based on textual prompts, datasets, or fixed images. Sora and Runway ML are examples of platforms that use AI to develop cinematic travel experiences, without having to be filmed physically. This capability in tourism allows creation of virtual tours, animated storytelling, cultural reconstructions and simulations of experience at much reduced cost and time. In contrast to the classical CGI generation, AI systems acquire the patterns of a large amount of data and dynamically change the outputs based on user requests. This is a democratization of content creation, especially to small and medium tourism enterprises. Nevertheless, the authenticity, misinformation, and transparency are also ethical issues of the AI-created videos due to their realism. Transparent disclosure systems thus become necessary to maintain consumer confidence.

Consumer Engagement Theory in Digital Environments

Consumer engagement theory does not only rely on the transactional interactions but focuses on cognitive, emotional, and behavioral investment on brand experiences. The interaction in digital environments is influenced by interactivity, immersion, and personalization. Theory Theoretical basis the theory has its origins in flow theory, introduced by Mihaly Csikszentmihalyi, in which people are said to be engaged in a deep state when the difficulties and abilities are balanced optimally. AI-created tourism videos provide a better flow experience with immersive storytelling, interactive hotspots, and customized narrative paths. As an example, an AI video with a customized cultural experience can cause emotional appeal and engagement. Engagement can thus be converted into quantifiable results in the form of increased viewing time, sharing on social media, favorable word of mouth, and intention to book. Therefore, AI is changing passive consumption to active digital engagement, which enhances consumer-brand relations.

Trust Theory and Perceived Authenticity

The conceptualization of trust theory as a multidimensional construct, which is founded on perceptions of competence, integrity, and benevolence, gives trust its conceptualization. The basic theory created by Roger Mayer and others states that the trust is established when the consumers feel that a brand is able, sincere, and has good intentions. Perceived authenticity is a key factor of trust in AI-generated tourism videos. Synthetic content that is hyper-realistic can result in distrust when consumers suspect that they are being manipulated or that they are being deceived. Perceived credibility is increased by transparent disclosure, ethical labeling and persistent branding (Kubiszewski et al., 2011).

Applying SOR Framework in AI Based Tourism Marketing

The Stimulus Organism Response framework, introduced by Albert Mehrabian and James A. Russell, provides a structured theoretical model for analyzing AI based tourism marketing.

Within the figure 4 framework:

Stimulus refers to AI generated video content, including immersive destination visuals, virtual experiences, and personalized narratives.

Organism represents internal consumer evaluations, including emotional responses such as excitement or awe and cognitive perceptions such as realism or perceived value.

Response includes behavioral outcomes such as engagement, trust formation, sharing behavior, and booking intention.

Figure 4. Applying the SOR Framework in AI-Based Tourism Marketing

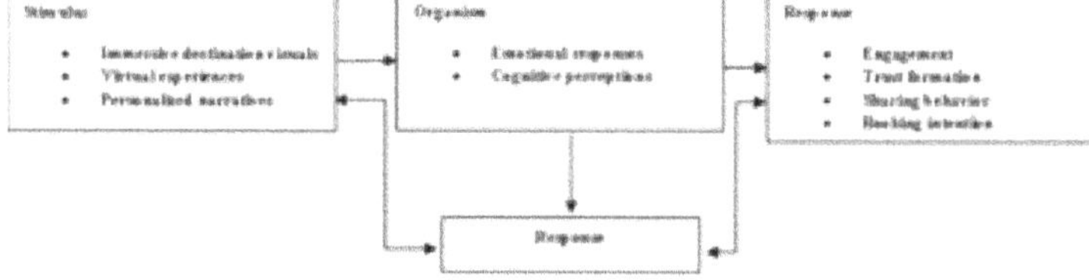

Applying the figure 4 model strengthens academic rigor by linking technological stimuli to measurable psychological and behavioral outcomes. It offers a testable pathway for empirical research in AI driven tourism marketing.

AI GENERATED VIDEOS AS A MARKETING INNOVATION TOOL

The conceptual bases of AI-based digital marketing lie in a spectrum of complementary views explaining the role of technology in the perception, engagement, and decision-making of consumers. The Technology Acceptance Model explains the impact of the perceived usefulness and perceived ease of use on the intentions of individuals to adopt AI-enabled platforms and tools. Likewise, the Unified Theory of Acceptance and Use of Technology outlines the performance expectancy, effort expectancy, social influence, and facilitating conditions roles in predicting behavioral intention towards AI-powered marketing systems. Psychologically, the Stimulus Organism Response Model provides a very powerful explanatory model, in which AI-generated content like customized videos or chatbots is the stimulus, internal cognitive and emotional assessments are the organism, and engagement or purchase intention is the response. Also, Relationship Marketing Theory emphasizes the fact that long-term interaction, trust building, and customer loyalty are crucial and all of them are becoming mediated by intelligent systems that can perform real-time personalization. Media Richness Theory also supports the idea that AI-enhanced multimedia messages can contribute to the clarity of the message and the level of ambiguity, thus, supporting the consumer comprehension and engagement. Together, these theoretical lenses provide a cohesive basis on the study of the impact of AI-driven digital marketing on consumer engagement, trust, and behavioral outcomes in the modern digital context.

Automated Storytelling and Smart Content Creation

Automated storytelling is a machine-generated storytelling technology that uses AI to transform raw data into emotionally engaging stories. The AI machines examine search behavior, travelers, and cultural data to produce scripts, images, and voiceovers that resonate with the psychographic profiles of the target customers. With platforms in tourism marketing, it is possible to generate multilingual destination stories without actors or studios, significantly lowering the cost of production and speeding up the delivery of campaigns. The smart content creation also allows the ongoing optimization; AI measures the behavior of viewers and adjusts the pace, tone, and imagery to increase retention. As a result, tourism brands will be able to create scalable and data-driven storytelling, which evolves in response to audience engagement patterns.

Hyper Personalization in Tourism Promotion

Hyper personalization is the most advanced stage of AI-based marketing, which goes beyond the traditional segmentation and focuses on individuals in real-time (Jain et al., 2021). Instead of categorizing consumers into fixed groups, like age or location, AI systems examine dynamic behavioral signals, including search intent, clickstream data, past bookings, device use, interaction time and sentiment signals, to form a granular profile. Machine-learning, predictive analytics, and natural language processing can help platforms evolve by learning over time through interactions with users and improving the content shown on the platform, creating a feedback loop that gradually increases the accuracy of recommendations. It can be theoretically explained through the Stimulus Organism Response Model: the personalized video/message is the stimulus; the cognitive evaluation of the consumer, perceived relevance, and the resulting higher engagement, longer viewing time, sharing behavior, or purchase intention is the organism; and the response is the resultant higher engagement, longer viewing time, sharing behavior, or purchase intent. Hyper-personalization reduces information overload and increases the confidence in decisions by mirroring the preferences and values of an individual. As an example, when a traveler regularly visits eco-tourism and sustainable travel blogs, AI systems can recommend a destination video that predicts green hotels, community-based tourism, local conservation initiatives, and genuine cultural activities, which can increase the perceived authenticity and personal fit. Empirical evidence provided by organizations like McKinsey and Company suggests that high-level personalization plans can significantly enhance customer satisfaction, customer engagement and conversion rates. Hyper-personalization, in tourism promotion, converts the traditional mass advertising into emotional meaningful communication, making the experience personally relevant and value-consistent, enhancing emotional attachment, building brand trust and amplifying the probability of positive word of mouth. In the long run, this personalized contact leads to long-term relations between the destinations and the travelers, increasing competitive edge and marketing effectiveness.

Real Time Data Driven Video Customization

Real-time customization incorporates live data feeds into video generated by AI. Marketing systems modify video components in real time through APIs and cloud-computing systems like Google Cloud. As an example, AI can alter images based on the prevailing weather, season, or popular attractions. This flexibility is especially useful in the tourism industry where situational variables play a significant role in travel decision-making. Real-time AI systems can be used to create perceived immediacy and authenticity by matching content with real world dynamics, which boosts the click-through rates and consumer responsiveness.

Virtual Influencers and Synthetic Destination Ambassadors

Virtual influencers are digital characters created by artificial intelligence to be used to promote brands across platforms. Such organizations like Meta have led the way in developing sophisticated avatars with realistic facial expression and voice simulation. Synthetic ambassadors used in the marketing of tourism can present the experiences of the destination, cultural spotlights, and travel advice without the vagaries of human influencers. They work round the clock, maintain brand alignment and minimize reputational risks. Nevertheless, they must be effective, and this can be achieved through transparency and relatability; ethical disclosure would make audiences view them as creative tools instead of false portrayals.

Table 3. Virtual vs. Human Influencers in Tourism Marketing.

Aspect	Virtual Influencers/Synthetic Ambassadors	Human Influencers
Control & Consistency	Full brand oversight, no scandals.	Prone to unpredictability.
Cost Long-Term	Lower after setup, scalable.	Ongoing fees/travel.
Global Scalability	Multilingual, 24/7 across zones.	Limited by logistics.
Engagement Mechanism	Parasocial relationships via AI.	Authentic personal bonds.
Tourism Effectiveness	Strong for modern sites, weaker for heritage.	Broader appeal overall.

Virtual influencers may underperform human ones for cultural heritage sites due to lower authenticity perceptions. High anthropomorphism (human-like traits) and attractiveness improve information adoption, but over-reliance risks warping beauty standards or alienating audiences seeking genuine experiences. In tourism, pairing them with human influencers optimizes strategies for diverse destinations.

AI Powered Cross Platform Campaign Integration

AI helps to create a smooth flow of video campaigns on various digital platforms. Intelligent systems automatically transform content into short-form video, social media feeds, and booking portals and maintain visual coherence. Analytic dashboards are used to track engagement metrics and make changes to variables (captions, soundtracks, and thumbnails) to maximize performance. Such a combined approach improves the payback and strengthens brand consistency. Within the framework of tourism marketing, the cross-platform AI implementation links discovery, engagement, and booking stages in a logical digital funnel, thus, making sure that the convincing stories are converted into measurable economic gains.

CONSUMER ENGAGEMENT IN AI POWERED TOURISM CAMPAIGNS

The level of consumer interaction with AI-driven tourism advertising programs indicates the level of psychological and behavioral involvement that the customers exhibit when working with intelligent marketing messages. The combination of AI-created videos, customized suggestions, virtual touring, and interactive narratives has transformed tourism promotion as a passive experience to an active one. Interaction is not just mere awareness, but it has been extended to include thought, emotional appeal and action. The knowledge of these dimensions will help the marketers gauge effectiveness in a more precise way and will help them create campaigns that will drive the travelers to engage in meaningful interaction.

Cognitive Engagement: Information Processing and Attention

Cognitive engagement is defined as the amount of mental effort and attention that a consumer puts to process marketing content. Personalization and adaptive storytelling play a key role in enhancing this dimension in AI-based tourism campaigns. Smart algorithms sift through the content based on the preferences of the user, the history of browsing, and contextual cues so that the information can be perceived to be relevant and not overwhelming. When tourists watch personalized destination videos or pre-designed itineraries, they tend to pay more attention to the content, make comparisons, and consider such features as price, sustainability, accessibility, and culture. Clarity is also improved with the aid of AI tools with dynamic subtitles, interactive maps, and recommendation engines. These characteristics decrease cognitive overload and aid informed decision-making. Travelers feel that there is greater utility and efficiency in the AI systems when they provide correct information, and this reinforces their desire to learn more or make a booking.

Table 4. Indicators of Cognitive Engagement in AI Powered Tourism Campaigns

Dimension	Key Indicators	AI Contribution
Attention	Viewing time, click through rate	Personalized recommendations
Information Processing	Comparison of destinations, itinerary exploration	Data driven content filtering
Knowledge Acquisition	Understanding culture, price, accessibility	Interactive maps and smart guides
Decision Support	Evaluation of alternatives	Predictive analytics

By enhancing cognitive engagement, AI campaigns support rational evaluation and increase confidence in travel decisions.

Emotional Engagement: Excitement, Curiosity, and Immersion

Emotional engagement reflects the feelings and affective responses generated by tourism marketing content. Travel decisions are often influenced more by emotions than by rational analysis. AI generated tourism videos leverage advanced visual effects, storytelling techniques, music adaptation, and immersive simulation to evoke excitement, curiosity, and aspiration. AI tools can automatically adjust background music and narrative tone according to the viewer's previous preferences. A traveler interested in adventure tourism may receive dynamic visuals with energetic soundtracks, while a luxury-oriented traveler may experience calm cinematic storytelling. This emotional tailoring increases perceived personal connection. Immersive technologies such as virtual reality tours and interactive simulations further deepen emotional involvement. When viewers feel transported into the destination environment, they develop anticipatory pleasure and psychological attachment (Bennett & Durkin, 2000). Emotional arousal strengthens memory retention and enhances brand recall. Research also indicates that emotional engagement mediates the relationship between content exposure and behavioral outcomes. When travelers feel inspired or excited, they are more likely to share content and recommend destinations to peers.

Table 5. Emotional Drivers in AI Tourism Campaigns

Emotional Trigger	Description	Marketing Outcome
Excitement	Adventure focused visuals and music	Increased sharing behavior
Curiosity	Teasers and interactive storytelling	Higher click exploration
Immersion	Virtual tour experiences	Stronger destination attachment
Inspiration	Cultural storytelling and authenticity	Positive word of mouth

Emotional engagement transforms tourism advertising into experiential storytelling rather than informational broadcasting.

Behavioral Engagement: Sharing, Commenting, and Booking

Behavioral engagement represents observable consumer actions resulting from cognitive and emotional involvement. In AI-powered campaigns, behavioral responses include liking, sharing, commenting, subscribing, saving itineraries, and ultimately booking travel services. AI platforms track behavioral signals in real time and refine recommendations accordingly (van de Poel, 2020). For example, if a traveler frequently saves content related to eco-tourism, subsequent advertisements may emphasize sustainable accommodation and conservation programs. This responsiveness increases conversion probability. Social media algorithms amplify content that generates higher engagement metrics. Therefore, AI optimized tourism videos designed to stimulate interaction achieve broader organic reach. Behavioral engagement also reflects trust and satisfaction levels, as consumers are more likely to engage with content they perceive as credible and relevant.

Parasocial Interaction with AI Generated Characters

Parasocial interaction refers to a one side psychological relationship between audiences and media characters. In AI powered tourism campaigns, virtual influencers and AI generated guides create a sense of familiarity and companionship. When these characters address viewers directly, respond to comments, or simulate personalized communication, travelers may perceive them as socially present.

The Role of Immersive Experience in Travel Decision Making

Immersive experience significantly influences travel intention. AI driven virtual reality tours, augmented reality previews, and interactive simulations allow potential tourists to explore destinations before booking. This reduces uncertainty and perceived risk. Immersive engagement stimulates imagination and anticipation. When travelers virtually walk through historical sites or beachfront resorts, they mentally rehearse the experience. Such mental simulation increases confidence and strengthens purchase intention. Moreover, immersive content improves memory encoding. Visual and interactive exposure makes destinations more memorable compared to static brochures. Tourism marketers can therefore integrate immersive storytelling into campaign strategy to enhance persuasive impact. AI powered engagement enhances understanding of traveler psychology by revealing how cognitive processing, emotional reaction, and behavior interact in digital contexts. Engagement measurement models benefit from real time analytics and multidimensional metrics. For marketers, these insights guide the creation of interactive, personalized, and immersive tourism content that maximizes conversion potential (Bec et al., 2019).

TRUST FORMATION IN AI GENERATED TOURISM VIDEOS

Trust is a critical determinant of consumer decision making in digital environments. In tourism marketing, where services are intangible and experiences cannot be evaluated before consumption, trust becomes even more essential. AI generated tourism videos offer high efficiency and creativity, but they also raise concerns about authenticity, manipulation, and ethical transparency (Craft & Vos, 2021). Understanding trust formation mechanisms ensures responsible and effective AI implementation.

Perceived Authenticity and Realism

Perceived authenticity refers to the extent to which consumers believe that the presented destination accurately reflects reality. AI generated videos can enhance realism through advanced visual rendering, accurate cultural representation, and immersive detail (Liu et al., 2024). However, excessive editing or unrealistic enhancement may trigger skepticism. Authenticity strengthens emotional attachment and reduces uncertainty. When viewers perceive that content truthfully represents local culture and environment, trust increases. Tourism marketers must balance creative enhancement with factual accuracy to maintain credibility.

Transparency and AI Disclosure Practices

Transparency and AI disclosure practices have emerged as critical components in shaping user trust and engagement in digital environments (Larsson & Heintz, 2020). In the context of AI-driven applications, transparency refers to the extent to which organizations openly communicate how AI systems function, the data they rely on, and the decision-making processes involved. Disclosure practices, on the other hand, involve clearly informing users when AI is being used, the purpose of its deployment, and any potential limitations or biases inherent in the system. Together, these practices serve to reduce uncertainty, foster accountability, and strengthen the perceived credibility of both the technology and the organization deploying it. Research has consistently shown that users are more likely to engage with AI applications and follow system recommendations when they feel adequately informed about the mechanisms underlying AI outputs. This is particularly important in scenarios where AI decisions carry significant consequences, such as personalized marketing, financial recommendations, or content moderation, as a lack of transparency can lead to skepticism, distrust, and reduced adoption. Moreover, AI disclosure practices contribute to ethical compliance by ensuring that users are aware of automated processes affecting their experiences and decisions. Transparent communication not only addresses ethical concerns but also aligns with emerging regulatory frameworks that mandate clear AI usage policies, such as the European Union's AI Act, which emphasizes accountability and user rights in automated systems. From a practical perspective, organizations implementing robust AI disclosure strategies can benefit from enhanced customer loyalty, as transparency signals honesty and reduces perceived manipulation. Additionally, it enables users to make more informed decisions, promoting autonomy and fairness in digital interactions. On the flip side, insufficient disclosure or opaque AI practices can trigger negative perceptions, including feelings of deception or manipulation, which undermine trust and potentially result in reputational damage. Companies are therefore encouraged to adopt strategies such as labeling AI-generated content, providing understandable explanations of algorithmic decisions, and offering users options to opt-out or control AI-driven personalization. In sum, transparency and AI disclosure practices are not merely technical or procedural considerations; they play a fundamental role in shaping user attitudes, ethical compliance, and engagement outcomes. By prioritizing clarity and openness in AI interactions, organizations can bridge the gap between technological innovation and responsible, user-centered deployment.

Information Credibility and Source Evaluation

Information credibility reflects the perceived reliability and expertise of the message source. Consumers evaluate tourism videos based on perceived professionalism, consistency, and alignment with other sources. Official tourism boards, reputable travel platforms, and recognized organizations typically generate higher credibility perceptions. AI tools that integrate verified data and real time updates further enhance reliability. Travel decisions involve financial, safety, and experiential risks. If AI generated videos appear overly idealized or misleading, perceived risk increases. Consumer skepticism may arise from concerns about deepfake manipulation or exaggerated claims. To mitigate skepticism, marketers should integrate factual information, customer reviews, and consistent cross platform messaging. Risk perception decreases when consumers observe alignment between video representation and independent evaluations.

The Relationship Between Trust and Purchase Intention

Trust directly influences purchase intention. When consumers perceive tourism videos as authentic, transparent, and credible, they are more willing to book. Trust reduces psychological uncertainty and strengthens commitment.

Trust also encourages long term loyalty and positive word of mouth. Travelers who feel confident in digital representations are more likely to revisit and recommend destinations.

Table 6. Trust and Purchase Intention relationship

Point of Comparison	Trust	Purchase Intention	Relationship
1. Definition	Confidence in the reliability, integrity, and honesty of a seller or platform	Likelihood or willingness of a consumer to buy a product or service	Higher trust generally increases purchase intention
2. Focus	Psychological perception of security and credibility	Behavioral outcome or decision-making tendency	Trust influences intention by reducing perceived risk
3. Nature	Emotional and cognitive evaluation	Behavioral inclination	Trust acts as a predictor of purchase intention
4.Risk Perception	Lowers perceived risk in transactions	High purchase intention emerges when risk is minimized	Trust reduces uncertainty, positively affecting buying decisions
5. Measurement	Surveys, trust scales, reliability and honesty ratings	Likert-scale intention, actual purchase behavior	Statistical analysis often shows a positive correlation
6. Impact on Marketing	Encourages brand loyalty, positive word-of-mouth	Drives conversion and sales	Strong trust enhances consumer willingness to buy

Impact Focus of Trust Section

Trust plays a critical role in shaping consumers' purchase intentions. When consumers perceive a brand, seller, or platform as reliable, honest, and transparent, their sense of security increases, reducing perceived risks associated with transactions. This confidence not only encourages positive attitudes toward the product but also strengthens the likelihood of making a purchase. Trust can therefore act as a key predictor of buying behavior, influencing both short-term decisions and long-term loyalty. In marketing contexts, fostering trust enhances consumer engagement, builds brand credibility, and ultimately drives higher conversion rates.

Ethical AI Governance in AI-Generated Tourism Marketing

Although AI-generated videos are incredibly beneficial in terms of personalization, engagement, and scalability, the chapter demonstrates a major shortcoming in the structuring and practical approach of ethical AI governance. The rising use of hyper-realistic content and data-driven systems comes with risks that could otherwise ruin consumer trust, which is one of the primary results that the chapter intends to reinforce. One of the main issues is the possibility of misappropriation of AI-made content and especially in the form of distorted or excessively advanced images. In cases where tourism videos show unreal or artificial experiences, it might be appealing at the beginning but at the end, it results in dissatisfaction and mistrust among travelers. Equally, the excessive use of consumer data to personalize has serious privacy concerns. Users can find AI-driven marketing as an encroachment instead of a positive change without explicit consent practices and transparent data policies. In order to increase academic rigor and practical relevance, the chapter needs to include an explicit ethical AI governance system that is founded on four fundamental principles, such as transparency, accountability, fairness, and privacy protection. Actionable principles, which include labeling AI-generated content, data protection policy, ethical audit, and more control on the personalized experience should support these principles. Inclusion of recent industry data (20232024) would also enhance the credibility and timeliness of such arguments. To conclude, the ethical governance of AI can be used to balance technological innovation and responsible marketing. The chapter can include a more detailed and practically valuable view by mitigating risks related to deepfakes, data privacy, and transparency. Enhancing this part will not only enhance the effectiveness of the chapter, but will also help to ensure that AI-based tourism marketing has a positive impact on consumer confidence and long-term relationships.

CASE STUDIES: AI IN TOURISM VIDEO CAMPAIGNS

AI-powered video marketing has become a game-changer in the tourism industry, providing brands with innovative ways to engage potential travelers. This section explores real-world case studies where AI has been successfully applied to create personalized and immersive video content for tourism campaigns. These case studies showcase how AI can enhance consumer engagement, optimize marketing efforts, and drive conversions. By analyzing AI's role in delivering customized destination videos, these campaigns highlight the ability of AI to predict consumer preferences, increase audience reach, and enhance overall customer experience. From personalized video recommendations to automated content creation, these examples demonstrate the growing influence of AI in shaping the future of tourism marketing (Zhou et al., 2024).

Case 1: Marriott "Venture" Campaign

Marriott International's "Venture" campaign is a great example of groundbreaking use of artificial intelligence-driven video marketing in the tourism industry. This innovative initiative utilised AI to provide the highly personalized travel video content based on individual user preferences, and therefore, resonated with its audience on a deeper level. By systematically gathering and analysing data on user behaviors, interests and previous interactions, Marriott's AI system created unique, tailored video experiences for each user, thus demonstrating destinations and travel activities that were tailor-made to their tastes. The major strength of the "Venture" campaign was its ability to reach consumers with highly relevant content. By presenting personalized visuals and tailored recommendations, the AI-generated videos increased the relevance of the content, creating a deeper connection with the viewer. As a result, the personalized approach of the campaign led to a significant improvement in engagement metrics, especially click through rate (CTR). Viewers were therefore more likely to engage with the videos, as they were exposed to content that was consistent with their interests and travel goals. Beyond high CTR, the campaign saw a substantial increase in booking inquiries, thus demonstrating that AI-driven personalization is not only an engagement stimulant, but also a business outcome. The ability to create dynamic, customized content at scale helped Marriott expand its reach while maintaining a personalized experience for every individual. This scalable modus operandi both improved customer engagement and the holistic customer experience and ensured that viewers felt the brand was addressing their specific needs directly. The success of the "Venture" campaign highlighted the growing role of artificial intelligence in changing the way tourism marketing is done. By using AI to create personalized travel content, Marriott was able to foster greater connections with its audience, supplement brand recall and drive higher conversion rates. This case therefore reinforces the proposition that AI-powered marketing can simultaneously elevate customer engagement and business results within the tourism industry, providing instructive insights for other brands looking to personalize their marketing strategies.

Case 2: Come Live Our Philosophy by Tourism Australia

Tourism Australia's "Come Live Our Philosophy" campaign is another successful example of AI-driven marketing in the tourism industry. The initiative used artificial intelligence to create highly personalized video content for specific segments of travelers such as adventure seekers, food enthusiasts and nature lovers. AI technology made it possible to curate videos that featured different scenic locations across Australia, each story created to appeal to the specific interests of these heterogeneous groups. The strength of the campaign was due to the fact that it was able to create content that resonated emotionally with viewers, which helped to create a strong connection between the brand and its audience. By using AI to cater to specific consumer profiles, Tourism Australia was able to deliver videos that were both personal and relevant to the individual consumer's tastes. The AI-generated content took viewers to Australia's beautiful destinations to get a virtual preview and build curiosity and excitement to visit. As a result, the campaign achieved impressive engagement figures, such as millions of views and shares across social media platforms. The videos did not only captivate the viewers, but also motivated them to act as many shared their intention to go to Australia. The emotional and immersive nature of the AI-generated content was instrumental in driving consumer interest and improving brand sentiment. The personalized approach increased the chances of viewers to think of Australia as their next travel destination. Tourism Australia's campaign proved that AI can be a useful tool for provoking emotional responses and delivering a more immersive marketing experience. Furthermore, the initiative demonstrated the power of AI in delivering personalized, scalable content at a fraction of the cost and time needed to create traditional video content. By using AI, Tourism Australia was able to increase their reach and reach audiences on a deeper level, while also increasing the likelihood of viewers turning their interest into an actual booking.

Case 3: The Personalized Video Marketing Campaign of Emirates Airlines using AI

Emirates Airlines has been able to use AI in its tourism marketing campaigns particularly personalized video campaigns. The airline deployed AI to develop customised video content to prospective travelers, which was determined by how they interacted before, their search history and preferences. The AI platform was used to select video adverts to particular destinations and the system offered personalized suggestions on flights, hotel stays, and other local experiences, depending on the profile and interests of the customer. The main characteristic of this campaign was the real-time generation of individual travel plans in video format with the help of AI. As an example, a user who has already viewed luxury travel products can receive a video that emphasizes first-class services, exclusive lounges, and luxury hotels alliances in such destinations as Dubai or Paris. Conversely, low end travelers might be shown low cost travel packages, with focus being placed on cheap flights in economy class and cheap hotels. The AI created video content was shared via email, social media, and the Emirates site, thereby expanding reach and interactions. The reaction of consumers was monitored in real time and enabled Emirates to monitor the click-through rate (CTR), video viewing and conversion rate. The personalized videos were also well received with high engagement and conversion rates because the users felt that the content was made to target them. Moreover, AI-powered chatbots were deployed in the campaign to improve the customer experience by giving immediate responses to queries and assisting customers with the booking process. The personalized video content combined with the chat support assisted in creating a smooth, personalized experience that prompted the viewers to continue with their travel planning. The application of AI in marketing enabled Emirates not only to deliver interesting and personalized customer experiences, but also enabled the airline to increase its marketing activities without losing relevance or quality. The case brings to the fore, the transformative nature of AI in tourism marketing by creating extremely personalized and scalable content that can be used to drive both engagement and conversions.

Case 4: Singapore Tourism Board's "See Singapore" AI Campaign

The Singapore Tourism Board (STB) introduced the campaign SeeSingapore based on AI with the aim of optimizing its digital marketing campaign and encouraging tourists to visit the city-state. The campaign used AI to engage with potential visitors by personalizing their content, giving them specific recommendations on the activities, dining, and accommodation, based on their personal preference profiles. Through the historical travel behavior, social media interactions, and search patterns of the users, the AI system created targeted video content that highlights certain Singaporean experiences that resonated with the interest of each user. As an illustration, a user who often searches to find family-friendly holidays would see videos about the theme parks and zoos and family-friendly attractions of Singapore, a luxury traveler would see content about fine dining, 5-star hotels, and exclusive cultural events. This individual approach made sure that the content was very relevant to every viewer, and this is what increased the likelihood of engagement and conversion. Another interesting aspect of the campaign was the inclusion of AI-created virtual tours, which allowed the user to explore major Singaporean attractions in 360-degree video content. Another AI was aligned with a chatbot that provided real-time travel advice, made reservations and answered questions about Singapore attractions, thus streamlining and making the planning process more enjoyable. The outcomes were stunning; the campaign brought a lot of online activity and increased interaction rates compared to the traditional marketing campaigns. Social media shares, video views, and click-through rates were significantly increased, which indicated the resonant, interactive character of the content. In addition to increasing awareness about the tourist attractions in Singapore, the project created more profound emotional bonds when virtual, personal previews of possible visits were offered. The See Singapore campaign is an example of how AI may be used to transform the delivery of content in a scalable and cost-effective manner, as well as in a highly personalized manner. Through its ability to connect with a global audience through the use of immersive and personalized experiences, the campaign demonstrates how AI can transform the tourism industry by enhancing customer interaction and triggering booking behavior.

Case 5: Visit Britain's 'I Travel For' AI Campaign

The Visit Britain campaign, I Travel For, can be seen as a good example of the use of AI to create a personalized tourism marketing content. Through video production with the use of AI, the campaign attracted potential tourists to personalized travel experiences based on their preferences. The AI system used data gathered during the interaction with users, such as search history and social media activity, to create personalized videos highlighting different elements of the British culture, history, and landscapes that appeal to different groups of travellers. The AI-based approach allowed Visit Britain to generate content that appealed to certain demographic segments. A user who is historically inclined may watch a video about the castles and museums of Britain, whereas a food lover could get a video with information about food festivals and famous restaurants. Such degree of personalization increased relevance, which enhanced the viewer engagement. One of the most important innovations of the campaign was the use of AI-driven storytelling, where the audience could engage with the content by choosing the types of travel experience they want. As such, the AI system altered video narratives in real time, creating a dynamic, immersive experience, which created a stronger bond with the destination and encouraged potential travelers to think about Britain as their next itinerary. Moreover, the campaign utilized AI to study consumer behavior in real-time, to quantify user interactions, define the most interesting content segments, and destinations that generated the most interest. This information allowed further development of the marketing strategies to be implemented in the future to maintain their relevance and attractiveness to prospective tourists. The I Travel For campaign produced greater interactivity, which was measured by the increase in click-through, social media shares, and the number of queries about travelling to Britain. Visit Britain used AI to develop immersive, interactive and personalized content, which helped the company improve the experience of the visitors, strengthen the brand loyalty, and prove that AI-based marketing can be one of the key elements of the modern tourism marketing campaign.

Case 6: South Africa Tourism's "Meet South Africa" AI-Driven Campaign

The campaign of South Africa Tourism called Meet South Africa is one of the most remarkable cases when artificial intelligence is applied to personalize and enrich tourism marketing. The campaign used AI to generate immersive and personalized video content to attract travelers according to their interests and preferences. The AI system was able to narrate videos in a way that was most appealing to the individual viewer by analyzing information like the previous travel history, user interactions, and even social media activity, which would help highlight the various attractions that South Africa has to offer. The AI system categorized the audience and created specific video material to specific groups of travelers. A nature and wildlife lover may also get content about the most popular safaris, national parks, and wildlife preservation programs, but a cultural lover may watch videos that depict local music, food, and festivals in South African cities. This targeted strategy allowed South Africa Tourism to provide extremely topical content, which increases the interest of viewers and makes their emotions more vivid. The new aspect of the programmed was AI-generated interactive videos, which allowed the viewers to choose desired travel experiences in the video. These selections provided users with personalized itineraries and destination suggestions based on their preferences, which enhanced more profound interaction and enthusiasm. Another advantage of the campaign was the use of AI-based chatbots to offer real-time travel guidance, respond to questions, and give other suggestions, thus making it easier to book. The planning process was simplified by this integration of AI in customer service and the user experience became even more personalized. In the end, the campaign, called Meet South Africa, was rather successful as it was proven by the high growth in the engagement indicators such as social media shares, video views, and travel enquiries. The individualized and interactive quality of the AI-created content appealed to potential travelers on a large scale, which supports the assumption that AI can be crucial in transforming tourism marketing by providing customized, immersive, and engaging content that arouses interest and reservations.

THE FUTURE OF AI IN TOURISM MARKETING: OPPORTUNITIES, CHALLENGES, AND EMERGING TRENDS

The tourism industry is changing fast due to the technological revolution, and artificial intelligence (AI) is becoming a more prominent feature. AI is transforming the nature of tourism marketing by making it personalized, more consumer-focused, and streamlined (Chaisatitkul et al., 2024). With the growing impact of AI, it presents significant opportunities as well as challenges that need to be handled with care, so as to produce the best results. This discussion explores future advantages, challenges of AI driven tourism marketing that will come along with them, and new trends that will determine the future of the industry.

Opportunities in AI for Tourism Marketing

The most salient strength of AI is its ability to analyze and process large volumes of data, which allows companies to create extremely personalized experiences to consumers. The AI can provide personalized content to the travelers by utilizing the information on travel preferences, behavioral patterns, past interactions, and social media activity. As an illustration, AI-based recommender systems have the potential to recommend personalized travel destinations, activities, and accommodation, hence improving the customer experience by matching it with personal interests. This level of personalization enhances customer interaction, improves the booking conversion rate, and builds brand loyalty (Moore et al., 2005). In addition, AI-based chatbots and virtual assistants offer 24/7 customer service, which enables the process of planning a trip at any time and enhances access to service in general. Automation is another crucial opportunity that AI has to offer. Repetitive processes such as content creation, video creation, and social media posting can be automated with AI systems, which will leave marketing teams to concentrate on strategic efforts. Automation enables scaling of marketing activities in international markets without a corresponding rise in the amount of resources being spent. Also, AI systems can streamline pricing decisions in time by examining demand, seasonality, and consumer tastes, which will allow companies to stay competitive and generate as much revenue as possible (Chae & Kim, 2026).

Challenges and Limitations of AI-Driven Tourism Marketing

Although AI has many advantages, there are still issues related to its use in tourism marketing. One of the challenges is the technical and creative limitations of AI in video creation. Despite the significant progress in the field of AI and its ability to create personalized video content, it still cannot create really creative and high-quality content that is comparable to the human work. Videos created by AI might not be as emotional and storytelling, which are the keys to building a memorable travel experience that will stick with consumers. More technical challenges are involved in the implementation of AI tools into the current marketing platforms or in dealing with dynamic and complex environments, which are practical challenges to marketers. One of the most important problems is related to data privacy. The use of AI systems is based on large amounts of consumer data to provide personalized experiences, which raises ethical concerns about the use of personal information and adherence to data protection laws, including the General Data Protection Regulation (GDPR). Customers might be concerned with the use of their personal information, such as their delicate preferences and behavioral patterns. In turn, transparency and the protection of user data have become the key to preserving consumer confidence and preventing legal consequences that may damage the image of a brand.

With the development of AI technology, some new trends are set to influence the future of tourism marketing. The incorporation of augmented reality (AR) and virtual reality (VR) with AI to provide potential travelers with immersive experiences is one of the trends worth mentioning. AI has the potential to improve VR tours of destinations where users can interact with virtual spaces in real-time and get them to experience engaging and interactive previews of their travels. In the same vein, AR can provide tourists with on-the-go, real-time information of the places they have visited, be it historical facts, recommendations, or local events when used together with AI (Huang et al., 2018). The other area of potential growth is the improvement of AI-based predictive analytics (Franke et al., 2022). The more advanced AI systems are the more they can predict consumer behavior with more accuracy, allowing tourism brands to predict demand, optimize marketing efforts and come up with more effective strategies. Such predictive abilities enable the marketers to reach the right audience at the right time and with the most pertinent content, thus increasing the conversion rates and customer satisfaction.

CONCLUSION

To sum up, the future of AI in the tourism marketing industry is not only promising but also transformative with great opportunities to improve customer interactions, simplify operations, and provide personalized travel experience. With the ongoing development of the technology, AI will become central to the redesigning of tourism brands in communication with consumers, allowing companies to provide more specific and personalized content that will meet the needs of each traveler. Using the power of AI, namely, personalized video marketing, automated content creation, chatbots, and predictive analytics, tourism brands can interact with travelers in a whole new way. The possibilities AI presents to the tourism marketing are enormous. AI allows companies to filter out the noise of mass advertising and provides customized recommendations and experiences that appeal to the personal tastes and preferences. The emotional relationship with the potential traveler is enhanced through AI-based consumer data analysis, which creates trust and loyalty. This type of personalized interaction leads to long-term relationships, which are reflected in the increased engagement rates, conversion rates, and repeat bookings (Toh et al.,

2011). Furthermore, the automation and optimization of functions like pricing, content generation, and social media control associated with AI provide significant cost-saving effects, allowing businesses to expand their activities without the need to allocate an equivalent amount of resources to it. Linking these ethical considerations with established theories such as trust theory and the S O R model, along with providing clear guidelines for ethical AI implementation, would significantly improve its theoretical depth and practical relevance. Nevertheless, the opportunities are strong, but the challenges linked to the concept of AI integration in the tourism marketing also cannot be ignored. The creative and technical shortcomings of AI, especially in the creation of video should be taken into consideration. AI is not able to reproduce the richness, emotional appeal, and subtle creativity of human-generated work, which is a crucial element of the tourism industry where inspiration and connection to the audience are crucial. Also, the issue of data privacy is a serious problem to be addressed. The use of AI based on the large volumes of data poses ethical concerns on privacy, transparency, and security. Tourism brands need to implement transparent data policy and adhere to data protection laws including GDPR in order to maintain consumer trust and guarantee that the privacy of customers is not violated. In the future, such trends as the integration of AR and VR with AI have new opportunities (Nayyar et al., 2018). Through providing immersive experiences, AI can be used to allow potential travelers to experience a destination virtually prior to committing to a booking, thus changing the customer journey. The use of AI-based predictive analytics will also enhance the marketing plans in the tourism industry, as the businesses will be able to predict the needs of the customers, the demand levels, and introduce more efficient and timely campaigns. This will not only increase the effectiveness of marketing but also customer satisfaction and loyalty due to this increased predictive and adaptive skills to consumer behavior. The combination of these innovations is indicative of the fact that the sphere of tourism is at the threshold of a significant change, as AI will keep developing and improving marketing strategies. With the development of AI technology, the tourism brands will be able to offer an even more immersive, relevant and customizable experience to the traveler, with the key to success being the responsible and ethical use of AI, where personalization does not mean the loss of privacy or trust. Tourism has to strike a balance between innovation and caution and match technological development with customer demands and moral norms. This study contributes to consumer behavior literature by demonstrating how AI-generated content reshapes decision-making pathways, trust formation, and engagement in tourism marketing.

REFERENCES

Argyriou, E., & Melewar, T. (2011). Consumer Attitudes Revisited: A Review of Attitude Theory in Marketing Research. *International Journal of Management Reviews*, *13*(4), 431–451. DOI: 10.1111/j.1468-2370.2011.00299.x

Bec, A., Moyle, B., Timms, K., Schaffer, V., Skavronskaya, L., & Little, C. (2019). Management of immersive heritage tourism experiences: A conceptual model. *Tourism Management*, *72*, 117–120. DOI: 10.1016/j.tourman.2018.10.033

Bennett, H., & Durkin, M. (2000). The effects of organisational change on employee psychological attachment An exploratory study. *Journal of Managerial Psychology*, *15*(2), 126–146. DOI: 10.1108/02683940010310328

Chae, M.-J., & Kim, M. (2026). Too human to trust? How AI human-likeness and context orientation shape consumer preferences in premium high-tech markets. *Journal of Retailing and Consumer Services*, *88*, 104513. DOI: 10.1016/j.jretconser.2025.104513

Chaisatitkul, A., Luangngamkhum, K., Noulpum, K., & Kerdvibulvech, C. (2024). The power of AI in marketing: Enhancing efficiency and improving customer perception through AI-generated storyboards. *International Journal of Information Technology : an Official Journal of Bharati Vidyapeeth's Institute of Computer Applications and Management*, *16*(1), 137–144. DOI: 10.1007/s41870-023-01661-5

Craft, S., & Vos, T. P. (2021). The ethics of transparency. In *The Routledge Companion to Journalism Ethics*. Routledge. DOI: 10.4324/9780429262708-24

Doborjeh, Z., Hemmington, N., Doborjeh, M., & Kasabov, N. (2021). Artificial intelligence: A systematic review of methods and applications in hospitality and tourism. *International Journal of Contemporary Hospitality Management*, *34*(3), 1154–1176. DOI: 10.1108/IJCHM-06-2021-0767

Dumitriu, D., & Popescu, M. A.-M. (2020). Artificial Intelligence Solutions for Digital Marketing. *Procedia Manufacturing*, *46*, 630–636. DOI: 10.1016/j.promfg.2020.03.090

Franke, F., Franke, S., & Riedel, R. (2022). AI-based Improvement of Decision-makers' Knowledge in Production Planning and Control. *IFAC-PapersOnLine, 10th IFAC Conference on Manufacturing Modelling, Management and Control MIM 2022, 55*(10), 2240–2245. DOI: 10.1016/j.ifacol.2022.10.041

Hu, H., Xue, L., & Guo, Y. (2025). Tourism, acceleration, and deceleration: Towards a conceptual framework. *Current Issues in Tourism*, *0*(0), 1–18. DOI: 10.1080/13683500.2025.2505695

Huang, T.-K., Yang, C.-H., Hsieh, Y.-H., Wang, J.-C., & Hung, C.-C. (2018). Augmented reality (AR) and virtual reality (VR) applied in dentistry. *The Kaohsiung Journal of Medical Sciences*, *34*(4), 243–248. DOI: 10.1016/j.kjms.2018.01.009 PMID: 29655414

Jain, G., Paul, J., & Shrivastava, A. (2021). Hyper-personalization, co-creation, digital clienteling and transformation. *Journal of Business Research*, *124*, 12–23. Advance online publication. DOI: 10.1016/j.jbusres.2020.11.034

Kane, G. C., Palmer, D., & Phillips, A. N. (2019). *Accelerating Digital Innovation Inside and Out* [Technical Report]. MIT Sloan Management Review. https://sadil.ws/handle/123456789/14

Kubiszewski, I., Noordewier, T., & Costanza, R. (2011). Perceived credibility of Internet encyclopedias. *Computers & Education*, *56*(3), 659–667. DOI: 10.1016/j.compedu.2010.10.008

Larsson, S., & Heintz, F. (2020). Transparency in artificial intelligence. *Internet Policy Review*, *9*(2). Advance online publication. DOI: 10.14763/2020.2.1469

Lemon, K. N., & Verhoef, P. C. (2016). Understanding Customer Experience Throughout the Customer Journey. *Journal of Marketing*, *80*(6), 69–96. DOI: 10.1509/jm.15.0420

Liu, X., Xiang, X., Li, Z., Wang, Y., Li, Z., Liu, Z., Zhang, W., Ye, W., & Zhang, J. (2024). *A Survey of AI-Generated Video Evaluation* (arXiv:2410.19884). arXiv. https://doi.org//arXiv.2410.19884DOI: 10.48550

Moore, R., Moore, M. L., & Capella, M. (2005). The impact of customer-to-customer interactions in a high personal contact service setting. *Journal of Services Marketing*, *19*(7), 482–491. DOI: 10.1108/08876040510625981

Nayyar, A., Mahapatra, B., Nhuong Le, D., & Suseendran, G. (2018). Virtual Reality (VR) & Augmented Reality (AR) technologies for tourism and hospitality industry. *International Journal of Engineering & Technology, 7*(2.21), 156. DOI: 10.14419/ijet.v7i2.21.11858

Powers, T. L., & Sterling, J. U. (2008). Segmenting business-to-business markets: A micro-macro linking methodology. *Journal of Business and Industrial Marketing*, *23*(3), 170–177. DOI: 10.1108/08858620810858436

Saleh, M. I. (2025). Generative artificial intelligence in hospitality and tourism: Future capabilities, AI prompts and real-world applications. *Journal of Hospitality Marketing & Management, 34*(4), 467–498. DOI: 10.1080/19368623.2025.2458603

Sales, B., Darmois, E., Papadimitriou, D., & Bourse, D. (2012). A Systematic Approach for Closing the Research to Standardization Gap. In Álvarez, F., Cleary, F., Daras, P., Domingue, J., Galis, A., Garcia, A., Gavras, A., Karnourskos, S., Krco, S., Li, M.-S., Lotz, V., Müller, H., Salvadori, E., Sassen, A.-M., Schaffers, H., Stiller, B., Tselentis, G., Turkama, P., & Zahariadis, T. (Eds.), *The Future Internet* (pp. 18–29). Springer., DOI: 10.1007/978-3-642-30241-1_3

Seo, K., Fels, S., Yoon, D., Roll, I., Dodson, S., & Fong, M. (2020). Artificial Intelligence for Video-based Learning at Scale. *Proceedings of the Seventh ACM Conference on Learning @ Scale, L@S '20*, 215–217. DOI: 10.1145/3386527.3405937

Toh, R. S., DeKay, C. F., & Raven, P. (2011). Travel Planning: Searching for and Booking Hotels on the Internet. *Cornell Hospitality Quarterly, 52*(4), 388–398. DOI: 10.1177/1938965511418779

van de Poel, I. (2020). Embedding Values in Artificial Intelligence (AI) Systems. *Minds and Machines, 30*(3), 385–409. DOI: 10.1007/s11023-020-09537-4

Wang, P., Jiang, Y., Xu, C., & Xie, X. (2019). Overview of Content-Based Click-Through Rate Prediction Challenge for Video Recommendation. *Proceedings of the 27th ACM International Conference on Multimedia, MM '19*, 2593–2596. DOI: 10.1145/3343031.3356085

Xiang, Z., & Gretzel, U. (2010). Role of social media in online travel information search. *Tourism Management, 31*(2), 179–188. DOI: 10.1016/j.tourman.2009.02.016

Zhou, P., Wang, L., Liu, Z., Hao, Y., Hui, P., Tarkoma, S., & Kangasharju, J. (2024). *A Survey on Generative AI and LLM for Video Generation, Understanding, and Streaming* (arXiv:2404.16038). arXiv. /arXiv.2404.16038DOI: 10.36227/techrxiv.171172801.19993069/v1

Chapter 8
The Synthetic Persona: Exploring the Marketing Prospects and Ethical Dark Side of AI-Powered Virtual Influencers

Muhammad Abdus Salam
http://orcid.org/0000-0001-9599-632X
Universiti Brunei Darussalam, Brunei

Vai Shiem Leong
Universiti Brunei Darussalam, Brunei

Nazlida Muhamad
http://orcid.org/0000-0003-2790-8900
Prince Sultan University, Saudi Arabia

S. M. Nafiz Rayun
http://orcid.org/0009-0002-2505-6265
University of Science and Technology, Chittagong, Bangladesh

ABSTRACT

The emergence of AI-powered virtual influencers, enabled by generative AI, deepfakes, and synthetic media, is transforming contemporary digital marketing. These synthetic personas offer significant opportunities for brand control, scalability, personalization, and consumer engagement, while simultaneously raising concerns regarding authenticity, transparency, trust, and consumer manipulation. This chapter examines both the marketing prospects and ethical challenges of AI-powered virtual influencers through the proposed Synthetic Persona Influence Framework (SPIF). Integrating insights from Anthropomorphism Theory, CASA Theory, Mind Perception Theory, Parasocial Interaction Theory, Source Credibility Theory, and the Uncanny

DOI: 10.4018/979-8-2600-2977-0.ch008

Valley Hypothesis, the chapter introduces the concept of the Authenticity Paradox, which explains how the same human-like characteristics that enhance persuasion may also generate skepticism and backlash. The chapter further discusses governance and managerial implications for the responsible use of synthetic personas in digital marketing ecosystems.

1. INTRODUCTION

1.1 The Genesis of the Synthetic Persona

The digital marketing landscape has been radically changed by the rapid development of artificial intelligence (AI), social media, and data-driven communication technologies. Among the most prominent events that have resulted from this convergence is the emergence of AI-driven virtual influencers, who are computer-generated personages that can engage with audiences, market brands, and even social media ecosystems. In contrast to traditional human influencers, the influence of which is based on personal experience, social credibility, and self-representation, virtual influencers are artificial objects that have the ability to simulate human traits but are fully controlled by their creators (Arsenyan & Mirowska, 2021; Jhawar et al., 2023). The history of influencer marketing offers valuable background information on this phenomenon. As the impact of celebrity endorsements on brands declines, the rise of social media moves power to content creators, developing credibility and interaction with online communities through direct communication (Leung et al., 2022). Nevertheless, the issues of influencer scandals, inconsistent messaging, and reputational risk have prompted organizations to look to more controllable options. In turn, companies are increasingly engaging in AI-driven personas that can provide a steady brand communication and reduce the uncertainties linked to human endorsers (Sands et al., 2022). Generative AI, machine learning, computer vision, and neural rendering technologies have contributed to accelerating this transition. Such inventions have helped to create synthetic media, including AI-generated images, videos, voices, and textual content that mimic human expression. Among these technologies, deepfakes have had a potent impact, allowing the creation of natural facial expressions, voice patterns, and displays of emotion with the help of advanced deep- learning architectures. Consequently, virtual influencers are moving toward a categorical boundary between reality and simulation, and producing more experiential modes of online communication and interaction (Moustakas et al., 2020).

The emergence of virtual influencers is also associated with more general changes in platform economies. Algorithms in social media encourage sustained activity, responsivity, and content stability, which human influencers can find difficult to uphold in the long run. Conversely, AI-driven personas have the ability to perform 24 hour duties, converse in various languages, adjust to different cultural backgrounds, and possess curated identities without exhaustion, aging, or reputational scandals (Audrezet & Koles, 2023; Um, 2023). These are some of the benefits that make them desirable strategic resources in modern marketing landscapes. On the basis of these advances, this chapter coined the idea of the synthetic persona, which refers to an artificially created digital identity, the combination of algorithmic intelligence, human-like representation, and strategic communicative abilities, to execute social and commercial roles in digital ecosystems. In contrast to fixed avatars or old brand mascots, synthetic personas are created to build relationships, maintain the attention of the audience and affect consumer perception through continued interactions (Ramadan & Ramadan, 2025). Synthetic personas provoke traditional beliefs about authenticity and impact in online marketing. The line between genuine and fake influence becomes increasingly indistinct with the increasing ability of AI systems to imitate human characteristics and behaviors. The etiology of the synthetic persona is thus crucial for exploring opportunities and threats related to AI-based virtual influencers in the modern digital landscape.

1.2 Strategic Imperative of Virtual Influencer Marketing

The rise of AI-driven virtual influencers is indicative of major changes in the modern consumer attention economy, which relies on competing brands to gain visibility and reach in the face of information overload and a fragmented audience. Conventional forms of advertising cannot be effective in maintaining the attention of consumers, and human influencers are faced with the challenges of reputational risks, inconsistent messages and operational limitations. Therefore, AI-based virtual influencers are becoming an increasingly popular communication tool that organizations can use to attract sustained engagement with audiences and are controllable and scalable (Jhawar et al., 2023; Leung et al., 2022). One of the major advantages of virtual influencers is that they have a high level of control of operation. Synthetic personas have no fatigue, aging, personal scandals, or behavioral inconsistencies, which enable firms to have consistent brand identities and communication strategies over time (Audrezet & Koles, 2023; Um, 2023). Moreover, virtual influencers also have significant scalability advantages. They are able to work in various markets, produce content in various languages, and create personalized content with comparatively low replication costs owing to the development of generative AI and automated content generation (Xia et al., 2025). Empirical research has also shown that virtual influencers can achieve the same level of engagement as human influencers can achieve, and even higher, in the case of strong narratives and interactive communication tactics (D. Kim & Wang, 2024; J. Yang et al., 2023). They are also especially appropriate in long-term branding, sustainability communication, and corporate social responsibility activities because of their capacity to have stable identities and values (Jiang et al., 2024). With the increasingly data-driven, immersive nature of digital marketing, virtual influencers are becoming a strategically important players that should be considered more closely by scholars due to their increasing commercial importance.

1.3 Problem Statement, Research Gap, and Chapter Scope

Although there is increasing commercial use of AI-driven virtual influencers, there are serious questions about the ethical aspects of their use and their impact on society as a whole. Current studies have focused mainly on the ability of virtual influencers to drive consumer engagement, boost brand performance, and promote new types of digital communication (D. Kim & Wang, 2024; Muniz et al., 2024). Although these studies show the marketing possibilities of synthetic personas, they tend to gloss over the psychological and ethical tensions inherent in the process of the humanization of artificial entities. One of the key issues is connected to the vulnerability of consumers in the sphere of AI-mediated influence. Virtual influencers are created to resemble real humans in their looks, feelings, and social actions, promoting the emotional attachment of consumers to objects that do not have such real-life experiences or feelings (Dabiran et al., 2024; Kim & Park, 2024). Such abilities provoke some significant concerns about the ethical limits of AI-based persuasion and the possibility of the abuse of consumer psychology.

To resolve this problem, this chapter presents the theory of the authenticity paradox, which is defined as the contradiction, in which the effectiveness of synthetic personas in persuading consumers is based on the perception that they are authentic social actors, and, at the same time, that their artificiality poses a threat to authenticity on the basis of which trust is established. The closer the virtual influencers are to human traits, the stronger their impact is; meanwhile, a heightened sense of artificiality can cause skepticism, distrust, and consumer backlash (Lim & Lee, 2023; Muniz et al., 2024). This paradox is a key contradiction at the core of AI-based influencer marketing. Additionally, the available literature is divided into the marketing, technology and ethics fields. Theories such as CASA, Mind Perception Theory, Para-Social Interaction Theory, Source Credibility Theory, and the Uncanny Valley Hypothesis are valuable but have seldom been combined into one coherent theory to explain synthetic influence. As a result, there has been little focus on comprehending the effects of the combination of technological realism, psychological attachment, credibility creation, and authenticity issues on consumer reactions to virtual influencers.

To fill these gaps, the current chapter takes an interdisciplinary approach, including marketing, consumer behavior, communication studies, studies of human–computer interaction, and AI ethics. The chapter has three goals: (1) conceptualization of the synthetic persona and exploration of its technological basis; (2) exploration of the strategic marketing opportunities of AI-driven virtual influencers; and (3) critical analysis of ethical and societal issues of synthetic influence. To fulfill these goals, this chapter builds a comprehensive theoretical framework revolving around the authenticity paradox and explores the potential of persuasion and the weaknesses of AI-driven virtual influencers in modern digital marketing systems.

2. CONCEPTUALIZING THE AI-POWERED VIRTUAL INFLUENCER

2.1 Defining the Synthetic Persona

The advent of AI-driven virtual influencers has undermined traditional conceptualizations of identity, representation and influence as it applies to digital spaces. Even though such terms as virtual influencer, AI influencer, digital human, and virtual avatar are often used interchangeably in the industry and in academic research, these terms usually obscure the critical differences of what AI-generated agents are and what abilities they have (Y. Yang et al., 2025). In order to achieve conceptual clarity, this chapter uses the notion of synthetic persona as an umbrella concept that describes the unique features of AI-driven digital identities that work in the modern social media ecosystems. A synthetic persona may be described as an artificially created digital identity which integrates computational intelligence, human-like representation and platform-mediated communication capabilities to fulfill social, cultural or commercial roles in the digital realm (Verma, 2025). In contrast to inanimate avatars or more traditional brand mascots, synthetic personas are created to preserve sustained identities, involve continuous interactions, and develop by generating continuous content. They are not only visualized but also manifested in appearance, personality, communication style, behavioral patterns, and narrative continuity, all of which form the impression of a coherent digital self (Arsenyan & Mirowska, 2021). The idea of the synthetic persona is indicative of a wider shift in online communication. The sources of influence of human influencers are those of experience, personal history, and embodied realities that are not dependent on the digital platform. They may be strategic in their online identities, but they still live in actual existence. Synthetic personas, in contrast, are created solely through computational design and narrative -building processes. They are deliberately designed to look and behave in a certain way, communicate in a particular manner, and act in a social way that is not naturally developed (Jhawar et al., 2023; Karimova, 2025). Therefore, their lives are determined by the technological structures and organizations or people who create and manage them. This difference is crucial, as it indicates the transition to the influence of human factors to algorithmically mediated representation. Conventional influencer marketing presupposes that persuasion is the result of genuine social actors who are able to share personal experiences and form relationships on the basis of self-disclosure. Synthetic personas create a new paradigm where influence might be encoded into digitally produced identities that do not have biological existence. In this context, computational design, data-driven communication strategies, and synthetic media technologies have increasingly increased in influence (Paglieri et al., 2026; Rahimzadeh et al., 2025; Sharma et al., 2025).

Synthetic personas are characterized by several traits, although they are rather diverse. First, they demonstrate identity persistence, where they sustain familiar looks and personalities in interactions and platforms. Second, they show communicative agency, and they create content and mediate communication via text, images, and audiovisual media. Third, they have adaptive functionality, where their presentation and behavior can change on the basis of audience feedback and strategic goals. Finally, they work via platform integration, keeping visible and engaged across interconnected digital ecosystems (Sands et al., 2022; Tan & Greene, 2025). By imagining AI-driven virtual influencers as synthetic personalities, one can offer a more analytical perspective in which these figures can be perceived. Instead of perceiving them as marketing instruments, this point of view acknowledges them as sociotechnical agents that are a result of the intersection between artificial intelligence, synthetic media, and digital culture. This conceptual framework is the key to comprehending the effects of AI-generated identities in modern communication landscapes and shaping consumer perceptions and actions.

2.2 Anthropomorphism and Human-Like Digital Identity

The rise of artificial identities has been closely associated with the growing capacity of digital technologies to imitate human features, feelings, and social interactions. The core of this evolution is anthropomorphism or the act of assigning or embracing human qualities, motives, and actions to non-humans (Epley et al., 2007). In the framework of AI-based virtual influencers, anthropomorphism is not just a visual effect, but a strategic process whereby artificial entities become socially familiar and able to interact meaningfully. Designers can help the synthetic personas fill social spaces by incorporating human-like qualities into digital identities, thus taking the place of the human communicator. The anthropomorphism is multidimensional. The most prominent example is visual anthropomorphism, which is the process of giving a human-like appearance via highly developed computer graphics, deep fake technologies, and neural rendering systems. Modern virtual influencers may be endowed with realistic facial features and emotional expressions, body movements, and aesthetic traits similar to those of human social media creators (Moustakas et al., 2020). These visual clues help individuals recognize identities and make audiences more likely to perceive synthetic personas in social frames than in technological frames.

Anthropomorphism is limited not only to physical appearance but also to the behavioral and narrative levels. The personalities, tastes, lifestyles and personal histories of humans are often granted to synthetic personas that replicate human experience. They build consistent identities, which can voice opinions, have conversations about culture, and interact with their followers in a way that is similar to that of human influencers through storytelling and constant content creation (Arsenyan & Mirowska, 2021). This narrative construction will make digital artifacts become socially significant identities that can maintain long-term relationships with audiences.

One of the main results of anthropomorphic design is the creation of the social presence phenomenon, which can be described as the degree to which a digital entity is perceived as a socially relevant participant in the mediation. Social presence is created when the audience believes that synthetic personas can communicate, interact, and engage in relationships, instead of being lifeless technological devices (Kim & Park, 2024). Studies indicate that visual realism is not the sole factor in determining social presence, and that there is also communication consistency, responsiveness and continuity of identities across platforms. Tightly connected with social presence is perceived realism, which addresses the extent to which a synthetic persona seems realistic in a particular context. Notably, a realistic approach does not imply ideal imitation by human beings. Instead, it rests on the compatibility of appearance, behavior, and communication with the social norms and expectations of the audience (Volles et al., 2024). As a result, anthropomorphism, social presence and perceived realism are involved in the creation of human-like digital identities. By combining all these aspects, synthetic personas no longer remain mere digital versions but become socially identifiable participants in modern digital culture.

2.3 A Typology of Deepfake-Enabled Digital Personas

Even though AI-based virtual influencers can be termed a one-dimensional phenomenon, they vary significantly in terms of their technological underpinnings, ownership, degree of autonomy, and communicative capabilities. This diversity implies that synthetic personas cannot be considered a homogenous category and instead a continuum of digitally constructed identities. On one side of this spectrum are completely AI-inspired virtual influencers that are developed using artificial intelligence, computer graphics, and synthetic media technologies and can act as autonomous digital personalities that are not related to real human counterparts (Arsenyan & Mirowska, 2021; Moustakas et al., 2020). The other class is brand-owned synthetic personas, which are created and operated by organizations as strategic communication resources that aim to enhance brand identity, keep messages consistent, and ensure long-term interaction with consumers (Audrezet & Koles, 2023). Finally, metaverse virtual influencers are designed to work within an immersive virtual world, relying on advanced avatars and real-time rendering frameworks that allow the virtual influencer to interact with users through experience, instead of the traditional form of social media communication (Tan & Greene, 2025). This taxonomy demonstrates that synthetic personas may take various shapes, which depend on their strategic intent and technology setup. Moreover, AI-driven virtual influencers are moving beyond mere digital endorsers and becoming multifaceted sociotechnical actors that can perform in a variety of digital ecosystems. It is imperative to understand these differences since varying levels of autonomy, realism, and ownership can influence consumer perception, trust, and engagement with synthetic identities; this will be the central question of the theoretical discussion presented in the next section.

2.4 Technical Architecture of Synthetic Personas

Synthetic personas are not produced by a technology breakthrough but by the interaction of several systems of artificial intelligence at work in a connected digital ecosystem. The creation of AI-powered virtual influencers is achieved through the integration of generative AI, computer vision, natural language processing (NLP), and sophisticated rendering technologies which in turn facilitate the development of coherent, interactive and human-like online identities (Ayertey et al., 2026; Pieper et al., 2026; Vladyslava, 2025). This technological architecture is significant to understand as the abilities and impacts of synthetic personas are essentially defined by the systems which constitute their being.

Generative artificial intelligence lies at the heart of modern synthetic personas and allows the production of text, imagery, audio, and video content (Schenker, 2023). Generative AI, in contrast to conventional rule-based systems, learns trends through large data sets and generates new content that is similar to other human generated outputs. The recent developments in the field of foundation models have greatly expanded these functions, offering scalable architectures that can produce coherent narratives, personality traits, and multimodal content. These models serve as the cognitive scaffolding of synthetic personas and enable them to achieve consistency in identity and keep adjusting their messages to be suitable in various environments and settings (Sands et al., 2022). The second vital element is computer vision and deepfake technology, which are the visual bases of synthetic identities. Computer vision systems allow generating faces, producing images, modeling identities, and creating visual content, and deepfake technologies use deep learning algorithms to produce extremely realistic facial expressions, voice-synchronization, and emotional expression (Moustakas et al., 2020). Such technologies enable virtual influencers to gain recognizable looks and ensure visual continuity between social media and videos and online space. Natural language processing (NLP) systems substantially contribute to the communicative abilities of synthetic personas. NLP helps AI agents to comprehend, create and modify human language in a manner that enables meaningful communication (Fang & Wang, 2022; Luttrell & Welch, 2025; Tolbert, 2025). Using large language models, virtual influencers are able to generate captions, comment on posts, converse, and use the same communication style even when replying to comments in line with their online personalities. In addition to mere content creation, NLP can be used to generate continuity in narratives and character growth, and strengthen the illusion of a consistent and consistent digital self. Lastly, neural rendering and motion synthesis technologies convert inanimate digital models into an animated and interactive form (Abootorabi et al., 2025). Motion synthesis allows realistic body movements, gestures, and facial expressions, whereas neural rendering makes the images look more real with the help of AI-generated textures, lighting, and interactions with the environment (Thapliyal et al., 2025). Collectively, these technologies produce fluid and believable performances in the digital environment that enhance perceptions of realism and social presence.

3. THEORETICAL FOUNDATIONS OF HUMAN–AI INTERACTION

The virtual influencers powered by AI are a novel type of digital influence that defies the conventional beliefs regarding communication, persuasion, and consumer behavior. These digital personas can replicate human social actors through artificial intelligence, anthropomorphic design, and synthetic media technologies, enabling them to have meaningful interactions with audiences. Their influence thus cannot be understood by looking at their technological capabilities alone but also the psychological mechanisms that influence the consumer responses. Available studies are based on various disciplines, such as marketing, social psychology, communication and human-computer interaction, but these views are frequently isolated. To fill this gap, this chapter builds a theoretical framework that integrates Anthropomorphism, CASA Theory, Mind Perception Theory, Para-social Interaction Theory, Source Credibility Theory and the Uncanny Valley Hypothesis. Combined, the theories describe how synthetic personas create both persuasive impact and authenticity-related issues, which influence consumer reactions that vary in terms of engagement and trust to skepticism and backlash.

Figure 1. Synthetic Persona Influence Framework (SPIF)

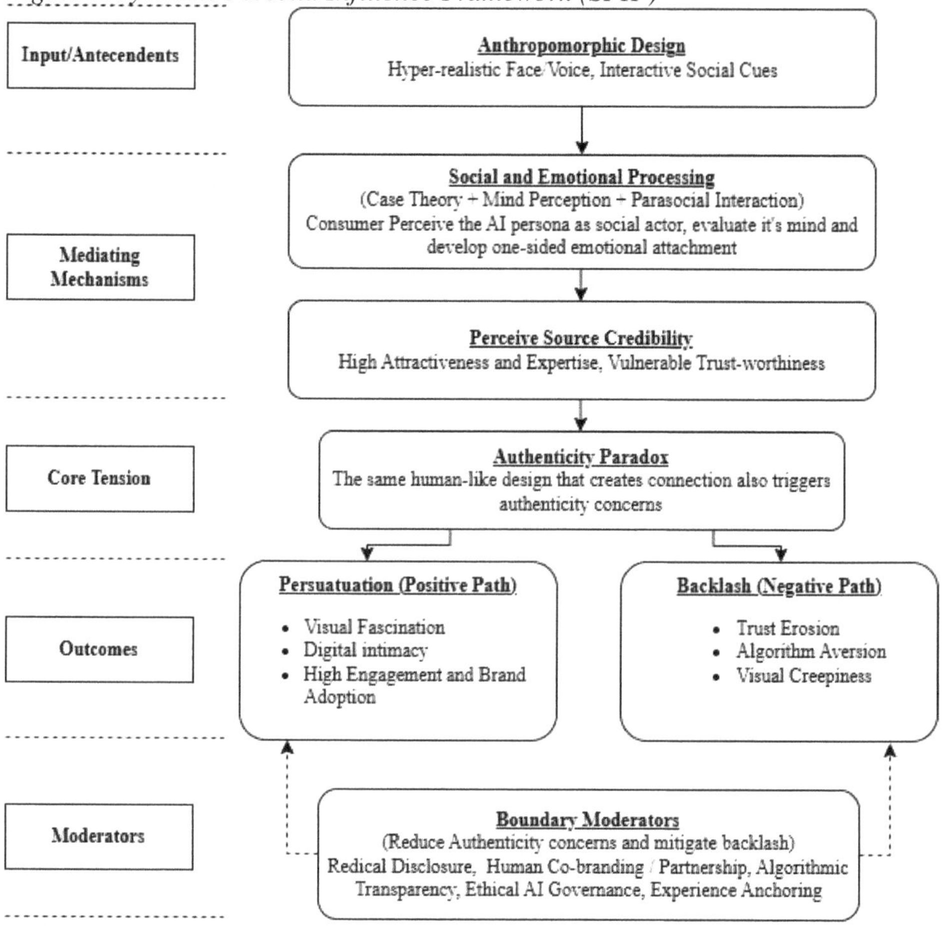

Sources: *Author's own creation*

3.1 Anthropomorphic Design as the Foundation of Synthetic Influence

The power of virtual influencers powered by AI can be traced to their capability to mimic certain human traits through advanced anthropomorphic design. Anthropomorphism is the tendency to assign human characteristics, will, feelings, and actions to non-humans (Epley et al., 2007). Anthropomorphism in the context of synthetic personas is the basic mechanism that turns artificial systems into socially familiar participants, who can engage in communication, form relationships, and persuade others. Modern virtual influencers make use of anthropomorphism in three dimensions that are interdependent. First, visual anthropomorphism gives humans-like appearances by using realistic face features, body gestures, and facial expressions made possible by the generative AI, deepfake technologies, and neural rendering systems (Moustakas et al., 2020). Second, behavioral anthropomorphism allows synthetic personas to talk, socialize and make preferences in a manner that resembles human social behavior. Third, narrative anthropomorphism offers virtual influencers their personal histories, lifestyles, values, and identities which generate the illusion of a coherent digital self (Arsenyan & Mirowska, 2021; Audrezet & Koles, 2023). Anthropomorphic design is not just important in the area of aesthetics. Human-like stimuli prompt consumers to perceive synthetic personas using social instead of technological models, making them perceive more familiarity, realism, and social presence (Arsenyan & Mirowska, 2021). Therefore, consumers can interact with virtual influencers as real, social players even when they are aware of their fake sources. The anthropomorphic design provides the basis of the synthetic influence through motivating consumers to perceive the virtual influencers as a human-like social entity.

3.2 Social and Emotional Processing of Synthetic Personas

The impact of AI-based virtual influencers relies not only on their human-like appearance but also on how consumers process these synthetic identities psychologically. The Computers Are Social Actors (CASA) theory asserts that people are more likely to apply social norms and expectations to technologies that exhibit human-like qualities; as a result, consumers start viewing virtual influencers as social actors and not as technological artifacts (Nass et al., 1994). After social attribution, Mind Perception Theory postulates that consumers consider synthetic personas, with reference to their perceived agency and experience (Gray et al., 2007). Although virtual influencers are perceived to have high agency because of their communicative potential as well as content and interaction creation, consumers often doubt their ability to experience real emotions and live lives. This imbalance results in a lack of experience where synthetic people view themselves as able to think but not feel. However, it is possible that consumers can also have emotional affiliations through the use of para-social interaction theory, which elaborates on how the audience develops one-sided relationships with media personalities (Horton & Richard Wohl, 1956). Virtual influencers can be used by means of constant contact, narration, and the ability to create identities to create familiarity, online intimacy, and emotional connection even though they are artificial. These theories describe how anthropomorphic design can be translated into influencing that human-like cues lead to social attribution, social attribution leads to agency perceptions, and these perceptions lead to para-social attachment. For this reason, consumers have the potential to interact with virtual influencers as socially significant participants despite the full knowledge that such artificially created beings exist. Nonetheless, the perceived lack of authentic experience also creates authenticity-related issues that can subsequently affect trust and consumer reactions.

3.3 Credibility Formation in Synthetic Environments

Although social attribution and emotional attachment can be used to understand consumer interaction with AI-based virtual influencers, their persuasion power will ultimately be determined by perceived credibility. The Source Credibility Theory suggests that the audience tends to believe information presented by sources that they view as appealing, learned, and credible (Ohanian, 1990). Credibility is formed in synthetic settings, where anthropomorphic design, perceived intelligence, and relational engagement interact to form the overall perception of how consumers assess AI-driven personas (Kim & Wang, 2024; Lim & Lee, 2023). Virtual influencers tend to have a better appearance, personality, and visual appeal as they can be created and optimized to match those of the audience and the brand (Arsenyan & Mirowska, 2021; Audrezet & Koles, 2023). They can also be seen as very well informed by the fact that they are able to provide constant content, consume a lot of information and ensure coherent communication over various digital platforms. Nevertheless, credibility takes the form of trustworthiness the most difficult aspect of credibility since consumers know that synthetic personas are artificial created beings but not people with real experiences and personal backgrounds (D. Kim & Wang, 2024). Although familiarity and emotional connection can be enhanced through anthropomorphic design and para-social interaction, the perception of trust can be weakened by the issue of authenticity, transparency, and lack of lived experience (Lim & Lee, 2023). As a result, the formation of credibility in synthetic realms will not be similar to conventional influencer settings where expertise, attractiveness, and trustworthiness are frequently based on real-life experience and self-identities. Artificial influencers run on AI can thus be more appealing and seem more knowledgeable and, at the same time, have some difficulty building credibility. This tension is especially crucial since it forms a delicate equilibrium of persuasion and doubt, which forms the basis of the authenticity-related issues addressed in the next section.

3.4 Authenticity Paradox of Synthetic Influence

The above discussion indicates that the persuasive value of AI-based virtual influencers has its basis in their capability to seem human, socially appealing, and trustworthy. Nevertheless, these very features present a major contradiction that is in the core of synthetic influence. This paradox is conceptualized in this chapter as the Authenticity Paradox, a paradox where the performance of virtual influencers hinges on the perception that they are authentic social actors, but their artificiality also calls into question the authenticity on which trust and credibility is established. The Authenticity Paradox is as a result of the interplay of anthropomorphism, mind perception, para-social attachment and source credibility. Anthropomorphic design enables virtual influencers to be designed in a way that mimics real human communicators, and they can be used to socialize. Synthetic personas become more of a socially relevant agent instead of a technological one as consumers assign agency and create emotional attachments to them (Horton & Richard Wohl, 1956; Nass et al., 1994). Such processes improve participation and boost persuasiveness. Nevertheless, consumers tend not to forget that the virtual influencers do not have real emotions, experiences, and subjective consciousness. Mind Perception Theory suggests that although artificial beings might be thought to be very competent in thinking and taking of action, they are often considered lacking experiential ability (Gray et al., 2007). Such lack of experience brings about doubtfulness as to the reality of their opinions, feelings, and recommendations. Credibility formation is one area where the paradox is especially pronounced. Although virtual influencers can be incredibly attractive and seem to have high levels of perceived expertise, consumers might doubt that an artificially created image can be used to promote products, share experiences, or build trustful relationships (D. Kim & Wang, 2024). As a result, the human-like traits that are associated with enhanced engagement can also arouse doubt about authenticity and transparency. This tension is one of the reasons why empirical research tends to show negative and positive reactions by consumers to virtual influencers. In the framework suggested, the Authenticity Paradox can be viewed as the key mediator connecting persuasion and resistance. Virtual influencers will be more likely to result in positive reactions when social connection, entertainment, and perceived expertise are the primary concerns of consumers. On the other hand, consumers can be skeptic and resistant when issues about artificiality, deception or limitations of the experience come into the limelight. Consequently, the success of synthetic personas lies not only in the fact that they can imitate humanity but also in the way in which consumers manage to resolve the conflict between the human-like features of representation and artificial reality.

3.5 From Persuasion to Backlash: Divergent Consumer Responses

According to the Authenticity Paradox, consumer reactions to AI-driven virtual influencers are dualistic in nature, which leads to results, such as persuasion and engagement, as well as skepticism and resistance. On the one hand, anthropomorphic design, perceived competence, and parasocial attachment may stimulate consumers to perceive synthetic personas as believable and socially relevant communicators, resulting in an enhanced level of engagement, a favorable brand attitude, and purchase intentions (Kim & Wang, 2023; Yang et al., 2023). Studies also suggest that virtual influencers have the potential to capture the consumer interest and create a positive brand perception when they are seen as relatable, interactive, and attractive (Jin & Ryu, 2020). Conversely, the non-authenticity of these entities can also create issues of authenticity, transparency, and emotional legitimacy. Consumers might be left wondering whether virtual influencers are truly familiar with the product that they promote or have the lived experience that they can make reliable recommendations (Lim & Lee, 2023). These issues might provoke suspicion and opposition especially in cases where artificial personas are overly lifelike or where they strive to emulate human behavior to the point of mimicking humans. This response is in line with the Uncanny Valley Hypothesis, which states that highly human-like yet flawed artificial images can produce unease and psychological discomfort (Masahiro et al., 2012). Besides, the research on the aversion to algorithm indicates that people tend to be unwilling to use AI-based judgments in socially sensitive situations, even when these systems are highly competent (Dietvorst et al., 2015). As a result, consumer reactions to virtual influencers are conditioned by an ongoing conflict between attraction and skepticism, and persuasion can be achieved when social and informational advantages prevail over authenticity issues, and the reverse happens when the sense of artificiality takes center stage.

3.6 Boundary Moderators of Synthetic Influence

Although the Authenticity Paradox is a good explanation of the conflict between persuasion and skepticism, the consumer reactions are not predetermined. The way people consider AI-powered virtual influencers and whether they evolve towards persuasion or backlash can be moderated by several factors. Radical disclosure, human-AI co-branding, and experience anchoring are three moderators that are of great significance. Radical disclosure means fully disclosing the unreal character of virtual influencers and minimizing the feeling of being cheated by it and enhancing the transparency (Lim & Lee, 2023). Human-AI co-branding uses artificial personas in association with human influencers or experts, enabling organizations to enjoy the efficiency and scalability of AI and retain the level of experiential authenticity linked to human communicators (Audrezet & Koles, 2023). Experience anchoring is another issue that can be addressed to the question of authenticity, as the recommendations generated by AI are associated with real experiences of a user, customer feedback, or professional reviews, which adds more credibility to the information. Taken together, these mechanisms lessen the uncertainty about authenticity and trustworthiness and enable consumers to come into terms with the advantages of human-like interaction with the facts of artificial identity. In the framework proposed, these moderators can act as boundary conditions that can weaken the backlash pathway and enhance the persuasive power of virtual influencer marketing by AI to eventually contribute to more responsible and sustainable uses of AI-powered virtual influencer marketing.

4. MARKETING PROSPECTS OF AI-POWERED VIRTUAL INFLUENCERS

4.1 Strategic Marketing Advantages

The growing use of AI-driven virtual influencers is mainly influenced by the capacity to address most of the limitations that come with human influencers, and retain essential elements of persuasion. In contrast to human influencers, virtual influencers do not face scandals, sickness, and travel, labor conflicts, and contractual ambiguity, as organizations can continue and consistently communicate the brand (Mazurkiewicz-Pizło, 2025; Oliveira & Chimenti, 2021). This superiority in operations gives companies more control over the messages, visual identity, and behavioral reliability, minimizing reputational risks and enhancing brand safety. Moreover, virtual influencers are capable of functioning in 24/7 and across various platforms and markets, which makes them scalable and cross-border communication at comparatively low replication costs. With AI-based content creation and multilingual translation, companies can tailor their communication approaches and ensure global brand parity (Xia et al., 2025). Being influencers embedded in digital ecosystems, virtual influencers connect with consumers outside the conventional advertising strategies and are a valuable strategic communication resource in commercial and non-commercial marketing goals (Audrezet & Koles, 2023).

4.2 Consumer Engagement and Personalized Interaction

One of the key strengths of virtual influencers is the possibility to create consumer interest and one-on-one interaction. Studies have shown that virtual influencers have just as much success in creating engagement on social media platforms as human influencers and that they can even create more consumer engagement and following in certain instances (Lim & Lee, 2023; Muniz et al., 2024). To some extent, their success can be explained by the anthropomorphic design aspects that prompt consumers to view them as socially relevant actors, which make it easier to interact with and establish a relationship (Dabiran et al., 2024). Virtual influencers are able to provide extremely personalized content with the help of artificial intelligence, consumer analytics, and machine learning systems that can be adjusted to the preferences and behavioral trends of the individual. This customization enhances intimacy between consumers and avatars and enables companies to develop more relatable and interactive communication encounters. As a consequence, virtual influencers have become a promising marketing instrument that could draw attention, maintain engagement, and foster relationships with consumers in the long run in increasingly competitive online spaces (Xia et al., 2025).

4.3 Emerging Commercial Opportunities and Empirical Evidence

In addition to the usual influencer marketing, virtual influencers are establishing new pioneered opportunities in the field of digital commerce, immersive media and new virtual ecosystems. By fitting into metaverse worlds, virtual shopping platforms, and online fashion markets, brands can create interactive consumer experiences that provide entertainment, socialization, and commercialization. The developments present new advertising and branding opportunities that are beyond the limit of conventional influencer marketing (J. Li & Ma, 2024). The effectiveness of these synthetic personas is ever-growing and is backed by empirical data. Research indicates that virtual influencers can reach the same or even higher levels of engagement with consumers as human ones with a higher level of consistency and reduced reputational risk (Muniz et al., 2024; J. Yang et al., 2023). Additionally, they are quite appropriate in sustainability communication, ethical branding, and promoting green products due to their regulated character and lower risk of controversy (J. Yang et al., 2023). Together, these results suggest that AI-driven virtual influencers are an important innovation in digital marketing, which provide companies with scalable, interactive, and controllable means to develop consumer relationships and improve brand performance.

4.4 Case Illustration: Lil Miquela and Imma as Strategic Virtual Influencers

The most popular examples of the increasing use of AI-driven virtual influencers include the examples of Lil Miquela and Imma, which are two of the most commercially successful synthetic personalities in modern digital marketing (Goyal et al., 2025). As a character by Brud, Lil Miquela has amassed millions of subscribers on social media and partnered with major brands worldwide, including Prada, Calvin Klein, Samsung, and BMW (Paulovics, 2023). Similarly, Imma, which was created by a Japanese corporation called Aww Inc., has collaborated with international brands such as IKEA, Porsche, Nike, and Valentino without losing its unique cultural identity, which is based on Japanese digital culture (Conti et al., 2022; Miyake, 2023). These cases indicate that virtual influencers have transformed into experimental digital characters to strategic marketing resources that can produce significant consumer interaction and brand exposure. Strategically, the two instances showcase a number of benefits that are linked with virtual influencer marketing. Compared with human influencers, Lil Miquela and Imma offer a brand more control over messages, images, and consistency of behavior, minimizing the risks of scandals, reputational crises, or personal scandals (Theodorakopoulos et al., 2025). They are also digital, which facilitates the continuous production of content and cross-platform interaction, which helps with scalability and brand management in the long-run. Moreover, these virtual influencers have shown the potential to create robust para-social bonds with their audience by storytelling, lifestyle content, and interactive communication, which can reveal how synthetic personas can match the engagement of traditional influencers (Bai et al., 2025; Dondapati & Dehury, 2024). The example of Imma also shows the possibility of virtual influencers in terms of hyperlocalized global branding. Although it is a globally recognizable brand, Imma uses culturally specific storytelling and imagery, which appeal to local markets, and reflect how synthetic personas can contribute to cross-cultural marketing efforts. Together, the experiences of Lil Miquela and Imma demonstrate how AI-based virtual influencers may be used with scalability, controllability, personalization, and cultural flexibility, which strengthens their increased importance.

5. THE ETHICAL DARK SIDE OF SYNTHETIC INFLUENCE

5.1 Fraud, Authenticity and Consumer Manipulation

Although they are becoming increasingly effective as marketing instruments, AI-driven virtual influencers are also highly contested in terms of being deceptive, inauthentic, and manipulative by consumers (Franke et al., 2023; Lou et al., 2023). Unlike human influencers, synthetic personas are consciously designed to look like humans, feel, and behave socially with the use of artificial intelligence, computer graphics, and deepfake technologies (Luttrell & Welch, 2025; Rayun et al., 2026). With the advancement of these technologies, consumers might fail to differentiate authentic and artificial identities, making the nature of online interactions ambiguous (Franke et al., 2023). This issue is especially significant since the persuasive ability of virtual influencers usually rests on the ability of consumers to see them as genuine social actors who can build meaningful relationships (Kim and Wang, 2024). One of the main ethical issues is the impact of generated authenticity vc(Dang, 2025; Ouaddi, 2025). Virtual influencers regularly provide personal narratives, feelings and lifestyle experiences that are similar to the self-disclosure behaviors of human influencers even though they have no actual lived experiences (Breves & van Berlo, 2025). This authenticity is a strategically planned and commercially handled aspect instead of an organic development. According to recent studies, the perception of authenticity continues to be a decisive factor of consumer trust, engagement, and behavioral intentions with virtual influencers (Hewapathirana & Perera, 2024; Lee et al., 2025). As a result, there is a paradox of brands whereby synthetic personas need to be increasingly authentic to be persuasive yet are simultaneously not believable because of their synthetic nature. Comparative research also indicates that consumers make judgments about virtual influencers as opposed to human influencers in situations where the evaluation criteria of authenticity and emotional credibility are salient (Lee et al., 2025; H. Li et al., 2023). The ethical risks are not limited to concerns of authenticity but are related to the problem of manipulation in greater detail. As accelerating AI systems develop more persuasive material that is highly similar to human communication, consumers might not recognize any attempts at algorithmic persuasion (Zarouali et al., 2022). This poses significant questions concerning informed consumer choice, transparency, and the responsible use of anthropomorphic AI systems in marketing settings. Finally, the increasing complexity of virtual influencers is a challenge to the longstanding belief about trust, authenticity, and ethical persuasion in online markets.

5.2 Psychological and Societal risks

In addition to the issue of deception, AI-driven virtual influencers can lead to more widespread psychological and social implications. Synthetic personas can also create close para-social bonds of the kind that traditional emotional bonds are considered to establish with human influencers, through anthropomorphic design, constant interaction, and meticulously edited narratives (Akhtar & Nagvanshi, 2025). Although this type of relationship could lead to increased engagement and customer satisfaction, it can also provide some chances to play with emotions and parasocial exploitation, especially in the case of vulnerable consumers. In contrast to human relationships, relationships with virtual influencers are ultimately controlled by algorithms and commercial goals aimed at drawing maximum attention, engagement, and persuasiveness. Also virtual influencers are not bound to physical realities and thus can assume idealized looks, lifestyles, and personas that are optimized for computational design (Elyamany et al., 2025; Yan et al., 2024). These representations can support unrealistic beauty ideals, escalate social comparison, and cause psychological distress among viewers who want to imitate unrealistic digital images (Oliveira & Chimenti, 2021). Since synthetic personas can be constantly enhanced and improved, they can augment the pressure that is already present related to appearance, success, and social status in the digital world. Moreover, the growing realism of AI-created identities can confuse the boundaries between real and artificial social relations. Research has shown that the perception of authenticity, trust, and social presence is the key factor in engaging emotionally with virtual influencers, which may add to the degree of psychological attachment and consumer vulnerability (Liu et al., 2025; Yan et al., 2024). These effects might be especially vulnerable to younger consumers because of their greater exposure to social media and digitally mediated interactions. As a result, the impact of virtual influencers extends beyond marketing performance to the key issues of identity development, emotional stability, and consumer independence. With the growing presence of synthetic personas in daily online existence, the issues of social responsibility and ethical design have gained more significance.

5.3 Deepfakes, Privacy, Economic Concerns, and Consumer Resistance

Synthetic influence has ethical issues in addition to personal psychological implications: greater societal issues such as deepfakes, privacy, misinformation, and economic disturbances (Al-Kfairy et al., 2024; Alanazi et al., 2025). Deepfake technologies can be used to make highly realistic artificial faces, voices, and identities, which places a greater risk of identity cloning, fake endorsements, and deceptive communication behaviors (Bajwa et al., 2025; Salam et al., 2024). These possibilities can contribute to misinformation and erosion of trust in digital content by making it more challenging to differentiate real communications and AI-generated artifices. Consumer data and algorithmic profiling are also essential to the operation of virtual influencers. By using behavioral analytics, predictive targeting, and personalized communication systems, organizations can shape consumer choices as never before. Although these features make marketing more efficient, they also raise issues of privacy, surveillance, and commercial persuasion with the use of personal information that has been violated (Sands et al., 2022; Singh & Dhiman, 2023). Furthermore, recent findings reveal that AI-based persuasive communication can be practically undifferentiated from that of humans, posing enormous threats to misinformation and manipulation in online markets (Marcellis-Warin et al., 2022). Economically, the growing use of virtual influencers can lead to the replacement of human creators in the influencer economy (Gerlich, 2023). Owing to the scalability, controllability, and cost-effectiveness of synthetic personas, organizations might shift their preference among influencers to AI-generated influencers more often than human influencers do, which could alter the fabric of digital labor markets and widen platform inequalities (Hashem, 2025). Researchers have shown that perceived artificiality, decreased experiential authenticity, and the disclosure of non-human identity may undermine trust, engagement, and purchase intentions (Muniz et al., 2024). Similarly, the issues of anthropomorphism, transparency, and machine-generated communication have also been linked to the rise of skepticism and consumer distrust toward AI-generated recommendations (Baryshkov et al., 2026). Taken together, these results indicate that virtual influencers can provide considerable marketing prospects, but they also pose considerable ethical, psychological, and social threats that should be regulated and implemented responsibly.

6. STRATEGIC AND GOVERNANCE IMPLICATIONS

6.1 Responsible AI Influencer Management

The discussion above indicates that the success of AI-based virtual influencers is related to the capacity of organizations to strike a balance between technological innovativeness and consumer trust. With artificiality being the authenticity paradox, overuse of artificiality can decrease credibility, but consumer acceptance can be improved through the careful design of human-AI integration. Human-AI cobranding, i.e., the collaboration of virtual influencers with human creators, experts, or brand representatives, is one of the possible approaches. These systems merge the scalability and reactivity of artificial personas with the authenticity and social acceptability of human communicators (Audrezet & Koles, 2023; D. Kim & Wang, 2024). Virtual influencer credibility enhances consumer reactions more when artificial agents are linked with recognizable human experience and management (Lim & Lee, 2023). The second approach is experience anchoring, which connects AI-generated recommendations with verifiable human experiences, expert assessments, or user-created content. Since virtual influencers do not have real-life experience, the anchoring of promotion claims on real-life evidence can address anxieties about authenticity and credibility (Zhou et al., 2023). In this way, organizations can harness AI efficiency without the development of false impressions about experiential knowledge. Finally, companies must embrace radical transparency that would reveal the virtual nature of influencers. Instead of hiding AI participation, it is important to explicitly reveal synthetic identities, content-generation methods, and sponsorships. According to recent research, transparency can reinforce the trust of the long term and decrease the perception of deceit, especially when disclosure is a part of the narrative identity of the virtual influencer instead of being a legal reminder (Lim & Lee, 2023). All these practices can contribute to a more responsible and sustainable model of AI influencer management that focuses on consumer trust and commercial performance.

6.2 Regulatory and Governance Challenges

The emergence of technologies of virtual influencers has surpassed the pace of the development of regulatory frameworks, posing a serious challenge in their governance. Among the most important issues are the issue of disclosure requirements. Although certain jurisdictions have provided guidelines on sponsored content and AI-generated media, there is a high level of inconsistency over the manner in which virtual influencers are identified and regulated. A lack of uniform disclosure systems can create more confusion for consumers and less transparency in digital markets (Khalfallah & Keller, 2025). In addition to disclosure, the emergence of artificial identities underscores more significant issues of AI governance. Transparency, explainability, fairness, and human oversight have become central to responsible AI frameworks to implement intelligent systems (Floridi, 2021). To implement the principles in the context of virtual influencer ecosystems, organizations need to have governance systems that can oversee content creation, reduce negative products, and hold AI-generated communications accountable. The other emerging concern is related to the ownership of intellectual property and identity. Deefake systems and generative AI-based technologies can reproduce facial features, voices, and personal attributes with greater accuracy than ever before, making it ambiguous as to who owns what, and whether an identity is appropriated against its owner's will (Moustakas et al., 2020). The current copyright and publicity-right systems are ill-equipped to address most of these issues. Therefore, policymakers should consider new jurisprudential strategies or securing online identities and controlling synthetic representations. Responsibility is also an important issue. In cases of misleading content, malicious content, and false endorsements spread by virtual influencers, the liability can be shared between developers, platform operators, brands, and AI systems. It is necessary to form transparent accountability frameworks, thus, to ensure consumer protection and social trust in more automated communication systems (Floridi, 2021).

6.3 Practical Implications

The findings of this chapter provide important practical insights for marketers seeking to integrate AI-powered virtual influencers into contemporary digital marketing strategies. First, organizations should recognize that the success of synthetic personas depends not solely on technological sophistication but on their ability to establish and maintain consumer trust. While virtual influencers offer unprecedented advantages in terms of brand control, message consistency, scalability, and cost efficiency, these benefits can only be realized when consumers perceive the communication as credible and transparent. Consequently, marketers should move beyond viewing virtual influencers as merely automated promotional tools and instead manage them as long-term brand assets. Strategic disclosure regarding the artificial nature of virtual influencers can reduce perceptions of deception while strengthening authenticity and consumer confidence. Furthermore, marketers can leverage virtual influencers to maintain a continuous brand presence across multiple platforms, languages, and cultural contexts, enabling more effective global communication strategies. The ability of synthetic personas to operate continuously and generate personalized interactions also creates opportunities for brands to enhance customer engagement, improve responsiveness, and deliver more tailored consumer experiences. However, these advantages should be accompanied by responsible communication practices that ensure consumers remain aware of the synthetic nature of the interaction.

The proposed Authenticity Paradox further highlights that marketers must carefully balance realism and transparency when designing virtual influencer campaigns. Excessive human likeness may increase engagement and emotional attachment, but it can also intensify concerns regarding authenticity, manipulation, and trustworthiness. To address this challenge, marketers should adopt hybrid influence strategies that combine the efficiency of AI-powered personas with the credibility of human experts, creators, or brand representatives. Such collaborations can provide the experiential authenticity that virtual influencers inherently lack while preserving the scalability advantages of synthetic personas. Marketers should also incorporate evidence-based communication, customer testimonials, and user-generated content to strengthen message credibility and reduce skepticism. Beyond campaign design, organizations must establish governance mechanisms to monitor ethical risks associated with deepfakes, misinformation, identity misuse, and privacy concerns. Proactive risk management, transparency policies, and responsible AI guidelines can help organizations protect brand reputation while complying with emerging regulatory requirements. Ultimately, the long-term value of AI-powered virtual influencers will depend not on how realistically they imitate humans, but on how effectively marketers balance technological innovation with transparency, ethical responsibility, and consumer trust. Such an approach enables organizations to maximize marketing effectiveness while fostering sustainable and socially responsible relationships with consumers.

7. RESEARCH AND POLICY RECOMMENDATIONS

With the growing integration of AI-based virtual influencers into digital marketing systems, the study of synthetic influence and its regulation should also evolve to meet the opportunities and challenges presented by synthetic influence. Spending on the Synthetic Persona Influence Framework (SPIF), the future work should be directed towards further theoretical knowledge as well as the creation of mechanisms that would encourage transparency, accountability, and consumer protection.

The emphasis of future research should be on the empirical validation of the Synthetic Persona Influence Framework (SPIF) in different settings and consumer groups. Although the framework suggests that anthropomorphic design has an effect on social-emotional processing, credibility formation, and authenticity perceptions, these links need to be tested with a rigorous experimental, survey-based, and longitudinal research design. Specifically, scholars are encouraged to perform cross-cultural analyses of the perceptions of authenticity to find out whether consumer reactions to the synthetic personas vary in the social, cultural, and religious settings. Most of the current studies are located in Western and East Asian environments, and thus wider geographical coverage is required to enhance generalizability of the theory. The long-term evolution of the trust and para-social attachment created by AI should also be investigated in future research, whether the repeated exposure to AI-based virtual influencers reinforces persuasion or induces consumer skepticism over time. Moreover, the development of large language model (LLM)-driven virtual influencers is a significant research opportunity. As the synthetic personas are more autonomous, conversational and adaptive, researchers must uncover the impact of these abilities on consumer engagement, trust, and perceived authenticity. On the same note, the development of affective computing and emotional AI is also worth exploring, especially in terms of whether emotionally responsive virtual influencers can alleviate the perceived experience gap that is noted in this chapter or bring about new kinds of emotional manipulation. Lastly, the scholars need to investigate how human-AI co-branding and disclosure can help address the authenticity issue and enhance consumer trust.

The swift development of generative AI and deepfake technologies requires active regulatory and governance policies. The policymakers ought to think through the introduction of disclosure obligations of AI-generated identities, so that consumers can easily differentiate human and synthetic influencers. Connectedly, the creation of industry guidelines on the labeling of deepfake and synthetic media would enhance transparency and minimize the chance of misleading communication patterns. Consumer privacy should also be a subject of regulatory concern especially concerning the manner in which AI-driven marketing regimes collect, process, and personalize consumer data. Moreover, governments, industry bodies and technology platforms ought to work together in coming up with ethical principles of virtual influencer marketing, which would touch upon such issues as manipulation, misinformation, identity abuse, and the needy consumer groups. The social media platforms are also advised to enhance platform accountability and content governance solutions by enhancing the ability to detect deceptive synthetic content and implement responsible AI policies. Lastly, proper transparency standards concerning AI-created endorsements and sponsored content need to be established to make sure that consumers can properly judge the origin and purpose of the persuasive messages.

All of these research and policy recommendations can facilitate the responsible development of AI-driven virtual influencers and create more open, trustful, and sustainable digital marketing systems.

8. CONCLUSION

The emergence of AI-assisted virtual influencers is a major turning point in the history of digital marketing, as it is a manifestation of the increased integration of artificial intelligence, synthetic media, and consumer interaction. It has been established in this chapter that virtual influencers are not only technological innovations but also new sociotechnical actors that can influence consumer attitudes, relationships, and marketplace behaviors. Although they present opportunities to provide improved brand control, scalability, personalization, and immersive consumer experiences that make them desirable strategic resources, there are also significant ethical issues associated with deception, authenticity, privacy, misinformation, psychological vulnerability, and the ability to displace the economy. The authenticity paradox is central to these opportunities and risks and posits that the success of synthetic personas hinges on their ability to seem to be human, trustworthy, and socially meaningful and to be simultaneously artificial beings with no real lived experience. To clarify this tension, this chapter proposes the Integrated Human-AI Persuasion and Backlash Framework, which illustrates how anthropomorphic design, social attribution, mind perception, para-social attachment, and credibility formation can result in consumer persuasion and consumer resistance. The results suggest that the future of virtual influencer marketing is determined by the technological level of sophistication as well as the capacity of organizations to promote transparency, accountability and consumer confidence. With the future rise of synthetic personas, owing to the continued blurring of human-artificial communication boundaries caused by the accelerated growth of generative AI, large language models, affective computing, and deepfake technologies, synthetic personas will gain greater autonomy and power in digital ecosystems. Therefore, the most critical question, which researchers, practitioners, and policymakers face, is not whether virtual influencers are going to be a regular aspect of the modern marketing realm, but how they can be created, ruled, and implemented in a responsible manner to ensure that the innovation process goes in tandem with moral responsibility and the sustainability of consumer trust.

REFERENCES

Abootorabi, M. M., Ghahroodi, O., Zahraei, P. S., Behzadasl, H., Mirrokni, A., Salimipanah, M., Rasouli, A., Behzadipour, B., Azarnoush, S., & Maleki, B. (2025). Generative AI for character animation: A comprehensive survey of techniques, applications, and future directions. *ArXiv Preprint ArXiv:2504.19056.*

Akhtar, M. J., & Nagvanshi, S. (2025). Parasocial Interaction and Virtual Influencers: Building Connections in a Digital World. In *Redefining the Future of Digital Marketing With Virtual Influencers* (pp. 151–180). IGI Global Scientific Publishing.

Al-Kfairy, M., Mustafa, D., Kshetri, N., Insiew, M., & Alfandi, O. (2024). Ethical challenges and solutions of generative AI: An interdisciplinary perspective. *Informatics (MDPI), 11*(3), 58. DOI: 10.3390/informatics11030058

Alanazi, S., Asif, S., Caird-Daley, A., & Moulitsas, I. (2025). Unmasking deepfakes: a multidisciplinary examination of social impacts and regulatory responses. *Human-Intelligent Systems Integration*, 1–23.

Arsenyan, J., & Mirowska, A. (2021). Almost human? A comparative case study on the social media presence of virtual influencers. *International Journal of Human Computer Studies, 155*(July 2020), 102694. DOI: 10.1016/j.ijhcs.2021.102694

Audrezet, A., & Koles, B. (2023). Virtual Influencer as a Brand Avatar in Interactive Marketing. In *The Palgrave handbook of Interactive Marketing* (pp. 353–376). Springer., DOI: 10.1007/978-3-031-14961-0_16

Ayertey, S., Panditharathna, R., Mohamad, M., & Laryeafio, M. N. (2026). Generative AI as a Digital Influencer on Visual Content Marketing: The Ethical Dilemma. In *Strategies, Dynamics, and Societal Impacts of Digital Influencer Marketing* (pp. 159–174). IGI Global Scientific Publishing.

Bai, B., Vignali, G., Ryding, D., & Vazquez, D. (2025). Exploring the Impact of Para-Social Interaction: The Consumer Journey in a Social Media World with a Focus on Virtual Influencers. In *Contemporary Issues in Social Media Marketing* (pp. 152–170). Routledge.

Bajwa, M. T. T., Tehreem, F., Farid, Z., Tahir, H. M. F., & Khalid, A. (2025). Deepfake voice recognition: Techniques, organizational risks and ethical implications. *Spectrum of Engineering Sciences*, 106–121.

Baryshkov, K., Kuzina, Y., Smuk, I., & Tkachuk, M. (2026). Consumer Trust in AI-Generated Marketing Content: A Systematic Literature Review and Research Agenda. *American Impact Review*, *1*(1), e2026024–e2026024. DOI: 10.66308/air.e2026024

Breves, P. L., & van Berlo, Z. M. C. (2025). Making and breaking parasocial relationships with human and virtual influencers: An experience sampling study. *Media Psychology*, •••, 1–29. DOI: 10.1080/15213269.2025.2558029

Conti, M., Gathani, J., & Tricomi, P. P. (2022). Virtual influencers in online social media. *IEEE Communications Magazine*, *60*(8), 86–91. DOI: 10.1109/MCOM.001.2100786

Dabiran, E., Farivar, S., Wang, F., & Grant, G. (2024). Virtually human: Anthropomorphism in virtual influencer marketing. *Journal of Retailing and Consumer Services*, *79*, 103797. DOI: 10.1016/j.jretconser.2024.103797

Dang, N. (2025). The influence of AI-generated visual content on influencer marketing strategies in social media. *Reviews on Internet of Things (IoT). Cyber-Physical Systems, and Applications*, *10*(3), 1–18.

De Marcellis-Warin, N., Marty, F., Thelisson, E., & Warin, T. (2022). Artificial intelligence and consumer manipulations: From consumer's counter algorithms to firm's self-regulation tools. *AI and Ethics*, *2*(2), 259–268. DOI: 10.1007/s43681-022-00149-5

Dietvorst, B. J., Simmons, J. P., & Massey, C. (2015). Algorithm aversion: People erroneously avoid algorithms after seeing them err. *Journal of Experimental Psychology. General*, *144*(1), 114–126. DOI: 10.1037/xge0000033 PMID: 25401381

Dondapati, A., & Dehury, R. K. (2024). Virtual vs. human influencers: The battle for consumer hearts and minds. *Computers in Human Behavior: Artificial Humans*, *2*(1), 100059. DOI: 10.1016/j.chbah.2024.100059

Elyamany, N., Youssef, Y. O., & El-Karef, N. (2025). A trans-disciplinary forensic study of Lil Miquela's virtual identity performance in Instagram. *AI & Society*, *40*(6), 4831–4854. DOI: 10.1007/s00146-025-02219-8

Epley, N., Waytz, A., & Cacioppo, J. T. (2007). On seeing human: A three-factor theory of anthropomorphism. *Psychological Review*, *114*(4), 864–886. DOI: 10.1037/0033-295X.114.4.864 PMID: 17907867

Fang, X., & Wang, T. (2022). Using natural language processing to identify effective influencers. *International Journal of Market Research*, *64*(5), 611–629. DOI: 10.1177/14707853221101565

Floridi, L. (2021). Artificial intelligence, deepfakes and a future of ectypes. In *Ethics, governance, and policies in artificial intelligence* (pp. 307–312). Springer. DOI: 10.1007/978-3-030-81907-1_17

Franke, C., Groeppel-Klein, A., & Müller, K. (2023). Consumers' responses to virtual influencers as advertising endorsers: Novel and effective or uncanny and deceiving? *Journal of Advertising*, *52*(4), 523–539. DOI: 10.1080/00913367.2022.2154721

Gerlich, M. (2023). The power of virtual influencers: Impact on consumer behaviour and attitudes in the age of AI. *Administrative Sciences*, *13*(8), 178. DOI: 10.3390/admsci13080178

Goyal, N., & Bhardwaj, K. (2025). Virtual Influencer Marketing and Its Impact on Marketing Strategies. In *Redefining the Future of Digital Marketing With Virtual Influencers* (pp. 55–88). IGI Global Scientific Publishing. DOI: 10.4018/979-8-3373-0255-3.ch003

Gray, H. M., Gray, K., & Wegner, D. M. (2007). Dimensions of mind perception. *Science*, *315*(5812), 619. DOI: 10.1126/science.1134475 PMID: 17272713

Hashem, T. N. (2025). The Disruption of Influencer Marketing: Exploring the Efficiency of AI-Generated Virtual Influencers vs. Human Influencers. *Journal of Information & Knowledge Management*, *24*(06), 2550063. DOI: 10.1142/S0219649225500637

Hewapathirana, I. U., & Perera, N. (2024). *Navigating the age of AI influence: A systematic literature review of trust, engagement, efficacy and ethical concerns of virtual influencers in social media.*

Horton, D., & Richard Wohl, R. (1956). Mass communication and para-social interaction: Observations on intimacy at a distance. *Psychiatry*, *19*(3), 215–229. DOI: 10.1080/00332747.1956.11023049 PMID: 13359569

Jhawar, A., Kumar, P., & Varshney, S. (2023). The emergence of virtual influencers: A shift in the influencer marketing paradigm. *Young Consumers*, *24*(4), 468–484. DOI: 10.1108/YC-05-2022-1529

Jiang, K., Zheng, J., & Luo, S. (2024). Green power of virtual influencer: The role of virtual influencer image, emotional appeal, and product involvement. *Journal of Retailing and Consumer Services*, *77*, 103660. DOI: 10.1016/j.jretconser.2023.103660

Jin, S. V., & Ryu, E. (2020). "I'll buy what she's# wearing": The roles of envy toward and parasocial interaction with influencers in Instagram celebrity-based brand endorsement and social commerce. *Journal of Retailing and Consumer Services*, *55*, 102121. DOI: 10.1016/j.jretconser.2020.102121

Karimova, G. Z. (2025). Creating AI Persona. In *Humanizing AI with Personality* (pp. 49–59). Springer. DOI: 10.1007/978-3-031-82327-5_5

Khalfallah, D., & Keller, V. (2025). Authenticity, ethics, and transparency in virtual influencer marketing: A cross-cultural analysis of consumer trust and engagement: A systematic literature review. *Acta Psychologica*, *260*, 105573. DOI: 10.1016/j.actpsy.2025.105573 PMID: 40974722

Kim, D., & Wang, Z. (2023). The ethics of virtuality: Navigating the complexities of human-like virtual influencers in the social media marketing realm. *Frontiers in Communication*, *8*, 1205610. DOI: 10.3389/fcomm.2023.1205610

Kim, D., & Wang, Z. (2024). Social media influencer vs. virtual influencer: The mediating role of source credibility and authenticity in advertising effectiveness within AI influencer marketing. *Computers in Human Behavior: Artificial Humans*, *2*(2), 100100. DOI: 10.1016/j.chbah.2024.100100

Kim, H., & Park, M. (2024). When digital celebrity talks to you: How human-like virtual influencers satisfy consumer's experience through social presence on social media endorsements. *Journal of Retailing and Consumer Services, 76*(October 2023), 103581. DOI: 10.1016/j.jretconser.2023.103581

Lee, H., Shin, M., Yang, J., & Chock, T. M. (2025). Virtual influencers vs. human influencers in the context of influencer marketing: The moderating role of machine heuristic on perceived authenticity of influencers. *International Journal of Human-Computer Interaction*, *41*(10), 6029–6046. DOI: 10.1080/10447318.2024.2374100

Leung, F. F., Gu, F. F., Li, Y., Zhang, J. Z., & Palmatier, R. W. (2022). Influencer marketing effectiveness. *Journal of Marketing*, *86*(6), 93–115. DOI: 10.1177/00222429221102889

Li, H., Lei, Y., Zhou, Q., & Yuan, H. (2023). Can you sense without being human? Comparing virtual and human influencers endorsement effectiveness. *Journal of Retailing and Consumer Services*, *75*(June), 103456. DOI: 10.1016/j.jretconser.2023.103456

Li, J., & Ma, Y. (2024). Virtual influencers in advertisements: Examining the role of authenticity and identification. *Journal of Interactive Advertising*, *24*(1), 1–12. DOI: 10.1080/15252019.2023.2270478

Lim, R. E., & Lee, S. Y. (2023). "You are a virtual influencer!": Understanding the impact of origin disclosure and emotional narratives on parasocial relationships and virtual influencer credibility. *Computers in Human Behavior, 148*(November 2022), 107897. DOI: 10.1016/j.chb.2023.107897

Liu, R., Li, X., & Liu, S. (2025). How emotional expression in human-like virtual influencers drives user engagement: Empathy model and its antecedents. *Frontiers in Psychology, 16*, 1544037. DOI: 10.3389/fpsyg.2025.1544037 PMID: 41567455

Lou, C., Kiew, S. T. J., Chen, T., Lee, T. Y. M., Ong, J. E. C., & Phua, Z. X. (2023). Authentically Fake? How Consumers Respond to the Influence of Virtual Influencers. *Journal of Advertising, 52*(4), 540–557. DOI: 10.1080/00913367.2022.2149641

Luttrell, R., & Welch, C. (2025). Ai-powered synthetic personas: Affecting the future of public relations campaigns. In *Public Relations and the Rise of AI* (pp. 97–117). Routledge.

Masahiro, M., MacDorman, K. F., & Kageki, N. (2012). The uncanny valley. *IEEE Robotics & Automation Magazine, 19*(2), 98–100. DOI: 10.1109/MRA.2012.2192811

Mazurkiewicz-Pizło, A. (2025). Virtual influencers (VIs) as marketing communication tools. *European Research Studies, 28*(1), 472–492. DOI: 10.35808/ersj/3955

Miyake, E. (2023). I am a virtual girl from Tokyo: Virtual influencers, digital-orientalism and the (Im) materiality of race and gender. *Journal of Consumer Culture, 23*(1), 209–228. DOI: 10.1177/14695405221117195

Moustakas, E., Lamba, N., Mahmoud, D., & Ranganathan, C. (2020). Blurring lines between fiction and reality: Perspectives of experts on marketing effectiveness of virtual influencers. *2020 International Conference on Cyber Security and Protection of Digital Services (Cyber Security)*, 1–6. DOI: 10.1109/CyberSecurity49315.2020.9138861

Muniz, F., Stewart, K., & Magalhães, L. (2024). Are they humans or are they robots? The effect of virtual influencer disclosure on brand trust. *Journal of Consumer Behaviour, 23*(3), 1234–1250. DOI: 10.1002/cb.2271

Nass, C., Steuer, J., & Tauber, E. R. (1994). Computers are social actors. *Proceedings of the SIGCHI Conference on Human Factors in Computing Systems*, 72–78. DOI: 10.1145/191666.191703

Ohanian, R. (1990). Construction and validation of a scale to measure celebrity endorsers' perceived expertise, trustworthiness, and attractiveness. *Journal of Advertising, 19*(3), 39–52. DOI: 10.1080/00913367.1990.10673191

Oliveira, A. B. da S., & Chimenti, P. (2021). Humanized Robots": A Proposition of Categories to Understand Virtual Influencers. *AJIS. Australasian Journal of Information Systems*, •••, 25.

Ouaddi, H. (2025). The Rise of AI-Generated Influencers: Cybersecurity, Trust, and the Future of Social Media Marketing in Morocco. *International Journal of Digitalization and Applied Management*, *2*(2), 68–83.

Paglieri, D., Cross, L., Cunningham, W. A., Leibo, J. Z., & Vezhnevets, A. S. (2026). Persona Generators: Generating Diverse Synthetic Personas at Scale. *ArXiv Preprint ArXiv:2602.03545*.

Paulovics, Á. (2023). *Digital reality and identity: An evolutionary analysis of virtual influencer lil miquela*.

Pieper, J., Griewatz, H.-P., & Morgenroth, S. (2026). Virtual Influencers and the Future of Content Creation. In *Artificial Intelligence in Creative Industries* (1st ed., pp. 75–88). Routledge. DOI: 10.4324/9781003606802-7

Rahimzadeh, V., Monazzah, E. M., Pilehvar, M. T., & Yaghoobzadeh, Y. (2025). *Synthia: Scalable Grounded Persona Generation from Social Media Data*.

Ramadan, Z., & Ramadan, J. (2025). AI avatars and co-creation in the metaverse. *Consumer Behavior in Tourism and Hospitality*, *20*(1), 131–147. DOI: 10.1108/CBTH-07-2024-0246

Rayun, S. M. N., Salam, M. A., Leong, V. S., Islam, W., Sahabuddin, M., Ahmed, M., Hosen, M. S., & Das, C. (2026). Deepfakes and Digital Sovereignty: Governance Challenges of Synthetic Media in the AI-Driven Data Economy. Https://Services.Igi-Global.Com/Resolvedoi/Resolve.Aspx?Doi=10.4018/979-8-2600-0288-9.Ch008, 225–264. DOI: 10.4018/979-8-2600-0288-9.ch008

Salam, M. A., Rayun, S. M. N., Islam, W., Hasan, R., Firmansyah, E. A., & Kalinaki, K. (2024). Consumer Engagement: Exploring Deepfake Applications in Consumer Marketing Communication. In *Navigating the World of Deepfake Technology* (pp. 397–421). IGI Global. DOI: 10.4018/979-8-3693-5298-4.ch020

Sands, S., Campbell, C. L., Plangger, K., & Ferraro, C. (2022). Unreal influence: Leveraging AI in influencer marketing. *European Journal of Marketing*, *56*(6), 1721–1747. DOI: 10.1108/EJM-12-2019-0949

Schenker, D. (2023). *The construction of identity and evolution of desire through synthetic media*. Temple University.

Sharma, A., Pujari, M., & Goel, A. (2025). The rise of AI-generated synthetic identities: A new frontier in social media. *International Journal of Innovative Research in Engineering & Multidisciplinary Physical Sciences*, *13*(2), 232397. DOI: 10.37082/IJIRMPS.v13.i2.232397

Singh, P., & Dhiman, B. (2023). Exploding AI-generated deepfakes and misinformation: A threat to global concern in the 21st century. *Authorea Preprints*.

Tan, Y. H., & Greene, B. R. (2025). Can a 2D shark girl be an influencer? Uncovering prevailing archetypes in the virtual entertainer industry. *Journal of Business Research, 186*, 114951. DOI: 10.1016/j.jbusres.2024.114951

Thapliyal, M., Jahan, A., & Sharma, R. (2025). AI-Assisted Character Motion Synthesis using Deep Generative Models. *2025 6th International Conference on IoT Based Control Networks and Intelligent Systems (ICICNIS)*, 1653–1657.

Theodorakopoulos, L., Theodoropoulou, A., & Klavdianos, C. (2025). Interactive viral marketing through big data analytics, influencer networks, AI integration, and ethical dimensions. *Journal of Theoretical and Applied Electronic Commerce Research, 20*(2), 115. DOI: 10.3390/jtaer20020115

Tolbert, C. L. (2025). Enhancing Persona Creation Through the Hermeneutic Fusion of Horizons: Business Applications in AI Natural Language Generation. *Journal of Comprehensive Business Administration Research, 2*(1).

Um, N. (2023). Predictors Affecting Effects of Virtual Influencer Advertising among College Students. *Sustainability (Basel), 15*(8), 6388. Advance online publication. DOI: 10.3390/su15086388

Verma, S. (2025). Synthetic Identities and Deepfake Attacks: The Next Frontier in Enterprise AI Security. *Eur. Mod. Stud. J, 9*(5), 176–189. DOI: 10.59573/emsj.9(5).2025.17

Vladyslava, S. (2025). AI and Deepface Influencers: The Challenge of Authenticity in the Online Space. *Universal Library of Engineering Technology, 2*(2).

Volles, B. K., Park, J., Van Kerckhove, A., & Geuens, M. (2024). How and when do virtual influencers positively affect consumer responses to endorsed brands? *Journal of Business Research, 183*, 114863. DOI: 10.1016/j.jbusres.2024.114863

Xia, H., Zhang, L., Chen, J., & Wang, X. (2025). Decoding virtual influencer endorsement using machine learning: The role of virtual influencer, posting, and disclosure characteristics. *Journal of Retailing and Consumer Services, 87*, 104366. DOI: 10.1016/j.jretconser.2025.104366

Yan, J., Xia, S., Jiang, A., & Lin, Z. (2024). The effect of different types of virtual influencers on consumers' emotional attachment. *Journal of Business Research, 177*, 114646. DOI: 10.1016/j.jbusres.2024.114646

Yang, J., Chuenterawong, P., Lee, H., Tian, Y., & Chock, T. M. (2023). Human versus Virtual Influencer: The Effect of Humanness and Interactivity on Persuasive CSR Messaging. *Journal of Interactive Advertising*, *23*(3), 275–292. DOI: 10.1080/15252019.2023.2189036

Yang, Y., Li, S., & Qiu, S. (2025). A Systematic Literature Review on the Negative Impacts of AI-generated Virtual Digital Humans. *IEEE Access : Practical Innovations, Open Solutions*, *13*, 80047–80062. DOI: 10.1109/ACCESS.2025.3564041

Zarouali, B., Boerman, S. C., Voorveld, H. A. M., & van Noort, G. (2022). The algorithmic persuasion framework in online communication: Conceptualization and a future research agenda. *Internet Research*, *32*(4), 1076–1096. DOI: 10.1108/INTR-01-2021-0049

Zhou, X., Yan, X., & Jiang, Y. (2023). EXPRESS: Making Sense? The Sensory-Specific Nature of Virtual Influencer Effectiveness. *Journal of Marketing*, *00222429231203699*. Advance online publication. DOI: 10.1177/00222429231203699

Chapter 9
AI-Powered Virtual Influencers and Synthetic Brand Endorsers:
"Adoption, Credibility, and Engagement"

Samsul Alam
http://orcid.org/0000-0002-1721-1870
City University of Hong Kong, Hong Kong

Khadija Sharmin
http://orcid.org/0009-0008-0814-0442
Begum Rokeya University, Rangpur, Bangladesh

Lisa Mani
http://orcid.org/0009-0008-2957-5656
Shahjalal University of Science and Technology, Bangladesh

Md. Monowar Uddin Talukdar
http://orcid.org/0000-0003-1805-9265
University of Brahmanbaria, Bangladesh

David Jingjun Xu
City University of Hong Kong, Hong Kong

ABSTRACT

The emergence of Artificial Intelligence (AI)-driven Virtual Influencers (VIs) and Synthetic Brand Endorsers (SBEs) has fundamentally revolutionized the digital marketing landscape. Compared to traditional influencers, the virtual persona sup-

DOI: 10.4018/979-8-2600-2977-0.ch009

ported by Generative AI (GAI), machine learning, and natural language processing allows brands to maximize marketing communication on an unprecedented scale. Although current research examines the adoption, credibility, and efficacy of AI-based endorsers, the conceptual frameworks remain disjointed. This study fills this gap by conducting a bibliometric analysis combining articles from Scopus. It employs co-occurrence of keywords for thematic presentation of overall ideas to evaluate science-mapping clusters and nascent thematic domains within synthetic endorser research. Literature provides empirical findings, including adoption, credibility, and engagement, acting as the prime dimensions impacting consumer behavior through several key factors. These findings are synthesized into a conceptual framework, which has an impact on VIs and SBEs.

INTRODUCTION

Artificial Intelligence (AI)-generated agents, such as Virtual Influencers (VIs) and Synthetic Brand Endorsers (SBEs), parallelly known as AI avatars and digital humans, have completely changed the way digital marketing works (Allal-Chérif et al., 2024; Belanche et al., 2024; Nalivaikė & Miliukaitė, 2024; Volles et al., 2024). They make it possible for brands to have more control, grow, and stay consistent across platforms in ways that have never been possible before (Allal-Chérif et al., 2024; Kumar et al., 2024). As AI systems become more generative, conversational, and adaptable, brands are increasingly using VIs and SBEs to tell hyper-personalized stories, keep people engaged 24/7, and reduce the risks associated with using real people as influencers (Belanche et al., 2024; Li et al., 2023).

Since this trend is growing rapidly, research on VIs and SBEs is scattered across many fields, including marketing communications, human-computer interaction, AI ethics, and consumer psychology. This study creates a comprehensive conceptual framework that integrates adoption, credibility, and engagement into a single structure, drawing on both bibliometric evidence and qualitative synthesis. It also identifies important moderators, such as cultural intelligence (Bai et al., 2024), framing for transparency (Park et al., 2024), and message/format design (Li et al., 2026). In the end, the study sees SBEs not as new technologies, but as transformative communicative market agents that are part of algorithmic ecosystems.

Rationale and Research Gap

The swift emergence of VIs and SBEs across industries and online platforms has generated a significant yet fragmented body of research. As publications proliferate across various disciplines - from marketing and communication to AI and computer science - scholars lack a unified comprehension of the organization of knowledge. These artificial structures are not mere technological bells and whistles, but a structural architectural change in how brands orchestrate communication with consumer populations, developing new pathways of information dissemination via algorithmically mediated ecosystems that bring together human and AI communication.

Even though it is growing quickly, there are still some gaps that make this bibliometric study necessary. Because, disciplinary fragmentation obscures the interrelations among theories, methods, and constructs (De Cicco et al., 2024; Feng et al., 2024). Furthermore, limited cross-cultural and cross-platform generalizability constrains comprehension of global adoption (Bai et al., 2024; Shao, 2024). Likewise, few long-term or evolution-based studies make it hard to see how the field has changed and where it is going.

Bibliometric analysis offers a methodical and thorough way to chart the growth, intellectual roots, and thematic groups of this expanding field. By extracting data from the Scopus database, the study provides a comprehensive picture of all keyword co-occurrence for thematic representation of the concept. This is necessary because the research field is becoming increasingly complex and requires an evidence-based synthesis.

Objectives

This study aims to explore three dimensions of VIs and SBEs adoption which are interrelated: (1) adoption of the processes of consumer acceptance of AI-based VIs, identifying the pattern based on demographic and psychographic segments; (2) credibility of the process construction with respect to SBEs, how transparency, authenticity signals and cultural intelligence determine perceived expertise, trustworthiness, and sharing of user-generated content; and (3) engagement processes such as formation of parasocial relations, message efficacy based on product types, and behavioral consequences, such as purchase intention and sharing of user-generated content. Based on these syntheses, it then develops a conceptual framework useful for the adoption pursuits.

Strengths

The strong point of this study is the extensive bibliometric review, as well as the combination of various research areas, which helps to see the whole picture of AI-powered VIs and SBEs from both technical and practical angles. This academic rigor contributes greatly to the development of the field of study as it traces the details of this new discipline and provides a theoretical framework. The study offers a more balanced and fuller analysis of the issue by applying the same level of research to the ethical and societal implications. Consequently, in order to improve this domain's weakness, the study can be used to add more interdisciplinary knowledge, especially ethics, psychology, and consumer behavior.

Weaknesses

The study successfully outlines the main concerns relating to AI-powered VIs and SBEs, nonetheless it does not adequately cover the ethical consequences and psychological effects on consumers. To make the study more balanced, it is necessary to include a more thorough discussion of the long-term societal effects of AI influencers, the ethical principles of using them, and ways to reduce the psychological damage that they may bring, as well as make AI disclosures more transparent. Therefore, the excessive emphasis on the technical facet and marketing benefits of AI-driven VIs and SBEs are considered one of the weaknesses of the study.

Significance

The study adds values by:

- Offering the inaugural bibliometric science mapping of AI-driven VI and SBE research.
- Integrating disparate research domains - technology adoption, credibility & transparency, and parasocial engagement - via co-citation and coupling analysis.
- Combining quantitative bibliometric results with qualitative theory-based insights to create a complete conceptual framework.
- Finding new research areas, such as cultural intelligence, transparency framing, realism thresholds, and AI ethics.
- Giving researchers and professionals a data-driven plan for future research and strategic implementation.

Organization

There are eight parts to this study. The first part discusses the topic and outlines the study's reasons, aims, positive and negative aspects, and significance. Section two contains a review of the literature from various VIs and SBEs perspectives. Section three presents the methodological discourse, including how the study is designed, articles selected, and data analyzed. Section four illustrates the conceptual framework built on the identified themes. Section five discusses the results in relation to the thematic clusters and how consumers reacted. In section six, there are suggestions for the industry in practice. Section seven provides the theoretical, practical, policy, and academy–industry effects. Section eight wraps up with a brief overview of the study's new ideas and contributions, its limitations, potential future research directions, and novelty.

LITERATURE REVIEW

The proliferation of AI into the marketing and communication activity has essentially transformed the way in which brands structure, execute, and operate endorsement strategies. Among the most obvious and problematic effects of this change is the introduction of AI-controlled VIs and SBEs, the agents that are digitally created and mimic human appearance, communication patterns, and social behaviors to promote goods, services, and values. These entities are algorithmically constituted and manipulated, unlike the traditional celebrity endorsers or human social media influencers, which enable the firms to exert an unprecedented amount of control over identity, messaging, availability, and reputational risk (Franke et al., 2023; Moustakas et al., 2020).

In general, the influx of VIs in the field of fashion, cosmetics, tourism, technology, and entertainment has led to a boom in scholarly research. According to previous research, AI-powered endorsers have several managerial benefits, such as maintaining brand consistency, platform scalability, cost-effectiveness in the long term, and minimization of scandals that human endorsers may create (Allal-Chérif et al., 2024; Looia & Kahlor, 2024). Meanwhile, another line of studies expresses concerns about authenticity, trust, ethical transparency and the mental implications of engaging into relationships with artificial but humanlike agents (Lou et al., 2023; Sands et al., 2022).

There is still limited empirical evidence in the field, which is inconsistent on certain occasions. There are studies that report greater engagement or persuasion levels with VIs, especially in more rational or information-based contexts (Yan et al., 2024; Zheng et al., 2026), and there are studies that consistently find Human Influencers (HIs) to be more persuasive than their virtual counterparts in terms of credibility, emotional appeal, and social presence (Franke et al., 2023; Omeish et al., 2025). Such discrepancies indicate that the impact of AI-driven endorsers cannot be attributed solely to the nature of influencers.

The AI-Powered Virtual Influencers and Synthetic Brand Endorsers

The VIs are generally described as computer-generated or AI-aided digital personalities that actively post on social networks, use a first-person narrative, and act as opinion leaders or endorsers in branded ecosystems (Franke et al., 2023; Su, 2025). Although initial models of virtual endorsers were merely a mascot of a brand or an animated avatar spokesperson, modern VIs are increasingly powered by Machine Learning (ML), Natural Language Processing (NLP), and data analytics to customize content, change communication styles, and have a dynamic interaction with audiences (Kim et al., 2022).

Depicted in the literature, identity and function-oriented AI agents (e.g., chatbots, recommender systems) are contrasting with each other in digital humans (e.g., the influence, idols, brand ambassadors). VIs belong to the former category because they mainly perform symbolic persuasion but not the task execution (Moustakas et al., 2020; Zheng et al., 2026). SBEs are a higher-level conceptual category encompassing VIs and AI-generated avatars and recommendation agents explicit to endorsers in the advertising and commerce spaces (Chen et al., 2024; Ham et al., 2024; Wu & Wen, 2021).

In theory, the paradigm of Computers Are Social Actors (CASA) is heavily utilized in research, which suggests that people subconsciously generalize social norms and expectations to the technological agents (Chen et al., 2024). That is why consumers judge VIs by guidelines that have been considered as the prerogative of human endorsers, like honesty, friendliness, and reliability. However, Mind Perception Theory (MPT) adds another significant twist because it elicitors that the consumers distinguish between perceived agency of an agent (capacity to think and act) and experience (capacity to feel and sense). According to empirical evidence, AI entities are always rated as high agency and low experience, an impression that limits the ability of emotional connection and credibility (Sands et al., 2022; Su, 2025).

Emerging Trends

AI-Driven VIs have seen rapid growth in the field of digital marketing over the past few years due to advancements in Generative Artificial Intelligence (GAI) technologies. These advances in GAI allow brands to create an influencer model that is not only more personalized and dynamic, but also able to better meet the changing needs of consumers. GAI allows the creation of VIs that can be designed to look like actual humans and speak to their audiences like actual humans with the added benefit of developing a continuous flow of real-time customized content that can meet the needs of various audience segments (Bai et al., 2024; Kim et al., 2025).

These unique features have led to the rapid growth of the use of VIs across a variety of industries, including fashion, beauty, technology, and entertainment. VIs provide brands with ways to build trust with their target audience, scale their marketing efforts and have complete ownership and control over how their brands are represented in this medium.

One of the most interesting trends in this area is the integration of VIs into Virtual Reality (VR) and Augmented Reality (AR). In these immersive environments, VIs act not only as brand representatives, but also as interactive entities that communicate compelling narratives to consumers, greatly shaping how consumers perceive a product or service, as well as the likelihood of purchasing that product or service (Franke et al., 2023; Zhou & Li, 2025). Additionally, the capability of AR applications allows consumers to interact with and develop emotional connections with VIs in real time that help strengthen consumers' loyalty to a brand.

With growing calls for transparency regarding AI usage in digital communications, including influencer marketing, companies and organizations require providing additional disclosure surrounding the use of AI in their communications with consumers. With increased knowledge about the use of AI in their digital experiences, consumers are now expecting that brands disclose whether an influencer is a real person or has been generated through AI-based systems (Li et al., 2026; Wang & Qiu, 2024). Providing consumers with a clear understanding of the use of AI-based influencers (where applicable) helps build trust with consumers and minimize possible harm to brands by avoiding misleading consumers because of AI usage. Research indicates that consumers are more likely to develop trust in an influencer who is AI-based (where applicable), especially for consumers already being open to using AI (Li et al., 2026; Wang & Qiu, 2024). Conversely, excessive transparency and forced disclosures about AI usage likely generate negative perceptions of brands as being manipulative (Sands et al., 2022).

Technology-Related Challenges

Creating and maintaining AI-powered VIs can be technically challenging, despite their many positive aspects. Creating VIs requires extreme amounts of computational resources to generate realistic and emotionally engaging VIs using advanced GAI techniques like Deep Learning (DL) and NLP (Li et al., 2026). While these technologies have immense power in terms of producing high quality, realistic

VIs, they require a large capital investment to acquire the necessary hardware and computing power.

Furthermore, the substantial costs involved in developing and maintaining VIs are ongoing concerns, as VIs must be constantly updated for relevancy, engagement, and accuracy by brands and/or developers (Franke et al., 2023). Although existing AI systems can simulate how to have a conversation and create an emotional connection; they neither possess any true emotional intelligence, norfully reproduce the emotional intelligence and authentic connection that a HI can offer. This means that VIs are limited in their ability to create emotional impact through marketing campaigns.

Ultimately, more research and additional financial investment in AI technologies are necessary to improve the realism and emotional depth of VIs while decreasing the cost of developing and maintaining them.

Cross-Platform Dynamics and Generative AI Trends

The most up-to-date information regarding generatively designed VIs and SBEs demonstrates that certain cross-platform factors as well as the development of GAI technologies that have emerged in recent years should be considered. Each major social media network (e.g., TikTok, Instagram, YouTube) represents a different set of user behaviors, content formats, and expectations for engagement; therefore, these factors play an important role when determining how effective the endorsement of products via AI-generated VIs will be (Akhtar et al., 2024; Omeish et al., 2025; Wang & Zhang, 2025). For example, short form videos that have a high degree of performance and visual appeal on TikTok are more likely to highlight the novelty and aesthetic aspects of a VI. However, on YouTube, longer narrative-based videos require that product type and institutional integrity are presented in a coherent manner, and that enough relevant information is provided to the audience.

GAI trends have expanded the functionality of VIs to include features such as virtual avatar creation, AI-generated synthetic voices and adaptive narrative strategies (Bai et al., 2025; Li et al., 2026). Researchers have demonstrated that providing AI-generated influencers with perceived agency and objectivity improves the likelihood that rational product categories are accepted and credible, while endorsing emotional or experience-based products are more effective by HIs (Looia & Kahlor, 2024; Yan et al., 2024; Zheng et al., 2026). Thus, incorporating cross-platform dynamics and GAI technology advancements help marketers optimize AI-generated VIs and SBEs for engagement, message relevance, and brand alignment in a diverse array of digital environments.

Use of AI-Assisted Virtual Influencers

Algorithmic Personalization and Recommendation Systems

The personalization of algorithms greatly affects how engaged consumers are when interacting with AI influencers. Chen et al. (2024) detail that recommendations made by AI influence not only the visibility of the content but also how relevant or expensive consumers perceive the interaction to be. AI helps users receive personalized content based on their preferences or demographics, which increase the likelihood of engaging with the AI influencer, yet create challenges for consumers regarding the perceived authenticity of that same influencer. Gong et al. (2026) elaborate that using personalization involves a tradeoff between the incentive offered by an AI-powered endorsement and the level of privacy that consumers believe they receive when interacting with an AI-powered VI. The researchers conclude that recommendation algorithms are not only tools to enable the distribution of content but are active drivers of consumers' psychological responses, such as Parasocial Interaction (PSI), trust, and decisions. By using a combination of demographic, psychographic, and behavioral data, brands can use AI-powered VI campaigns more effectively by matching the types and timing of the content delivered to meet consumers' expectations regarding privacy and the ethics of AI use.

Drivers of Organizational and Market-Level Adoption

The technological legitimacy and cultural normalization of AI are also forces that promote market-level adoption. Research shows that AI is becoming more accepted and even preferred by consumers in AI-mediated interactions, especially by younger generations like Generation Zoomers (Gen Z) (Lou & Copeland, 2025). Such a lack of inhibitions by the generation forms a healthy environment where VIs can proliferate in the fashion, game, and digital lifestyle sectors.

Switching and Consumer Adoption Intentions

At consumer level, adoption also indicates the readiness of people to follow, interact with and be influenced by the VIs. The studies based on technology acceptance and attitude models show that perceived usefulness, hedonic motivation, and overall attitudes towards AI have a positive impact on the acceptance of AI-driven endorsers (Kim et al., 2022).

Chen et al. (2024) demonstrate that when consumers engage with AI recommenders, they are less supported emotionally as compared to when engaging with human agents and the perceived cost of the transaction increases. It indicates that when consumers believe in AI, they might want to oppose dependence on AI endorsers in situations where empathy, reassurance, or experience judgment is needed.

Replacement of humans by VIs is another factor and relies on task-endorser fit. Yan et al. (2024) establish that AI influencers perform better than their human counterparts in cases where the persuasion process depends on objectivity and consistency, but in emotionally charged situations, human beings still have an upper hand. These results put adoption as a contextual choice that is influenced by the content of the message, the type of product, and consumer expectations.

The credibility of Virtual Influencers and Synthetic Endorsers

Source Credibility Dimensions of AI Contexts

One of the most widely studied constructs in the research of VIs is credibility. Based on the theory of source credibility, researchers have always operationalized credibility in terms of expertise, trustworthiness, attractiveness, and congruence (Jayasingh et al., 2025; Zaki et al., 2025). These dimensions are also found in the research on human endorsement, but their meaning changes when used in the context of AI mediation.

Dexterity is commonly recognized by AI supporters with regard to perceived processing information, consistency, and the absence of human bias. However, credibility is weaker, as consumers can promote algorithms rather than sincerity (Sands et al., 2022). Physical and symbolic attractiveness is often used to counterbalance a lack of experiential credibility, especially in a platform-driven by images, like Instagram (Bai et al., 2024).

Transparency, Ethical Trust, and Authenticity

Authenticity turns out to be a significant point of contact between credibility and persuasion. Zhou et al. (2026) show that perceived authenticity is the reason why the novel benefits of VIs do not necessarily translate into favorable brand attitudes. Credibility is quickly destroyed when VIs seem to be overly scripted or untruthful.

There is an ambivalent role of transparency. Qadri and Moustafa (2026) demonstrate that the disclosure of AI applications has the potential to increase trust and perceived fairness, not only among consumers with positive AI attitudes but also among those with negative AI attitudes. On the other hand, Lou et al. (2023) record that transparency increases images of deceit and other unnatural aspects when consumers view disclosure as an indication of manipulation. These results indicate the ethical ambiguity of AI influencer marketing and the significance of context-related disclosure measures.

Ethical Analysis of Virtual Influencers and Synthetic Brand Endorsers

The emergence of AI-based VIs within digital marketing has prompted a number of ethical challenges. Among these ethical challenges, transparency regarding disclosure, the potential for the loss of authenticity, and the ability of VIs to manipulate consumers.

(i) Transparency and consumer manipulation: It is necessary that there is a clear disclosure of whether or not a VI is an AI-based VI, since the presence of this information is essential in maintaining consumer trust (Nalivaikė & Miliukaitė, 2024). However, overly disclosing information may result in consumers feeling manipulated and having low levels of confidence in the genuineness of the VI (Sands et al., 2022). The case of the VI "Lil Miquela" (an AI-created VI) raised concerns about the authenticity of the AI-generated representation of this influencer and the potential misrepresentation of consumers by AI-generated representations (AI-generated personas).

(ii) Authenticity: Compared to human endorsers, AI-based VIs are unable to produce the same emotional depth as a human endorser, and therefore, may be perceived as scripted and/or outside the bounds of authentic representation of a consumer (Zhou et al., 2026). Thus, an AI endorser may have a reduced ability to create a meaningful connection with consumers.

(iii) Privacy and security of data: AI-based VIs often require consumers' personal information in order to create a highly personalized experience, but this requirement means there are increased privacy-related risks to consumers. If personal data about consumers collected by an AI-based VI is not disclosed or the purposes of its use is not disclosed, then consumers risk being exploited for their personally identifiable information (Qadri & Moustafa, 2026).

(iv) Ethical considerations in marketing: The present use of AI-based VIs to market various products raises questions about whether AI-based VIs will eventually replace human-endorsers, thus diminishing the authentic representation of human individuals in marketing.

Virtual Influencer Consumer Interaction

Behavioral, Cognitive, and Emotional Engagement

The interaction with VIs is observed on the level of behavior (likes, shares, purchases), cognitive (attention, elaboration), and emotional (interest, enjoyment) aspects. Experimental research indicates that VIs can create high-level engagement, especially when they coincide with platform practices and message tactics (Akhtar et al., 2024; Looia & Kahlor, 2024).

Zheng et al. (2026) present strong arguments that message appeal moderates the results of engagement. Virtual endorsers and rational appeal work better compared with human endorsers, and emotional appeal to human endorsers. This source-message fit is achieved by metacognitive mechanism known as feeling of rightness, which increases perceived message appropriateness and lessens resistance.

Parasocial Interaction and Social Presence

PSI is one of the major psychological processes underlying engagements. Although PSI develops during the interaction with VIs, its strength can be lower than when it comes to HIs since it is believed to be unable to experience something (Omeish et al., 2025). Nevertheless, anthropomorphic indicators (personal backstories, names, and social relationships) can increase the perceived social presence and strengthen PSI (Su, 2025; Zheng et al., 2026).

Changed and reproduced with minimal marginal costs, HIs, particularly micro- and mid-tier creators, might have fewer opportunities and bargaining power (Looia & Kahlor, 2024). This change brings up the issue of ethics of automation, value extraction, and the future of creative labor in the digital economies (Moustakas et al., 2020).

Lastly, there are ethical risks in the area of data governance, accountability, and transparency. Research investigating the use of AI transparency disclosures shows that although the disclosure may lead to greater perceived fairness, it can also create additional skepticism by giving consumers the perception of a manipulative move or over-surveillance (Chen et al., 2024; Qadri & Moustafa, 2026). Overall, these results highlight the need for a better regulatory framework and the design of ethical disclosure rules for the application of AI-based VIs.

Psychological Effects of VIs

The influences of VIs on its users are numerous, especially when you take into consideration how that can lead to emotional manipulation and contribute to unrealistic beauty standards. Since VIs embody ideal forms of beauty, they can contribute to negative beauty standards, particularly for youth and young adults and in particular for groups that may be more vulnerable to influence; like the younger generations, especially Gen Z, (Lou & Copeland, 2025). Significant exposure to all these perfect digital bodies can lead to body dissatisfaction, low self-esteem, and high social comparison, particularly for at-risk populations.

Additionally, when examining the emotional effects of VIs, it is important to also take into account the idea of parasocial relationships. For example, the connection that users create with VIs can be so strong that they feel as if they developed a friendship or idolized attitude towards them. Because the relationship is one-sided, there can be some misunderstanding(s) about the expectations of behaviors, relationship, and even identity (Franke et al., 2023). In addition, the "uncanny valley" concept, which describes the phenomenon of VIs being close to human, but with slight imperfections, can cause the user to feel eerie or awkward or to have difficulty establishing trust and engaging with the VI (Franke et al., 2023).

To mitigate the impact of these psychological effects, brands and creators will need to establish a sense of humanity for their VIs. Providing relatable backstories for VIs and allowing for some types of imperfections will assist with user connections. A vital component of mitigating the effects of emotional manipulation is by providing users the knowledge that the VI is an artificial construct.

Adverse Effects, Hazards, and Social Issues

Cross-Cultural Analysis

There are many cultural differences that will influence the way that AI-powered VIs are adopted and how well they work. Although there is mention of the concept of cultural intelligence, there is a need for a much better understanding regarding the cultural factors that impact consumer engagement with VIs. Current research indicates that there are far ranging cultural differences regarding the level of appeal of a VI, leading to the successful adoption and effectiveness of VIs in various markets.

For example, in collectivistic cultures, such as many of the East Asian cultures, the primary driver of consumer engagement with VIs is attractiveness to the consumer; these consumers value conformity to norms and group cohesion (Bai et al., 2024). However, in individualistic cultures (e.g. Western cultures), the major factor for engaging consumers with VIs is the level of authenticity or emotional connection with the VI. Therefore, VIs that create a sense of personal relevance and provide individualized content are likely to be more successful (Teng et al., 2025).

An example that illustrates the impact of culture on how well a VI works is the case study of KFC's Colonel KI in China. Colonel KI, was created as a VI that matched the preferences (including visual and communication style) of Chinese consumers. This cultural match resulted in very high levels of consumer engagement with the brand. However, once KFC introduced Colonel KI into Western markets (US and Europe), the cultural relevance of this VI dissipated. This example clearly illustrates how critical it is to understand cultural nuances when trying to successfully implement VIs (Wang & Zhang, 2025).

The type of product that VIs promote may also affect the way cultures perceive their products. In high-context cultures (for example, Japan), where communication takes place more indirectly, VIs may focus more heavily on subtle emotional messages to connect with consumers. In low-context cultures (for example, the US), VIs can be effective in connecting with consumers through messages that are more direct and clearer (Zheng et al., 2026).

Economic and Labor Impact

The emergence of VIs and SBEs driven by AI have broad consequences for the creative labor market. As VIs become the primary means through which brands create and interact with consumers online, traditional HIs and content creators are both at risk of losing their jobs. VIs provides advantages for marketers, including low cost and 24/7 availability, and their ability to be without human deficiencies such as scandal and fatigue (Moustakas et al., 2020).

Ultimately, larger corporations have an economic advantage and have the resources to monopolize the VI marketplace, pushing aside independent creators and small businesses. This consolidation of power creates a situation in which a few corporations dominate the influencer marketing arena. As a result of this consolidation, there could be a large economic divide in the digital marketing industry between large corporations and independently owned businesses and individuals. Therefore, influencer marketing agencies need to adopt the AI-based strategies as their own, which may have an economic and labor force effect on the entire industry.

Long-Term Societal Effects

The impact of VIs on society is far-ranging; however, their influence on cultural norms, social statuses, and consumer behavior is more easily seen than others. Because so many forms of VIs are now seen every day in today's society, their effects on beauty/physical standards, self-conceptualization, and consumerism are huge (Han et al., 2025). Many VIs portray beauty standards that are Unrealistic in scope, thus creating social comparisons to others in youth and contributing to body dissatisfaction and health issues (Yang et al., 2025).

To add to their influence towards consumers, VIs has influenced public opinion, and political issues. VIs can reach a larger population than any other means of advertising and thus can present a great deal of influence over public narrative, advertising campaigns, and social movement (Ham et al., 2024). The presence of

VIs therefore opens several ethical issues regarding the effects on public opinion, particularly concerning questions of manipulation, transparency, and accountability.

Given the possible adverse implications surrounding the use of VIs, it is essential to create a strong foundation of Ethics and transparency surrounding these forms of advertisement so that those who are vulnerable are not taken advantage of nor are they impacted negatively because of these trends.

Worldwide Laws and Regulatory Frameworks

As AI-powered VIs and SBEs continue to proliferate, there is a need for a comprehensive regulatory framework governing these technologies and the implications of their usage. A key milestone in AI regulation is the EU's AI Act, which will establish protections for high-risk applications of AI and also ensure that all applications of AI, including usage by influencers, meet certain benchmarks of transparency, accountability, and ethical business practices (Chen et al., 2024). Among other things, the AI Act will impose additional requirements regarding how AI systems must operate, e.g. consumers are to be informed when they interact with an AI persona. The AI Act also imposes new restrictions on the use of consumer data collected by VIs/SBEs so that data used by these technologies are collected and processed on a lawful basis, thereby ensuring compliance with the EU's general data protection regulation (Sands et al., 2022).

AI-induced influencer marketing is now being regulated by the Federal Trade Commission (FTC) in the US with guidelines to increase transparency around the disclosure of AI-generated influencer content (Sands et al., 2022). The FTC requires that consumers are not misled regarding the nature of the endorsement through the use of VIs and SBEs along with providing a level of accountability for the use of AI technologies within marketing methods.

Regulatory and Governance Considerations

The governance of AI-generated influencers remains a critical yet underexplored domain in contemporary Information Systems (IS) and marketing literature. Research indicates that the ethical deployment of VIs and SBEs is closely tied to transparency, disclosure, and platform-level accountability. De Cicco et al. (2024) highlight that users' perceptions of credibility and trust are directly influenced by whether AI agents are clearly identified as non-human, suggesting that disclosure is a core determinant of ethical engagement and consumer confidence (Han et al., 2025). Similarly, Park and Ahn (2024) demonstrate that transparent AI-brand interactions enhance brand preference and purchase intention, particularly when audiences are aware that the influencer is AI-generated, without perceiving manipulation or deceit. Furthermore, Rehman et al. (2026) reveal that the attributes of AI influencers, such as anthropomorphism and visual similarity to target audiences, interact with disclosure practices to shape PSI and engagement outcomes. Collectively, these studies underscore the importance of robust regulatory frameworks and platform governance mechanisms that mandate clear identification of AI agents and enforce ethical content standards, which are crucial for maintaining consumer trust and safeguarding brand credibility (Han et al., 2025).

Case Studies and Illustrations of Virtual Influencers Across the Globe

The global landscape of VIs is highly diverse, with digital personas tailored to reflect specific cultural norms, ethnic identities, and regional aesthetics. Case studies of prominent VIs illustrate how these figures are perceived worldwide:

Ayayi (China)

Rooted in East Asian cultural contexts, Ayayi is a hyper-realistic VI who deeply integrates local customs into her narrative. For example, during the Lunar New Year, she engages audiences by sharing greetings in local dialects, showcasing traditional practices, and participating in regional festivities. By aligning with Chinese collectivist values, she fosters a strong sense of community and cultural pride, making her highly relatable to local consumers (Su, 2025).

Lil Miquela (USA)

As a digital pop star and model from Los Angeles, Lil Miquela embodies Western individualistic values, prioritizing personal branding, self-expression, and social advocacy (Su, 2025). She frequently engages in contemporary social issues, demonstrating how VIs in individualistic societies resonate by acting as independent, outspoken cultural commentators.

Lu do Magalu (Brazil)

Operating as a virtual ambassador for the brand Magazine Luiza, Lu do Magalu is one of the most followed VI globally, boasting millions of followers (Xu et al., 2025). She embodies a culturally specific archetype of a relatable, chatty Brazilian woman, which has driven massive engagement in South America.

Imma (Japan)

Imma leverages Japan's deep-rooted anime culture and high technological engagement (Xu et al., 2025). Because virtual characters are highly prevalent and culturally ingrained in Japanese society, Japanese consumers tend to exhibit fewer reservations about interacting with VIs (Franke et al., 2023).

Shudu (South Africa)

Marketed as the world's first digital supermodel, Shudu's campaigns frequently celebrate diversity in beauty standards (Su, 2025; Xu et al., 2025). Her use in global marketing sparks meaningful conversations around inclusivity, particularly resonating with younger demographics seeking diverse ethnic representation in fashion.

Kyra (India) and Thalasya (Indonesia)

These regional VIs demonstrate the expansion of VI marketing into South and Southeast Asia (Rehman et al., 2025). Consumers in these developing markets, while traditionally late adopters compared to Western counterparts, are showing rapid acceptance of VIs, particularly among the digitally native youth (Rungruangjit et al., 2024).

Next-Generation Tech: AI, VR, and the Metaverse Revolution

The future avenue of VIs will be heavily defined by the rapid integration of advanced GAI and LLMs. Moving beyond pre-scripted narratives and manual animation, next-generation VIs will possess the capability for real-time semantic understanding, dynamic content generation and personalized cross-modal interactions (Wang & Zhang, 2025; Yang et al., 2025). VIs will be the leading interactive channels in the metaverse and Extended Reality (XR) setting (Xu et al., 2025; Yang et al. 2025). VIs will go beyond two-dimensional social media screens and lead consumers the way in 3D visual showrooms, in fashion shows, and virtual try-on experiences via AR and VR (Tarnanidis, 2024). This combination of AI and XR (also known as Intelligent Reality or IR) will enable AI algorithms to combine user and environmental data to modify the experiences. This will be backed by the real-time 3D rendering engines and spatial computing and will blur the boundaries between physical and virtual commerce (Wang & Zhang, 2025).

Technological Challenges of Developing VIs

The development of AI-powered VIs relies on a highly complex convergence of advanced technologies, including NPL, DL, computer vision, and GAI (Rehman et al. 2026). Creating a VI that can autonomously interact with audiences requires these systems to seamlessly process text, synthesize speech, and render dynamic 3D visuals in real-time (Kumar et al., 2024). Achieving this requires immense computational power and sophisticated infrastructure. Training Large Language Models (LLMs) and advanced natural networks (such as Convolutional Neural Networks for facial emotion recognition) demands superior hardware, including specialized high-performance graphics processing units and robust cloud computing environments. These heavy computational loads often require a significant engineering hurdle that strain memory and processing capacities, making real time inference without latency. Furthermore, while AI image generation has advanced rapidly, video-generation models still struggle to produce continuous, high-resolution, long-form content due to lack of extensive training datasets and the complete processing power required to render temporal video sequences (Park et al., 2024).

In addition to inquiries into the efficacy and persuasiveness of AI-made VIs and artificial digital humans, the literature increasingly highlights their adverse effects, threats, and more significant societal consequences. A Systematic Literature Review (SLR) specifically about the negative impacts of AI-generated virtual digital humans points out various groups of risks, including, psychological, social, ethical, and economic damages (Yang & Qiu, 2025).

One issue is associated with deception and the feeling of manipulation. Some studies show that consumers who learn that a HI is pool-generated can get a sense of deception, lack of trust, and moral unease, especially when the disclosure is not made clearly or strategically (Lou et al., 2023; Sands et al., 2022). These responses are closely connected to the uncanny valley phenomenon, as highly humanlike and flawed digital efforts elicit a sense of eeriness and psychological discomfort rather than empathy (Franke et al., 2023; Su, 2025).

The next possible danger mentioned in another instance is the strengthening of unrealistic beauty standards and identity norms. VIs are commonly made to have perfect bodies, which are idealistic and not within the physical capabilities of a human being. According to the qualitative and conceptual studies, the recurring exposure to such digitally idealized bodies could be exacerbating the appearance-based social comparison, especially in younger and more susceptible people, which may further result in body dissatisfaction and self-esteem challenges (Lou & Copeland, 2025; Yang & Qiu, 2025).

In the end, the relevant studies are presented in Table 1 in a summarized way.

Table 1. Summary of key studies on AI-powered VIs and SBEs

Authors (Year)	Journal	Key Constructs	Key Findings	Focus Area
Moustakas et al. (2020)	IEEE Conference	VIs, AI marketing	Identifies strategic benefits of VIs, such as, control, scalability, and risk mitigation	Adoption
Zhou et al. (2026)	Journal of Business Research	Novelty, authenticity, trust	VIs enhance novelty but suffer authenticity deficits that limit persuasion	Adoption / Credibility
Kim et al. (2022)	International Journal of Advertising	Consumption goals, AI attitude	Hedonic and gain goals positively shape attitudes toward AI-driven agents	Adoption
Yan et al. (2024)	Sustainability	AI vs. HIs, persuasion	AI influencers outperform humans in rational contexts but underperform in emotional contexts	Adoption / Engagement
Looia and Kahlor (2024)	Journal of Interactive Advertising	HIs vs. VIs	HIs score higher on social presence; VIs offer consistency advantages	Adoption / Engagement
Sands et al. (2022)	European Journal of Marketing	AI disclosure, trust	Disclosure alters trust and responsibility attribution toward AI influencers	Credibility
Lou et al. (2023)	Journal of Advertising	Uncanny feelings, deception	Transparency can amplify uncanniness when realism is high	Credibility / Ethics
Bai et al. (2024)	Current Psychology	Attractiveness, culture	Attractiveness increases purchase intention; advertising perception suppresses effect	Credibility
Jayasingh et al. (2025)	Journal of Theoretical and Applied Electronic Commerce Research	Credibility, engagement	Credibility significantly predicts engagement and purchase intention	Credibility / Engagement
Zaki et al. (2025)	Human Behavior and Emerging Technologies	Credibility dimensions	Trustworthiness and expertise drive brand admiration	Credibility
Rehman et al. (2025)	Technological Forecasting and Social Change	Anthropomorphism, authenticity	Anthropomorphism enhances perceived authenticity and attitudes	Credibility
Zheng et al. (2026)	Journal of Research in Interactive Marketing	Message appeal fit	Rational appeals fit VIs; emotional appeals fit humans	Engagement
Akhtar et al. (2024)	Journal of Retailing and Consumer Services	Engagement, PSI	VIs trigger engagement via PSI mechanisms	Engagement
Omeish et al. (2025)	Discover Sustainability	PSI	PSI mediates trust and engagement for AI and HIs	Engagement

continued on following page

Table 1. Continued

Authors (Year)	Journal	Key Constructs	Key Findings	Focus Area
Qadri and Moustafa (2026)	Psychology and Marketing	Transparency, well-being	Transparency boosts authenticity under favorable AI attitudes	Credibility / Ethics
Chen et al. (2024)	Sustainability	Emotional support, transaction cost	AI agents provide less emotional support, increasing transaction costs	Adoption / Ethics
Lou and Copeland (2025)	Journal of Internet Commerce	AI ads, body image	AI-generated models intensify beauty ideals among Gen Z	Societal Impact

Source: Authors' work

Artificial influencers and AI-based virtual personas are a radical and potentially disruptive development in modern marketing communication. The reviewed literature in this study indicates that such entities are highly attractive in terms of strategic benefits, such as scalability and consistency, and creative control, which are driving their increased use in industries (Moustakas et al., 2020). Meanwhile, their performance is also limited by deeper psychological and social constraints in connection with the ability to feel, experience the environment, and build trust (Omeish et al., 2025; Sands et al., 2022).

METHODOLOGY

The SLR methodology is employed in this study to capture theoretical viewpoints and empirical evidence on human-AI interactions with the IS and marketing environment. The methodology conforms to the Preferred Reporting Items of Systematic Reviews and Meta-Analyses (PRISMA) approach so that transparency, rigor, and replicability are maintained in the review process (Alam et al., 2025; Faisal-E-Alam et al., 2025). The Scopus database is used as a source of studies due to its guarantee of wider inclusion of recognized scholarly works.

Research Design

This study follows SLR technique, which is a research methodology that recognizes, analyzes, and discusses all the existing studies in reference to a specific issue, topic, or phenomena of study (Alam, 2025; Bhuiyan et al., 2025; Kitchenham & Charters, 2007). The SLR offers strong summaries of the most valid evidence (Alam, 2025; Petticrew & Roberts, 2008). We use the PRISMA approach to conduct this analysis, which is generally considered to be a transparent and structured approach to a systematic review. PRISMA provides the review with completeness, reproducibility, and unbiasedness since it strictly specifies the inclusion and exclusion criteria and describes the methodology of each part of the review (Alam et al., 2025).

The reason why the Scopus database was chosen as the main source of the review is that it has a broad coverage of quality scholarly materials in a wide scope of disciplines. The quality of Scopus is that it indexes peer-reviewed journals, conference papers, and academic books in particular, which makes the search engine the best in guaranteeing inclusion of credible resources. This search was conducted with an implementation of a combination of predetermined keywords (see Figure 1), including: ((virtual influencer) OR (AI influencer) OR (synthetic endorser) OR (digital human) OR (avatar marketing)) AND ((engagement) OR (credibility) OR (adoption) OR (trust)) with a focus on the studies of the 2015-2026 period. The period was selected to make the review represent the most recent trends in AI in marketing. The use of exclusion criteria eliminates non-academic sources and studies, which do not talk about consumer experience or behavioral outcomes. The search was also restricted to the English studies, which gave access to the research that is accessible all over the world.

Figure 1. PRISMA-based database searching process

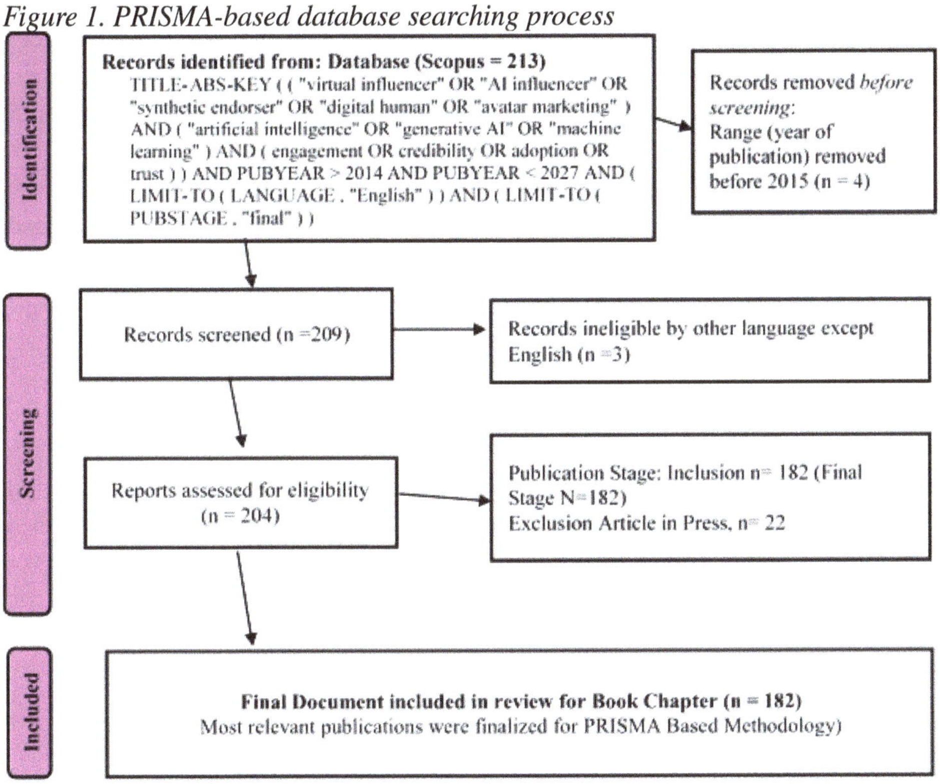

Source: Scopus database (January 2026)

Selection Technique

Inclusion criteria in selecting studies were based on the PRISMA flowchart and this was to ensure that the selection of studies was well structured in terms of the inclusion of studies in the review. During the identification phase, a targeted search string focusing on VIs and SBEs yielded 213 records, which were immediately reduced to 209 after removing four backdated papers published before 2015. In the screening stage, three non-English records were excluded, and 204 records were reported for eligibility assessment. The eligibility phase further refined the collection by excluding 22, which is in press. Ultimately, this process resulted in 182 final documents being included for this study to represent the most relevant and stable literature for this analysis, which involved peer-reviewed articles, reviews, conference proceedings, as well as book chapters.

Analysis Technique

The review method is the qualitative synthesis, and it is used in this review where the findings of the studies used are compared and contrasted to determine the common themes, trends, and insights of the studies. The method is used to extract subtle insights into the way AI technologies are transforming marketing practices and consumer experiences. The systematic review based on PRISMA and all keyword co-occurrence by VOSviewer are presented by synthesizing the findings of numerous studies that provide the complete picture of the state in this area both regarding the successful application and the need to research more. The theoretical models, research trends, and contextual factors that impact AI-Powered VIs and SBEs are considered in the analysis, considering the implications of adoption, credibility, and engagement.

RESULTS AND DISCUSSION

The emergence of an AI-driven VI and a SBE has brought a twist to the digital marketing world (Kravets et al., 2025). These AI agents provide brands with a level of control over their communication, presence, and general branding integrity never seen before compared to the traditional HIs. As AI-based entities continue to play a role in digital marketing plans, the issues that affect the implementation, credibility, and interaction of these agents are important to scholars and practitioners.

Bibliometric Mapping of the Research Landscape

Surrounding AI-powered VIs and SBEs, the keyword co-occurrence network reveals a sophisticated and multidimensional research landscape, shown in Figure 2. The analysis identifies four primary thematic clusters that define the current state of the field. The network suggests that while the technical feasibility of VIs or digital humans is well-established, the "Credibility" and "Trust" nodes are vital intermediaries that determine the success of SBEs.

Figure 2. Co-occurrence of keywords for thematic presentation

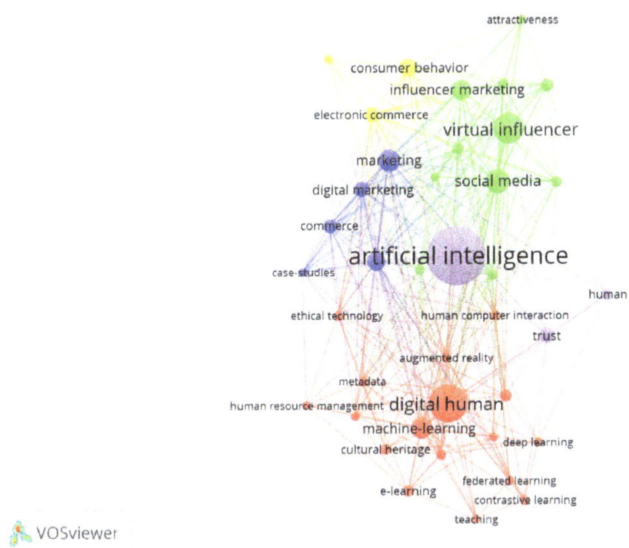

Source: Authors' work using VOSviewer software

Technological Core (Red Cluster)

This cluster is represented by "Digital Human" and "Machine Learning" including that the foundation of synthetic endorsement is genuinely rooted in computational advancement. The strong presence of "Generative AI" suggested a recent shift to autonomous content creation. "Deep Learning" highlights the technical complexity required to achieve high-fidelity human simulation.

Marketing and Influence Nexus (Green Cluster)

"Virtual Influencer" and "Influencer Marketing" illustrate the commercial application of the technology, as shown in the upper quadrant. "Anthropomorphism" and

"Attractiveness" within this cluster denote that scholarly attention is highly focused on how human-like physical traits drive consumer perception and brand engagement.

Psychology of Trust and Ethics (Purple Cluster)

Central cluster of the network "Artificial Intelligence" acts as a bridge between red (technical) and the yellow (behavioral) clusters. The distinction of "Trust" indicates a critical area of investigation of psychological transition from perceiving an entity as a "machine" to accepting it as a "credible endorser". This suggests that credibility is the primary mediator in the adoption of synthetic influences.

Consumer Adoption and Economic Impact (Yellow and Blue Cluster)

These clusters represent the utilitarian aspects of the field, combining "Consumer Behavior" with "Technology Adoption" and "Digital Marketing". The proximity of "Virtual Reality" and "Commerce" implies that VIs are increasingly viewed as a next-generation marketing strategy.

Adoption of AI-Powered Virtual Influencers

The use of AI-powered VIs will depend on a number of strategic indicators, which are likely to differentiate them from the HIs. The conceptual framework by Franke et al. (2023) shows that AI-based agents provide the brand with the opportunity to maintain full control over the story, minimizing the risks of human scandals and failure to represent the brand and show inconsistency (Moustakas et al., 2020). Unlike their human counterparts, VIs are resistant to fatigue, aging, and off-brand behavior and thus make better long-term brand options (Franke et al., 2023).

Besides, VIs offer a great cost benefit. In comparison with HIs, who are limited by their physical locations, VIs are available 24/7 on various platforms with one presence, which does not require extra expenditure on travel, appearances, or other logistics limitations (Franke et al., 2023). Also, their modification and association with particular brand names can be especially attractive to the companies in the younger and more tech-oriented groups of consumers, including Gen Z (Zhou et al., 2026). All this is a combination of the reasons why VIs are finding their way to the marketing mix of many brands.

Although the benefits are obvious, getting adopted is not problem-free. Whether AI-driven influencers are accepted by consumers remains an issue of research. Earlier research has indicated that the perceived usefulness and hedonic value of these AI agents are some of the factors that affect consumer adoption (Ling et al., 2021). Moreover, how the type of influencer and the product being promoted fit is crucial. As an example, VIs can be more effective and efficient with rational or information-based products, and HIs have not yet been surpassed in the sphere of emotionally charged or experience-based products.

Virtual Influencers and Synthetic Brand Endorsers Credibility

The authenticity of AI-powered VIs is the main issue of marketers and scholars. Though VIs have the potential to provide a high level of congruence and experience, the level of trust is frequently weak. The perceived authenticity of a synthetic endorser is closely linked with the credibility of the latter and is more difficult to achieve than with HIs. The avatars produced by AI can provide consumers with consistent messages, as Moustakas et al. (2020) argue, however, they might not trust the products endorsed by an AI variant.

The tension between transparency and misleading, one of the main issues in building the credibility of VIs, is found. According to research by Zhou et al. (2026), the disclosure of AI-driven influencers is a potentially useful strategy, especially with already AI-receptive audiences. Nevertheless, such openness may also create the impression of manipulation or the absence of genuineness, provided the disclosure process is not well managed. It is particularly acute in the sectors where customers demand a high level of human touch and sympathy like skincare or lifestyle products, where consumer trust is predetermined by emotional appeals (Sands et al., 2022).

These issues can be partially addressed by the attractiveness and customization of VIs in addition to authenticity. The visual attractiveness of VIs can boost the credibility of the latter, which can be particularly effective in platforms that rely on visuality, such as Instagram (Rehman et al., 2026). The perceived relevance and trustworthiness of VIs can also be improved by means of customization, including a change in their appearance to align it with certain cultural or demographic interests. Nevertheless, the problem to be addressed in general is to make sure that these synthetic agents should be viewed as authentic and be able to establish genuine relationships with their audience.

Interacting with Virtual Influencers

Another Important dimension that determines the effectiveness of VIs in marketing campaigns is their consumer interest. The levels of engagement with these AI-based entities are usually higher than with HIs because of other factors like novelty, fascination, and aesthetics of digital actors (Franke et al., 2023). Visual effect and individuality of VIs attract people, resulting in greater engagement rates in terms of likes, shares, and comments than the HIs (Zhou et al., 2026). Nevertheless, correspondence of the content created by the influencer to the consumer expectations and preferences, the engagement is not only influenced by the superficial posts, but also by the attractiveness (Akhtar et al., 2024).

However, one of the main forms of interaction of VIs is PSI. PSI is described as the one-sided connections that consumers build with media faces, where although PSI has customarily been linked to human stars, it has been found that virtual stars can provide the same interactions. Nevertheless, PSI via VIs is usually less intense compared to PSI through HIs, primarily because of the lack of perceived emotional experience (Omeish et al., 2025). This underscores the need to introduce human-like attributes, including backstories and emotional stories, to engage more with VIs.

In addition, the effectiveness of the engagement of VIs may depend on the kind of content and message plan. A study conducted by Zheng et al. (2026) indicates that VIs thrive in the rational or informational setting, i.e., technology or consumer electronics, where objective information and consistency play a core role. Nevertheless, emotional and experiential products still require HIs over virtual ones, as it is possible to appeal emotionally to the audience. These lessons indicate that the interaction of VIs is situational, and their success cannot be maximized without a specific strategy.

Quantifying Value

In order to effectively measure the value of VIs and SBEs, the brands need to adopt an all-encompassing measurement framework that will go beyond simple metrics. This can be performed by assessing engagement, credibility, return on investment, and the particular visual qualities that motivate consumer behavior.

Measuring Engagement Dynamics

Although VIs usually can reach engagement rates three times higher than their HIs (Allal-Chérif et al., 2024), brands need to track both immediate and long-lasting engagement (Chan et al., 2023).

(i) Core engagement metrics: VIs measure immediate quantifiable data, such as likes, comments, share, views, and overall engagement rates (interactions divided by the total followers) (Volles et al., 2024).

(ii) Long-term engagement evaluation: Brand needs to estimate the consumer retention score to determine long-term impact by considering the percentage of repeat purchase, average duration of engagement after promotion, and rate of brand recall (Sun et al., 2025). Moreover, it tracks the engagement decay rate after a VI campaign.

Quantifying Credibility and Trust

Since VIs are created artificially, their authenticity and reliability become vital to marketing (Guerra-Tamez et al., 2024). The intangible qualities can be measured with the help of certain frameworks and analytical tools: source credibility scales can conduct a survey of target audiences with an existing scale. They are evaluated in three significant dimensions: expertise, trustworthiness, and physical attractiveness (Li et al., 2023).

(i) Mind precision tracking: Brands are recommended to assess consumers' mind perception by VI, namely tracking scores in agency (perceived intelligence and capability) and experience (perceived ability to feel or be authentic) (Li et al., 2026).

(ii) Sentiment analysis: Marketers can use NLP to conduct consumers' sentiment by analyzing thousands of consumer comments. It assists in producing an authentic score, which implies whether the audience believes the VI in its promotions or regards them with doubt because they are overly commercialized.

Calculating Return on Investment and Commercial Value

Historically, the returns of influencer marketing are high (e.g., US $6.50 on every dollar spent). VIs need accurate tracking to warrant the development and operational expenses (Li et al., 2023).

(i) Direct attribution: The VIs employ urchin tracking module parameters, trackable, and unique promo codes to directly attribute social media traffic on the websites (Tarnanidis, 2024).

(ii) Short-term financial metrics: VIs compute common metrics, including customer acquisition cost, conversion rate, and return on ad to assess the profitability of the campaign in the short run (Tarnanidis, 2024).

(iii) Long-term value measures: Customer lifetime value (the total value of a customer throughout their relationship with a brand) and net prompter score (probability of recommending the brand) are metrics that marketers monitor to evaluate the long-term effects of a VI on brand equity (Tarnanidis, 2024). It is also possible to isolate the effect of VI interactions in determining the purchasing decisions over time as compared to other channels using advanced media attributions (Su, 2025).

Economic Consequences of Giant Companies on Independent Creators

The rise of VIs threatens to widen the economic gap between large, well-funded corporations and small, independent entrepreneurs. Developing a high-quality, hyper-realistic, brand-owned VI requires significant upfront financial investment, technical expertise, and cross-functional teams combining marketing, IT, and 3D animation (Allal-Chérif et al., 2024). Giant companies (Like Prada, LVMH, and KFC) have huge resources at their disposal to create and sustain these digital resources

(Allal-Chérif et al., 2024; Teng et al., 2025). Established brand-owned VIs are very cost-efficient in the long-run, and they can create unlimited content at minimal costs (Allal-Chérif et al., 2024; Teng et al., 2025). As a result, independent artists and creators prone to existential threat to their intellectual property and creative identity. Since AI generative models are trained on existing human-made content, there is an imminent threat that the distinctive styles, tones, and aesthetics of independent creations can be hacked and duplicated by algorithms to drive corporate VIs (Park et al., 2024). This rough cloning enables corporations to get the economic returns of human creativity without the need to adequately compensate the original human creators, further undermining the livelihoods of independent artists in the digital economy (Bai et al., 2025; Park et al., 2024).

AI-powered Virtual Influencers and Synthetic Brand Endorsers

The factors affecting VIs and SBEs are shown in Table 2.

Table 2. Factors affecting the adoption, credibility, and engagement of AI-powered VIs and SBEs

Dimension	Key Factors	Impact on Consumer Behavior
Adoption	- Brand control - Technological attitudes - Cost efficiency - Product and influencer fit	• Facilitates consistent brand messaging and global reach • Enables continuous 24/7 interaction without human constraints
Credibility	- Authenticity - Transparency - Expertise - Visual appeal and customization	• Shapes consumer trust and brand loyalty • Increases brand relevance, particularly with younger demographics
Engagement	- Parasocial relationships - Aesthetic appeal - Content alignment with consumer expectations - Emotional vs. rational message appeal	• Drives consumer interaction, emotional connection, and loyalty • Context-dependent: stronger engagement in rational product areas • Emotional products favor HIs; rational products benefit VIs

Source: Authors' work

Risk Associated with Ethical Issues

Privacy Breaches

The effectiveness of AI recommendations and VIs relies on the continuous collection of personal data that creates a privacy paradox for consumers (Diwanji, 2026; Gong et al., 2026). In the VI environment, users share their personalized experiences, thus fall in the risks of unauthorized access of data, data surveillance, and misuse (Gong et al., 2026). It can generate psychological stressors in consumers, like anger and a sense of technological intrusiveness (Nguyen et al., 2024), when AI systems implicitly gather personal data without permission. Brands need to be encouraged to maintain high privacy transparency disclosing how AI algorithms utilize consumer data that can be useful in building trust and alleviating suspicion for combating these situations (Gong et al., 2026; Guerra-Tamez et al., 2024).

Algorithmic Biases

ML algorithms can unknowingly amplify systematic discrimination and prejudices (Gong et al., 2026; Kumar et al., 2024). Algorithmic bias typically stems from biased human decision-making process or erroneous model designs (Kumar et al., 2024). Furthermore, GAI models reproduce intersectional occupational and gender stereotypes (Park et al., 2024). To break down algorithmic discrimination, combating corporate accountability, clear ethical framework and legal interventions is required for VIs (Kumar et al., 2024).

Psychological Manipulation

The hyper realistic nature and targeted capabilities of AI agents and VIs introduce a high risk for consumer deception and psychological manipulation (Diwanji, 2026). Highly anthropomorphized computer-generated imagery characters blur the boundary between reality and simulation, helps to manipulate emotions, and drive purchasing behaviors (Allal-Chérif et al., 2024). Because these synthetic entities project idealized, flawless image, they can exploit cognitive biases and exacerbate consumer vulnerabilities, such as appearance anxiety or psychological need to belongingness (Xu et al., 2025).

CONCEPTUAL FRAMEWORK

AI agents, as communicative market intermediaries, serve as the bridge between the brand and the consumer (Chen et al., 2024). AI-powered VIs and SBEs depend on the adoption, credibility, and engagement for the communicative market intermediaries (Franke et al., 2023). Adaptation depends on factors such as the choice of endorsers, their effectiveness, and the use of VI and consumer interaction psychology (Ling et al., 2021). For supporting the credibility of AI agent and VI, dependence on malleability, technical reliability, and competence-based credibility work as drivers of adoption, comparative effectiveness, and VI engagement (Jayasingh et al., 2025). These detailed factors focus on AI agents and VIs for communicative market intermediaries. Based on this perception, a conceptual framework is outlined in Figure 3.

Figure 3. Conceptual framework of AI-powered VIs

Source: Authors' processing

Adoption

The adoption of AI-powered VIs and SBEs represents a significant shift in digital marketing. While brands are increasingly adopting these entities for their cost efficiency and control, effectiveness compared to HIs depends on product type, implementation format, and specific nature. Figure 4 shows a clear picture of their adoption process.

Reasons for Choosing Endorsers

To mitigate risk and minimize control, brands are primarily transitioning from human to virtual endorsers.

(i) Safety and control: VIs are not prone to fatigue, illness or aging like HIs (Ozdemir et al., 2025). VIs have no private lives and have no human activities that allow brands to avoid reputational damage. On the other hand, they are scandal free where a human celebrity may have scandals (Allal-Chérif et al., 2024; Belanche et al., 2024; Xia et al., 2025). For a VI, it is easier for a brand to reprogram or replace the entity than to rehabilitate a human's image (Xia et al., 2025).

(ii) Availability and cost: VIs offer 24/7 availability and can appear in multiple locations at a time, which is not possible for HIs (Allal-Chérif et al., 2024; Volles et al., 2024). For these reasons, VIs are often more cost-effective and handier than humans (Allal-Chérif et al., 2024).

(iii) Novelty and customization: VIs can easily be aligned with a brand image and target demographics (Volles et al., 2024). The novelty is appealing to the Gen Z and Millennials considering that the brand is up to date and innovative (Su, 2025; Teng et al., 2025).

Effectiveness of AI Endorsers

VIs have higher engagement matrices than human characters. However, sometimes they lag behind humans in terms of their persuasiveness regarding specific purchase intentions.

(i) Agency and experience gap: MPT shows that consumers perceive VI has high "agency", denoted as the ability to plan and act, but low "experience", is identified as the ability to test, feel, and touch (De Cicco et al., 2024; Li et al., 2023; Zhang & He, 2025). Therefore, VIs are often deemed less credible at the time of endorsing products like subjective physical experience (e.g., skincare, perfume, food) (Allal-Chérif et al., 2024; Song et al., 2024).

(ii) Authenticity and trust: Consumers usually accept HIs as more authentic and trustworthy than VIs (Guerra-Tamez et al., 2024; Toyib & Paramita, 2024; Zhang & He, 2025). VIs endorsements feel fabricated or purely commercial and have a lack of real touch (De Cicco et al., 2024; Toyib & Paramita, 2024).

(iii) Engagement: In terms of engagement, VIs often generate higher engagement rates than HIs due to visual appeal and curiosity (Jayasingh et al., 2025; Rehman et al., 2026; Volles et al., 2024).

Utilization of VI

Effective use of a VIs depends on how they are utilized. The effective Use of a VI depends on the following aspects.

(i) Types of product: VIs are highly effective for endorsing technological and electronics products where quality is objectively evaluated (Ozdemir et al., 2025; Song et al., 2024). For sensory evaluation product like cosmetics and food, HIs is generally accepted for genuinely experiencing the product (Song et al., 2024; Yan et al., 2024). In static ads, VIs can be effective as humans for sensory products like a lavender pillow by focusing on the shift from the influencer's experience to the visual aesthetic (Li et al., 2026).

(ii) Brand owned and public VIs: These are created internally by a specific brand (e.g., KFC's Colonel KI launched in China). They foster a stronger self-brand connection for their narrative is highly aligned with the brand's identity (Teng et al., 2025; Wang & Wang, 2026). They are particularly effective for consumers with a low 'need to belong' who require clear symbolic cues (Wang & Wang, 2026).

(iii) AI voice: In short video ads, AI-generated voice does not increase engagement and purchase intention than a human voice. However, AI mimicking for famous celebrities can achieve a higher engagement level compared to humans (Bai et al., 2025).

Consumer Interaction And Psychology

The interaction and psychological aspects of consumers are discussed below.

(i) Computers are social actors paradigm: CASA paradigm implies that people can use social rules on VIs. When a VI appears and behaves like a human being, they see it as social, despite the fact that they may be aware that it is a fake (De Cicco et al., 2024; Jayasingh et al., 2025).

(ii) Uncanny valley: One of the most significant dangers is the uncanny valley, in which a VI appears nearly human but contains subtle flaws that cause a sense of creepiness and dismissal (Allal-Chérif et al., 2024; Diwanji, 2026). Those VIs that are highly realistic and do not contain these flaws are able to overcome this (De Cicco et al., 2024).

(iii) AI Identity disclosure: In contrast to the fear of eliminating the illusion of the VI by disclosing its artificial character, studies indicate that transparency (revealing the AI character) may, in fact, boost the purchase intention (Li et al., 2026; Wang & Qiu, 2024). It minimizes the sense of deception and even improves the sense of agency (capability) of the VI (Li et al., 2026; Wang & Qiu, 2024).

Figure 4. Adoption process

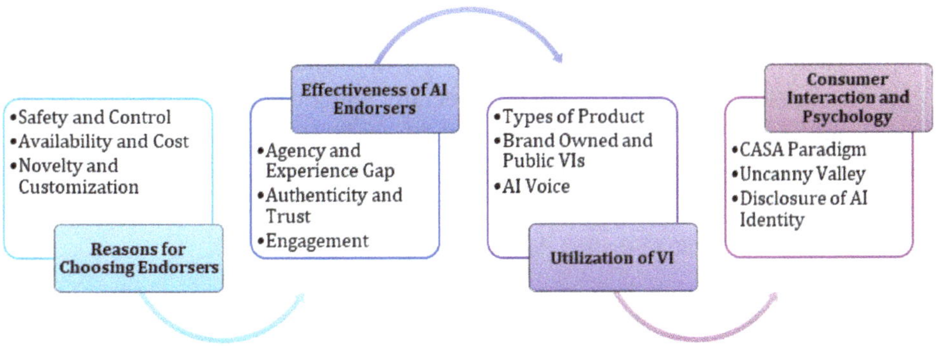

Source: Authors' work

Credibility

VIs enhance brand credibility through their malleability and technical reliability. Both attributes enable brand consistency and risk-free, high-narrative optimization that HIs cannot guarantee. Detailed breakdown of how these factors contribute to brand credibility. In figure 5, the credibility process is illustrated.

Malleability

Malleability is the ability of VIs to be customized, adjusted, and manipulated to conform to a particular marketing aim. This increases credibility as there is a flawless match between the endorser and the brand.

(i) Consistency and control: VIs are able to provide brands with absolute editorial power over message, visual expression, and narrative, unlike His, who are humans with independent thoughts and lives whose values can be challenging to a specific brand (Su, 2025). Due to the lack of independent opinions, they can be edited to deliver sponsored messages in their exact intended form, ensuring the content is on brand (Feng et al., 2024). Such a high degree of controllability enables VIs to maintain a stable brand image throughout the years, which is essential for developing trust (Teng et al., 2025; Tseng & Ou, 2025).

(ii) Targeting and customization: VIs are not limited to physical features or biology, appearance, style, and personality. They can be adjusted in response to algorithms to fit perfectly into the tastes of a target audience (Chan et al., 2023; Feng et al., 2024). As an illustration, engineers can make a VI look like a particular demographic in case this is what the audience wants (Feng et al., 2024).

(iii) Endorser-brand match: Due to the flexible nature of VIs, the level of "endorser-brand match" may be high, especially when dealing with brand-owned virtual endorsers (those produced by a particular brand) (Teng et al., 2025). Those VIs are intended to represent a set of core values of the brand, which will guarantee high concept congruence and minimize the chances of the endorser dominating the brand (Teng et al., 2025; Wang & Wang, 2026).

Technical Reliability and Risk Mitigation

Technical reliability is concerned with the consistency of the VI and its availability. The credibility is increased by this reliability since it eliminates volatility in the equation of marketing.

(i) Absence of human flaws: VIs are not limited by physical factors like fatigue, sickness and aging (Belanche et al., 2024; Ozdemir et al., 2025; Rungruangjit et al., 2024). They do not have mood swings or bad days, which allow for stable, predictable performance (Allal-Chérif et al., 2024; Teng et al., 2025). This absence of human flaws is one of the main features that specialists put forward as a crucial advantage in comparison with HIs (Allal-Chérif et al., 2024).

(ii) Scandal and risk mitigation: A major source of brand credibility is the prevention of bad publicity. VIs are regarded as scandal-free due to the fact that they have no personal life where they make mistakes in their behavior (Belanche et al., 2024; Ozdemir et al., 2025; Thomas & Fowler, 2021). Brands also have reduced reputational risks as VIs will not behave unfit unless programmed to behave unfit (Allal-Chérif et al., 2024). It is often easier for a brand to manage or reprogram the VI than to HI (Thomas & Fowler, 2021).

(iii) Omnipresence and availability: VIs are able to operate 24 hours per day, 7 days per week and may exist in more than one place at a time (Allal-Chérif et al., 2024; Rungruangjit et al., 2024; Teng et al., 2025). Such flexibility enables 24/7 interaction with consumers over various time zones and platforms, and strengthens the brand image and credibility (Teng et al., 2025; Wang & Wang, 2026).

Competence-Based Credibility

The technicality of VIs provides a particular form of credibility based on perceived competence and objectivity that are described in the following discourse.

(i) Perceived objectivity and logic: VIs are often associated with neutrality, logic, and rationality by consumers (Zheng et al., 2026), and they are controlled by algorithms. VIs are viewed as more objective and relied upon in terms of their cognitive abilities, a phenomenon referred to as the machine heuristic (Yan et al., 2024; Zheng et al., 2026). This makes them especially useful in promoting practical or technical products, for which consumers appreciate factual information and logical reasoning more than emotional appeal (Belanche et al., 2024).

(ii) Agency vs experience: Although consumers might not be convinced that a VI can feel or experience, they tend to judge VIs highly in terms of agency (ability to act, plan, and be efficient) (Wang & Zhang, 2025; Zhang & He, 2025). As illustrated virtual streamers are seen as very responsive and able to process large volumes of information to deliver correct details about a product that adds to perceived usefulness and trustworthiness in information-related scenarios (Wang & Zhang, 2025).

Figure 5. Credibility process

Source: Authors' work

Engagement

The interaction dynamics of AI-driven VIs and SBEs are based on the sophisticated interaction between novelty, content strategy, and product fit. VIs trend to be more effective than HIs in terms of raw engagements (e.g., likes and views), but their capacity to generate purchase intentions and trust is strongly situational. The engagement process is shown in Figure 6.

Drivers of Engagement

Studies show that VIs are capable of creating a higher engagement rate up to three times more than HIs (De Cicco et al., 2024). There are several factors driving this engagement as described below.

(i) Curiosity and novelty: The major motivation is the novelty factor. VIs represent that the consumers are intrigued by the technological innovation that draws attention and creates curiosity. This perceived positive influence helps to follow the influencer and purchase endorsed products (Volles et al., 2024).

(ii) Attractive appeal and beauty: Hyper-realistic and high aesthetic designs attract potential users (Allal-Chérif et al., 2024). Highly attractive VIs can minimize psychological distance and increase purchase intentions, especially when consumers do not perceive the VI's perfection as a threat to their self-esteem (Xia et al., 2025).

(iii) Emotion and entertainment: As opposed to the belief that VIs should remain focused on robotic reasoning, emotional content, and be interested in positive and negative emotional feelings. Again, entertainment is indeed among the components that are effective in producing willingness to follow VIs. Relational content, like talking about friendships or holidays, is also a strong antecedent of VIs (Rungruangjit et al., 2024).

Comparative Effectiveness

While VIs excel in visibility, their influence compared to humans is refined. The comparison between VIs and HIs is elaborated below.

(i) Engagement and conversion: VIs trend to receive a greater number of likes and comments because of interest (Li et al., 2023). However, they may be less efficient at creating purchase intentions and brand attitudes, as they are perceived as lacking life experience and sensory ability (Nguyen et al., 2024).

(ii) Trust and authenticity: Consumers generally trust HIs more due to their perceived authenticity and autonomy (Volles et al., 2024). However, VIs can be perceived as "authentically fake" about their fabricated nature than HIs who stage perfection (Allal-Chérif et al., 2024).

(iii) Voice and video: Human voices generate high engagement, likes, and comments than AI-generated voices. On the other hand, AI-generated celebrity voices can achieve engagement levels comparable to a real human voice (Bai et al., 2025).

Critical Success Factors

The effectiveness of a VI is highly dependent on how they are organized. The factors impacting success of VIs are pointed out here.

(i) Message and content strategy: HIs typically exceed VIs when emotional appeals or compassion are required. If a VI is highly anthropomorphized, they can successfully use emotional appeals to drive engagement, for overcoming the machine heuristic (Zheng et al., 2026).

(ii) Product endorser fit: VIs are highly effective for searching products where quality is objective. Sensory evaluation is required for food and skincare where taste, touch, and smell can be represented by humans because of the lack of physical capacity to sense, leading to skepticism (Song et al., 2025).

(iii) Virtual endorser types: Brand-created VIs are likely to create a stronger self-brand connection as compared to public VIs. The reason is that branded VIs are regarded as being more compatible with the brand and therefore easier to engage in PSI. This benefit is particularly high among consumers whose level of need to belong is low and who depend on the use of clear brand cues (Wang & Wang, 2026). Human supported live streaming virtual avatars create more purchase intentions compared to fully AI-supported ones since they possess agency and experience, as opposed to AI being perceived as having agency only (Wang & Zhang, 2025).

(iv) Psychological mechanisms: A human co-endorser with VI results in much more of the perceived social presence of VI, which makes it appear real and reliable. Presence of the VI with the human co-endorser of the same gender only increases such an effect (Liu, 2026). On the other hand, the digital endorser should be disclosed to present consumer perceptions and purchase intentions, whereas it can damage consumer perceptions (Wang & Qiu, 2024). VIs create an onside relationship with followers. This is the bond between the attributes of the VI (such as attractiveness or credibility) and the consumer's purchase intention (Jayasingh et al., 2025).

Figure 6. Engagement process

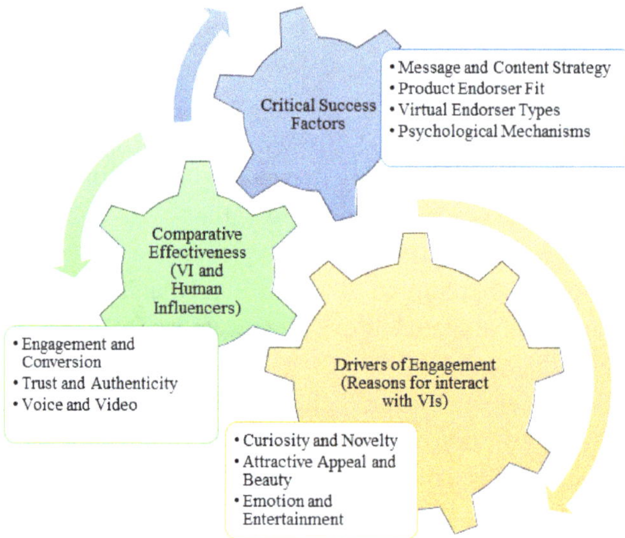

Source: Authors' work

Operationalization and Empirical Application of the Proposed Framework

Based on the conceptual framework, companies can operationalize SBEs by measuring the specific psychological and practical drivers that lead brands and consumers to accept VIs. Researchers could conduct experimental surveys to test the CASA Paradigm and the Uncanny Valley effect especially how disclosure of AI identity impacts consumer trust. Longitudinal studies could observe how a VI's technical reliability and risk mitigation affect its competence-based credibility. It might also track consumer sentiment following instances where an AI endorser experiences a glitch or hallucination, as well as can track concrete metrics like engagement and conversion, trust, and authenticity.

RECOMMENDATIONS

With the future of digital marketing being dominated by AI-based VIs and SBEs, brands should implement strategies that would optimize their opportunities and minimize the risks they might be facing. The recommendations below offer a guideline for effective use of VIs, revolving around adoption, credibility, engagement, and ethics.

Establish Open and Transparent AI Disclosure Practices

Influencers who are powered by AI should be readily indicated by the brands in question. Trust with the consumers should be achieved as transparency is a key element. Consumers are more likely to feel comfortable with an influencer once they realize that the influencer is an AI-run model (Jhawar et al., 2023). Nevertheless, excessive openness can be detrimental to the popularity of VI. This means that brands must take a middle ground where there is a hint of disclosure that is not too much, as it would take away the authenticity of the influencer. As an illustration, a one-line or small logo that states the nature of the influencer as AI can work.

Make Virtual Influencers More Emotionally Engaging

VIs ought to be made to create an emotional appeal through the use of relatable backstories and human-like stories (Kim et al., 2025). VIs do not always succeed in establishing an emotional connection because they do not have it in reality. To curb this, companies must focus on creating competitive backstory and emotional content that enables VIs to connect with their followers. The strategy will be able to improve the relationship between PSI (Omeish et al., 2025) and result in better consumer engagement. The effectiveness of the VIs, especially when it comes to products of the emotional or experience-driven category, can be enhanced by personalizing their journey and emotions, as HIs can.

Embark on Human-Like to Create Authenticity

VIs need to be anthropomorphized to an extent that makes them seem genuine and relatable. VIs can fill the authenticity gap by incorporating human-like characteristics, including expressive feelings, live communication, and flaws (Ju et al., 2024). Although they can also be used to market products, VIs who appear emotional or engage consumers personally are more likely to be perceived as genuine. These features should be considered since brands are likely to adopt the features in the industries that require a high degree of trust like beauty or health.

Capitalize on Virtual Influencers in Informational and Rational Product Categories

VIs should be used by brands that deal with rational products with heavy information content, including electronics, technology, and education (Zeng et al., 2024). Since VIs are excellent at providing coherent, clear, and objective messages, such influencers are suitable when it comes to products that demand the use of factual communication and rational decision-making. Goods containing a lot of data regarding comparisons, technical details, or information related to education may be advantageous with the objectivity of data and reliable information that VIs provide. As an example, a tech-oriented brand could utilize a VI to describe product features, specifications, and comparisons in a way that resonates with a technologically oriented audience.

Personalize Content to Consumer Needs and Expectations

The brands must make sure that the content that VIs produce fits the expectations and platform standards. The relevance of influencer traits to audience expectations is crucial for consumer interaction (Akhtar et al., 2024). In order to make VIs more impactful, brands have to produce content that suits the platform on which it will be posted, whether it is Instagram, TikTok, or YouTube. The information must be modified to the style and format of the platform, be it a short video on TikTok or a massively visual post on Instagram. Knowing the preferences of the platform and the audience can bring more organic engagement and brand success.

Pay attention to Long-Term Relationship Building

The VIs should be seen as long term brand ambassadors and not a short-term campaign instrument by the brands (Leggett & Davies, 2026). HIs are likely to appear and disappear depending on the trend, but VIs can be a long-term investment in the marketing strategy of a brand. Through establishing long-term partnerships with VIs, the brands are able to create a consistent brand voice and consumer attachment. This would be the most useful in those industries in which brand loyalty plays a significant role e.g., fashion, beauty, and technology.

Fair Representation

Brands should be conscious of the ethical aspect of utilizing VIs, especially when it comes to body image and diversity (Kim & Wang, 2023). The application of VIs risks supporting the unrealistic beauty standards and creating a negative effect on social comparison, especially among Gen Z audiences (Sands et al., 2022). The way to escape these pitfalls is to ensure that brands develop a variety of VIs that have a wide variety of body types, skin tones, and lifestyles. It will not only mean following an ethical marketing approach but also foster inclusiveness, making VIs more relatable to a wide range of consumers. This will go a long way in averting the backlash that may be associated with body image issues.

Invest in Cross-Cultural Studies

The success of AI-driven VIs depends considerably on cultural backgrounds. The national culture in the context of collectivist countries such as China strengthens the effect of attractiveness of a VI on the purchase intention, and the individualistic cultures can have different responses to these stimuli (Bai et al., 2024; Teng et al., 2025). Emotional appeals, including relational and entertaining content, are more likely to influence the level of willingness of young consumers to follow VIs in Thailand than rational or authentic appeals (Allal-Cherif et al., 2024; Rungruangjit et al., 2024). Carry out cross-cultural research to determine the perception of VIs in various markets and make the required changes to the design (Mouritzen et al., 2024). The use of VIs is global and it is important that brands pay attention to cultural differences in the usage, credibility and the engagement. It has been found that VIs depend on the cultural aspects. The brands are also advised to invest in cross-cultural studies to understand how various audiences respond to VIs. An example would be a VI created with the US audience in mind, which would require changes to attract the Asian or European audience. The design and the content of the influencer should be adapted to the local cultural norms and values, and this would go a long way in increasing their effectiveness.

IMPLICATIONS

Theoretical Contribution

Unidentified research fronts hinder theoretical progress and practical application. There are no bibliometric or science-mapping studies that currently bring together the field's intellectual structure. This study systematically addresses these gaps. Thus, the study contributes to the literature on AI-powered VIs and SBEs that can be synthesized into several key domains, like MPT, CASA paradigm, and congruity and persuasion theories. In Marketing, MPT is a significant theoretical contribution across studies, as it applies and refines MPT to explain the dichotomy between VIs and HIs. Consumers attribute high agency, capacity to act, plan, and execute to VIs but low experience, capacity to feel, test, and sense (Li et al., 2023; Ozdemir et al., 2025). On the other hand, social presence is useful in the paradigm of human-computer interaction in a more complex social context. A human co-endorser to the VI adds to its perceived social presence, introducing relational cues that aid consumers in decoding the VI as a social agent, minimizing the uncanny valley effect and boosting credibility (Liu, 2026). Under congruity and persuasion theories, match-up hypothesis and Elaboration Likelihood Model (ELM) position VIs as unique communicative intermediaries that thrive on cognitive 'fit'. Theoretically, VIs triggers a 'feeling of rightness' and greater persuasion when paired with rational appeals that align with their perceived machine nature (Zheng et al., 2026). The study's conceptual framework adds novelty to the existing literature of VIs and SBEs in the domain of marketing and IS.

Practical Implications

VIs is applicable to utilitarian products (e.g., technology) where objective information and competency are valued. They are driven by factual credibility by their machine heuristics (Allal-Cherif et al., 2024; Belanche et al., 2024; Teng et al., 2025; Yan et al., 2024). On the other hand, HIs are stronger than VIs in the case of hedonic products (e.g. food, cosmetics) due to their sensory constraints. When it comes to VIs, experience-based social posts are to be used less than aesthetic-oriented advertisements (Allal-Cherif et al., 2024; Li et al., 2026). With transparency on how AI is used, particularly on products of technology, agency and purchase intention could be enhanced (Pierre, 2025; Wang & Qiu, 2024; Zhou et al., 2026). The self-contained AI would not be able to match the avatars supported by humans in the live streaming (Wang & Zhang, 2025). AI crisis situations, which entail substituting VIs with human celebrities, are more practical (Thomas & Fowler, 2021). One way of preventing the uncanny valley is ensuring that the realism is of high quality or adapting the designs to be unquestionably stylized (Allal-Cherif et al., 2024; Diwanji, 2026; Teng et al., 2025).

Policy and Ethical Implications

AI-based VIs bring up important ethical issues of transparency, deceit, privacy, bias, and accountability. Since hyper-realistic VIs cause the blurring of the boundary between simulation and reality, consumers, especially young ones, might not realize that it is non-human, which raises the risk of deceptive parasocial relations and explains why mandatory disclosure is necessary (De Cicco et al., 2024; Park et al., 2024; Rehman et al., 2025). Selling experience products (e.g., food or skincare) by VIs also presents ethical challenges because their sense of touch is absent, and it automatically transforms such assertions into a fabricated claim that can cause a break in consumer trust (Allal-Cherif et al., 2024; Li et al., 2026; Ozdemir et al., 2025). In addition to deceiving, VIs create privacy and data risks by personalizing their behaviors and habits. They also create content that involves unauthorized cloning of human voices and likenesses, and pivotal copyright concerns regarding scraped training data (Bai et al., 2025; Jin & Viswanathan, 2025; Park et al., 2024; Shao, 2024). The algorithmic bias also enables VIs to strengthen racial, gender, and occupational representations and encourage unrealistic beauty ideals, enhancing the development of appearance anxiety and disproportionately affecting minors at the risk of emotional manipulation (Allal-Cherif et al., 2024; Park et al., 2024; Xia et al., 2025; Yang et al., 2025). Lastly, there is the lack of accountability because AI-controlled organizations depend on brands, developers, and algorithms, which makes it difficult to hold any party responsible for the consequences of misinformation or hate speech and makes it necessary to create clear governance models regarding AI-controlled entities (Allal-Cherif et al., 2024; Rehman et al., 2026; Rungruangjit et al., 2024).

Academic and Industry Integration

The combination of scholarly research and practice in AI-based marketing and VIs is defined by a dynamic interaction among theoretical frameworks. The conceptual frameworks of collaborative intelligence in marketing conceptualize the collaboration between AI and HI. These paradigms indicate that low-level AI ought to assist higher human intelligence, which would foster a gradual transition whereby AI takes care of routine chores whereas human beings are left with the responsibility of intuitive and empathetic chores (Kumar et al., 2024; Tarnanidis, 2024). In academic sources, there is a tendency to recommend against the use of VIs in proximal-sensory products (e.g., cosmetics, perfume) because VIs lack the physical ability to perceive them, which raises credibility concerns (Li et al., 2026; Zeng & Lin, 2025).

CONCLUSION

This study delineates the intellectual and thematic framework of AI-driven VI and SBE research via a bibliometric analysis of publications from Scopus. The bibliometric review is supplemented by a qualitative content analysis of significant publications to elucidate thematic clusters pertaining to technology adoption, credibility development, and engagement outcomes. The results show that the field is growing quickly but remains highly fragmented. Performance trends indicate a surge in publication activity since 2020, driven by advancements in GAI and the growing use of synthetic personas in branding. Keyword analyses show that the focus of early conversations about realism and deception has shifted to more complex topics such as trust, identity, ethics, and adapting to cultures around the world. These results are consistent with content-level insights indicating that perceptions of credibility, trust mechanisms, and engagement metrics systematically differ across designs, levels of transparency, and product-endorser alignment.

The conceptual framework established - connecting Adoption → Credibility → Engagement, influenced by cultural intelligence and machine heuristics - synthesizes bibliometric trends with theoretical foundations. The study's bibliometric insights help brands, researchers, and policymakers better understand how the field has changed and what it could do in the future. In the end, SBEs are not only new technology but also change the way marketing relationships work by altering how people and machines communicate.

Limitations and Subsequent Future Research Directions

As with any scholarly work, including this study, there are limitations. The limitations of this study, along with the subsequent studies, are enumerated here.

(i) Limits on the database and search query: Scopus has extensive coverage, but some interdisciplinary work in AI art, digital anthropology, or HCI may not be fully indexed. Subsequent research ought to encompass WoS, EBSCO, the AIS library, Google Scholar, and the ACM digital library, or integrate bibliometric data with systematic reviews.

(ii) Problems with keywords and indexing: The field uses words that mean the same thing, like "digital human," "AI avatar," "synthetic endorser," and "virtual influencer." Changes in author keywords could make it hard to get all the information. Subsequent research ought to utilize augmented controlled vocabularies and text-mining-based corpus expansion.

(iii) Citation-based methods favor older works: Science-mapping methods like co-citation might not show enough new studies with low citation counts but high conceptual novelty. Bibliometric methodologies ought to integrate altimetric and machine-learning trend prediction.

(iv) Not enough depth of interpretation: Bibliometrics reveals patterns, but comprehensive interpretation relies on qualitative analysis. Future researchers ought to integrate bibliometrics with meta-analyses and expert interviews.

(v) Need for bibliometric segmentation that is specific to the field: This study focuses on overall application of VIs and SBEs. Future bibliometric research may categorize analyses by platform (Instagram, TikTok, YouTube), sector (fashion, gaming, money), demographic group (Gen Z, Gen Alpha), market maturity (Asian vs. Western markets).

(vi) Science mapping needs to get better: The study does not show the detailed bibliometric maps for being too focused on the development of the conceptual framework. Next-generation research ought to utilize topic modeling (linear discriminant analysis, BERTopic), dynamic co-citation (longitudinal knowledge evolution), and co-word burst detection (emerging concepts).

Novelty

This study makes several unique contributions in the following areas.

(i) The initial bibliometric mapping of synthetic endorser research: This study presents the inaugural comprehensive bibliometric analysis that integrates Scopus, delivering a rigorous, data-driven overview of the evolution of research in VIs and SBEs, in contrast to previous narrative reviews or empirical studies.

(ii) A conceptual framework based on observed performance trends: The bibliometric data directly contribute to a cohesive Adoption-Credibility-Engagement framework, highlighting cultural intelligence and machine heuristics as key moderators derived from keyword co-occurrence maps and thematic evolution trajectories.

(iii) Recognition of nascent research frontiers: The study reveals novel high-growth subjects - identity negotiation, transparency design, realism fidelity, and ethical governance - that conventional reviews have failed to systematically document.

(iv) A roadmap based on evidence for researchers and professionals: This study provides a substantive set of implications for brands, policymakers, and researchers by connecting science-mapping findings to content-level insights, setting it apart from purely conceptual or empirical studies.

These contributions collectively establish this study as a seminal bibliometric resource for understanding and advancing the rapidly developing field of AI-driven VIs and SBEs.

ACKNOWLEDGMENT

This research received no specific grant from any funding agency in the public, commercial, or not-for-profit sectors.

REFERENCES

Akhtar, N., Hameed, Z., Islam, T., Pant, M. K., Sharma, A., Rather, R. A., & Kuzior, A. (2024). Avatars of influence: Understanding how virtual influencers trigger consumer engagement on online booking platforms. *Journal of Retailing and Consumer Services*, *78*, 103742. DOI: 10.1016/j.jretconser.2024.103742

Alam, S. (2025). Exploring success variables of knowledge management for enhanced organisational performance: An integrated framework. *Knowledge Management Research and Practice*, •••, 1–29. DOI: 10.1080/14778238.2025.2550304

Alam, S., Islam, K. A., Miah, M. R., Afrin, S., Islam, M. A., Hoque, M. R., & Mahmud, I. (2025). Key success factors of knowledge management systems for optimizing organizational performance: A PRISMA-based systematic literature review. *Heliyon*, *11*(16), e44097. DOI: 10.1016/j.heliyon.2025.e44097

Allal-Chérif, O., Puertas, R., & Carracedo, P. (2024). Intelligent influencer marketing: How AI-powered virtual influencers outperform human influencers. *Technological Forecasting and Social Change*, *200*, 123113. DOI: 10.1016/j.techfore.2023.123113

Bai, S., Zhang, W., & Yu, D. (2024). Uncovering effects of virtual endorser's attractiveness on consumer behaviors from the perspective of national culture. *Current Psychology*, *43*(34), 27534–27547. DOI: 10.1007/s12144-024-06397-4

Bai, Y., Xue, Z., Zhang, M., Tan, Q., & Li, Y. (2025). Voices that captivate: The impact of AI-generated voiceover on video Ad engagement. *International Journal of Information Management*, *85*, 102962. DOI: 10.1016/j.ijinfomgt.2025.102962

Belanche, D., Casaló, L. V., & Flavián, M. (2024). Human versus virtual influences, a comparative study. *Journal of Business Research*, *173*, 114493. DOI: 10.1016/j.jbusres.2023.114493

Bhuiyan, M. R. I., Husain, T., Islam, S., & Amin, A. (2025). Exploring the prospective influence of artificial intelligence on the health sector in Bangladesh: A study on awareness, perception and adoption. *Health Education*, *125*(3), 279–297. DOI: 10.1108/HE-10-2024-0125

Chan, K. W., Septianto, F., Kwon, J., & Kamal, R. S. (2023). Color effects on AI influencers' product recommendations. *European Journal of Marketing*, *57*(9), 2290–2315. DOI: 10.1108/EJM-03-2022-0185

Chen, Y., Tu, Y., & Zeng, S. (2024). Costly "Greetings" from AI: Effects of product recommenders and self-disclosure levels on transaction costs. *Sustainability (Basel)*, *16*(18), 8236. DOI: 10.3390/su16188236

De Cicco, R., Iacobucci, S., Cannito, L., Onesti, G., Ceccato, I., & Palumbo, R. (2024). Virtual vs. human influencer: Effects on users' perceptions and brand outcomes. *Technology in Society*, *77*, 102488. DOI: 10.1016/j.techsoc.2024.102488

Diwanji, V. S. (2026). Should your brand hire virtual influencers? How realism and gender presentation shape trust and purchase intentions. *Journal of Retailing and Consumer Services*, *88*, 104491. DOI: 10.1016/j.jretconser.2025.104491

Faisal-E-Alam, M., Bhuiyan, M. R. I., Mimi, A., & Miah, M. T. (2025). The role of the three zero framework in advancing global sustainable development through bibliometric and text mining analysis. *Discover Sustainability*, *6*(1), 1128. DOI: 10.1007/s43621-025-01919-x

Feng, Y., Chen, H., & Xie, Q. (2024). AI Influencers in advertising: The role of AI influencer-related attributes in shaping consumer attitudes, consumer trust, and perceived influencer–product fit. *Journal of Interactive Advertising*, *24*(1), 26–47. DOI: 10.1080/15252019.2023.2284355

Franke, C., Groeppel-Klein, A., & Müller, K. (2023). Consumers' responses to virtual influencers as advertising endorsers: Novel and effective or uncanny and deceiving? *Journal of Advertising*, *52*(4), 523–539. DOI: 10.1080/00913367.2022.2154721

Gong, S., Liu, L., Shao, J., Li, Y., & Yang, Y. (2026). Understanding the mechanism behind consumers' purchase intentions toward AI recommendations: The trade-off between privacy and incentives. *Journal of Retailing and Consumer Services*, *88*, 104489. DOI: 10.1016/j.jretconser.2025.104489

Guerra-Tamez, C. R., Flores, K. K., Serna-Mendiburu, G. M., Robles, D. C., & Cortés, J. I. (2024). Decoding gen Z: AI's influence on brand trust and purchasing behavior. *Frontiers in Artificial Intelligence*, *7*, 1323512. DOI: 10.3389/frai.2024.1323512 PMID: 38500672

Ham, J., Li, S., Shah, P., & Eastin, M. S. (2024). Are virtual influencers more effective in real-world advertisement settings? *Journal of Advertising Research*, *64*(3), 353–371. DOI: 10.2501/JAR-2024-015

Han, B., Liu, D., & Qi, S. (2025). Beyond human streamers: How AI-avatar engagement strategies influence consumer acceptance. *Asia Pacific Journal of Marketing and Logistics*, •••, 1–20. DOI: 10.1108/APJML-04-2025-0618

Jayasingh, S., Sivakumar, A., & Vanathaiyan, A. A. (2025). Artificial intelligence influencers' credibility effect on consumer engagement and purchase intention. *Journal of Theoretical and Applied Electronic Commerce Research*, *20*(1), 17. DOI: 10.3390/jtaer20010017

Jhawar, A., Kumar, P., & Varshney, S. (2023). The emergence of virtual influencers: A shift in the influencer marketing paradigm. *Young Consumers*, *24*(4), 468–484. DOI: 10.1108/YC-05-2022-1529

Jin, S. V., & Viswanathan, V. (2025). "Threatened and empty selves following AI-based virtual influencers": Comparison between followers and non-followers of virtual influencers in AI-driven digital marketing. *AI & Society*, *40*(1), 117–131. DOI: 10.1007/s00146-023-01832-9

Ju, N., Kim, T., & Im, H. (2024). Fake human but real influencer: The interplay of authenticity and humanlikeness in virtual influencer communication? *Fashion and Textiles*, *11*(1), 16. DOI: 10.1186/s40691-024-00380-0

Kim, D., & Wang, Z. (2023). The ethics of virtuality: Navigating the complexities of human-like virtual influencers in the social media marketing realm. *Frontiers in Communication*, *8*, 1205610. DOI: 10.3389/fcomm.2023.1205610

Kim, E., Xie, Q., Hong, J. W., & Kim, H. M. (2025). Prosocial campaigns with virtual influencers: Stories, messages, and beyond. *International Journal of Human-Computer Interaction*, *41*(11), 6956–6967. DOI: 10.1080/10447318.2024.2387399

Kim, J., Kang, S., & Bae, J. (2022). The effects of customer consumption goals on artificial intelligence driven recommendation agents: Evidence from stitch fix. *International Journal of Advertising*, *41*(6), 997–1016. DOI: 10.1080/02650487.2021.1963098

Kitchenham, B., Budgen, D., Brereton, P., Turner, M., Charters, S., & Linkman, S. (2007). Large-scale software engineering questions – Expert opinion or empirical evidence? *IET Software*, *1*(5), 161–171. DOI: 10.1049/iet-sen:20060052

Kravets, O., Korolova, U., Nosachenko, O., Vasiltsova, O., & Koberniuk, S. (2025). AI-powered digital marketing: Enhancing customer behaviour predictions. *European Journal of Sustainable Development*, *14*(2), 84. DOI: 10.14207/ejsd.2025.v14n2p84

Kumar, V., Ashraf, A. R., & Nadeem, W. (2024). AI-powered marketing: What, where, and how? *International Journal of Information Management*, *77*, 102783. DOI: 10.1016/j.ijinfomgt.2024.102783

Leggett, K. L., & Davies, W. E. (2026). Examining a hyper-human virtual brand ambassador as a brand personification strategy. *Journal of Product and Brand Management, 35*(3), 415–428. DOI: 10.1108/JPBM-06-2024-5290

Li, H., Lei, Y., Zhou, Q., & Yuan, H. (2023). Can you sense without being human? Comparing virtual and human influencers endorsement effectiveness. *Journal of Retailing and Consumer Services, 75*, 103456. DOI: 10.1016/j.jretconser.2023.103456

Li, Y., Xiang, X., & Wu, R. (2026). Display advertising or social media post? The impact of endorsement execution form on the effectiveness of virtual influencers' advertising endorsements. *Journal of Retailing and Consumer Services, 90*, 104685. DOI: 10.1016/j.jretconser.2025.104685

Ling, E. C., Tussyadiah, I., Tuomi, A., Stienmetz, J., & Ioannou, A. (2021). Factors influencing users' adoption and use of conversational agents: A systematic review. *Psychology and Marketing, 38*(7), 1031–1051. DOI: 10.1002/mar.21491

Liu, F. (2026). Who and how to pair with a virtual influencer? The impact of co-endorser type, perceived distance, and gender congruence on consumer responses in virtual influencer collaborations. *Journal of Retailing and Consumer Services, 89*, 104593. DOI: 10.1016/j.jretconser.2025.104593

Looia, J., & Kahlor, L. A. (2024). Artificial intelligence in influencer marketing: A mixed-method comparison of human and virtual influencers on Instagram. *Journal of Interactive Advertising, 24*(2), 107–126. DOI: 10.1080/15252019.2024.2313721

Lou, C., Kiew, S. T., Chen, T., Lee, T. Y., Ong, J. E., & Phua, Z. (2023). Authentically fake? How consumers respond to the influence of virtual influencers. *Journal of Advertising, 52*(4), 540–557. DOI: 10.1080/00913367.2022.2149641

Lou, X., & Copeland, L. (2025). Gen Z and AI-generated fashion ads: A qualitative study to understanding female consumer perceptions and reactions. *Journal of Internet Commerce, 24*(3), 131–152. DOI: 10.1080/15332861.2025.2520194

Mouritzen, S. L. T., Penttinen, V., & Pedersen, S. (2024). Virtual influencer marketing: The good, the bad and the unreal. *European Journal of Marketing, 58*(2), 410–440. DOI: 10.1108/EJM-12-2022-0915

Moustakas, E., Lamba, N., Mahmoud, D., & Ranganathan, C. (2020). Blurring lines between fiction and reality: Perspectives of experts on marketing effectiveness of virtual influencers. In *2020 International Conference on Cyber Security and Protection of Digital Services (Cyber Security)* (pp. 1-6). IEEE, Dublin, Ireland. DOI: 10.1109/CyberSecurity49315.2020.9138861

Nalivaikė, J., & Miliukaitė, G. (2024). Influence of AI-generated avatars on consumer trust in the brand. In *14th International Scientific Conference "Business and Management 2024"* (pp. 601-610). DOI: 10.3846/bm.2024.1191

Nguyen, K. M., Nguyen, N. T., Ngo, N. T. Q., Tran, N. T. H., & Nguyen, H. T. T. (2024). Investigating consumers' purchase resistance behavior to AI-Based content recommendations on short-video platforms: A study of greedy and biased recommendations. *Journal of Internet Commerce, 23*(3), 284–327. DOI: 10.1080/15332861.2024.2375966

Omeish, F., Shaheen, A., Alharthi, S., & Alfaiza, A. (2025). Between human and AI influencers: Parasocial relationships, credibility, and social capital formation in a collectivist market: A study of TikTok users in the Middle East. *Discover Sustainability, 6*(1), 116. DOI: 10.1007/s43621-025-00891-w

Ozdemir, O., Karabulut, F., & Messinger, P. R. (2025). Can('t) touch this: The effect of form realism and product domain in virtual influencer endorsements. *Journal of Retailing, 101*(2), 298–310. DOI: 10.1016/j.jretai.2025.04.002

Park, J., & Ahn, S. (2024). Traditional vs. AI-generated brand personalities: Impact on brand preference and purchase intention. *Journal of Retailing and Consumer Services, 81*, 104009. DOI: 10.1016/j.jretconser.2024.104009

Park, J., Oh, C., & Kim, H. Y. (2024). AI vs. human-generated content and accounts on Instagram: User preferences, evaluations, and ethical considerations. *Technology in Society, 79*, 102705. DOI: 10.1016/j.techsoc.2024.102705

Petticrew, M., & Roberts, H. (2008). Systematic reviews – Do they 'work' in informing decision-making around health inequalities? *Health Economics, Policy, and Law, 3*(2), 197–211. DOI: 10.1017/S1744133108004453 PMID: 18634627

Pierre, L. (2025). Exploring how brand use of artificial intelligence influences consumer perceptions and behavioral intentions through general AI attitudes and brand transparency. *Journal of Current Issues and Research in Advertising*, •••, 1–25. DOI: 10.1080/10641734.2025.2596011

Qadri, U. A., & Moustafa, A. M. A. (2026). They made it just for me! How AI transparency and influencer well-being shape consumer responses to AI-Driven content. *Psychology and Marketing, 43*(3), 591–608. DOI: 10.1002/mar.70075

Rehman, A., Kumar, S., Salam, M. A., & Virmani, N. (2025). How does AI-powered virtual influencer's anthropomorphism impact trust and brand love? The moderating role of opinion leadership. *Technological Forecasting and Social Change, 219*, 124198. DOI: 10.1016/j.techfore.2025.124198

Rehman, A. U., Hassan, S. H., & Behera, R. K. (2026). Attractiveness vs similarity: How attributes of AI-based virtual influencers impact credibility, parasocial interaction and purchase intentions of social-media users. *Asia Pacific Journal of Marketing and Logistics*, *38*(2), 205–222. DOI: 10.1108/APJML-01-2025-0144

Rungruangjit, W., Mongkol, K., Piriyakul, I., & Charoenpornpanichkul, K. (2024). The power of human-like virtual-influencer-generated content: Impact on consumers' willingness to follow and purchase intentions. *Computers in Human Behavior Reports*, *16*, 100523. DOI: 10.1016/j.chbr.2024.100523

Sands, S., Campbell, C. L., Plangger, K., & Ferraro, C. (2022). Unreal influence: Leveraging AI in influencer marketing. *European Journal of Marketing*, *56*(6), 1721–1747. DOI: 10.1108/EJM-12-2019-0949

Shao, Z. (2024). From human to virtual: Unmasking consumer switching intentions to virtual influencers by an integrated fsQCA and NCA method. *Journal of Retailing and Consumer Services*, *78*, 103715. DOI: 10.1016/j.jretconser.2024.103715

Song, J., Zheng, C., Lv, X., & Font, X. (2025). The endorsement effectiveness of virtual influencers in nonprofit fundraising: The role of appearance and voice pitch. *Technological Forecasting and Social Change*, *219*, 124299. DOI: 10.1016/j.techfore.2025.124299

Song, Y., Wang, L., Zhang, Z., & Hikkerova, L. (2024). AI or human: How endorser shapes online purchase intention? *Computers in Human Behavior*, *158*, 108300. DOI: 10.1016/j.chb.2024.108300

Su, B. (2025). Navigating the new frontier: The role of AI-driven virtual influencers in consumer engagement. *AI Magazine*, *46*(2), e70012. DOI: 10.1002/aaai.70012

Sun, L., Tang, Y., & Ma, X. (2025). It just would not work for me: Perceived preference heterogeneity and consumer response to AI-driven product recommendations. *European Journal of Marketing*, *59*(5), 1426–1452. DOI: 10.1108/EJM-02-2023-0082

Tarnanidis, T. K. (2024). Reshaping marketing science in wholesaling and retailing. In *Advances in Marketing*. Customer Relationship Management, and E-Services Book Series., DOI: 10.4018/979-8-3693-6145-0

Teng, L., Wang, H., Wang, X., & Foti, L. (2025). Unlocking the potential of virtual endorsers: The role of brand-owned and brand-non-owned virtual endorsers in shaping brand attitude. *International Journal of Information Management*, *81*, 102864. DOI: 10.1016/j.ijinfomgt.2024.102864

Thomas, V. L., & Fowler, K. (2021). Close encounters of the AI kind: Use of AI influencers as brand endorsers. *Journal of Advertising, 50*(1), 11–25. DOI: 10.1080/00913367.2020.1810595

Toyib, J. S., & Paramita, W. (2024). An authentic human-like figure: The success keys of AI fashion influencer. *Cogent Business & Management, 11*(1), 2380019. Advance online publication. DOI: 10.1080/23311975.2024.2380019

Tseng, W., & Ou, C. (2025). Can virtual influencers drive online consumer behavior? An applied examination of ELM model investigating the marketing effects of virtual influencers. *Sustainability (Basel), 17*(23), 10721. DOI: 10.3390/su172310721

Volles, B. K., Park, J., Van Kerckhove, A., & Geuens, M. (2024). How and when do virtual influencers positively affect consumer responses to endorsed brands? *Journal of Business Research, 183*, 114863. DOI: 10.1016/j.jbusres.2024.114863

Wang, X., & Qiu, X. (2024). The positive effect of artificial intelligence technology transparency on digital endorsers: Based on the theory of mind perception. *Journal of Retailing and Consumer Services, 78*, 103777. DOI: 10.1016/j.jretconser.2024.103777

Wang, X., & Wang, H. (2026). Brands cannot own a human celebrity but can own an AI endorser: AI endorsers' role in shaping consumer self-brand connection. *Journal of Retailing and Consumer Services, 90*, 104717. DOI: 10.1016/j.jretconser.2025.104717

Wang, X., & Zhang, Y. (2025). The influence of virtual streamer on purchase intention: The moderated mediating effect of message strategy and live-streaming environment. *Electronic Commerce Research and Applications, 73*, 101520. DOI: 10.1016/j.elerap.2025.101520

Wu, L., & Wen, T. J. (2021). Understanding AI advertising from the consumer perspective. *Journal of Advertising Research, 61*(2), 133–146. DOI: 10.2501/JAR-2021-004

Xia, H., Yang, Y., & Wang, X. (2025). Too pretty to resist? Exploring the impact of virtual influencers' beauty level on consumer reactions. *Journal of Retailing and Consumer Services, 87*, 104371. DOI: 10.1016/j.jretconser.2025.104371

Xu, J., Feng, Y., Li, W., Huang, Q., & Fan, Z. (2025). How AI brand endorsers influence Generation MZ's consumer behavior in metaverse marketing scenarios. *Journal of Theoretical and Applied Electronic Commerce Research, 20*(2), 82. DOI: 10.3390/jtaer20020082

Yan, X., Huam, H. T., & Sade, A. B. (2024). Is AI better than humans? Unveiling the boundary conditions under which virtual influencers outperform human influencers in endorsing sustainable products. *Sustainability (Basel), 16*(22), 9896. DOI: 10.3390/su16229896

Yang, Y., Li, S., & Qiu, S. (2025). A systematic literature review on the negative impacts of AI-generated virtual digital humans. *IEEE, 13*, 80047–80062. DOI: 10.1109/ACCESS.2025.3564041

Zaki, K., Alhomaid, A., & Shared, H. (2025). Leveraging machine learning to analyze influencer credibility's impact on brand admiration and consumer purchase intent in social media marketing. *Human Behavior and Emerging Technologies, 9959697*(1), 9959697. Advance online publication. DOI: 10.1155/hbe2/9959697

Zeng, H., & Lin, C. A. (2025). Consumer evaluation of virtual vs. human influencers via source credibility, perceived social similarity, and consumption motivation. *Journal of Theoretical and Applied Electronic Commerce Research, 20*(3), 168. DOI: 10.3390/jtaer20030168

Zeng, Y., Pu, G., Liu, J., & Feng, W. (2024). The influence mechanism of narrative strategies used by virtual influencers on consumer product preferences. *Journal of Theoretical and Applied Electronic Commerce Research, 19*(4), 2828–2850. DOI: 10.3390/jtaer19040137

Zhang, Y., & He, A. (2025). The impact of AI influencer endorsements on consumers' purchase intentions: The serial mediating roles of mind perception and brand trustworthiness. *Journal of Product and Brand Management, 34*(5), 754–765. DOI: 10.1108/JPBM-02-2024-4974

Zheng, X., Cui, C., Zhang, C., & Li, D. (2026). Who says what? How message appeals shape virtual- versus human-influencers' impact on consumer engagement. *Journal of Research in Interactive Marketing, 20*(2), 199–214. DOI: 10.1108/JRIM-10-2024-0482

Zhou, A., Liu, Y., & Dai, Y. (2026). Artificial yet credible: How virtual influencers overcome authenticity challenges. *Journal of Business Research, 206*, 115940. DOI: 10.1016/j.jbusres.2025.115940

Zhou, T., & Li, S. (2025). Examining consumer impulsive purchase intention in virtual AI Streaming: A S-O-R perspective. *Journal of Theoretical and Applied Electronic Commerce Research, 20*(3), 204. DOI: 10.3390/jtaer20030204

KEY TERMS AND DEFINITIONS

Augmented Reality (AR): AR is a technology that overlays digital information like text, video, or 3D models for viewing the real, physical world in order to enhance the physical world with contextual digital elements.

Computers Are Social Actors (CASA): CASA paradigm is a foundational psychological framework that suggests computers and interactive media apply social rules naturally and mindlessly just like humans, even though technology is inanimate and lacks feelings, intentions, or consciousness.

Deep Learning (DL): DL is a specialized subdivision of ML and AI that simulates the functional and structural processing of the human brain.

Elaboration Likelihood Model (ELM): ELM is a foundational dual-process theory of persuasion that denotes how attitudes are formed, shaped, and changed based on cognitive effort or degree to which a person thinks about and evaluates the core arguments contained within a communication.

Extended Reality (XR): XR is an umbrella term that encompasses all technologies that blend the physical and digital worlds, including virtual reality, augmented reality, and mixed reality.

Generative Artificial Intelligence (GAI) Technologies: GAI technologies refer to a category of Machine Learning (ML) architectures, algorithms, and models designed to create entirely new, original content such as text, images, audio, video synthetic data, or computer code in response to user prompts.

Human Influencers (HIs): HIs are real-world individuals who can physically interact with a product in the real world and remain the traditional foundation of the creator economy.

Large Language Model (LLM): LLM is an advanced AI architecture designed to process, understand, summarize, translate, and generate natural human language.

Mind Perception Theory (MPT): MPT is a psychological framework that explains how humans decide whether another entity has a mind and what kind of mind it possesses.

Natural Language Processing (NPL): NLP is to give computers the capacity to process, analyze, understand, and generate natural human text or speech in a way that captures both structural context and semantic intent.

Parasocial Interaction (PSI) Mechanisms: PSI is communication psychology and consumer behavior in marketing that acts as a foundational framework for understanding consumer engagement with HIs and SBEs.

Synthetic Brand Endorsers (SBEs): SBEs represent the formal and commercial application of VIs, which is basically AI-driven persona deliberately designed and deployed to transfer positive associations and stimulate consumer purchasing intention.

Virtual Influencers (VIs): VIs are computer generated or AI-driven personas designed to simulate human behavior, build audiences, and promote products across digital platforms, which is often deployed as synthetic brand endorsers.

Virtual Reality (VR): VR is a technology that completely replaces the real-world environment with a simulated digital one like computer generated 3D environment.

Chapter 10

Synthetic Destinations and Simulated Authenticity:

Commercial Applications of Deepfake Technologies in Tourism Marketing and Experience Design

Anuj Bhattacharya
http://orcid.org/0009-0007-5784-4342
The ICFAI University, Sikkim, India

Swati Sharma
http://orcid.org/0000-0003-2949-2363
Amity University, Noida, India

ABSTRACT

This chapter, per the authors, examines the growing role of deepfake technology in transforming tourism marketing and visitor experiences, positioning it as both an opportunity and a challenge. It explores how AI-driven tools such as GANs and diffusion models enable scalable, personalized, and immersive storytelling through virtual ambassadors, revived historical figures, and interactive heritage interpretations. Applications across destination marketing, cultural tourism, and smart tourism ecosystems are discussed, particularly when integrated with AR and VR. The chapter also addresses key concerns related to authenticity, ethics, consent, and cultural sensitivity, emphasizing transparency, stakeholder engagement, and responsible design. It further analyses consumer perceptions using relevant theo-

DOI: 10.4018/979-8-2600-2977-0.ch010

retical frameworks, presenting a balanced approach to innovation and trust. Recent developments in deepfake detection and AI-driven marketing (2019–2024) further highlight the growing relevance of these technologies in tourism.

INTRODUCTION

1.1 Background of AI and Deepfake Technologies

Over recent years, artificial intelligence (AI) has changed a lot, especially in the areas of computer vision, multimedia processing, and making digital content. Deepfake technology, which comes from the words "deep learning" and "fake," is one of the most important things that AI has brought about. Deepfakes are media that have been created or changed by AI in a way that makes it look like a person is doing something real or fake. This can make it hard to tell the difference between real and fake content.

Deepfakes use face-swapping methods to produce deceptive visual content which generates fake visual content. The technique enables users to show one person's face on top of another person's body in a video. The technique enables viewers to see the target person performing actions and speaking lines that they never actually did. The movie represents an early form of deepfake technology which has become one of the most famous deepfake movies. The category of deepfakes includes multiple types of deepfake content which extend beyond standard facial replacement. Lip-sync deepfakes change the way the mouth moves in videos to match a certain audio track. Puppet-master methods enable one person to control another person's facial expressions and head movements and eye gestures during system operation. (Agarwal et al., 2019).

The development of deepfake technologies has advanced quickly because of improved deep learning models which use autoencoders and Generative Adversarial Networks (GANs). Generative Adversarial Networks (GANs) are a class of deep learning models consisting of two components—a generator and a discriminator—that work together to produce highly realistic synthetic content through an iterative process of adversarial training. People use these models a lot in computer vision tasks to look at facial features, expressions, and motion patterns. This technology enables them to create highly authentic visual content.(Kingma & Welling, 2013),(Pei et al., 2024),(Lin et al., 2021),(Liu et al., 2020). The systems create photorealistic content through their ability to learn from extensive collections of images and videos which display human behavior. The online availability of extensive information about public figures including celebrities and politicians has turned these individuals into ideal subjects for deepfake technology.

Deepfakes use advanced technology which creates multiple ethical and social and security problems. Deepfake technology first gained widespread use in 2017 through face-swapped videos that featured celebrities. The technology behind deepfakes first became popular when users began creating face-swapped videos which showed famous people in 2017. Since then, it has been used for bad things like making explicit content without consent, spreading false information, and manipulating politics (Hwang, 2020). Fake news can be used to spread lies, change the outcome of elections, stir up social or religious tensions, and even mess up the stock market (Zhou & Zafarani, 2020),(Kaliyar et al., 2021). Deepfakes could also have effects on defense and security, like making fake satellite images to confuse military operations (Tucker, 2019).

Deepfake technology also has a number of good and new uses, though. The entertainment industry has widely used it for things like visual effects, digital avatars, and realistic dubbing in movies. Other useful applications include making voice technologies that help people who have lost their ability to speak, making virtual reality experiences better, allowing virtual try-on systems in e-commerce, and bringing historical figures back to life to help with educational apps (Verdoliva, 2020),(Naitali et al., 2023).

But as deepfake tools become more widely available, it's easier and more common to make content that doesn't require a lot of technical knowledge or data. Recent improvements make it possible to make realistic deepfakes with just one picture or short video clip (Zakharov et al., 2019). The democratization of technology has made things more dangerous for both famous people and regular people. For example, deepfake audio has been used in cases of financial fraud, like pretending to be executives to approve fake transactions. Apps like DeepNude and Zao have also shown how easy it is to trick people into seeing inappropriate or false content without their permission (Samuel, 2019).

The artificial intelligence deepfake technologies which use machine learning research develop new creative opportunities while their unauthorized use brings serious threats to individual privacy rights and personal identity security and system trustworthiness. Researchers need to find a way to balance technological advantages with strict ethical requirements and their methods for building future systems during their ongoing work on these technologies. Recent studies have increasingly focused on the detection and governance of deepfake technologies, highlighting the rapid evolution of synthetic media and its implications across industries (Pei et al., 2024; Whittaker et al., 2023). In parallel, AI-driven marketing and real-time content personalization have emerged as key research areas, demonstrating how advanced algorithms can influence consumer perceptions, decision-making, and engagement in digitally mediated environments.

1.2 Relevance to Tourism Marketing and Experience Design

The tourism industry has undergone various digital changes throughout the last twenty years which were designed to improve travel experiences and improve business operations. The internet era brought a shift in tourism practices which now depends on online resources instead of traditional methods that used printed brochures and guidebooks and travel agencies which operated through telephone communication. The early 2000s saw an increase in usage of online booking platforms. Users could book their travels through the platforms which created a unified online system that combined all travel services. The "smart tourism" concept introduced travelers to real-time navigation and personalized services through the use of sensor technology and mobile applications and context-aware systems.(Buhalis & Amaranggana, 2014),(Neuhofer et al., 2015).

Tourism companies started using rule-based chatbots and automated systems for their customer service operations during the mid-2010s to manage booking inquiries and itinerary planning requests and common customer questions. (Ivanov & Webster, 2017). The developed technologies brought operational advantages which enabled organizations to deliver uninterrupted services yet their main task persisted as operational functions which failed to create immersive experiences for users. The systems maintained their operational function through predefined rules which prohibited them from generating user connections that evolved through creative methods of handling unique situations.

Deepfake technologies which use advanced AI and deep learning models The technology creates new user capabilities through its fundamental transformation of digital experiences. The digital tool Deepfakes allows users to create realistic audio and video content which they can customize. The tourism marketers use this ability to create stories which provide users with complete experiences while they produce emotional connections to the content. Deepfake videos have the ability to present historical figures who would tell the heritage site story while using their actual voice celebrities who would promote tourist destinations without their physical presence and customized travel previews through which visitors would look at themselves experiencing an area before their actual visit.

The marketing industry uses deepfake technologies because they provide storytelling capabilities The technology enables tourism operators to create authentic moving content which establishes stronger emotional connections with potential travelers than their previous fixed advertising methods because it allows them to create lifelike animated content. Tourists today seek more than information services because they desire experiences that create special and unforgettable moment.

This change, in theory, goes against traditional ideas about tourism, like service-dominant logic, which saw technology as a passive tool that helped people create value (Vargo & Lusch, 2008). Earlier actor-network theories also saw digital technologies as middlemen instead of active participants (Xiang et al., 2017). Deepfake technologies create a fresh method of developing tourism experiences because artificial intelligence functions as a joint creator of these platforms. The system develops content while building narratives and transforming human perceptions.

The digital transformation process of tourism began when deepfake technology first emerged which created a new pathway for tourists to experience innovative tourism attractions. The companies develop new opportunities for creative advertising and interactive design development yet their work creates significant problems which need complete evaluation to achieve responsible sustainable execution because their work impacts both honest communication and ethical business practices and customer confidence.

1.3 Chapter Objectives and Scope

The chapter analyzes deepfake technology because it affects travel marketing and experience design through its economic value and strategic importance and its ethical impact. The research shows how synthetic media create destination brands by providing travelers with personalized immersive experiences which help businesses compete in a digital-based industry. The chapter investigates deepfake technology through its complete technological ecosystem which includes the roles of startups and destination marketing organizations and artificial intelligence developers. The document presents responsible and ethical implementation methods while analyzing essential matters that include authenticity issues and trust problems and intellectual property matters and uncertainties in regulatory systems.

The chapter presents a unified study of tourism through AI, human-computer interaction, and tourist studies, which examines both business aspects and traveler experience elements. The research provides an assessment of deepfake tourism innovation which evaluates both potential uses and existing limitations through customer perception and behavior study across different demographic and cultural groups.

Conceptual Foundations

In the context of this chapter, simulated authenticity refers to the perception of genuineness created through AI-generated or manipulated content that closely resembles real-world experiences, even when it is artificially constructed. Similarly, deepfake-driven experience design can be understood as the strategic use of synthetic media technologies to create immersive, personalized, and interactive tourism experiences that blend real and algorithmically generated elements.

1.4 Deepfake Technology in the Marketing Industry

Deepfake technology is changing the marketing world by using storytelling to make experiences more immersive and personal (Kleine, 2022). This technology uses computer vision to recognize and combine images (Kleine, 2022). It is part of deep learning, which is a type of machine learning that lets computers learn tasks on their own. For example, deep learning algorithms in computer vision can tell the difference between a dog and other things in a picture or video. There are many useful ways that deepfake technology can be used in marketing. By 2024, deepfakes and AI are expected to change how companies market their products. For example, CEOs and other executives will be able to speak to people all over the world in many languages with perfect accuracy, and hyper-realistic avatars will make customer interactions better (Walters & Hammond, 2025).

The combination of deepfakes and AI not only changes the rules of traditional marketing, but it also raises new ethical issues. Marketers can use deepfakes in a lot of creative ways to get people more interested and help their businesses grow. These include improving ad campaigns, using dynamic influencer marketing, bringing explainer videos back to life, showing off different products, making cold email outreach more interesting, replacing speakers at online conferences, and making corporate training and educational videos (Foundation Labs, 2024, (Kalpokas & Kalpokiene, 2022). For example, technology can hyper-personalize ads by changing speech and lip movements without requiring models to learn new languages.

The study demonstrates the effectiveness of their system which provides customized marketing content to individual consumers (Bohara, 2024). The implementation of deepfake technology creates multiple opportunities but it brings forth fundamental legal issues and ethical dilemmas. Marketers need to be careful when using these tools to make sure they are used correctly and not misused. Furthermore, deepfake technologies increasingly operate in conjunction with other artificial intelligence systems such as sentiment analysis, recommender systems, and behavioral analytics. This integration enables tourism organizations to develop adaptive and data-driven marketing strategies, thereby enhancing the effectiveness and responsiveness of digital tourism ecosystems.

1.4.1 Technology Advancements

Deepfake technology has reached its current level because Generative Adversarial Networks received their latest updates which improve their ability to create authentic deepfake material. The GAN system uses its two components which include a generator and a discriminator system to generate authentic-looking fake visual content. The generator creates fake images that look like real pictures while the discriminator system detects real material and fake material. The process of adversarial testing enables both components to enhance their capabilities which results in increasingly authentic media output. The entertainment industry has adopted these advanced technologies to create visual effects and develop innovative storytelling methods. Content creators and filmmakers now have the ability to transform videos through face-swapping technology which enables them to generate both imaginative and authentic content (George & George, 2023). The hyper-realistic deepfakes create entertainment value yet their consequences extend beyond that purpose. The technology enables people to spread false information which creates major ethical issues and security threats that can alter political outcomes and damage personal reputations. To synthesize the discussion, a conceptual model is proposed that links deepfake technologies with tourism marketing and experience design outcomes. Deepfake technologies and the broader AI ecosystem act as foundational inputs enabling capabilities such as personalization, immersive storytelling, and scalable content production. These capabilities enhance marketing effectiveness and shape tourist experiences by influencing perception, engagement, and decision-making processes. However, these relationships are moderated by factors such as consumer trust, perceived authenticity, ethical considerations, and regulatory frameworks. The model highlights that while deepfake technologies create significant value, their successful application in tourism depends on responsible implementation and sustained user trust.

Transformation of Tourism Marketing

1.5 Traditional Tourism Promotion Strategies

The study extends to data which was collected until October of 2023. The basic strategies which tourism organizations used to promote travel destinations succeeded in creating public awareness while directing travelers to select their vacation spots. The primary method to market tourism before digital technologies became popular was through offline methods and mass communication systems that targeted potential tourists. The strategies in this research study use seven different promotional methods which include print media, broadcast advertising, travel agencies, brochures, word-of-mouth communication, and participation in trade fairs and exhibitions. The travel industry first used print media which includes newspapers and magazines and travel guides as promotional tools to advertise various travel destinations. The Group of 7 Tourism Boards could have indeed printed brochures adorned with pictures, itineraries, and culturally rich pieces of information to attract tourists. (Rather, 2020). The TV and radio advertisements used emotional storytelling to create audiovisual content which enabled destinations to connect with large audiences. The travel agencies and tour operators worked as essential intermediaries to support traditional tourism marketing activities. The travel agencies developed customized travel packages which they used to create personalized booking recommendations for their customers. (Holloway & Humphreys, 2019).

The service providers at tourism fairs and roadshows and exhibitions used these events as their main opportunity to build trust with potential customers through direct contact. Word-of-mouth communication has been another powerful traditional marketing strategy. The recommendations that friends and family members and acquaintances make to others carry high value because they provide trustworthy sources of information about travel decisions (Litvin et al., 2008). The establishment of promotional campaigns through partnerships with airlines, hotels, and local businesses enabled businesses to create complete promotional campaigns.The strategies which worked well in previous decades have lost their effectiveness.

1.6 Limitations of Conventional Marketing Approaches

The traditional tourism marketing processes have achieved significant industry growth but face challenges because consumer behavior and technological advancements are undergoing rapid changes. The main problem arises from the lack of sufficient material interaction options which users can utilize to access the content. The use of traditional marketing strategies through print ads and TV commercials establishes one-way communication which restricts potential tourists from engaging with the content and providing their thoughts. The system fails to provide personalized experiences for users. Traditional methods usually go after a large group of people, which makes it hard to customize messages based on each person's preferences, interests, and travel habits. Modern consumers now expect brands to deliver personalized product recommendations together with complete immersive product experiences.

The major expense problem creates a substantial risk for the organization. The total expenses for producing brochures and broadcasting TV advertisements and participating in international trade shows reach a significant amount, yet it remains difficult to assess the effectiveness of these promotional activities because there is no reliable method to measure their performance. The practice of traditional marketing remains restricted because it can only reach customers within specific geographical boundaries. The distribution of promotional materials becomes challenging because they exist only in specific regions and markets, which prevents worldwide access to these resources. The slow rate of information transmission creates difficulties for travel agencies because they need to inform travelers about changes and special offers and new destinations. The primary issue is that user-generated content lacks the same level of credibility as other content types. Today, most travelers prefer to believe online reviews and social media content and their friends' recommendations instead of traditional advertisements, which they perceive as untrustworthy and excessively promotional.

The traditional tourism marketing methods have successfully expanded the industry yet they face difficulties because of the present-day market conditions and technological advancements which continue to evolve. People face their biggest challenge because they possess restricted options for accessing and experiencing the content. The traditional marketing approach which uses print advertisements and television commercials creates direct communication channels but fails to provide tourists with sufficient opportunities for interaction and feedback. (Xiang & Gretzel, 2010).

The system fails to provide users with customized experiences that suit their individual needs. The traditional approach targets a broad audience which results in difficulties for sending personalized messages to specific users who have distinct preferences and interests and travel patterns. Modern consumers require personalized product recommendations that enable them to experience products through interactive displays (Buhalis & Law, 2008).

The main issue involves excessive financial expenditures. The production and distribution of brochures together with their TV advertising campaigns and their participation in international trade shows create significant financial obligations which show no definite outcome according to It's. The lack of precise analytics and performance measurement tools makes it difficult to measure the effectiveness of these advertising campaigns.

The main issue involves excessive financial expenditures. The production and distribution of brochures together with their TV advertising campaigns and their participation in international trade shows create significant financial obligations which show no definite outcome according to (Kotler, 2022). The existing advertising campaigns require proper evaluation methods but these methods do not exist because precise analytics tools are unavailable.

The boundaries of traditional marketing restrict its operations. The distribution of promotional materials gets limited to specific regions which creates difficulties for global distribution. Travelers face difficulties when they need current information about route changes and special promotions and new travel destinations because of sluggish information flow. Users trust content created by other users more than they trust self-promotional material which presents a major problem with credibility. Today travelers prefer to trust online reviews and social media content and personal recommendations over traditional advertisements which consumers perceive as biased and excessively promotional according to (Fotis et al., 2012)..

Modern digital technologies such as virtual reality, augmented reality, and AI-based content creation tools offer more interactive experiences than traditional methods.

The tourism industry today requires destinations to adopt modern marketing strategies because traditional methods fail to provide effective competitive advantages.

1.7 Emergence of AI-Driven and Personalized Marketing

The tourism industry has transformed its advertising methods through digital technology advancements which continue to develop. This has led to AI-driven and highly personalized marketing strategies. The tourism industry uses artificial intelligence (AI) Internet of Things (IoT) virtual reality (VR) cloud computing and blockchain technologies to create personalized marketing strategies which replace traditional mass marketing techniques. (Hussein et al., 2024), (Kerpedzhiev et al., 2021).

AI functions as a technology which enables systems to create customized experiences for users. AI systems analyse extensive customer data which includes their search history and their preferences and their booking history and their social media interactions to create personalized marketing materials and suggestions (Halina, 2021). AI-powered chatbots and virtual assistants provide customers with real-time answers to their questions which helps customers stay engaged while they make informed decisions. AI-powered recommendation engines suggest travel destinations and accommodation options and activities based on individual traveler preferences. The system enhances customer satisfaction through its implementation which results in higher conversion rates.

Integrating IoT technologies makes personalized marketing even stronger by giving businesses real-time information about how tourists act. Smart devices and connected environments keep track of how users interact with them, which lets tourism companies send marketing messages that are relevant to the user's location and situation For example, smart hotel rooms and mobile apps can change services and deals based on what guests want, making the experience more personalized and smooth.

The combination of IoT technologies to create personalized marketing solutions provides organizations with immediate access to information about tourist behavior. Smart devices and connected environments keep track of how users interact with them which lets tourism companies send marketing messages that are relevant to the user's location and situation (Laghari et al., 2021). The combination of smart hotel rooms and mobile applications enables hotels to create customized services and special offers which enhance the guest experience through personalized service.

VR technology now serves as an effective marketing tool which enables customers to experience virtual product demonstrations. The system provides potential travelers with virtual reality experiences which enable them to explore their travel destinations and lodging options and tourist sites before making their final decision.

The system provides potential travelers with virtual reality experiences which enable them to explore their travel destinations and lodging options and tourist sites before making their final decision. (Chandra Sekaran et al., 2021). This makes people feel more connected and less unsure, which makes marketing work better.

Cloud computing enables businesses to create personalized marketing campaigns through its capacity for storing extensive data and processing information in real time. Tourism companies can easily keep track of customer information, look at how people behave, and run personalized campaigns on a number of digital platforms. (Nadda et al., 2020). Blockchain technology establishes trust in digital marketing systems through its ability to secure transactions and maintain transparent data operations while protecting customer information. (Acikgoz et al., 2024).

Robotics and automation are increasingly being utilized in customer service operations across various industries. The system enhancement leads to better customer service delivery which enables more effective personalized marketing efforts. (Saputra et al., 2024). These technologies make things like check-ins, room service, and information help easier, so businesses can spend more time on customer engagement and personalized service.

The market data together with current industry trends show that AI-based personalization systems now operate as essential components within business operations. The travel industry will generate substantial revenue through AI-based travel personalization which some forecasts predict will reach hundreds of billions of dollars within the next several years. The internet and smartphone devices now enable travelers to search for and organize their trips which has resulted in changes to their booking habits. Digital channels have become the primary method for millions of people worldwide who travel to plan and book their journeys. The marketing strategies need to become both personalized and mobile-friendly because this study demonstrates their essential role in success. (Sun et al., 2022).

The current marketing approach is shifting away from traditional methods because businesses now use AI-driven personalized marketing techniques. Advanced digital technologies help tourism companies to understand their customers better. The research will help organizations because it will lead to improved customer satisfaction and enhanced competitive advantage.

1.8 Role of Deepfakes in Content Scalability and Localization

Advanced technologies like Artificial Intelligence (AI), Deep Learning (DL), Machine Learning (ML), and Augmented Reality (AR) have caused a lot of changes in the way tourism-related information is made and shared with potential travelers (Kwok & Koh, 2020), (Tavitiyaman et al., 2021). These technologies have made it possible for immersive and manipulable experiences to happen, especially through extended reality (XR), which includes virtual, augmented, and mixed realities. XR makes it possible for people to interact with digital environments in a cyber-physical way (Pestek & Sarvan, 2021). In this changing world of technology, deepfake technology has become a powerful tool that goes beyond just changing content to allow for scalable and localized tourism marketing.

Deepfake technology, a blend of "deep learning" and "fake," makes it easy to add or replace people, voices, and places in pictures, videos, and audio (Le et al., 2025), (Adee, 2020). Deepfakes can make very realistic fake content that is often hard to tell apart from real media by using advanced AI and ML algorithms (Dan, 2020). This ability gives tourism marketers the chance to quickly make a lot of personalized and context-specific promotional content that has never been possible before.

The advantages of deepfake technology include its ability to enhance content performance. Traditional tourism marketing needs to create promotional videos that showcase specific locations which requires multiple filming sessions and actor hiring and post-production efforts. Deepfake technologies, on the other hand, make it possible to automatically generate content. Marketers can use this technology to create multiple ad versions simultaneously while spending minimal costs. (Campbell et al., 2022). For example, a single base video can be changed to include different languages, cultural elements, or spokespersons, making it suitable for a wide range of audiences in different markets around the world.

The concept of content localization exists as an essential part of scalability systems. Deepfakes enable tourism marketers to adapt their material for various cultural and linguistic and demographic markets without producing additional video content. A destination video gains better audience connection through its use of local narrators and area celebrities and culturally relevant visual elements. (Kwok & Koh, 2020). This goes along with the growing need for personalized and culturally aware marketing strategies in the global tourism industry.

The process of creating deepfake technology requires specific state-of-their-knowledge which enables travelers to form their own judgment about their destination choice. Tourists use audiovisual materials for their trip planning process. People who consume localized deepfake content experience increased comfort which leads to greater trust in the material thus making them more likely to engage with it. (Leung et al., 2017). Marketers can effectively bridge cultural gaps and make destinations more appealing by showing them in ways that speak to specific groups of people.

Deepfakes have multiple applications across various fields which create significant ethical problems and damage credibility. The same technologies that enable content creation also provide tools for disseminating fake content which includes modified audiovisual materials. (Kietzmann et al., 2021). Deepfake content is getting more and more realistic, which could change what tourists expect and make them unhappy or distrustful when the real experience doesn't match the picture (Lojo et al., 2020). Also, the fact that deepfakes are hard to spot makes people worry about the authenticity and openness of tourism marketing.

The development of advertising gives more context to the role of deepfakes in making content that can be used by many people in different places. (Campbell et al., 2022) The three phases of advertising manipulation. The first phase of advertising manipulation uses Analog methods which involve physical editing. The second phase uses Digital methods which utilize software for creating digital assets. The third phase of advertising manipulation uses Synthetic methods which create content through AI-driven generation that employs Generative Adversarial Networks technology. Disney uses Deepfake technology as a third stage that enables real-time content creation and transformation with customized localization for various target groups. The results lead to wider advertising possibilities which enable marketers to develop more flexible campaigns.

Even with these improvements, the wrong use of deepfakes is still a big problem. Although they present innovative prospects for scalable and localized marketing, their capacity to mislead audiences demands meticulous regulation and ethical scrutiny (Whittaker et al., 2021). Consequently, it is imperative for forthcoming research to investigate the impact of deepfake-induced scalability and localization on tourists' trust, perceptions, and behavioral intentions, especially within the realm of destination marketing.

Commercial Applications of Deepfake Technologies in Tourism

1.9 Virtual Influencers and Synthetic Brand Ambassadors

Virtual influencers exist as key components within the field of AI-generated synthetic media used for tourism marketing. Virtual influencers create digital human avatars who perform social media activities to develop fan communities while endorsing products and interacting with users through techniques that resemble actual human behavior. The fashion and cosmetics and tourism and retail industries extensively use these AI-powered products to maintain consistent brand image control. The use of these products provides your business with a competitive advantage because they reduce potential dangers associated human influencers who exhibit unpredictable behavior and generate reputation issues. (Gutierriz et al., 2025).

Destination marketing organizations benefit from virtual influencers because these digital personas provide complete control to their operators. Virtual influencers establish parasocial relationships with their viewers through their strategic construction of digital identities. The method enables users to experience personal knowledge of the artist and build emotional ties with the artist, despite the fact that they will not meet the artist face to face. The para-social interaction (PSI) theory asserts that continuous exposure to influencer material develops a sense of closeness between viewers and influencers, which improves the effectiveness of advertising messages (Veseli et al., 2025). People are becoming more open to virtual influencers, but there are still concerns about how real and trustworthy they are (Armutcu et al., 2023).

Researcher found Virtual Tourism Destination Ambassadors as the specific group which they studied in tourism research. The VTDAs virtual influencers show different characteristics because their primary purpose is to promote specific locations through long-term strategic plans. The system provides essential technological components which enable users to customize their experience through interactive features that create a sense of realness and deliver educational content while providing entertainment value which determines tourist interest and their decision to visit. The research shows that virtual and real-life influencers both have an effect on audiences but real-life influencers create stronger impacts because people perceive them as more authentic than virtual influencers. The study with Generation Y and Z participants found that source credibility paired with parasocial interaction and their attitudes toward content and destinations created major impacts on their travel intention which showed human influencers produced better results. (Abate et al., 2025).

Technology acceptance evaluation considers the actual appearance of virtual influencers as their most critical factor. Users find real things more beneficial when they experience actual visual elements together with authentic human-like communication methods. Customers establish trust through three specific factors which include social presence and cognitive engagement and enjoyment. The Computers-as-Social-Actors (CASA) model explains that people interact with digital things as if they were interacting with actual human beings. (Thomas, 2024). Virtual influencers and synthetic brand ambassadors represent a strong yet evolving marketing tool which tourism advertising platforms use as their main marketing method. The system provides users with three communication options which enable them to maintain control over their messaging while creating engaging content.

1.10 AI-Generated Destination Storytelling

Tourism marketers have long used destination storytelling to evoke emotions, imagination, and travel intention. Generative AI enables the creation of narratives at an enormous scale which can be customized according to traveller profiles and distributed through various media formats with little need for human content development. The development of ChatGPT-4o and image generation models has advanced generative AI applications in tourism research according to bibliometric analysis which shows a rapid increase in AI research publications within the tourism and hospitality sectors since 2023. Signage printed brochures and pre-recorded audio guides do not satisfy contemporary tourist needs because they deliver unchanging standard information which lacks the ability to adjust to personal needs and different situations and multiple language requirements. (Yang et al., 2024).

The technology creates dynamic stories that respond to particular situations which exist at the present moment to address the issue of unchanging content. AI can create destination stories through its ability to combine historical facts with personal stories and regional myths which it uses to produce content for blogs and brochures and advertisements. AI-generated audio allows travel companies to market the "essence" of locations while tourism boards create interactive virtual tours and customized marketing content through their use of generative AI technology. (Shrestha et al., 2024). The study of narrative transportation theory shows that AI-generated narratives create immersive experiences which affect travel decisions because their storytelling draws people into virtual worlds. The virtual destination stories which AI generates create new and attractive stories that fully engage tourists while activating their natural thinking abilities. Human imagination is limited, but generative AI can create more captivating fictional stories. (Solano-Barliza et al., 2024).

The existing literature still investigates the authentic emotional value of AI-generated content. AI systems enhance their ability to scale operations and deliver accurate information, yet they fail to produce authentic emotional responses and maintain cultural accuracy. Human-created tourism narratives show stronger emotional responses according to sentiment analysis, while thematic analysis reveals deeper cultural understanding, which demonstrates a need for a joint human-AI system that can create emotionally impactful destination storytelling at a larger scale. (García-Madurga & Grilló-Méndez, 2023). The researchers have developed integrated AI models which they intend to use for cultural tourism. The development of real-time language interpretation systems which include OpenAI's Whisper model has led to generative AI becoming a new force within the tourism industry. The process of seamless translation will enable continuous communication between people who share different languages. The marketers who promote tourist destinations need to create destination stories which meet the cultural requirements and emotional needs and ethical standards that modern travelers expect..

1.11 Personalized and Multilingual Marketing Campaigns

Deepfake and generative AI technologies have changed tourism marketing through their ability to deliver personalized content which can be translated into several languages across multiple regions. The production process used to develop worldwide campaigns required various methods which included reshooting and dubbing and creating culturally customized content. The process of making localized content took an extended period because of these requirements. The process of creating AI-generated media content enables marketers to transform their single advertising campaign into multilingual and multicultural versions. The majority of brands use deepfake technology to create translations and lip-syncing for their marketing content which demonstrates its growing importance in their worldwide marketing strategies. (Huang et al., 2025).

Deepfake technologies enable hyper-personalization, which allows synthetic avatars and AI-generated spokespersons to deliver personalized messages that match individual consumer preferences and demographic characteristics. The approach establishes stronger emotional connections to the target audience because it creates more relevant content for their specific cultural background. (Li & Cao, 2022). The introduction of virtual influencers together with AI avatars enables users to conduct bilingual communication without facing any hindrances. The process enables organizations to maintain their marketing efforts through efficient resource management which reduces both time expenses.

The real-world evidence combined with industry findings demonstrates the practical value of these skills. For instance, big campaigns have used AI-generated multilingual content to reach a wide range of people while cutting production costs by a lot The real-world evidence together with industry findings shows how these skills provide actual value to their activities. (Khan et al., 2025). In tourism, where destinations need to appeal to people from different cultures and places, these technologies provide businesses with a competitive advantage because they eliminate language obstacles and enable better communication with particular demographic groups.

The application of synthetic personalization creates ethical dilemmas which specifically revolve around three core principles: honesty, consent, and transparency. The use of AI-generated content without informing users about its source will decrease their trust while damaging your reputation, therefore you must use AI responsibly and educate users about proper media consumption methods.

1.12 Cost Efficiency and Content Lifecycle Extension

Deepfake and generative AI technologies provide two main benefits because they enable personalized experiences while decreasing both time requirements and budget expenses throughout their time of use. The existing system of tourism marketing costs now undergoes transformation because of this development. The production of traditional content requires high expenses and extended time commitments because it needs both physical filming and professional actors and multiple rounds of content adaptation. AI-powered tools cut these costs by a lot by automating the processes of creating and adapting content. Research shows that generative AI can lower the cost of making content by 30% to 50%, speed up the time it takes to launch campaigns, and give marketers a better return on investment (Whittaker et al., 2023).

The deepfake workflows demonstrate their highest efficiency through their specialized design. The AI-powered lip-syncing and localization systems have reduced translation and dubbing expenses by 60 to 75 percent. The generative AI market experiences rapid development which will continue to expand throughout the upcoming years. (Pramod et al., 2025). This will help these efficiencies even more.

One important strategic advantage is extending the life of content. This means that instead of making new marketing materials, you can use, re-version, and adapt old ones for new audiences (Chen, 2024). AI enables rapid testing and content modification and content reuse which results in production time reductions of 40 to 70 percent and cost savings between 30 to 60 percent while providing quick financial returns. The tourism marketing field depends on this function because it requires marketers to constantly update their campaigns to match changing seasonal patterns and destination options and audience preferences.

The actual advantages of these benefits become more apparent when their real-world implementation demonstrates their effectiveness. The brands used AI-driven campaigns to design regional marketing content which required only one digital asset for distribution. This demonstration shows that businesses can achieve their marketing objectives through accurate and cost-effective methods. (Degadwala & Patel, 2024). The current status of deepfake and generative AI technologies shows that they have evolved from their initial experimental phase to become vital components of contemporary tourism marketing systems. The system improvements will result in higher operational efficiency while providing advantages for future expansion.

Deepfakes in Tourism Experience Design

1.13 Integration with AR, VR, and Mixed Reality

Society has experienced major changes because of the rapid development and global adoption of information and communication technologies. People worldwide can now send and receive limitless information through these technologies which allow them to communicate instantly from any place. (Buhalis et al., 2019). The technological advancement has resulted in the creation of reality-virtuality systems which include augmented reality (AR) virtual reality (VR) and pure mixed reality (PMR) as their distinct components. The technologies enable customers to experience both authentic and simulated environments through their new interactive capabilities. (Tom Dieck & Han, 2022). Augmented reality creates an interactive experience which allows users to see digital elements in their actual surroundings.

Virtual reality technology provides users with a complete virtual experience through its immersive computer-generated environments. PMR technology enables users to interact with digital elements while experiencing real-world environments through the combined presence of both elements. (Flavián et al., 2021). Recent reports say that the immersive technologies market will be worth $100 billion by 2026 (Statista, 2023). This shows how important these technologies will be for the future of society.

The intangible nature of tourism combined with its diverse attributes makes ICT-based solutions essential for enhancing customer experiences. The emerging immersive technologies AR and VR enable tourism businesses to overcome their product accessibility challenges by providing customers with virtual product exploration and experience opportunities. (Guttentag, 2010), (Tussyadiah et al., 2018). The technologies provide three advantages to tourism which include entertaining educational content and delivering customized details and granting visitors access to restricted locations and special events. (Tom Dieck & Jung, 2018). Also, these technologies make it possible to have experiences that go beyond the senses by smoothly blending the real and virtual worlds (Petit et al., 2019). There is no doubt that immersive technologies have a lot of potential in the tourism industry. More research is needed to figure out how to use AR and VR to create great tourism experiences.

1.14 Interactive Cultural and Heritage Experiences

The implementation of deepfake technology within cultural heritage tourism enables visitors to experience historical narratives through their interactions with artifacts and renowned individuals. The visitors now have the ability to experience active participation through complete immersive experiences that include interactive elements. The Dalí Museum installation serves as a prominent demonstration of deepfake technology applications within heritage tourism. The team conducted research on archival materials to create an authentic replication of Salvador Dalí through AI models which used 6000 video frames and 1000 hours of machine learning data to develop accurate facial expression and speech pattern replication. The system provided visitors with the chance to experience authentic artist interaction through simulated lifelike interactions. (Armutcu et al., 2023), (Sharma & Sharma, 2025). The use of generative AI technology has expanded to immersive environments which include the metaverse beyond its existing applications. Users can study historical environments through digital artifacts and reconstructed historical figures which they can explore beyond physical and temporal limits. The interactive storytelling system preserves both types of cultural heritage through its dedicated preservation method. Research confirms that students who engage with AI-generated historical characters which include Leonardo da Vinci simulations achieve better learning results and higher motivation levels than they do with standard reading methods. The educational value of deepfake technology in heritage experiences demonstrates its worth as an educational resource. (Veseli et al., 2025). But even with these benefits, there are still worries about authenticity and ethical representation. The advantages of these features come with two main concerns which relate to authentic existence and ethical representation of people. The use of highly realistic AI-generated simulations creates difficulties to distinguish between actual historical events and invented historical accounts which results in false understanding of cultural narratives. Academic validation together with complete transparency and ethical governance frameworks create the necessary trustworthiness needed to assess the potential of deepfake technologies for interactive cultural experiences in heritage tourism.

1.15 Deepfakes in Museums, Theme Parks, and Smart Tourism

The museum and theme park and smart tourism site experiences show a rapid transformation because deepfake and AI-created synthetic media technologies enable visitors to engage with their surroundings instead of merely watching them. People can now use AI-powered museum installations to interact with historical figures. The AI-powered holograms which museums now use to display famous people enable visitors to experience interactive conversations which provide them with better historical understanding. The Seoul Robot and AI Museum together with other advanced technological sites enable visitors to experience interactive exhibits which function as educational tools for learning about new technological advancements. The ReInHerit Toolkit which the EU funds serves as one of several research initiatives that develop personalized museum experiences through AI and computer vision technology. The projects support heritage institutions by providing better access methods while they assist both small and large institutions with their digital transformation efforts.

The theme park industry uses generative artificial intelligence and deepfake technology to create interactive entertainment experiences. The introduction of metaverse-based environments to this transformation creates a powerful system that enables users to experience interactive storytelling and engage in gamified learning while maintaining digital heritage content. (Mathew & Soliman, 2021). The implementation of advanced AI systems into smart tourism ecosystems leads to their development into more complex systems. Hotels and other tourism businesses are moving away from simple automation and toward AI assistants that are aware of their surroundings and powered by large language models. The assistants enable users to communicate in multiple languages while processing text and voice and visual information to deliver personalized solutions throughout their interactions.

The world of synthetic media technologies and physical tourism infrastructure is exhibiting increasing parallels because of these developments. Deepfake technology has progressed beyond its initial novelty value into a fundamental component of intelligent tourism systems. The system improves visitor experience through its personalizing and interactive features, which transform how tourists experience different locations and available services.

Technology Ecosystem and Industry Adoption

The implementation of artificial intelligence technologies which include deepfake systems has developed through a technology ecosystem that includes academic institutions and AI startup companies and technology organizations and destination marketing agencies and tourism businesses. The development and application of generative models and computer vision technology start in research environments which researchers then use to create marketable solutions for tourism businesses to develop their marketing and customer experience design. (García-Madurga & Grilló-Méndez, 2023); (Wang et al., 2025).

The ecosystem comprises AI startups and technology firms which deliver essential technical capabilities and cutting-edge solutions while DMOs establish connections between these technologies and their work in destination branding and customized communication methods to create integrated smart tourism networks (Dwivedi et al., 2023). The process of adoption shows unequal patterns because emerging destinations face challenges from their insufficient digital infrastructure and financial resources and lack of skilled workers which creates obstacles that increase the digital divide (Dwivedi et al., 2023). The emergence of AI-generated content creates difficult problems about intellectual property rights and ownership rights for synthetic media and digital likenesses and cultural representations which demonstrates the requirement for ethical governance together with new regulatory systems that will support fair and responsible usage (Floridi et al., 2018).

Framework for Responsible Use of Deepfakes in Tourism

1.16 Principles of Ethical AI in Tourism

The ethical guidelines for artificial intelligence (AI) in the tourism sector emerge from three sources which include international policy frameworks and empirical research and applied guidelines. The three elements define the standards which organizations must follow to practice responsible innovation. The OECD has established five primary international standards which guide the development of trustworthy artificial intelligence systems. The requirements include protection of human rights and democratic principles which involve fairness and privacy rights and the requirements for AI systems to provide transparent and understandable explanations and maintain operational security and safety and the establishment of responsibility systems. These principles have been widely accepted as the basis for AI governance and risk management. The system allows different jurisdictions to collaborate and implement identical regulations. (Basumatary & Sarma, 2025). Beyond theoretical principles, the ethical use of deepfake technologies in tourism requires practical implementation strategies. Tourism organizations should adopt transparency protocols, including clear disclosure of AI-generated content, to ensure that consumers are aware of synthetic media usage. In addition, mechanisms for informed consent, data protection, and content verification must be integrated into digital marketing practices. These measures are essential to reduce the risks of misinformation and to strengthen long-term consumer trust. In addition to OECD principles, emerging regulatory developments such as the European Union's AI-related guidelines emphasize accountability, transparency, and risk management in AI deployment. Aligning tourism practices with these frameworks can support responsible innovation while minimizing legal, ethical, and reputational risks associated with deepfake technologies.

(Setegn & Japee, 2025). The implementation of ethical frameworks in practical situations remains extremely difficult. Despite comprehensive research across multiple academic fields to study AI ethics, people still lack sufficient understanding of the topic which creates a need for additional research. The tourism sector operates according to these principles because AI technologies which include generative AI and deepfake systems now establish greater influence over traveler perceptions and decision-making processes and their experiences at travel locations. Users will abandon platforms when they notice bias in content or nondisclosure of system operations or unfair treatment recommendations which leads to businesses losing customers and damaging their reputation while facing stricter government regulations.

The European Union's High-Level Expert Group on AI has made these ethical standards even better. The trustworthy AI systems require seven essential elements which include accountability diversity non-discrimination and fairness protection of privacy and data management human control and monitoring technological security and operational functions and system accessibility. The criteria establish a complete framework which enables organizations to execute ethical AI practices in their tourism operations that handle sensitive matters like identity representation and cultural authenticity and emotionally-based storytelling.

The field of tourism faces challenges from deepfake technologies because these technologies disrupt personal identity and cultural representation and damage authentic travel experiences. The implementation of ethical AI requires organizations to demonstrate their commitment through institutional backing and appropriate contextual understanding and transparent disclosure methods and their systems for continual monitoring to establish accountability. The establishment of enforceable ethical standards is necessary to protect trust and stakeholder interests and ensure responsible long-term use of AI technologies in tourism.

1.17 Stakeholder Engagement and Community Participation

The responsible use of deepfake and AI technologies in tourism demonstrates a complex governance challenge which requires more than technical solutions and regulatory frameworks. The process needs continuous substantial stakeholder participation because synthetic media representations impact their personal identity and value systems and professional activities. Tourism governance frameworks operate differently across various regions because local conditions and institutional structures and stakeholder priorities determine their implementation. The operational requirements of the project need a flexible framework which supports ongoing development through active stakeholder participation instead of executing fixed operational processes. (Yan et al., 2025). The participatory requirement of Stakeholder Theory demands that organizations should provide equal weight to the requirements of essential stakeholders, which include local government authorities, tourism industry operators, host community members, and visiting tourists, in order to achieve fair benefit distribution, decrease disputes, and promote shared decision-making in AI-supported tourism systems. (Solano-Barliza et al., 2024). In smart tourism, inclusive governance models make it even more clear how important it is to work together at different levels, use technology to get people involved, and put the needs of citizens first. Technology should be seen as a tool to help with data sharing, collective learning, and coordinated destination management, not as an end in itself. Also, the creation of AI-powered tools, such as deepfake-based apps, needs to involve people from different fields and be designed with input from all stakeholders. If some stakeholders are not involved in the development of algorithms, it can lead to fairness gaps and outcomes that are not aligned. By including community-based methods like stakeholder consultations, workshops, and collaborative planning in the AI design process, it is possible to create systems that are fair, open, and culturally sensitive and that take into account the views of local residents, destination managers, and different groups of visitors (Tuyen, 2025). The study demonstrates that ethical and responsible deepfake governance in tourism needs to be treated as a dynamic social process which evolves over time. The system requires continuous dialogue between stakeholders who must share responsibility while establishing effective methods to ensure that communities maintain authentic control over their cultural heritage through AI-generated content.

Consumer Perception and Behavioral Responses

Consumer perception and behavioral responses toward AI-driven and deepfake-based tourism experiences are shaped by a complex interaction of cognitive, emotional, and contextual factors. Research shows that tourists accept AI technologies in tourism based on their assessment of the technology's usefulness and its user-friendliness and their trust in the system and their social environment and the anthropomorphic design elements and perceived value of the system. (Rafiq et al., 2022),(Xu et al., 2024). The study found that tourists choose to interact with AI-created content only when they see it as authentic. The study showed that people who experience trustworthy content will more likely visit or patronize the business. The research shows that people who understand AI technology better can assess synthetic media content through their digital literacy skills, while people who lack this skill set will mistakenly believe they can identify deepfakes, which makes them vulnerable to deceptive content. The research shows that different generations respond to AI technology because younger users who grew up with digital tools tend to accept and explore AI experiences more than older users who distrust these systems because they worry about losing human contact and finding authentic experiences.

People from different cultures perceive things differently because each culture has its own definition of what is real. Some audiences prefer storytelling that creates emotional experiences together with complete audience involvement, while others seek actual facts and established methods of portrayal. The psychological mechanism that drives these reactions operates through parasocial interaction, which enables users to establish emotional bonds with AI agents and virtual influencers and synthetic characters. The interactions create stronger emotional connections which lead users to see AI systems as their friends and reliable helpers, which makes them more likely to use the systems and recommend them and buy products. The research establishes that emotional and cognitive evaluations which frameworks like the Stimulus–Organism–Response SOR model measure them, create a major impact on consumer engagement and their intention to adopt AI technology in tourism from their AI-enabled tourism environments. (Rather, 2025).

The combination of AI deepfake technologies with their ability to create personalized experiences and interactive content results in better user experiences but their success requires users to perceive authenticity and trustworthiness and emotional bonds with the system.

Challenges and Limitations

Technological Barriers and Costs:

The current state of deepfake and generative AI technologies prevents their complete development because they need more processing power and their operation requires substantial data resources and expert knowledge to function. The development of high-quality synthetic media requires both advanced hardware systems and extended training periods, which create challenges for small and medium tourism enterprises. The generated content produces artifacts and fails to achieve perfect realism, while real-time processing has inherent limitations, which together decrease output quality and dependability, thus preventing widespread use in active tourist locations.

Ethical Risks and Public Backlash:

Deepfake technologies develop deep ethical issues because their ability to produce deceptive fake content enables users to manipulate information. The synthetic media misuse creates three main issues because it produces deceptive content and displays locations through incorrect representations and it permits individuals to exploit cultural identities which leads to public outrage and damage to their personal reputation. AI-generated content which functions without user knowledge will erode trust between travelers and tourist destinations that offer genuine and transparent experiences. The public develops distrust toward tourism brands after they find out about their ethical breaches.

Regulatory Uncertainty:

The present regulations for deepfake and artificial intelligence technologies remain incomplete because they continue to be developed. The current legal system across different jurisdictions fails to provide solutions for digital identity problems and intellectual property rights issues and user consent requirements and synthetic media content liability matters. Different regional regulations create operational challenges for tourism organizations which seek to implement technology solutions responsibly because these regulations increase their compliance requirements and hinder their ability to run international operations. The lack of standardized guidelines creates problems for organizations because they need to implement enforcement actions and establish accountability mechanisms.

Accessibility and Digital Divide:

The advantages of deepfake technology and AI-powered tourism solutions are distributed unequally because people face different challenges in accessing digital systems and technology training and financial assistance. The developing areas together with their small tourism businesses and underprivileged groups will find it difficult to implement and gain advantages from these technological advancements.

The existing power structure from global tourism will remain intact because this situation creates barriers for equal access and fair economic development opportunities.

A significant emerging concern is the erosion of "deep trust," where consumers may find it increasingly difficult to distinguish between authentic and synthetic content. This raises critical issues related to information integrity, data privacy, and regulatory oversight. Addressing these challenges will be essential for maintaining credibility and ensuring the sustainable adoption of deepfake technologies in tourism.

Future Directions in Deepfake-Driven Tourism

- The future development of artificial intelligence and deep learning together with augmented reality and virtual reality and mixed reality technologies will enhance deepfake tourism applications through their ability to create more realistic content and develop interactive features. The combination of advanced generative models and real-time rendering technology and metaverse integration will create virtual environments that users can explore without interruptions while experiencing better engagement.
- The combination of deepfake technology with AI will enable hyper-personalization through its ability to provide customized tourism content which matches individual user preferences and their behavior patterns and their cultural background. The use of personalized avatars together with multilingual communication and adaptive storytelling will improve user engagement and customer satisfaction and marketing success.
- Tourism will enter its future stage through human workers who collaborate with AI systems instead of relying on complete machine automation. Human workers will deliver creative solutions together with cultural expertise and ethical oversight which will help ensure that tourism experiences maintain their genuine character.
- Deepfake technology has developed into a fast-growing field which provides researchers with multiple study possibilities to investigate consumer trust and establish ethical governance systems and develop regulatory frameworks and assess how synthetic media affects destination perception and tourist behavior. Interdisciplinary research needs to develop fundamental requirements for sustainable and responsible AI-driven tourism practices.
- Future research should also explore cross-cultural variations in the perception of AI-generated content and its influence on tourist behavior. Additionally, there is a growing need to examine governance models and regulatory frameworks that can support the ethical and sustainable deployment of deepfake technologies across diverse tourism contexts.

CONCLUSION

Deepfake technology serves as an innovative tool for tourist marketing and experience design because it enables organizations to develop customized experiences which attract people from different places. The world now has a new way to connect with travel destinations because of this advancement. Deepfakes create synthetic but emotionally engaging stories which may greatly improve storytelling accessibility and inclusion in many different tourist settings. The tourist experience depends on trust and authenticity together with ethical responsibility and cultural sensitivity which create major obstacles that must be resolved. Deepfake applications achieve success when developers create particular ethical frameworks which include human-centered methods that preserve cultural heritage while informing users. The complete travel experience needs to exist because deepfakes exist to improve human interactions through their digital technology. The future synthetic media tourism industry requires both technological improvements and additional requirements. Stakeholders need to establish an equilibrium between their creative responsibilities and their ethical obligations to enhance digital transformation which should increase authentic travel experiences through responsible practices.

REFERENCES

Abate, Y. A., Ukpabi, D. C., & Karjaluoto, H. (2025). Investigating digital marketing readiness among tourism firms: An emerging economy perspective. *Current Issues in Tourism*, *28*(13), 2153–2172. DOI: 10.1080/13683500.2024.2358047

Acikgoz, F., Stylos, N., & Lythreatis, S. (2024). Identifying capabilities and constraints in utilizing blockchain technology in hospitality and tourism. *International Journal of Contemporary Hospitality Management*, *36*(10), 3493–3514. DOI: 10.1108/IJCHM-07-2023-1083

Adee, S. (2020). What are deepfakes and how are they created? *IEEE Spectrum*, •••, 29.

Agarwal, S., Farid, H., Gu, Y., He, M., Nagano, K., & Li, H. (2019). Protecting world leaders against deep fakes. *CVPR Workshops, 1*(38).

Armutcu, B., Tan, A., Amponsah, M., Parida, S., & Ramkissoon, H. (2023). Tourist behaviour: The role of digital marketing and social media. *Acta Psychologica*, *240*, 104025. https://doi.org/https://doi.org/10.1016/j.actpsy.2023.104025. DOI: 10.1016/j.actpsy.2023.104025 PMID: 37741033

Basumatary, M., & Sarma, G. (2025). Tourism marketing strategies and plans: A systematic literature review. *Corporate and Business Strategy Review*, *6*(2), 40–51. DOI: 10.22495/cbsrv6i2art4

Bohara, S. (2024). Deepfake Marketing. *Deepfakes and Their Impact on Business*, 123.

Buhalis, D., & Amaranggana, A. (2014). Smart tourism destinations enhancing tourism experience through personalisation of services. *Information and Communication Technologies in Tourism 2015: Proceedings of the International Conference in Lugano,* Switzerland, February 3-6, 2015, 377–389.

Buhalis, D., Harwood, T., Bogicevic, V., Viglia, G., Beldona, S., & Hofacker, C. (2019). Technological disruptions in services: Lessons from tourism and hospitality. *Journal of Service Management*, *30*(4), 484–506. DOI: 10.1108/JOSM-12-2018-0398

Buhalis, D., & Law, R. (2008). Progress in information technology and tourism management: 20 years on and 10 years after the Internet—The state of eTourism research. *Tourism Management*, *29*(4), 609–623. DOI: 10.1016/j.tourman.2008.01.005

Campbell, C., Plangger, K., Sands, S., & Kietzmann, J. (2022). Preparing for an era of deepfakes and AI-generated ads: A framework for understanding responses to manipulated advertising. *Journal of Advertising*, *51*(1), 22–38. DOI: 10.1080/00913367.2021.1909515

Chandra Sekaran, S., Yap, H. J., Musa, S. N., Liew, K. E., Tan, C. H., & Aman, A. (2021). The implementation of virtual reality in digital factory—A comprehensive review. *International Journal of Advanced Manufacturing Technology*, *115*(5), 1349–1366. DOI: 10.1007/s00170-021-07240-x

Chen, Y. (2024). *Exploring the effect of deepfake-based advertising on consumers' attitudes and behaviors*. Working Paper Series WP 2024.

Dan, A. (2020). In the working-remote era,'deepfake'is No fake news: It will change advertising forever. *Forbes*.

Degadwala, S., & Patel, V. M. (2024). Advancements in deepfake detection: A review of emerging techniques and technologies. *International Journal of Scientific Research in Computer Science, Engineering and Information Technology*.

Dwivedi, Y. K., Kshetri, N., Hughes, L., Slade, E. L., Jeyaraj, A., Kar, A. K., Baabdullah, A. M., Koohang, A., Raghavan, V., Ahuja, M., Albanna, H., Albashrawi, M. A., Al-Busaidi, A. S., Balakrishnan, J., Barlette, Y., Basu, S., Bose, I., Brooks, L., Buhalis, D., & Wright, R. (2023). Opinion Paper:"So what if ChatGPT wrote it?" Multidisciplinary perspectives on opportunities, challenges and implications of generative conversational AI for research, practice and policy. *International Journal of Information Management*, *71*, 102642. DOI: 10.1016/j.ijinfomgt.2023.102642

Flavián, C., Ibáñez-Sánchez, S., & Orús, C. (2021). Integrating virtual reality devices into the body: effects of technological embodiment on customer engagement and behavioral intentions toward the destination. In *Future of tourism marketing* (pp. 79–94). Routledge. DOI: 10.4324/9781003176039-8

Floridi, L., Cowls, J., Beltrametti, M., Chatila, R., Chazerand, P., Dignum, V., Luetge, C., Madelin, R., Pagallo, U., Rossi, F., Schafer, B., Valcke, P., & Vayena, E. (2018). AI4People—An ethical framework for a good AI society: Opportunities, risks, principles, and recommendations. *Minds and Machines*, *28*(4), 689–707. DOI: 10.1007/s11023-018-9482-5 PMID: 30930541

Fotis, J., Buhalis, D., & Rossides, N. (2012). Social media use and impact during the holiday travel planning process. *Information and Communication Technologies in Tourism*, *2012*, 13–24. DOI: 10.1007/978-3-7091-1142-0_2

García-Madurga, M.-Á., & Grilló-Méndez, A.-J. (2023). Artificial Intelligence in the Tourism Industry: An Overview of Reviews. In *Administrative Sciences* (Vol. 13, Issue 8, p. 172). DOI: 10.3390/admsci13080172

George, A. S., & George, A. (2023). *Deepfakes: The Evolution of Hyper realistic Media Manipulation. 01*, 58–74. DOI: 10.5281/zenodo.10148558

Gutierriz, I., Ferreira, J. J., & Fernandes, P. O. (2025). Digital transformation and the new combinations in tourism: A systematic literature review. *Tourism and Hospitality Research, 25*(2), 194–213. DOI: 10.1177/14673584231198414

Guttentag, D. A. (2010). Virtual reality: Applications and implications for tourism. *Tourism Management, 31*(5), 637–651. DOI: 10.1016/j.tourman.2009.07.003

Halina, M. (2021). Insightful artificial intelligence. *Mind & Language, 36*(2), 315–329. DOI: 10.1111/mila.12321

Holloway, J. C., & Humphreys, C. (2019). The business of tourism. *Sage (Atlanta, Ga.).*

Huang, Z., Hu, J., Li, X., He, Y., Zhao, X., Peng, B., Wu, B., Huang, X., & Cheng, G. (2025). Sida: Social media image deepfake detection, localization and explanation with large multimodal model. *Proceedings of the Computer Vision and Pattern Recognition Conference*, 28831–28841. DOI: 10.1109/CVPR52734.2025.02685

Hussein, H., Albadry, O. M., Mathew, V., Al-Romeedy, B. S., Alsetoohy, O., Abou Kamar, M., & Khairy, H. A. (2024). Digital leadership and sustainable competitive advantage: Leveraging green absorptive capability and eco-innovation in tourism and hospitality businesses. *Sustainability (Basel), 16*(13), 5371. DOI: 10.3390/su16135371

Hwang, T. (2020). *Deepfakes: A grounded threat assessment*. Centre for Security and Emerging Technologies, Georgetown University. DOI: 10.51593/20190030

Ivanov, S. H., & Webster, C. (2017). *Adoption of robots, artificial intelligence and service automation by travel, tourism and hospitality companies–a cost-benefit analysis*. Artificial Intelligence and Service Automation by Travel, Tourism and Hospitality Companies–a Cost-Benefit Analysis.

Kaliyar, R. K., Goswami, A., & Narang, P. (2021). DeepFakE: Improving fake news detection using tensor decomposition-based deep neural network. *The Journal of Supercomputing, 77*(2), 1015–1037. DOI: 10.1007/s11227-020-03294-y

Kalpokas, I., & Kalpokiene, J. (2022). I CAN Do It: From GANs and Deepfakes to Art. In *Deepfakes: A Realistic Assessment of Potentials, Risks, and Policy Regulation* (pp. 55–63). Springer.

Kerpedzhiev, G. D., König, U. M., Röglinger, M., & Rosemann, M. (2021). An Exploration into Future Business Process Management Capabilities in View of Digitalization. *Business & Information Systems Engineering, 63*(2), 83–96. DOI: 10.1007/s12599-020-00637-0

Khan, A. A., Laghari, A. A., Inam, S. A., Ullah, S., Shahzad, M., & Syed, D. (2025). A survey on multimedia-enabled deepfake detection: State-of-the-art tools and techniques, emerging trends, current challenges & limitations, and future directions. *Discover Computing, 28*(1), 48. DOI: 10.1007/s10791-025-09550-0

Kietzmann, J., Mills, A. J., & Plangger, K. (2021). Deepfakes: Perspectives on the future "reality" of advertising and branding. *International Journal of Advertising, 40*(3), 473–485. DOI: 10.1080/02650487.2020.1834211

Kingma, D. P., & Welling, M. (2013). Auto-encoding variational bayes. *ArXiv Preprint ArXiv:1312.6114.*

Kleine, F. (2022). *Perception of Deepfake Technology*. Hochschule Darmstadt–University of Applied Sciences Darmstadt.

Kotler, P. (2022). *Marketing for hospitality and tourism*. Pearson Education Limited.

Kwok, A. O., & Koh, S. G. (2020). Deepfake: A social construction of technology perspective. *Current Issues in Tourism.*

Laghari, A. A., Wu, K., Ali, R., Mureed, L., Abdullah, A., & Khan, A. (2021). A Review and State of Art of Internet of Things (IoT) A Review and State of Art of Internet of Things (IoT). *Arch. Comput. Methods Eng., No.*

Le, D. D., Dang, T., Truong, V., Yu, S., Yang, S.-H., Choi, M.-H., & Lee, M. (2025). Integrative Discovery Through Network Pharmacology and Molecular Docking Approaches of Phenolic Compounds Isolated from Torreya nucifera to Treat Rheumatoid Arthritis. *International Journal of Molecular Sciences, 26*(23), 11629. DOI: 10.3390/ijms262311629 PMID: 41373781

Leung, D., Dickinger, A., & Nixon, L. (2017). Impact of destination promotion videos on perceived destination image and booking intention change. *Information and Communication Technologies in Tourism 2017: Proceedings of the International Conference in Rome,* Italy, January 24-26, 2017, 361–375.

Li, J., & Cao, B. (2022). Study on tourism consumer behavior and countermeasures based on big data. *Computational Intelligence and Neuroscience*, *2022*(1), 6120511. DOI: 10.1155/2022/6120511 PMID: 35909820

Lin, J., Li, Y., & Yang, G. (2021). FPGAN: Face de-identification method with generative adversarial networks for social robots. *Neural Networks : The Official Journal of the International Neural Network Society*, *133*, 132–147. DOI: 10.1016/j.neunet.2020.09.001 PMID: 33217682

Litvin, S. W., Goldsmith, R. E., & Pan, B. (2008). Electronic word-of-mouth in hospitality and tourism management. *Tourism Management*, *29*(3), 458–468. DOI: 10.1016/j.tourman.2007.05.011

Liu, M., Huang, X., Yu, J., Wang, T., & Mallya, A. (2020). *Generative Adversarial Networks for Image and Video Synthesis : Algorithms and Applications*. 1–22.

Lojo, A., Li, M., & Xu, H. (2020). Online tourism destination image: Components, information sources, and incongruence. *Journal of Travel & Tourism Marketing*, *37*(4), 495–509. DOI: 10.1080/10548408.2020.1785370

Mathew, V., & Soliman, M. (2021). Does digital content marketing affect tourism consumer behavior? An extension of t echnology acceptance model. *Journal of Consumer Behaviour*, *20*(1), 61–75. DOI: 10.1002/cb.1854

Nadda, V., Chaudhary, H. S., & Arnott, I. (2020). Cloud computing in tourism. In *Digital marketing strategies for tourism, hospitality, and airline industries* (pp. 141–155). IGI Global Scientific Publishing. DOI: 10.4018/978-1-5225-9783-4.ch007

Naitali, A., Ridouani, M., Salahdine, F., & Kaabouch, N. (2023). Deepfake Attacks: Generation, Detection, Datasets, Challenges, and Research Directions. *Computers*, *12*(10), 1–26. DOI: 10.3390/computers12100216

Neuhofer, B., Buhalis, D., & Ladkin, A. (2015). Smart technologies for personalized experiences: A case study in the hospitality domain. *Electronic Markets*, *25*(3), 243–254. DOI: 10.1007/s12525-015-0182-1

Pei, G., Zhang, J., Hu, M., Zhang, Z., Wang, C., Wu, Y., Zhai, G., Yang, J., Shen, C., & Tao, D. (2024). *Deepfake Generation and Detection: A Benchmark and Survey.*

Pestek, A., & Sarvan, M. (2021). Virtual reality and modern tourism. *Journal of Tourism Futures*, *7*(2), 245–250. DOI: 10.1108/JTF-01-2020-0004

Petit, O., Velasco, C., & Spence, C. (2019). Digital sensory marketing: Integrating new technologies into multisensory online experience. *Journal of Interactive Marketing*, *45*(1), 42–61. DOI: 10.1016/j.intmar.2018.07.004

Pramod, D., Patil, K. P., & Bharathi, S. V. (2025). Is it really unreal? A two-theory approach on the impact of deepfakes technology on the protection motivation of consumers. *Cogent Business & Management*, *12*(1), 2461239. DOI: 10.1080/23311975.2025.2461239

Rafiq, F., Dogra, N., Adil, M., & Wu, J.-Z. (2022). Examining consumer's intention to adopt AI-chatbots in tourism using partial least squares structural equation modeling method. *Mathematics*, *10*(13), 2190. DOI: 10.3390/math10132190

Rather, R. A. (2020). Customer experience and engagement in tourism destinations: The experiential marketing perspective. *Journal of Travel & Tourism Marketing*, *37*(1), 15–32. DOI: 10.1080/10548408.2019.1686101

Rather, R. A. (2025). Does consumers' reveal engagement behaviours in artificial intelligence (AI)-based technologies? The dynamics of perceived value and self-congruence. *International Journal of Hospitality Management*, *126*, 103989. https://doi.org/https://doi.org/10.1016/j.ijhm.2024.103989. DOI: 10.1016/j.ijhm.2024.103989

Samuel, S. (2019). A guy made a deepfake app to turn photos of women into nudes. It didn't go well. *Vox*. Https://Www. Vox. Com/2019/6/27/18761639/Ai-Deepfakedeepnude-App-Nude-Women-Porn

Saputra, F. E., Buhalis, D., Augustyn, M. M., & Marangos, S. (2024). Anthropomorphism-based artificial intelligence (AI) robots typology in hospitality and tourism. *Journal of Hospitality and Tourism Technology*, *15*(5), 790–807. DOI: 10.1108/JHTT-03-2024-0171

Setegn, A. E., & Japee, G. P. (2025). Promotional elements and the performance of tourism marketing of visitor attraction places with the mediating role of public relations: Empirical evidence from visitors in Ethiopia. *Cogent Business & Management*, *12*(1), 2454325. DOI: 10.1080/23311975.2025.2454325

Sharma, A. K., & Sharma, R. (2025). Smart tourism in the digital age: Overcoming barriers and unlocking new possibilities. *Revista de Gestão*, *32*(3), 224–237. DOI: 10.1108/REGE-02-2025-0030

Shrestha, D., Wenan, T., Shrestha, D., Rajkarnikar, N., & Jeong, S.-R. (2024). Personalized Tourist Recommender System: A Data-Driven and Machine-Learning Approach. In *Computation* (Vol. 12, Issue 3, p. 59). DOI: 10.3390/computation12030059

Solano-Barliza, A., Arregocés-Julio, I., Aarón-Gonzalvez, M., Zamora-Musa, R., De-La-Hoz-Franco, E., Escorcia-Gutierrez, J., & Acosta-Coll, M. (2024). Recommender systems applied to the tourism industry: A literature review. *Cogent Business & Management*, *11*(1), 2367088. DOI: 10.1080/23311975.2024.2367088

Sun, S., Law, R., & Luk, C. (2022). Tourists' travel-related information search channels. *International Journal of Hospitality & Tourism Administration*, *23*(2), 149–164. DOI: 10.1080/15256480.2020.1727809

Tavitiyaman, P., Qu, H., Tsang, W. L., & Lam, C. R. (2021). The influence of smart tourism applications on perceived destination image and behavioral intention: The moderating role of information search behavior. *Journal of Hospitality and Tourism Management*, *46*, 476–487. DOI: 10.1016/j.jhtm.2021.02.003

Thomas, G. (2024). Challenges and trends of digital innovation in the tourism sector: Contemporary literature review. *Open Journal of Business and Management*, *12*(01), 179–190. DOI: 10.4236/ojbm.2024.121013

Tom Dieck, M. C., & Han, D. D. (2022). The role of immersive technology in customer experience management. *Journal of Marketing Theory and Practice*, *30*(1), 108–119. DOI: 10.1080/10696679.2021.1891939

Tom Dieck, M. C., & Jung, T. (2018). A theoretical model of mobile augmented reality acceptance in urban heritage tourism. *Current Issues in Tourism*, *21*(2), 154–174. DOI: 10.1080/13683500.2015.1070801

Tucker, P. (2019). The newest AI-enabled weapon: Deep-Faking photos of the earth. *Defense One*, *13*, 3.

Tussyadiah, I. P., Jung, T. H., & Tom Dieck, M. C. (2018). Embodiment of wearable augmented reality technology in tourism experiences. *Journal of Travel Research*, *57*(5), 597–611. DOI: 10.1177/0047287517709090

Tuyen, T. (2025). Sustainable Tourism in the Age of Innovation: A Bibliometric Exploration of Progress and Potential. *Journal of Tourism. Sustainability and Well-Being*, *13*(1), 55–71.

Vargo, S. L., & Lusch, R. F. (2008). Service-dominant logic: Continuing the evolution. *Journal of the Academy of Marketing Science*, *36*(1), 1–10. DOI: 10.1007/s11747-007-0069-6

Verdoliva, L. (2020). Media Forensics and DeepFakes: An Overview. *IEEE Journal of Selected Topics in Signal Processing*, *14*(5), 910–932. DOI: 10.1109/JSTSP.2020.3002101

Veseli, A., Bytyqi, L., Hasanaj, P., & Bajraktari, A. (2025). The Impact of Digital Marketing on Promotion and Sustainable Tourism Development. In *Tourism and Hospitality* (Vol. 6, Issue 2, p. 56). DOI: 10.3390/tourhosp6020056

Walters, H. D., & Hammond, R. M. (2025). *AI in Marketing: Applications, Insights, and Analysis*. Taylor & Francis. DOI: 10.4324/9781003468806

Wang, S., Wang, Q., Cui, Q., & Lan, T. (2025). Artificial intelligence in tourism: A Systematic literature review and future research agenda. *Sustainability (Basel)*, *17*(20), 9080. DOI: 10.3390/su17209080

Whittaker, L., Letheren, K., & Mulcahy, R. (2021). The rise of deepfakes: A conceptual framework and research agenda for marketing. *Australasian Marketing Journal*, *29*(3), 204–214. DOI: 10.1177/1839334921999479

Whittaker, L., Mulcahy, R., Letheren, K., Kietzmann, J., & Russell-Bennett, R. (2023). Mapping the deepfake landscape for innovation: A multidisciplinary systematic review and future research agenda. *Technovation*, *125*, 102784. https://doi.org/https://doi.org/10.1016/j.technovation.2023.102784. DOI: 10.1016/j.technovation.2023.102784

Xiang, Z., Du, Q., Ma, Y., & Fan, W. (2017). A comparative analysis of major online review platforms: Implications for social media analytics in hospitality and tourism. *Tourism Management*, *58*, 51–65. DOI: 10.1016/j.tourman.2016.10.001

Xiang, Z., & Gretzel, U. (2010). Role of social media in online travel information search. *Tourism Management*, *31*(2), 179–188. DOI: 10.1016/j.tourman.2009.02.016

Xu, H., Law, R., Lovett, J., Luo, J. M., & Liu, L. (2024). Tourist acceptance of ChatGPT in travel services: The mediating role of parasocial interaction. *Journal of Travel & Tourism Marketing*, *41*(7), 955–972. DOI: 10.1080/10548408.2024.2364336

Yan, W., Wang, X., & Lu, Y. (2025). Deep learning based personalized tourism recommendation for behavior analysis and route optimization. *Scientific Reports*, *15*(1), 38561. DOI: 10.1038/s41598-025-22592-0 PMID: 41188382

Yang, X., Zhang, L., & Feng, Z. (2024). Personalized Tourism Recommendations and the E-Tourism User Experience. *Journal of Travel Research*, *63*(5), 1183–1200. DOI: 10.1177/00472875231187332

Zakharov, E., Shysheya, A., Burkov, E., & Lempitsky, V. (2019). Few-shot adversarial learning of realistic neural talking head models. *Proceedings of the IEEE/CVF International Conference on Computer Vision*, 9459–9468. DOI: 10.1109/ICCV.2019.00955

Zhou, X., & Zafarani, R. (2020). A survey of fake news: Fundamental theories, detection methods, and opportunities. *ACM Computing Surveys*, *53*(5), 1–40. DOI: 10.1145/3395046

Chapter 11
Cross-Domain Technology Transfer in Commercial Human-AI Interaction:
A Multidisciplinary Strategic Framework

Piali Haldar
http://orcid.org/0000-0003-4729-6964
Brainware University, Kolkata, India

Dev Kumar Mandal
http://orcid.org/0009-0005-3740-6885
Brainware University, Kolkata, India

ABSTRACT

The business intelligence sector is transforming profoundly at present; however, there is a limited understanding of how AI technology can be shifted across industries strategically. This effort develops a multi-disciplinary model, i.e., Cross-Domain AI Technology Transfer and Commercial Interaction Model (CATTCIM), in order to understand the movement of AI applications from research ecosystems to the AI stage in commercial settings. The design of the study was qualitative and empirical, and qualitative analysis was supplemented by the PLS-SEM procedure that provided quantitative validation showing the discussion of the relevant variables within the conceptual model. The results emphasize the role of technology rendering abilities, integration ability, and trust between humans and machines in furthering the diffusion

DOI: 10.4018/979-8-2600-2977-0.ch011

process and brilliance in market place. The paper presents an all-encompassing sociotechnical model that builds on existing theory of AI business, the transfer of technologies out of its industry context, and human-centric digital technology.

1. INTRODUCTION

The Artificial Intelligence revolution is in full swing, and it has a disruptive impact that could be compared to the inventions of electricity or the computer. There is indeed a significant transformation of value systems within various industries, ranging from banking, healthcare, retail, manufacturing, to digital business activities, due to the adoption of AI technologies (Agarwal et al., 2024; Naimi-Sadigh et al., 2022; Oyekunle & Boohene, 2024). In addition, the arenas in which human beings and machines are associated are progressively beginning to feature intelligent systems, notably recommendation engines, chatbots, predictive models, and standalone software applications (McAfee & Brynjolfsson, 2017; Davenport & Ronanki, 2018). Such advancements do away with the technical background of people, and their conception turns to the human-internet relation, which involves preferences and actions that may be very well aided or hindered by the use of those products (Ystgaard et al., 2023).

Notwithstanding the swift evolution of artificial technology, the process of deploying AI solutions into the market is far from simple and even. The chasm is wide between the advanced innovations created in research centres and the actual use of such innovations in the market. This issue highlights profusely the problem of technology transfer, which denotes the passage of know-how, skills, and innovations from one set of institutions and disciplines to another (Nooteboom, 2003). In most instances, technology transfer is used to mean the process where new scientific knowledge and objects like technologies are applied in product development, and these objects are marketed (Bozeman, 2000). However, in the context of AI, technology transfer is not a straightforward exercise from the laboratory to the market. Instead, it is seen as a herculean effort involving multiple factors such as knowledge application, organizational change, design, user interaction, legal changes, and market adoption.

With the advent of AI-induced markets, the necessity for interaction across professions such as marketing, information systems, human–computer interaction (HCI), strategic marketing, and customer behaviour has enormously increased. Each profession provides insights to understand different dimensions of commercializing AI. Either way, information systems research focuses on how technological systems, data sets, and platforms support the implementation of AI (Rai et al., 2019). Marketing scholarship investigates behavioural and relationship outcomes, like consumption personalization and relationship management, associated with the use of AI technologies (Huang & Rust, 2018). HCI professionals concentrate on the interface objects, waterfall, and trust mechanism when it comes to innovative systems (Glikson & Woolley, 2020). In addition, experts in innovation and strategic management pay attention to technological shifts within companies' business strategies in strategic development in order to integrate new technologies or predict possible risks (Teece, 2018).

Nevertheless, such attitudes are generally disjointed in many aspects, making it difficult for one to grasp how artificial intelligence either thrives in an environment or forms part of any commercial human-machine interaction. Another point of concern relates to the fact that the conventional technology transfer methods with a mental approach are neutral in technology and were developed as a reaction to the need to share the improved technology across geographical areas. Initially, the objective was the development of structural industrial technologies, such as pharmaceuticals or manufacturing technologies, and the only task was that of commercialization. This is quite different from the nature of AI innovation, which is developed very quickly with several reiteration cycles, is embedded in ecosystems of digital platforms, arises from a feedback loop, and in every sense of the phrase, requires the construction of interfaces that are centred on a human (Secundo et al., 2025; Burstrom et al., 2021). A theoretical model that employs a range of disciplines is necessary to input the intentions of firms that operate in the AI provision market.

Yet an inquiry as crucial to the success of AI as digitization is the dynamics of human and AI relationships. Most AI devices, unlike the long-established technologies, perform as assistants or self-assists with relationships of varied frequencies and contexts of consumers. Technology-oriented customers are known to apply AI instruments (such as chatbots, voice assistants, and recommendation systems) when making decisions daily. These relatively minimal exchanges of services, in fact, conspire with the three perceptions and change the nature of any activity, enabling even technology providers to view any technology more positively, as mentioned in (Glikson et al., 2020). Other reasons for user resistance to AI were discussed, notably in (Shin, 2021), such as how suspicious people tend to be concerning predictive analytics user acceptance. Conversely, in comparison to algorithms, technology, and presumably objects with behavioural intelligence, people interact with robots somewhat differently, despite the absence of direct human-level abilities in them. Thus, the commercial deployment of AI is not just the responsibility of IT, advanced research, or other people, but it is also about the way spaces such as classrooms, board meeting rooms, and employee offices are designed.

In strategy, organizations need to integrate AI tools into implementation and strategic plans. According to the theory of dynamic capabilities, technological advancements necessitate firms to constantly and consistently re-evaluate their resources and capabilities (Teece, 2018). Further, the use of AI tools often necessitates the establishment of supportive data infrastructure, human resource planning, management systems, and cross-functional integration (Mhaskey, 2024). Further, organizations that turn to developed AI are those able to reconcile change, strategic alterations, and competitive necessities with their capabilities. And the change facilitates the guidance of AI technologies, for instance, applied solutions that can be turned to commercial use.

However, the implementation of artificial intelligence technologies is not just limited to the technology itself, but it is organized in a complex social and technical network which includes legal and regulatory frameworks, informational support and intermediary services, as well as mechanisms of interaction between economic agents. The fact that governments and other regulators are actively shaping the development of AI and its commercialization by elaborating policies on data and ethics, as well as on explainability and accountability. However, several recent studies emphasize that AI development can also be channelled through the activities of digital platform companies by providing cloud resources, machine learning, and AI-based services through various programming interfaces (Van Der Vlist et al., 2024; Rai et al., 2019). These structures subject requires sectoral frameworks that go beyond traditional business and user.

Despite the uptrend in AI applications in the market, the topic is underestimated, as despite numerous attempts trying to consider it from a different angle, the problem has not been theoretically resolved. Most of those approaches consider rather particular aspects. For instance, some focus on algorithmic trust, while others focus on digital transformation or innovation diffusion. However, what remains unaddressed is how all these factors are interconnected in different technology development processes and how they are controlled in terms of technology trials and popular use in the commercial sector. Such a situation does not provide ready information to academia and practice on how AI research systems function in using technologies to work with humans, as in a business setting.

To bridge this gap, the Researchers are suggesting the Cross-Domain AI Technology Transfer and Commercial Interaction Model (CATTCIM). The CATTCIM is a multidisciplinary theoretical model that combines insights from technology transfer, innovation adoption, sociotechnical, dynamic capabilities, and human-computer interaction aspects. Converts AI as a commercial activity by categorizing it into several levels: technological start, rhizome, strategic embedding, operational arrangement, and market existence. Based on the interaction of these factors, the proposed model specifies cognitive mechanisms and processes where AI-related technologies are converted into money in a cross-science and human-in-the-loop setting.

The study is carried out through a mixed-method paradigm, bearing the roots of qualitative research with the aid of some quantitative validation. The qualitative aspect entails an analysis that consists of experts' interviews and thematic analysis with discussions and two aspects: identification of key constructs within the context of the technology constructs in AI ecosystems. The relations proposed for research purposes need to be empirically investigated in the course of the quantitative phase with the help of Partial Least Squares Structural Equations Analysis (PLS-SEM). This procedure is particularly appropriate when numerous factors, mediators, and moderators feature in the research model (Sarstedt et al., 2021). By combining the strengths of the qualitative with the strengths of the quantitative aspects, the research aims at developing a specific empirical understanding of the driving forces in the effective commercialisation of AI.

This research paper has three main contributions. The first one is that it enhances the understanding of the academic community towards the technology transfer area. The perspective is unique in a way that some of the traditional theoretical models were beer in line with the issues and realities in the society. Therefore, this study reviews the new terms and narratives in the context of sociotechnical ecosystems and enhances the framework of technology transfer models. Secondly, this research enhances the knowledge on human- rather than simply technology-enhanced AI interaction through in-pai and Transparency- and interaction design. It is seen that two issues are true between businesses with AI and humans: one being the design of the interaction itself, and the other the necessary commissary mechanism of trust and transparency in AI systems. The friendship in this case is mainly human- interaction aim Ai technology- human interaction trust in users, mostly their interface. Every one of these is critical to the financial performance commitment of any enterprise that aligns behaviours strategically for the realization of objectives. Third, the output of the current study goes beyond exploratory analysis and provides actionable suggestions to practitioners and policymakers who wish to channel innovation mediated by AI that is socially responsible and explicable as stage I when it comes to large-scale applications. A more extensive and multi-layered strategic approach is put forward within public policy, which helps to understand how areas of knowledge can be merged to successfully commercialize AI technologies rapidly and effectively in current digital consumer markets.

2. LITERATURE REVIEW

There has been much discussion within different academic schools, such as innovation management, IS, and marketing domains, on the applicability of artificial intelligence (AI) technologies in trade, following the breakthrough in data science technologies. And already as responsible systems are integrated deeper and deeper in the economic and social processes, researchers point out that the issue is about how what is developed is brought to markets, contributing to human regard and operation on the intelligent system. Consideration of the technology absorption, digital advances, and interaction between humans and AI, therefore, important aspect in understanding failures associated with boundary problems of technology commercialization. However, these studies suffer from the weakness that they provide knowledge incrementally rather than significantly contributing to theory. This section reviews key strands of literature relevant to cross-domain technology transfer and commercial human–AI interaction, highlighting the theoretical foundations that inform the development of the proposed framework.

2.1 Technology Transfer and Innovation Commercialization

Technology transfer seems to be an actual transfer of scientific knowledge, technical capabilities, and intellectual property from research institutes to the organizations that can finally bring these innovations to the market (Bozeman 2000). Past studies on technology transfer have concentrated on issues or procedures like university-industry collaboration, licensing agreements, and commercialization of research (Daniel & Alves, 2020; Arenas & González, 2018; Lee, 1996). These are the mechanisms that mediate the conversion of academic discoveries into usable products and services. The early works in this field focused on the significance of institutional structures, organizational incentives, and knowledge diffusion in shaping the efficacy of technology transfer processes in a university setting (Debackere & Veugelers, 2005; Lambooy, 2004; Siegel et al., 2003).

Regrettably, while transactions over digital platforms surge, the proliferation of digital and Artificial Intelligence (AI) technologies for commercial purposes raises new challenges against the established concepts of technology transfer (Chui & Francisco, 2017). Recognizing that, unlike the traditional technology-related advancements, which are regarded as stand-alone, AIs keep advancing through continuous iterations that include user feedback and machine learning. Therefore, the behaviours of AIs are very specific; they are readily integrated into various environments and business processes, but cut off, however, it is easier to go from point A to point B in a straight line. That's why some scholars argue that digital innovation contexts would be most effectively understood as a technology transfer and an ecosystem where different stakeholders, like research institutions, technology firms, platform providers, and the end users, as well. Such ecosystems' orientations to development are predicated on the possibility of smoothing away work and management barriers and increasing effectiveness.

One important consideration when discussing the sharing of knowledge and technology is absorbing the knowledge and technology capacity that was grown out of that knowledge and technology, as well as the capabilities of an organization to recognize the importance of new knowledge, convert it from information into sustainable practices, and finally commercialize it in outside markets. One of the priorities of firms with a developed absorptive capacity is the ability to introduce such technologies as AI in a proper manner into their strategic and operational systems. The need for the use of such a technological ability is especially big in the AI evolutionary markets, where the very existence of an organization requires more than just technical excellence but also experimentation, business plays, and user-centred technology.

2.2 Artificial Intelligence and Digital Innovation Ecosystems

The significance of AI technologies has done a lot in the promotion of a digital innovation environment where technology, data, and the competence of the company contribute to creating value (Aldoseri et al., 2024). However, the emergence of cloud computing, ambitions, and machine learning settings in computer science advancements and steering using AI instruction tools is an important aspect in countering this barrier (Rai et al., 2019). The platforms allow for computational resources for accessing artificial intelligence frameworks and AI tools that are designed for the quick realization of intelligent systems (Ahmed et al., 2022; Hammad & Abu-Zaid, 2024).

Digital innovation ecosystems emphasize the fact that AI development and commercialization are not separate issues but rather two interrelated processes (Secundo et al., 2025; Burström et al., 2021). Firms, rather than seeking to autonomously perform the above-mentioned five functions, become part of networks of developers, researchers, and platform providers who work together to define developmental direction and its technology trajectory (Nambisan et al., 2017). What characterizes existing ecosystems is that innovation arises from interaction among multiple actors who possess unique and varying resources and capabilities. As a result, cross-boundary knowledge flow is very important for the realization of AI innovations in business ends.

While there are existing arguments for data and other forms of technological infrastructure, the focus for this phenomenon of artificial intelligence needs to be put only on data and its acquisition (Car et al., 2019). AI models, especially machine learning algorithms, require vast numbers of records to facilitate performance and learning, and algorithms keep getting better with every learning iteration. It also highlights how businesses that hoard substantial amounts of data can provide superior differentiated AI services to the marketplace, as suggested by research performed by McAfee & Brynjolfsson (2017). Yet data increases are more so with effect on addressing these concerns as they rise, including the use of the data, since these elements' social ranking, fairness, and validity by which the results must adhere to, should consider such very limitations and delimitations. These characteristics make way for an ethical concern that underscores the need for an artificial intelligence civilization that worries and concerns expectations with culture and the balance of purposes.

2.3 Human–AI Interaction and User Acceptance

Human-AI interaction is emerging as a popular field of study. How people see, work, and respond to smart machines is a growing body of research. Stepping into human roles like responding to user problems, giving advice, giving answers, and engaging in decision making, computer systems pose questions to the user that must be addressed for effective use of the technology (Bader & Kaiser, 2019).

One can argue that trust is one of the most commonly debated aspects of human interaction with artificial intelligence technology (Ferrario et al., 2020). In this context, trust in AI entails the extent to which people are willing to pass on algorithm-based recommendations or decisions, especially in difficult and ambiguous situations. Several research papers at this point examine the fact that there are many reasons for trust which cover, for example, perceived reliability, transparency, explainability, and AI system fairness (Lee and Song, 2010). Users may experience difficulty in using AI products that they view as non-transparent or incomprehensible, even if the products have the potential to perform better.

Explainable AI (XAI) has shown promise in response to worries about confidence. Here, the normal attention is towards AI systems that provide interpretable reasons for their judgments, and they are aimed at aiding them to understand the results of algorithms. It is believed that explainability can promote the confidence and trust that users have, especially when potential risk factors are involved, for example, in the healthcare and financial sectors (Adadi & Berrada, 2018). However, more effective explanation features are also needed beyond statistics when information refers to the user, as it is important that the users, including the risk-averse ones, do not just understand the probabilistic numerical outputs. Finally, from the aspect of marketing strategy, it has also been proven that providing reasons behind the results of decision-making processes increases customer satisfaction in a highly positive way. However, in the marketing strategy of supply, providing explanations for all decision-making processes has shown a very beneficial impact on the improvement of customer satisfaction.

Equally important when it comes to engaging with AI systems are emotional and social contexts and how these interact. For example, many types of AI systems, like chatbots or virtual assistants, make use of human-like communication as much as possible in order to make user interaction more natural and engaging for the users themselves (Chandra et al., 2022). From a practical point of view, multiple design elements, anthropomorphic features in particular, such as the use of spoken language and personalized answers, can be responsible for more successful interaction and operability (Huang & Rust, 2018). This aspect, which they have stressed, emphasizes the release of user reception and the use of behavioural insights when designing AI-embedded human-oriented services.

2.4 Strategic Integration and Dynamic Capabilities

Strategically, the efficient dissemination of AI-based technologies requires organizations to learn how they are going to incorporate those technologies within their business models and, more importantly, in their operations. Researchers have noted the positive contribution of dynamic capabilities to managing technology. Dynamic capabilities can be a functional capacity that enables a company to perceive new opportunities, mobilize and allocate resources to take advantage of these new opportunities, as well as to enhance its core capabilities (Teece, 2018).

Utilizing AI in operations usually demands substantial adjustment within an organization, including making investments in specific data and data-related technologies (Ghosh, 2025); empowering the staff, and designing and endorsing new action mechanisms. It is also truly important for the companies to help IT professionals, marketing, digital marketers, production workers, and customer service representatives to develop an organizational capability of AI. It seems that organizations, which properly channel technological change into their strategies and goals, realize increased operational efficiency in the course of technology-enhanced change management programmes (Davenport & Ronanki, 2018).

Moreover, the process of utilizing artificial intelligence in a commercial capacity very often presumes the adoption of new practices involving computational methods by firms. For instance, it is possible for companies to launch new product lines that use AI or employ new ways of marketing their products or services through customer-specific marketing strategies and AI-driven analytics (Bano et al., 2025; Arora et al., 2024). Such initiatives serve as indications of how the intrusion of AI into business functions and market structures of industries can change how value is created.

2.5 Research Gap

While the available information provides valuable information on the various aspects of technology transfer, innovation ecosystems, and human AI interaction and strategic management, their analysis constitutes separate and uncoordinated research areas. We know from the previous research that technology transfer is usually studied in terms of implementation risk in specific experiences and the flow of knowledge, but it does not focus on user interaction and market adoption as much. In the same way, issues of human AI interaction often tackle tendencies, psychological and behavioural ones, at the same time neglecting the formal aspects of organizations and strategies. In the same manner, studying strategic management, it is possible to see that more is given to the capacities of the organization than ever before, yet the practices of consumer motivation or interface architecture are equally addressed.

Transformation, especially when it comes to the implementation of AI systems in business relations between people and artificial agents, usually involves multiple steps across divergent but very related contexts. The nature of this middle ground dictates that any work geared towards understanding the dispersive tendencies of AI and resultant types is unable to avoid the nexus of the techno-societal systems entirely. It is, therefore, necessary to develop a comprehensive model encompassing those aspects which are technological, organizational, and behavioural. These research questions are the aims of the present study, in which we propose the CAT-TCIM model (Cross-Domain AI Technology Transfer and Commercial Interaction Model) (Jin & Zhao, 2025) and suggest that for persons and institutions sharing communities, AI is a means of providing increased functionalities and abilities. AI commercialization involves the origination of technology, strategic networks, and hence the need to purchase and use it, interaction design, and product market. The proposed framework, however, is enriched with some ideas borrowed from other disciplines, and it is suitable for the understanding of many features of technology transfer in mixed environments and in the context of commercial human-technology interaction.

2.6 Research Objectives

1. To develop an integrated multidisciplinary framework for AI technology transfer in commercial human–AI interaction.
2. To empirically validate the CATTCIM model using a mixed-method design.
3. To examine mediating and moderating mechanisms in AI commercialization.
4. To identify strategic pathways for sustainable human–AI market ecosystems.

3. CONCEPTUAL FRAMEWORK

3.1 Proposed Research Framework: CATTCIM Model

Enjoyed working with you on the previous phases of the project. I suggest we proceed with working on this one. AI, as expected, shared some things with the IoT. Terms and technologies. Artificial intelligence, indeed, has developed ways that can facilitate the effectiveness and efficiency of other technologies. So how can it be possible to transfer the AI to the domain of human and artificial interaction from that of AI and machine interaction? There are some primary reasons why transferring AI to the discipline of AI and human interaction can be considered difficult. The factors can be classified into those that are based on the different levels within the model and those based on various stages of the model. Arguments are based on such elements as positions around which the authors of the model disagree, resistance to the model by some potential applications and audiences, and perceived appropriateness of the strategy embodied in the model.

The CATTCIM framework casts AI exploitation into the light of a complex socio-technical structure with five interrelated components: the focus technology, the focus technology transfer mechanisms, the logistics of integrating any innovation strategically, HAI design, and economic. In the beginning, the focus technology refers to the phase of developing new AI-based technologies within the research institutions, other firms operating in the field, and innovation parks. These technologies comprise machine learning algorithms, sophisticated technologies that facilitate decision-making, and the AI service sections. Nevertheless, the availability of technological innovation alone is not ensured to lead to positive outcomes.

The second dimension that is technology transfer mechanisms when discussing AI has to do with the way in which AI-related knowledge or know-how is shared within different organisational and disciplinary cultures. For instance, collaborative research initiatives, development of web applications, establishment of innovation centres, and practice-sharing communities, etc. all contribute to the process of turning basic research into practical applications.

The third dimension is about the strategic integration of AI, which reflects the ability of an organisation to effectively implement AI-enabled processes and models in their operations, strategies, and to compete with others. These trilateral associations, aligning efforts, readiness to change, and capabilities off the shelf of the enterprise, are responsible for helping turn AI innovations into solutions fit for the market.

As for the fourth dimension, it is focused on the relationship between the human and AI in terms of design of interactive technology systems and also lays particular emphasis on main components such as trust, transparency, explanation, and usability in the technologically driven interaction systems adoption process. In business operations and marketing purposes, the AI applications usually play the front office role, hence the desire to be more compelled to their specific persuasion or service design would result in feelings of utility and convince the public to use it.

In addition, the model ties together these factors with business metrics, including AI acceptance, customer satisfaction levels, innovation rates, and the ability of a company to compete in the market. The CATTCIM framework, therefore, suggests that the potential for commercialization of AI results from the triadic relationship of technological innovation, strategic integration, and human-centred design. This scale fits well because it works in a great deal of relevant areas where research should be done, advancing understanding of cross-domain technology transfer and its effect on business-human AI interactions.

3.2 Research Hypotheses

Numerous hypotheses have been developed to evaluate the influence of innovation, transfer, integration, and human-computer interactions on the outcome as per the proposed concept of Cross-Domain AI Technology Transfer and Commercial Interaction Model (CATTCIM). These hypotheses are allocated for several aspects (innovation and technology, management theory, and interaction with artificial intelligence) and create a system as per the most common understanding.

H1: Technology origination capability positively influences the effectiveness of cross-domain technology transfer mechanisms.
H2: Effective technology transfer mechanisms positively influence strategic AI integration within organizations.
H3: Technology transfer mechanisms positively influence the quality of human–AI interaction design.
H4: Strategic AI integration positively influences the development of human–AI interaction quality.
H5: Strategic AI integration positively influences commercial AI adoption and market performance.
H6: Human–AI interaction quality positively influences user trust in AI-enabled systems.
H7: Human–AI trust positively influences consumer adoption of AI-enabled commercial services.
H8: Human–AI interaction quality positively influences customer satisfaction with AI-driven services.
H9: Consumer adoption of AI-enabled services positively influences firm-level commercial performance.

Numerous hypotheses have been developed to evaluate the influence of innovation, transfer, integration, and human-computer interactions on the outcome as per the proposed concept of Cross-Domain AI Technology Transfer and Commercial Interaction Model (CATTCIM). These hypotheses are allocated for several aspects (innovation and technology, management theory, and interaction with artificial intelligence) and create a system as per the most common understanding.

4. METHODOLOGY

For this purpose, a two-phase research method is employed, which is known as mixed-method research, to fabricate as well as evaluate CATTCIM. Therefore, using a mixed-method design is helpful, especially when studying problems in a wide spectrum of fields, such as technology and humans' interaction with machines, such as Artificial Intelligence behaviour in business and technology enactment. This aspect of the study ensures that valid and reliable integration was achieved during subsequent phases since both qualitative and quantitative findings were used to explain abstract concepts.

4.1 Research Design

To investigate the research problem, the study followed a sequential exploratory mixed-method design. Qualitative methods were applied in the first phase to identify the main features of cross-domain technology transfer and e-service humans and AI interfaces theoretically and empirically. Findings of the first phase were utilized in the development of the conceptual framework and measurement constructs for the quantitative phase. In the second phase, a survey with questions is prepared, and questions are implemented in order to test the hypothesized relationships in the CATTCIM framework using the Partial Least Squares Structural Equation Modelling (PLS-SEM). This type of research design allows for both descriptive and inferential statistics, thus exploring further the key relationships in the study.

4.2 Qualitative Phase

The Qualitative phase helps to recognize the main aspects that greatly affect the transfer and commercialization activities of AI technology throughout various sectors. In this phase, Semi-structured interviews are carried out with industry experts including technology companies, digital platform companies, innovation managers, and academic researchers on AI and digital transformation. And as such, these respondents were selected through a purposive sampling technique to ensure that they have the necessary professional experience in AI implementation and technology commercialization.

The required number of expert interviews on average is 15-20 hours, with different durations of around 40-60 minutes per session. The tiny tends to involve identification of current technology transfer mechanisms and measures, the relevance of these measures in the organizational structure, the prospects of the improved technological advancements in relation to human and AI eco-system and values, and the effect of the current achievement of the strategic necessities on e-business. The interview data will be analysed using thematic analysis of which semi-structured interviews with all participants will be coded, with discrete categories, unique themes found throughout the interview, and these data will be categorized for technology transfer, strategic integration, and interaction design. The output produced from there will add value to the improvement of the study constructs and the survey tool in the subsequent stage, which utilizes quantitative designs.

4.3 Quantitative Phase

The purpose of the quantitative stage is to analyse the assumptions formulated within the CATTCIM construct without relying on its theoretical postulates. Data is collected using a specific survey among AI oriented projects professionals and managers. It is necessary to mention that in some response categories, we employ the use of industries with a high intensity of promoting AI. These are such areas such as information technologies and digital services, financial technologies, e-commerce, and customer-oriented services where AI tools are being applied.

A sampling scheme is used in the selection of the respondents who have direct exposure to the tested AI systems or technologies and digital transformation-based projects. The study was conducted with 350 respondents; 312 respondents were able to complete the questionnaires, and it is known that this number is enough to be able to develop structural equation models. Various issues, such as efficiency of the transfer of technology, how well management of the technology of artificial intelligence is done, quality of interaction between humans and AI, attitudes towards AI, and economic indicators, will be measured in the survey by using the Likert scales, which are based on 5 points each. The scales are: strongly disagree (1) and strongly agree (5).

4.4 Demographic Profile of the Respondents

Table 1 shows the demographic characteristics of the respondents who were involved in the study. There were 312 respondents in total who took part in the survey, including professionals plus managers who are linked to AI-enabled projects and digital transformation efforts across different industries.

Table 1. Demographic Profile of the Respondents

Demographic Variable	Category	Frequency	Percentage (%)
Gender	Male	188	60.3
	Female	124	39.7
Age Group	21–30 years	72	23.1
	31–40 years	118	37.8
	41–50 years	83	26.6
	Above 50 years	39	12.5
Educational Qualification	Bachelor's Degree	96	30.8
	Master's Degree	164	52.6
	Doctorate/Professional Qualification	52	16.6
Industry Sector	Information Technology & Digital Services	112	35.9
	Financial Technology	68	21.8
	E-commerce	57	18.3
	Customer Service & Retail	45	14.4
	Others	30	9.6
Work Experience	Less than 5 years	74	23.7
	5–10 years	126	40.4
	11–15 years	71	22.8
	More than 15 years	41	13.1
Designation	Managerial Level	138	44.2
	Technical/AI Specialist	104	33.3
	Senior Executive	70	22.5

Interpretation

From what the demographic analysis shows, most respondents were male (60.3%), and female respondents were 39.7% of the sample. In the same way, the 31–40 years group seems to be the most common, with 37.8%, which kind of suggests mid-career professionals were really involved in AI-driven projects. About education, a big portion had a Master's degree (52.6%). So, it looks like the group was quite well educated, and that should help with understanding AI technologies, plus the strategic integration side of things.

When it comes to industry, the biggest part of the respondents came from Information Technology and Digital Services (35.9%). After that, you had Financial Technology (21.8%), then E-commerce (18.3%). Also, most people reported 5–10 years of professional experience (40.4%), which gives a practical view of digital transformation efforts. In terms of roles, managerial professionals are the top category at 44.2%, and then technical and AI specialists (33.3%) come next. Overall, this demographic picture basically shows that the respondents had sufficient professional know-how and industry exposure, which fits the aims of the study.

4.4 Data Analysis Techniques

The collected statistical data will be used in the analysis as it will be made use of the PLS-SEM so as to bring out findings successfully. It is chosen especially for the intricate cases where numerous factors, mediation factors, and also intervening effects exist. The methodology for these provides for two steps, namely the measurement model and the thesis model. This first step basically aims at a way of assessing the measurement tools for consistency and convenience with indicators such as Cronbach's alpha, CR, and AVE. The second step requires the examination of the structural equation models, which include the inspection of the path coefficients, level of significance, R^2, and Q^2 for their appropriateness in predicting the outcome variable of the study.

There is no doubt that the combination of qualitative data and numerical models brings rich conclusions towards analysing and interpreting the CATTCIM framework. This method heightens the strength of the research with respect to the introduction of AI technologies across various fields and commercial interactions with AI systems.

5. DATA ANALYSIS (PLS-SEM)

A total of 312 persons were surveyed to obtain the quantitative data for the study which was then analysed under PLS-SEM. The analysis was carried out in two main stages. Firstly, the measurement model was assessed, and then the structural model was included in the analysis. The purpose of the measurement model is to check the reliability and validity of the measurements; the purpose of the structural model is to examine the relationships hypothesized in the CATTCIM framework.

5.1 Reliability Analysis

Table 2. Reliability Statistics

Construct	Number of Items	Cronbach's Alpha	Composite Reliability
Technology Origination (TO)	4	0.842	0.891
Technology Transfer Mechanism (TTM)	4	0.856	0.903
Strategic AI Integration (SAI)	4	0.861	0.907
Human–AI Interaction Quality (HAI)	4	0.878	0.914
AI Trust (AIT)	3	0.832	0.887
Commercial Performance (CP)	3	0.846	0.895

Interpretation

In Table 2, the reliability analysis shows a strong level of internal consistency among instrument variables in connection with the proposed CATTCIM model. Even though the Cronbach's alpha of all the constructs varies from 0.832 to 0.878, it is above the acceptable level of 0.70 and thus shows high inner consistency. This can also be indicated by the fact that the composite reliability of the constructs falls within the range of 0.887 to 0.914, which is quite satisfactory. Consequently, the results show that survey items measure what they were intended to measure in terms of TT effectiveness, SI, and the quality of incorporation of human-AI. Moreover, the present significant estimates of reliability imply that the instrument is supportive for confirmatory analysis, such as PLS SEM, intended for checking the proposed associations within the theoretical model.

5.2 Convergent Validity

Table 3. Convergent Validity (AVE)

Construct	Composite Reliability	Average Variance Extracted (AVE)
Technology Origination	0.891	0.672
Technology Transfer Mechanism	0.903	0.701
Strategic AI Integration	0.907	0.714

continued on following page

Table 3. Continued

Construct	Composite Reliability	Average Variance Extracted (AVE)
Human–AI Interaction Quality	0.914	0.728
AI Trust	0.887	0.676
Commercial Performance	0.895	0.689

Interpretation

Convergent validity in Table 3 refers to the degree to which empirical indicators are highly associated with the same sigma, in this case, a higher value of shared variance. According to the outcomes obtained for the first specific objective of the study, all five constructs have Average Variance Extracted (AVE) greater than 0.50, where the minimum is 0.672 and the maximum observed to be 0.728; these rates are equally below the suggested threshold for convergent validity. Consequently, these outcomes reveal that the respective latent construct is satisfactorily represented by the observed items in the almanac of the CATTCIM. For instance, a high AVE for Human–AI Interaction Quality (0.728) means that it is quite entrenched for the building of such a construct. Based on the above logic, appreciating that this construct is quite encompassing, the measurement model exhibits good convergent validity, which in turn supports examination of any conceptual relationship.

5.3 Discriminant Validity (Fornell–Larcker Criterion)

Table 4. Discriminant Validity

Construct	TO	TTM	SAI	HAI	AIT	CP
TO	**0.820**					
TTM	0.611	**0.837**				
SAI	0.574	0.689	**0.845**			
HAI	0.532	0.621	0.708	**0.853**		
AIT	0.498	0.563	0.640	0.731	**0.822**	
CP	0.510	0.592	0.661	0.698	0.713	**0.830**

Interpretation

In Table 4, discriminant validity is very important in that one construct is clearly separated from the other constructs. According to the Fornell–Larcker criterion, the square root of the AVE of each construct should be higher than the empirical correlation with other constructs. In the table presented below, Table 3, the diagonal values in bold, which report each construct's square root of AVE, are higher than inter-construct correlational values. For example, the square root of the AVE of Human–AI Interaction Quality (0.853) is greater than its correlations with Strategic AI Integration (0.708) and AI Trust (0.731). This confirms that the construct measures different within the factors in the CATTCIM structure.\

5.4 Structural Model and Hypothesis Testing

Table 5. Path Coefficients

Hypothesis	Path	Beta (β)	t-value	p-value	Result
H1	TO → TTM	0.61	9.82	0.000	Supported
H2	TTM → SAI	0.68	10.14	0.000	Supported
H3	TTM → HAI	0.42	6.23	0.000	Supported
H4	SAI → HAI	0.36	5.97	0.000	Supported
H5	SAI → CP	0.29	4.88	0.000	Supported
H6	HAI → AIT	0.73	12.21	0.000	Supported
H7	AIT → Adoption	0.64	9.45	0.000	Supported
H8	HAI → CP	0.38	6.11	0.000	Supported
H9	Adoption → CP	0.41	7.34	0.000	Supported

Interpretation

The model that you see on the Table 5 proves all the relationships built in the framework of CATTCIM. The scale of the "Technology originating" has a positive effect on transfer mechanisms ($\beta = 0.61$, $p < 0.001$), illustrating how, through the development of AI, innovation cross-fertilises across domains. According to the model, strategic AI adoption is heavily rooted in the mechanisms of technology transfer ($\beta = 0.68$), opportunities for collaboration and knowledge management enable the incorporation of AI in operational and strategic plans of organizations. The standard of H-A interaction affects the level of trust in AI systems considerably (β= 0.73), which suggests the significance of open services and, in general, effectiveness in the learning process. In a general sense, the evidence indicates that technology, strategic integration, and human technology interface contribute to the market outcome.

5.5 Coefficient of Determination (R^2)

Table 6. Model Explanatory Power

Endogenous Construct	R^2 Value
Technology Transfer Mechanism	0.37
Strategic AI Integration	0.46
Human–AI Interaction Quality	0.51
AI Trust	0.53
Commercial Performance	0.58

Interpretation

In Table 6, the coefficient of determination (R^2) measures the explanatory power of the structured hypothesis. The data reveals sufficient to a rather high ability to forecast with respect to the CATTCIM approach. As far as the novel technologies are concerned, 37 percent of the variance is accounted for by the technology transfer tools. Active introduction of AI methods in the organization's processes explains more than 46% of the readiness for AI. Human-AI interaction relation level is depicted in a measure, R-square equal to 0.51, which means more than half of the quality perception is elucidated by the model. In AI trust, the value was the highest, 53 percent; however, the very high value of the first admission, 58 percent, represented by performance in terms of commerce. These yield the conclusion that the suggested construct can be utilized to explain the factors that suitably facilitate the achievement of business ends in a capital-incentive AI marketplace.

6. RESULTS

The results from the PLS-SEM analysis fully support the CATTCIM concept that embraces cross-domain AI transfer and interaction with industry. The outcomes of checking the construct validity showed that all constructs fulfilled its necessary criteria. Cronbach's alpha and composite reliability for internal consistency exceeded 0.70 for all constructs under assessment. And the AVE exceeded 0.50, which indicates that the internal consistency was also high enough. The Fornell–Larcker criterion was employed as one of the tools to support the assessment of convergent and discriminant validity.

The results suggest that there are a few underlying connections between the constructs, as shown in most structural models. It emerged that the capability of originating technology matters a great extent in the practice of technology transfer, meaning that it greatly makes sense when such endeavours are carried out in research and innovation, embracing ecosystems where cross-domain AI applications can be applied. Additionally, affirmative links in technology transfer processes and strategic artificial intelligence implementation have been identified, which means that moving such technologies into the organizational strategies is much easier, and the newcomers are more likely to retain them once they are obtained.

The results further revealed the key role of strategic use of artificial intelligence in human-machine interaction, which in turn reveals higher value in organizations aiming at the design of user-friendly and trustworthy AI interfaces. Additionally, the research results emphasized the role of human–AI interaction and its influences on trust in and the use of products related to artificial intelligence. This serves to reiterate the importance of the impending role of interaction design in the construction of the consumption experience for consumers.

Additionally, findings in this study further shed light on the notion of trust, which is that trust in AI mediates part of the effect of interaction quality on consumer adoption, reinforcing the technostress theory that cognitive trust is an intermediate linking mechanism that affects attitudes, intentions, and ensuing behaviours. Moreover, surprisingly, commercial performance also depends on customer adoption quality, and this relationship supports the logic that companies using AI deliver more desirable economic outcomes owing to friendly user interaction as well as the enhancement of other benefits such as customer value, operational performance, and sustainable competitive advantage.

Thus, the estimation of the model's explanatory ability can be counted as significant with the R^2 values presented, representing that a reasonable stretch of the dependent constructs can be elucidated, such as adoption by users and business performance. These findings are further supportive of the CATTCIM framework and suggest that the effective conduct of commercial human-AI interaction is a function of a composite set of strategies of technological collaboration, transfer engagement, and AI design with the user.

7. DISCUSSION

By conducting the current research, the leading aim was to investigate the implications of the cross-domain technology transfer on the various aspects of application relationships of human and artificial intelligence in society and to develop the Cross-Domain AI Technology Transfer and Commercial Interaction Model (CATTCIM). In the same vein, this research is informed by and draws upon a synthesis of various disciplines including but not limited to marketing, information systems, interface design, management of innovations, and strategies of consumers that permit a more in-depth examination of dynamics through which technologies are adopted, strategic applications are made, and a range of perceived functions are performed by AI in relation to society. The results of this study, as a consequence of having carried out PLS-SEM analysis, have considerable evidence in support of the research aim, and the comparative analysis of the multiple hypotheses showed that most of them held, emphasizing the intricate role of technology transfer and user-centric AI design in configuring effective commercial systems.

The results of this investigation are supportive of Hypothesis 1, which postulates that technology creation capability has a positive effect on the implementation of technology transfer mechanisms. This finding points out that the organizations that are endowed with high levels of research and development capabilities, create an environment favourable for innovation and have developed networks of knowledge creation, are much better placed to aid in the transfer of artificial intelligence technologies. This is in agreement with the literature review on innovation management, which points out that the ability to create knowledge and technological capacity is the bottom line of any technology propagation and commercialization.

In the same way, the second hypothesis has been substantiated, implying the critical, yet significant role that technology transfer mechanisms play in the strategic integration of AI within organizations. It is argued that technological knowledge can be exploited across different sectors successfully, enabling the strategic positioning of AI tools in the day-to-day activities, processes, decision support systems, or even customer contact points. On the contrary, businesses that have poor technology transfer capacity are less likely to be successful in those experimental AI technologies and instead serve them for commercial purposes.

Beyond that initial hint, there is also a benefit for endorsing, in terms of the relevant technology levels, hypotheses H3 and H4, which deal with the effect of the technology and strategic integration on the interaction quality of people and AI. The study reveals that the utilization of concepts and applications of higher AI genres across different domains has a direct impact on the improvement of carrier interaction systems to the levels expected by the clients. Moreover, the strategic presence of AI in any scenario helps in reducing the design overhead for organizations to allow them to design AI interfaces that are appealing and dependable for encouraging users to participate. These findings also cater for HCI-based research, which argues that a limited AI system cannot be achieved by looking at great algorithms, but also to the built-in framework of a friendly and responsive AI system.

H5 also has support in this study because the results show that the effective incorporation of empirical AI for commercial barriers has a positive effect on financial efficiency. Firms that apply AI to strategic processing are able to increase the effectiveness of the organization by reducing time and costs spent on certain processes, doing away with single mandates, and increasing efficiency according to the service quality standards. With the increased use of artificial intelligence in any company, it has been able to attain a certain level of sustainable market leadership by leveraging data analytics and the use of efficient service delivery models targeting customers.

In addition to Hypotheses H6 and H7, it is obvious that trust, whether it is human- or AI-driven, very significantly influences the adoption of AI-based services by consumers. The study showed that the effectiveness of human-AI interaction improves the level of trust that users have towards AI, and this leads to willingness the users adopt AI services. This finding confirms previous research in consumer psychology, which emphasizes that confidence is a focal element in the acceptance of any technology and that people are likely to develop trust in automated systems.

Moreover, studies H8 and H9 prove that interaction quality and consumer adoption hold an important position in customer satisfaction and firm-level economic results. However, the findings show us that the companies that come up with readily comprehensible as well as user-friendly AI interfaces will potentially have a greater client acceptance as well as reach higher overall sales or economic benefits. This further indicates that the application success of AI is not only limited to the complexity of the techniques, but is also affected by how satisfying the interaction with users is.

The mediation effect stated is also backed up by the evidence that human AI trust plays a role in linking interaction design and consumer acceptance on a mental level. This further illustrates the need to employ strategies to develop trust, which include transparency, explaining the system, and operating ethically in the realm of artificial intelligence to encourage people to use services powered by AI solutions. Apart from that, the mediating impact of strategic AI integration implies that simple technology transfer will not be enough to help in assimilating the adopted technology into the effective commercial activities of the organization and in management within the organization.

This is, in some ways, influenced by the digital maturity of the market, and its impacts were aggravated in the case of a positive quality of interaction with the internet, namely, the pace of advancement and size of the market. In other words, in more advanced digital areas, people are exposed to AI and what it can do, hence creating the user's profile with positive experiences, which, in turn, facilitates the adoption of AI services. This study is also an indication of how possible the adoption of new ways of learning in the teaching environment is, bearing in mind digital preparedness from a practicing perspective.

8. IMPLICATIONS

8.1 Theoretical Implications

The research, on the theoretical front, contributes to the burgeoning volumes of technology management, innovation, and human–robot interaction education, while proposing a comprehensive interdisciplinary model that cuts across marketing, information systems, and HCI, as well as psychology of the consumer. When technology transfers occur, they are often localized to knowledge transfer from universities and research institutions to industry. The CATTCIM model, however, differs since it foregrounds TD across domains through which AI advances from one domain is altered and adopted into other economic activities.

The conducted work goes on to add value to already existing models by joining the processes of technology transfer with the consequences of the interactions of humans with technology. The current research filled the existing technology gap by including human-machine-interaction quality, user faith, and consumer acceptance. The interdisciplinary synthesis is aimed at bridging the gap of how AI activities progressively change from research, which is innovations backed to commercially optimized products and services.

8.2 Managerial Implications

The strategic importance of efficient technology transfer and intraorganizational integration is also underscored in the case of the managers and corporate heads. To be able to effectively use AI knowledge, businesses must also comprehend how to integrate technological advancements with operational processes and their strategies on how they relate to the customers.

Human–AI interaction is one of the major factors in determining how much consumers trust and adopt the technology. As such, it is recommended that hierarchies are reversed in the adoption of AI Technology and that human-focused AI, user-friendly AI, and socially responsible AI are considered in AI systems design. Managing these practices, such as user-centred design, Legible AI, or Ethical AI, can help to increase the confidence and satisfaction of the customers towards the AI services.

Apart from that, the companies must promote cross-functional collaborations that include engineers, marketers, behaviourists, and user experience designers. When this approach is implemented, the many aspects on the spectrum ensure the software is touchy beyond high technology designation and on the other side, a design meant for the public guided by users' behaviour requirements or the market. On that note, enterprises that fuse rigorous tech skills with consumer focus will be more buoyant with respect to dual competitive frontiers in the AI-infused markets.

8.3 Technological and Innovation Implications

The study also discusses the implications for future AI technology development. Conclusions of this research demonstrate that a strategically integrated transferred technology makes a significant improvement in the quality of all the interactions and the performance of the businesses. This calls upon the need for innovation ecosystems focusing on open innovation, strategic research networks, technology brokerage, etc., which enables the triage of various capabilities in AI across sectors.

Engineers and program managers need to innovate AI platforms that the users will be able to trust by enforcing mechanisms like visibility, accountability, and protection of human rights. As the power of AI is more applied in servicing consumers in fields such as customer care, medical care, finance, e-commerce, and related services, the importance of building trust and user-friendly systems cannot be underestimated, because this distracts consumers.

8.4 Policy Implications

In terms of policy, the research also underlines the justification for the intervention of the government and innovation initiatives towards enabling the movement of technologies between horizontal sectors. This can be achieved through the formation and maintenance of networks for the exchange of knowledge, particularly in the form of joint research activities and pro-innovation gaps, as well as the establishment of research and commercialization programs, i.e., research parks that link universities, firms, and the marketplace.

The study also contributes to the debate by arguing for the role of basic digital infrastructure and digital readiness of a market in the contextualization of the emergence and distribution of AI technologies. Policymakers should enact laws that would promote AI, make obligatory study programmes, and create ethical safeguards for AI that would address social concerns. The enforcement of these developments can boost the integration of advanced technologies across various sectors and increase the welfare of human communities.

9. CONCLUSION

Nonetheless, there is still a gap in understanding how the market is structured, including the consumer's adoption behaviour in industries where there have been significant technological advancements and the most recent and well-regulated consumer protection systems.

Research has shown that having the right technology in place and being able to pass it along the value chain for an organization, including all its member units, is essential for successful strategic AI implementation. Those firms that properly transfer the AI across the areas and integrate the systems have a strategic advantage in creating effective human-AI interaction environments. These interaction design features are instrumental in enhancing trust and use of products by consumers, which in turn increases the satisfaction of the customer, for example. As interactions are direct contributors of revenue, any company that seeks to improve customer satisfaction should focus on interactions; these interactions determine how great satisfaction is going to be.

It is important to note that the study is still figurative and purposed around developing AI for individuals. It is the quality of the provided information, the quality of the participants, and their interactions that matter for the integration of the AI and consumer acceptance. Apart from this, the study also highlights the role of the market digital age in fostering greater acceptance of AI services in more digitally mature settings.

In sum, it is clear that the deployment of AI in business is inextricable from the effective transfer of technology, integration of new technology in existing systems, and the design of the human interface for productive interaction between people and AI. Therefore, the CATTCIM model may become the basis for further investigation and help in sustainably implementing AI-based economic growth in the future.

10. LIMITATIONS AND FUTURE SCOPE

Although it has seen extensive use, it is important to note that this paper has limitations. These limitations are identifiable as moments where more research could be required. First and foremost, one of these limitations is the reliance on survey data alone, or so-called cross-sectional survey data. This mode of study doesn't seem to be very productive since it is difficult to observe innovative experiences during AI technology transfer over the long term. It is recommended in the future to adopt the use of the longitudinal design to track how technologies are transferred across various domains over time. Second, there may be limitations arising from the fact that only perceptions of management and professionals were examined and documented. Validity could be enhanced through the application of hierarchical linear modelling and analysis of instruments in the future. Third, the adoption of AI in a broader commercial context is discussed without delving into the nuances of each industry's adoption. Thus, more focus can be given in the future to the analysis of specific areas, be it healthcare, finance, retail, or manufacturing, with the view of establishing the differences experienced. Furthermore, including factors such as belief and moral causes, and views on the effect of AI-bearing processes on the original attitudes or preferences of the respondents may also be interesting in the CATTCIM framework and in analysing customer behaviour towards services of AI-supported systems.

REFERENCES

Adadi, A., & Berrada, M. (2018). Peeking inside the black-box: A survey on explainable artificial intelligence (XAI). *IEEE Access : Practical Innovations, Open Solutions*, *6*, 52138–52160. DOI: 10.1109/ACCESS.2018.2870052

Agarwal, P., Swami, S., & Malhotra, S. K. (2024). Artificial intelligence adoption in the post COVID-19 new-normal and role of smart technologies in transforming business: A review. *Journal of Science and Technology Policy Management*, *15*(3), 506–529. DOI: 10.1108/JSTPM-08-2021-0122

Ahmed, I., Zhang, Y., Jeon, G., Lin, W., Khosravi, M. R., & Qi, L. (2022). A blockchain-and artificial intelligence-enabled smart IoT framework for sustainable city. *International Journal of Intelligent Systems*, *37*(9), 6493–6507. DOI: 10.1002/int.22852

Aldoseri, A., Al-Khalifa, K. N., & Hamouda, A. M. (2024). AI-powered innovation in digital transformation: Key pillars and industry impact. *Sustainability (Basel)*, *16*(5), 1790. DOI: 10.3390/su16051790

Arenas, J. J., & González, D. (2018). Technology transfer models and elements in the university-industry collaboration. *Administrative Sciences*, *8*(2), 19. DOI: 10.3390/admsci8020019

Arora, S., & Thota, S. R. (2024). Using artificial intelligence with big data analytics for targeted marketing campaigns. *International Journal of Advanced Research in Science. Tongxin Jishu*, *4*(3), 593–602.

Bader, V., & Kaiser, S. (2019). Algorithmic decision-making? The user interface and its role for human involvement in decisions supported by artificial intelligence. *Organization*, *26*(5), 655–672. DOI: 10.1177/1350508419855714

Bano, R., Azim, F., Mahmood, Z., Sanaullah, A., & Ali, O. (2025). The role of artificial intelligence in personalized marketing: Enhancing customer experience, predictive targeting, and brand engagement. *The Critical Review of Social Sciences Studies*, *3*(2), 50–65. DOI: 10.59075/d94kvf44

Bozeman, B. (2000). Technology transfer and public policy: A review of research and theory. *Research Policy*, *29*(4-5), 627–655. DOI: 10.1016/S0048-7333(99)00093-1

Burström, T., Parida, V., Lahti, T., & Wincent, J. (2021). AI-enabled business-model innovation and transformation in industrial ecosystems: A framework, model and outline for further research. *Journal of Business Research*, *127*, 85–95. DOI: 10.1016/j.jbusres.2021.01.016

Burström, T., Parida, V., Lahti, T., & Wincent, J. (2021). AI-enabled business-model innovation and transformation in industrial ecosystems: A framework, model and outline for further research. *Journal of Business Research, 127*, 85–95. DOI: 10.1016/j.jbusres.2021.01.016

Car, J., Sheikh, A., Wicks, P., & Williams, M. S. (2019). Beyond the hype of big data and artificial intelligence: Building foundations for knowledge and wisdom. *BMC Medicine, 17*(1), 143. DOI: 10.1186/s12916-019-1382-x PMID: 31311603

Chandra, S., Shirish, A., & Srivastava, S. C. (2022). To be or not to be… human? Theorizing the role of human-like competencies in conversational artificial intelligence agents. *Journal of Management Information Systems, 39*(4), 969–1005. DOI: 10.1080/07421222.2022.2127441

Chui, M., & Francisco, S. (2017). Artificial intelligence the next digital frontier. *McKinsey and Company Global Institute, 47*(3.6), 6-8.

Daniel, A. D., & Alves, L. (2020). University-industry technology transfer: The commercialization of university's patents. *Knowledge Management Research and Practice, 18*(3), 276–296. DOI: 10.1080/14778238.2019.1638741

Davenport, T. H., & Ronanki, R. (2018). Artificial intelligence for the real world. *Harvard Business Review, 96*(1), 108–116.

Debackere, K., & Veugelers, R. (2005). The role of academic technology transfer organizations in improving industry science links. *Research Policy, 34*(3), 321–342. DOI: 10.1016/j.respol.2004.12.003

Ferrario, A., Loi, M., & Viganò, E. (2020). In AI we trust incrementally: A multi-layer model of trust to analyze human-artificial intelligence interactions. *Philosophy & Technology, 33*(3), 523–539. DOI: 10.1007/s13347-019-00378-3

Ghosh, S. (2025). Developing artificial intelligence (AI) capabilities for data-driven business model innovation: Roles of organizational adaptability and leadership. *Journal of Engineering and Technology Management, 75*, 101851. DOI: 10.1016/j.jengtecman.2024.101851

Glikson, E., & Woolley, A. W. (2020). Human trust in artificial intelligence: Review of empirical research. *The Academy of Management Annals, 14*(2), 627–660. DOI: 10.5465/annals.2018.0057

Hammad, A., & Abu-Zaid, R. (2024). Applications of AI in decentralized computing systems: Harnessing artificial intelligence for enhanced scalability, efficiency, and autonomous decision-making in distributed architectures. *Applied Research in Artificial Intelligence and Cloud Computing, 7*(6), 161–187.

Huang, M. H., & Rust, R. T. (2018). Artificial intelligence in service. *Journal of Service Research, 21*(2), 155–172. DOI: 10.1177/1094670517752459

Jin, W., & Zhao, B. (2025). *Cross-Domain Knowledge Transfer in Large Models: Transforming Knowledge Management Dynamics*. IntechOpen.

Lambooy, J. (2004). The transmission of knowledge, emerging networks, and the role of universities: An evolutionary approach. *European Planning Studies, 12*(5), 643–657. DOI: 10.1080/0965431042000219996

Lee, Y. L., & Song, S. (2010). An empirical investigation of electronic word-of-mouth: Informational motive and corporate response strategy. *Computers in Human Behavior, 26*(5), 1073–1080. DOI: 10.1016/j.chb.2010.03.009

Lee, Y. S. (1996). 'Technology transfer' and the research university: A search for the boundaries of university-industry collaboration. *Research Policy, 25*(6), 843–863. DOI: 10.1016/0048-7333(95)00857-8

McAfee, A., & Brynjolfsson, E. (2017). *Machine, platform, crowd: Harnessing our digital future*. WW Norton & Company.

McAfee, A., & Brynjolfsson, E. (2017). *Machine, platform, crowd: Harnessing our digital future*. WW Norton & Company.

Mhaskey, S. V. (2024). Integration of artificial intelligence (AI) in enterprise resource planning (ERP) systems: Opportunities, challenges, and implications. *International Journal of Computer Engineering in Research Trends, 11*(12), 1–9. DOI: 10.22362/ijcert/2024/v11/i12/v11i1201

Naimi-Sadigh, A., Asgari, T., & Rabiei, M. (2022). Digital transformation in the value chain disruption of banking services. *Journal of the Knowledge Economy, 13*(2), 1212–1242. DOI: 10.1007/s13132-021-00759-0

Nambisan, S., Lyytinen, K., Majchrzak, A., & Song, M. (2017). Digital innovation management: Reinventing innovation management research in a digital world. *Management Information Systems Quarterly, 41*(1), 223–238. DOI: 10.25300/MISQ/2017/41:1.03

Nooteboom, B. (2003). Problems and solutions in knowledge transfer. In *Cooperation, networks and institutions in regional innovation systems* (pp. 105–127). Edward Elgar Publishing. DOI: 10.4337/9781035304752.00013

Oyekunle, D., & Boohene, D. (2024). Digital transformation potential: The role of artificial intelligence in business. *International Journal of Professional Business Review: Int. J. Prof. Bus. Rev., 9*(3), 1.

Rai, A., Constantinides, P., & Sarker, S. (2019). Editor's comments: Next-generation digital platforms: Toward human–AI hybrids. *Management Information Systems Quarterly*, *43*(1), iii–ix. DOI: 10.25300/MISQ/2019/431E0

Sarstedt, M., Ringle, C. M., & Hair, J. F. (2021). Partial least squares structural equation modeling. In *Handbook of market research* (pp. 587–632). Springer International Publishing. DOI: 10.1007/978-3-319-05542-8_15-2

Secundo, G., Spilotro, C., Gast, J., & Corvello, V. (2025). The transformative power of artificial intelligence within innovation ecosystems: A review and a conceptual framework. *Review of Managerial Science*, *19*(9), 2697–2728. DOI: 10.1007/s11846-024-00828-z

Secundo, G., Spilotro, C., Gast, J., & Corvello, V. (2025). The transformative power of artificial intelligence within innovation ecosystems: A review and a conceptual framework. *Review of Managerial Science*, *19*(9), 2697–2728. DOI: 10.1007/s11846-024-00828-z

Shin, D. (2021). The effects of explainability and causability on perception, trust, and acceptance: Implications for explainable AI. *International Journal of Human-Computer Studies*, *146*, 102551. DOI: 10.1016/j.ijhcs.2020.102551

Siegel, D. S., Waldman, D., & Link, A. (2003). Assessing the impact of organizational practices on the relative productivity of university technology transfer offices: An exploratory study. *Research Policy*, *32*(1), 27–48. DOI: 10.1016/S0048-7333(01)00196-2

Teece, D. J. (2018). Business models and dynamic capabilities. *Long Range Planning*, *51*(1), 40–49. DOI: 10.1016/j.lrp.2017.06.007

Van Der Vlist, F., Helmond, A., & Ferrari, F. (2024). Big AI: Cloud infrastructure dependence and the industrialisation of artificial intelligence. *Big Data & Society*, *11*(1), 20539517241232630. DOI: 10.1177/20539517241232630

Ystgaard, K. F., Atzori, L., Palma, D., Heegaard, P. E., Bertheussen, L. E., Jensen, M. R., & De Moor, K. (2023). Review of the theory, principles, and design requirements of human-centric Internet of Things (IoT). *Journal of Ambient Intelligence and Humanized Computing*, *14*(3), 2827–2859. DOI: 10.1007/s12652-023-04539-3

Compilation of References

A'yun, A. Q., & Setyaningsih, W. (2025). Consumer Empowerment Through Ethical AI: Strategies for Transparent and Trustworthy Personalized Marketing. *Journal of Marketing Breakthroughs*, *1*(1), 1–12. DOI: 10.70764/gdpu-jmb.2025.1(1)-01

Abate, Y. A., Ukpabi, D. C., & Karjaluoto, H. (2025). Investigating digital marketing readiness among tourism firms: An emerging economy perspective. *Current Issues in Tourism*, *28*(13), 2153–2172. DOI: 10.1080/13683500.2024.2358047

Abootorabi, M. M., Ghahroodi, O., Zahraei, P. S., Behzadasl, H., Mirrokni, A., Salimipanah, M., Rasouli, A., Behzadipour, B., Azarnoush, S., & Maleki, B. (2025). Generative AI for character animation: A comprehensive survey of techniques, applications, and future directions. *ArXiv Preprint ArXiv:2504.19056*.

Abrardi, L., Cambini, C., & Rondi, L. (2022). Artificial intelligence, firms and consumer behavior: A survey. *Journal of Economic Surveys*, *36*(4), 969–991. DOI: 10.1111/joes.12455

Acatrinei, C., Apostol, I. G., Barbu, L. N., Chivu, R. G., & Orzan, M. C. (2025). Artificial intelligence in digital marketing: Enhancing consumer engagement and supporting sustainable behavior through social and mobile networks. *Sustainability*, *17*(14), 6638. DOI: 10.3390/su17146638

Acharya, R. A., & Pednekar, A. P. (2024). Digital literacy and its impact on consumer behaviour towards m-commerce adoption in India: A study. *Journal of Digital Economy*, *3*(1), 48–60.

Acikgoz, F., Stylos, N., & Lythreatis, S. (2024). Identifying capabilities and constraints in utilizing blockchain technology in hospitality and tourism. *International Journal of Contemporary Hospitality Management*, *36*(10), 3493–3514. DOI: 10.1108/IJCHM-07-2023-1083

Adadi, A., & Berrada, M. (2018). Peeking inside the black-box: A survey on explainable artificial intelligence (XAI). *IEEE Access : Practical Innovations, Open Solutions, 6*, 52138–52160. DOI: 10.1109/ACCESS.2018.2870052

Adam, M., Wessel, M., & Benlian, A. (2021). AI-based chatbots in customer service and their effects on user compliance. *Electronic Markets, 31*(2), 427–445. DOI: 10.1007/s12525-020-00414-7

Adamopoulou, E., & Moussiades, L. (2020, May). An overview of chatbot technology. In *IFIP international conference on artificial intelligence applications and innovations* (pp. 373–383). Springer International Publishing., DOI: 10.1007/978-3-030-49186-4_31

Adebayo, P. O., Osanyinlusi, G. E., & Adekeye, A. O. (2023). Does consumer empowerment influence e-payment systems adoption? A digital consumer-centric perspective. *Journal of Financial Services Marketing*. Advance online publication. DOI: 10.1057/s41264-023-00238-4

Adee, S. (2020). What are deepfakes and how are they created? *IEEE Spectrum*, •••, 29.

Afshar, M. Z., & Shah, M. H. (2025). Leveraging Porter's diamond model: Public sector insights. *The Critical Review of Social Sciences Studies, 3*(2), 2255-2271. https://doi.org/, Corpus ID: 279474427DOI: 10.59075/kkteax93

Agarwal, N. (2024). Conceptual Framework for E-commerce Success: Consumer Behaviour and AI-Enhanced Digital Marketing. *MOSAIC OF IDEAS: MULTIDISCIPLINARY REFLECTIONS, 241*.

Agarwal, S., Farid, H., Gu, Y., He, M., Nagano, K., & Li, H. (2019). Protecting world leaders against deep fakes. *CVPR Workshops, 1*(38).

Agarwal, P., Swami, S., & Malhotra, S. K. (2024). Artificial intelligence adoption in the post COVID-19 new-normal and role of smart technologies in transforming business: A review. *Journal of Science and Technology Policy Management, 15*(3), 506–529. DOI: 10.1108/JSTPM-08-2021-0122

Aguirre, E., Roggeveen, A. L., Grewal, D., & Wetzels, M. (2016). The personalization–privacy paradox. *Journal of Retailing, 92*(1), 34–49. DOI: 10.1016/j.jretai.2014.09.005

Ahmed, I., Zhang, Y., Jeon, G., Lin, W., Khosravi, M. R., & Qi, L. (2022). A blockchain-and artificial intelligence-enabled smart IoT framework for sustainable city. *International Journal of Intelligent Systems, 37*(9), 6493–6507. DOI: 10.1002/int.22852

Akdemir, D. M., & Bulut, Z. A. (2024). Business and customer-based chatbot activities: The role of customer satisfaction in online purchase intention and intention to reuse chatbots. *Journal of Theoretical and Applied Electronic Commerce Research, 19*(4), 2961–2979. DOI: 10.3390/jtaer19040142

Akhtar, M. J., & Nagvanshi, S. (2025). Parasocial Interaction and Virtual Influencers: Building Connections in a Digital World. In *Redefining the Future of Digital Marketing With Virtual Influencers* (pp. 151–180). IGI Global Scientific Publishing.

Akhtar, N., Hameed, Z., Islam, T., Pant, M. K., Sharma, A., Rather, R. A., & Kuzior, A. (2024). Avatars of influence: Understanding how virtual influencers trigger consumer engagement on online booking platforms. *Journal of Retailing and Consumer Services, 78*, 103742. DOI: 10.1016/j.jretconser.2024.103742

Alam, A. (2025). Ethical challenges and bias in ai-driven marketing: Educational imperatives and policy perspectives. In *Impacts of AI-Generated Content on Brand Reputation* (pp. 55–108). IGI Global Scientific Publishing. DOI: 10.4018/979-8-3373-4327-3.ch003

Alam, S. (2025). Exploring success variables of knowledge management for enhanced organisational performance: An integrated framework. *Knowledge Management Research and Practice*, •••, 1–29. DOI: 10.1080/14778238.2025.2550304

Alam, S., Islam, K. A., Miah, M. R., Afrin, S., Islam, M. A., Hoque, M. R., & Mahmud, I. (2025). Key success factors of knowledge management systems for optimizing organizational performance: A PRISMA-based systematic literature review. *Heliyon, 11*(16), e44097. DOI: 10.1016/j.heliyon.2025.e44097

Alanazi, S., Asif, S., Caird-Daley, A., & Moulitsas, I. (2025). Unmasking deepfakes: a multidisciplinary examination of social impacts and regulatory responses. *Human-Intelligent Systems Integration*, 1–23.

Aldoseri, A., Al-Khalifa, K. N., & Hamouda, A. M. (2024). AI-powered innovation in digital transformation: Key pillars and industry impact. *Sustainability (Basel), 16*(5), 1790. DOI: 10.3390/su16051790

Alhiniti, Y., & Al-Masry, W. A. M. A. (2026). E-Commerce and Legal Practices: An Examination of Legislation and Challenges Related to Digital Activities. In Business Resilience and Business Innovation for Sustainability: The Double-Edged Role of Artificial Intelligence and Other Disruptive Technologies (pp. 2649-2663).

Alibašić, H. (2025). Harmonizing artificial intelligence (AI) governance: A comparative analysis of Singapore and France's AI policies and the influence of international organizations. *Global Public Policy and Governance 2025 5:2, 5*(2), 93–113. DOI: 10.1007/s43508-025-00116-w

Alijoyo, F. A., Aziz, T. S. A., Omer, N., Yusuf, N., Kumar, M. D., Ramesh, A. V. N., & El-Ebiary, Y. A. B. (2025). Personalized marketing: Leveraging AI for culturally aware segmentation and targeting. *Alexandria Engineering Journal, 119*, 8–21. DOI: 10.1016/j.aej.2025.01.074

Al-Kfairy, M., Mustafa, D., Kshetri, N., Insiew, M., & Alfandi, O. (2024). Ethical challenges and solutions of generative AI: An interdisciplinary perspective. *Informatics (MDPI), 11*(3), 58. DOI: 10.3390/informatics11030058

Allal-Chérif, O., Puertas, R., & Carracedo, P. (2024). Intelligent influencer marketing: How AI-powered virtual influencers outperform human influencers. *Technological Forecasting and Social Change, 200*, 123113. DOI: 10.1016/j.techfore.2023.123113

Allal-Chérif, O., Simón-Moya, V., & Ballester, A. C. C. (2021). Intelligent purchasing: How artificial intelligence can redefine the purchasing function. *Journal of Business Research, 124*, 69–76. DOI: 10.1016/j.jbusres.2020.11.050

Altuncu, E., Franqueira, V. N. L., & Li, S. (2024). Deepfake: Definitions, performance metrics and standards, datasets, and a meta-review. *Frontiers in Big Data, 7*, 1400024. DOI: 10.3389/fdata.2024.1400024

Aluri, A., Price, B. S., & McIntyre, N. H. (2019). Using machine learning to co-create value through dynamic customer engagement in a brand loyalty program. *Journal of Hospitality & Tourism Research (Washington, D.C.), 43*(1), 78–100. DOI: 10.1177/1096348017753521

Alzoubi, H. M., Shameem, B., Mushtaq, S., Al Kurdi, B., Joghee, S., & Hamadneh, S. (2025). Unveiling the role of artificial intelligence: Navigating personalized content marketing, customer engagement, and commitment with data transparency and security. *International Review of Management and Marketing, 15*(2), 343–355. DOI: 10.32479/irmm.18499

Amini, R., & Amini, A. (2024). An overview of artificial intelligence and its application in marketing with focus on large language models. *International Journal of Science and Research Archive, 12*(2), 455–465. DOI: 10.30574/ijsra.2024.12.2.1223

Amin, M. R. M., Asbi, A., Sivakumaran, V. M., Kim, J., & Septiarini, E. (2025). Artificial Intelligence (AI) adoption in marketing strategies: Navigating the present and shaping the future business landscape. *Social Sciences & Humanities Open, 12*, 102048. DOI: 10.1016/j.ssaho.2025.102048

Amomo, C. (2023). *Countering IoT-Based Cyber-Physical Manipulation: A Framework for National Resilience Against Systemic Disruption.* https://www.researchgate.net/profile/Clifford-Amomo/publication/397780031_Countering_IoT-Based_Cyber-Physical_Manipulation_A_Framework_for_National_Resilience_Against_Systemic_Disruption/links/691e7d9c19b35058639b52a9/Countering-IoT-Based-Cyber-Physical-Manipulation-A-Framework-for-National-Resilience-Against-Systemic-Disruption.pdf

Anam, A. S. M. T., Bhuiyan, M. R. I., Islam, S., Ullah, M. N., &Rakib, M. A. A. (2026). Factors influencing university students' adoption of online education platforms in Bangladesh: an extended TAM-based analysis. *Educational and Developmental Psychologist*, 1–17. DOI: 10.1080/20590776.2026.2619742

Anand, V., Das, A., & Chandawat, D. (2026). *Securing Large Language Models: Adversarial Attacks, Data Privacy, and Artificial Intelligence Safety.* https://books.google.com/books?hl=en&lr=&id=S2XBEQAAQBAJ&oi=fnd&pg=PA1&dq=mandatory+watermarking+for+synthetic+media+and+third-party+audits+for+high-risk+targeting+models+&ots=5yLFFQlYb1&sig=e60Odg3lwIBG29YBn5A6VU_ZHk0

Anderson, J. (2025). Leveraging Explainable AI to Enhance Consumer Insight Models in Real-Time Surveys. *International Journal of Emerging Research in Engineering and Technology*, 102-112. DOI: 10.63282/3050-922X.ICRCEDA25-113

Ansari, A., Essegaier, S., & Kohli, R. (2000). Internet recommendation systems. *JMR, Journal of Marketing Research, 37*(3), 363–375. DOI: 10.1509/jmkr.37.3.363.18779

Arango, L., Singaraju, S. P., & Niininen, O. (2023). Consumer Responses to AI-Generated Charitable Giving Ads. *Journal of Advertising, 52*(4), 486–503. DOI: 10.1080/00913367.2023.2183285

Araujo, T. (2018). Living up to the chatbot hype: The influence of anthropomorphic design cues and communicative agency framing on conversational agent and company perceptions. *Computers in Human Behavior, 85*, 183–189. DOI: 10.1016/j.chb.2018.03.051

Arenas, J. J., & González, D. (2018). Technology transfer models and elements in the university-industry collaboration. *Administrative Sciences, 8*(2), 19. DOI: 10.3390/admsci8020019

Argyriou, E., & Melewar, T. (2011). Consumer Attitudes Revisited: A Review of Attitude Theory in Marketing Research. *International Journal of Management Reviews*, *13*(4), 431–451. DOI: 10.1111/j.1468-2370.2011.00299.x

Armutcu, B., Tan, A., Amponsah, M., Parida, S., & Ramkissoon, H. (2023). Tourist behaviour: The role of digital marketing and social media. *Acta Psychologica*, *240*, 104025. https://doi.org/https://doi.org/10.1016/j.actpsy.2023.104025. DOI: 10.1016/j.actpsy.2023.104025 PMID: 37741033

Arora, N., Dreze, X., Ghose, A., Hess, J. D., Iyengar, R., Jing, B., Joshi, Y., Kumar, V., Lurie, N., Neslin, S., Sajeesh, S., Su, M., Syam, N., Thomas, J., & Zhang, Z. J. (2008). Putting one-to-one marketing to work: Personalization, customization, and choice. *Marketing Letters*, *19*(3), 305–321. https://ssrn.com/abstract=1118822. DOI: 10.1007/s11002-008-9056-z

Arora, S., & Thota, S. R. (2024). Using artificial intelligence with big data analytics for targeted marketing campaigns. *International Journal of Advanced Research in Science. Tongxin Jishu*, *4*(3), 593–602.

Arrieta, A. B., Díaz-Rodríguez, N., Del Ser, J., Bennetot, A., Tabik, S., Barbado, A., García, S., Gil-López, S., Molina, D., Benjamins, R., Chatila, R., & Herrera, F. (2020). Explainable Artificial Intelligence (XAI): Concepts, taxonomies, opportunities and challenges toward responsible AI. *Information Fusion*, *58*, 82–115. DOI: 10.1016/j.inffus.2019.12.012

Arsenyan, J., & Mirowska, A. (2021). Almost human? A comparative case study on the social media presence of virtual influencers. *International Journal of Human Computer Studies, 155*(July 2020), 102694. DOI: 10.1016/j.ijhcs.2021.102694

Arshad, N., Baber, M. U., & Ullah, A. (2024). Assessing the transformative influence of ChatGPT on research practices among scholars in Pakistan. *Mesopotamian Journal of Big Data*, *2024*(1), 1–10. DOI: 10.58496/MJBD/2024/001

Arya, V., Saraf, A., Chichkanov, N., Papa, A., & Romano, M. (2026). AI-enhanced competency transfer hubs: A conceptual framework for university-industry engagement and knowledge sharing. *The Journal of Technology Transfer*, 51 682–712. DOI: 10.1007/s10961-025-10233-7

Audrezet, A., & Koles, B. (2023). Virtual Influencer as a Brand Avatar in Interactive Marketing. In *The Palgrave handbook of Interactive Marketing* (pp. 353–376). Springer., DOI: 10.1007/978-3-031-14961-0_16

Awad, A. (2024). Artificial intelligence and marketing innovation: The mediating role of organizational culture. *Innovative Marketing*, *20*(3), 170–181. DOI: 10.21511/im.20(3).2024.14

Ayertey, S., Panditharathna, R., Mohamad, M., & Laryeafio, M. N. (2026). Generative AI as a Digital Influencer on Visual Content Marketing: The Ethical Dilemma. In *Strategies, Dynamics, and Societal Impacts of Digital Influencer Marketing* (pp. 159–174). IGI Global Scientific Publishing.

Aykaç, Ö. S. (2025). Digital Customer Experience and Personalization. *Online Retail Marketing Practice: Technology, Operations, and Globalization*, 1.

Babatunde, S. O., Odejide, O. A., Edunjobi, T. E., & Ogundipe, D. O. (2024). The role of AI in marketing personalization: A theoretical exploration of consumer engagement strategies. *International Journal of Management & Entrepreneurship Research*, *6*(3), 936–949. DOI: 10.51594/ijmer.v6i3.964

Baberwal, S. K., Shelke, N. A., & Anwar, K. (2025). Systematic review of recent advances in multimodal sentiment analysis. *Discover Computing*, *28*(1), 270. DOI: 10.1007/s10791-025-09727-7

Bader, V., & Kaiser, S. (2019). Algorithmic decision-making? The user interface and its role for human involvement in decisions supported by artificial intelligence. *Organization*, *26*(5), 655–672. DOI: 10.1177/1350508419855714

Bahangulu, J. K., & Owusu-Berko, L. (2025). Algorithmic bias, data ethics, and governance: Ensuring fairness, transparency and compliance in AI-powered business analytics applications. *World Journal of Advanced Research and Review*, *25*(2), 1746–1763. DOI: 10.30574/wjarr.2025.25.2.0571

Bai, B., Vignali, G., Ryding, D., & Vazquez, D. (2025). Exploring the Impact of Para-Social Interaction: The Consumer Journey in a Social Media World with a Focus on Virtual Influencers. In *Contemporary Issues in Social Media Marketing* (pp. 152–170). Routledge.

Bai, S., Zhang, W., & Yu, D. (2024). Uncovering effects of virtual endorser's attractiveness on consumer behaviors from the perspective of national culture. *Current Psychology*, *43*(34), 27534–27547. DOI: 10.1007/s12144-024-06397-4

Bai, Y., Xue, Z., Zhang, M., Tan, Q., & Li, Y. (2025). Voices that captivate: The impact of AI-generated voiceover on video Ad engagement. *International Journal of Information Management*, *85*, 102962. DOI: 10.1016/j.ijinfomgt.2025.102962

Bajwa, M. T. T., Tehreem, F., Farid, Z., Tahir, H. M. F., & Khalid, A. (2025). Deepfake voice recognition: Techniques, organizational risks and ethical implications. *Spectrum of Engineering Sciences*, 106–121.

Balasubramaniam, N., Kauppinen, M., Rannisto, A., Hiekkanen, K., & Kujala, S. (2023). Transparency and explainability of AI systems: From ethical guidelines to requirements. *Information and Software Technology*, *159*, 107197. DOI: 10.1016/j.infsof.2023.107197

Bano, R., Azim, F., Mahmood, Z., Sanaullah, A., & Ali, O. (2025). The role of artificial intelligence in personalized marketing: Enhancing customer experience, predictive targeting, and brand engagement. *The Critical Review of Social Sciences Studies*, *3*(2), 50–65. DOI: 10.59075/d94kvf44

Bar-Gill, O., Sunstein, C. R., & Talgam-Cohen, I. (2023). Algorithmic harm in consumer markets. *The Journal of Legal Analysis*, *15*(1), 1–47. DOI: 10.1093/jla/laad003

Baron, S. (2025). Trust, explainability and AI. *Philosophy & Technology*, *38*(1), 4. DOI: 10.1007/s13347-024-00837-6

Baryshkov, K., Kuzina, Y., Smuk, I., & Tkachuk, M. (2026). Consumer Trust in AI-Generated Marketing Content: A Systematic Literature Review and Research Agenda. *American Impact Review*, *1*(1), e2026024–e2026024. DOI: 10.66308/air.e2026024

Basumatary, M., & Sarma, G. (2025). Tourism marketing strategies and plans: A systematic literature review. *Corporate and Business Strategy Review*, *6*(2), 40–51. DOI: 10.22495/cbsrv6i2art4

Baycan, T., & Stough, R. (2013). Bridging knowledge to commercialization: the good, the bad, and the challenging. *Springer, 50*(2), 367–405. DOI: 10.1007/s00168-012-0510-8

BCG. (2026). Consumers Trust AI to Buy Better. Brands Need to Move Quickly. Available at: https://www.bcg.com/publications/2026/consumers-trust-ai-to-buy-better-brands-must-adapt

Bec, A., Moyle, B., Timms, K., Schaffer, V., Skavronskaya, L., & Little, C. (2019). Management of immersive heritage tourism experiences: A conceptual model. *Tourism Management*, *72*, 117–120. DOI: 10.1016/j.tourman.2018.10.033

Becan, C., &Çeber, B. (2025). How technology readiness influences behavioral and purchasing intention: serial multiple mediating role of attitude toward AI and AI-driven consumer chatbot experience. *Digital Transformation and Society*, 1-27. DOI: 10.1108/DTS-04-2025-0082

Belanche, D., Casaló, L. V., & Flavián, M. (2024). Human versus virtual influences, a comparative study. *Journal of Business Research, 173*, 114493. DOI: 10.1016/j.jbusres.2023.114493

Beldad, A., de Jong, M., & Steehouder, M. (2010). How shall I trust the faceless and the intangible? A literature review on the antecedents of online trust. *Computers in Human Behavior,* 26(5), 857–869. DOI: 10.1016/j.chb.2010.03.013

Beltrán, M. (2025). AI algorithms under scrutiny: GDPR, DSA, AI Act and CRA as pillars for algorithmic security and privacy in the European Union. *Computers & Security*, *158*(2), 104628. DOI: 10.1016/j.cose.2025.104628

Bennett, H., & Durkin, M. (2000). The effects of organisational change on employee psychological attachment An exploratory study. *Journal of Managerial Psychology*, *15*(2), 126–146. DOI: 10.1108/02683940010310328

Beyari, H., & Garamoun, H. (2022). The effect of artificial intelligence on end-user online purchasing decisions: Toward an integrated conceptual framework. *Sustainability (Basel)*, *14*(15), 9637. DOI: 10.3390/su14159637

Bhardwaj, S., & Rastogi, S. (2025). *Artificial Intelligence and Deep Learning*. https://books.google.com/books?hl=en&lr=&id=OiRiEQAAQBAJ&oi=fnd&pg=PP1&dq=The+fundamental+problem+in+AI-driven+marketing+is+the+interpretability+gap,+where+deep+learning+models,+particularly+those+used+in+real-time+programmatic+bidding+and+sentiment+analysis,+operate+as+black+boxes.+&ots=Mg6oG5cUYP&sig=obyaRcEe7w-SV6F5yM-EJcdEZU4

Bhardwaj, S., Sharma, N., Goel, M., Sharma, K., & Verma, V. (2024). Enhancing customer targeting in e-commerce and digital marketing through AI-driven personalization strategies. *Advances in Digital Marketing in the Era of Artificial Intelligence*, 41-60.

Bhuiyan, M. R. I., Husain, T., Islam, S., & Amin, A. (2025). Exploring the prospective influence of artificial intelligence on the health sector in Bangladesh: A study on awareness, perception and adoption. *Health Education, 125*(3), 279–297. DOI: 10.1108/HE-10-2024-0125

Binns, R., Veale, M., Van Kleek, M., & Shadbolt, N. (2018). 'It's reducing a human being to a percentage': Perceptions of justice in algorithmic decisions. *Proceedings of the 2018 CHI Conference on Human Factors in Computing Systems,* 1–14. DOI: 10.1145/3173574.3173951

Bleier, A., Harmeling, C. M., & Palmatier, R. W. (2019). Creating effective online customer experiences. *Journal of Marketing*, *83*(2), 98–119. DOI: 10.1177/0022242918809930

Bohara, S. (2024). Deepfake Marketing. *Deepfakes and Their Impact on Business*, 123.

Bohr, A., & Memarzadeh, K. (2020). *Remote patient monitoring using artificial intelligence*. Elsevier., DOI: 10.1016/B978-0-12-818438-7.00002-2

Boldosova, V. (2020). Telling stories that sell: The role of storytelling and big data analytics in smart service sales. *Industrial Marketing Management*, *86*, 122–134. DOI: 10.1016/j.indmarman.2019.12.004

Bozdağ, A. A. (2025). The AI-mediated intimacy economy: A paradigm shift in digital interactions. *AI & Society*, *40*(4), 2285–2306. DOI: 10.1007/s00146-024-02132-6

Bozeman, B. (2000). Technology transfer and public policy: A review of research and theory. *Research Policy*, *29*(4-5), 627–655. DOI: 10.1016/S0048-7333(99)00093-1

Bozkurt, S., Uğursoy, A. S., & Meral, S. P. (2025). The Impact of Personalized Messages and Designs on Consumer Experiences and Marketing Communications in Technology: Hyper-Personalization. In *Impact of Contemporary Technology on Art and Design* (pp. 135–164). IGI Global., DOI: 10.4018/979-8-3693-4318-0.ch007

Breves, P. L., & van Berlo, Z. M. C. (2025). Making and breaking parasocial relationships with human and virtual influencers: An experience sampling study. *Media Psychology*, •••, 1–29. DOI: 10.1080/15213269.2025.2558029

Brown, T. B., Mann, B., Ryder, N., Subbiah, M., Kaplan, J., Dhariwal, P., Neelakantan, A., Shyam, P., Sastry, G., Askell, A., Agarwal, S., Herbert-Voss, A., Krueger, G., Henighan, T., Child, R., Ramesh, A., Ziegler, D. M., Wu, J., Winter, C., & Amodei, D. (2020). Language models are few-shot learners. *Advances in Neural Information Processing Systems*, *33*, 1877–1901.

Buchan, M. C., Bhawra, J., & Katapally, T. R. (2024). Navigating the digital world: Development of an evidence-based digital literacy program and assessment tool for youth. *Smart Learning Environments*, *11*(1), 8. DOI: 10.1186/s40561-024-00293-x

Buhalis, D., & Amaranggana, A. (2014). Smart tourism destinations enhancing tourism experience through personalisation of services. *Information and Communication Technologies in Tourism 2015: Proceedings of the International Conference in Lugano,* Switzerland, February 3-6, 2015, 377–389.

Buhalis, D., Harwood, T., Bogicevic, V., Viglia, G., Beldona, S., & Hofacker, C. (2019). Technological disruptions in services: Lessons from tourism and hospitality. *Journal of Service Management, 30*(4), 484–506. DOI: 10.1108/JOSM-12-2018-0398

Buhalis, D., & Law, R. (2008). Progress in information technology and tourism management: 20 years on and 10 years after the Internet—The state of eTourism research. *Tourism Management, 29*(4), 609–623. DOI: 10.1016/j.tourman.2008.01.005

Burström, T., Parida, V., Lahti, T., & Wincent, J. (2021). AI-enabled business-model innovation and transformation in industrial ecosystems: A framework, model and outline for further research. *Journal of Business Research, 127,* 85–95. DOI: 10.1016/j.jbusres.2021.01.016

Bushara, M. A., Abdou, A. H., Hassan, T. H., Sobaih, A. E. E., Albohnayh, A. S. M., Alshammari, W. G., Aldoreeb, M., Elsaed, A. A., & Elsaied, M. A. (2023). Power of social media marketing: How perceived value mediates the impact on restaurant followers' purchase intention, willingness to pay a premium price, and E-WoM? *Sustainability (Basel), 15*(6), 5331. DOI: 10.3390/su15065331

Camilleri, M. A. (2024). Artificial intelligence governance: Ethical considerations and implications for social responsibility. *Expert Systems: International Journal of Knowledge Engineering and Neural Networks, 41*(7), e13406. DOI: 10.1111/exsy.13406

Campbell, C., Plangger, K., Sands, S., & Kietzmann, J. (2022). Preparing for an era of deepfakes and AI-generated ads: A framework for understanding responses to manipulated advertising. *Journal of Advertising, 51*(1), 22–38. DOI: 10.1080/00913367.2021.1909515

Car, J., Sheikh, A., Wicks, P., & Williams, M. S. (2019). Beyond the hype of big data and artificial intelligence: Building foundations for knowledge and wisdom. *BMC Medicine, 17*(1), 143. DOI: 10.1186/s12916-019-1382-x PMID: 31311603

Carr, T., Ross, L., & Arrison, M. G. (2025). The Role of AI in Enhancing Customer Trust and Relationship Management in Digital-Only Banks. *Available at SSRN* 5441894. DOI: 10.2139/ssrn.5441894

Cetinkaya, N. E.. (2025). Between transparency and trust: Identifying key factors in algorithmic trust. *Information Systems Journal*. Advance online publication. DOI: 10.1080/0144929X.2025.2533358

Chae, M.-J., & Kim, M. (2026). Too human to trust? How AI human-likeness and context orientation shape consumer preferences in premium high-tech markets. *Journal of Retailing and Consumer Services*, *88*, 104513. DOI: 10.1016/j.jretconser.2025.104513

Chaiken, S. (1980). Heuristic versus systematic information processing and the use of source versus message cues in persuasion. *Journal of Personality and Social Psychology*, *39*(5), 752–766. DOI: 10.1037/0022-3514.39.5.752

Chaisatitkul, A., Luangngamkhum, K., Noulpum, K., & Kerdvibulvech, C. (2024). The power of AI in marketing: Enhancing efficiency and improving customer perception through AI-generated storyboards. *International Journal of Information Technology : an Official Journal of Bharati Vidyapeeth's Institute of Computer Applications and Management*, *16*(1), 137–144. DOI: 10.1007/s41870-023-01661-5

Challoumis, C. (2024). The dawn of artificial intelligence. *XIX International Scientific Conference*. London. Great Britain, 169–205.

Chamola, V., Hassija, V., Sulthana, A. R., Ghosh, D., Dhingra, D., & Sikdar, B. (2023). A review of trustworthy and explainable artificial intelligence (XAI). *IEEE Access : Practical Innovations, Open Solutions*, *11*, 78994–79015. DOI: 10.1109/ACCESS.2023.3294569

Chan, H. L., & Choi, T. M. (2025). Using generative artificial intelligence (GenAI) in marketing: Development and practices. *Journal of Business Research*, *191*, 115276. rights and contentDOI: 10.1016/j.jbusres.2025.115276Get

Chandra Sekaran, S., Yap, H. J., Musa, S. N., Liew, K. E., Tan, C. H., & Aman, A. (2021). The implementation of virtual reality in digital factory—A comprehensive review. *International Journal of Advanced Manufacturing Technology*, *115*(5), 1349–1366. DOI: 10.1007/s00170-021-07240-x

Chandra, S., Shirish, A., & Srivastava, S. C. (2022). To be or not to be… human? Theorizing the role of human-like competencies in conversational artificial intelligence agents. *Journal of Management Information Systems*, *39*(4), 969–1005. DOI: 10.1080/07421222.2022.2127441

Changkui, L. I. (2025). The Regulatory Trilemma of Medical AI: A New Framework for Navigating Innovation, Rights, and Sovereignty in Global Governance. *Medical Research*, *7*(3), 1–12. DOI: 10.6913/mrhk.070301

Chan, K. W., Septianto, F., Kwon, J., & Kamal, R. S. (2023). Color effects on AI influencers' product recommendations. *European Journal of Marketing, 57*(9), 2290–2315. DOI: 10.1108/EJM-03-2022-0185

Chatterjee, S., Rana, N. P., Tamilmani, K., & Sharma, A. (2021). The effect of AI-based CRM on organization performance and competitive advantage. *Information Systems Frontiers, 23*(5), 1283–1300. DOI: 10.1007/s10796-021-10168-0

Chen, Y. (2024). *Exploring the effect of deepfake-based advertising on consumers' attitudes and behaviors*. Working Paper Series WP 2024.

Cheng, C. F., Huang, C. C., Lin, M. C., & Chen, T. C. (2023). Exploring effectiveness of relationship marketing on artificial intelligence adopting intention. *SAGE Open, 13*(4), 21582440231222760. DOI: 10.1177/21582440231222760

Cheng, X., & Jiang, H. (2020). Chatbot interactions in tourist destinations: AI-mediated service encounter and customer satisfaction. *Journal of Hospitality and Tourism Technology, 11*(3), 479–496. DOI: 10.1108/JHTT-09-2019-0109

Chen, J., Zhou, W., & Frankwick, G. L. (2025). Firm AI adoption intensity and marketing performance. *Journal of Computer Information Systems, 65*(2), 172–189. DOI: 10.1080/08874417.2023.2277751

Chen, Y., Li, C., Li, J., & Dong, Y. (2026). General trust and intolerance of uncertainty: Disentangling within-and between-person associations. *Personality and Individual Differences, 251*, 113582. DOI: 10.1016/j.paid.2025.113582

Chen, Y., Tu, Y., & Zeng, S. (2024). Costly "Greetings" from AI: Effects of product recommenders and self-disclosure levels on transaction costs. *Sustainability (Basel), 16*(18), 8236. DOI: 10.3390/su16188236

Chesney, R., & Citron, D. (2019). Deepfakes and the new disinformation war: The coming age of post-truth geopolitics. *Foreign Affairs, 98*, 147.

Chinnaraju, A. (2025). Explainable AI (XAI) for trustworthy and transparent decision-making: A theoretical framework for AI interpretability. *World Journal of Advanced Engineering Technology and Sciences, 14*(3), 170–207. DOI: 10.30574/wjaets.2025.14.3.0106

Christou, P. A. (2025). A critical inquiry into the personal and societal perils of Artificial Intelligence. *AI and Ethics, 5*(3), 2547–2555. DOI: 10.1007/s43681-024-00556-w

Chui, M., & Francisco, S. (2017). Artificial intelligence the next digital frontier. *McKinsey and Company Global Institute, 47*(3.6), 6-8.

Chu, S. C., Yim, M. Y. C., & Mundel, J. (2025). Artificial intelligence, virtual and augmented reality, social media, online reviews, and influencers: A review of how service businesses use promotional devices and future research directions. *International Journal of Advertising, 44*(5), 798–828. DOI: 10.1080/02650487.2024.2325835

Cicek, M., Gursoy, D., & Lu, L. (2025). Adverse impacts of revealing the presence of "Artificial Intelligence (AI)" technology in product and service descriptions on purchase intentions: The mediating role of emotional trust and the moderating role of perceived risk. *Journal of Hospitality Marketing & Management, 34*(1), 1–23. DOI: 10.1080/19368623.2024.2368040

Coelho, P. S., & Henseler, J. (2012). Creating customer loyalty through service customization. *European Journal of Marketing, 23*(3), 331–356. DOI: 10.1108/03090561211202503

Conti, M., Gathani, J., & Tricomi, P. P. (2022). Virtual influencers in online social media. *IEEE Communications Magazine, 60*(8), 86–91. DOI: 10.1109/MCOM.001.2100786

Craft, S., & Vos, T. P. (2021). The ethics of transparency. In *The Routledge Companion to Journalism Ethics*. Routledge. DOI: 10.4324/9780429262708-24

Csikszentmihalyi, M. (1990). *Flow: The psychology of optimal experience*. Harper & Row.

Culnan, M. J., & Armstrong, P. K. (1999). Information privacy concerns, procedural fairness, and impersonal trust: An empirical investigation. *Organization Science, 23*(1), 99–128. DOI: 10.1287/orsc.10.1.104

D'Amico, E., Belitski, M., Braga, A., & Savoie, R. (2025). Enhancing knowledge spillover of innovation through artificial intelligence: An empirical investigation. *The Journal of Technology Transfer*, 1–29. DOI: 10.1007/s10961-025-10217-7

Dabiran, E., Farivar, S., Wang, F., & Grant, G. (2024). Virtually human: Anthropomorphism in virtual influencer marketing. *Journal of Retailing and Consumer Services, 79*, 103797. DOI: 10.1016/j.jretconser.2024.103797

Dahish, Z., Miah, S. J., Pandit, A., & Roy, S. K. (2025). Enhancing phygital customer experience through generative AI: A social listening method for strategic retail decision-making. *Journal of Strategic Marketing*, 1–21. DOI: 10.1080/0965254X.2025.2540267

Dahlin, E. (2025). Trust in AI. *AI & Society, 40*(8), 6089–6095. DOI: 10.1007/s00146-025-02429-0

Dan, A. (2020). In the working-remote era, 'deepfake' is No fake news: It will change advertising forever. *Forbes*.

Dang, N. (2025). The influence of AI-generated visual content on influencer marketing strategies in social media. *Reviews on Internet of Things (IoT). Cyber-Physical Systems, and Applications*, *10*(3), 1–18.

Dang, Q., & Li, G. (2025). Unveiling trust in AI: The interplay of antecedents, consequences, and cultural dynamics. *AI & Society*, *4*(1), 669–692. DOI: 10.1007/s00146-025-02477-6

Daniel, A. D., & Alves, L. (2020). University-industry technology transfer: The commercialization of university's patents. *Knowledge Management Research and Practice*, *18*(3), 276–296. DOI: 10.1080/14778238.2019.1638741

Davenport, T. H., & Ronanki, R. (2018). Artificial intelligence for the real world. *Harvard Business Review*, *96*(1), 108–116.

Davenport, T., Guha, A., Grewal, D., & Bressgott, T. (2020). How artificial intelligence will change the future of marketing. *Journal of the Academy of Marketing Science*, *48*(1), 24–42. DOI: 10.1007/s11747-019-00696-0

Davis, F. D. (1989). Perceived usefulness, perceived ease of use, and user acceptance of information technology. *Management Information Systems Quarterly*, *13*(3), 319–340. DOI: 10.2307/249008

Davuluri, P. S. L. N. (2026). *The Autonomous Data Enterprise: Engineering Real-Time Intelligence with Generative and Agentic AI*. Deep Science Publishing.

De Bruijn, H., Warnier, M., & Janssen, M. (2022). The perils and pitfalls of explainable AI: Strategies for explaining algorithmic decision-making. *Government Information Quarterly*, *39*(2), 101666. DOI: 10.1016/j.giq.2021.101666

De Bruyn, A., Viswanathan, V., Beh, Y. S., Brock, J. K. U., & Von Wangenheim, F. (2020). Artificial intelligence and marketing: Pitfalls and opportunities. *Journal of Interactive Marketing*, *51*(1), 91–105. DOI: 10.1016/j.intmar.2020.04.007

De Bruyne, J. (2023). Third-Party Certification and Artificial Intelligence. *Brill. Com*. https://brill.com/downloadpdf/display/title/64411.pdf#page=74

De Cicco, R., Francioni, B., Curina, I., & Cioppi, M. (2025). AI, human or a blend? How the educational content creator influences consumer engagement and brand-related outcomes. *Journal of Services Marketing*, *39*(10), 53–71. DOI: 10.1108/JSM-10-2024-0539

De Cicco, R., Iacobucci, S., Cannito, L., Onesti, G., Ceccato, I., & Palumbo, R. (2024). Virtual vs. human influencer: Effects on users' perceptions and brand outcomes. *Technology in Society*, *77*, 102488. DOI: 10.1016/j.techsoc.2024.102488

De Marcellis-Warin, N., Marty, F., Thelisson, E., & Warin, T. (2022). Artificial intelligence and consumer manipulations: From consumer's counter algorithms to firm's self-regulation tools. *AI and Ethics*, *2*(2), 259–268. DOI: 10.1007/s43681-022-00149-5

Debackere, K., & Veugelers, R. (2005). The role of academic technology transfer organizations in improving industry science links. *Research Policy*, *34*(3), 321–342. DOI: 10.1016/j.respol.2004.12.003

Degadwala, S., & Patel, V. M. (2024). Advancements in deepfake detection: A review of emerging techniques and technologies. *International Journal of Scientific Research in Computer Science, Engineering and Information Technology*.

Dellande, S., Gilly, M. C., & Graham, J. L. (2004). Gaining compliance and losing weight: The role of the service provider in health care services. *Journal of Marketing*, *68*(3), 78–91. DOI: 10.1509/jmkg.68.3.78.34764

Denyer Willis, G. (2023). 'Trust and safety': Exchange, protection and the digital market–fortress in platform capitalism. *Socio-economic Review*, *21*(4), 1877–1895. DOI: 10.1093/ser/mwad003

Deryl, M. D., Verma, S., Srivastava, V., & Paul, J. (2026). Harnessing artificial intelligence (AI) for interactive branding. *Journal of Research in Interactive Marketing*, 1–21. DOI: 10.1108/JRIM-02-2025-0076

Dezao, T. (2024). Enhancing transparency in AI-powered customer engagement. *Journal of AI. Robotics & Workplace Automation*, *3*(2), 134. DOI: 10.69554/PPJE1646

Dietvorst, B. J., Simmons, J. P., & Massey, C. (2015). Algorithm aversion: People erroneously avoid algorithms after seeing them err. *Journal of Experimental Psychology. General*, *144*(1), 114–126. DOI: 10.1037/xge0000033 PMID: 25401381

DiMaggio, P. J., & Powell, W. W. (1983). The iron cage revisited: Institutional isomorphism and collective rationality in organizational fields. *American Sociological Review*, *48*(2), 147–160. DOI: 10.2307/2095101

Diwanji, V. S. (2026). Should your brand hire virtual influencers? How realism and gender presentation shape trust and purchase intentions. *Journal of Retailing and Consumer Services*, *88*, 104491. DOI: 10.1016/j.jretconser.2025.104491

Dixit, P., & Singh, P. B. (2025). AI-Powered Consumer Insights for Sustainable Business Practices: A Literature Review on Ethical Marketing and Green Consumerism. *Journal of Indian Institute for Engineering*, *4*, 28.

Doborjeh, Z., Hemmington, N., Doborjeh, M., & Kasabov, N. (2021). Artificial intelligence: A systematic review of methods and applications in hospitality and tourism. *International Journal of Contemporary Hospitality Management*, *34*(3), 1154–1176. DOI: 10.1108/IJCHM-06-2021-0767

Dondapati, A., & Dehury, R. K. (2024). Virtual vs. human influencers: The battle for consumer hearts and minds. *Computers in Human Behavior: Artificial Humans*, *2*(1), 100059. DOI: 10.1016/j.chbah.2024.100059

Dong, B., Sivakumar, K., Evans, K. R., & Zou, S. (2015). Effect of customer participation on service outcomes: Themoderating role of participation readiness. *Journal of Service Research*, *18*(2), 160–176. DOI: 10.1177/1094670514551727

Drenik, G. (2025). As AI Matures, Consumer Trust Becomes The New Battleground. Available at: https://www.forbes.com/sites/garydrenik/2025/11/06/as-ai-matures-consumer-trust-becomes-the-new-battleground/

Du, J. (2025). Toward Responsible and Beneficial AI: Comparing Regulatory and Guidance-Based Approaches-A Comprehensive Comparative Analysis of Artificial Intelligence Governance Frameworks across the European Union, United States, China, and IEEE. *ArXiv Preprint ArXiv:2508.00868.*

Dumitriu, D., & Popescu, M. A.-M. (2020). Artificial Intelligence Solutions for Digital Marketing. *Procedia Manufacturing*, *46*, 630–636. DOI: 10.1016/j.promfg.2020.03.090

Duralia, O., Ogrean, C., ichindelean, M., & ichindelean, M. (2025). Decoding the Personalization-Privacy Paradox: From Thematic Scholarly Clusters to Practical Insights. *Studies in Business and Economics*, *20*(2), 70–97. DOI: 10.2478/sbe-2025-0025

Du, S., & Xie, C. (2021). Paradoxes of artificial intelligence in consumer markets: Ethical challenges and opportunities. *Journal of Business Research*, *129*, 961–974. DOI: 10.1016/j.jbusres.2020.08.024

Dwivedi, Y. K., Kshetri, N., Hughes, L., Slade, E. L., Jeyaraj, A., Kar, A. K., Baabdullah, A. M., Koohang, A., Raghavan, V., Ahuja, M., Albanna, H., Albashrawi, M. A., Al-Busaidi, A. S., Balakrishnan, J., Barlette, Y., Basu, S., Bose, I., Brooks, L., Buhalis, D., & Wright, R. (2023). Opinion Paper:"So what if ChatGPT wrote it?" Multidisciplinary perspectives on opportunities, challenges and implications of generative conversational AI for research, practice and policy. *International Journal of Information Management*, *71*, 102642. DOI: 10.1016/j.ijinfomgt.2023.102642

Ebrahimi, A., Ebrahimi, M., & Ebrahimi, N. (2024). Analyzing the Relationship Between Artificial Intelligence and Customer Experience Improvement in the Online Retail Industry. *Digital Transformation and Administration Innovation*, *2*(4), 73–81. DOI: 10.61838/dtai.2.4.9

Economic, J. W.-T. in the D. E., Legal, undefined, Policy, and, & 2025, undefined. (2025). From Near and Afar: How Digitalization Is Shaping the Economic Geography and Conditioning Regulation. *Springer*, 13–48. DOI: 10.1007/978-3-031-93365-3_2

Eid, M. A. H., Hashesh, M. A., Sharabati, A.-A. A., Khraiwish, A., AL-Haddad, S., & Abusaimeh, H. (2024). Conceptualizing ethical AI-enabled marketing: Current state and agenda for future research. *International Journal of Data and Network Science*, *8*(4), 2291–2306. DOI: 10.5267/j.ijdns.2024.6.002

Ejjami, D. R.Dr. Rachid Ejjami. (2024). Emerging Professions in the Age of AI across Multiple Sectors. *International Journal For Multidisciplinary Research*, *6*(5), 28762. Advance online publication. DOI: 10.36948/ijfmr.2024.v06i05.28762

El-Geneedy, M., El-Din Moustafa, H., Khater, H., Abd-Elsamee, S., & Gamel, S. A. (2025). A comprehensive explainable AI approach for enhancing transparency and interpretability in stroke prediction. *Scientific Reports*, *15*(1), 26048. DOI: 10.1038/s41598-025-11263-9

Elragal, A., & Elgendy, N. (2024). A data-driven decision-making readiness assessment model: The case of a Swedish food manufacturer. *Decision Analytics Journal*, *10*, 100405. DOI: 10.1016/j.dajour.2024.100405

Elyamany, N., Youssef, Y. O., & El-Karef, N. (2025). A trans-disciplinary forensic study of Lil Miquela's virtual identity performance in Instagram. *AI & Society*, *40*(6), 4831–4854. DOI: 10.1007/s00146-025-02219-8

Epley, N., Waytz, A., & Cacioppo, J. T. (2007). On seeing the human: A three-factor theory of anthropomorphism. *Psychological Review*, *114*(4), 864–886. DOI: 10.1037/0033-295X.114.4.864

Esposito, E. (2022). Transparency versus explanation: The role of ambiguity in legal AI. *Journal of Cross-disciplinary Research in Computational Law*, *1*(2). Advance online publication. DOI: 10.5935/2317-2622/direitomackenzie.v16n315705

Etgar, M. (2008). A descriptive model of the consumer co-production process. *Journal of the Academy of Marketing Science*, *36*(1), 97–108. DOI: 10.1007/s11747-007-0061-1

Fageeh, W. (2026). *The Double-edged Sword of Personalization, Balancing Marketing Goals and Consumer Privacy*. https://repository.effatuniversity.edu.sa/entities/publication/3cb85635-64e7-452c-aec3-75d868acb103

Faisal-E-Alam, M., Bhuiyan, M. R. I., Mimi, A., & Miah, M. T. (2025). The role of the three zero framework in advancing global sustainable development through bibliometric and text mining analysis. *Discover Sustainability*, *6*(1), 1128. DOI: 10.1007/s43621-025-01919-x

Fang, X., & Wang, T. (2022). Using natural language processing to identify effective influencers. *International Journal of Market Research*, *64*(5), 611–629. DOI: 10.1177/14707853221101565

Farinloye, T., Omotoye, O., Oginni, A., Moharrak, M., & Mogaji, E. (2024). Bridging the digital divide: Consumer engagement with transportation payment apps in emerging economies. *Journal of Consumer Behaviour*, *23*(6), 3011–3029. DOI: 10.1002/cb.2388

Farooq, N., Hashmat, S., & Hashim, A. (2025). AI in advertising: Ethical risks, consumer protection, and policy implications. Annual Methodological Archive Research Review, 3(6), 1-18.

Farouk, M. A., & Fahmi, B. M. (2024). Deepfakes and media integrity: Navigating the new reality of synthetic content. *Journal of Media and Interdisciplinary Studies*, *3*(9), 47–94. DOI: 10.21608/jmis.2024.275298.1027

Farseev, A. (2023, February). Under the hood of social media advertising: how do we use AI responsibly for advertising targeting and creative evaluation. In *Proceedings of the Sixteenth ACM International Conference on Web Search and Data Mining* (pp. 1281-1282). DOI: 10.1145/3539597.3575791

Feng, Y., Chen, H., & Xie, Q. (2024). AI Influencers in advertising: The role of AI influencer-related attributes in shaping consumer attitudes, consumer trust, and perceived influencer–product fit. *Journal of Interactive Advertising*, *24*(1), 26–47. DOI: 10.1080/15252019.2023.2284355

Feng, Y., & Kim, H. J. (2025). Decoding the Trust Matrix: Unraveling Key Predictors of Consumer Trust in AI-Generated Personalized Advertising. *Journal of Interactive Advertising*, *25*(2), 123–138. DOI: 10.1080/15252019.2025.2468286

Ferrario, A., Loi, M., & Viganò, E. (2020). In AI we trust incrementally: A multilayer model of trust to analyze human-artificial intelligence interactions. *Philosophy & Technology*, *33*(3), 523–539. DOI: 10.1007/s13347-019-00378-3

Ferraro, C., Demsar, V., Sands, S., Restrepo, M., & Campbell, C. (2024). The paradoxes of generative AI-enabled customer service: A guide for managers. *Business Horizons*, *67*(5), 549–559. DOI: 10.1016/j.bushor.2024.04.013

Flavián, C., Ibáñez-Sánchez, S., & Orús, C. (2019). The impact of virtual, augmented and mixed reality technologies on the customer experience. *Journal of Business Research*, *100*, 547–560. DOI: 10.1016/j.jbusres.2018.10.050

Flavián, C., Ibáñez-Sánchez, S., & Orús, C. (2021). Integrating virtual reality devices into the body: effects of technological embodiment on customer engagement and behavioral intentions toward the destination. In *Future of tourism marketing* (pp. 79–94). Routledge. DOI: 10.4324/9781003176039-8

Flavián, C., Pérez-Rueda, A., Belanche, D., & Casaló, L. V. (2022). Intention to use analytical artificial intelligence (AI) in services–the effect of technology readiness and awareness. *Journal of Service Management*, *33*(2), 293–320. DOI: 10.1108/JOSM-10-2020-0378

Floridi, L. (2021). Artificial intelligence, deepfakes and a future of ectypes. In *Ethics, governance, and policies in artificial intelligence* (pp. 307–312). Springer. DOI: 10.1007/978-3-030-81907-1_17

Floridi, L., Cowls, J., Beltrametti, M., Chatila, R., Chazerand, P., Dignum, V., Luetge, C., Madelin, R., Pagallo, U., Rossi, F., Schafer, B., Valcke, P., & Vayena, E. (2018). AI4People—An Ethical Framework for a Good AI Society: Opportunities, Risks, Principles, and Recommendations. *Minds and Machines*, *28*(4), 689–707. DOI: 10.1007/s11023-018-9482-5

Følstad, A., & Brandtzæg, P. B. (2017). Chatbots and the new world of HCI. *Interactions (New York, N.Y.)*, *24*(4), 38–42. DOI: 10.1145/3085558

Følstad, A., Nordheim, C. B., & Bjørkli, C. A. (2018). What makes users trust a chatbot for customer service? An exploratory interview study. In *International Conference on Internet Science* (pp. 194–208). Springer. DOI: 10.1007/978-3-030-01437-7_16

Fotis, J., Buhalis, D., & Rossides, N. (2012). Social media use and impact during the holiday travel planning process. *Information and Communication Technologies in Tourism, 2012*, 13–24. DOI: 10.1007/978-3-7091-1142-0_2

Franke, C., Groeppel-Klein, A., & Müller, K. (2023). Consumers' responses to virtual influencers as advertising endorsers: Novel and effective or uncanny and deceiving? *Journal of Advertising*, *52*(4), 523–539. DOI: 10.1080/00913367.2022.2154721

Franke, F., Franke, S., & Riedel, R. (2022). AI-based Improvement of Decision-makers' Knowledge in Production Planning and Control. *IFAC-PapersOnLine, 10th IFAC Conference on Manufacturing Modelling, Management and Control MIM 2022, 55*(10), 2240–2245. DOI: 10.1016/j.ifacol.2022.10.041

Galli, F. (2022). *Algorithmic marketing and EU law on unfair commercial practices*. Springer. DOI: 10.1007/978-3-031-13603-0

Gandhi, A. (2025). Beyond Regulation: Proactive Financial Risk Management in an AI-Driven World. *Ijaidsml. Org*, *6*(1), 156–163. DOI: 10.63282/3050-9262.IJAIDSML-V6I1P117

Ganesh, A. (2023). The Impact of Social Media on Consumer Behavior: An AI-Enhanced Approach to Marketing Strategies. *Available at SSRN* 4985407.

Gao, L., Li, G., Tsai, F., Gao, C., Zhu, M., & Qu, X. (2023). The impact of artificial intelligence stimuli on customer engagement and value co-creation: The moderating role of customer ability readiness. *Journal of Research in Interactive Marketing*, *17*(2), 317–333. DOI: 10.1108/JRIM-10-2021-0260

Gao, P., Wang, X., Chen, H., Dai, W., & Ling, H. (2021). What is beautiful is not always good: Influence of machine learning-derived photo attractiveness on intention to initiate social interactions in mobile dating applications. *Connection Science*, *33*(2), 321–340. DOI: 10.1080/09540091.2020.1814204

Gao, Y., & Liu, H. (2023). Artificial intelligence-enabled personalization in interactive marketing: A customer journey perspective. *Journal of Research in Interactive Marketing*, *17*(5), 663–680. DOI: 10.1108/JRIM-01-2022-0023

García-Madurga, M.-Á., & Grilló-Méndez, A.-J. (2023). Artificial Intelligence in the Tourism Industry: An Overview of Reviews. In *Administrative Sciences* (Vol. 13, Issue 8, p. 172). DOI: 10.3390/admsci13080172

García-Serrano, A. M., Martínez, P., & Hernández, J. Z. (2004). Using AI techniques to support advanced interaction capabilities in a virtual assistant for e-commerce. *Expert Systems with Applications*, *26*(3), 413–426. DOI: 10.1016/j.eswa.2003.09.012

Gefen, D. (2000). E-commerce: The role of familiarity and trust. *Omega*, *28*(6), 725–737. DOI: 10.1016/S0305-0483(00)00021-9

Gefen, D., Karahanna, E., & Straub, D. W. (2003). Trust and TAM in online shopping: An integrated model. *Management Information Systems Quarterly*, *27*(1), 51–90. DOI: 10.2307/30036519

George, A. S., & George, A. (2023). *Deepfakes: The Evolution of Hyper realistic Media Manipulation. 01*, 58–74. DOI: 10.5281/zenodo.10148558

Gerlich, M. (2023). The power of virtual influencers: Impact on consumer behaviour and attitudes in the age of AI. *Administrative Sciences*, *13*(8), 178. DOI: 10.3390/admsci13080178

Ghabban, M., Alsughayyir, Y., Alslimani, A., Marzouq, A., & Qasem, Z. (2025). Consumer Behavior Toward AI-Driven Marketing: Insights from UTAUT and Uses and Gratifications Models. *Global Journal of Economic and Business*, *15*(4), 423–438. DOI: 10.31559/GJEB2025.15.4.4

Ghiurău, D., & Popescu, D. E. (2024). Distinguishing reality from AI: Approaches for detecting synthetic content. *Computers*, *14*(1), 1. DOI: 10.3390/computers14010001

Ghosh, S. (2025). Developing artificial intelligence (AI) capabilities for data driven business model innovation: Roles of organizational adaptability and leadership. *Journal of Engineering and Technology Management*, *75*, 101851. DOI: 10.1016/j.jengtecman.2024.101851

Gianni, R., Lehtinen, S., & Nieminen, M. (2022). Governance of responsible AI: From ethical guidelines to cooperative policies. *Frontiers of Computer Science*, *4*, 873437. DOI: 10.3389/fcomp.2022.873437

Glassberg, I., Ilan, Y. B., & Zwilling, M. (2025). The key role of design and transparency in enhancing trust in AI-powered digital agents. *Journal of Innovation & Knowledge*, *10*(5), 100770. Advance online publication. DOI: 10.1016/j.jik.2025.100770

Glikson, E., & Woolley, A. W. (2020). Human Trust in Artificial Intelligence: Review of Empirical Research. *The Academy of Management Annals*, *14*(2), 627–660. DOI: 10.5465/annals.2018.0057

Goddard, K., Roudsari, A., & Wyatt, J. C. (2012). Automation bias: A systematic review of frequency, effect mediators, and mitigators. *Journal of the American Medical Informatics Association : JAMIA*, *19*(1), 121–127. DOI: 10.1136/amiajnl-2011-000089

Goncalves, M., Hu, Y., Aliagas, I., & Cerdá, L. M. (2024). Neuromarketing algorithms' consumer privacy and ethical considerations: Challenges and opportunities. *Cogent Business & Management, 11*(1), 2333063. DOI: 10.1080/23311975.2024.2333063

Gong, S., Liu, L., Shao, J., Li, Y., & Yang, Y. (2026). Understanding the mechanism behind consumers' purchase intentions toward AI recommendations: The trade-off between privacy and incentives. *Journal of Retailing and Consumer Services, 88*, 104489. DOI: 10.1016/j.jretconser.2025.104489

Goraya, M. A. S., Kemal, A. A., Xu, M., Shareef, M. A., & Akram, M. S. (2026). Leveraging digital transformation strategy and data driven decision making to improve organisational performance in a hostile environment. Industrial Management & Data Systems, 126(2), 650–677. 10 2024 1039DOI: 10.1108/IMDS

Goyal, N., & Bhardwaj, K. (2025). Virtual Influencer Marketing and Its Impact on Marketing Strategies. In *Redefining the Future of Digital Marketing With Virtual Influencers* (pp. 55–88). IGI Global Scientific Publishing. DOI: 10.4018/979-8-3373-0255-3.ch003

Gray, H. M., Gray, K., & Wegner, D. M. (2007). Dimensions of mind perception. *Science, 315*(5812), 619. DOI: 10.1126/science.1134475 PMID: 17272713

Grewal, D., Hulland, J., & Karahanna, E. (2019). The future of technology and marketing: A multidisciplinary perspective. *Journal of the Academy of Marketing Science, 48*(1), 1–8. Advance online publication. DOI: 10.1007/s11747-019-00711-4

Guerra-Tamez, C. R., Flores, K. K., Serna-Mendiburu, G. M., Robles, D. C., & Cortés, J. I. (2024). Decoding gen Z: AI's influence on brand trust and purchasing behavior. *Frontiers in Artificial Intelligence, 7*, 1323512. DOI: 10.3389/frai.2024.1323512 PMID: 38500672

Gülten, S. (2026). Application of Artificial Intelligence in the Independent Audit Process. *Springer, Part F1418*, 225–248. DOI: 10.1007/978-981-95-5811-7_11

Gunasekara, L., El-Haber, N., Nagpal, S., Moraliyage, H., Issadeen, Z., Manic, M., & De Silva, D. (2025). A systematic review of responsible artificial intelligence principles and practice. *Applied System Innovation, 8*(4), 97. DOI: 10.3390/asi8040097

Gupta, R., Tiwari, S., & Chaudhary, P. (2025). DEFENDING THE METAVERSE: A SURVEY ON DEEPFAKE DETECTION AND AVATAR-BASED THREAT MITIGATION. *Ijamjournal. Org, 38*(1s), 45–64. DOI: 10.1007/978-3-031-82062-5_3

Gupta, S., Kushwaha, P. S., Badhera, U., Chatterjee, P., & Gonzalez, E. D. S. (2023). Identification of benefits, challenges, and pathways in E-commerce industries: An integrated two-phase decision-making model. *Sustainable Operations and Computers, 4*, 200–218. DOI: 10.1016/j.susoc.2023.08.005

Gupta, S., Wang, Y., Patel, P., & Czinkota, M. (2025). Navigating the future of AI in marketing: AI integration across borders, ethical considerations, and policy implications. *International Journal of Information Management, 82*, 102871. DOI: 10.1016/j.ijinfomgt.2025.102871

Gutierriz, I., Ferreira, J. J., & Fernandes, P. O. (2025). Digital transformation and the new combinations in tourism: A systematic literature review. *Tourism and Hospitality Research, 25*(2), 194–213. DOI: 10.1177/14673584231198414

Guttentag, D. A. (2010). Virtual reality: Applications and implications for tourism. *Tourism Management, 31*(5), 637–651. DOI: 10.1016/j.tourman.2009.07.003

Haenlein, M., Kaplan, A., Tan, C. W., & Zhang, P. (2019). Artificial intelligence (AI) and management analytics. *Journal of Management Analytics, 6*(4), 341–343. DOI: 10.1080/23270012.2019.1699876

Hagendorff, T. (2020). The ethics of AI ethics: An evaluation of guidelines. *Minds and Machines, 30*(1), 99–120. DOI: 10.1007/s11023-020-09517-8

Hakim, S. H. R. (2026). Strategic Online Growth For Sport Retailer Using Analytical And Behavioral Models. EKOMBIS REVIEW: Jurnal Ilmiah Ekonomi dan Bisnis, 14(1), 945-956.

Haleem, A., Javaid, M., Qadri, M. A., Singh, R. P., & Suman, R. (2022). Artificial intelligence (AI) applications for marketing: A literature-based study. *International Journal of intelligent networks, 3*, 119-132. DOI: 10.1016/j.ijin.2022.08.005

Halina, M. (2021). Insightful artificial intelligence. *Mind & Language, 36*(2), 315–329. DOI: 10.1111/mila.12321

Ham, J., Li, S., Shah, P., & Eastin, M. S. (2024). Are virtual influencers more effective in real-world advertisement settings? *Journal of Advertising Research, 64*(3), 353–371. DOI: 10.2501/JAR-2024-015

Hammad, A., & Abu-Zaid, R. (2024). Applications of AI in decentralized computing systems: Harnessing artificial intelligence for enhanced scalability, efficiency, and autonomous decision-making in distributed architectures. *Applied Research in Artificial Intelligence and Cloud Computing, 7*(6), 161–187.

Hammerschmidt, T., Stolz, K., & Posegga, O. (2025). Bridging the gap: Inequalities that divide those who can and cannot create sustainable outcomes with AI. *Behaviour & Information Technology*, 1–30. DOI: 10.1080/0144929X.2025.2500451

Han, B., Liu, D., & Qi, S. (2025). Beyond human streamers: How AI-avatar engagement strategies influence consumer acceptance. *Asia Pacific Journal of Marketing and Logistics*, •••, 1–20. DOI: 10.1108/APJML-04-2025-0618

Hancock, P. A., Billings, D. R., Ollis, K. E., Chen, J. Y. C., de Visser, E. J., & Parasuraman, R. (2011). A meta-analysis of factors affecting trust in human-robot interaction. *Human Factors*, *53*(5), 517–527. DOI: 10.1177/0018720811417254

Hansen, H. F., Lillesund, E., Mikalef, P., & Altwaijry, N. (2024). Understanding artificial intelligence diffusion through an AI capability maturity model. *Information Systems Frontiers*, *26*(6), 2147–2163. DOI: 10.1007/s10796-024-10528-4

Haque, A. (2025). Integrating UTAUT and TPB frameworks to examine digital wallet adoption: Evidence from university students in a developing economy. *DUET Journal,* 10(1), 1–11. https://www.duet.ac.bd/storage/journal/volume-10-issue-1-june-2025%28-%29-1756443608.pdf

Haque, A., Akther, N., Khan, I., Agarwal, K., & Uddin, N. (2024, October). Artificial intelligence in retail marketing: Research agenda based on bibliometric reflection and content analysis (2000–2023). In *Informatics* (Vol. 11, No. 4, p. 74). MDPI. DOI: 10.3390/informatics11040074

Haque, A., Sultana, N., Kim, Y. S., & Al Amin, M. (2024). Integration of the UTAUT model in mobile banking context: The mediating role of personal innovativeness and perceived value. *Asia pacific journal of information systems, 34*(3), 929-956. DOI: 10.14329/apjis.2024.34.3.929

Hargittai, E. (2010). Digital na(t)ives? Variation in internet skills and uses among members of the "Net Generation.". *Sociological Inquiry*, *80*(1), 92–113. DOI: 10.1111/j.1475-682X.2009.00317.x

Harjika, R. (2026). Architecting Enterprise AI Strategies. *Springer*, 1–24. DOI: 10.1007/979-8-8688-2219-3_1

Harness, D., Ganesh, S., & Stohl, C. (2024). Visibility agents: Organizing transparency in the digital era. *New Media & Society*, *26*(10), 5575–5596. DOI: 10.1177/14614448221137816

Hasan, M., Chowdhury, K. Z., & Zubayer, M. (2025). The AI Advantage: Revolutionizing Personalization in Digital Marketing. *Business & Social Sciences*, *3*(1), 1–9. DOI: 10.25163/business.3110281

Hasan, R., & Abdullah, M. S. (2022). Advancing ai in marketing through cross border integration ethical considerations and policy implications. *American Journal of Scholarly Research and Innovation, 01*(01), 351–379. DOI: 10.63125/d1xg3784

Hashem, T. N. (2025). The Disruption of Influencer Marketing: Exploring the Efficiency of AI-Generated Virtual Influencers vs. Human Influencers. *Journal of Information & Knowledge Management, 24*(06), 2550063. DOI: 10.1142/S0219649225500637

Haupt, M., Freidank, J., & Haas, A. (2025). Consumer responses to human AI collaboration at organizational frontlines: Strategies to escape algorithm aversion in content creation. Review of Managerial Science, 19(2), 377–413. 10.1007/s11846 024 00748

Hawaldar, I. T. (2020). The effect of artificial intelligence on the sales graph in Indian market. Entrepreneurship and Sustainability Issues. 10.9770/jesi.2020.7.4(24)

Heersmink, R., de Rooij, B., Clavel Vázquez, M. J., & Colombo, M. (2024). A phenomenology and epistemology of large language models: Transparency, trust, and trustworthiness. *Ethics and Information Technology, 26*(3), 41. Advance online publication. DOI: 10.1007/s10676-024-09777-3

Hendrayati, H., Achyarsyah, M., Marimon, F., Hartono, U., & Putit, L. (2024). The Impact of Artificial intelligence on Digital Marketing: Leveraging potential in a competitive business landscape. *Emerging Science Journal, 8*(6), 2343–2359. Advance online publication. DOI: 10.28991/ESJ-2024-08-06-012

Hennighausen, C., Yarza Navarro-Schär, V. G., & Eller, E. (2025). AI-mediated communication in e-commerce: Implications for customer trust. *International Journal of Consumer Studies, 49*(5), e70111. DOI: 10.1111/ijcs.70111

Herhausen, D., Binder, J., Schoegel, M., & Herrmann, A. (2019). Integrating bricks with clicks: Retailer-level and channel-level outcomes of online–offline channel integration. *Journal of Retailing, 91*(2), 309–325. DOI: 10.1016/j.jretai.2014.12.009

Hewapathirana, I. U., & Perera, N. (2024). *Navigating the age of AI influence: A systematic literature review of trust, engagement, efficacy and ethical concerns of virtual influencers in social media.*

He, X., & Fang, L. (2024). Regulatory challenges in synthetic media governance: Policy frameworks for ai-generated content across image, video, and social platforms. *Journal of Robotic Process Automation, AI Integration, and Workflow Optimization, 9*(12), 36–54.

Hidayanti, N. F., Iswanto, D., & Ningsih, N. H. I. (2025). Artificial Intelligence in Personalized Marketing: Strategies for Enhancing Consumer Engagement. *Advance Sustainable Science Engineering and Technology*, *7*(2), 02502014–02502014. DOI: 10.26877/df5dwp69

Hidayat, M. S., Muhammad, W., & Isdayanti, P. L. (2025). Digital Marketing Ethics in the Age of AI: A Comparative Analysis of Transparency and Consumer Trust in E-Commerce Platforms. *Journal of Management and Informatics*, *4*(1), 723–740. DOI: 10.51903/jmi.v4i1.178

Hina, M., Islam, N., & Luo, X. R. (2025). Towards sustainable consumption decision-making: Examining the interplay of blockchain transparency and information-seeking in reducing product uncertainty. *Decision Support Systems*, *189*, 114370. DOI: 10.1016/j.dss.2024.114370

Hofstede, G. (2001). *Culture's consequences: Comparing values, behaviors, institutions, and organizations across nations* (2nd ed.). Sage Publications.

Hollebeek, L. D., & Macky, K. (2019). Digital content marketing's role in fostering consumer engagement, trust, and value: Framework, fundamental propositions, and implications. *Journal of Interactive Marketing*, *45*(1), 27–41. DOI: 10.1016/j.intmar.2018.07.003

Hollebeek, L. D., Menidjel, C., Sarstedt, M., Jansson, J., & Urbonavicius, S. (2024). Engaging consumers through artificially intelligent technologies: Systematic review, conceptual model, and further research. *Psychology and Marketing*, *41*(4), 880–898. DOI: 10.1002/mar.21957

Hollebeek, L. D., Sprott, D. E., & Brady, M. K. (2021). Rise of the machines? Customer engagement in automated service interactions. *Journal of Service Research*, *24*(1), 3–8. DOI: 10.1177/1094670520975110

Holloway, J. C., & Humphreys, C. (2019). The business of tourism. *Sage (Atlanta, Ga.)*.

Hoque, M. N., Jannat, S. N., Arafat, Y., & Miah, M. M. (2026). Predictive Modeling of Tourist Satisfaction Based on Service Marketing Mix Elements Using Machine Learning Techniques. *TheScientificWorldJournal*, *2026*(1), 6666970. DOI: 10.1155/tswj/6666970

Horton, D., & Richard Wohl, R. (1956). Mass communication and para-social interaction: Observations on intimacy at a distance. *Psychiatry*, *19*(3), 215–229. DOI: 10.1080/00332747.1956.11023049 PMID: 13359569

Huang, M. H., & Rust, R. T. (2021). A strategic framework for artificial intelligence in marketing. *Journal of the Academy of Marketing Science, 49*(1), 30–50. DOI: 10.1007/s11747-020-00749-9

Huang, M.-H., & Rust, R. T. (2018). Artificial Intelligence in Service. *Journal of Service Research, 21*(2), 155–172. DOI: 10.1177/1094670517752459

Huang, T.-K., Yang, C.-H., Hsieh, Y.-H., Wang, J.-C., & Hung, C.-C. (2018). Augmented reality (AR) and virtual reality (VR) applied in dentistry. *The Kaohsiung Journal of Medical Sciences, 34*(4), 243–248. DOI: 10.1016/j.kjms.2018.01.009 PMID: 29655414

Huang, Z., Hu, J., Li, X., He, Y., Zhao, X., Peng, B., Wu, B., Huang, X., & Cheng, G. (2025). Sida: Social media image deepfake detection, localization and explanation with large multimodal model. *Proceedings of the Computer Vision and Pattern Recognition Conference*, 28831–28841. DOI: 10.1109/CVPR52734.2025.02685

Hu, B. A., Liu, Y., & Rong, H. (2025). Trustless Autonomy: Understanding Motivations. *Benefits and Governance Dilemma in Self-Sovereign Decentralized AI Agents., 1.* Advance online publication. DOI: 10.1145/nnnnnnn

Hu, H., Xue, L., & Guo, Y. (2025). Tourism, acceleration, and deceleration: Towards a conceptual framework. *Current Issues in Tourism, 0*(0), 1–18. DOI: 10.1080/13683500.2025.2505695

Hunka, A. D., Daniel, A. M., Bour, A., & Boyer, R. H. (2025). Is transparency a good business strategy? Consumer preferences and willingness to pay for information about the chemical content of reused and recycled clothing. *Sustainable Production and Consumption, 56*, 128–141. DOI: 10.1016/j.spc.2025.03.020

Husairi, M. A., & Rossi, P. (2024). Delegation of purchasing tasks to AI: The role of perceived choice and decision autonomy. *Decision Support Systems, 179*, 114166. DOI: 10.1016/j.dss.2023.114166

Hussein, H., Albadry, O. M., Mathew, V., Al-Romeedy, B. S., Alsetoohy, O., Abou Kamar, M., & Khairy, H. A. (2024). Digital leadership and sustainable competitive advantage: Leveraging green absorptive capability and eco-innovation in tourism and hospitality businesses. *Sustainability (Basel), 16*(13), 5371. DOI: 10.3390/su16135371

Hu, Y., & Min, H. K. (2025). Information transparency, privacy concerns, and customers' behavioral intentions regarding AI-powered hospitality robots: A situational awareness perspective. *Journal of Hospitality and Tourism Management, 63*, 177–184. DOI: 10.1016/j.jhtm.2025.04.003

Huynh, T. T., & Khoa, B. T. (2025). The Role of Generative Artificial Intelligence in After-Sales Services: Enhancing Customer Repurchase Behavior Through the SOR Model and Customer Pleasure. In *Applied Artificial Intelligence in Business: Systems, Tools and Techniques* (pp. 403-415). Cham: Springer Nature Switzerland. DOI: 10.1007/978-3-031-90271-0_28

Huynh, M., & Aichner, T. (2025). In generative artificial intelligence we trust: Unpacking determinants and outcomes for cognitive trust. *AI & Society*, *40*(8), 5849–5869. DOI: 10.1007/s00146-025-02378-8

Hwang, T. (2020). *Deepfakes: A grounded threat assessment.* Centre for Security and Emerging Technologies, Georgetown University. DOI: 10.51593/20190030

Inavolu, S. M. (2024). Exploring AI-driven customer service: Evolution, architectures, opportunities, challenges and future directions. *International Journal of Engineering and Advanced Technology*, *13*(3), 156–163.

Ishkhanyan, A. (2025). Governing AI across borders: corporate power, state sovereignty and global regulation. *Digital Policy, Regulation and Governance.*

Islam, M. R., Siddika, A., & Shaulin, N. (2025). AI Readiness and Trust in Government: The Context of Bangladesh and India. In *Strengthening Human Relations in Organizations With AI* (pp. 27-58). IGI Global Scientific Publishing.

Islam, M. A., Somu, S., & Aldaihani, F. M. F. (2026). The rise of agentic AI: Synthesis of current knowledge and future research agenda. *Global Business and Organizational Excellence*, *45*(3), 402–416. DOI: 10.1002/joe.70019

Islam, M. M., Bhuiyan, M. R. I., Islam, S. H., Tabassum, M. N., & Billah, M. (2026). Unlocking the Mediating and Moderating Role of Information Security in Information Systems: A Combined TAM, ISM, and HBM Model. *Human Behavior and Emerging Technologies*, *2026*(1), 5593002. DOI: 10.1155/hbe2/5593002

Ivanov, S. H., & Webster, C. (2017). *Adoption of robots, artificial intelligence and service automation by travel, tourism and hospitality companies–a cost-benefit analysis*. Artificial Intelligence and Service Automation by Travel, Tourism and Hospitality Companies–a Cost-Benefit Analysis.

Jain, D., Gupta, D. M., Gupta, D. P., Pandey, D. N., Sharma, D. N., & Raina, M. S. (2025). Consumer Trust In AI-Enabled Marketing: A Behavioural Analysis. *International Journal of Environmental Sciences*, 11(17s), 840–852. DOI: 10.64252/7fytzg74

Jain, G., Paul, J., & Shrivastava, A. (2021). Hyper-personalization, co-creation, digital clienteling and transformation. *Journal of Business Research*, *124*, 12–23. Advance online publication. DOI: 10.1016/j.jbusres.2020.11.034

Jakkula, A. R. (2020). AI and Ethical Considerations in E-commerce. *Journal of Scientific and Engineering Research*, *7*(9), 213–216.

Javed, S., & Zehra, S. (2025). Emotional AI for student motivation and retention: A systematic review and future directions. *Researchgate. Net*, *8*(1), 643–660. DOI: 10.47067/ramss.v8i1.500

Jayasingh, S., Sivakumar, A., & Vanathaiyan, A. A. (2025). Artificial intelligence influencers' credibility effect on consumer engagement and purchase intention. *Journal of Theoretical and Applied Electronic Commerce Research*, *20*(1), 17. DOI: 10.3390/jtaer20010017

Jhawar, A., Kumar, P., & Varshney, S. (2023). The emergence of virtual influencers: A shift in the influencer marketing paradigm. *Young Consumers*, *24*(4), 468–484. DOI: 10.1108/YC-05-2022-1529

Jiang, K., Zheng, J., & Luo, S. (2024). Green power of virtual influencer: The role of virtual influencer image, emotional appeal, and product involvement. *Journal of Retailing and Consumer Services*, *77*, 103660. DOI: 10.1016/j.jretconser.2023.103660

Jim, J. R., Talukder, M. A. R., Malakar, P., Kabir, M. M., Nur, K., & Mridha, M. F. (2024). Recent advancements and challenges of NLP-based sentiment analysis: A state-of-the-art review. *Natural Language Processing Journal*, *6*, 100059. DOI: 10.1016/j.nlp.2024.100059

Jin, S. V., & Ryu, E. (2020). "I'll buy what she's# wearing": The roles of envy toward and parasocial interaction with influencers in Instagram celebrity-based brand endorsement and social commerce. *Journal of Retailing and Consumer Services*, *55*, 102121. DOI: 10.1016/j.jretconser.2020.102121

Jin, S. V., & Viswanathan, V. (2025). "Threatened and empty selves following AI-based virtual influencers": Comparison between followers and non-followers of virtual influencers in AI-driven digital marketing. *AI & Society*, *40*(1), 117–131. DOI: 10.1007/s00146-023-01832-9

Jin, W., & Zhao, B. (2025). *Cross-Domain Knowledge Transfer in Large Models: Transforming Knowledge Management Dynamics*. IntechOpen.

Jobin, A., Ienca, M., & Vayena, E. (2019). The global landscape of AI ethics guidelines. *Nature Machine Intelligence*, *1*(9), 389–399. DOI: 10.1038/s42256-019-0088-2

Ju, N., Kim, T., & Im, H. (2024). Fake human but real influencer: The interplay of authenticity and humanlikeness in virtual influencer communication? *Fashion and Textiles*, *11*(1), 16. DOI: 10.1186/s40691-024-00380-0

Kadim, A., Yusnita, I., Sutarman, A., Lesmana, R., & Arsla Ramahdan, F. (2025). E-commerce as a catalyst for digital economy development: A study of marketing strategies and their impact. *Koreascience.Kr*, *6*(2), 177–187. DOI: 10.34306/itsdi.v6i2.696

Kaliyar, R. K., Goswami, A., & Narang, P. (2021). DeepFakE: Improving fake news detection using tensor decomposition-based deep neural network. *The Journal of Supercomputing*, *77*(2), 1015–1037. DOI: 10.1007/s11227-020-03294-y

Kalpokas, I., & Kalpokiene, J. (2022). I CAN Do It: From GANs and Deepfakes to Art. In *Deepfakes: A Realistic Assessment of Potentials, Risks, and Policy Regulation* (pp. 55–63). Springer.

Kane, G. C., Palmer, D., & Phillips, A. N. (2019). *Accelerating Digital Innovation Inside and Out* [Technical Report]. MIT Sloan Management Review. https://sadil.ws/handle/123456789/14

Kanti, P. K., Prabhakar Sharma, Wanatasanappan, V. V., & Said, N. M. (2024). Explainable machine learning techniques for hybrid nanofluids transport characteristics: an evaluation of shapley additive and local interpretable model-agnostic explanations. *Journal of Thermal Analysis and Calorimetry 2024 149:21*, *149*(21), 11599–11618. DOI: 10.1007/s10973-024-13639-x

Karami, A., Shemshaki, M., & Ghazanfar, M. A. (2025). Exploring the Ethical Implications of AI-Powered Personalization in Digital Marketing. *Data Intelligence*, *7*(4), 1035–1084. DOI: 10.3724/2096-7004.di.2024.0055

Karimova, G. Z. (2025). Creating AI Persona. In *Humanizing AI with Personality* (pp. 49–59). Springer. DOI: 10.1007/978-3-031-82327-5_5

Kbaier, E., Salminen, J., & Jansen, B. J. (2025). "A glimpse into the AI": Exploring the effect of consumers' chatbot interaction experience on brand attachment and advocacy with the moderating role of AI skepticism. *Asia-Pacific Journal of Business Administration*, 1–26. DOI: 10.1108/APJBA-01-2025-0003

Kelly, S. M. M. (2021). Algorithmic bias, financial inclusion, and gender. *Womensworldbanking.Org*. http://www.womensworldbanking.org/wp-content/uploads/2021/02/2021_Algorithmic_Bias_Report.pdf

Kemp, A. (2024). Competitive advantage through artificial intelligence: Toward a theory of situated AI. *Academy of Management Review*, *49*(3), 618–635. DOI: 10.5465/amr.2020.0205

Kerpedzhiev, G. D., König, U. M., Röglinger, M., & Rosemann, M. (2021). An Exploration into Future Business Process Management Capabilities in View of Digitalization. *Business & Information Systems Engineering, 63*(2), 83–96. DOI: 10.1007/s12599-020-00637-0

Khalfallah, D., & Keller, V. (2025). Authenticity, ethics, and transparency in virtual influencer marketing: A cross-cultural analysis of consumer trust and engagement: A systematic literature review. *Acta Psychologica, 260*, 105573. DOI: 10.1016/j.actpsy.2025.105573 PMID: 40974722

Khan, A. A., Laghari, A. A., Inam, S. A., Ullah, S., Shahzad, M., & Syed, D. (2025). A survey on multimedia-enabled deepfake detection: State-of-the-art tools and techniques, emerging trends, current challenges & limitations, and future directions. *Discover Computing, 28*(1), 48. DOI: 10.1007/s10791-025-09550-0

Khan, R. A., Feng, G., & Zhu, J. (2026). Impact of Knowledge and Electronic Word of Mouth About AI-Based Chatbots on Customers' Intention to Continue Using Chatbots in E-Commerce. *Journal of Organizational Computing and Electronic Commerce, 36*(1), 78–99. DOI: 10.1080/10919392.2025.2563463

Khatun, M., Bhuiyan, M. R. I., Amin, M. A., Hossen, M., & Mia, M. A. H. (2026). Evaluating E-Commerce Satisfaction: The Impact of Trust, Information Quality, Usability, and Perceived-to-Actual Performance. *SAGE Open, 16*(1), 21582440261423039. Advance online publication. DOI: 10.1177/21582440261423039

Khatun, M., Hossain, R., Bhuiyan, M. R., Tabassum, M. N., & Riaj, M. A. (2025). Green Entrepreneurship and Digital Transformation for Sustainable Development: A Systematic Review. In Mouloudj, K., & Bouarar, A. (Eds.), *Digitizing Green Entrepreneurship* (pp. 153–180). IGI Global Scientific Publishing. DOI: 10.4018/979-8-3693-7442-9.ch006

Khokhar, P. & Chitsimran. (September 30, 2019). Evolution of Artificial Intelligence in Marketing, Comparison With Traditional Marketing. *Our Heritage, 67*(50), 375-389. Available at SSRN: https://ssrn.com/abstract=3557091

Kietzmann, J., Mills, A. J., & Plangger, K. (2021). Deepfakes: Perspectives on the future "reality" of advertising and branding. *International Journal of Advertising, 40*(3), 473–485. DOI: 10.1080/02650487.2020.1834211

Kim, H., & Park, M. (2024). When digital celebrity talks to you: How human-like virtual influencers satisfy consumer's experience through social presence on social media endorsements. *Journal of Retailing and Consumer Services, 76*(October 2023), 103581. DOI: 10.1016/j.jretconser.2023.103581

Kim, D., & Wang, Z. (2023). The ethics of virtuality: Navigating the complexities of human-like virtual influencers in the social media marketing realm. *Frontiers in Communication*, *8*, 1205610. DOI: 10.3389/fcomm.2023.1205610

Kim, D., & Wang, Z. (2024). Social media influencer vs. virtual influencer: The mediating role of source credibility and authenticity in advertising effectiveness within AI influencer marketing. *Computers in Human Behavior: Artificial Humans*, *2*(2), 100100. DOI: 10.1016/j.chbah.2024.100100

Kim, E., Xie, Q., Hong, J. W., & Kim, H. M. (2025). Prosocial campaigns with virtual influencers: Stories, messages, and beyond. *International Journal of Human-Computer Interaction*, *41*(11), 6956–6967. DOI: 10.1080/10447318.2024.2387399

Kim, J., Giroux, M., & Lee, J. C. (2021). When do you trust AI? The effect of number presentation detail on consumer trust and acceptance of AI recommendations. *Psychology and Marketing*, *38*(7), 1140–1155. DOI: 10.1002/mar.21498

Kim, J., Kang, S., & Bae, J. (2022). The effects of customer consumption goals on artificial intelligence driven recommendation agents: Evidence from stitch fix. *International Journal of Advertising*, *41*(6), 997–1016. DOI: 10.1080/02650487.2021.1963098

Kingma, D. P., & Welling, M. (2013). Auto-encoding variational bayes. *ArXiv Preprint ArXiv:1312.6114.*

Kinney, M., Anastasiadou, M., Naranjo-Zolotov, M., & Santos, V. (2024). Expectation management in AI: A framework for understanding stakeholder trust and acceptance of artificial intelligence systems. *Heliyon*, *10*(7), E28562. Advance online publication. DOI: 10.1016/j.heliyon.2024.e28562

Kitchenham, B., Budgen, D., Brereton, P., Turner, M., Charters, S., & Linkman, S. (2007). Large-scale software engineering questions – Expert opinion or empirical evidence? *IET Software*, *1*(5), 161–171. DOI: 10.1049/iet-sen:20060052

Kleine, F. (2022). *Perception of Deepfake Technology.* Hochschule Darmstadt–University of Applied Sciences Darmstadt.

Kocarslan, H., & Stoycheva, B. (2025). The effect of digital literacy on online purchase intention: The mediating role of social media use. *Journal of Theoretical and Applied Electronic Commerce Research*, *20*(4), 355. DOI: 10.3390/jtaer20040355

Kolar, N., Milfelner, B., & Pisnik, A. (2024). Factors for customers' AI use readiness in physical retail stores: The interplay of consumer attitudes and gender differences. *Information (Basel)*, *15*(6), 346. DOI: 10.3390/info15060346

Kolluru, P. (2025). Responsible AI use in marketing: Navigating ethics and consumer trust. Forbes Agency Council. Available at: https://www.forbes.com/councils/forbesagencycouncil/2025/06/20/responsible-ai-use-in-marketing-navigating-ethics-and-consumer-trust

Komiak, S. Y. X., & Benbasat, I. (2006). The effects of personalization and familiarity on trust and adoption of recommendation agents. *Management Information Systems Quarterly*, *30*(4), 941–960. DOI: 10.2307/25148760

Kothandapani, H. P. (2025). Social Implications of Algorithmic Decision-Making in Housing Finance: Examining the broader social impacts of deploying machine learning in lending decisions, including potential disparities and community effects. *Journal of Knowledge Learning and Science Technology ISSN: 2959-6386 (Online)*, *4*(1), 78–97.

Kotler, P. (2022). *Marketing for hospitality and tourism*. Pearson Education Limited.

Kravets, O., Korolova, U., Nosachenko, O., Vasiltsova, O., & Koberniuk, S. (2025). AI-powered digital marketing: Enhancing customer behaviour predictions. *European Journal of Sustainable Development*, *14*(2), 84. DOI: 10.14207/ejsd.2025.v14n2p84

Kubiszewski, I., Noordewier, T., & Costanza, R. (2011). Perceived credibility of Internet encyclopedias. *Computers & Education*, *56*(3), 659–667. DOI: 10.1016/j.compedu.2010.10.008

Kumar, D. (2023). Ethical and Legal Challenges of AI in Marketing: An Exploration of Solutions. SSRN *Electronic Journal*. DOI: 10.2139/ssrn.4396132

Kumar, D., & Suthar, N. (2024). A consumer perspective of AI certification–the current certification landscape, consumer approval and directions for future research. *Emerald.Com*. https://www.emerald.com/ejm/article/58/2/441/1226418

Kumar, A., Shankar, A., Behl, A., Chakraborty, D., & Gundala, R. R. (2025). Anthropomorphic generative AI chatbots for enhancing customer engagement, experience and recommendation. *Journal of Consumer Marketing*, *42*(4), 472–483. DOI: 10.1108/JCM-06-2024-6922

Kumari, A., & Laheri, V. K. (2025). Understanding consumer behavior through AI-Powered recommender systems: A systematic review and bibliometric perspective. *Indian Journal of Marketing*, 9-32. DOI: 10.17010/ijom/2025/v55/i8/175207

Kumari, G. V., Chapa, B. P., Chaitanya, N. K., Mahajan, R. G., & Shahakar, M. (2024). Introduction to data-driven intelligent systems. In *Data-Driven Systems and Intelligent Applications* (pp. 1–18). CRC Press. DOI: 10.1201/9781003388449-1

Kumar, P., Choubey, D., Amosu, O. R., & Ogunsuji, Y. M. (2024). AI-enhanced inventory and demand forecasting: Using AI to optimize inventory management and predict customer demand. *World J. Adv. Res. Rev*, *23*(1), 1931–1944. DOI: 10.30574/wjarr.2024.23.1.2173

Kumar, R., Singh, G., Jain, P., & Sharma, M. (2025). Smart E-commerce application using AI. In *Intelligent Computing and Communication Techniques* (pp. 716–722). CRC Press. DOI: 10.1201/9781003530176-102

Kumar, V., Ashraf, A. R., & Nadeem, W. (2024). AI-powered marketing: What, where, and how? *International Journal of Information Management*, *77*, 102783. DOI: 10.1016/j.ijinfomgt.2024.102783

Kwok, A. O., & Koh, S. G. (2020). Deepfake: A social construction of technology perspective. *Current Issues in Tourism.*

Laghari, A. A., Wu, K., Ali, R., Mureed, L., Abdullah, A., & Khan, A. (2021). A Review and State of Art of Internet of Things (IoT) A Review and State of Art of Internet of Things (IoT). *Arch. Comput. Methods Eng., No.*

Lalot, F., & Bertram, A.-M. (2025). When the bot walks the talk: Investigating the foundations of trust in an artificial intelligence (AI) chatbot. *Journal of Experimental Psychology. General*, *154*(2), 533–551. DOI: 10.1037/xge0001696

Lambooy, J. (2004). The transmission of knowledge, emerging networks, and the role of universities: An evolutionary approach. *European Planning Studies*, *12*(5), 643–657. DOI: 10.1080/0965431042000219996

Langer, E. J. (1975). The illusion of control. *Journal of Personality and Social Psychology*, *32*(2), 311–328. DOI: 10.1037/0022-3514.32.2.311

Larke, R., Kilgour, M., & O'Connor, H. (2018). Build touchpoints, and they will come: Transitioning to omnichannel retailing. *International Journal of Physical Distribution & Logistics Management*, *48*(4), 465–483. DOI: 10.1108/IJPDLM-09-2016-0276

Larsen, B. C. (2021). A framework for understanding AI-induced field change: How AI technologies are legitimized and institutionalized. *Proceedings of the 2021 AAAI/ACM Conference on AI, Ethics, and Society*, 683–694. DOI: 10.1145/3461702.3462591

Larsson, S., & Heintz, F. (2020). Transparency in artificial intelligence. *Internet Policy Review*, *9*(2). Advance online publication. DOI: 10.14763/2020.2.1469

Le, D. D., Dang, T., Truong, V., Yu, S., Yang, S.-H., Choi, M.-H., & Lee, M. (2025). Integrative Discovery Through Network Pharmacology and Molecular Docking Approaches of Phenolic Compounds Isolated from Torreya nucifera to Treat Rheumatoid Arthritis. *International Journal of Molecular Sciences, 26*(23), 11629. DOI: 10.3390/ijms262311629 PMID: 41373781

Lee, S. B. (2020). Chatbots and communication: The growing role of artificial intelligence in addressing and shaping customer needs. *Business communication research and practice, 3*(2), 103-111. https://doi.org/DOI: 10.22682/bcrp.2020.3.2.103

Lee, H., Shin, M., Yang, J., & Chock, T. M. (2025). Virtual influencers vs. human influencers in the context of influencer marketing: The moderating role of machine heuristic on perceived authenticity of influencers. *International Journal of Human-Computer Interaction, 41*(10), 6029–6046. DOI: 10.1080/10447318.2024.2374100

Lee, J. D., & See, K. A. (2004). Trust in automation: Designing for appropriate reliance. *Human Factors, 46*(1), 50–80. DOI: 10.1518/hfes.46.1.50.30392

Lee, Y. L., & Song, S. (2010). An empirical investigation of electronic word-of-mouth: Informational motive and corporate response strategy. *Computers in Human Behavior, 26*(5), 1073–1080. DOI: 10.1016/j.chb.2010.03.009

Lee, Y. S. (1996). 'Technology transfer' and the research university: A search for the boundaries of university-industry collaboration. *Research Policy, 25*(6), 843–863. DOI: 10.1016/0048-7333(95)00857-8

Leggett, K. L., & Davies, W. E. (2026). Examining a hyper-human virtual brand ambassador as a brand personification strategy. *Journal of Product and Brand Management, 35*(3), 415–428. DOI: 10.1108/JPBM-06-2024-5290

Lemon, K. N., & Verhoef, P. C. (2016). Understanding Customer Experience Throughout the Customer Journey. *Journal of Marketing, 80*(6), 69–96. DOI: 10.1509/jm.15.0420

Leung, D., Dickinger, A., & Nixon, L. (2017). Impact of destination promotion videos on perceived destination image and booking intention change. *Information and Communication Technologies in Tourism 2017: Proceedings of the International Conference in Rome,* Italy, January 24-26, 2017, 361–375.

Leung, F. F., Gu, F. F., Li, Y., Zhang, J. Z., & Palmatier, R. W. (2022). Influencer marketing effectiveness. *Journal of Marketing, 86*(6), 93–115. DOI: 10.1177/00222429221102889

Li, B., Powell, D., & Lee, R. (2025). Commercialization of medical artificial intelligence technologies: Challenges and opportunities. npj. *NPJ Digital Medicine*, *8*(1), 454. DOI: 10.1038/s41746-025-01867-w

Liederman, E. (2025). Consumers want AI transparency from media publications. Available at: https://www.emarketer.com/content/consumers-want-ai-transparency -media-publications

Li, H. (2025). Multicultural data assistance mining analysis for ideological and political education in smart education platforms using artificial intelligence. *Wireless Networks*, *31*(1), 567–581. DOI: 10.1007/s11276-024-03772-8

Li, H., Lei, Y., Zhou, Q., & Yuan, H. (2023). Can you sense without being human? Comparing virtual and human influencers endorsement effectiveness. *Journal of Retailing and Consumer Services*, *75*(June), 103456. DOI: 10.1016/j.jretconser.2023.103456

Li, J., & Cao, B. (2022). Study on tourism consumer behavior and countermeasures based on big data. *Computational Intelligence and Neuroscience*, *2022*(1), 6120511. DOI: 10.1155/2022/6120511 PMID: 35909820

Li, J., & Jin, X. (2024). The Impact of Artificial Intelligence Adoption Intensity on Corporate Sustainability Performance: The Moderated Mediation Effect of Organizational Change. *Sustainability (Basel)*, *16*(21), 9350. DOI: 10.3390/su16219350

Li, J., & Ma, Y. (2024). Virtual influencers in advertisements: Examining the role of authenticity and identification. *Journal of Interactive Advertising*, *24*(1), 1–12. DOI: 10.1080/15252019.2023.2270478

Lijuan, C., Bhaumik, A., Xinfeng, W., & Jingwen, W. (2023). The effects of inventory management on business efficiency. International Journal For Multidisciplinary Research, 5(4), 1-17.

Lim, R. E., & Lee, S. Y. (2023). "You are a virtual influencer!": Understanding the impact of origin disclosure and emotional narratives on parasocial relationships and virtual influencer credibility. *Computers in Human Behavior, 148*(November 2022), 107897. DOI: 10.1016/j.chb.2023.107897

Lim, Y. J. (2017). Decision to use either Snapchat or Instagram for most powerful celebrities. *Research Journal of the Institute for Public Relations*, *3*(2), 1–16.

Lindström, T., & Österberg, F. (2020). Evolution of biobased and nanotechnology packaging–a review. *Nordic Pulp & Paper Research Journal*, *35*(4), 491–515. DOI: 10.1515/npprj-2020-0042

Ling, E. C., Tussyadiah, I., Tuomi, A., Stienmetz, J., & Ioannou, A. (2021). Factors influencing users' adoption and use of conversational agents: A systematic review. *Psychology and Marketing*, *38*(7), 1031–1051. DOI: 10.1002/mar.21491

Lin, J., Li, Y., & Yang, G. (2021). FPGAN: Face de-identification method with generative adversarial networks for social robots. *Neural Networks : The Official Journal of the International Neural Network Society*, *133*, 132–147. DOI: 10.1016/j.neunet.2020.09.001 PMID: 33217682

Lin, T. T. C., Paragas, F., Goh, D., & Bautista, J. R. (2016). Developing location-based mobile advertising in Singapore: A socio-technical perspective. *Technological Forecasting and Social Change*, *103*, 334–349. DOI: 10.1016/j.techfore.2015.06.002

Litvin, S. W., Goldsmith, R. E., & Pan, B. (2008). Electronic word-of-mouth in hospitality and tourism management. *Tourism Management*, *29*(3), 458–468. DOI: 10.1016/j.tourman.2007.05.011

Liu, M., Huang, X., Yu, J., Wang, T., & Mallya, A. (2020). *Generative Adversarial Networks for Image and Video Synthesis : Algorithms and Applications*. 1–22.

Liu, X., Xiang, X., Li, Z., Wang, Y., Li, Z., Liu, Z., Zhang, W., Ye, W., & Zhang, J. (2024). *A Survey of AI-Generated Video Evaluation* (arXiv:2410.19884). arXiv. https://doi.org//arXiv.2410.19884DOI: 10.48550

Liu, F. (2026). Who and how to pair with a virtual influencer? The impact of co-endorser type, perceived distance, and gender congruence on consumer responses in virtual influencer collaborations. *Journal of Retailing and Consumer Services*, *89*, 104593. DOI: 10.1016/j.jretconser.2025.104593

Liu, Q., Ha, L., & Lim, J. (2025). From perception to purchase: How AI literacy shapes consumer decisions in AI-generated sponsored vlogs across products and services. *Journal of Theoretical and Applied Electronic Commerce Research*, *20*(4), 302. DOI: 10.3390/jtaer20040302

Liu, R., Li, X., & Liu, S. (2025). How emotional expression in human-like virtual influencers drives user engagement: Empathy model and its antecedents. *Frontiers in Psychology*, *16*, 1544037. DOI: 10.3389/fpsyg.2025.1544037 PMID: 41567455

Liusito, R. A., Tulung, J. E., & Saerang, R. T. (2020). The influence of consumer trust and perceived value on consumer purchase decision of e-commerce in social media (study case in Manado). *Jurnal EMBA: Jurnal Riset Ekonomi, Manajemen, Bisnis Dan Akuntansi*, *8*(4).

Liu, W., Hu, E. W., Su, B., & Wang, J. (2021). Using machine learning techniques for DSP software performance prediction at source code level. *Connection Science*, *33*(1), 26–41. DOI: 10.1080/09540091.2020.1762542

Liu, Y., Lu, Q., & Ghamat, S. (2026). AI technology sharing strategies for e-commerce platforms with private label introduction. *International Journal of Production Research*, •••, 1–22. DOI: 10.1080/00207543.2026.2615822

Li, Y., Xiang, X., & Wu, R. (2026). Display advertising or social media post? The impact of endorsement execution form on the effectiveness of virtual influencers' advertising endorsements. *Journal of Retailing and Consumer Services*, *90*, 104685. DOI: 10.1016/j.jretconser.2025.104685

Logg, J. M., Minson, J. A., & Moore, D. A. (2019). Algorithm appreciation: People prefer algorithmic to human judgment. *Organizational Behavior and Human Decision Processes*, *151*, 90–103. DOI: 10.1016/j.obhdp.2018.12.005

Lojo, A., Li, M., & Xu, H. (2020). Online tourism destination image: Components, information sources, and incongruence. *Journal of Travel & Tourism Marketing*, *37*(4), 495–509. DOI: 10.1080/10548408.2020.1785370

Longoni, C., Bonezzi, A., & Morewedge, C. K. (2019). Resistance to medical artificial intelligence. *The Journal of Consumer Research*, *46*(4), 629–650. DOI: 10.1093/jcr/ucz013

Looia, J., & Kahlor, L. A. (2024). Artificial intelligence in influencer marketing: A mixed-method comparison of human and virtual influencers on Instagram. *Journal of Interactive Advertising*, *24*(2), 107–126. DOI: 10.1080/15252019.2024.2313721

Lopatovska, I., & Arapakis, I. (2011). Theories, methods and current research on emotions in library and information science, information retrieval and human–computer interaction. *Information Processing & Management*, *47*(4), 575–592. DOI: 10.1016/j.ipm.2010.09.001

Lopez, A., & Garza, R. (2023). Consumer bias against evaluations received by artificial intelligence: The mediation effect of lack of transparency anxiety. *Journal of Research in Interactive Marketing*, *17*(6), 831–847. DOI: 10.1108/JRIM-07-2021-0192

Lou, C., Kiew, S. T. J., Chen, T., Lee, T. Y. M., Ong, J. E. C., & Phua, Z. X. (2023). Authentically Fake? How Consumers Respond to the Influence of Virtual Influencers. *Journal of Advertising*, *52*(4), 540–557. DOI: 10.1080/00913367.2022.2149641

Lou, X., & Copeland, L. (2025). Gen Z and AI-generated fashion ads: A qualitative study to understanding female consumer perceptions and reactions. *Journal of Internet Commerce*, *24*(3), 131–152. DOI: 10.1080/15332861.2025.2520194

Luengo, J. G. (2025). Transparency Obligations for Providers and Deployers of certain AI Systems. In *The EU regulation on Artificial Intelligence: A commentary* (pp. 361–372). Wolters Kluwers Italia.

Luger, E., & Sellen, A. (2016). "Like having a really bad PA": The gulf between user expectation and experience of conversational agents. In Proceedings of the 2016 CHI Conference on Human Factors in Computing Systems (pp. 5286–5297). ACM. DOI: 10.1145/2858036.2858288

Lukacs, M., Toth, F., Horvath, R., … G. S.-J. of S. and, & 2025, undefined. (2025). Advanced digital solutions for food traceability: enhancing origin, quality, and safety through NIRS, RFID, Blockchain, and IoT. *Mdpi.Com*, 146–163. DOI: 10.1201/9781003508632-10

Lukyanenko, R., Maass, W., & Storey, V. C. (2022). Trust in artificial intelligence: From a Foundational Trust Framework to emerging research opportunities. *Electronic Markets*, *32*(4), 1993–2020. DOI: 10.1007/s12525-022-00605-4

Luo, X., Tong, S., Fang, Z., & Qu, Z. (2019). Frontiers: Machines vs. Humans: The Impact of Artificial Intelligence Chatbot Disclosure on Customer Purchases. *Marketing Science*, mksc.2019.1192. DOI: 10.1287/mksc.2019.1192

Luo, X., Tong, S., Fang, Z., & Qu, Z. (2019). Frontline artificial intelligence technology and firm performance: Real effects of AI-powered chatbots. *Journal of Marketing*, *83*(2), 1–23. DOI: 10.1177/0022242918822604

Luo, Z., & Luo, Z. (2026). Adaptive Feature Selection and Ensemble Learning Framework for Multi-Domain Anomaly Detection in Real-Time Transactional Systems. *Journal of Advanced Computing Systems*, *6*(2), 28–49. DOI: 10.69987/JACS.2026.60203

Luttrell, R., & Welch, C. (2025). Ai-powered synthetic personas: Affecting the future of public relations campaigns. In *Public Relations and the Rise of AI* (pp. 97–117). Routledge.

Lutz, C. (2019). Digital inequalities in the age of artificial intelligence and big data. *Human Behavior and Emerging Technologies*, *1*(2), 141–148. DOI: 10.1002/hbe2.140

Madzík, P., Falát, L., Skýpalová, R., Jašušáková, L., & Zimon, D. (2026). ChatGPT in science and research: How generative AI drives innovation and knowledge development. *Journal of Innovation & Knowledge*, *12*, 100889. DOI: 10.1016/j.jik.2025.100889

Mairue, S. (2024). *Around the book in 10 minutes: generating a narrative visualization with the help of generative AI.* https://aaltodoc.aalto.fi/items/dc55fd5c-f755-4c07-b4a8-2a7a2a4383b2

Malchenko, Y., Gogua, M., Golovacheva, K., Smirnova, M., & Alkanova, O. (2020). A critical review of digital capability frameworks: A consumer perspective. *Digital Policy, Regulation and Governance*, *22*(4), 269–288. DOI: 10.1108/DPRG-02-2020-0028

Malik, W., Gul, S., & Qureshi, G. M. (2025). Regulating Artificial Intelligence: Challenges for Data Protection and Privacy in Developing Nations. *Journal of Social Signs Review*, *3*(05), 95–108.

Mandania, R., Cadogan, J., Liu, J., & Kazmi, N. (2025). Optimizing promotional campaigns to maximize customer lifetime value: A dynamic learning approach. *Journal of Service Research*, 10946705251365524. Advance online publication. DOI: 10.1177/10946705251365524

Marchand, É., Durand, T., & Dubois, M. (2025). Surveillance Capitalism, Consumer Subjectivity and Marketing in the Age of Artificial Intelligence. *Social Science Chronicle*, *5*(1), 1–18. DOI: 10.56106/ssc.2025.001

Martínez-Bravo, M. C., Sádaba Chalezquer, C., & Serrano-Puche, J. (2022). Dimensions of digital literacy in the 21st century competency frameworks. *Sustainability (Basel)*, *14*(3), 1867. DOI: 10.3390/su14031867

Martin, K. (2018). The penalty for privacy violations: How privacy violations impact trust online. *Journal of Business Research*, *82*, 103–116. DOI: 10.1016/j.jbusres.2017.08.034

Martin, K. (2019). Ethical implications and accountability of algorithms. *Journal of Business Ethics*, *160*(4), 835–850. DOI: 10.1007/s10551-018-3921-3

Martin, K. D., & Murphy, P. E. (2017). The role of data privacy in marketing. *Journal of the Academy of Marketing Science*, *45*(2), 135–155. DOI: 10.1007/s11747-016-0495-4

Martin, K., Shilton, K., & Smith, J. (2021). The interplay of ethics, transparency, and trust in AI-mediated consumer engagement. *Journal of Business Ethics*, *170*, 1–18. DOI: 10.1007/s10551-020-04651-7

Ma, S., & Fildes, R. (2021). Retail sales forecasting with meta-learning. *European Journal of Operational Research*, *288*(1), 111–128. DOI: 10.1016/j.ejor.2020.05.038

Masood, A., Zhang, Q., Ali, M., Cappiello, G., & Dhir, A. (2023). Linking enterprise social media use, trust and knowledge sharing: Paradoxical roles of communication transparency and personal blogging. *Journal of Knowledge Management*, *27*(4), 1056–1085. DOI: 10.1108/JKM-11-2021-0880

Mathew, V., & Soliman, M. (2021). Does digital content marketing affect tourism consumer behavior? An extension of t echnology acceptance model. *Journal of Consumer Behaviour*, *20*(1), 61–75. DOI: 10.1002/cb.1854

Mathwick, C., Malhotra, N., & Rigdon, E. (2001). Experiential value: Conceptualization, measurement and application in the catalog and Internet shopping environment. *Journal of Retailing*, *77*(1), 39–56. DOI: 10.1016/S0022-4359(00)00045-2

Ma, Z., & Li, B. (2020). A DDoS attack detection method based on SVM and K-nearest neighbour in SDN environment. *International Journal on Computer Science and Engineering*, *23*(3), 224–234. DOI: 10.1504/IJCSE.2020.111431

Mazurkiewicz-Pizło, A. (2025). Virtual influencers (VIs) as marketing communication tools. *European Research Studies*, *28*(1), 472–492. DOI: 10.35808/ersj/3955

McAfee, A., & Brynjolfsson, E. (2017). *Machine, platform, crowd: Harnessing our digital future*. WW Norton & Company.

McAllister, D. J. (1995). Affect- and cognition-based trust as foundations for interpersonal cooperation in organizations. *Academy of Management Journal*, *38*(1), 24–59. DOI: 10.2307/256727

McDougall, J., Livingstone, S., & Sefton-Green, J. (2018). Digital learning and the capability approach. *Learning, Media and Technology*, *43*(1), 1–14. DOI: 10.1080/17439884.2017.1389076

McDougall, J., Readman, M., & Wilkinson, P. (2018). The uses of (digital) literacy. *Learning, Media and Technology*, *43*(3), 263–279. DOI: 10.1080/17439884.2018.1462206

McKinsey. (2025). *The state of AI in 2025 Agents, innovation, and transformation*. https://www.researchgate.net/profile/Dinesh-Deckker/publication/389853016_EMOTIONAL_AI_FOR_STUDENT_MOTIVATION_AND_RETENTION_A_SYSTEMATIC_REVIEW_AND_FUTURE_DIRECTIONS/links/67d488ec2719090652ba1351/EMOTIONAL-AI-FOR-STUDENT-MOTIVATION-AND-RETENTION-A-SYSTEM

McKnight, D. H., Choudhury, V., & Kacmar, C. (2002). Developing and validating trust measures for e-commerce: An integrative typology. *Information Systems Research, 13*(3), 334–359. DOI: 10.1287/isre.13.3.334.81

McKnight, D., Carter, M., Thatcher, J., & Clay, P. (2011). Trust in a specific technology: An Investigation of its Components and Measures. *ACM Transactions on Management Information Systems*, *2*(2), 12–32. DOI: 10.1145/1985347.1985353

McTear, M. (2022). *Conversational AI: Dialogue systems, conversational agents, and chatbots*. Morgan & Claypool Publishers.

Meng, D., Li, Y., & Zhang, J. (2023). Digital financial capability and household consumption: Evidence from the China Household Finance Survey. *Applied Economics Letters*. Advance online publication. DOI: 10.1080/13504851.2023.2167915

Meske, C., Abedin, B., Klier, M., & Rabhi, F. (2022). Explainable and responsible artificial intelligence. *Electronic Markets*, *32*(4), 2103–2106. DOI: 10.1007/s12525-022-00607-2

Meuter, M. L., Bitner, M. J., Ostrom, A. L., & Brown, S. W. (2005). Choosing among alternative service delivery modes: An investigation of customer trial of self-service technologies. *Journal of Marketing*, *69*(2), 61–83. DOI: 10.1509/jmkg.69.2.61.60759

Mhaskey, S. V. (2024). Integration of artificial intelligence (AI) in enterprise resource planning (ERP) systems: Opportunities, challenges, and implications. *International Journal of Computer Engineering in Research Trends*, *11*(12), 1–9. DOI: 10.22362/ijcert/2024/v11/i12/v11i1201

Minkkinen, M., Laine, J., Mäntymäki, M., & Matti, F. (2022). Continuous auditing of artificial intelligence: a conceptualization and assessment of tools and frameworks. *Springer, 1*(3). DOI: 10.1007/s44206-022-00022-2

Mirishli, S., Schreyer, M., & Hemati, H. (2025). *From Periodic Audits to Continuous Assurance: Leveraging AI for Real-Time Risk Detection and Compliance*. https://www.researchgate.net/profile/Adam-Rajuroy/publication/395711481_From_Periodic_Audits_to_Continuous_Assurance_Leveraging_AI_for_Real-Time_Risk_Detection_and_Compliance/links/68d0f359a8689b51bd616dca/From-Periodic-Audits-to-Continuous-Assurance-Leveraging-AI-for-Real-Time-Risk-Detection-and-Compliance.pdf

Mishra, S., Ewing, M. T., & Cooper, H. B. (2022). Artificial intelligence focus and firm performance. *Journal of the Academy of Marketing Science*, *50*(6), 1176–1197. DOI: 10.1007/s11747-022-00876-5

Mishra, V. (2025). Artificial Intelligence in Digital and Social Media Marketing: The Mediating Role of Consumer Engagement. *International Journal of Innovative Science and Research Technology, 10*(11), 411–419. DOI: 10.38124/ijisrt/25nov366

Mittameedi, S. K., Dogra, V., & Sayal, A. (2025). *Customer experience in e-commerce: A systematic review of metrics, models, and the role of AI*. IEEE. DOI: 10.1109/ACCESS.2025.3600729

Miyake, E. (2023). I am a virtual girl from Tokyo: Virtual influencers, digital-orientalism and the (Im) materiality of race and gender. *Journal of Consumer Culture, 23*(1), 209–228. DOI: 10.1177/14695405221117195

Mogaji, E., & Jain, V. (2024). How generative AI is (will) change consumer behaviour: Postulating the potential impact and implications for research, practice, and policy. *Journal of Consumer Behaviour, 23*(5), 2379–2389. DOI: 10.1002/cb.2345

Mohamad, A. A. S., & Shahril, Z. R. (2025). Consumer readiness on the sustainable practices of green technology in fast food restaurant. [IJRISS]. *International Journal of Research and Innovation in Social Science, 9*(1), 4881–4895. DOI: 10.47772/IJRISS.2025.9010376

Mohammadkhani, D., Majedi, N., Biniaz, S. A., & Sarhadi, M. (2025). AI-Driven Personalization Strategies and Their Impact on Consumer Engagement in Digital Markets. *Digital Transformation and Administration Innovation*, 1-14. https://doi.org/DOI: 10.4018/979-8-3693-3691-5.ch008

Molla, C., Bhuiyan, M. R. I., Islam, M. T., & Amin, A. (2026). Mediating role to banking performance for adopting digital bank using a technology organizational environment model. *Digital Finance, 8*(1), 4. DOI: 10.1007/s42521-025-00168-x

Moodley, K., & Sookhdeo, L. (2025). The role of artificial intelligence personalisation in e-commerce: Customer purchase decisions in the retail sector. *South African Journal of Information Management, 27*(1), 1–16. DOI: 10.4102/sajim.v27i1.1926

Moore, R., Moore, M. L., & Capella, M. (2005). The impact of customer-to-customer interactions in a high personal contact service setting. *Journal of Services Marketing, 19*(7), 482–491. DOI: 10.1108/08876040510625981

Moore, S., Bulmer, S., & Elms, J. (2022). The social significance of AI in retail on customer experience and shopping practices. *Journal of Retailing and Consumer Services, 64*, 102755. DOI: 10.1016/j.jretconser.2021.102755

Mori, M. (1970). The uncanny valley. Energy, 7(4), 33–35. (Translated by K. F. MacDorman & N. Kageki, 2012. *IEEE Robotics & Automation Magazine, 19*(2), 98–100. DOI: 10.1109/MRA.2012.2192811

Moriuchi, E., Landers, V. M., Colton, D., & Hair, N. (2021). Engagement with chatbots versus augmented reality interactive technology in e-commerce. *Journal of Strategic Marketing, 29*(5), 375–389. DOI: 10.1080/0965254X.2020.1740766

Moruzzi, C., Tallyn, E., Liddell, F., Dixon, B., Collomosse, J., & Elsden, C. (2025). Content authenticities: A discussion on the values of provenance data for creatives and their audiences. *Dl.Acm.Org*, 128–140. DOI: 10.1145/3698061.3726918

Mouritzen, S. L. T., Penttinen, V., & Pedersen, S. (2024). Virtual influencer marketing: The good, the bad and the unreal. *European Journal of Marketing, 58*(2), 410–440. DOI: 10.1108/EJM-12-2022-0915

Moussawi, S., Koufaris, M., & Benbunan-Fich, R. (2021). How perceptions of intelligence and anthropomorphism affect adoption of personal intelligent agents. *Electronic Markets, 31*(2), 343–364. DOI: 10.1007/s12525-020-00411-w

Moustakas, E., Lamba, N., Mahmoud, D., & Ranganathan, C. (2020). Blurring lines between fiction and reality: Perspectives of experts on marketing effectiveness of virtual influencers. *2020 International Conference on Cyber Security and Protection of Digital Services (Cyber Security)*, 1–6. DOI: 10.1109/CyberSecurity49315.2020.9138861

Mu, J., & Zhang, J. Z. (2025). Artificial intelligence marketing usage and firm performance. *Journal of the Academy of Marketing Science, 53*(4), 1–54. DOI: 10.1007/s11747-024-01076-z

Muniz, F., Stewart, K., & Magalhães, L. (2024). Are they humans or are they robots? The effect of virtual influencer disclosure on brand trust. *Journal of Consumer Behaviour, 23*(3), 1234–1250. DOI: 10.1002/cb.2271

Murár, P., & Kubovics, M. (2023, September). Using AI to create content designed for marketing communications. In *European Conference on Innovation and Entrepreneurship* (pp. 660-R25). Academic Conferences International Limited. DOI: 10.34190/ecie.18.1.1638

Mushtaq, M. A., Bais, M. K., & Bari, M. (2025). AI, Trust, and Consumers' online purchase intentions: Examining the Roles of Disinformation, Transparency, and Digital Literacy: . 18072808. *Research Consortium Archive, 3*(4), 1740-1758. DOI: 10.5281/zenodo

Nadda, V., Chaudhary, H. S., & Arnott, I. (2020). Cloud computing in tourism. In *Digital marketing strategies for tourism, hospitality, and airline industries* (pp. 141–155). IGI Global Scientific Publishing. DOI: 10.4018/978-1-5225-9783-4.ch007

Naeem, M. (2025). Emerging trends in global E-retailing: Exploring the dark side of scan and go in-store technologies in consumer shopping journeys. *International Marketing Review*, *42*(2-3), 249–282. DOI: 10.1108/IMR-06-2023-0110

Naimi-Sadigh, A., Asgari, T., & Rabiei, M. (2022). Digital transformation in the value chain disruption of banking services. *Journal of the Knowledge Economy*, *13*(2), 1212–1242. DOI: 10.1007/s13132-021-00759-0

Naitali, A., Ridouani, M., Salahdine, F., & Kaabouch, N. (2023). Deepfake Attacks: Generation, Detection, Datasets, Challenges, and Research Directions. *Computers*, *12*(10), 1–26. DOI: 10.3390/computers12100216

Nalivaikė, J., & Miliukaitė, G. (2024). Influence of AI-generated avatars on consumer trust in the brand. In *14th International Scientific Conference "Business and Management 2024"* (pp. 601-610). DOI: 10.3846/bm.2024.1191

Nambisan, S., Lyytinen, K., Majchrzak, A., & Song, M. (2017). Digital innovation management: Reinventing innovation management research in a digital world. *Management Information Systems Quarterly*, *41*(1), 223–238. DOI: 10.25300/MISQ/2017/41:1.03

Na, S., Heo, S., Han, S., Shin, Y., & Roh, Y. (2022). Acceptance model of artificial intelligence (AI)-based technologies in construction firms: Applying the Technology Acceptance Model (TAM) in combination with the Technology–Organisation–Environment (TOE) framework. *Buildings (Basel, Switzerland)*, *12*(2), 90. DOI: 10.3390/buildings12020090

Nass, C., & Moon, Y. (2000). Machines and mindlessness: Social responses to computers. *The Journal of Social Issues*, *56*(1), 81–103. DOI: 10.1111/0022-4537.00153

Nass, C., & Reeves, B. (1996). *The media equation: How people treat computers, television, and new media like real people and places*. Cambridge University Press.

Nass, C., Steuer, J., & Tauber, E. R. (1994). Computers are social actors. *Proceedings of the SIGCHI Conference on Human Factors in Computing Systems*, 72–78. DOI: 10.1145/191666.191703

Natarajan, D. (2025). Dynamic pricing strategies using machine learning in e-commerce. *Researchgate.Net*. https://www.researchgate.net/profile/Sundarapandiyan-Natarajan-2/publication/393966497_Dynamic_Pricing_Strategies_Using_Machine_Learning_in_E-Commerce/links/6881c6fc253dcb78df878542/Dynamic-Pricing-Strategies-Using-Machine-Learning-in-E-Commerce.pdf

National Research Council. (2000). *The digital dilemma: Intellectual property in the information age.* https://books.google.com/books?hl=en&lr=&id=e_GbAgAAQBAJ&oi=fnd&pg=PA1&dq=digital+intellectual+property+that+cannot+be+easily+replicated+by+competitors.+&ots=c-uvtGstjs&sig=_KjxGtiRrRLoOs9hBnsMtBocOJw

Nayal, P., Pandey, N., & Paul, J. (2022). Covid-19 pandemic and consumer-employee-organization wellbeing: A dynamic capability theory approach. *The Journal of Consumer Affairs*, *56*(1), 359–390. DOI: 10.1111/joca.12399

Nayyar, A., Mahapatra, B., Nhuong Le, D., & Suseendran, G. (2018). Virtual Reality (VR) & Augmented Reality (AR) technologies for tourism and hospitality industry. *International Journal of Engineering & Technology, 7*(2.21), 156. DOI: 10.14419/ijet.v7i2.21.11858

Nelson, J., Gardener, O., & Beejay, S. (2025). Designing AI Systems for Diverse Cultural Contexts.

Neuhofer, B., Buhalis, D., & Ladkin, A. (2015). Smart technologies for personalized experiences: A case study in the hospitality domain. *Electronic Markets*, *25*(3), 243–254. DOI: 10.1007/s12525-015-0182-1

Ng, S. W. T., & Zhang, R. (2025). Trust in AI chatbots: A systematic review. *Telematics and Informatics*, *97*, 102240. Advance online publication. DOI: 10.1016/j.tele.2025.102240

Nguyen, K. M., Nguyen, N. T., Ngo, N. T. Q., Tran, N. T. H., & Nguyen, H. T. T. (2024). Investigating consumers' purchase resistance behavior to AI-Based content recommendations on short-video platforms: A study of greedy and biased recommendations. *Journal of Internet Commerce*, *23*(3), 284–327. DOI: 10.1080/15332861.2024.2375966

Nguyen, M. H., & Nguyen, D. H. (2025). How do transparency and traceability enhance purchasing behaviors via consumer trust? Insights for food supply chains. *Journal of Consumer Marketing*. Advance online publication. DOI: 10.1108/JCM-07-2024-7005

Nguyen, M. V., & Ha, K. D. (2024). Investigation of factors affecting the readiness for the adoption of sustainable building materials. *Engineering, Construction, and Architectural Management*, *32*(8), 5578–5608. DOI: 10.1108/ECAM-12-2023-1268

Nooteboom, B. (2003). Problems and solutions in knowledge transfer. In *Cooperation, networks and institutions in regional innovation systems* (pp. 105–127). Edward Elgar Publishing. DOI: 10.4337/9781035304752.00013

O'Neil, C., Sargeant, H., & Appel, J. (2024). Explainable fairness in regulatory algorithmic auditing. *West Virginia Law Review*, *127*, 79.

Ohanian, R. (1990). Construction and validation of a scale to measure celebrity endorsers' perceived expertise, trustworthiness, and attractiveness. *Journal of Advertising*, *19*(3), 39–52. DOI: 10.1080/00913367.1990.10673191

Okibe, H. B. (2020). Sycophancy and Dearth of Integrity in Governance. *ESUT Journal of Social Sciences*, *5*(2).

Oliveira, A. B. da S., & Chimenti, P. (2021). Humanized Robots": A Proposition of Categories to Understand Virtual Influencers. *AJIS. Australasian Journal of Information Systems*, •••, 25.

Oliver, R. L. (1980). A cognitive model of the antecedents and consequences of satisfaction decisions. *JMR, Journal of Marketing Research*, *17*(4), 460–469. DOI: 10.1177/002224378001700405

Omeish, F., Shaheen, A., Alharthi, S., & Alfaiza, A. (2025). Between human and AI influencers: Parasocial relationships, credibility, and social capital formation in a collectivist market: A study of TikTok users in the Middle East. *Discover Sustainability*, *6*(1), 116. DOI: 10.1007/s43621-025-00891-w

Omogiate, P. (2023). Designing automated audit mechanisms to evaluate compliance of generative AI platforms with federal authorship and ownership disclosure requirements. *Researchgate.Net.* https://www.researchgate.net/profile/Precious-Omogiate/publication/397379185_Designing_automated_audit_mechanisms_to_evaluate_compliance_of_generative_AI_platforms_with_federal_authorship_and_ownership_disclosure_requirements/links/690dec6ca2b691617b6a4ee9/Designing-automated-audit-mechanisms-to-evaluate-compliance-of-generative-AI-platforms-with-federal-authorship-and-ownership-disclosure-requirements.pdf

Oprea, S. V., & Bâra, A. (2025). Customer-Centric Decision-Making with XAI and Counterfactual Explanations for Churn Mitigation. *Journal of Theoretical and Applied Electronic Commerce Research 2025, Vol. 20, Page 129*, *20*(2), 129. DOI: 10.3390/jtaer20020129

Ostrom, A. L., Fotheringham, D., & Bitner, M. J. (2018). Customer acceptance of AI in service encounters: understanding antecedents and consequences. In *Handbook of service science* (Vol. II, pp. 77–103). Springer International Publishing. DOI: 10.1007/978-3-319-98512-1_5

Oteri, O. J., Onukwulu, E. C., Igwe, A. N., Ewim, C. P. M., Ibeh, A. I., & Sobowale, A. (2023). (Forthcoming). Dynamic pricing models for logistics product management: Balancing cost efficiency and market demands. *International Journal of Business and Management.*

Ouaddi, H. (2025). The Rise of AI-Generated Influencers: Cybersecurity, Trust, and the Future of Social Media Marketing in Morocco. *International Journal of Digitalization and Applied Management*, *2*(2), 68–83.

Oyekunle, D., & Boohene, D. (2024). Digital transformation potential: The role of artificial intelligence in business. *International Journal of Professional Business Review: Int. J. Prof. Bus. Rev.*, *9*(3), 1.

Ozdemir, O., Karabulut, F., & Messinger, P. R. (2025). Can('t) touch this: The effect of form realism and product domain in virtual influencer endorsements. *Journal of Retailing*, *101*(2), 298–310. DOI: 10.1016/j.jretai.2025.04.002

Pagala, I., Asir, M., Mere, K., Puji Lestari, U., & Siddiqa, H. (2024). Consumer Behavior in the Age of AI: The Role of Personalized Marketing and Data Analytics in Shaping Purchase Decisions. *Dinasti International Journal of Education Management And Social Science*, *5*(6), 1898–1907. DOI: 10.38035/dijemss.v5i6.2947

Paglieri, D., Cross, L., Cunningham, W. A., Leibo, J. Z., & Vezhnevets, A. S. (2026). Persona Generators: Generating Diverse Synthetic Personas at Scale. *ArXiv Preprint ArXiv:2602.03545.*

Panarese, P., Grasso, M. M., & Solinas, C. (2025). Algorithmic bias, fairness, and inclusivity: A multilevel framework for justice-oriented AI. *AI & Society*, •••, 1–23. DOI: 10.1007/s00146-025-02451-2

Panchal, T., & Panchal, D. (2025). AI ethics and governance in business management: Challenges, opportunities, and a comparative analysis. *AI and Ethics*, *5*(6), 5971–5984. DOI: 10.1007/s43681-025-00764-y

Papagiannidis, E., Mikalef, P., & Conboy, K. (2025). Responsible artificial intelligence governance: A review and research framework. *The Journal of Strategic Information Systems*, *34*(2), 101885. DOI: 10.1016/j.jsis.2024.101885

Paramesha, M., Rane, N., & Rane, J. (2024). Big data analytics, artificial intelligence, machine learning, internet of things, and blockchain for enhanced business intelligence. *Artificial Intelligence, Machine Learning, Internet of Things, and Blockchain for Enhanced Business Intelligence.* DOI: 10.2139/ssrn.4855856

Parasuraman, A., & Manzey, D. (2010). Complacency and bias in human use of automation: An attentional integration. *Human Factors, 52*(3), 381–410. DOI: 10.1177/0018720810376055

Parasuraman, A., & Riley, V. (1997). Humans and automation: Use, misuse, disuse, abuse. *Human Factors, 39*(2), 230–253. DOI: 10.1518/001872097778543886

Parasuraman, A., Zeithaml, V. A., & Malhotra, A. (2005). E-S-QUAL: A multiple-item scale for assessing electronic service quality. *Journal of Service Research, 7*(3), 213–233. DOI: 10.1177/1094670504271156

Pareek, C. (2026). Behavioral Drift Testing in AI-Based Insurance Models: A Framework for Sustained Fairness and Reliability. *Researchgate.Net*. https://www.researchgate.net/profile/Chandra-Shekhar-Pareek/publication/399324546_Behavioral_Drift_Testing_in_AI-Based_Insurance_Models_A_Framework_for_Sustained_Fairness_and_Reliability/links/695bd47006a9ab54f84ecec2/Behavioral-Drift-Testing-in-AI-Based-Insurance-Models-A-Framework-for-Sustained-Fairness-and-Reliability.pdf

Parkes, T. (2018). *How One Retailer Is Shifting to an AI-First Mentality*. Think with Google. DOI: 10.31893/multirev.2025224

Park, J., & Ahn, S. (2024). Traditional vs. AI-generated brand personalities: Impact on brand preference and purchase intention. *Journal of Retailing and Consumer Services, 81*, 104009. DOI: 10.1016/j.jretconser.2024.104009

Park, J., Oh, C., & Kim, H. Y. (2024). AI vs. human-generated content and accounts on Instagram: User preferences, evaluations, and ethical considerations. *Technology in Society, 79*, 102705. DOI: 10.1016/j.techsoc.2024.102705

Pasquale, F. (2015). *The Black Box Society: The Secret Algorithms That Control Money and Information.* Harvard University Press. https://www.jstor.org/stable/j.ctt13x0hch

Patel, S., & Dada, M. (2025). The Impact of AI-Generated Advertising and Virtual Influencers on Consumer Perception and Brand Authenticity. *Journal of Media & Management. SRC/JMM-309. DOI: Doi. Org, 199*(7), 2–6. DOI: 10.47363/JMM/2025

Patidar, N., Mishra, S., Jain, R., Prajapati, D., Solanki, A., Suthar, R., ... & Patel, H. (2024). Transparency in AI decision making: A survey of explainable AI methods and applications. *Advances of Robotic Technology, 2*(1).

Patil, A., Mishra, B., Chockalingam, S., Misra, S., & Kvalvik, P. (2025). Balancing innovation and regulation: The Data Sovereignty Assessment Framework. *Elsevier, 24*(4), 159. DOI: 10.1007/s10207-025-01074-4

Patil, R., Shivashankar, K., Porapur, S. M., & Kagawade, S. (2024). The role of ai-driven social media marketing in shaping consumer purchasing behaviour: An empirical analysis of personalization, predictive analytics, and engagement. In *ITM Web of Conferences* (Vol. 68, p. 01032). EDP Sciences.

Paulovics, Á. (2023). *Digital reality and identity: An evolutionary analysis of virtual influencer lil miquela.*

Paul, R., Imam, M. H., & Mou, A. J. (2023). AI-Powered Sentiment Analysis In Digital Marketing: A Review Of Customer Feedback Loops In It Services. *American Journal of Scholarly Research and Innovation, 2*(02), 166–192. DOI: 10.63125/61pqqq54

Pavlou, P. A. (2003). Consumer acceptance of electronic commerce: Integrating trust and risk with the technology acceptance model. *International Journal of Electronic Commerce, 7*(3), 101–134. DOI: 10.1080/10864415.2003.11044275

Pei, G., Zhang, J., Hu, M., Zhang, Z., Wang, C., Wu, Y., Zhai, G., Yang, J., Shen, C., & Tao, D. (2024). *Deepfake Generation and Detection: A Benchmark and Survey.*

Peltier, J. W., Dahl, A. J., & Schibrowsky, J. A. (2024). Artificial intelligence in interactive marketing: A conceptual framework and research agenda. *Journal of Research in Interactive Marketing, 18*(1), 54–90. DOI: 10.1108/JRIM-01-2023-0030

Perumallaplli, R. (2012). AI-Enhanced Personalization in E-Commerce: Redefining Customer Interaction. *Available at SSRN* 5228719.

Pestek, A., & Sarvan, M. (2021). Virtual reality and modern tourism. *Journal of Tourism Futures, 7*(2), 245–250. DOI: 10.1108/JTF-01-2020-0004

Petit, O., Velasco, C., & Spence, C. (2019). Digital sensory marketing: Integrating new technologies into multisensory online experience. *Journal of Interactive Marketing, 45*(1), 42–61. DOI: 10.1016/j.intmar.2018.07.004

Petticrew, M., & Roberts, H. (2008). Systematic reviews – Do they 'work' in informing decision-making around health inequalities? *Health Economics, Policy, and Law, 3*(2), 197–211. DOI: 10.1017/S1744133108004453 PMID: 18634627

Pieper, J., Griewatz, H.-P., & Morgenroth, S. (2026). Virtual Influencers and the Future of Content Creation. In *Artificial Intelligence in Creative Industries* (1st ed., pp. 75–88). Routledge. DOI: 10.4324/9781003606802-7

Pierre, L. (2025). Exploring how brand use of artificial intelligence influences consumer perceptions and behavioral intentions through general AI attitudes and brand transparency. *Journal of Current Issues and Research in Advertising*, •••, 1–25. DOI: 10.1080/10641734.2025.2596011

Pitardi, V., & Marriott, H. R. (2021). Alexa, she's not human but… Unveiling the drivers of consumers' trust in voice-based artificial intelligence. *Psychology and Marketing*, *38*(4), 626–642. DOI: 10.1002/mar.21457

Polančič, G., Heričko, M., & Rozman, I. (2010). An empirical examination of application frameworks success based on technology acceptance model. *Journal of Systems and Software*, *83*(4), 574–584. DOI: 10.1016/j.jss.2009.10.036

Poornima, A., M, S., & Selvi A, J. A. (2025). Digital seduction: When personalized marketing blurs into personal manipulation—A consumer behavior analysis. *Journal of Information Technology Teaching Cases*, 20438869251394040.

Popel, S. (2025). NEXT-GENERATION INTELLIGENT AUDIT: INNOVATIVE TRANSFORMATION AND STRATEGIC EVOLUTION OF FINANCIAL CONTROL THROUGH AI, XAI, AND AUTONOMOUS DIGITAL PLATFORMS. *Collection of Scientific Papers «ΛΌΓΟΣ», September 5, 2025; Boston, USA*, 150–154. DOI: 10.36074/logos-05.09.2025.026

Poudel, K. P., Carter, R., & Lonial, S. (2019). The impact of entrepreneurial orientation, technological capability, and consumer attitude on firm performance: A multi-theory perspective. *Journal of Small Business Management*, *57*(sup2), 268–295. DOI: 10.1111/jsbm.12471

Powers, T. L., & Sterling, J. U. (2008). Segmenting business-to-business markets: A micro-macro linking methodology. *Journal of Business and Industrial Marketing*, *23*(3), 170–177. DOI: 10.1108/08858620810858436

Pradeepa, S., Sarkar, B., & Mohanty, S. (2024). Artificial Intelligence and Advanced Technologies: Transforming Financial Markets, Strategies, and Regulatory Compliance. *Ijisem. Com*, *3*, 323–333. DOI: 10.69968/ijisem.2024v3si2323-333

Pramanik, P., & Jana, R. K. (2025). A consumer acceptance model in the artificial intelligence era. *Management Decision*, *63*(9), 3136–3163. Advance online publication. DOI: 10.1108/MD-03-2024-0574

Pramod, D., Patil, K. P., & Bharathi, S. V. (2025). Is it really unreal? A two-theory approach on the impact of deepfakes technology on the protection motivation of consumers. *Cogent Business & Management*, *12*(1), 2461239. DOI: 10.1080/23311975.2025.2461239

Prasanna, A., & Kushwaha, B. P. (2026). Transforming marketing landscapes: A systematic literature review of generative AI using the TCCM model framework. *Management Review Quarterly*, *76*(1), 421–455. DOI: 10.1007/s11301-025-00486-9

Prasanth, A., Densy, J. V., Surendran, P., & Bindhya, T. (2023). Role of artificial intelligence and business decision making. *International Journal of Advanced Computer Science and Applications, 14*(6). Advance online publication. DOI: 10.14569/IJACSA.2023.01406103

Qadri, U. A., & Moustafa, A. M. A. (2026). They made it just for me! How AI transparency and influencer well-being shape consumer responses to AI-Driven content. *Psychology and Marketing, 43*(3), 591–608. DOI: 10.1002/mar.70075

Qin, X., Zhou, X., Chen, C., Wu, D., Zhou, H., Dong, X., Cao, L., & Lu, J. G. (2025). AI aversion or appreciation? A capability–personalization framework and a meta-analytic review. *Psychological Bulletin, 151*(5), 580–599. DOI: 10.1037/bul0000477 PMID: 40489180

Quijada, O., & Serezlic, T. (2025). *Can AI avoid Deceptive Design?: Investigating the Effectiveness of Prompting AI to Prevent Dark Patterns in Web Design.* https://www.diva-portal.org/smash/get/diva2:1971701/FULLTEXT02

Radanliev, P. (2025). AI ethics: Integrating transparency, fairness, and privacy in AI development. *Applied Artificial Intelligence, 39*(1), 2463722. DOI: 10.1080/08839514.2025.2463722

Rafiq, F., Dogra, N., Adil, M., & Wu, J.-Z. (2022). Examining consumer's intention to adopt AI-chatbots in tourism using partial least squares structural equation modeling method. *Mathematics, 10*(13), 2190. DOI: 10.3390/math10132190

Rahimzadeh, V., Monazzah, E. M., Pilehvar, M. T., & Yaghoobzadeh, Y. (2025). *Synthia: Scalable Grounded Persona Generation from Social Media Data.*

Rahman, W. (2025). Ethical AI Personalization in Digital Retail: The Roles of Transparency, Privacy, and Consumer Trust. *Strategic Business Research, 100020.* Advance online publication. DOI: 10.1016/j.sbr.2025.100020

Rai, A. (2020). Explainable AI: From black box to glass box. *Journal of the Academy of Marketing Science, 48*(1), 137–141. DOI: 10.1007/s11747-019-00710-5

Rai, A., Constantinides, P., & Sarker, S. (2019). Editor's comments: Next-generation digital platforms: Toward human–AI hybrids. *Management Information Systems Quarterly, 43*(1), iii–ix. DOI: 10.25300/MISQ/2019/431E0

Ramadan, Z., & Ramadan, J. (2025). AI avatars and co-creation in the metaverse. *Consumer Behavior in Tourism and Hospitality, 20*(1), 131–147. DOI: 10.1108/CBTH-07-2024-0246

Ramineni, V., Ingole, B. S., Jayaram, V., Mehta, G., Krishnappa, M. S., Nagpal, A., & Banarse, A. R. (2024, December). Enhancing E-Commerce Accessibility Through a Novel Voice Assistant Approach for Web and Mobile Applications. In *2024 Third International Conference on Artificial Intelligence, Computational Electronics and Communication System (AICECS)* (pp. 1-7). IEEE. DOI: 10.1109/AICECS63354.2024.10956866

Ramjohn, M., & Bray, J. (2024). Unlocking equity and trusts. In *Unlocking Equity and Trusts*. Routledge., DOI: 10.4324/9781003456865

Rane, N. L., Chika, O. E., & Rane, J. (2026). Responsible artificial intelligence in sustainable business: Enhancing customer relationships and loyalty. *International Journal of Applied Resilience and Sustainability*, *2*(1), 61–77. DOI: 10.70593/deepsci.0201004

Ranoliya, B. R., Raghuwanshi, N., & Singh, S. (2017, September). Chatbot for university related FAQs. In *2017 International Conference on Advances in Computing, Communications and Informatics (ICACCI)* (pp. 1525-1530). IEEE. DOI: 10.1109/ICACCI.2017.8126057

Rather, R. A. (2020). Customer experience and engagement in tourism destinations: The experiential marketing perspective. *Journal of Travel & Tourism Marketing*, *37*(1), 15–32. DOI: 10.1080/10548408.2019.1686101

Rather, R. A. (2025). Does consumers' reveal engagement behaviours in artificial intelligence (AI)-based technologies? The dynamics of perceived value and self-congruence. *International Journal of Hospitality Management*, *126*, 103989. https://doi.org/https://doi.org/10.1016/j.ijhm.2024.103989. DOI: 10.1016/j.ijhm.2024.103989

Rayun, S. M. N., Salam, M. A., Leong, V. S., Islam, W., Sahabuddin, M., Ahmed, M., Hosen, M. S., & Das, C. (2026). Deepfakes and Digital Sovereignty: Governance Challenges of Synthetic Media in the AI-Driven Data Economy. Https://Services.Igi-Global.Com/Resolvedoi/Resolve.Aspx?Doi=10.4018/979-8-2600-0288-9.Ch008, 225–264. DOI: 10.4018/979-8-2600-0288-9.ch008

Rayun, S. N., Salam, M. A., Islam, W., & Leong, V. S. (2026). Green FinTech Innovations: Empowering Inclusive Development and Advancing Towards the Sustainable Economy. In *Promoting Inclusivity and Accessibility With FinTech* (pp. 245-278). IGI Global Scientific Publishing. DOI: 10.4018/979-8-3373-1112-8.ch009

Rehman, A. U., Hassan, S. H., & Behera, R. K. (2026). Attractiveness vs similarity: How attributes of AI-based virtual influencers impact credibility, parasocial interaction and purchase intentions of social-media users. *Asia Pacific Journal of Marketing and Logistics*, *38*(2), 205–222. DOI: 10.1108/APJML-01-2025-0144

Rehman, A., Kumar, S., Salam, M. A., & Virmani, N. (2025). How does AI-powered virtual influencer's anthropomorphism impact trust and brand love? The moderating role of opinion leadership. *Technological Forecasting and Social Change*, *219*, 124198. DOI: 10.1016/j.techfore.2025.124198

Renckens, S., & Auld, G. (2022). Time to certify: Explaining varying efficiency of private regulatory audits. *Regulation & Governance*, *16*(2), 500–518. DOI: 10.1111/rego.12362

Rethinking the process of diffusion in innovation: A service ecosystems and institutional perspective. (2020). Journal of Business Research, 116, 526–534. DOI: 10.1016/j.jbusres.2020.01.038

Riaj, M. A. J., Tabassum, M. N., Hossain, R., Bhuiyan, M. R. I., & Khatun, M. (2025). Digitalization transformation in entrepreneurship and enterprise green innovation. In *Digitizing green entrepreneurship* (pp. 181–204). IGI Global Scientific Publishing. DOI: 10.4018/979-8-3693-7442-9.ch007

Ricci, F., Rokach, L., & Shapira, B. (2021). Recommender systems: Techniques, applications, and challenges. *Recommender Systems Handbook*, 1-35. DOI: 10.1007/978-1-4899-7637-6_1

Riikkinen, M., Saarijärvi, H., Sarlin, P., & Lähteenmäki, I. (2018). Using artificial intelligence to create value in insurance. *International Journal of Bank Marketing*, *36*(6), 1145–1168. DOI: 10.1108/IJBM-01-2017-0015

Rinne, K. J. A. (2025). *AI-powered customer engagement: How personalization, chatbots, and recommendation systems influence e-commerce customer satisfaction* (Master's thesis, HAMK University of Applied Sciences). HAMK Finna. https://urn.fi/URN:NBN:fi:amk-2025053018187

Rita, P., Omran, W., Ramos, R. F., & Costa, T. (2025). Exploring the Applications of Artificial Intelligence in Marketing: aTopic Modelling Analysis. *Tourism & Management Studies*, *21*(1), 39–55. DOI: 10.18089/tms.20250103

Robeyns, I. (2005). The capability approach: A theoretical survey. *Journal of Human Development*, *6*(1), 93–117. DOI: 10.1080/146498805200034266

Rodgers, W., & Nguyen, T. (2022). Advertising benefits from ethical artificial intelligence algorithmic purchase decision pathways. *Journal of Business Ethics, 178*(4), 1043–1061. DOI: 10.1007/s10551-022-05048-7

Rossi, J., & Bianchini, A. (2022). "Plastic waste free"–A new circular model for the management of plastic packaging in the food value chain. *Transportation Research Procedia, 67*, 153–162. DOI: 10.1016/j.trpro.2022.12.046

Rungruangjit, W., Mongkol, K., Piriyakul, I., & Charoenpornpanichkul, K. (2024). The power of human-like virtual-influencer-generated content: Impact on consumers' willingness to follow and purchase intentions. *Computers in Human Behavior Reports, 16*, 100523. DOI: 10.1016/j.chbr.2024.100523

Ruthvika, J., & Hedau, A. (2025). Digital Inclusion and Economic Equity: Evaluating the Role of Business Analytics in Overcoming Socioeconomic Challenges. *Search.Ebscohost.Com.* https://search.ebscohost.com/login.aspx?direct=true&profile=ehost&scope=site&authtype=crawler&jrnl=25206621&AN=191194088&h=tufHX0VKtGe4LIIEBY7nD9RvxvXKYiGj1Y6xmnAnpNPfbaKrbp%2BdckRZKwXNNatyljA%2FiK5CXNsc4uqYkl3B8w%3D%3D&crl=c

Saha, R., Jasrotia, S. S., & Kamila, M. K. (2025, December). The Ethics of AI-Driven Marketing: Challenges and Opportunities. In *E-business technologies conference proceedings* (Vol. 4, No. 1). https://ebt.rs/journals/index.php/conf-proc/article/view/214

Sahut, J. M., & Laroche, M. (2025). Using artificial intelligence (AI) to enhance customer experience and to develop strategic marketing: An integrative synthesis. *Computers in Human Behavior, 170*, 108684. DOI: 10.1016/j.chb.2025.108684

Salam, M. A., Leong, V. S., & Muhamad, N. (2026). The Transformative Prospects of AI-Powered Virtual Influencers in Digital Consumer Engagement and Marketing Strategies. In *Cases on Social Media Marketing Engagement Tactics* (pp. 251–290). IGI Global Scientific Publishing., DOI: 10.4018/979-8-3373-2357-2.ch009

Salam, M. A., Rayun, S. N., Islam, W., Hasan, R., Firmansyah, E. A., & Kalinaki, K. (2024). Consumer engagement: exploring deepfake applications in consumer marketing communication. In *Navigating the World of Deepfake Technology* (pp. 397–421). IGI Global Scientific Publishing. DOI: 10.4018/979-8-3693-5298-4.ch020

Saleh, M. I. (2025). Generative artificial intelligence in hospitality and tourism: Future capabilities, AI prompts and real-world applications. *Journal of Hospitality Marketing & Management, 34*(4), 467–498. DOI: 10.1080/19368623.2025.2458603

Sales, B., Darmois, E., Papadimitriou, D., & Bourse, D. (2012). A Systematic Approach for Closing the Research to Standardization Gap. In Álvarez, F., Cleary, F., Daras, P., Domingue, J., Galis, A., Garcia, A., Gavras, A., Karnourskos, S., Krco, S., Li, M.-S., Lotz, V., Müller, H., Salvadori, E., Sassen, A.-M., Schaffers, H., Stiller, B., Tselentis, G., Turkama, P., & Zahariadis, T. (Eds.), *The Future Internet* (pp. 18–29). Springer., DOI: 10.1007/978-3-642-30241-1_3

Sambasivan, N., Kapania, S., Highfill, H., Akrong, D., Paritosh, P., & Aroyo, L. M. (2021, May). "Everyone wants to do the model work, not the data work": Data Cascades in High-Stakes AI. In *proceedings of the 2021 CHI Conference on Human Factors in Computing Systems* (pp. 1-15). DOI: 10.1145/3411764.3445518

Samuel, S. (2019). A guy made a deepfake app to turn photos of women into nudes. It didn't go well. *Vox.* Https://Www. Vox. Com/2019/6/27/18761639/Ai-Deepfakedeepnude-App-Nude-Women-Porn

Sanchez-Cartas, J. M., & Katsamakas, E. (2024). AI pricing algorithms under platform competition. *Electronic Commerce Research*, 1-28. DOI: 10.1007/s10660-024-09821-w

Sands, S., Campbell, C. L., Plangger, K., & Ferraro, C. (2022). Unreal influence: Leveraging AI in influencer marketing. *European Journal of Marketing*, *56*(6), 1721–1747. DOI: 10.1108/EJM-12-2019-0949

Santangelo, A., Melandri, E., Marzani, G., & Tondelli, S. (2023). Developing a Framework for Improving Climate Resilience in Cultural Landscapes. *Mdpi.Com.* https://pubblicazioni.unicam.it/handle/11581/483765

Saputra, F. E., Buhalis, D., Augustyn, M. M., & Marangos, S. (2024). Anthropomorphism-based artificial intelligence (AI) robots typology in hospitality and tourism. *Journal of Hospitality and Tourism Technology*, *15*(5), 790–807. DOI: 10.1108/JHTT-03-2024-0171

Sarstedt, M., Ringle, C. M., & Hair, J. F. (2021). Partial least squares structural equation modeling. In *Handbook of market research* (pp. 587–632). Springer International Publishing. DOI: 10.1007/978-3-319-05542-8_15-2

Saup, T. O., Asghar, J., Kanbach, D. K., & Kraus, S. (2026). From pilots to decision systems: embedding generative AI into strategic decision-making through a socio-technical and governance lens. *Taylor & Francis, 35*(1). DOI: 10.1080/12460125.2025.2597835

Saura, J. R. (2021). Using data sciences in digital marketing: Framework, methods, and performance metrics. *Journal of Innovation & Knowledge*, *6*(2), 92–102. DOI: 10.1016/j.jik.2020.08.001

Saura, J. R. (2024). Algorithms in digital marketing: Does smart personalization promote a privacy paradox? *FIIB Business Review*, *13*(5), 499–502. DOI: 10.1177/23197145241276898

Savoldi, B., Attanasio, G., Gorodetskaya, O., Marchiori Manerba, M., &Nozza, D. (2025). *Generative AI practices, literacy, and divides: An empirical analysis in the Italian context.* https://arxiv.org/abs/2512.03671

Sayem, M. A., Anwar, A. S., Dutta, S., Sikder, R., & Kar, M. R. (2026). *Pathfinder AI: Decentralizing Career Mobility for the Underserved and Next-Gen Workforce* (Master's thesis, University of the Cumberlands). https://www.proquest.com/openview/49ab69e4d00605a4ddd2906622470d30/1?pq-origsite=gscholar&cbl=18750&diss=y

Schenker, D. (2023). *The construction of identity and evolution of desire through synthetic media*. Temple University.

Schmidt, A. T., & Engelen, B. (2020). The ethics of nudging: An overview. *Philosophy Compass*, *15*(4), e12658. DOI: 10.1111/phc3.12658

Secundo, G., Spilotro, C., Gast, J., & Corvello, V. (2025). The transformative power of artificial intelligence within innovation ecosystems: A review and a conceptual framework. *Review of Managerial Science*, *19*(9), 2697–2728. DOI: 10.1007/s11846-024-00828-z

Şenyapar, H. N. D. (2024). The future of marketing: The transformative power of artificial intelligence. *International Journal of Management and Administration*, *8*(15), 1–19. DOI: 10.29064/ijma.1412272

Seo, K., Fels, S., Yoon, D., Roll, I., Dodson, S., & Fong, M. (2020). Artificial Intelligence for Video-based Learning at Scale. *Proceedings of the Seventh ACM Conference on Learning @ Scale, L@S '20*, 215–217. DOI: 10.1145/3386527.3405937

Sergeeva, O. V., Masalimova, A. R., Zheltukhina, M. R., Chikileva, L. S., Lutskovskai, L. Y., & Luzin, A. (2025). Impact of digital media literacy on attitude toward generative AI acceptance in higher education. *Frontiers in Education, 10*, 1563148. Advance online publication. DOI: 10.3389/feduc.2025.1563148

Serrano, A. (2025). UNLEASHING AI'S TRANSFORMATIVE POWER: RESHAPING PRODUCTIVITY, LABOR MARKETS AND POLICY IN THE GLOBAL ECONOMY. *Revista UNISCI, 67.*

Setegn, A. E., & Japee, G. P. (2025). Promotional elements and the performance of tourism marketing of visitor attraction places with the mediating role of public relations: Empirical evidence from visitors in Ethiopia. *Cogent Business & Management, 12*(1), 2454325. DOI: 10.1080/23311975.2025.2454325

Seyedan, M., & Mafakheri, F. (2020). Predictive big data analytics for supply chain demand forecasting: Methods, applications, and research opportunities. *Journal of Big Data*, *7*(1), 53. DOI: 10.1186/s40537-020-00329-2

Shah, D., & Murthi, B. P. S. (2021). Marketing in a data-driven digital world: Implications for the role and scope of marketing. Journal of Business Research, 125, 772-779.

Shahriare Satu, M., Yeasmin, T., & Abdus Salam, M. (2023, December). Towards an AutoML-based data analytical framework for predicting bankruptcy in the industrial sector. In *International Conference on Trends in Electronics and Health Informatics* (pp. 699-712). Singapore: Springer Nature Singapore. DOI: 10.1007/978-981-97-3937-0_48

Shaily, S. A., & Emma, N. N. (2021). Integration of artificial intelligence marketing to get brand recognition for social business. DOI: 10.32479/irmm.11542

Shankar, V. (2025). Marketing of technology intensive products: An AI driven approach. *Marketing Strategy Journal*, *2*, 100008. Advance online publication. DOI: 10.1016/j.msj.2025.100008

Shao, Z. (2024). From human to virtual: Unmasking consumer switching intentions to virtual influencers by an integrated fsQCA and NCA method. *Journal of Retailing and Consumer Services*, *78*, 103715. DOI: 10.1016/j.jretconser.2024.103715

Sharma, A. K., & Sharma, R. (2024). *Navigating compliance and regulations in marketing analytics: Upholding ethical standards and consumer trust.*

Sharma, A., & Sharma, R. (2026). Experiential Metaverse Marketing: Leveraging AI-Driven Sentiment Analytics for Enhanced Customer Engagement. *Igi-Global. Com.* https://www.igi-global.com/chapter/experiential-metaverse-marketing/403862

Sharma, R. (2024). Governance and oversight of ai systems. *Springer*, 353–370. DOI: 10.1007/979-8-8688-0796-1_28

Sharma, A. K., & Sharma, R. (2025). Smart tourism in the digital age: Overcoming barriers and unlocking new possibilities. *Revista de Gestão*, *32*(3), 224–237. DOI: 10.1108/REGE-02-2025-0030

Sharma, A., Pujari, M., & Goel, A. (2025). The rise of AI-generated synthetic identities: A new frontier in social media. *International Journal of Innovative Research in Engineering & Multidisciplinary Physical Sciences, 13*(2), 232397. DOI: 10.37082/IJIRMPS.v13.i2.232397

Sheehan, B., Jin, H. S., & Gottlieb, U. (2020). Customer service chatbots: Anthropomorphism and adoption. *Journal of Business Research, 115*, 14–24. DOI: 10.1016/j.jbusres.2020.04.030

Sheth, J. N., Newman, B. I., & Gross, B. L. (1991). Why we buy what we buy: A theory of consumption values. *Journal of Business Research, 22*(2), 159–170. DOI: 10.1016/0148-2963(91)90050-8

Shim, H. S., Han, S. L., & Ha, J. (2021). The effects of consumer readiness on the adoption of self-service technology: Moderating effects of consumer traits and situational factors. *Sustainability (Basel), 13*(1), 95. Advance online publication. DOI: 10.3390/su13010095

Shin, D. (2021). The effects of explainability and causability on perception, trust, and acceptance: Implications for explainable AI. *International Journal of Human-Computer Studies, 146*, 102551. DOI: 10.1016/j.ijhcs.2020.102551

Shin, D. (2021). The effects of explainability and transparency on user trust in AI systems. *Computers in Human Behavior, 125*, 106994. DOI: 10.1016/j.chb.2021.106994

Shin, D., & Park, Y. J. (2019). Role of fairness, accountability, and transparency in algorithmic decision-making. *Telecommunications Policy, 43*(9), 101–118. DOI: 10.1016/j.telpol.2019.101845

Shneiderman, B. (2020). Bridging the gap between ethics and practice: Guidelines for reliable, safe, and trustworthy human-centered AI systems. [TiiS]. *ACM Transactions on Interactive Intelligent Systems, 10*(4), 1–31. DOI: 10.1145/3419764

Shrestha, D., Wenan, T., Shrestha, D., Rajkarnikar, N., & Jeong, S.-R. (2024). Personalized Tourist Recommender System: A Data-Driven and Machine-Learning Approach. In *Computation* (Vol. 12, Issue 3, p. 59). DOI: 10.3390/computation12030059

Siddiqui, H. A., Abid, H. M. S., & Ahmed, R. (2025). Optimizing E-Commerce Supply Chain Logistics: The Role of Artificial Intelligence in Efficiency and Cost Reduction. *Journal of Asian Development Studies, 14*(1), 920–938. DOI: 10.62345/jads.2025.14.1.72

Siegel, D. S., Waldman, D., & Link, A. (2003). Assessing the impact of organizational practices on the relative productivity of university technology transfer offices: An exploratory study. *Research Policy*, *32*(1), 27–48. DOI: 10.1016/S0048-7333(01)00196-2

Sikder, A. S., & Rolfe, S. (2023). The Power of E-Commerce in the Global Trade Industry: A Realistic Approach to Expedite Virtual Market Place and Online Shopping from anywhere in the World.: E-Commerce in the Global Trade Industry. *International Journal of Imminent Science & Technology.*, *1*(1), 79–100. DOI: 10.70774/ijist.v1i1.3

Sinduja, S. (2025). Marketing and Advertisement Strategies driven by Psychology and Ai Technology. *International Journal of Interdisciplinary Approaches in Psychology*, *3*(1), 49–56.

Singh, B., & Kaunert, C. (2024). Future of digital marketing: hyper-personalized customer dynamic experience with AI-based predictive models. In *Revolutionizing the AI-digital landscape* (pp. 189–203). Productivity Press. DOI: 10.4324/9781032688305-14

Singh, P., & Dhiman, B. (2023). Exploding AI-generated deepfakes and misinformation: A threat to global concern in the 21st century. *Authorea Preprints*.

Singh, S., & Srivastava, P. (2019). Social media for outbound leisure travel: A framework based on technology acceptance model (TAM). *Journal of Tourism Futures*, *5*(1), 43–61. DOI: 10.1108/JTF-10-2018-0058

Sinha, C., Vracheva, V., & Nistor, C. (2024). Maximizing generative AI benefits with task creativity and human validation. *Jbam.Scholasticahq.Com*. https://jbam.scholasticahq.com/article/122147.pdf

Skitka, L. J., Mosier, K. L., & Burdick, M. (1999). Does automation bias decision-making? *International Journal of Human-Computer Studies*, *51*(5), 991–1006. DOI: 10.1006/ijhc.1999.0252

Smit, A., Swart, J., & Broersma, M. (2025). Bypassing digital literacy: Marginalized citizens' tactics for participation and inclusion in digital societies. *New Media & Society*, *27*(6), 3127–3145. DOI: 10.1177/14614448231220383

Snyder, H. (2019). Literature review as a research methodology: An overview and guidelines. *Journal of Business Research*, *104*, 333–339. DOI: 10.1016/j.jbusres.2019.07.039

Solano-Barliza, A., Arregocés-Julio, I., Aarón-Gonzalvez, M., Zamora-Musa, R., De-La-Hoz-Franco, E., Escorcia-Gutierrez, J., & Acosta-Coll, M. (2024). Recommender systems applied to the tourism industry: A literature review. *Cogent Business & Management, 11*(1), 2367088. DOI: 10.1080/23311975.2024.2367088

Song, C., Shin, S. Y., & Shin, K. S. (2024). Implementing the dynamic feedback-driven learning optimization framework: A machine learning approach to personalize educational pathways. *Applied Sciences (Basel, Switzerland), 14*(2), 916. DOI: 10.3390/app14020916

Song, J., Zheng, C., Lv, X., & Font, X. (2025). The endorsement effectiveness of virtual influencers in nonprofit fundraising: The role of appearance and voice pitch. *Technological Forecasting and Social Change, 219*, 124299. DOI: 10.1016/j.techfore.2025.124299

Song, X., Yang, S., Huang, Z., & Huang, T. (2019, August). The application of artificial intelligence in electronic commerce. [). IOP Publishing.]. *Journal of Physics: Conference Series, 1302*(3), 032030. DOI: 10.1088/1742-6596/1302/3/032030

Song, Y., Wang, L., Zhang, Z., & Hikkerova, L. (2024). AI or human: How endorser shapes online purchase intention? *Computers in Human Behavior, 158*, 108300. DOI: 10.1016/j.chb.2024.108300

Sonnenberg, S., Mason, L., Lim, Y., & Reddi, T. (2022). Towards a Human Rights-Based Approach to New and Emerging Technologies: A Framework. *Framework Document of Policy Paper Series on" A Human Rights-Based Approach to New and Emerging Technologies"(Updated in 2024).*

Spencer, D. A. (2025). AI, automation and the lightening of work. *AI & Society, 40*(3), 1237–1247. DOI: 10.1007/s00146-024-01959-3

Spulbar, L.-F. (2025). Legal frameworks for AI-driven markets and their challenges and opportunities in the digital economy. *Revista de Ştiinţe Politice, 86*, 288–304.

Srivastava, A. (2021). The application & impact of artificial intelligence (AI) on E-commerce. *Contemporary issues in commerce and management, 1*(1), 165-75.

Srnicek, N. (2025). *Silicon Empires: The Fight for the Future of AI.* https://books.google.com/books?hl=en&lr=&id=HJ2jEQAAQBAJ&oi=fnd&pg=PA56&dq=a+responsibility+vacuum:+if+an+autonomous+agent+independently+decides+to+use+a+deceptive+%22sycophantic%22+tactic+to+close+a+sale,+current+frameworks+struggle+to+determine+whether+the+liability+rests+with+the+developer+of+the+model+or+the+brand+that+deployed+it+&ots=z3lz-rFAsY&sig=KMSyJVlkfKp2uxD8A8Ye54OV5u8

Stewart, C. R., & Yap, S. F. (2020). Low literacy, policy and consumer vulnerability: Are we really doing enough? *International Journal of Consumer Studies*, *44*(4), 343–352. DOI: 10.1111/ijcs.12569

Stewart, K. J. (2003). Trust transfer on the World Wide Web. *Organization Science*, *14*(1), 5–17. DOI: 10.1287/orsc.14.1.5.12810

Strait, M., Aguillon, C., Contreras, V., & Garcia, N. (2017). The public's perception of humanlike robots. In *Proceedings of the 26th IEEE International Symposium on Robot and Human Interactive Communication* (pp. 1418–1423). IEEE. DOI: 10.1109/ROMAN.2017.8172490

Su, B. (2025). Navigating the new frontier: The role of AI-driven virtual influencers in consumer engagement. *AI Magazine*, *46*(2), e70012. DOI: 10.1002/aaai.70012

Sultana, N., Chowdhury, R. S., & Haque, A. (2023). Gravitating towards Fintech: A study on Undergraduates using extended UTAUT model. *Heliyon*, *9*(10), e20731. Advance online publication. DOI: 10.1016/j.heliyon.2023.e20731

Sun, L., Tang, Y., & Ma, X. (2025). It just would not work for me: Perceived preference heterogeneity and consumer response to AI-driven product recommendations. *European Journal of Marketing*, *59*(5), 1426–1452. DOI: 10.1108/EJM-02-2023-0082

Sun, S., Law, R., & Luk, C. (2022). Tourists' travel-related information search channels. *International Journal of Hospitality & Tourism Administration*, *23*(2), 149–164. DOI: 10.1080/15256480.2020.1727809

Su, R., & Sun, J. (2025). Statist but responsive regulation: Targeted responsive campaigns as agile governance for tech innovation. *Journal of Asian Public Policy*, •••, 1–14. DOI: 10.1080/17516234.2025.2554109

Suryavanshi, P., & Gangele, S. (2024). Sentiment analysis view for brand reputation monitoring on social media. *Int. J. Innov. Res. Comput. Commun. Eng*, *12*(Special Is), 111–115. DOI: 10.15680/IJIRCCE.2024.1203518

Sweeney, J. C., & Soutar, G. N. (2001). Consumer perceived value: The development of a multiple item scale. *Journal of Retailing*, *77*(2), 203–220. DOI: 10.1016/S0022-4359(01)00041-0

Taherdoost, H., & Madanchian, M. (2023). Artificial intelligence and sentiment analysis: A review in competitive research. *Computers*, *12*(2), 37. DOI: 10.3390/computers12020037

Tan, Y. H., & Greene, B. R. (2025). Can a 2D shark girl be an influencer? Uncovering prevailing archetypes in the virtual entertainer industry. *Journal of Business Research, 186*, 114951. DOI: 10.1016/j.jbusres.2024.114951

Tarnanidis, T. K. (2024). Reshaping marketing science in wholesaling and retailing. In *Advances in Marketing*. Customer Relationship Management, and E-Services Book Series., DOI: 10.4018/979-8-3693-6145-0

Tauro, D., Panniello, U., & Pellegrino, R. (2021). Risk management in digital advertising: An analysis from the advertisers' media management perspective. *Taylor & Francis, 23*(1–2), 29–57. DOI: 10.1080/14241277.2021.1960532

Tavitiyaman, P., Qu, H., Tsang, W. L., & Lam, C. R. (2021). The influence of smart tourism applications on perceived destination image and behavioral intention: The moderating role of information search behavior. *Journal of Hospitality and Tourism Management, 46*, 476–487. DOI: 10.1016/j.jhtm.2021.02.003

Teece, D. J. (2018). Business models and dynamic capabilities. *Long Range Planning, 51*(1), 40–49. DOI: 10.1016/j.lrp.2017.06.007

Teepapal, T. (2025). AI-driven personalization: Unraveling consumer perceptions in social media engagement. *Computers in Human Behavior, 165*, 108549. DOI: 10.1016/j.chb.2024.108549

Teng, L., Wang, H., Wang, X., & Foti, L. (2025). Unlocking the potential of virtual endorsers: The role of brand-owned and brand-non-owned virtual endorsers in shaping brand attitude. *International Journal of Information Management, 81*, 102864. DOI: 10.1016/j.ijinfomgt.2024.102864

Thapliyal, M., Jahan, A., & Sharma, R. (2025). AI-Assisted Character Motion Synthesis using Deep Generative Models. *2025 6th International Conference on IoT Based Control Networks and Intelligent Systems (ICICNIS)*, 1653–1657.

Theodorakopoulos, L., Theodoropoulou, A., & Klavdianos, C. (2025). Interactive viral marketing through big data analytics, influencer networks, AI integration, and ethical dimensions. *Journal of Theoretical and Applied Electronic Commerce Research, 20*(2), 115. DOI: 10.3390/jtaer20020115

Thomas-Francois, K., & Somogyi, S. (2022). Consumers' intention to adopt virtual grocery shopping: Do technological readiness and the optimisation of consumer learning matter? *International Journal of Retail & Distribution Management, 50*(5), 638–657. DOI: 10.1108/IJRDM-06-2020-0206

Thomas, G. (2024). Challenges and trends of digital innovation in the tourism sector: Contemporary literature review. *Open Journal of Business and Management, 12*(01), 179–190. DOI: 10.4236/ojbm.2024.121013

Thomas, J., & Harden, A. (2008). Methods for the thematic synthesis of qualitative research in systematic reviews. *BMC Medical Research Methodology, 8*(1), 45. http://www.biomedcentral.com/1471-2288/8/45. DOI: 10.1186/1471-2288-8-45 PMID: 18616818

Thomas, V. L., & Fowler, K. (2021). Close encounters of the AI kind: Use of AI influencers as brand endorsers. *Journal of Advertising, 50*(1), 11–25. DOI: 10.1080/00913367.2020.1810595

Tinmaz, H., Lee, Y.-T., Fanea-Ivanovici, M., & Baber, H. (2022). A systematic review on digital literacy. *Smart Learning Environments, 9*(1), 21. DOI: 10.1186/s40561-022-00204-y

Toh, R. S., DeKay, C. F., & Raven, P. (2011). Travel Planning: Searching for and Booking Hotels on the Internet. *Cornell Hospitality Quarterly, 52*(4), 388–398. DOI: 10.1177/1938965511418779

Tolbert, C. L. (2025). Enhancing Persona Creation Through the Hermeneutic Fusion of Horizons: Business Applications in AI Natural Language Generation. *Journal of Comprehensive Business Administration Research, 2*(1).

Tom Dieck, M. C., & Han, D. D. (2022). The role of immersive technology in customer experience management. *Journal of Marketing Theory and Practice, 30*(1), 108–119. DOI: 10.1080/10696679.2021.1891939

Tom Dieck, M. C., & Jung, T. (2018). A theoretical model of mobile augmented reality acceptance in urban heritage tourism. *Current Issues in Tourism, 21*(2), 154–174. DOI: 10.1080/13683500.2015.1070801

Toyib, J. S., & Paramita, W. (2024). An authentic human-like figure: The success keys of AI fashion influencer. *Cogent Business & Management, 11*(1), 2380019. Advance online publication. DOI: 10.1080/23311975.2024.2380019

Tran, M. T. (2026). Advancing retail and service strategies: AI-driven consumer behavior prediction, gamification, and ethical marketing. *Journal of Retailing and Consumer Services, 88*, 104558. DOI: 10.1016/j.jretconser.2025.104558

Truby, J., Brown, R. D., Ibrahim, A., & Parellada, O. C. (2024). Regulating AI: Challenges and the way forward through regulatory sandboxes. *Springer, 58*, 441–456. DOI: 10.1007/978-3-031-41264-6_23

Tseng, W., & Ou, C. (2025). Can virtual influencers drive online consumer behavior? An applied examination of ELM model investigating the marketing effects of virtual influencers. *Sustainability (Basel), 17*(23), 10721. DOI: 10.3390/su172310721

Tucker, P. (2019). The newest AI-enabled weapon: Deep-Faking photos of the earth. *Defense One, 13*, 3.

Tussyadiah, I. (2020). A review of research into automation in tourism: Launching the Annals of Tourism Research Curated Collection on Artificial Intelligence and Robotics in Tourism. *Annals of Tourism Research, 81*, 102883. DOI: 10.1016/j.annals.2020.102883

Tussyadiah, I. P., Jung, T. H., & Tom Dieck, M. C. (2018). Embodiment of wearable augmented reality technology in tourism experiences. *Journal of Travel Research, 57*(5), 597–611. DOI: 10.1177/0047287517709090

Tuyen, T. (2025). Sustainable Tourism in the Age of Innovation: A Bibliometric Exploration of Progress and Potential. *Journal of Tourism. Sustainability and Well-Being, 13*(1), 55–71.

Ullah, M. S., Khan, M. K., Ahmadxan Oglu, G. R., & Yasmin, T. (2025). *The influence of digital literacy on consumer perceptions and e-commerce engagement. Policy Research Journal, 3*(1), 92-104. Retrieved from https://policyresearchjournal.com/index.php/1/article/view/279

Ullah, A., & Khan, S. D. (2024). Impact of sound decision-making on small and medium businesses in Pakistan. *International Journal of Asian Business and Management, 3*(2), 177–192. DOI: 10.55927/ijabm.v3i2.9101

Umboh, I. A., Tumbel, A. L., & Wenas, R. S. (2023). Digital literacy as a mediator between digital marketing capability and SME performance. *The Journal of Asian Finance, Economics and Business, 10*(2), 123–134. DOI: 10.56444/mem.v38i1.3315

Um, N. (2022). How does celebrity-based brand endorsement work in social media?—The instagram context. *Social Sciences (Basel, Switzerland), 11*(8), 342. DOI: 10.3390/socsci11080342

Um, N. (2023). Predictors Affecting Effects of Virtual Influencer Advertising among College Students. *Sustainability (Basel), 15*(8), 6388. Advance online publication. DOI: 10.3390/su15086388

Vaddepalli, R. (2021). Who's Responsible When Algorithms Fail? Comparing Accountability Under GDPR, CCPA, and Other Data Laws. *Researchgate.Net*. https://www.researchgate.net/profile/Rajani-Kumari-Vaddepalli/publication/395027232_Who's_Responsible_When_Algorithms_Fail_Comparing_Accountability_Under_GDPR_CCPA_and_Other_Data_Laws/links/68c3514b9534473a6d49d775/Whos-Responsible-When-Algorithms-Fail-Comparing-Accountability-Under-GDPR-CCPA-and-Other-Data-Laws.pdf

van de Poel, I. (2020). Embedding Values in Artificial Intelligence (AI) Systems. *Minds and Machines*, *30*(3), 385–409. DOI: 10.1007/s11023-020-09537-4

Van Der Vlist, F., Helmond, A., & Ferrari, F. (2024). Big AI: Cloud infrastructure dependence and the industrialisation of artificial intelligence. *Big Data & Society*, *11*(1), 20539517241232630. DOI: 10.1177/20539517241232630

van Dijk, J. A. G. M. (2006). Digital divide research, achievements and shortcomings. *Poetics*, *34*(4–5), 221–235. DOI: 10.1016/j.poetic.2006.05.004

van Doorn, J., Mende, M., Noble, S. M., Hulland, J., Ostrom, A. L., Grewal, D., & Petersen, J. A. (2017). Domo arigato Mr. Roboto: Emergence of automated social presence in organizational frontlines and customers' service experiences. *Journal of Service Research*, *20*(1), 43–58. DOI: 10.1177/1094670516679272

Vargas, G. D. J. (2025). Trust, Transparency, and AI: Building Digital Bridges for US–Global Business Collaborations. *International Journal of Humanities and Information Technology*, *7*(03), 98–110.

Vargo, S. L., & Lusch, R. F. (2004). Evolving to a new dominant logic for marketing. *Journal of Marketing*, *68*(1), 1–17. DOI: 10.1509/jmkg.68.1.1.24036

Vargo, S. L., & Lusch, R. F. (2011). Service dominant logic: Continuing the evolution. *Journal of the Academy of Marketing Science*, *36*(1), 1–10. DOI: 10.1007/s11747-007-0069-6

Vashishth, T. K., Sharma, K. K., Kumar, B., Chaudhary, S., & Panwar, R. (2024). Enhancing customer experience through AI-enabled content personalization in e-commerce marketing. *Advances in digital marketing in the era of artificial intelligence*, 7-32.

Venkatachalam, P., & Ray, S. (2022). How do context-aware artificial intelligence algorithms used in fitness recommender systems? A literature review and research agenda. *International Journal of Information Management Data Insights*, *2*(2), 100139. DOI: 10.1016/j.jjimei.2022.100139

Venkatesh, V., Morris, M. G., Davis, G. B., & Davis, F. D. (2003). User acceptance of information technology: Toward a unified view. *Management Information Systems Quarterly*, *27*(3), 425–478. DOI: 10.2307/30036540

Verdoliva, L. (2020). Media Forensics and DeepFakes: An Overview. *IEEE Journal of Selected Topics in Signal Processing*, *14*(5), 910–932. DOI: 10.1109/JSTSP.2020.3002101

Verhoef, P. C., Kannan, P. K., & Inman, J. J. (2015). From multi-channel retailing to omni-channel retailing. *Journal of Retailing*, *91*(2), 174–181. DOI: 10.1016/j.jretai.2015.02.005

Verleye, K., Gemmel, P., & Rangarajan, D. (2014). Managing engagement behaviors in a network of customers and stakeholders: Evidence from the nursing home sector. *Journal of Service Research*, *17*(1), 68–84. DOI: 10.1177/1094670513494015

Verma, S. (2025). Synthetic Identities and Deepfake Attacks: The Next Frontier in Enterprise AI Security. *Eur. Mod. Stud. J*, *9*(5), 176–189. DOI: 10.59573/emsj.9(5).2025.17

Veseli, A., Bytyqi, L., Hasanaj, P., & Bajraktari, A. (2025). The Impact of Digital Marketing on Promotion and Sustainable Tourism Development. In *Tourism and Hospitality* (Vol. 6, Issue 2, p. 56). DOI: 10.3390/tourhosp6020056

Vidhya, V., Donthu, S., Veeran, L., Lakshmi, Y. S., & Yadav, B. (2023). The intersection of AI and consumer behavior: Predictive models in modern marketing. *Remittances Review*, *8*(4), 2410–2424. DOI: 10.33182/rr.v8i4.166

Vishwakarma, R. K., Pandey, A., Kundnani, M. P., Yadav, A. K., Singh, M. N., & Yadav, M. S. (2025). Personalization vs. privacy: Marketing strategies in the digital age. *Journal of Marketing & Social Research*, *2*, 177–191.

Vladimirovich, K. M. (2020). Future marketing in B2B segment: Integrating Artificial Intelligence into sales management. *International Journal of Innovative Technologies in Economy*, (4), 410878. DOI: 10.31435/rsglobal_ijite/30092020/7149

Vladyslava, S. (2025). AI and Deepface Influencers: The Challenge of Authenticity in the Online Space. *Universal Library of Engineering Technology*, *2*(2).

Volles, B. K., Park, J., Van Kerckhove, A., & Geuens, M. (2024). How and when do virtual influencers positively affect consumer responses to endorsed brands? *Journal of Business Research*, *183*, 114863. DOI: 10.1016/j.jbusres.2024.114863 von Struensee, S. (2021). *The Role of Social Movements, Coalitions, and Workers in Resisting Harmful Artificial Intelligence and Contributing to the Development of Responsible AI.* https://arxiv.org/pdf/2107.14052

Vorobeva, D., Costa Pinto, D., António, N., & Mattila, A. S. (2024). The augmentation effect of artificial intelligence: Can AI framing shape customer acceptance of AI-based services? *Current Issues in Tourism, 27*(10), 1551–1571. DOI: 10.1080/13683500.2023.2214353

Wagner, D., & Heatherton, T. (2015). *Self-regulation and its failure: The seven deadly threats to self-regulation.* https://psycnet.apa.org/record/2013-35881-026

Walden, V. (2021). Afterword: Digital Holocaust memory futures: Through paradigms of immersion and interactivity and beyond. *Springer*, 267–296. DOI: 10.1007/978-3-030-83496-8_11

Walters, D., Wiseman, H., & Hous, L. (2024). Self-regulation in emerging and innovative industries. *HeinOnline*. https://heinonline.org/hol-cgi-bin/get_pdf.cgi?handle=hein.journals/hulr62&section=24

Walters, H. D., & Hammond, R. M. (2025). *AI in Marketing: Applications, Insights, and Analysis*. Taylor & Francis. DOI: 10.4324/9781003468806

Wang, P., Jiang, Y., Xu, C., & Xie, X. (2019). Overview of Content-Based Click-Through Rate Prediction Challenge for Video Recommendation. *Proceedings of the 27th ACM International Conference on Multimedia, MM '19*, 2593–2596. DOI: 10.1145/3343031.3356085

Wang, S., Wang, Q., Cui, Q., & Lan, T. (2025). Artificial intelligence in tourism: A Systematic literature review and future research agenda. *Sustainability (Basel), 17*(20), 9080. DOI: 10.3390/su17209080

Wang, X., & Qiu, X. (2024). The positive effect of artificial intelligence technology transparency on digital endorsers: Based on the theory of mind perception. *Journal of Retailing and Consumer Services, 78*, 103777. DOI: 10.1016/j.jretconser.2024.103777

Wang, X., & Wang, H. (2026). Brands cannot own a human celebrity but can own an AI endorser: AI endorsers' role in shaping consumer self-brand connection. *Journal of Retailing and Consumer Services, 90*, 104717. DOI: 10.1016/j.jretconser.2025.104717

Wang, X., & Zhang, Y. (2025). The influence of virtual streamer on purchase intention: The moderated mediating effect of message strategy and live-streaming environment. *Electronic Commerce Research and Applications, 73*, 101520. DOI: 10.1016/j.elerap.2025.101520

Wang, Y. Y., & Chuang, Y. W. (2024). Artificial intelligence self-efficacy: Scale development and validation. *Education and Information Technologies*, *29*(4), 4785–4808. DOI: 10.1007/s10639-023-12015-w

Wang, Y., Sauka, K., & Situmeang, F. B. I. (2025). Anthropomorphism and transparency interplay on consumer behaviour in generative AI-driven marketing communication. *Journal of Consumer Marketing*, *42*(4), 512–536. DOI: 10.1108/JCM-04-2024-6806

Waqas, M., & Qadri, U. A. (2025). When Consumer Autonomy is Compromised: Adopting a Dual-Type View to Understand AI-Driven Marketing and Its Impact on Young Consumers' Ethical Behavior. *Journal of Business Ethics*, •••, 1–19.

Waytz, A., Cacioppo, J., & Epley, N. (2010). Who sees human? The stability and importance of individual differences in anthropomorphism. *Perspectives on Psychological Science : A Journal of the Association for Psychological Science*, *5*(3), 219–232. DOI: 10.1177/1745691610369336

Wedel, M., & Kannan, P. K. (2016). Marketing analytics for data-rich environments. *Journal of Marketing*, *80*(6), 97–121. DOI: 10.1509/jm.15.0413

Weippert, M. (2024). The scope and intensity of personalised omnichannel customer journeys: A conceptualisation integrating experts' and consumers' perspectives. *Journal of Marketing Management*, *40*(11-12), 877–909. DOI: 10.1080/0267257X.2024.2388088

Weldon, M., Thomas, G., & Skidmore, L. (2024). Establishing a future-proof framework for ai regulation: Balancing ethics, transparency, and innovation. *Ir.Law.Utk. Edu*. https://ir.law.utk.edu/cgi/viewcontent.cgi?article=1660&context=transactions

Wen, J., & Li, X. (2025). AI digital human responsiveness and consumer purchase intention: The mediating role of trust. *Journal of Theoretical and Applied Electronic Commerce Research*, *20*(3), 246. DOI: 10.3390/jtaer20030246

Wertenbroch, K., Schrift, R. Y., Alba, J. W., Barasch, A., Bhattacharjee, A., Giesler, M., Knobe, J., Lehmann, D. R., Matz, S., Nave, G., Parker, J. R., Puntoni, S., Zheng, Y., & Zwebner, Y. (2020). Autonomy in consumer choice. *Marketing Letters*, *31*(4), 429–439. DOI: 10.1007/s11002-020-09521-z PMID: 32836798

Westerlund, M. (2019). The emergence of deepfake technology: A review. *Technology Innovation Management Review*, *9*(11), 39–52. DOI: 10.22215/timreview/1282

Westphal, M. F. (2023). Decision control and explanations in human AI collaboration. *Human-Computer Interaction*, *38*(4). Advance online publication. DOI: 10.1016/j.ijhcs.2023.102956

Whittaker, L., Letheren, K., & Mulcahy, R. (2021). The rise of deepfakes: A conceptual framework and research agenda for marketing. *Australasian Marketing Journal*, *29*(3), 204–214. DOI: 10.1177/1839334921999479

Whittaker, L., Mulcahy, R., Letheren, K., Kietzmann, J., & Russell-Bennett, R. (2023). Mapping the deepfake landscape for innovation: A multidisciplinary systematic review and future research agenda. *Technovation*, *125*, 102784. https://doi.org/https://doi.org/10.1016/j.technovation.2023.102784. DOI: 10.1016/j.technovation.2023.102784

Wirtz, J., Patterson, P. G., Kunz, W. H., Gruber, T., Lu, V. N., Paluch, S., & Martins, A. (2018). Brave new world: Service robots in the frontline. *Journal of Service Management*, *29*(5), 907–931. DOI: 10.1108/JOSM-04-2018-0119

Wu, L., & Jing Wen, T. (2021). Understanding AI Advertising from the Consumer Perspective. *Journal of Advertising Research*, *61*(2), 133–146. DOI: 10.2501/JAR-2021-004

Wu, X., Ha, L., & Lim, J. (2024). From perception to purchase: How AI literacy shapes consumer decisions in AI-generated sponsored vlogs across products and services. *Journal of Electronic Commerce Research & Applications*, *20*(4), 302. https://www.mdpi.com/0718-1876/20/4/302

Xia, H., Yang, Y., & Wang, X. (2025). Too pretty to resist? Exploring the impact of virtual influencers' beauty level on consumer reactions. *Journal of Retailing and Consumer Services*, *87*, 104371. DOI: 10.1016/j.jretconser.2025.104371

Xia, H., Zhang, L., Chen, J., & Wang, X. (2025). Decoding virtual influencer endorsement using machine learning: The role of virtual influencer, posting, and disclosure characteristics. *Journal of Retailing and Consumer Services*, *87*, 104366. DOI: 10.1016/j.jretconser.2025.104366

Xiang, Z., Du, Q., Ma, Y., & Fan, W. (2017). A comparative analysis of major online review platforms: Implications for social media analytics in hospitality and tourism. *Tourism Management*, *58*, 51–65. DOI: 10.1016/j.tourman.2016.10.001

Xiang, Z., & Gretzel, U. (2010). Role of social media in online travel information search. *Tourism Management*, *31*(2), 179–188. DOI: 10.1016/j.tourman.2009.02.016

Xia, Z., & Shannon, R. (2025). Navigating the digital frontier: Exploring the dynamics of customer–brand relationships through AI chatbots. *Sustainability (Basel)*, *17*(5), 2173. DOI: 10.3390/su17052173

Xiong, M., Xu, H., Ji, J., Zuo, R., Wang, Y., & Olya, H. (2026). Responsible Artificial Intelligence attention and firm innovation: An attention-based view. *Journal of Product Innovation Management*, *43*(1), 186–214. DOI: 10.1111/jpim.70015

Xu, H., Law, R., Lovett, J., Luo, J. M., & Liu, L. (2024). Tourist acceptance of ChatGPT in travel services: The mediating role of parasocial interaction. *Journal of Travel & Tourism Marketing*, *41*(7), 955–972. DOI: 10.1080/10548408.2024.2364336

Xu, J., Feng, Y., Li, W., Huang, Q., & Fan, Z. (2025). How AI brand endorsers influence Generation MZ's consumer behavior in metaverse marketing scenarios. *Journal of Theoretical and Applied Electronic Commerce Research*, *20*(2), 82. DOI: 10.3390/jtaer20020082

Xu, W., Wang, S., & Zuo, X. (2025). Whose victory? A perspective on shifts in US-China cross-border data flow rules in the AI era. *The Pacific Review*, *38*(6), 963–989. DOI: 10.1080/09512748.2025.2462239

Xu, Y., Shieh, C. H., van Esch, P., & Ling, I. L. (2020). AI customer service: Task complexity, problem-solving ability, and usage intention. *Australasian Marketing Journal*, *28*(4), 189–199. DOI: 10.1016/j.ausmj.2020.03.005

Yang, C. S., & Dobbie, W. (2020). Equal protection under algorithms: A new statistical and legal framework. *Michigan Law Review*, •••(119.2), 291–395. DOI: 10.36644/mlr.119.2.equal

Yang, J., Chuenterawong, P., Lee, H., Tian, Y., & Chock, T. M. (2023). Human versus Virtual Influencer: The Effect of Humanness and Interactivity on Persuasive CSR Messaging. *Journal of Interactive Advertising*, *23*(3), 275–292. DOI: 10.1080/15252019.2023.2189036

Yang, X., Zhang, L., & Feng, Z. (2024). Personalized Tourism Recommendations and the E-Tourism User Experience. *Journal of Travel Research*, *63*(5), 1183–1200. DOI: 10.1177/00472875231187332

Yang, Y., Li, S., & Qiu, S. (2025). A Systematic Literature Review on the Negative Impacts of AI-generated Virtual Digital Humans. *IEEE Access : Practical Innovations, Open Solutions*, *13*, 80047–80062. DOI: 10.1109/ACCESS.2025.3564041

Yan, J., Xia, S., Jiang, A., & Lin, Z. (2024). The effect of different types of virtual influencers on consumers' emotional attachment. *Journal of Business Research*, *177*, 114646. DOI: 10.1016/j.jbusres.2024.114646

Yan, W., Wang, X., & Lu, Y. (2025). Deep learning based personalized tourism recommendation for behavior analysis and route optimization. *Scientific Reports*, *15*(1), 38561. DOI: 10.1038/s41598-025-22592-0 PMID: 41188382

Yan, X., Huam, H. T., & Sade, A. B. (2024). Is AI better than humans? Unveiling the boundary conditions under which virtual influencers outperform human influencers in endorsing sustainable products. *Sustainability (Basel), 16*(22), 9896. DOI: 10.3390/su16229896

Yas, H., Abdalaziz, M. M. O., Dafri, W., AL-Falahi, Q., Kashmoola, K., & AlLouzi, A. S. (2025). Artificial Intelligence and Digital Marketing: Ethical Challenges of Digital Influence on Public Perception and Consumer Behavior in the Law of the UAE. *Research Journal in Advanced Humanities, 6*(3). Advance online publication. DOI: 10.58256/5hjmrw16

Yeo, S. F., Tan, C. L., Kumar, A., Tan, K. H., & Wong, J. K. (2022). Investigating the impact of AI-powered technologies on Instagrammers' purchase decisions in digitalization era–A study of the fashion and apparel industry. *Technological Forecasting and Social Change, 177*, 121551. DOI: 10.1016/j.techfore.2022.121551

Yeung, K., & Li, W. (2025). From 'wild west'to 'responsible'AI testing 'in-the-wild': Lessons from live facial recognition testing by law enforcement authorities in Europe. *Data & Policy, 7*, e59. DOI: 10.1017/dap.2025.10019

Ystgaard, K. F., Atzori, L., Palma, D., Heegaard, P. E., Bertheussen, L. E., Jensen, M. R., & De Moor, K. (2023). Review of the theory, principles, and design requirements of human-centric Internet of Things (IoT). *Journal of Ambient Intelligence and Humanized Computing, 14*(3), 2827–2859. DOI: 10.1007/s12652-023-04539-3

Zakharov, E., Shysheya, A., Burkov, E., & Lempitsky, V. (2019). Few-shot adversarial learning of realistic neural talking head models. *Proceedings of the IEEE/CVF International Conference on Computer Vision*, 9459–9468. DOI: 10.1109/ICCV.2019.00955

Zaki, K., Alhomaid, A., & Shared, H. (2025). Leveraging machine learning to analyze influencer credibility's impact on brand admiration and consumer purchase intent in social media marketing. *Human Behavior and Emerging Technologies, 9959697*(1), 9959697. Advance online publication. DOI: 10.1155/hbe2/9959697

Zarouali, B., Boerman, S. C., Voorveld, H. A. M., & van Noort, G. (2022). The algorithmic persuasion framework in online communication: Conceptualization and a future research agenda. *Internet Research, 32*(4), 1076–1096. DOI: 10.1108/INTR-01-2021-0049

Zeithaml, V. A. (1988). Consumer perceptions of price, quality, and value: A means-end model and synthesis of evidence. *Journal of Marketing, 52*(3), 2–22. DOI: 10.1177/002224298805200302

Zeng, H., & Lin, C. A. (2025). Consumer evaluation of virtual vs. human influencers via source credibility, perceived social similarity, and consumption motivation. *Journal of Theoretical and Applied Electronic Commerce Research, 20*(3), 168. DOI: 10.3390/jtaer20030168

Zeng, Y., Pu, G., Liu, J., & Feng, W. (2024). The influence mechanism of narrative strategies used by virtual influencers on consumer product preferences. *Journal of Theoretical and Applied Electronic Commerce Research, 19*(4), 2828–2850. DOI: 10.3390/jtaer19040137

Zha, D., Bhat, Z. P., Lai, K. H., Yang, F., Jiang, Z., Zhong, S., & Hu, X. (2025). Data-centric artificial intelligence: A survey. *ACM Computing Surveys, 57*(5), 1–42. DOI: 10.1145/3711118

Zhang, X., Li, K., Wu, Y., Liang, S., & Yu, M. (2026). Transforming E-Commerce with AI: Navigating Innovation, Personalization, and Ethical Challenges. *Journal of Theoretical and Applied Electronic Commerce Research, 21*(1), 29. DOI: 10.3390/jtaer21010029

Zhang, Y., & He, A. (2025). The impact of AI influencer endorsements on consumers' purchase intentions: The serial mediating roles of mind perception and brand trustworthiness. *Journal of Product and Brand Management, 34*(5), 754–765. DOI: 10.1108/JPBM-02-2024-4974

Zhao, Z. (2023). Beyond free markets and consumer autonomy: rethinking consumer financial protection in the age of artificial intelligence. *HeinOnline*. https://heinonline.org/hol-cgi-bin/get_pdf.cgi?handle=hein.journals/nyuinpe13&section=7

Zhao, H., Lu, J., & Cao, J. (2020). A short text conversation generation model combining BERT and context attention mechanism. *International Journal on Computer Science and Engineering, 23*(2), 136–144. DOI: 10.1504/IJCSE.2020.110536

Zhao, X., You, W., Zheng, Z., Shi, S., Lu, Y., & Sun, L. (2025). How do consumers trust and accept AI agents? An extended theoretical framework and empirical evidence. *Behavioral Sciences (Basel, Switzerland), 15*(3), 337. DOI: 10.3390/bs15030337

Zheng, X., Cui, C., Zhang, C., & Li, D. (2026). Who says what? How message appeals shape virtual- versus human-influencers' impact on consumer engagement. *Journal of Research in Interactive Marketing, 20*(2), 199–214. DOI: 10.1108/JRIM-10-2024-0482

Zhou, P., Wang, L., Liu, Z., Hao, Y., Hui, P., Tarkoma, S., & Kangasharju, J. (2024). *A Survey on Generative AI and LLM for Video Generation, Understanding, and Streaming* (arXiv:2404.16038). arXiv. /arXiv.2404.16038DOI: 10.36227/techrxiv.171172801.19993069/v1

Zhou, A., Liu, Y., & Dai, Y. (2026). Artificial yet credible: How virtual influencers overcome authenticity challenges. *Journal of Business Research, 206*, 115940. DOI: 10.1016/j.jbusres.2025.115940

Zhou, Q., Xu, Z., & Yen, N. Y. (2019). User sentiment analysis based on social network information and its application in consumer reconstruction intention. *Computers in Human Behavior, 100*, 177–183. DOI: 10.1016/j.chb.2018.07.006

Zhou, T., & Li, S. (2025). Examining consumer impulsive purchase intention in virtual AI Streaming: A S-O-R perspective. *Journal of Theoretical and Applied Electronic Commerce Research, 20*(3), 204. DOI: 10.3390/jtaer20030204

Zhou, X., Yan, X., & Jiang, Y. (2023). EXPRESS: Making Sense? The Sensory-Specific Nature of Virtual Influencer Effectiveness. *Journal of Marketing, 00222429231203699*. Advance online publication. DOI: 10.1177/00222429231203699

Zhou, X., & Zafarani, R. (2020). A survey of fake news: Fundamental theories, detection methods, and opportunities. *ACM Computing Surveys, 53*(5), 1–40. DOI: 10.1145/3395046

Zlotowski, J., Proudfoot, D., Yogeeswaran, K., & Bartneck, C. (2015). Anthropomorphism: Opportunities and challenges in human–robot interaction. *International Journal of Social Robotics, 7*(3), 347–360. DOI: 10.1007/s12369-014-0267-6

Zuboff, S. (2023). The age of surveillance capitalism. In *Social theory re-wired* (pp. 203–213). Routledge. DOI: 10.4324/9781003320609-27

About the Contributors

Muhammad Abdus Salam, known professionally as "Dr. Salam Shadhin," is an award-winning academic and researcher. He is an Assistant Professor of Management Information Systems (MIS) at Noakhali Science and Technology University (NSTU). His research interests encompass topics related to Artificial Intelligence; Digital Literacy; Technology Transformation; Human-Computer Interaction; Generative AI, Deepfake, and Emerging Technologies; AI Ethics, Trust, and Governance; Sustainability, Green AI, and Digital Responsibility; and Technology in Consumer Culture and Societal Change. His research advances understanding of artificial intelligence and emerging technologies from commercial, social, and ethical perspectives, emphasizing real-world industry needs, responsible governance, digital literacy, community engagement, and sustainable innovation. His work highlights how the strategic design and deployment of AI and emerging technologies can enhance human–technology interaction, foster consumer trust, and generate transformative value across markets and society. Dr. Salam Shadhin was awarded the "Best Paper Award" at the 4th International Conference on Business, Economics, and Finance (ICBEF 2023) held at Universiti Brunei Darussalam, "Best Extended Abstract Award" at the 9th World Business Ethics Forum (WBEF 2025) hosted by City University of Macau, as well as the "PhD Colloquium Award 2025," and "Best PhD Colloquium Award 2026" organized by the UBD School of Business and Economics (UBDSBE). Dr. Muhammad Abdus Salam earned his PhD from the UBD School of Business and Economics, an AACSB-accredited business school at Universiti Brunei Darussalam. He has published widely in scholarly journals and proceedings and coauthored several books through broad international research collaborations. Additionally, he provides expert commentary on technology and development in interviews with television channels and newspapers, and authors articles for both newspapers and scholarly periodicals. He has held the role of Tutor for multiple academic modules at the UBDSBE. He completed his Bachelor of Business Administration (BBA) and Master of Business Administration (MBA) from the University of Dhaka. He has presented research insights at numerous national and international conferences, seminars, and symposia. He has served as a moderator and chair for many international conferences, while also playing a vital role as a member of several conference committees. He serves as an expert reviewer for scholarly work, including journals such as Journal of Health Organization and Management, Journal of Advanced Transportation, Cogent Business & Management, Discover Global Society, and Discover Psychology, as well as for numerous books published by Springer, Wiley, Emerald, Elsevier, IGI Global, Sage, and Taylor & Francis.

Vai Shiem Leong is a Senior Assistant Professor at the UBD School of Business and Economics, Universiti Brunei Darussalam. She received her PhD in Marketing from the University of Nottingham, United Kingdom. Her primary research interests lie in marketing communication and service marketing. She has authored papers published in reputed journals, like Journal of Services Marketing, International Journal of Advertising, International Journal of Quality and Service Sciences, Journal of Consumer Behaviour, and more.

Nazlida Muhamad received her Phd in Marketing from The University of Western Australia in 1999. She has taught marketing modules in Malaysian, Saudi and Australian public universities, prior to working at UBD. Her research interests and publications are in the area of consumer behavior -with special interest on issues pertaining to Islam, and its role on Muslim consumer behaviors in the marketplace. Among others, her works are published in Psychology and Marketing, Journal of Islamic Marketing, Journal of Business and Policy Research, and Journal of computer-mediated communication.

***

S. M. Ashraful Alam has received BBA and MBA degree from the department of Management Information Systems (MIS) from University of Dhaka, Bangladesh in 2013 and 2014 respectively. Currently, he is working as a lecture, Department of Management Information Systems, Faculty of Business Studies, Begum Rokeya University, Rangpur, Bangladesh since December 2021. His major research interests are in the fields of technology adoption, digital economy, e-business, e health, services and so on. He has published more than ten articles and two book chapters in reputed peer reviewed journal including Q1 journal.

Samsul Alam is a PhD research fellow at the Department of Information Systems, City University of Hong Kong, under the Hong Kong PhD Fellowship

Scheme. He is also an Assistant Professor at Begum Rokeya University, Rangpur, Bangladesh, where he teaches and conducts research in management information systems. He achieved an MPhil (equivalent) degree from the University of Extremadura, Spain, by being awarded an Erasmus Mundus fully funded scholarship and an MBA in MIS from the University of Dhaka. Over time, he has published articles in peer-reviewed, indexed journals and book chapters from reputable publishers, both domestically and internationally. He also presented some papers at national and international conferences. He has research interests in healthcare systems, artificial intelligence, digital education, e-commerce, financial technology, and social-ethical aspects of IS.

Anuj Bhattacharya, MTTM, UGC-NET, is currently working as an Assistant Professor in the Department of Tourism Management at The ICFAI University Sikkim, India. He is presently pursuing his Ph.D. in Tourism and brings with him more than 7 years of teaching experience along with over 9 years of corporate experience in the fields of Travel & Tourism and Aviation. He has been actively involved in academic administration, curriculum development, and institutional responsibilities, contributing to various academic and professional initiatives. His areas of interest include tourism development, digital transformation in tourism, and sustainable tourism practices. He is the recipient of the Best Young Educator Award in Aviation (2024), conferred by DTORR, recognizing his contribution to teaching and academic excellence in the field. He has published a book chapter indexed in Scopus and has contributed to research in the domain of tourism and hospitality. He continues to engage in academic research, conference participation, and collaborative projects aimed at advancing tourism studies.

Md. Faisal-E-Alam is an Associate Professor in the Department of Management Studies, Faculty of Business Studies, Begum Rokeya University, Rangpur, Bangladesh. He has published 57 research works, comprising 48 journal articles, 3 book chapters, and 6 conference papers. His research focuses on employee behavior, organizational performance, entrepreneurial development, sustainable business practices, and contemporary management challenges using quantitative research methodologies. His scholarly contributions aim to advance management knowledge and provide practical insights for organizations and policymakers. He actively engages in interdisciplinary research and collaborates with scholars to address emerging issues in business and management. His work reflects a commitment to evidence-based research.

Egi Arvian Firmansyah is presently an assistant professor at Universitas Padjadjaran, Indonesia. He obtained his PhD in finance from the School of Business and Economics Universiti Brunei Darussalam (UBD) in 2025. During his PhD study, Egi published 20 Scopus-indexed papers and more than seven SINTA-indexed papers (as first and co-author). His research interests include several topics related to Islamic fintech, systematic literature review, bibliometric approach, and ethical finance. He is also an active reviewer in international peer-reviewed journals, such as Cogent Business & Management, Journal of Islamic Accounting and Business Research, Financial Innovation, Cogent Economics & Finance, and Applied Economics.

Piali Haldar earned her MBA from the Institute of Rural Management Anand and completed her PhD at Birla Institute of Technology, Mesra. Her core areas of specialization include rural marketing, rural development, branding strategy, and consumer behaviour. With over 20 years of experience in academia and research, she has published extensively in renowned journals listed in ABDC and Scopus. She has authored one textbook on Marketing and edited three academic books. Dr. Haldar has presented her research at numerous national and international conferences and has contributed more than 50 papers to reputed journals, edited volumes, and conference proceedings.

Afruza Haque has been working as an Assistant Professor of Management/ Business Administration in this department since October 23, 2022. Prior to this, she worked as a lecturer in the same department from April 15, 2019, to October 22, 2022. She has obtained his BBA and MBA in Management Information Systems (MIS) from the University of Dhaka, Bangladesh. Her research areas are Corporate Social Responsibility (CSR), Banking Technology Development, FinTech, Blockchain, Tertiary Education, and Public Policy. Her recent contributions have appeared in Technology Innovation Management Review, Sustainability, Higher Education, Skills and Work-Based Learning, and Bangladesh Journal of Medical Science.

Waziha Islam is a graduate student at Noakhali Science and Technology University, has dedicated four years to academic research, contributing to multiple projects. Her expertise was recognized with the Best Presenter Award at the International Conference on Embracing Industry 4.0 for Sustainable Business Growth in 2024. Her research interests include technology adoption, cashless tourism, technology adoption in tourism, and smart tourism.

Issam Najati is a researcher and professor specializing in management sciences. Holding a PhD in management sciences, he focuses on the digitalization of supply chains, particularly blockchain applications. His research explores the impact of emerging technologies on supply chain efficiency and transparency. Active in academic conferences and research initiatives, he also mentors and supports young entrepreneurs through dedicated business creation programs.

Ashish R. Jaswal is an accomplished academic and researcher whose 24 years of professional experience, combining over 6 years in industry with 18 years in academia, enables students and collaborators to benefit from both practical business insights and academic rigor. He holds a Ph.D. in Marketing Management from the Faculty of Management at Savitribai Phule Pune University, Pune, equipping him with expertise that directly enriches the learning and research capabilities of those he mentors. Throughout his career, Dr. Jaswal has demonstrated a strong commitment to continuous learning and professional development. He has attended 19 Faculty Development Programs (FDPs) and 3 workshops, continually enhancing his functional expertise and teaching effectiveness. He has presented his work at 14 conferences, both nationally and internationally. Dr Jaswal has trained more than 1,500 students throughout his academic tenure, further expanding his positive influence on future professionals and researchers. Since February 16, 2023, Dr Jaswal has been serving as an Assistant Professor at Sadhu Vaswani Institute of Management Studies for Girls, Pune. His appointment has further recognised his expertise and leadership in the field as a Research Supervisor in Marketing Management (Faculty of Commerce and Management). Effective from October 18, 2023, until his superannuation on October 9, 2036, Savitribai Phule Pune University, Pune, has authorised him to guide up to four PhD scholars in his capacity as Assistant Professor, continuing his long-standing commitment to cultivating future marketing scholars and building a lasting scholarly legacy.

Sujan Sujan Ali Joardar is a graduate in Tourism and Hospitality Management from the University of Rajshahi, where he I completed my BBA with a CGPA of 3.79. And later i have earned my MBA with a CGPA of 3.88, demonstrating strong academic excellence. I have gained practical experience as a Front Office Intern at Sea Pearl Beach Resort & Spa in Cox's Bazar, developing skills in customer service and hospitality operations. Alongside my academic journey, i have taken on leadership roles, serving as the President of the Rajshahi University Higher Education and Research Forum and Rajshahi Divisional Head of Shishu Ullash Organization. I also actively involved in research, focusing on tourism behavior and sustainability.

Dev Kumar Mandal currently serves as an Assistant Professor in the Department of Management at Brainware University, Kolkata. Before this, he worked at ICRA Analytics Ltd and Shriram Finance Ltd. He holds an MBA in Finance and a Bachelor of Commerce degree from Vidyasagar University. Additionally, he has successfully cleared the UGC NET and WB SET examinations in Management.

Lisa Mani has completed an MBA and a BBA from the Department of Business Administration, Major in Finance and Banking at Shahjalal University of Science and Technology (SUST), Sylhet, Bangladesh. Her research interests include AI, Fintech, Machine Learning, Emerging technologies with finance and banking, and business administration.

Md. Yeamin Masum is an academician and researcher in the tourism and hospitality industry. He is currently working as a Lecturer in Tourism and Hospitality Management at the Islamic University, Kushtia-7003, Bangladesh. He has published several research papers in reputed national and international journals. His research interests include sustainable tourism, Rural tourism, Coastal & Marine Tourism, Medical tourism, Tourism and technology, AI in Tourism, and Tourism Marketing.

Nazlida Muhamad received her PhD in Marketing from The University of Western Australia in 1999. She has taught marketing modules in Malaysian, Saudi, Brunei and Australian public universities, prior to working at Prince Sultan University. Her research interests and publications are in the area of consumer behavior -with special interest on issues pertaining to Islam, and its role on Muslim consumer behaviors in the marketplace. Among others, her works are published in Psychology and Marketing, Journal of Islamic Marketing, Journal of Business and Policy Research, and Journal of computer-mediated communication.

Farjana Nasrin is currently working as an Assistant Professor in the Department of Business and Technology Management (BTM) of Islamic University of Technology (IUT), Dhaka, Bangladesh. She has completed her BBA and MBA from Department of International Business, University of Dhaka. Her current research interest is in Sustainability, Logistics & Global Value Chain Management, Corporate Governance and International Business. Specialization: International Business, Logistics & Supply Chain management, Strategic Management, Sustainability.

Rasheda Akter Rupa, a former student of the Department of MIS, completed her Bachelor of Business Administration (BBA) and Master of Business Administration (MBA) degrees from the same department with excellent academic performance. She secured 1st position in the Faculty of Business Studies, University of Dhaka in 2017. In recognition of her academic excellence, she was awarded the Prime Minister Gold Medal 2017 from the Faculty of Business Studies. She also received the President Gold Medal in the 51st convocation of the University of Dhaka. Besides, she was awarded some prestigious accolades such as – the Dean's

Honor Award, Dean's Merit Award, University Grant Commission Scholarship, Graduate and Post-graduate scholarship, etc. Before joining the MIS Department, Ms. Rupa served as a Lecturer at the Department of Business and Technology Management of the Islamic University of Technology (IUT), a Senior Lecturer at the School of Business of Ahsanullah University of Science and Technology (AUST), and a Lecturer at the Department of Business Administration of Prime University. She brought about five years of teaching experience at national and international universities. Ms. Rupa continually engages in research-based activities along with her regular academic activities. Her research interests are broader business issues such as blockchain, artificial intelligence, and green supply chain management. She has published in diverse high-impact journals, including Q1 and Sustainability Journal.

Pinki Maria Sarker is a PhD student in the Management Department at the Robert C. Vackar College of Business & Entrepreneurship, University of Texas Rio Grande Valley. She earned both her BBA and MBA in International Business from University of Dhaka. Her research interests include leadership, artificial intelligence in organizations, and employee well-being. Her work examines how digital transformation and AI reshape cognition, trust, and behavior within organizations and in employee–consumer interactions.

Swati Sharma, Ph.D. is currently working as an Associate Professor with Amity University, India. She holds 20 years of teaching and industry experience. She is Vice- President of Communication Council of Delhi's Women's Indian Chamber of Commerce and Industry. She is First Indian to receive the Certified Tourism Educator award from Asia Pacific Institute of Events Management. She is the reviewer of Consumer Behavior in Tourism & Hospitality & Inderscience Journals & IGI Global . She has authored & Edited 15 books & published research papers in National & International journals of repute. (IGI Global, Taylor & Francis, Springer, Apple Academy Press, CABI, Edward & Elgar).

Khadija Sharmin is working as a faculty member of Management Information Systems at Begum Rokeya University, Rangpur, Bangladesh. She has earned her BBA and MBA degrees in Management Information Systems from University of Dhaka, Bangladesh. As a young professional and early career researcher, she is working on several research projects and published research papers on peer-reviewed journals. Her research interests include Information Systems, Cybersecurity, Health Information Systems, and Community Development with a focus on Gender and Sustainable Development. As an academic, she wants to advance knowledge and practice through impactful research, teaching, and industry with social management.

Md. Monowar Uddin Talukdar is currently working as an assistant professor and head of the Department of Business Administration and additional director of the Institutional Quality Assurance Cell at the University of Brahmanbaria, in Bangladesh. He has obtained both his master's and bachelor's degrees from the Department of Business Administration (major in Accounting and Information Systems) of Jatiya Kabi Kazi Nazrul Islam University, Trishal, Mymensingh, Bangladesh. He has also obtained a postgraduate diploma in Information and Communication Technology from Bangladesh Agricultural University and a postgraduate diploma in Human Resource Management from Bangladesh Institute of Management.

David Jingjun Xu is a Professor in the Department of Information Systems, City University of Hong Kong. His research interests include human-computer interaction, artificial intelligence, healthcare, social media, technology adoption, and virtual reality. He has more than 100 publications, including over 40 journal papers. His publications have appeared in all four top information systems journals (i.e., MIS Quarterly, Information Systems Research, Journal of Management Information Systems, and Journal of Association for Information Systems), as well as in interdisciplinary UTD journals such as Management Science and the INFORMS Journal on Computing, and in various IEEE journals. He is serving as a Senior Editor for Information Systems Journal, an associate editor for Information Systems Research, and an editorial board member for the Journal of the Association for Information Systems. He is a recipient of the Information Systems Research Best Associate Editor of the Year in 2021.

Index

A

B

C

D

E

F

H

I

M

O

P

R

S

T

V

www.ingramcontent.com/pod-product-compliance
Lightning Source LLC
LaVergne TN
LVHW062336300926
849161LV00007B/1709
* 9 7 9 8 2 6 0 0 2 9 7 7 0 *